AERIAL LANDBIRDS
pp. 212–242

Hummingbirds
pp. 212–232

Swifts
pp. 234–236

Swallows
pp. 238–242

SONGBIRDS
pp. 244–432

Ovenbirds
pp. 244–258

Tapaculo
p. 276

Antbirds
pp. 260–270

Antthrushes
p. 272

Antpittas
p. 274

Cotingas and
Allies
pp. 276–280

Tityras, Becards
pp. 280–284

Manakins
pp. 286–288

Flycatchers
pp. 290–324

SONGBIRDS
pp. 244–432

Mimids
p. 326

Thrushes
pp. 326–332

Dipper
p. 334

Silkies, Waxwing
p. 334

Wrens
pp. 336–344

Gnatwrens,
Gnatcatchers
p. 346

Vireos
pp. 348–352

Warblers
pp. 354–374

Chat, Thrush-tanager
p. 374

Sparrows
pp. 376–386

Finches
pp. 386–390

Seedeaters, Grassquits
pp. 392–396

Grosbeaks, Buntings
pp. 396–404

Tanagers
pp. 406–420

Icterids
pp. 422–432

Birds of
Costa Rica

Dale Dyer and Steve N. G. Howell

Princeton University Press

Princeton and Oxford

Dale: For my parents, Dwight and Emily Dyer

Published by Princeton University Press
41 William Street, Princeton, New Jersey 08540
99 Banbury Road, Oxford OX2 6JX

press.princeton.edu

Library of Congress Cataloging-in-Publication Data
Names: Howell, Steve N. G., author. | Dyer, Dale (Artist), illustrator.
Title: Birds of Costa Rica / Dale Dyer and Steve N.G. Howell.
Description: First edition. | Princeton, New Jersey : Princeton University Press, [2023] | Series: Princeton field guides | Includes bibliographical references and index.
Identifiers: LCCN 2022030128 (print) | LCCN 2022030129 (ebook) | ISBN 9780691203355 (pbk. acid-free paper) | ISBN 9780691243351 (ebook)
Subjects: LCSH: Birds—Costa Rica—Identification. | BISAC: NATURE / Birdwatching Guides | TRAVEL / Central America
Classification: LCC QL687.C8 H69 2023 (print) | LCC QL687.C8 (ebook) | DDC 598.097286—dc23/eng/20220719
LC record available at https://lccn.loc.gov/2022030128
LC ebook record available at https://lccn.loc.gov/2022030129

British Library Cataloging-in-Publication Data is available

Cover Credit: Resplendent Quetzals, by Dale Dyer

This book has been composed in Adobe Garamond Pro

Printed on acid-free paper. ∞

Typeset and designed by D & N Publishing, Wiltshire, UK

Printed in Italy

10 9 8 7 6 5 4 3 2 1

CONTENTS

PREFACE AND ACKNOWLEDGMENTS

Imagine a relatively small chunk of land wedged into a tropical isthmus connecting two large continental reservoirs of bird diversity; a chunk fronting two major oceans and dissected by high mountain ranges and active volcanoes; a chunk exposed to the effects of major glaciations that caused sea level to rise and fall, separating and isolating the surrounding landmasses to create environments conducive to speciation. And then call it Costa Rica. Over 900 species of birds (in about 87 families) have been recorded in Costa Rica, with a land area of about 51,000 km², smaller than many US states. The avian riches of the country range from brilliant Scarlet Macaws in verdant lowland rainforests to tiny Volcano Hummingbirds on windswept high mountain tops.

Birding visitors to Costa Rica have been well served by the seminal guide co-authored by former long-term residents Gary Stiles and Alexander Skutch (1989), a guide built upon many years of exploring the country, combined with a summary of the literature, notably the pioneering work on avian distribution by Paul Slud (1964). More recently, an updated handy field guide by Richard Garrigues and Robert Dean (2007, 2014) has helped many more visitors appreciate the birdlife of Costa Rica; and Costa Rican species are treated in *Birds of Central America* (Vallely & Dyer 2018), the plates from which form the basis for the present work. We are fortunate to have had such a wealth of prior literature to build upon, and we thank all those involved in earlier works. While this book is laid out as a field guide to help people identify birds in the field, it also serves as an updated compendium of the remarkable avian biodiversity of Costa Rica. In terms of labor division, Dyer painted all of the plates, and Howell had primary responsibility for the text.

As part of the mammoth task of illustrating the birds of Central America, Dyer visited Costa Rica and other Central American countries annually during 2007–2016. Howell first visited Costa Rica in 1986, as part of a five-year odyssey traveling and birding throughout Mexico and Central America; he visited several more times through the mid-1990s, including leading tours to most parts of the country, and started revisiting in the 2010s, after becoming distracted in the interim by the birds of Mexico and Chile. Between us and our many months of field work in Costa Rica and neighboring regions, we have gained field experience with all but a handful of the species included.

Fieldwork is only part of the equation, however, and a book such as this is the product of many people. In particular, for their long-term support of our work we thank the personnel at the Department of Ornithology of the American Museum of Natural History, especially Paul Sweet, Bentley Bird, Peter Capainolo, and curators Joel Cracraft, Brian Tilston Smith, and George Barrowclough; the personnel at WINGS, especially Greg Greene, Matt Brooks, and Will Russell; and all at the Palomarin Field Station of Point Blue (formerly PRBO), especially Diana Humple, Mark Dettling, Megan Elrod, and Renée Cormier.

Our taxonomic research was aided greatly by the herculean effort of the *Handbook of the Birds of the World* team in producing their illustrated checklists, including numerous vocal analyses by Peter Boesman; and the work of the North American Classification Committee and South American Classification Committee of the American Ornithological Society, and the International Ornithologists' Union in maintaining their checklists and providing references. The sound archives of the Macaulay Library at the Cornell Lab of Ornithology (www.macaulaylibrary.org) and Xeno-canto (www.xeno-canto.org) are fantastic resources that also helped immeasurably with our work, and we thank the many recordists who have uploaded useful recordings to these platforms.

For help with questions concerning the status and distribution of Costa Rican birds, and for help in the field, we thank Rosa Argueda S., Harry Barnard, Dick Cannings, Rafael Campos, Enrique Gómez, Keith Hansen, Richard C. Hoyer, Patrick O'Donnell, José Alberto Perez A. (CopeArte), Simon Perkins, Peter Pyle, Henry Sandi Amador, Fabrice Schmitt, and especially Luke Seitz and James R. Zook. Others who helped in various ways were J. Van Remsen, Michael L. P. Retter, and especially Dennis Jongsomjit of Point Blue, who created the base maps used for the introduction and for the species range maps. The book benefited from review by James R. Zook and Tom Johnson, and any remaining errors are our responsibility. Last, but far from least, we thank the remarkable Robert Kirk and team at Princeton University Press; admirably diligent copy editor Annie Gottlieb; and David Price-Goodfellow and team at D & N Publishing, for their care in bringing *Birds of Costa Rica* to fruition.

HOW TO USE THIS BOOK

Area and Species Covered

In this guide to field identification we cover bird species found regularly in mainland Costa Rica, on inshore islands, and over marine waters that can be reached comfortably within a day trip (out to about 50km, or 30 miles, from shore). Oceanic birds of far offshore waters that few people get to visit are not included, and neither are very rare and vagrant species unlikely to be seen in Costa Rica (for completeness, these are listed in the appendices). In a few cases, such as when a rare species is similar to a regularly occurring one, we have included rare and poorly known species on the plates to encourage clarification of status; in some cases, plate design considerations influenced the inclusion or omission of rarer species. Costa Rican species, plus those found in neighboring countries, are covered in the recent *Birds of Central America* (Vallely & Dyer 2018), which serious students should consult for further information. Our baseline taxonomy is that of IOC (Gill et al. 2021), except for oceanic birds, where we follow Howell & Zufelt (2019). Our cutoff date for species coverage and inclusion is December 2021.

Format

The inside front cover and first three pages comprise pictorial contents to help you get to the right group of birds. Putting a bird into the correct group of species is an important first step in any identification process—if you are trying to identify a duck by looking among hawks, well, as they say, 'You can't get there from here.' Birds are arranged in a user-friendly field-guide sequence (basically, waterbirds, then landbirds) following Howell et al. (2012) rather than in a phylogenetic order, which is often unsuited to field identification (Yoon 2009).

Plates

We have tried to group species on plates by similarity in appearance integrated with shared geographic distribution and habitat—thus, similar species likely to be found together are usually on the same plate or on adjacent plates. Species on a plate are shown at the same scale, except in a few cases where a line divides the plate into different scales; this should be obvious by consulting the lengths given in the facing-page text.

When different ages and sexes are shown, images for a species are arranged with juveniles and immatures on the left, adults on the right (usually females, then males). An image with no label for age or sex indicates simply an 'adult' bird in which sexes look similar (many first-year songbirds are not distinguishable from adults after molting out of their briefly held juvenile plumage). When shown, juveniles and immatures are labeled as such, as are males and females. Well-defined seasonal plumages (mainly for northern migrants) are often followed by month spans to indicate when these plumages are typically seen.

Family and Genus Accounts

Each family, plus some genera and other species groups, starts with a short account summarizing features common to the family or group. The number of regularly occurring species in each family is noted in parentheses; a plus sign (+) indicates additional species in that family have been recorded in Costa Rica, noted in the appendices.

Species Accounts

These start with English and scientific names, plus length (and sometimes wingspan) in cm; length is bill tip to tail tip, measured from museum specimens laid on their back with no undue stretching applied. An asterisk (*) preceding the species name refers you to taxonomic comments in Appendix C.

The use of parentheses in an English or scientific name indicates an alternative name, such as Charming (Beryl-crowned) Hummingbird, where the more informative name Beryl-crowned Hummingbird is sometimes used, as by Stiles & Skutch (1989); or *Tangara (Thraupis) palmarum* for Palm Tanager, where some authors place this species in the genus *Tangara*, others in the genus *Thraupis*. Because names are changing so frequently we have used parentheses only for what we consider the most widely known (or sometimes more appropriate) names. For example, Smoky-brown Woodpecker has been transferred among four (!) different genera in recent years, and different authorities still place it in at least two genera.

To convey the frequently ambiguous nature of taxonomy we sometimes employ brackets in both the English and scientific names. These brackets indicate relatedness (or traditionally perceived relatedness) for taxa that fall either into the gray zone of uncertainty or into the realm of proposed new splits (see Appendix C). If a taxon has a widely used English name, or if its original name is evident from the English name, we use brackets only in the scientific name, as in Northern Collared Trogon *Trogon [collaris] puella*, or Central American Sharpbill *Oxyruncus [cristatus] frater*; the name in brackets is simply the chronologically first-named taxon, which may be called the parent species. If the taxon has a potentially unfamiliar English name we also include the former (parent) English name in brackets, as with Veraguas [Brown-throated] Parakeet *Eupsittula [pertinax] ocularis* or Hick's [Variable] Seedeater *Sporophila [corvina] ophthalmica*. We do this also for some relatively recent splits that are widely agreed upon but likely unfamiliar to many users, such as Gartered [Violaceous] Trogon *Trogon [violaceus] caligatus* and Morelet's [White-collared] Seedeater *Sporophila [torqueola] morelleti*. Although sometimes a little cumbersome, we believe that the information provided by this method is preferable to simply dumping a load of new and potentially confusing names on the reader with no explanation.

Lengths simply give an idea of relative size; note that every species varies slightly to strikingly in length (most books provide simply an 'average' length, which can be quite misleading). Moreover, because area is a square of length, a bird 10% 'larger' (= longer) than another can appear appreciably bigger in the field, e.g., a bird 10cm long can appear 20% 'bigger' than a bird with similar proportions that is 9cm long ($10 \times 10 = 100 cm^2$, vs. $9 \times 9 = 81 cm^2$).

The species account text then covers points relevant to identification (hereafter, ID), which can include aspects of habitat, seasonal occurrence, abundance, and behavior, as well as the more conventional ID criteria of plumage, structure, and voice. Similar-looking species often segregate by geography and habitat, or by season, which can streamline ID vs. looking for minor plumage or structural differences (e.g., Blue-chested vs. Charming Hummingbirds, Louisiana vs. Northern Waterthrushes, Red-throated vs. Middle American Ant-tanagers). Habitat descriptions are usually broad-brush, and behavioral notes are limited to features that can assist with ID.

Sounds can be very helpful for ID. They are notoriously difficult to describe, but at least some description may help in several ways: 1) to ID a bird from something seen poorly but heard well; 2) to prompt the memory, including comparison with similar sounds; 3) to tell you what a bird *does not* sound like, often helpful when seeking a species—don't follow up on high lisping twitters if the bird you are seeking makes low-pitched rattles.

We use accents to indicate emphasis or a point of rising inflection, as in *peé-eer*; and CAPITAL letters to indicate loud or strongly emphasized phrases, as in PEE-eer. As a rule, only the most typical and frequently heard vocalizations are described; almost all species make myriad other sounds, especially in the breeding season. Sound descriptions are based on the personal experience of Howell unless stated otherwise, including reference to the online sound libraries of the Macaulay Library (www.macaulaylibrary.org) and Xeno-canto (www.xeno-canto.org). This section is omitted if a species is typically silent in Costa Rica.

Although many sounds can be found online and on apps, beware of potential geographic as well as individual variation, not to mention the possibility of misidentified sound files (especially in the Macaulay Library, whose utility, sadly, is being diluted by burgeoning poor-quality recordings added by well-meaning eBird users). Moreover, vocalizations on commercial CDs in particular can be of birds agitated in response to playback vs. birds giving vocalizations more typically heard in the field.

Status: Statements made here should be used in conjunction with the maps. Species are assumed to be resident unless stated otherwise. Migrants include *winter migrants* (mainly visitors from North America), *transient migrants* (passing through to/from North and South America), *summer migrants* (visiting Costa Rica in summer to breed), and simply *nonbreeding (nonbr.) migrants* that may occur year-round (such as wide-ranging pelagic species, or shorebirds that may remain in Costa Rica during their first summer rather than returning north to breed). Understandably confusing to many visitors from the Northern Hemisphere, the wet summer months in Costa Rica are often called 'winter' by local residents—a legacy from Spanish settlers coming from a Mediterranean climate, where the winters were rainy, the summers dry and sunny.

Date and elevational ranges are by necessity broad-brush guidelines, and elevation is often simply a proxy for habitat. Thus, a resident species found at 500–1500m would not be too surprising if encountered at 350m or 1600m (especially if in similar habitat), but it would be unusual at sea level or 2000m. Also note that cloud forest and other humid montane habitats occur at appreciably lower elevations on the volcanoes of the Guanacaste Cordillera than in the Talamanca Mountains, and that many species inhabiting humid foothill forest tend to occur at lower elevations on the Caribbean slope than on the

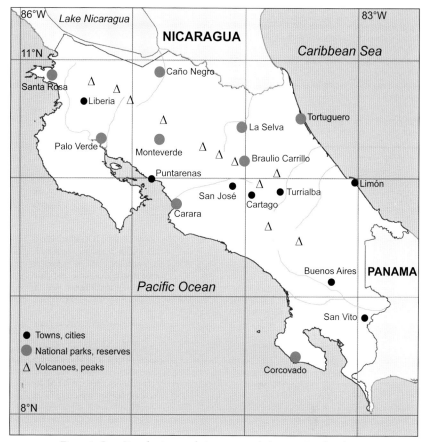

Figure 1. *Costa Rica, showing population centres and places mentioned in the text.*

less humid Pacific slope. Likewise, for a bird described as occurring from mid-March to September, an occurrence in early March or early October would not be exceptional, whereas an occurrence in January would be highly unusual. World range is summarized in parentheses at end of the Status section.

Abundance terms are by necessity subjective, as well as relative and averaged out over several years; migrants, especially transients, may be common one week, rare the next, depending on local weather conditions. Abundance tends to vary across a species' range (often a species is less numerous at the edge of its range), or by habitat and elevation. Apparent abundance can also be affected by time of year (species are often most conspicuous when singing in spring, and thus seem commoner at that season than when quiet, retiring, and molting in late summer and fall), and also by observer familiarity (some species are rarely seen but often heard, and will appear rare or even absent to somebody who doesn't recognize the vocalizations). Habitat can also influence real or perceived abundance: species of open habitats are more conspicuous, and often more numerous, than species of forested habitats, where greater species diversity is balanced by fewer individuals of any given species. And simply by virtue of lifestyle, common hawks are numerically less numerous than common tanagers.

That said, most species are (relatively) fairly common in appropriate habitat and season within their mapped range. Many species, however, especially those of forests, are now absent from much of their mapped range courtesy of habitat modification by humans; and even species that should be common in open and modified habitats are oddly scarce in large areas of the deforested Caribbean lowlands, presumably thanks to pesticides and other anthropogenic factors.

Common: encountered (seen or heard) on ostensibly all days *in range and habitat/season*, often in relatively large numbers. For example, Black Vulture, Great Kiskadee, Blue-gray Tanager.

Fairly common: encountered (seen or heard) on most or all days *in range and habitat/season*, but in smaller numbers than common species. For example, Gray Hawk, Northern Ochre-bellied Flycatcher, White-shouldered Tanager.

Uncommon: not usually encountered (seen or heard) on most days *in range and habitat/season*, and then only in small numbers. For example, Hook-billed Kite, Sepia-capped Flycatcher, White-winged Tanager. Also used for species encountered on most days *in range and habitat/season*, but only in very small numbers because of limited or specialized habitat; for example, Fasciated Tiger Heron, Green-fronted Lancebill.

Scarce: species that appear rare, perhaps more due to their behavior or to observer coverage than to actual rarity, such as Masked Duck, Audubon's Shearwater; or to population reduction through habitat change and hunting, as for Great Curassow in much of its range.

Rare: species that occur in low density, missed far more often than encountered (seen or heard) on a day in the field and perhaps only encountered a few times a year. For example, Tiny Hawk, Great Jacamar.

Very rare: not usually encountered every year, and should be documented carefully. For example, Gray-bellied Hawk, Brown-banded Martin.

Irregular: Abundance varies appreciably between years, not necessarily annual in occurrence. For example, Green-winged Teal, Tree Swallow, Myrtle Warbler.

Range Maps

In a country as topographically complex as Costa Rica, where lowland valleys cut far into high mountains, elevations can change greatly across a few kilometers, and it is impossible to show truly accurate bird distribution on a tiny range map; moreover, for reasons not readily discernible to humans, a species may be fairly common in one valley and absent from an adjacent but seemingly equally suitable valley. Hence, the range maps are by necessity simplified and often extrapolated, but a quick glance at them should give a good idea of whether you are in the right place and season, and the common patterns of distribution should soon become second nature (Figure 3). The maps are based on peer-reviewed literature, specimens, our own field experience, and eBird (but see below).

Maps should be used in conjunction with the Status sections of the species accounts. For example, a quick visual check of, say, p. 172 shows immediately that Yellow-billed and Black-billed Cuckoos are widespread transient migrants (usually absent from the highest mountains); Mangrove Cuckoo is a widespread nonbreeding migrant at low and mid-elevations (check the account for seasonality); Groove-billed Ani occurs widely as a resident breeding species; and Smooth-billed Ani occurs as a resident breeding species only on the south Pacific slope.

Because seasonal occurrence can be complex at a local level, and is poorly known in many cases, we map only the primary seasonal status, with notes in the text about local differences; for example, Yellow-billed Cuckoo is mapped as a transient migrant and Mangrove Cuckoo as a nonbreeding migrant, but the text notes that Yellow-billed can occur rarely in winter on the Pacific slope and that Mangrove may breed locally along the Pacific coast.

Most resident tropical species do not wander much, but migrants might on occasion be found well outside the mapped ranges. Distribution can also be dynamic, as for many species that favor open and disturbed habitats and whose ranges are expanding north and upslope to higher elevations. Maps are not included for very rare migrants and also do not usually show areas of very rare occurrence, where a species is not to be expected; this information may be covered in the text. Thus, the lack of a range map usually indicates a species unlikely to be encountered.

A note on eBird (see www.ebird.org). Based on the infinite number of monkeys theorem, this popular resource has great potential and was extremely helpful in creating the range maps. However, for numerous taxa in Costa Rica and elsewhere in Middle America we often found at least 10–20% of *documented* (by photo or sound recording) eBird reports to be misidentified (in some cases more than 50% misidentified; exceptionally 100% when only one or two reports existed). This is not a commentary on the gallant eBird reviewers, who have volunteered for this thankless, Sisyphean task, but simply an inevitable consequence of the sheer volume of unfiltered input far exceeding the foreseeable capacity for proofing. Hence, eBird can give misleading impressions of distributional and seasonal occurrence patterns, and should be used with caution (Figure 4). When our maps or range statements do not agree with eBird it is usually because we discount unverified or inaccurate reports rather than having overlooked them. Undoubtedly this will lead to errors of omission for some species, and we encourage users to document records outside the mapped ranges.

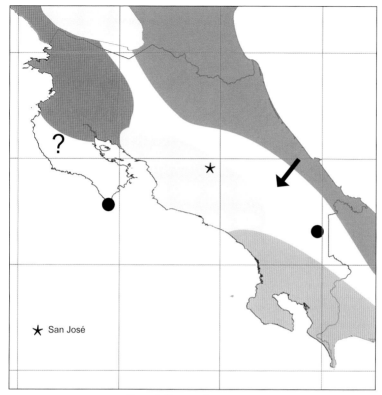

Figure 2. *Key to species range maps.*

○ Resident breeding species; breeding sites may be rather local for some species, especially colonial waterbirds

○ Seasonal breeding migrant, usually in summer; breeding sites may be rather local for some species, especially colonial waterbirds

○ Seasonal nonbreeding migrant, usually in winter but may be year-round for some species, especially waterbirds

○ Transient migrant

● Breeding colony or isolated population

? Occurrence possible or reported, status in need of elucidation or confirmation

→ Direction of range expansion

12

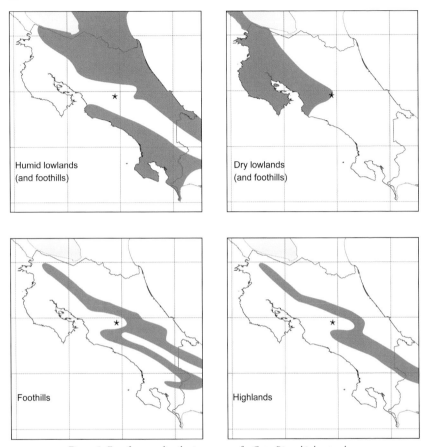

Figure 3. Four frequent distribution patterns for Costa Rican birds, at a glance; remember, the asterisk indicates San José, a useful point of reference.

Figure 4. Groove-billed Ani is not known to occur on the south Pacific slope of Costa Rica, yet the eBird map (left, accessed 21 October 2021) would suggest it does, and not rarely. However, when reports with documentation were examined (right), only three photos existed—all very good—and all showed typical Smooth-billed Anis, the expected species. Hopefully, this map will have been corrected by the time you read this, but such errors are not rare.

Bird Topography

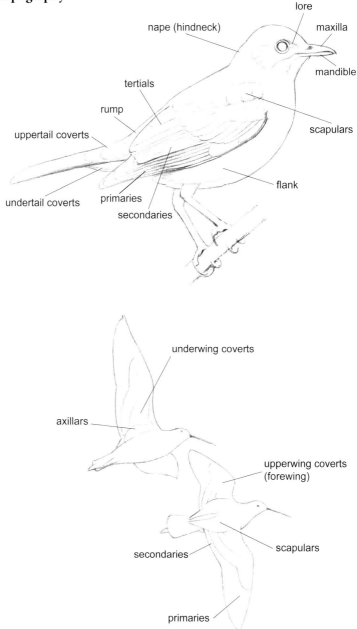

Figure 5. *Most terms we use should be self-explanatory, especially in reference to the plates. Some of the more important and potentially unfamiliar terms are illustrated above.*

Abbreviations and Some Terms Explained

We have limited the use of abbreviations and have tried to use widely understood terms for geography, habitat, bird topography, and such. Nonetheless, a few terms may be unfamiliar to some users and are explained below (also see Figure 5).

We use cen. for central, and n., s., ne. for north, south, northeast, etc. (capitalized for major regions, as in N Pacific or S America, etc.); I. for island, and Is. for islands. For months we use 3 letters: Jun = June, Sep = September, etc. For plumages we use nonbr. for nonbreeding, juv. for juvenile (a bird in its first non-downy = juvenile plumage) and imm. for immature (any non-adult plumage). We use WS for wingspan. Finally, in some places we use ID for identification and the Latin abbreviation cf. for compare with.

Bamboo Woody perennial grass that grows in dense mats or stands; flowers and seeds at long and unpredictable intervals, sometimes of many decades.

Central Mountains (Mts.) Collectively the four massifs along the northern edge of the Central Valley, namely the Viejo, Poás, Barva, and Turrialba/Irazú Volcanoes.

Cere A bare leathery patch of skin into which the nostrils open; mainly seen on hawks and falcons, often brightly colored.

Cloud Forest Humid evergreen broadleaf forest growing mainly on ridgetops where cloud forms and provides moisture throughout the year; often dense, with impressive tree ferns and loaded with epiphytes.

Culmen The upper ridge of the maxilla.

Dry Forest Deciduous forest, with an obvious dry season when trees look dead and gray for several months; but in the rainy season appears green and lush.

Elfin Forest Stunted cloud forest (usually <5m tall) sculpted by wind on ridgetops; typically tangled, mossy, and impenetrable.

Gallery Forest Corridors of humid forest growing along watercourses, usually in otherwise dry or scrubby habitats.

Heliconia Genus of herbaceous flowering plants with long broad leaves (suggestive of banana leaves) growing in successional and swampy habitats, the ornate and colorful flowers attractive to hermits and other hummingbirds; also known as wild plantain or *platanillo*.

Holarctic Temperate regions of North America and Eurasia.

Humid Forest Evergreen broadleaf forest without a marked dry season; includes rainforest in lowlands and foothills, and cloud forest.

Lore(s) The area between a bird's eye and the base of its bill; dark lores or pale lores can greatly influence facial expression.

Mandible The lower half of the bill; sometimes called lower mandible.

Mangroves Specialized evergreen plant community permanently or periodically inundated with salt or brackish water; can be low and scrubby or tall and forest-like, some species with stilt roots.

Maxilla The upper half of the bill; sometimes called upper mandible.

Neotropical Of New World tropical regions.

Northern Mountains (Mts.) Collectively the Guanacaste and Tilarán Cordilleras.

Northwest Lowlands (nw. lowlands) Includes the north Pacific slope and adjacent areas of the north Caribbean slope, east to the Caño Negro region.

Overslurred Of a sound that rises then falls; overslurs may be brief and sharp, as in *píp*, or drawn-out, as in *peeéer*.

Pantropical Of tropical regions worldwide.

Páramo Above timberline, a low wet vegetation dominated by bamboo, cushion plants, grasses, low shrubs.

Pelagic Offshore, deeper marine waters beyond the continental shelf; also used for pelagic trips—ventures offshore in boats to seek oceanic birds not normally seen from land.

Rainforest Humid evergreen broadleaf forest with tall trees, many with buttress roots, and a fairly open understory that includes low palms.

Savanna Natural grassland with scattered trees and bushes, growing mainly on poorer soils.

Second Growth Successional-stage shrubby and wooded habitats typical of disturbed areas, roadsides; trees generally smaller and canopy lower than in undisturbed forest.

Speculum Iridescent panel on the upper surface of the secondaries in various duck species.

Underslurred Of a sound that falls then rises; see 'overslurred.'

Verbena Popular ornamental bush (usually with magenta flowers) favored by many hummingbirds.

***Figure 6.** Ornamental plantings of verbena bushes (inset of flowers at right) are often frequented by coquettes, Snowcap, and other smaller hummingbirds. Heredia Province, October 2021.*

BIOGEOGRAPHY

Birds and their habitats are not distributed randomly, and a basic understanding of how geography and climate shape the distribution of habitat types—and consequently bird distribution—can help you to both find and identify species. While there is still much to learn about the finer points of distribution and seasonal occurrence of birds in Costa Rica, here we offer an overview of the physical geography, climate, and habitat to give a sense of bird distribution in this remarkable country.

Geography

Centered at 10°N and 84°W, toward the southern end of Central America, Costa Rica is oriented roughly from northwest to southeast and fronts both the Pacific Ocean and the Caribbean Sea. In the far north, just south of Lake Nicaragua, there is no clear division between Pacific and Caribbean lowlands, but south from there a series of mountain ranges separates the two coastal slopes, influencing the climate and with it the vegetation and bird distribution.

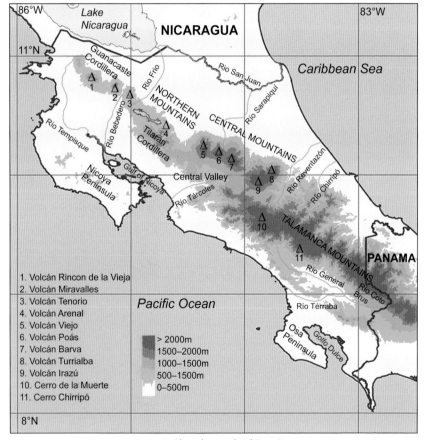

Figure 7. *Physical geography of Costa Rica.*

The Pacific coastal plain is overall rather narrow, whereas the Caribbean lowlands are very broad in the north, tapering down as they reach the Panama border in the south. An important inland extension of the Pacific slope is known as the Central Valley, ostensibly the watershed of the Tárcoles River, where slightly higher elevations (mainly 1000–1400m) and cooler temperatures are more agreeable to human settlement and where the capital city of San José is situated.

Costa Rica's spine of mountain ranges, increasing in height from northwest to southeast, comprises the Northern Mountains (including the Guanacaste and Tilarán Cordilleras, reaching 1600–2000m); the Central Mountains (volcanic massifs reaching 2700–3400m and essentially ringing the Central Valley, including the Poás, Barva, and Irazú Volcanoes); and the imposing wall of the Talamanca Mountains, which continues into western Panama and reaches 3800m at Cerro Chirripó, the highest peak in Costa Rica.

Spurs projecting from the Pacific side of the Talamancas form parallel south coastal mountain ranges that rise to about 1500m and enclose two interior valleys, El General Valley to the north and Coto Brus Valley to the south, which drain out into the Pacific via the Térraba River.

Climate and Habitat

Costa Rica lies in the latitude of the northeasterly trade winds, which blow in across warm Caribbean waters and bring rain throughout most of the year, helping make the Caribbean lowlands wet and green year-round. All else being equal, lowland swamp forest and rainforest would cover these lowlands, but all is not equal. Today, the Caribbean lowlands of Costa Rica constitute an environmental disaster akin to the English countryside, and have been mostly cleared by humans for agriculture, particularly cattle, sugar cane, pineapples, and bananas.

Many classic neotropical groups are well represented among birds typical of the original lowland habitats, including parrots, toucans, motmots, puffbirds, jacamars, woodcreepers, antbirds, and manakins. Some species are widespread, ranging from South America north to southern Mexico, such as Scaled Pigeon, Great Potoo, Collared Aracari, Black-cheeked Woodpecker, White-necked Jacobin, and Great Antshrike. Others are endemic to southern Central America (Honduras to Panama), such as Black-eared Wood Quail, Snowy Cotinga, Streak-crowned Antvireo, Tawny-chested Flycatcher, and Black-throated Wren. La Selva Biological Station, in the northern Caribbean lowlands, protects one of the few remaining areas of lowland rainforest in Costa Rica.

Sadly, however, forest reserves such as La Selva Biological Station exist only as small, far-flung islands in an expanding ocean of deforested and cut-over rolling lowlands, which, although deceptively green in aspect, are often rather lacking in birds, thanks to pesticides or other unseen human forces. In some areas, a few rainforest species of canopy and mid-levels—such as Short-billed Pigeon, Northern Mealy Amazon, Slaty-tailed Trogon, and Southern Black-faced Grosbeak—seem able to persist, at least for now, in tree-scattered agricultural and pasture lands, especially those with remnant forest corridors along watercourses; but understory and ground-dwelling species, not so much.

Reaching the mountains, moisture-laden air from the Caribbean rises and cools, dropping more rain and producing a very wet Caribbean foothill zone, where the steep terrain is not as amenable to agriculture or settlement. This narrow zone is thus relatively well forested but conversely not as easy to access as the lowlands. These humid foothill forests mark the northern limit for numerous species typical of the Andean foothills of northwestern South America, such as Green-fronted Lancebill, Red-headed Barbet, Brown-billed Scythebill, Red-faced Spinetail, Rufous-rumped Antwren, and Rufous-breasted Antthrush. They are also home to several species endemic to Central America, such as Snowcap, Lattice-tailed Trogon, Black-hooded Antthrush, Bare-necked Umbrellabird, Gray-headed Piprites, and Blue-and-gold Tanager. Braulio Carrillo National Park, only a short distance north of San José, offers access to this rich habitat zone.

With increasing elevation, temperatures cool and a temperate highland flora takes over, including cloud forest locally and, in the Central and Talamanca Mountains, extensive humid oak forest and bamboo. At the highest and coolest elevations, forest gives way to an open, wet shrubby habitat known as páramo. Long isolated from the highlands of northern Central America and eastern Panama, the highlands of Costa Rica and adjacent Panama are a major center of avian endemism. Some of the endemics are common and widespread, seen relatively easily, such as Fiery-throated and Volcano Hummingbirds, Prong-billed Barbet, Sooty Thrush, Long-tailed Silky, Collared Whitestart, and Sooty-capped Bush-tanager. Others are more local or elusive, including Silvery-throated Jay, Silvery-fronted Tapaculo, Ochraceous Pewee, Timberline Wren, Wrenthrush, and Peg-billed Finch. Access to this high-elevation habitat is easily achieved along the Pan-American Highway south of Cartago where it passes along the spine of Cerro de la Muerte.

Figure 8. *Costa Rica's Caribbean coast mostly comprises sandy beaches, often important nesting areas for sea turtles but relatively depauperate for waterbirds. Tortuguero National Park. Limón Province, July 2021.*

Figure 9. *Seasonally flooded forest borders the waterways of Tortuguero National Park. Limón Province, July 2021.*

Figure 10. *Costa Rica's Pacific coast is mostly rocky, often fringed with mangroves and scattered beaches. Puntarenas Province, October 2021.*

Figure 11. *Mangroves grow along much of the Pacific coast, some tall and extensive around river mouths (as here), others low and sparse. Tárcoles River, Puntarenas Province, October 2021.*

Figure 12. *Away from national parks and private reserves, which represent isolated islands of forest, most of the Caribbean slope lowlands are deforested, comprising an ocean of pasture, crops, and scattered trees. This rolling green landscape is often notably depauperate for birdlife. Alajuela Province, July 2021.*

Figure 13. *Not all agriculture is bad for birds. Rice fields can provide surrogate wetlands for crakes and other wading birds (such as these Jabirus), as well as for various seed-eating songbirds. Guanacaste Province, July 2021.*

Figure 14. *Large areas of the north Pacific lowlands have been deforested for agriculture, especially cattle ranching. In the background, clouds from the wet Caribbean slope spill through the pass adjacent to Volcán Miravalles. Guanacaste Province, July 2021.*

Figure 15. *The northwest lowlands include some extensive wetlands, at least in the wet season; in the background, hills of the Nicoya Peninsula are green with summer rains. Palo Verde National Park, Guanacaste Province, July 2021.*

Figure 16. *Very wet evergreen forest cloaks the steep foothills rising from the Caribbean lowlands; Braulio Carrillo National Park (550m elevation). Limón Province, July 2021.*

Figure 17. *Lush second growth with plants such as Heliconia and Cecropia often grows along roadsides and forest edge. In the absence of pesticides, such areas can be full of birds. Alajuela Province, October 2021.*

Figure 18. *Towering montane rainforest on slopes above the Coto Brus Valley. Zona Protectora Las Tablas (1600m). Puntarenas Province, April 2014.* © James R. Zook.

Figure 19. *Lowland rainforest (and bordering second growth on the left) on the Osa Peninsula (100m elevation). Puntarenas Province, October 2021.*

24

Figure 20. *Seasonally dry forest, here in the middle of the dry season; cf. same site in Figure 22. Guanacaste Province, February 2009.* © *James R. Zook.*

Figure 21. *Lowland rainforest understory is typically rather open, often featuring a diversity of palms (100m elevation). Heredia Province, October 2021.*

Figure 22. *Seasonally dry forest, here towards the end of the wet season; cf. same site in Figure 19. Guanacaste Province, November 2009.* © James R. Zook.

Figure 23. *Montane rainforest and cloud forest understory is denser and mossier than that of lowland rainforest, with numerous bromeliads and tree ferns. Tapantí National Park (1300m elevation). Cartago Province, October 2021.*

Figure 24. *Much of Costa Rica comprises rugged mountainous terrain, here the Volcán Irazú–Turrialba massif viewed from the east across the Reventazón drainage. Cartago Province, July 2021.*

Figure 25. *As with the lowlands, most of the mid-elevation slopes around the Central Valley have been cleared for agriculture, including large areas of sun coffee, a virtual ecological desert. Alajuela Province, July 2021.*

Figure 26. *Higher elevations of the Talamanca Mountains still have extensive areas of oak cloud forest mixed with stands of bamboo. San José Province (2800m elevation), July 2021.*

Figure 27. *Above treeline in the highest mountains one finds areas of páramo, a wet, shrubby and heath-like vegetation mixed with low bamboo. San José Province (3300m elevation), July 2021.*

Much of the mid-elevation and highland landscape, mainly on the slightly drier Pacific slopes of the mountains, has been cleared for cattle, coffee (mostly without shade trees, and thus another ecological desert), and human settlement. With clearing and climate warming, the Central Valley of Costa Rica increasingly acts as a corridor for species of cut-over and second-growth habitats to spread between Pacific and Caribbean slopes.

In the north of Costa Rica, the trade winds continue blowing across the relatively low mountains but have mostly dried out by the time they reach the Pacific slope. For about half the year this results in a sunny and windy dry season (roughly November to April) before the sun moves north and shifts wind patterns, allowing for a summer rainy season (roughly May to November). The original habitat of the north Pacific lowlands was mainly deciduous forest, or dry forest, with taller trees along watercourses, but today the region is largely deforested, mainly for cattle, sugar cane, and rice. Santa Rosa National Park protects a good example of the seasonally dry forest, which extends north to western Mexico, along with species such as Yellow-naped Amazon, Lesser Ground Cuckoo, Cinnamon Hummingbird, White-throated Magpie-Jay, Banded Wren, and Streak-backed Oriole. Deforestation of the relatively low passes between the volcanoes of the Guanacaste Cordillera, presumably in tandem with a warming climate, has enabled sundry species of more open lowland habitats—such as Double-striped Thick-knee and Yellow-headed Caracara—to expand their ranges across to the Caribbean slope.

Wetter forest, especially in the Pacific-slope foothills of the Northern Mountains, hosts a slightly different avifauna, including Rufous-necked Wood Rail (as a breeder, at least), Tody Motmot, Long-tailed Manakin, and White-eared Ground Sparrow, while open windswept slopes with rocky outcrops mark the southern range limit of Rock Wren and Rusty Sparrow. The peaks and higher slopes of the Nicoya Peninsula, rarely visited by birders, also have some wetter forest, along with a selection of birds typical of humid forest and edge habitats, including Little Tinamou, White Hawk, Ruddy and Violaceous Quail-Doves, Red-lored Amazon, White-necked Jacobin, Plain Xenops, Blue Seedeater, an enigmatic population of 'Vermiculated Screech Owl,' and, at least seasonally, Three-wattled Bellbird and Mountain Elaenia.

On higher ridges and peaks of the Northern Mountains, cooling air forms mist or cloud for much of the year, supporting lush wet forests known as cloud forests (or elfin forests, where stunted by wind), which can be rather abruptly demarcated from adjacent dry forest habitats on the Pacific slope. By virtue of topography, these cloud forests occur at appreciably lower elevations than those on the much higher Talamanca Mountains. The cloud forests of the Monteverde Biological Reserve exemplify this habitat, home to the iconic Resplendent Quetzal and Three-wattled Bellbird along with numerous species endemic to the highlands of Costa Rica and Panama, such as Black Guan, Bare-shanked Screech Owl, and Golden-browed Chlorophonia.

Large seasonal wetlands exist locally on the north Pacific slope and adjacent Caribbean slope, notably in the lower Tempisque River and Bebedero River drainages (which encompass Palo Verde National Park) and around Caño Negro, south of the inland sea of Lake Nicaragua. These wetlands host numerous wading birds, including a population of Jabirus, variable numbers of wintering waterfowl from North America, and the regionally endemic Nicaraguan Grackle.

On the south Pacific slope of Costa Rica, the Talamanca Mountains inland are so high that they mostly block the trade winds and create vortices whereby moisture-laden winds blow onshore and create a wetter environment year-round; the dry season here is mainly January to March, much shorter than in the north, and much of the lowland forest has an evergreen aspect similar to the Caribbean slope. Hence this region shares many bird species with the humid Caribbean lowlands; at the same time, its isolation from other wet forests has also resulted in a high degree of endemism centered around Golfo Dulce. Corcovado National Park is an increasingly isolated refuge for regional endemics that include numerous counterparts to Caribbean-slope species, such as Skutch's Screech Owl, Fiery-billed Aracari, White-crested Coquette, Charming Hummingbird, Yellow-billed Cotinga, and Black-cheeked Ant-tanager, this last species found only in Costa Rica.

The relatively dry interior valleys of the south Pacific slope host a number of species not found elsewhere in Costa Rica, including Ocellated Crake, Bran-colored Flycatcher, Northern Grassfinch, and Panama Thrush-tanager. As elsewhere in the country, however, the south Pacific lowlands are being increasingly deforested, creating a gateway for species of more open habitats to spread north from Panama, such as Savanna Hawk, Pearl Kite, Cayenne Lapwing, and Veraguas Parakeet.

The drier north Pacific slope and wetter south Pacific slope merge fairly abruptly in the vicinity of Carara National Park, helping explain the remarkable avian diversity found there. Species that replace one another on the central Pacific slope include Gray and Gray-lined Hawks, Black-headed and Baird's

Trogons, Hoffmann's and Red-crowned Woodpeckers, and Northern and Central American Beardless Tyrannulets.

Much of the Pacific coast is rocky, alternating with sandy beaches, and there are extensive areas of mangroves, home to Mangrove Rail, Panama Flycatcher, Mangrove Vireo, and the endemic Mangrove Hummingbird. Mainly in the Gulf of Nicoya, large areas of intertidal mudflats, along with bordering salt ponds, are attractive to migrant shorebirds and other waterbirds. Quite different, most of the Caribbean coast comprises steep sandy beaches backed by coconut plantations and in some places swamp forest, as found in Tortuguero National Park on the northern Caribbean coast.

Costa Rica's marine avifauna is not overly well known, but its secrets are slowly yielding to a small cadre of pioneering seabird enthusiasts. Pacific offshore waters are home to several widespread tropical seabirds, mainly boobies and terns, plus seasonally to migrants from distant regions—such as Tahiti and Parkinson's Petrels, plus Christmas and Galapagos Shearwaters from breeding grounds to the south; and Wedge-tailed Shearwater, Black and Least Storm Petrels from the north. Caribbean waters are poor in pelagic species, home to some boobies and terns, plus the occasional tropicbird or shearwater.

To summarize, the main terrestrial regions in Costa Rica are the Pacific slope (including the drier north Pacific slope, Central Valley, and wetter south Pacific slope); the highlands (comprising the Northern, Central, and Talamanca Mountains); and the Caribbean slope, including the wet Caribbean foothills. Because Costa Rica is such a small country, even a short visit may allow the visitor opportunity to sample most of these regions and habitats—and with them a remarkable diversity of birds.

TAXONOMY

Taxonomy is the science of classifying and naming things. For better or worse we are living in exciting if frustrating taxonomic times, as knowledge of avian taxonomy grows by leaps and bounds. Species are being shifted from one family to another, and families are being moved around to reflect their relatedness, despite the fact that it is inherently impossible to portray the multidimensional process of evolution in a linear list. One of the most heavily affected categories in this molecular revolution is that of genus, and the changes there are almost impossible to keep up with. Species, on the other hand, that elusive taxonomic level of most interest to birders, are being relatively ignored in all this higher-level work, where the focus is shifting toward genetic lineages, which may or may not reflect the more traditional concept of biological species (Howell 2021).

Taxonomy and Species

For professional ornithologists, let alone birders, it can be challenging if not impossible to keep pace with changing taxonomy and new names. With the advent of multiple bodies producing world lists, each with its own differing view of how species should be defined, the inconsistencies of what is treated as a species, or isn't, add to the challenge. For example, Plain Wren *Thryothorus modestus* of Stiles & Skutch (1989) became Plain Wren *Cantorchilus modestus* in Garrigues & Dean (2014), and has since been split by some authors into three species, including Isthmian Wren *Cantorchilus elutus*, which at first glance is not immediately connected to the Plain Wren of old.

If it helps, when thinking about different species concepts you might consider that the important word is *concept*, not *species*. That is, regardless of how humans define a species, it basically comes down to a matter of opinion, with no right or wrong (Howell 2021).

For this guide, we have tried to address the species status of Costa Rican birds in terms of related taxa in North America, Central America, and in some cases South America or Eurasia when we have relevant experience. The ability to travel worldwide and observe birds, combined with literature and museum work, including sound analysis, has enabled us to offer opinions about many taxa. We evaluated species status on a case-by-case basis and with reference to how closely related taxa are treated. Our taxonomic review of Costa Rican birds revealed over 100 taxa that could represent 'new' species but which are not widely recognized as such, ranging from painfully obvious and in dire need of splitting to weakly differentiated and poorly known (Howell & Dyer 2022). We refer interested readers to that paper, the conclusions of which are summarized in Appendix C.

Ideally, a species' English name should be simple, informative, and preferably memorable. 'Golf Foxtrot Lima,' we hear you respond to this sentiment. New names proposed here have for the most part attempted to disrupt the status quo as little as possible; most reflect geographic or plumage features, and a few commemorate persons who described the species or who have made major contributions to Costa Rican ornithology.

Many if not all of the splits we adopt or suggest here will undoubtedly become 'official' in the future. We hope that drawing attention to them acts as a laxative on the taxonomic constipation manifested by some committees and speeds the rate at which ignorance and inertia fall victim to reality. If nothing else, our insights may help humans more meaningfully catalogue the burgeoning environmental 'anthropogenocide' being inflicted on our planet.

And for birders who just want a simple answer to know what they can count on their lists? Well, there is none. We make no apologies for the realistic if sometimes ambiguous course we have adopted because, as the relationship page on some websites might say: 'It's complicated.' Birders who keep lists can choose one of several options to follow, although it's a bit like different religions. The thinking person realizes sooner or later that these different checklists, or species concepts, can't all be right, but often there's some comfort, or convenience, in following one or the other.

SPECIES
ACCOUNTS

CORMORANTS (PHALACROCORACIDAE; 1 SPECIES) Worldwide family of rather large diving birds with long, hook-tipped bills, fully webbed feet. Ages differ, sexes similar; adult appearance attained in 2–3 years.

NEOTROPIC CORMORANT *Phalacrocorax brasilianus* 64–70cm. Only cormorant in Costa Rica, but cf. slightly larger and longer-tailed Anhinga, which has sharply pointed bill, very long and pale-tipped tail. Widespread in varied wetland habitats, from ponds and rivers to mangroves and inshore coastal waters. Roosts on trees, rocky islets, sandbars; often perches with wings outstretched. Flies with fairly quick wingbeats, brief glides, often in lines and Vs like waterfowl or ibises. Locally in flocks of 100s. Imm. can fade to mostly whitish below. SOUNDS: Guttural grunts and croaks in interactions and when nesting. STATUS: Fairly common to common locally in lowlands, smaller numbers inland along rivers and at lakes; mostly below 1500m. (Americas.)

ANHINGAS (ANHINGIDAE; 1 SPECIES) Small pantropical family of long-necked, long-tailed diving waterbirds with sharply pointed bills, fully webbed feet. Ages/sexes differ; adult appearance attained in about 3 years. Wing molt synchronous, unlike gradual wing molt of cormorants.

ANHINGA *Anhinga anhinga* 84–94cm, WS 109–119cm. Varied wetland habitats, from small wooded ponds to lakes, rivers, mangroves. Distinctive, but cf. Neotropic Cormorant, which is often in the same areas. Perches on trees over water, often with wings outstretched, and soars readily on thermals. Flies with deep strong wingbeats, alternated with glides on flattish wings, the long tail usually spread slightly. Often swims with only neck above the surface, jerking along, hence a local name 'snakebird' (cormorants can also do this, however). Juv. has dirty buff head and neck, brown belly, duller upperwing panels than adult; 2nd-year like duller adult. Breeding male develops pale puffy plumes on head and neck, bright blue eyering. SOUNDS: Rasping and creaky short croaks, often in slightly stuttering or descending series. STATUS: Fairly common to uncommon locally on both slopes to 1000m, rarely wandering higher. (Tropical Americas.)

DUCKS (ANATIDAE; 12+ SPECIES) Familiar worldwide family usually associated with water. Ages differ slightly to distinctly; most species attain adult appearance within 1st year. Sexes similar in whistling ducks, different in other ducks (nonbr. males resemble females in late summer, but this plumage not typically seen in Costa Rica). A few other northern migrant ducks occur as irregular and rare winter visitors as far south as Costa Rica (Appendix B).

MUSCOVY DUCK *Cairina moschata* 66–87cm male>female. Large, very heavy-bodied duck of wetlands with adjacent cover, from forest streams to mangroves; perches readily in trees. Feeds by dabbling, often while wading in shallows. Distinctive, but widely domesticated; wild birds usually wary, mainly seen in flight. Signs of feral origin include extensively pink face (vs. mostly dark on wild birds) and variable white patches on head and body; black-bodied feral birds typically distinguished by mixed black-and-white on the largest upperwing and underwing coverts (vs. solidly white on wild birds). Male appreciably larger than female, obvious when together; juv. dark overall, usually with white spot on forewing. SOUNDS: Low quacks and hisses, rarely heard. STATUS: Scarce (mostly) to locally fairly common (in more remote and protected areas) on both slopes, mainly below 1200m; feral birds possible anywhere. (Tropical Americas.)

NEOTROPIC CORMORANT

imm.

adults

imm.

adults

ANHINGA

females

males

breeding colors

imm.

females

MUSCOVY DUCK

male

domestic and feral birds variable

34

*BLACK-BELLIED WHISTLING DUCK *Dendrocygna autumnalis* 46–51cm. Distinctive, long-legged, boldly patterned duck with coral-red bill. Varied freshwater and brackish habitats, from lakes and roadside ditches to flooded fields, mangroves. Mostly feeds by night, roosting by day in vegetation, often in trees. Flocks locally may be in 1000s. In flight, note bold white stripe on upperwing, dark underwing. Juv. duller overall with grayish bill, ghosting of adult plumage pattern; like adult within a few months. SOUNDS: High piping whistles, usually in short series of notes, mainly given in flight. STATUS: Fairly common to locally common on both slopes; small numbers increasingly seen inland, locally to 1500m. (Mexico and s. US to S America.)

FULVOUS WHISTLING DUCK *Dendrocygna bicolor* 48–54cm. Distinctive, long-legged, overall tawny duck found in freshwater and brackish habitats, from lakes and roadside ditches to flooded fields, mangroves; mostly feeds at night. Often in small flocks, mixing readily with more numerous Black-bellied Whistling Duck. In flight, note solidly dark wings, white U at tail base. SOUNDS: Nasal, slightly hoarse, usually 2-syllable whistles, distinct from high piping of Black-bellied Whistling Duck. STATUS: Uncommon locally in nw. lowlands; very rare to rare wanderer elsewhere. (Tropical Americas, Africa, Asia.)

DABBLING DUCKS (6+ species). All are winter migrants to Costa Rica, overall declining there as birds remain farther north in winter; recent pulses (since 2010) of larger numbers probably related to droughts in sw. US and Mexico. Best identified by overall size and shape, wing patterns in flight; also note bill shape and color, leg color. Takeoff typically direct from water, without a running start, and often vocalize when disturbed. Formerly all species placed in genus *Anas*.

NORTHERN PINTAIL *Anas acuta* 51–58cm. Winter migrant to varied wetland habitats, especially shallow freshwater. Feeds mainly by dabbling and up-ending. Elegant and long-necked with tapered tail, slender blue-gray bill, grayish legs. Adult male distinctive (imm. male resembles adult by early winter); other plumages overall paler and grayer than most dabbling ducks (but can be stained rusty in fall–early winter, cf. Fulvous Whistling Duck), best identified by overall shape, bill shape and color, wing pattern: underwings dusky overall, upperwing has broad white trailing edge to speculum. SOUNDS: Male gives high rolled *wirrrh*; female a slightly reedy quacking *kwerrk*. STATUS: Uncommon and local late Oct–early Mar in nw. lowlands, rare and irregular elsewhere; to 1500m. (Holarctic; winters to Cen America.)

GREEN-WINGED TEAL *Anas [crecca] carolinensis* 35–38cm. Rare winter migrant to varied wetland habitats, especially with muddy shallows. Feeds mainly by dabbling. Small, compact, and overall dark, with grayish legs. Adult male distinctive (imm. male resembles adult by mid-winter); female told by small size, buffy to whitish streak at sides of undertail coverts, dark upperwing with buffy leading edge to speculum. Cf. Blue-winged and Cinnamon Teal, which have larger bills, yellowish legs, pale blue forewing panels. SOUNDS: Male gives high, reedy, piping *kreek*; female a low rough quack. STATUS: Very rare and irregular Nov–Mar in nw. lowlands; exceptional elsewhere, mainly on Pacific slope. (Breeds N America, winters to Cen America.)

AMERICAN WIGEON *Mareca (Anas) americana* 43–51cm. Winter migrant to wetlands, lakes, adjacent flooded and grassy fields; often in small flocks. Feeds by grazing and dabbling. Note fairly stocky shape with small blue-gray bill tipped black, pointed tail, gray legs; white forewing of adult male striking in flight. Adult male distinctive (imm. male resembles adult by early winter); female told by small gray bill, overall ruddy plumage with grayer head and neck, rather plain breast and sides. SOUNDS: Male has high breathy whistle, *whiih*, often doubled or in short series; female a low grunting quack. STATUS: Uncommon to rare and local late Oct–early Apr in nw. lowlands; very rare elsewhere, occasionally to 1500m in Central Valley. (Breeds N America, winters to Cen America.)

BLACK-BELLIED WHISTLING DUCK

juv.

FULVOUS WHISTLING DUCK

NORTHERN PINTAIL

females

male (Oct–Jun)

females

male (Oct–Jun)

GREEN-WINGED TEAL

AMERICAN WIGEON

females

males (Oct–Jun)

BLUE-WINGED TEAL *Spatula (Anas) discors* 38–41cm. Commonest winter migrant duck in Costa Rica, found in varied wetland habitats, from lakes, small ponds, and flooded fields to quiet rivers and salt ponds; locally in flocks of 100s. Feeds mainly by dabbling and up-ending. Small and rather sleek, with yellowish legs. Adult male distinctive (imm. male resembles adult by mid-winter); female cold-toned with whitish spot at base of bill, dark eyestripe. Cf. much rarer Cinnamon Teal, Green-winged Teal. SOUNDS: Male gives slightly reedy, piping *pseep*; female a low quack. STATUS: Fairly common to locally common mid-Sep to Apr in nw. lowlands, a few earlier and into May; small numbers can occur elsewhere almost throughout, exceptionally to 3000m. (Breeds N America, winters to n. S America.)

CINNAMON TEAL *Spatula (Anas) cyanoptera* 38–41cm. Rare winter migrant to varied wetland habitats, most likely to be found among flocks of Blue-winged Teal. Feeds mainly by dabbling and up-ending. Small but rather stocky, with yellowish legs, relatively spatulate bill. Adult male distinctive (imm. male resembles adult by mid-winter); other plumages similar to Blue-winged Teal but warmer brown overall (beware other ducks stained rusty) with plainer face (no distinct dark eyestripe), more spatulate bill. Female Northern Shoveler has bigger bill, white tail sides. Cf. Green-winged Teal. SOUNDS: Male gives quiet crackling rattle, mainly in display; female a low quack. STATUS: Rare and irregular Oct–Mar in nw. lowlands; exceptional elsewhere, mainly on Pacific slope. (Americas.)

NORTHERN SHOVELER *Spatula (Anas) clypeata* 43–51cm. Winter migrant to wetland habitats, from lakes and sewage ponds to marshes with open water, salt ponds. Feeds mainly by dabbling. Note big head, long spatulate bill, orange legs. Adult male distinctive; female identified by big bill (longer than head); also note white tail sides. Imm. male resembles adult by late winter; many winter males 'messy,' with whitish crescent forward of eyes. SOUNDS: Male gives low muffled grunts; female a quiet quack. STATUS: Uncommon Oct–Apr in nw. lowlands and Central Valley, rare and irregular elsewhere; to 1500m. (Holarctic; winters to Cen America.)

SCAUPS (GENUS *AYTHYA*) (2+ species). Diving ducks that occur as winter migrants; like dabbling ducks, generally declining in Costa Rica as birds remain farther north in winter. Best identified by overall size and shape, head and bill patterns, wing patterns in flight. Unlike dabbling ducks, patter across water to takeoff. Mostly silent in winter, and spend much time sleeping.

LESSER SCAUP *Aythya affinis* 38–43cm. Winter migrant to ponds, lakes, other wetland habitats with open water; sometimes in flocks, occasionally 100s. Note slightly peaked hindcrown (can sleek down when diving to produce rounded head), blue-gray bill tipped black; broad white wingstripe on secondaries becomes pale gray on primaries. Male told from Ring-necked Duck by pale gray back, plainer bill; female by head and bill pattern, white wingstripe. STATUS: Uncommon to irregularly fairly common and local Nov–Mar (a few from Oct and into Apr) in nw. lowlands and Central Valley, to 1500m; scarce and irregular elsewhere. (Breeds N America, winters to n. S America.)

RING-NECKED DUCK *Aythya collaris* 41–46cm. Winter migrant to ponds, lakes, other wetland habitats with open water, often in more vegetated, less open situations than Lesser Scaup. Note slender bill with white subterminal band, relatively long tail; in flight shows broad, poorly contrasting grayish wingstripe. Male distinctive, with black back (imm. male resembles adult by late winter); female best told by grayish head sides with narrow white spectacles, diffuse whitish patch at base of bill, wing pattern; cf. Lesser Scaup. STATUS: Uncommon and local late Oct–Mar in nw. lowlands; very rare and irregular elsewhere. (Breeds N America, winters to Cen America.)

Blue-winged Teal

females

male (Oct–Jun)

Cinnamon Teal

females

male (Oct–Jun)

Northern Shoveler

male (Jun–Mar)

females

male (Oct–Jun)

Lesser Scaup

male (Oct–Jun)

females

Ring-necked Duck

male (Oct–Jun)

females

MASKED DUCK *Nomonyx (Oxyura) dominicus* 33–38cm. Rarely encountered denizen of freshwater wetlands with emergent vegetation, from lake edges and small ponds to roadside ditches. Found as singles or small groups, usually not associated with other species. Often mostly hidden in vegetation, at least during daytime; emerges at night on more open water to feed. Feeds by diving; rarely seen in flight (mainly dawn and dusk) but can spring into air, like a teal. Breeding male distinctive; female/imm. and nonbr. male have distinctive buff face cut by 2 horizontal dark stripes (beware similarity to ducklings of Black-bellied Whistling Duck, often found in same areas). Usually silent. STATUS: Scarce and local (nomadic?) on both slopes, mainly nw. lowlands, Central Valley, and s. Pacific slope; might show up anywhere, mainly below 1500m. (Tropical Americas.)

GREBES (PODICIPEDIDAE; 2+ SPECIES) Cosmopolitan family of small to fairly large diving waterbirds; rarely seen in flight. Ages differ; like adult in 1st year; sexes similar in plumage, but male averages bigger bill.

LEAST GREBE *Tachybaptus dominicus* 21–24cm. Small, dark grayish grebe of varied fresh and brackish habitats, from ponds and roadside ditches to fairly open lakes and mangroves; favors areas with emergent vegetation for cover, but sometimes out on open water. Found as singles or small groups, at times associating with appreciably bulkier Pied-billed Grebe. Note slender dark bill, golden eyes; broad white wingstripe rarely seen. SOUNDS: 'Song' a rapid, slightly pulsating, purring trill, recalling White-throated Crake but slightly lower, burrier; also a quacking *kwrek*, and bleating *eirhk!* Juv. has high, insistent, piping whistles. STATUS: Uncommon to fairly common but rather local on both slopes, to 1500m. (Tropical Americas.)

PIED-BILLED GREBE *Podilymbus podiceps* 28–33cm. Distinctive, chunky small grebe with stout pale bill. Found in varied wetland habitats, from roadside ditches and ponds to slow-moving rivers. Singles or small groups, at times associating loosely with other waterbirds, especially American Coot, Least Grebe. Breeding adult has ivory bill with black band; juv. bill appreciably more slender, dull pinkish overall. Narrow white trailing edge to wings rarely seen. SOUNDS: Complex 'song' a variable series of hollow clucks, coos, and grunts (can be given at night); also a rapid-paced, bleating chatter in greeting, and single quiet clucks. STATUS: Uncommon to scarce and local on both slopes, to 1500m; more widespread Sep–Apr. (Americas.)

FINFOOTS (HELIORNITHIDAE; 1 SPECIES) Distinctive, small pantropical family. Despite the name, Sungrebes favor shady areas, are not closely related to grebes, and do not dive to feed. Ages/sexes differ slightly (male cares for young); attains adult appearance in 1st year.

SUNGREBE *Heliornis fulica* 27–29cm. Small, easily overlooked swimming bird of unpolluted, typically slow-moving waterways with overhanging vegetation, including mangroves; can disperse to isolated lakes and ponds. Found as singles or pairs, usually swimming near shady cover. Picks for food on emergent and hanging vegetation and makes brief skittering dashes to snatch food near water surface. Flies readily when disturbed, pattering along the surface for takeoff; flight strong and low over water, when broad rounded tail conspicuous. Roosts on branches over water. Cheeks tawny on adult female, white on male; female bill and eyering flush red in breeding season. Juv. has whitish cheeks (tinged buff on female), duller bill than adult, pinkish-banded feet (yellowish on adult). SOUNDS: Often quiet, but at times utters a sharp clucking *wek!* and (in territorial interactions?) a short series of (usually 4) barking clucks, *kwek! kwek! kwek! kw'eh.* 'Song' a series of far-carrying, hollow hoots, *ook, ook,...*, usually 1 about every 4 secs, sometimes faster paced. STATUS: Uncommon to fairly common on Caribbean slope, scarce in s. Pacific lowlands; locally to 800m. (Tropical Americas.)

MASKED DUCK

breeding male
(year-round)

females

nonbr. male
(year-round)

duckling of
Black-bellied
Whistling Duck

LEAST GREBE

juv. (year-round)

nonbr.
(year-round)

breeding
(year-round)

PIED-BILLED GREBE

juv. (year-round)

nonbr.
(year-round)

breeding
(year-round)

SUNGREBE

breeding
female

male

40

PETRELS (PROCELLARIIDAE; 8+ SPECIES) Worldwide family of mostly medium-size, superficially gull-like seabirds with long narrow wings, webbed feet, hook-tipped bills with nostrils encased in a tube at top. Ages/sexes similar. Mostly silent at sea. No species breeds in Costa Rica.

WEDGE-TAILED SHEARWATER *Ardenna pacifica* 43–47cm, WS 99–109cm. Commonest large shearwater off Pacific coast, but rarely seen from land. Locally in flocks of 100s that mix in feeding and rafting flocks with boobies, terns, other shearwaters. In calm, flight typically unhurried with wings pressed forward slightly and crooked; wingbeats shallow and easy, interspersed with glides on slightly arched wings; wheels higher in strong winds but usually not steeply. Most birds white-bodied but small numbers of dark morphs occur. Note light build with small head, relatively broad crooked wings, long tapered tail, grayish bill (small numbers of both morphs have pinkish bill with darker tip); cf. bigger and bulkier Pink-footed Shearwater. STATUS: Fairly common to common nonbr. migrant, mainly Nov–Apr, smaller numbers May–Oct. (Tropical Pacific and Indian Oceans.)

PINK-FOOTED SHEARWATER *Ardenna creatopus* 45–48cm, WS 110–118cm. Pacific, offshore. Singles or small groups passing by, or mixed with flocks of Wedge-tailed Shearwaters. Typically flies with languid wingbeats and easy glides; can wheel high and steeply when windy. Larger and bulkier than Wedge-tailed with bigger head, broader wings held less crooked in flight, shorter and broader, less tapered tail; note pink bill with black tip. Underparts and underwings white overall with variable dusky markings, rarely mostly dusky. STATUS: Uncommon to rare nonbr. migrant, mainly Apr–May, Sep–Nov. (Breeds Dec–May in Chile, migrant to NE Pacific.)

PARKINSON'S PETREL *Procellaria parkinsoni* 41–46cm, WS 112–123cm. Pacific, offshore. Large dark petrel that scavenges at fishing boats; likely to be found as singles or small groups, not usually with rafts of shearwaters. Flies with easy smooth wingbeats and buoyant glides in calm to light winds, with wheeling glides and bouts of loose flapping in moderate winds. Distinctive, with very dark plumage, pale creamy bill with dusky to blackish tip, black legs and feet. STATUS: Scarce to seasonally uncommon nonbr. migrant, mainly Mar–Oct, usually well offshore. (Breeds Nov–May in New Zealand, migrant to tropical E Pacific.)

GALAPAGOS PETREL *Pterodroma phaeopygia* 39–42cm, WS 99–110cm. Pacific, offshore. Distinctive, medium-large petrel with long narrow wings, tapered tail, variable dark hood, and boldly patterned underwings. In light winds, flies with languid wingbeats and long shearing glides on slightly bowed wings; in stronger winds, wheels and banks but not steeply, with little flapping. Sometimes associates with feeding flocks of boobies, terns, shearwaters. STATUS: Scarce nonbr. migrant, possible year-round, usually well offshore. (Breeds year-round in Galapagos, ranges in tropical E Pacific.)

TAHITI PETREL *Pseudobulweria rostrata* 38–42cm, WS 101–108cm. Pacific, offshore. Distinctive, fairly large petrel with very long narrow wings, tapered tail, very stout black bill; note white body contrasting with dark underwings (sometimes showing paler median stripe). In light winds, flies with languid wingbeats and long shearing glides on wings held out rather straight from body; in stronger winds, wheels and banks but not steeply, with little flapping. Feeds by scavenging, thus not usually with feeding flocks. STATUS: Scarce to uncommon nonbr. migrant, mainly Mar–Nov, usually well offshore. (Tropical Pacific.)

light morphs

WEDGE-TAILED SHEARWATER

dark morph

PINK-FOOTED SHEARWATER

PARKINSON'S PETREL

GALAPAGOS PETREL

TAHITI PETREL

42

AUDUBON'S SHEARWATER *Puffinus lherminieri* 30–33cm, WS 65–74cm. Caribbean, offshore. Only small black-and-white shearwater to be expected off Caribbean coast. Likely to be seen as singles, on occasion in small groups; may associate with feeding flocks of boobies and terns. In light winds, flies low to water with quick stiff wingbeats and short glides; in stronger winds can wheel for longer periods but not steeply. Note relatively long tail, dark undertail coverts. STATUS: Scarce nonbr. migrant, seasonal status poorly known. (Breeds Caribbean region, ranges in tropical w. Atlantic.)

GALAPAGOS SHEARWATER *Puffinus subalaris* 28–31cm, WS 63–70cm. Pacific, offshore. Only small black-and-white shearwater regular off Pacific coast, where can occur in sizeable rafts and feeding flocks with Wedge-tailed Shearwaters, terns, boobies. Flight quick and low to water with fluttery wingbeats, brief glides; often raises head in flight. Note cleanly demarcated dark/white border to face and neck sides, narrow whitish spectacles, dark undertail coverts. Underwing coverts whitish on most birds but dark overall on others (these may represent cryptic species; study needed). Cf. vagrant Black-vented Shearwater (Appendix B). STATUS: Irregularly fairly common to common nonbr. migrant, year-round. (Breeds year-round in Galapagos, ranges in tropical E Pacific.)

CHRISTMAS SHEARWATER *Puffinus nativitatis* 33–38cm, WS 83–92cm. Pacific, offshore. Usually found as singles, sometimes with feeding and rafting flocks of Wedge-tailed and Galapagos Shearwaters. Flight usually rather low with quick stiff wingbeats, short glides, but can wheel higher in strong winds. Note small size, overall rather uniform, dark chocolate-brown plumage, slender black bill, ample tail; cf. larger but more lightly built dark-morph Wedge-tailed Shearwater; vagrant Sooty Shearwater (Appendix B). STATUS: Scarce nonbr. migrant, mainly Mar–Oct. (Tropical Pacific.)

NORTHERN STORM PETRELS (HYDROBATIDAE; 3+ SPECIES) Widespread
family of very small oceanic birds rarely seen from mainland; mostly silent away from breeding grounds. In Costa Rica, known only from Pacific waters. Ages/sexes similar. Several other species occur farther offshore (Appendices A–B) but not likely to be found regularly on day trips.

BLACK STORM PETREL *Halocyptena (Hydrobates) melania* 21.5–23cm; WS 50–55cm. Very large dark storm petrel with deeply forked tail; often feeds and rafts with Least Storm Petrel. Flight typically strong and unhurried, with deep languid wingbeats and easy sailing glides; in strong winds can bank in low arcs. Note deeply forked tail, big feet (which often dangle), blackish plumage. Farther offshore, cf. Markham's and dark-rumped Leach's Storm Petrels (Appendix B). STATUS: Fairly common to common nonbr. migrant, most numerous Oct–May; rarely may be seen from shore. (E Pacific.)

LEAST STORM PETREL *Halocyptena (Hydrobates) microsoma* 13.5–15cm; WS 32–36cm. Distinctive, tiny dark storm petrel with rather short, tapered tail; often feeds and rafts with much larger Black Storm Petrel. Flight typically quick, with little or no gliding and deep, slightly clipped wingbeats that can suggest a mini Black Storm Petrel. STATUS: Fairly common to common nonbr. migrant, most numerous Nov–May; rarely may be seen from shore. (E Pacific.)

PERUVIAN [WEDGE-RUMPED] STORM PETREL *Halocyptena (Hydrobates) [tethys] kelsalli* 14.5–15.5cm; WS 33–37cm. No other white-rumped storm petrel regular over warmer nearshore waters, but cf. Galapagos, Leach's, and Wilson's Storm Petrels (Appendix B): note big white rump patch (at rest, white can be all but hidden), flight manner. Often associates with Least and Black Storm Petrels; flies with deep wingbeats and only brief glides, much like Least. STATUS: Uncommon to fairly common nonbr. migrant, most numerous May–Nov. (Tropical E Pacific.)

AUDUBON'S SHEARWATER

GALAPAGOS SHEARWATER

dark-winged

white-winged

CHRISTMAS SHEARWATER

BLACK STORM PETREL

LEAST STORM PETREL

PERUVIAN STORM PETREL

44

FRIGATEBIRDS (FREGATIDAE; 1+ SPECIES) Very large but lightweight, mostly black seabirds with long crooked wings, deeply forked tails that can be held closed in a point. Ages/sexes differ; adult male has inflatable red throat pouch in display; adult appearance attained in about 5–6 years.

MAGNIFICENT FRIGATEBIRD *Fregata magnificens* 90–110cm, WS 200–240cm. Pacific and Caribbean coastal and inshore waters; often around fishing harbors, roosting on ship rigging, in mangroves at river mouths; does not alight on water; ranges inland a short distance to drink fresh water and splash-bathe at small lakes, rivers. Flight easy and buoyant with slow deep wingbeats, frequent effortless soaring, often in kettles high overhead; plucks food from sea surface with long hooked bill and also pirates terns, boobies, other seabirds. No similar species occur in coastal Costa Rica (Great Frigatebird breeds far offshore on Cocos I.). Adult male wholly glossy black with distensible red throat balloon inflated mainly in display; female has black head, white chest; juv./1st-cycle has white head and body with pointed black patches at breast sides. Complex age/sex plumage progression to adult plumage: 2nd-cycle has mostly white head and body; 3rd-cycle starts to fill in with black on head and belly; 4th-cycle like adult with variable whitish mottling in black areas; 5th-cycle ostensibly like adult. **SOUNDS:** Soft wheezy warbling and bill rattling, mostly in display. **STATUS:** Fairly common to common along both coasts; breeds very locally on islands off Pacific coast; very rare wanderer well inland, mainly in stormy weather. (Tropical Americas and Galapagos.)

PELICANS (PELECANIDAE; 2 SPECIES) Small worldwide family of very large, heavy-bodied aquatic birds with long bills and distensible throat pouches. Difficult to misidentify. Ages differ, sexes similar; attain adult appearance in about 3 years. Some seasonal change in adult appearance. Adults mostly silent, rarely uttering grunts and hisses; begging nestlings can be noisy.

BROWN PELICAN *Pelecanus occidentalis* 112–137cm, WS 190–255cm. Essentially unmistakable large dark waterbird of coastal and inshore waters, river mouths, adjacent lagoons, mangroves; nests on inshore islands. Often rests on sandbars and beaches with gulls, terns, cormorants, other waterbirds, also perches on pilings, boats, in mangroves. Singles and lines fly low over the waves, gliding easily between bouts of measured flapping; at times sails and soars high overhead. Feeds by plunge-diving, twisting abruptly on entry into the water. Adult silvery gray above, dark below; nonbr. plumage has white head and neck, dull eyes; breeding plumage has dark brown hindneck, eye becomes white; post-breeding adult has white crown spotted dusky. Juv/1st-year dark brown overall with white belly, broad white median stripe on dark underwing; 2nd-year like messy adult. **STATUS:** Fairly common to common along both coasts and over inshore waters, especially Pacific where breeds locally; rare and irregular inland. (Americas.)

AMERICAN WHITE PELICAN *Pelecanus erythrorhynchos* 145–165cm, WS 240–290cm. Very rare winter migrant. Huge, mostly white waterbird that could occur at lakes, wetlands, coastal lagoons. Essentially unmistakable, but at long range in flight, cf. Wood Stork. Singles or groups feed while swimming and submerging bill, not by diving. Soars readily, at times in kettles with other waterbirds and vultures. 1st-year has paler, more pinkish face, bill, and legs than adult, extensive black on inner secondaries and greater coverts, faint dusky wash to upperwing coverts. 2nd/3rd-year has brighter, more orangey face, bill, legs, less black on upperwings than 1st-year, often develops dark mottling on upperwing coverts. **STATUS:** Very rare and irregular nonbr. migrant to both slopes, mainly nw. lowlands, Dec–Apr. (Breeds N America to Mexico, winters to Cen America.)

MAGNIFICENT FRIGATEBIRD

adult males

1st-year

adult female

BROWN PELICAN

adults

1st-years

nonbr.

breeding

AMERICAN WHITE PELICAN

nonbr.

46

BOOBIES (SULIDAE; 6 SPECIES) Small worldwide family of large, streamlined, plunge-diving oceanic birds. Ages differ, sexes similar or differ in face and bill colors, voice; attain adult appearance in 2–4 years. Vocal mostly on breeding grounds but can be heard in feeding interactions.

BREWSTER'S BROWN BOOBY *Sula [leucogaster] brewsteri* 68–75cm, WS 135–153cm. Pacific inshore waters. Commonest and most frequently seen coastal booby, sometimes enters harbors, perches on boats, pilings; nests colonially and roosts on inshore rocks and islands. Often joins feeding flocks with terns, shearwaters. Adult distinctive, with sharply demarcated clean white belly, solidly brown upperparts; male crown pale milky, at times extending to most of neck, face slaty bluish; female face pale yellow, bill pale pinkish. Juv. has ghosting of adult pattern, whitish underwing coverts contrast with darker body. Older imm. has body variably mottled whitish and brown. **SOUNDS:** Male gives high wheezy whistles, female gruff brays. **STATUS:** Fairly common to common off and along Pacific coast, breeding locally, including Cocos I. (Tropical E Pacific.)

BLUE-FOOTED BOOBY *Sula nebouxii* 71–79cm, WS 148–166cm. Pacific inshore waters; often seen from shore; regularly roosts with Brewster's Brown Booby on inshore rocks. Often circles high and feeds by steep plunge dives, unlike lower, shallower-angle dives typical of Brewster's Brown. Relatively large with fairly slender grayish bill, distinctive white hindneck and rump patches, white center and tip of tail; also note white back scalloping. Bright blue feet develop in 2nd year; feet grayish on juv. Cf. Brewster's Brown Booby, imm. Nazca and Masked Boobies. **STATUS:** Irregular, rare to uncommon nonbr. migrant year-round to Pacific coast, including Gulf of Nicoya. (E Pacific.)

MASKED BOOBY *Sula dactylatra* 73–81cm, WS 150–170cm. Pacific and Caribbean offshore waters, unlikely to be seen from land. Mostly well offshore, alone or with feeding flocks of other boobies, terns, shearwaters. All ages have stout yellowish bill (rich yellow on some Pacific adults, cf. Nazca Booby), dark face, extensively white underwings, black tail (rarely some white at base on adults). Imms. variable, most have broad white neck collar, often some white on back and rump; however, some Pacific imms. are wholly dark above, not safely told from juv. Nazca; adult bill colors start to show in 2nd or 3rd year. Also cf. Blue-footed Booby, white morph Red-footed Booby. **STATUS:** Uncommon nonbr. migrant year-round to Pacific offshore waters, rare in nearshore waters; rarely reported off Caribbean coast. (Tropical oceans worldwide.)

NAZCA [MASKED] BOOBY *Sula [dactylatra] granti* 73–81cm, WS 150–170cm. Pacific, offshore waters, unlikely to be seen from land. Habits much like Masked Booby but tends to favor shelf waters vs. deeper offshore waters of Masked, and thus more likely to be encountered on day trips. Adult has diagnostic pinkish-orange bill (beware, apparent orange vs. yellow bill colors can be affected greatly by lighting), usually some white on base of central tail feathers; imm. not safely told from darker imm. Masked until white in central tail or adult bill colors start to show, but averages thicker black underwing margins; older imm. more often has dark shawl on neck sides vs. clean white neck of Masked. **STATUS:** Uncommon to fairly common nonbr. migrant year-round in Pacific waters. (E Pacific, breeds mainly on Galapagos.)

BREWSTER'S BROWN BOOBY

male

1st-year

juv.

female

adult male

BLUE-FOOTED BOOBY

adults

juv.

adult

juv.

MASKED BOOBY

adult

adults

juv.

juvs.

NAZCA BOOBY

juv.

adult

juv.

adult

48

ATLANTIC BROWN BOOBY *Sula leucogaster* 68–75cm, WS 135–153cm. Caribbean; mainly offshore but may be seen from land near Limón. Usually singles or small groups, feeding or rafting on water. Slightly larger and bulkier than Red-footed Booby, with heavier flight, less crooked wings; imm. body darker than whitish underwing coverts (reverse of imm. and brown morph Red-footed) and upperparts solidly brown, lacking white tail tip often shown by imm. Red-footed. Cf. imm. Masked Booby. Adult male has yellow face, ivory to pale greenish bill; female has pale yellow face, pinkish bill. **SOUNDS:** Male gives high wheezy whistles, female gruff brays. **STATUS:** Uncommon in Caribbean waters; small colony on islets near Uvita I. (Tropical Atlantic.)

RED-FOOTED BOOBY *Sula sula* 66–76cm, WS 130–150cm. Pacific and Caribbean, offshore; only exceptionally seen from land. Mostly alone or with feeding flocks of other boobies, terns, shearwaters; often curious around boats and ships, roosts on rigging. Smallest, most lightly built booby with highly variable plumage. Diagnostic bright red feet develop in 2nd year, pinkish on juv. (rarely pinkish on juv. brown boobies). Note crooked wings, long tail, maneuverable flight. Imm. and brown morph told from brown boobies by structure, paler body contrasting with dark underwings; imm. bill often pinkish with dark tip, tail usually has white tip. On all adults note pale bluish bill, pink throat patch. White-tailed morphs occur in Caribbean, dark-tailed morphs in Pacific; Cocos I. population almost all brown morphs. Cf. adult Masked and Nazca Boobies. **STATUS:** Uncommon to fairly common year-round in Pacific waters, usually well offshore; birds over nearer shore waters mainly imms; small colony found in 2000s on inshore islet near mouth of Sierpe River (and breeds commonly on Cocos I.). Very rare on Caribbean coast (mainly storm-blown). (Tropical oceans worldwide.)

TROPICBIRDS (PHAETHONTIDAE; 1+ SPECIES) Small family of spectacular plunge-diving seabirds found worldwide in tropical oceans. Ages differ, sexes similar; adult appearance attained in about 2 years.

RED-BILLED TROPICBIRD *Phaethon aethereus* 43–50cm (+ streamers), WS 97–110cm. Pacific, offshore. Spectacular, heavy-bodied oceanic bird, overall gleaming white with black leading wedge to outer wing, narrow dark barring on back. Cf. Royal Tern (p. 54). Flies with hurried, ungraceful wingbeats and plunge-dives from high up, causing a 'whale-blow splash' of water. Often rests on water, tail streamers curved up like a rooster; at times attracted to boats and ships, when appears magically overhead then disappears. Adult has red bill, long tail streamers; juv. has yellowish bill, short tail tipped black. 2nd-year like adult with orange-red bill, shorter tail streamers. Mostly silent at sea. **STATUS:** Uncommon nonbr. visitor year-round to Pacific waters, usually well offshore; may also occur rarely off Caribbean coast. (Tropical Americas and Atlantic.)

ATLANTIC BROWN BOOBY

male

1st-years

adult females

RED-FOOTED BOOBY

older imm.
white morph

1st-years (all morphs similar)

dark-tailed
adults

white-tailed adults

RED-BILLED TROPICBIRD

1st-year

adults

50

JAEGERS (STERCORARIIDAE; 3+ SPECIES) Small family of rather gull-like oceanic birds that feed mainly by pirating other birds, especially gulls, terns, shearwaters. Ages differ, sexes similar with females averaging larger. Adult plumage attained in about 3 years. ID of imms. can be very difficult, best to focus on structure and a few key plumage features, especially shape of any tail projections, extent and pattern of white wing flashes. Known as skuas in Old World.

POMARINE JAEGER (SKUA) *Stercorarius pomarinus* 44–51cm (+ 6–11cm adult tail projections). Pacific and Caribbean, offshore. Largest jaeger, chases mainly large shearwaters and gulls, less often terns. Direct flight rather heavy and steady, with powerful wingbeats; chases rarely prolonged and aerobatic. Sometimes scavenges at fishing boats; can be found with rafting flocks of shearwaters. Note relatively big head and bill, broad wings, and broad, blunt-tipped tail projections. All ages can be dark overall with reduced white wing flashes; adult dark morph uncommon. 1st-year has heavily barred underwings, 2nd-year has reduced barring on underwing coverts, 3rd-year and older typically have solidly dark underwing coverts. STATUS: Uncommon to fairly common nonbr. migrant to Pacific waters, mainly Aug–Apr; usually well offshore. Probably uncommon Sep–Apr in Caribbean, but few records. (Breeds n. Eurasia and N America, winters widely at sea.)

PARASITIC JAEGER (ARCTIC SKUA) *Stercorarius parasiticus* 40–44cm (+ 6–10cm adult tail projections). Pacific and Caribbean, mainly offshore; unlike other jaegers, regularly seen from shore. Chases mainly terns, smaller gulls. Flight strong and direct, suggesting a falcon; chases often persistent and aerobatic. Note relatively small head, slender bill, sharply pointed tail projections, crescent of white primary shafts on upperwing. All ages can be dark overall with reduced white wing flashes; adult dark morph fairly common. Juv. often relatively rusty-toned, unlike colder-toned juv. Pomarine and Long-tailed. Ageing as in Pomarine Jaeger. STATUS: Uncommon to fairly common nonbr. migrant to Pacific waters, mainly Aug–Oct, Mar–Apr, small numbers in winter; scarce off Caribbean coast. (Breeds n. Eurasia and N America, winters widely at sea.)

LONG-TAILED JAEGER (SKUA) *Stercorarius longicaudus* 37–41cm (+ 14–21cm adult tail projections). Pacific, offshore. Smallest, most lightly built jaeger; chases mainly terns, small gulls, phalaropes, storm petrels. Flight strong but graceful, with buoyant wingbeats, suggests a smaller tern. Note relatively short neck, small bill, only 2–3 white primary shafts on upperwing, finely pointed tail projections of older imm. and adult; juv. has relatively long but bluntly-tipped tail points. Juv./1st-year can be dark overall, but adult only has light morph. Ageing as in Pomarine Jaeger. STATUS: Scarce nonbr. migrant, usually well offshore, mainly Aug–Nov, Mar–May. (Breeds n. Eurasia and N America, winters at sea mainly in S Hemisphere.)

GULLS (LARIDAE; 5+ SPECIES) Worldwide family of familiar web-footed birds often found near water. Ages differ, sexes similar but males average larger, bigger-billed. Adult appearance attained in 2 years for smaller species (hence, 2-year gulls), up to 4 years or longer in large species (4-year gulls); 2nd- and 3rd-year plumages highly variable, intermediate between 1st-year and adult. Seasonal variation mainly in head pattern, bill color and pattern. Few species regular in Costa Rica, but several species occur as vagrants or rare migrants (Appendix B). Varied crowing and mewing calls mainly in interactions, mentioned only when obviously useful for ID.

SABINE'S GULL *Xema sabini* 32–35cm. Pacific, offshore. Small, boldly marked 2-year gull rarely seen from land. Singles or small groups, sometimes in association with feeding groups of terns, other gulls, shearwaters. Flight direct and buoyant, rather tern-like. Distinctive and striking in flight with gleaming white triangles on upperwings; also note forked tail. Adult attains dark slaty hood in late winter; juv. molts over 1st winter into adult-like plumage with partial dark hood or hindneck patch. STATUS: Uncommon nonbr. migrant offshore, mainly Aug–Nov, Mar–May. (Breeds n. Eurasia and N America, winters mainly S Hemisphere.)

POMARINE JAEGER

juv.
(Oct–Mar)

adults

breeding
(Apr–Oct)

dark adult

nonbr.
(Aug–Mar)

PARASITIC JAEGER

adults

breeding
(Apr–Oct)

juv.
(Aug–Mar)

dark adult

nonbr.
(Aug–Mar)

LONG-TAILED JAEGER

nonbr.
(Aug–Mar)

breeding
(Apr–Oct)

adults

juvs.
(Aug–Mar)

SABINE'S GULL

breeding
(Mar–Sep)

juvs.
(Aug–Nov)

adults

nonbr.
(Sep–Apr)

LAUGHING GULL *Leucophaeus atricilla* 38–43cm. Medium-size, long-winged 3-year gull with dark bill and legs. Commonest gull in Costa Rica, found on beaches, at river mouths, coastal lagoons, harbors, dumps, over inshore waters; rarely inland along rivers, at lakes; locally in flocks of 100s, even low 1000s. Often with flocks of terns, other gulls. Fairly distinctive, but cf. smaller, more compact, and smaller-billed Franklin's Gull. Adult has slaty-gray upperparts, blackish hood with narrow white eye-arcs in breeding plumage, when bill and legs become reddish. Nonbr. and imm. have smudged dusky mask through eyes, blackish to dark red legs and bill. Juv. dark brown overall with scaly pale edgings above, solidly black tail band; soon attains gray back, whiter head and underparts. 2nd-year like dull adult with more black in wing-tip, sometimes black in tail. SOUNDS: Varied, nasal laughing and yelping cries; 1st-year has high-pitched whistles. STATUS: Fairly common to common nonbr. migrant to both coasts; main numbers Sep–Apr, smaller numbers through summer; rare and irregular inland, mainly fall–winter. (Breeds N America to Caribbean, winters to S America.)

FRANKLIN'S GULL *Leucophaeus pipixcan* 35–38cm. Medium-small 3-year gull with dark bill and legs. Mainly coastal, but also ranges inland and over inshore waters; spring migrant flocks can number 100s, streaming into lines of 1000s as they pass by; otherwise, singles or flocks occur at river mouths, harbors, coastal lagoons, inland at lakes and flooded fields. Associates readily with Laughing Gulls, terns, other waterbirds. Slightly smaller, more lightly built than Laughing Gull, with smaller bill, more rounded wing-tips, thicker white eye-arcs; spring adults often have strong pink blush to underparts (Laughing can have pale blush). Adult wing-tip boldly patterned black-and-white, unlike Laughing; imm./nonbr. plumages have distinctive blackish half-hood. Black tail band of 1st-winter Franklin's does not reach to tail sides, but 1st-year Laughing often attains some white tail feathers. SOUNDS: Yelping and laughing calls higher, more mewing than crowing calls of Laughing Gull. STATUS: Common to fairly common Mar–May along and off Pacific coast, uncommon to fairly common Oct–Nov; scarce and irregular in winter. Rare at any season on Caribbean coast. (Breeds N America, winters S America.)

RING-BILLED GULL *Larus delawarensis* 44–52cm. Rare medium-size 3-year gull with pale gray back. Mainly coastal, at river mouths, beaches, coastal lagoons. Usually single imms. in association with flocks of other gulls, terns. Adult distinctive (but very rare in Costa Rica), with yellow legs, pale eyes, neat black bill ring (no red on bill). 1st-year rather pale overall, with pinkish legs, whitish underwings, clean-cut black/white tail pattern, pale gray inner primaries; cf. 2nd-year Smithsonian Gull. 2nd-year resembles duller adult with more black in wing-tip, often some black on tail, greenish-yellow legs. STATUS: Rare and irregular nonbr. migrant to both coasts, mainly Nov–Apr. (Breeds N America, winters to Cen America.)

*SMITHSONIAN (AMERICAN HERRING) GULL *Larus [argentatus] smithsonianus* 56–67cm. Large 4-year gull with pink legs, pale gray back; male appreciably larger and bigger-billed than female. Usually single imms. or small numbers with flocks of other waterbirds at harbors, river mouths, lagoons, beaches. Adult distinctive (but very rare in Costa Rica), with pink legs, black wing-tips, pale eyes, variable dusky streaking on head and neck in nonbr. 1st-year mottled brownish overall, often with paler head, paler panel on inner primaries in flight, variable pinkish at base of bill. The only regularly occurring large gull in Costa Rica, but cf. Appendix B. 2nd- and 3rd-years highly variable; 2nd-year pattern resembles smaller 1st-year Ring-billed Gull but messier, lacks clean black/white tail pattern of Ring-billed. STATUS: Rare to uncommon nonbr. migrant to both coasts, mainly Nov–Apr. (Breeds N America, winters to Cen America.)

LAUGHING GULL

1st-years

breeding
(Jan–Aug)

adults

nonbr.
(Jul–Mar)

FRANKLIN'S GULL

1st-years

breeding
(Mar–Aug)

adults

nonbr.
(Aug–Mar)

breeding
(Feb–Aug)

RING-BILLED GULL

adults

1st-years
(Sep–Jul)

nonbr.
(Aug–Mar)

older imms.

breeding
(Feb–Aug)

adults

SMITHSONIAN GULL

1st-years
(Sep–Jul)

nonbr.
(Aug–Mar)

TERNS (LARIDAE; 13+ SPECIES) Worldwide group of waterbirds that resemble gulls but have pointed bills, shorter legs, and typically are smaller, more graceful, with forked tails. Unlike gulls, rarely alight on water, mostly feed by plunge-diving for small fish. Ages differ, sexes similar but males average larger, bigger-billed. Adult appearance attained in 2–3 years; imm. plumages typically resemble nonbr. adults. Seasonal variation mainly in head pattern.

*SANDWICH TERN *Thalasseus sandvicensis* 34–36cm (+ 2.5cm adult tail streamers). Pacific and Caribbean coasts, at beaches, river mouths, coastal lagoons, over inshore waters. Often in flocks with other terns, gulls, skimmers. Distinctive, medium-size tern with shaggy crest, white body, slender black bill tipped yellow on adult, black legs. 1st-year bill black with little or no pale tip; dark spots and chevrons on juv. back soon replaced with plain pale gray. Cf. Gull-billed Tern. SOUNDS: Grating, screechy and rasping calls, such as *krriik* and *krrek*, distinct from smaller *Sterna* terns but much like Elegant Tern; 1st-year has high piping whistles. STATUS: Fairly common to common nonbr. migrant on both coasts, mainly Sep–May; smaller numbers of imms. occur through summer. (Breeds N Atlantic, winters to S Atlantic.)

ELEGANT TERN *Thalasseus elegans* 35–37cm (+ 4–5cm adult tail streamers). Pacific. Fairly large tern of marine waters, rocky and sandy coastlines, river mouths. Often found with other terns, gulls, skimmers, when groups of Elegants can bunch up tightly and be lost easily among much taller Royal Terns. Appreciably smaller and more lightly built than Royal Tern but size can be difficult to judge on lone birds; note much finer bill of Elegant, variable in color (orange-red to yellow) but often paler at tip (vs. uniform orange on Royal); longer and shaggier crest, which joins with eye in nonbr./imm. plumages (vs. eye often surrounded by white on Royal). Often has pink blush to underparts, unlike Royal and Sandwich Terns; legs rarely orange, mainly on imms. SOUNDS: Grating, screechy, and rasping calls much like Sandwich Tern, generally higher, scratchier than Royal Tern; 1st-year has high piping whistles. STATUS: Scarce to uncommon nonbr. migrant along and off Pacific coast, mainly Sep–Nov, Feb–Apr; rare at other seasons. (Breeds Mexico and s. California, winters S America.)

ROYAL TERN *Thalasseus maximus* 43–48cm (+ 5cm adult tail streamers). Large, orange-billed tern of varied coastal habitats, from rocky headlands and sandy beaches to river mouths, inshore waters, coastal lagoons. Often in feeding and roosting flocks with other terns, gulls, skimmers. Slightly smaller and more lightly built than Caspian Tern, with narrower, more angled wings, and longer tail, shaggier cap, uniform orange bill (rarely orange-red); lacks solidly dark underside to wing-tip of Caspian; imm./nonbr. plumages have large 'bald' white forehead, unlike Caspian. Cf. smaller, finer-billed Elegant Tern. Legs rarely orange, mainly on imms. SOUNDS: Adult has clucking *krehk* and laughing *kewh-eh*; also grating and screechy calls similar to Elegant Tern; 1st-year has high piping whistles. STATUS: Fairly common to common nonbr. migrant on both coasts, mainly Sep–May; smaller numbers of imms. occur through summer. (Americas.)

CASPIAN TERN *Hydroprogne caspia* 51–57cm. Largest tern in the world, a nonbr. migrant to coastal lagoons, tidal flats, river mouths, rarely over open ocean. Often rests with groups of gulls, other terns, mainly as singles. Bulky and broad-winged, lacks long tail streamers. Wingbeats relatively shallow and gull-like. Note overall size and bulk, very stout red bill with black ring near tip, dark underside to primaries; juv. has orange bill with dark near tip. Imm./nonbr. have densely black-streaked crown, lacking large 'bald' white crown patch of other terns. Cf. Royal Tern. SOUNDS: Adult has deep throaty *rahrr*, quite distinct from other terns and may suggest a heron; 1st-year has high lisping whistles. STATUS: Uncommon to rare and local nonbr. migrant on Pacific coast, mainly Sep–Apr in Gulf of Nicoya; a few imms. may occur through summer; very rare on Caribbean coast. (Worldwide except S America.)

SANDWICH TERN

breeding
(Mar–Jul)

1st-year

nonbr.
(Jul–Mar)

ELEGANT TERN

breeding
(Jan–Aug)

nonbr.
(Aug–Feb)

ROYAL TERN

1st-year

breeding
(Jan–Jul)

nonbr.
(Jul–Feb)

CASPIAN TERN

1st-year

breeding
(Mar–Sep)

nonbr.
(Sep–Mar)

LEAST TERN *Sternula antillarum* 21–23cm. Tiny tern of inshore marine waters, beaches, river mouths. Feeds mainly over inshore waters; often rests on beaches with other terns, smaller gulls, shorebirds. Flies with hurried deep wingbeats and plunge-dives steeply from moderate heights. Tiny size distinctive—barely larger than a Sanderling. SOUNDS: Varied, slightly sneezy and squeaky calls, typically 2-syllable, *chírit* and *kree-it*. STATUS: Uncommon to seasonally fairly common nonbr. migrant over inshore Pacific waters, especially Gulf of Nicoya, mainly Sep–Apr; a few imms. may occur through summer. Rare and irregular on Caribbean coast. (Breeds N America to Mexico, winters w. Mexico and s. Caribbean to n. S America.)

COMMON TERN *Sterna hirundo* 29–32cm (+ 2.5cm adult tail streamers). Coastal and offshore winter migrant, often resting at beaches, river mouths, coastal lagoons, harbors; feeds mainly over inshore marine waters. Singles to locally in flocks of 100s off Pacific coast, often mixed with other terns (especially American Black Tern). On nonbr./imm. note partial black cap with white forecrown, blackish leading edge to wing (shows at rest as dark shoulder bar). Breeding adult has red bill with small dark tip, pale smoky wash to body. Post-juv. plumages often have dark wedge on trailing edge of primaries (can be indistinct in spring, and also shown by 2nd-year Forster's). Wing molt occurs fall–winter, in Costa Rica. SOUNDS: High sharp *kiik*, suggesting Long-billed Dowitcher. STATUS: Fairly common to common Aug–May along and off Pacific coast, smaller numbers of imms. occur locally in summer. Uncommon spring and fall on Caribbean coast, scarce in winter. (Breeds n. Eurasia and N America, winters to S Hemisphere.)

ARCTIC TERN *Sterna paradisaea* 30–33cm (+ 3–5cm adult tail streamers). Pacific, offshore transient migrant. Singles rarely found resting on beaches with other terns, when note very short legs of Arctic. Stockier than Common Tern, with shorter neck, longer wings, and often stronger, more clipped wingbeats. On adult, note uniform translucent primaries with narrow black trailing edge, smoky-gray body; bill slightly shorter than Common (can have black tip on 2nd-summer and fall adult). Juv. has whitish secondaries (dark on Common) contrasting with darker leading edge of wing, but lacks contrasting black shoulder bar. Wing molt in S Hemisphere, not in Costa Rica. STATUS: Probably a regular migrant Aug–Nov, Apr–May far off Pacific coast, rarely wandering to within range of day trips; scattered coastal records mainly Oct–Nov. (Breeds n. Eurasia and N America, winters S Hemisphere.)

FORSTER'S TERN *Sterna forsteri* 32–36cm (+ 6–7.5cm adult tail streamers). Scarce winter migrant to estuaries, coastal lagoons, harbors, beaches, wetlands; not usually offshore. Likely to be found as single birds, often resting with other terns, gulls, shorebirds. Slightly larger and bigger-billed than Common Tern; nonbr./imm. plumages have distinctive broad black mask on white head, orange-red legs; cf. Gull-billed Tern. Breeding adult has silvery upperwings, whitish body, orange-red bill with extensive black tip, long tail streamers; wing molt in fall, completes before winter. Cf. Common Tern. SOUNDS: Hard clipped *kik!* STATUS: Rare and irregular nonbr. migrant to n. Pacific coast, mainly Nov–Feb in Gulf of Nicoya; very rare on Caribbean coast. (Breeds N America, winters to Cen America.)

GULL-BILLED TERN *Gelochelidon nilotica* 33–36cm. Medium-size, rather stocky tern of coastal lagoons, salt ponds, beaches, flooded fields, lakes; not over open ocean. Feeds by swooping down to snatch prey (crabs and such) from ground, not by diving into water. Associates readily with resting groups of other terns, gulls, skimmers. Distinctive: note habits, thick black bill, relatively long legs, short tail, very pale gray upperparts (no white rump), tapered and swept-back wings. Cf. nonbr./imm. Forster's Tern, Sandwich Tern. SOUNDS: Nasal laughing and mellow barking calls, mainly in flight, *ku-wek* and *ket-e-wek*, etc. STATUS: Uncommon and local nonbr. migrant on both coasts, mainly Sep–May, a few imms. may occur in summer. (Worldwide.)

LEAST TERN

1st-year

breeding

breeding
(Mar–Sep)

nonbr.
(Aug–Feb)

COMMON TERN

1st-year

breeding

breeding
(Mar–Sep)

nonbr.
(Sep–Mar)

breeding
(Apr–Oct)

ARCTIC TERN

1st-year

nonbr.

breeding
(Mar–Aug)

FORSTER'S TERN

nonbr.
(Aug–Mar)

nonbr.

breeding
(Feb–Aug)

nonbr.
(Aug–Mar)

GULL-BILLED TERN

*AMERICAN BLACK TERN *Chlidonias [niger] surinamensis* 23–25cm. Small tern of inshore marine waters, adjacent beaches, river mouths, coastal lagoons. Flocks of 100s occur off Pacific coast, often associating with other terns (especially Common). Flight buoyant and slightly floppy, swooping to pick food from near water surface; often rests on flotsam, sea turtles. Very small size, dusky gray upperparts, dark spur on sides of breast, and habits distinctive; birds in full breeding plumage rare in Costa Rica. SOUNDS: Quiet piping whistles; quacking *kek* in alarm. STATUS: Fairly common to common Sep–May over Pacific inshore and shelf waters, small numbers of imms. may occur in summer. Uncommon to fairly common spring and fall off and along Caribbean coast. (Breeds N America, winters Mexico to S America.)

WESTERN BRIDLED TERN *Onychoprion [anaethetus] melanopterus* 33–36cm (+ 5–6.5cm adult tail streamers). Marine waters, rarely seen from shore. Nests on inshore rocky islets. Singles or small groups occur with feeding flocks of boobies, shearwaters, other terns. Flight buoyant and graceful, swooping to pick from surface; often rests on flotsam. Adult has dark gray-brown upperparts, extensively white tail and underwings, long white brow, cf. Sooty Tern. SOUNDS: Varied braying and clucking calls. STATUS: Uncommon to fairly common off Pacific coast, breeding locally Mar–Aug in northwest. Scarce off Caribbean coast, mainly fall. (Tropical Americas and Atlantic.)

SOOTY TERN *Onychoprion fuscatus* 36–39cm (+ 6.5–7.5cm adult tail streamers). Offshore waters; very unlikely to be seen from land. Feeds over schooling tuna or dolphins with shearwaters, boobies, noddies. Adult clean black-and-white with extensive dark on underside of primaries, cf. Western Bridled Tern. Juv. distinctive: note whitish underwing coverts; cf. Common Brown Noddy. SOUNDS: Clucking *wed-a-wek*; juv. gives high lisping whistles. STATUS: Scarce year-round off Pacific coast, mainly well offshore; exceptional on Caribbean coast (storm-blown). (Pantropical.)

COMMON BROWN NODDY *Anous stolidus* 36–42cm. Marine waters, unlikely to be seen from shore. Often with feeding flocks of boobies, other terns, shearwaters. Flight typically low to the water, swooping to pick from the surface; transiting flight low and direct, when can suggest small jaeger. Rests on flotsam, sea turtles. Habits and uniform dark brown plumage distinctive; adult has variable whitish forecrown. Rarely vocal away from breeding grounds. STATUS: Uncommon to fairly common Apr–Nov over Pacific waters, mainly offshore (breeds Cocos I.); may nest locally on rocky inshore islets; rare in winter. Rare on Caribbean coast (mainly storm-blown). (Pantropical.)

SKIMMERS (LARIDAE; 1 SPECIES) Small pantropical group, sometimes treated as a distinct family. Resemble large angular terns with deep bills that have the elongated mandible adapted to aerial foraging by 'skimming' it through the water surface. Ages differ, attaining adult appearance in 1st year; sexes similar but male has appreciably larger bill.

BLACK SKIMMER *Rynchops niger* 43–45.5cm, WS 115–123cm. Distinctive, angular, and boldly patterned waterbird of river mouths, tidal flats, salt ponds, coastal lagoons, beaches. Often rests with gulls and terns, usually in closely spaced groups. Flocks typically fly in rather compact, wheeling formation. Feeds in flight, mainly at night, by slicing elongated mandible through water surface and snapping shut on contact with food. Breeding plumage has solidly black hindneck; juv. has pale edgings to upperparts. Comprises 2 groups that may represent species: **American Black Skimmer** *R. [n.] niger* with extensive white on tail and wings, white underwing coverts; **Amazonian Black Skimmer** *R. [n.] cinerascens* with mostly dark tail, narrow white trailing edge to wings, dusky underwings. SOUNDS: Nasal laughing and barking clucks, mainly in flight, including at night. STATUS: **American** is fairly common but very local nonbr. migrant Sep–May on Pacific coast (mainly Gulf of Nicoya), scarce inland in nw. lowlands and on Caribbean coast; a few birds oversummer locally. **Amazonian** is scarce and irregular nonbr. migrant May–Oct on s. Pacific coast. (Americas.)

AMERICAN BLACK TERN

nonbr.
(Jul–Mar)

breeding
(Apr–Aug)

WESTERN BRIDLED TERN

juvs.
(Jun–Oct)

breeding
(Feb–Sep)

juvs.
(Jun–Nov)

SOOTY TERN

breeding
(year-round)

adult

1st-year

adult

COMMON BROWN NODDY

breeding
(Mar–Aug)

BLACK SKIMMER

American

nonbr.
(Aug–Mar)

Amazonian

THICK-KNEES (BURHINIDAE; 1 SPECIES) Small family of large terrestrial 'shorebirds' found worldwide in warmer climates. Ages differ slightly, sexes similar; like adult in 1st year; despite the name, 'knees' not especially thick.

DOUBLE-STRIPED THICK-KNEE *Burhinus bistriatus* 45–50cm. Large, cryptic, long-legged nocturnal bird of grassland, savanna, ranchland with scattered trees and bushes; usually not close to human habitation. Usually in pairs or small groups; spends the day standing or sitting quietly, often in the shade of bushes, fence posts. Runs well and fast, in preference to flying. No truly similar species in Costa Rica, but at night cf. imm. Yellow-crowned Night Heron (p. 82), which can be well away from water. Juv. has subtly different head pattern without pronounced double stripes, soon like adult. **SOUNDS:** Heard mainly at night, sometimes in day when alarmed. Far-carrying, clipped barks and clucks, often in persistent, fairly rapid series, *kyeh-kyeh...*; at a distance might suggest frogs. **STATUS:** Fairly common but often local on n. Pacific slope; smaller numbers spreading e. into n. Caribbean lowlands and w. Central Valley, also s. along Pacific slope; rarely to 1000m. (Mexico to S America.)

STILTS AND AVOCETS (RECURVIROSTRIDAE; 2 SPECIES) Small worldwide family of elegant, long-legged shorebirds found in warmer climates. Ages/sexes differ slightly; adult appearance attained in 1st year; avocet has seasonal plumage changes.

BLACK-NECKED STILT *Himantopus mexicanus* 36–41cm. Essentially un-mistakable, visually elegant but vocally irritating large shorebird with improbably long, hot-pink legs. Breeds at salt ponds, shallow lagoons; ranges to varied wetland habitats, less frequent in freshwater and on open coasts. Often in flocks, associating readily with other shorebirds, and breeds colonially. Male has glossy black back and wings, breast often flushes pink on breeding birds; female and imm. have brownish back; juv. has weaker dark head and neck pattern, whitish trailing edge to secondaries; like adult in 1st year. **SOUNDS:** Varied, often persistent yapping and clucking calls, especially when nesting, have earned the nickname 'Marsh Poodle.' Also high piping *piik*, reminiscent of Long-billed Dowitcher. **STATUS:** Fairly common to common nonbr. migrant on both slopes and locally inland, mainly Aug–Apr; breeds locally, mainly in nw. lowlands; to 1500m. (Americas.)

AMERICAN AVOCET *Recurvirostra americana* 40–43cm. Elegant and essentially unmistakable migrant shorebird with fine upcurved bill, boldly pied plumage. Feeds by sweeping bill side-to-side through water. Usually singles, rarely small groups, at shallow lakes, salt ponds, other wetland habitats, associating readily with other large shorebirds, especially stilts. Sexes similar, but male has straighter bill than female; breeding plumage attained Feb–Apr. Juv. (Aug–Oct) has rusty tinge to head and hindneck, like nonbr. adult by early winter. **SOUNDS:** Overslurred piping *kleéh*, singly or in series, at times persistently repeated. **STATUS:** Rare and irregular nonbr. migrant to nw. lowlands, mainly Aug–Apr. (Breeds N America to Mexico, winters to Cen America.)

DOUBLE-STRIPED THICK-KNEE

BLACK-NECKED STILT

juv.

female

male

AMERICAN AVOCET

nonbr. female
(Aug–Apr)

breeding male
(Feb–Aug)

OYSTERCATCHERS (HAEMATOPODIDAE; 1 SPECIES) Small worldwide
family of large stocky shorebirds with laterally compressed, bright orange-red bills, thick pink legs. Ages differ slightly, sexes similar; adult appearance attained in 2nd year.

AMERICAN OYSTERCATCHER *Haematopus palliatus* 40.5–45.5cm. Distinctive, large, boldly patterned shorebird of sandy beaches, coastal lagoons, rocky coasts, mudflats. Found as singles, pairs, occasionally small flocks at high-tide roosts. Juv. has duller eyes and legs, black-tipped bill, faint pale buff edgings to upperparts; often retains dark on bill tip through 1st year. SOUNDS: Loud piping and screaming calls, *Wheeh* and *h'wheek*, often run into shrill, at times prolonged piping chatters; sharp *keek* in alarm near nest. STATUS: Uncommon but local breeder on Pacific coast; more widespread Aug–May when also scarce locally on Caribbean coast. (Americas.)

PLOVERS (CHARADRIIDAE; 8+ SPECIES) Worldwide family of small to large
shorebirds. Big eyes and short bills attest to visual hunting strategy, unlike probing and picking of sandpipers. Most migrants show seasonal variation; residents similar year-round. Ages usually differ, with juv. resembling nonbr.; attain adult appearance in 1st year. Sexes usually differ slightly, at least in breeding plumage, with males having more extensive black on face and underparts.

*CAYENNE [SOUTHERN] LAPWING *Vanellus [chilensis] cayennensis* 34–36cm. Large, spectacular shorebird of open areas, from ranchland with scattered ponds to soccer fields in rural towns; wetlands, riverbanks, lakeshores. Flies with unhurried bowed wingbeats suggesting a heron. No similar species in Costa Rica: note wispy crest, black chest shield, big white wing panels in flight. Juv. has duller eyes and legs, shorter crest, pale scaly edgings to upperparts; like adult in 1–2 months. SOUNDS: Can be noisy, including at night (cf. Double-striped Thick-knee): varied strident barks, yaps, and shrieking cries, mainly when disturbed and in display. STATUS: Uncommon to fairly common, mainly below 1800m but with records to 3000m or higher. First recorded Costa Rica in mid-1990s and still expanding its range. (S America, spreading to Cen America.)

BLACK-BELLIED (GRAY) PLOVER *Pluvialis squatarola* 26.5–28cm. Large bulky migrant plover of varied coastal habitats, from sandy beaches to mudflats, coastal lagoons, rocky areas; also inland to nearby fields; rarely inland lakeshores. Locally in flocks, associating readily with other shorebirds. Note large bulk, stout bill; in flight note white rump, white wingstripe, black 'armpits,' cf. American Golden Plover. Attains breeding plumage Feb–Apr. Juv. (Sep–Jan) resembles neat version of nonbr. plumage, with streaked breast, finely spangled upperparts. SOUNDS: Melancholy slurred whistles, *heéueeh* and *chweéee*; typically lower, more drawn-out than American Golden Plover. STATUS: Fairly common to common Aug–May on both coasts, scarce inland in nw. lowlands; small numbers oversummer locally. (Breeds n. Eurasia and N America, winters almost worldwide.)

AMERICAN GOLDEN PLOVER *Pluvialis dominica* 24–25.5cm. Medium-size, long-winged transient migrant plover found in grassland, farmland, at lakeshores, less often open beaches, rarely mudflats and rocky shorelines. Singles and small groups, often with Black-bellied Plovers. Smaller and slimmer than Black-bellied, with slender bill, mostly dark upperparts (narrow whitish wingstripe), dusky underwings; lacks small hind toe of Black-bellied. Juv. and nonbr. plumages rather dull above, not golden, with contrasting dark cap and whitish eyebrow. Attains breeding plumage Apr–May, at staging areas mainly n. of Costa Rica. SOUNDS: Varied plaintive whistles including fairly mellow *ch'weít* and flutier, more rolled *chweél*. STATUS: Uncommon Mar–early May, scarce Sep–early Dec, in coastal lowlands on both slopes, locally inland to 1500m, exceptionally in highlands; most numerous on Pacific slope. (Breeds N America, winters S America.)

American Oystercatcher

Cayenne Lapwing

Black-bellied Plover

nonbr.
(year-round)

breeding.
(Mar–Aug)

juv.
(Sep–Jan)

nonbr.
(Mar–May)

American Golden Plover

juv. (Sep–Dec)

64

SEMIPALMATED PLOVER *Charadrius semipalmatus* 16.5–17.5cm. Small migrant plover of varied coastal habitats from beaches and tidal mudflats to flooded fields, mangroves, salt ponds. Often in flocks, feeding in well-spaced arrays but roosting more tightly, often with other shorebirds. Note orange legs, wet-sand tone to upperparts, stubby, orange-based bill. Breeding plumage has black mask and breast band. Nonbr. resembles juv. SOUNDS: Upslurred, slightly plaintive *ch'wieh* and sharper *ch'wiet!* Nasal bickering chatters in feeding interactions. STATUS: Fairly common to locally common Aug–May on both coasts, especially Pacific, where small numbers oversummer; uncommon to fairly common locally inland, where more widespread in migration, to 1500m. (Breeds N America, winters to S America.)

WILSON'S PLOVER *Charadrius wilsonia* 18–19cm. Small but big-billed plover of coastal habitats, from sandy beaches to lagoon shores, salt ponds, mangrove mudflats, rocky coasts; often breeds in areas with gravel. Mainly feeds by running down small crabs. Often in groups. Note heavy black bill, pinkish legs. Male has black head and breast markings, female dark brown. Pacific coast birds average darker above; Caribbean coast birds often distinctly paler than Semipalmated Plover. SOUNDS: Sharp high *piik!* and clipped *pri-dik*; dry, buzzy, bickering chatters in interactions. STATUS: Uncommon to fairly common locally on both coasts, breeding on Pacific coast mainly around Gulf of Nicoya; more widespread in fall–winter. (Americas.)

COLLARED PLOVER *Charadrius collaris* 14–15cm. Dainty plover of varied coastal habitats from beaches and river mouths to lagoons, salt flats; also inland on gravel and sand bars in rivers, lakeshores. Note neat, narrow black collar, rusty cheeks, fine dark bill, pinkish legs; lacks whitish hindneck collar of other small ringed plovers. Pairs or small groups often keep apart from flocks of other small plovers. Juv. plumage held briefly; no distinct seasonal change in adult appearance. SOUNDS: Clipped sharp *pik*, suggesting Wilson's Plover; mellow rolled *krip* that can run into chatters. STATUS: Uncommon and local on both slopes, mainly in coastal lowlands but locally to 500m; rare and irregular visitor to Central Valley. (Mexico to S America.)

SNOWY PLOVER *Charadrius nivosus* 15–16cm. Small, pale migrant plover of sandy beaches, coastal lagoons, salt ponds. Singles or a few birds, often associating with other small plovers. Feeds mainly by chasing down sandflies. Note partial breast band, dull pinkish-gray legs, slender dark bill. Pacific coast birds pale sandy brown above, Caribbean coast birds average paler, more silvery. Male has bolder black head and breast markings than female. SOUNDS: Quiet rolled *prrit* in flight. STATUS: Rare and irregular Sep–early Apr on n. Pacific coast, very rare elsewhere on both coasts. (Americas.)

KILLDEER *Charadrius vociferus* 24–25.5cm. Relatively large, long-tailed, and often noisy ringed plover, with distinctive double black breast band, bright rusty rump and long, dark-tipped tail. Often away from water, in plowed fields, grassland, other open habitats; rarely open beaches or tidal mudflats. Regularly in flocks, separate from other ringed plovers. Slight age/sex/seasonal variation; chick has single black breast band, soon attains adult-like plumage. SOUNDS: Varied wailing and screaming cries, singly or in series; in display flight a repeated, onomatopoeic *kill-deéu....* STATUS: Uncommon nonbr. migrant on both slopes, especially Pacific, mainly Sep–Mar, to 1500m; local breeding resident, mainly in and around Central Valley. (Americas.)

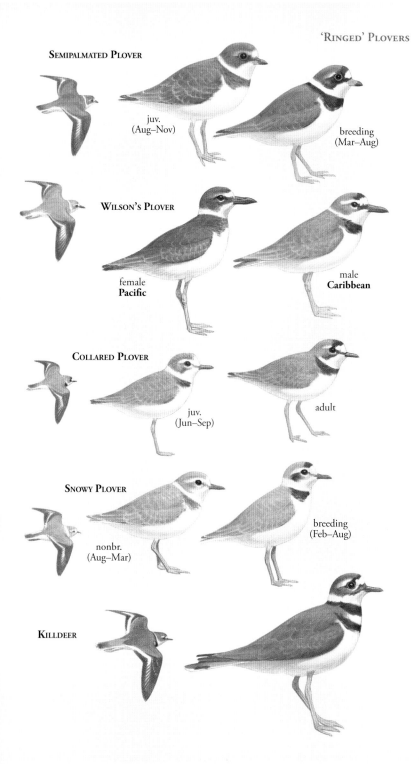

'RINGED' PLOVERS

SEMIPALMATED PLOVER

juv.
(Aug–Nov)

breeding
(Mar–Aug)

WILSON'S PLOVER

female
Pacific

male
Caribbean

COLLARED PLOVER

juv.
(Jun–Sep)

adult

SNOWY PLOVER

nonbr.
(Aug–Mar)

breeding
(Feb–Aug)

KILLDEER

SANDPIPERS (SCOLOPACIDAE; 29+ SPECIES) Fairly large, worldwide family of shorebirds. Mainly tactile feeders, picking and probing as they walk. Ages differ, sexes similar or may differ in breeding plumage; adult appearance usually attained in 1st year, but may not breed till 2 or 3 years; imms. of many species remain on nonbr. grounds through 1st summer. ID can be challenging, but species often associate together, which can help greatly— compare size, shape, bill shape, and behavior of an unfamiliar species with other species you know; voice also useful.

*WHIMBREL *Numenius phaeopus* 35.5–43cm. Large brown migrant sandpiper with long decurved bill, found on beaches, rocky coasts, at river mouths, salt ponds, estuaries; also nearby fields. Singly or in small loose groups, larger flocks locally in migration; feeds by probing. Cf. rare Long-billed Curlew. Ages/sexes similar, bill becomes mostly to wholly black on breeding adults. SOUNDS: In flight, fairly rapid series of overslurred piping whistles, *pee-pee-pee...*, 6–9 notes/sec. Quavering fluty whistles in territorial interactions. STATUS: Fairly common to uncommon Sep–Apr on both coasts, especially Pacific; more widespread and numerous in migration, Aug–Oct, Mar–early May, when scarce inland in north. Small numbers oversummer locally, mainly Pacific coast. (Breeds n. N America, winters to S America.)

LONG-BILLED CURLEW *Numenius americanus* 45.5–58.5cm. Rare migrant. Very large, buffy-brown sandpiper with very long decurved bill (appreciably shorter on 1st-year). Occurs on tidal mudflats, beaches, at river mouths, salt ponds; feeds by probing. Appreciably larger than Whimbrel (obvious in direct comparison) with warmer plumage tones, cinnamon underwings, plainer face, longer bill. When sleeping, cf. slightly smaller Marbled Godwit. Ages/sexes similar, but female distinctly longer-billed than male. SOUNDS: Slightly shrieky hoarse *reeip* and slurred rising *hooriep* in flight; plaintive quavering whistles and bubbling choruses. STATUS: Rare and local late Aug–Apr on Pacific coast, mainly Gulf of Nicoya; exceptional elsewhere, including Caribbean coast. (Breeds w. N America, winters to Cen America.)

UPLAND SANDPIPER *Bartramia longicauda* 28–30.5cm. Medium-size transient migrant sandpiper of grassy habitats, fields, airports, usually not around water. Singly or in small groups, at times associating loosely with other grassland shorebirds. Note cryptic plumage, long tail, slender straight bill, yellowish legs; nothing really similar, but cf. plain-breasted Buff-breasted Sandpiper of similar habitats. Ages/sexes similar. SOUNDS: Mainly in flight, including at night, a liquid whistled *wh-whit* and rippling *whi-whi-whuit*. STATUS: Uncommon Aug–Oct, Mar–May in Central Valley and on Pacific slope, scarce on Caribbean Slope. (Breeds N America, winters S America.)

MARBLED GODWIT *Limosa fedoa* 38–46cm. Large buffy-brown migrant sandpiper with long pinkish bill tipped dark. Mainly found at estuaries, salt marshes, coastal lagoons, sandy beaches; feeds by probing, often while wading in fairly deep water. Cf. rare Long-billed Curlew, especially when sleeping. Breeding plumage has variable barring on underparts. SOUNDS: Nasal, slightly crowing or laughing calls, *ah-ha* and *ahk*. STATUS: Uncommon to fairly common Aug–May on Pacific coast, more widespread and numerous in migration; a few oversummer locally; very rare on Caribbean coast. (Breeds N America, winters to Cen America.)

WILSON'S SNIPE *Gallinago delicata* 25–26.5cm. Cryptic, medium-size, long-billed migrant sandpiper of grassy marshes, lakeshores, other vegetated wetlands; not in open situations. Mostly seen feeding at marsh edges early and late in day or when flushed from vegetation, usually as singles or loose aggregations. Flushed flight strong and erratic, often towering before dropping back to cover. All plumages similar, with striped face, bold buffy back stripes. SOUNDS: Usually utters low rasping *zzhek* when flushed. STATUS: Uncommon to scarce Oct–Apr on both slopes, to 1500m; rarely to 3000m during migration. (Breeds N America, winters to n. S America.)

WHIMBREL

LONG-BILLED CURLEW

juv.
(Aug–Oct)

adult

UPLAND SANDPIPER

MARBLED GODWIT

breeding
(Mar–Aug)

nonbr.
(Aug–Mar)

WILSON'S SNIPE

68

GENUS *TRINGA* (5 species). Medium-size to large sandpipers with fairly long, often colorful legs and overall straight bills; upperparts typically have fine pale spotting or spangling in nonbr. plumages, vs. paler edging and scaly look typical of *Calidris* sandpipers. Often bob head or whole body when alarmed and tend to be fairly wary, flying off with whistled or yelping calls.

SOLITARY SANDPIPER *Tringa solitaria* 20.5–21.5cm. Medium-size migrant sandpiper of freshwater ponds, lake edges, wetlands, not on open mudflats or beaches. Singles occur at small bodies of water, also small flocks during migration; does not associate strongly with other shorebirds. Often towers when flushed; wingbeats deep, quick, and swallow-like. Note dark upperparts, fairly long greenish legs, dark underwings in flight; cf. Lesser Yellowlegs, Spotted Sandpiper. **SOUNDS:** Slightly plaintive piping whistles in short series, *t-swee sweet* and *teet t-weet t-weet*; brighter and flutier than Spotted Sandpiper. **STATUS:** Uncommon to fairly common late Jul–early May on both slopes, to 1500m; locally to 3000m, mainly during migration. (Breeds N America, winters Mexico to S America.)

LESSER YELLOWLEGS *Tringa flavipes* 24–25.5cm. Medium-size, long-legged migrant sandpiper of freshwater and brackish habitats, from lakes and marshes to salt ponds, coastal lagoons; rarely on open mudflats and beaches. Locally in flocks. Feeds while walking and wading actively, picking at water surface; rarely swims. Greater Yellowlegs is larger and stouter-billed, about willet-size, vs. Lesser, which is about dowitcher-size; Greater also has louder, 'shouted' calls vs. mellower calls of Lesser. Cf. Solitary and Stilt Sandpipers. **SOUNDS:** Mellow whistled *tew* or *kyew*, often in short series suggesting Short-billed Dowitcher. **STATUS:** Fairly common to common Jul–May on Pacific slope, smaller numbers on Caribbean slope and inland to 1500m; more widespread in migration; a few oversummer locally. (Breeds N America, winters to S America.)

GREATER YELLOWLEGS *Tringa melanoleuca* 29.5–31.5cm. Large, long-legged migrant sandpiper of varied wetland habitats, from lakes and marshes to river mouths, salt ponds, coastal lagoons. Usually singles and small groups. Feeds while walking and wading, often actively dashing after prey and sweeping bill side-to-side, vs. more sedate picking of Lesser Yellowlegs; rarely swims. Cf. Willet, Lesser Yellowlegs. **SOUNDS:** Loud ringing whistle, usually trebled, *tchoo-tchoo-tchoo*; repeated sharp *tew* when agitated. **STATUS:** Fairly common to common Jul–May on both slopes, especially Pacific, locally inland to 1500m; more widespread in migration; a few oversummer locally. (Breeds N America, winters to S America.)

*WESTERN WILLET *Tringa [semipalmata] inornata* 33–35.5cm. Large, rather stocky migrant sandpiper of varied coastal habitats, from mudflats, beaches, and rocky coasts to salt ponds, river mouths, mangroves. Singles and groups associate readily with other shorebirds; feeds by picking and probing, often in shallow water. Willets as such are distinctive, but distinguishing the two species can be challenging (see below, under Eastern): note stout straight bill, whitish spectacles, gray legs; diagnostic wing pattern striking in flight. Juv. (Aug–Oct) like nonbr. with narrow, pale-dotted edgings to upperparts. **SOUNDS:** Noisy. Varied, mainly 3- or 4-note mellow to loud shrieking whistles, *kri-wih-wih* and *krri-WI-WI-wihr*; nasal inflected *kyeh'eh* and short series, *kyeh-yeh-yeh*; alarm a sharp yapping *kyih!* at times repeated steadily. **STATUS:** Fairly common Aug–May on Pacific coast, uncommon on Caribbean coast; small numbers oversummer locally. (Breeds w. N America, winters to S America.)

*EASTERN WILLET *Tringa semipalmata* 32–34.5cm. Very similar to Western Willet, but slightly smaller and stockier overall, with deeper, blunter bill, shorter legs; breeding plumage averages darker and browner, with pinkish tinge to bill and legs. **SOUNDS:** Calls similar to Western, but average higher, less husky. **STATUS:** Scarce (overlooked?) late Jan–Mar on both coasts, probably also Aug–Oct. (Breeds e. N America to Caribbean, winters S America.)

SOLITARY SANDPIPER

nonbr.
(Aug–Mar)

breeding
(Mar–Aug)

LESSER YELLOWLEGS

juv.
(Aug–Oct)

nonbr.
(Aug–Mar)

breeding
(Mar–Aug)

GREATER YELLOWLEGS

juv.
(Aug–Oct)

nonbr.
(Aug–Mar)

breeding
(Mar–Aug)

WESTERN WILLET

nonbr.
(year-round)

breeding
(Mar–Aug)

EASTERN WILLET

breeding
(Feb–Aug)

SPOTTED SANDPIPER *Actitis macularius* 16.5–18cm. Distinctive small migrant sandpiper of varied fresh and saltwater habitats from coastlines and highland rivers to estuaries and ponds, often with stony and rocky shores; perches readily on posts, mangrove branches. Usually single birds, rarely loose small groups, and typically apart from other shorebirds. Walks with almost constant bobbing of rear end; very rarely wades in water. Flight typically low over water with stiff flicking beats of bowed wings. Note habits, white spur at chest sides; breeding plumage has variable black spotting below; juv. (Aug–Oct) like nonbr. with narrow pale edgings to upperparts. **SOUNDS:** High, slightly plaintive to piping single notes and short phrases, *siit* and *see-wee-wee*, etc. **STATUS:** Fairly common but low-density Jul–May on both slopes, locally to 1800m. (Breeds N America, winters to S America.)

WANDERING TATTLER *Tringa incana* 24–25.5m. Distinctive, medium-size migrant sandpiper of rocky, often rugged, and wave-dashed coasts, rarely adjacent sandy beaches. Usually single birds, apart from other species except sometimes at roosts. Walks with frequent bobbing of rear end. Note straight, medium-length bill, fairly short yellowish legs, plain slaty-gray upperparts in flight; breeding plumage has heavy dark barring on underparts; juv. (Aug–Oct) like nonbr. with notched whitish spotting on upperparts. **SOUNDS:** Rapid, slightly ringing, overall slightly descending or overslurred series of (usually 4–7) short, high piping whistles, *tii-lii-lii-lii* and variations. **STATUS:** Uncommon Aug–May along rocky stretches of Pacific coast, more numerous in migration; a few oversummer locally. (Breeds N America, winters to n. S America and across Pacific.)

RUDDY TURNSTONE *Arenaria interpres* 22.5–24cm. Distinctive, chunky, medium-size migrant sandpiper of rocky coasts, sandy beaches, estuaries, coastal lagoons. Often in flocks, associating readily with other shorebirds. Pokes amid and overturns seaweed, stones, in search of prey. Note bright reddish-orange legs, dark breast patches, variegated upperparts; striking flight pattern. Breeding female has duskier head markings, duller upperparts than male; juv. (Aug–Oct) like nonbr. but with neat pale scaly edgings to upperparts, duller legs. **SOUNDS:** Sharp *kyew!* and relatively mellow rolled *dr-dr-dr*, can suggest Short-billed Dowitcher. **STATUS:** Fairly common to common Aug–May on both coasts, especially Pacific; more widespread in migration; small numbers oversummer locally. (Breeds n. Eurasia and N America, winters almost worldwide.)

SURFBIRD *Calidris virgata* 24–25.5cm. Medium-size, distinctive chunky migrant sandpiper of rocky coasts and breakwaters, adjacent sandy beaches and tidal flats. Sometimes in small flocks, associating readily with Ruddy Turnstone and other species. Larger and bulkier than turnstone, with stouter bill, short yellowish legs, distinct flight pattern. Juv. (Aug–Oct) like nonbr. but with neat pale scaly edgings to upperparts. **SOUNDS:** Quiet mellow *whe-whek...*, and higher *whik*, easily lost amid the sound of crashing waves. **STATUS:** Uncommon Aug–Nov, Mar–May, on Pacific coast, scarce in winter; imms. rarely over-summer. (Breeds N America, winters to S America.)

SANDERLING *Calidris alba* 18–19cm. A large 'small sandpiper' of sandy beaches, river mouths, estuaries, adjacent rocky coasts. Feeds by picking and probing; classic behavior is to run after receding waves on sandy beaches to pick for food, then race back ahead of incoming waves. Note overall pale plumage with darker shoulder patch, medium-length straightish bill, black legs; lacks hind toe of other small and medium-size sandpipers. Breeding plumage rarely seen in Costa Rica. **SOUNDS:** Bright sharp *kiip* or *plik*. **STATUS:** Fairly common Aug–Oct, Mar–May on both coasts, uncommon in winter; a few may remain locally in summer. (Breeds n. Eurasia and N America, winters s. in New World to S America.)

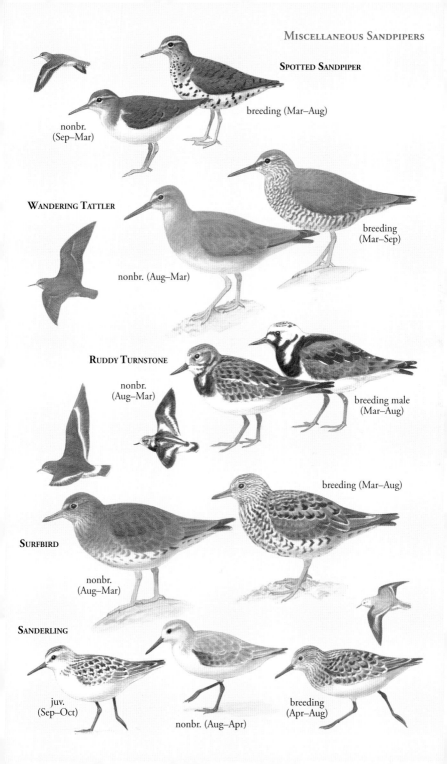

SPOTTED SANDPIPER

breeding (Mar–Aug)

nonbr.
(Sep–Mar)

WANDERING TATTLER

breeding
(Mar–Sep)

nonbr. (Aug–Mar)

RUDDY TURNSTONE

nonbr.
(Aug–Mar)

breeding male
(Mar–Aug)

breeding (Mar–Aug)

SURFBIRD

nonbr.
(Aug–Mar)

SANDERLING

juv.
(Sep–Oct)

nonbr. (Aug–Apr)

breeding
(Apr–Aug)

RED KNOT *Calidris canutus* 25.5–26.5cm. Medium-size, rather fat migrant sandpiper of tidal mudflats, beaches, river mouths, salt ponds. Winters locally in small compact flocks; elsewhere mainly singles, associating loosely with other sandpipers and often with Black-bellied Plovers. Feeds mainly by probing. Rather nondescript in winter, but nothing really similar in size and shape; body slightly larger than dowitchers, but bill obviously shorter. Breeding plumage may be seen briefly in spring, less often on worn fall migrants. SOUNDS: Nasal inflected *che'wet* and upslurred *wek* in flight. STATUS: Uncommon but local Aug–Apr around Gulf of Nicoya, rare elsewhere on Pacific coast, more widespread in migration; rare and local on Caribbean coast. (Breeds n. Eurasia and N America, winters s. in New World to S America.)

STILT SANDPIPER *Calidris himantopus* 20–21.5cm. Medium-size, rather long-legged migrant sandpiper of marshes, lakeshores, coastal lagoons, salt ponds; less often estuaries, beaches. Often in groups, locally 100s, feeding and roosting with Long-billed Dowitchers; less often singles mixed among other shorebirds. Feeds by probing while wading up to its belly, rear end typically raised steeply out of water. Nonbr. slightly smaller and paler gray than nonbr. Long-billed Dowitcher, with whitish brow, shorter black bill with slightly drooped tip; in flight note white rump, feet projecting well past tail tip. Cf. Lesser Yellowlegs. SOUNDS: Mostly silent; quiet grunting *greh* on occasion. STATUS: Uncommon to fairly common Aug–Oct, Mar–May, along Pacific coast, and locally in winter in nw. lowlands; very rare on Caribbean coast. (Breeds N America, winters Mexico to S America.)

SHORT-BILLED DOWITCHER *Limnodromus griseus* 24–28cm. Best identified by voice. Medium-size, long-billed sandpiper of coastal habitats, from tidal flats to salt ponds, river mouths, mangroves; also freshwater, mainly in migration. Often in flocks, associating with other shorebirds. Feeds mainly while wading, by rapid, steady, 'sewing-machine' probing, head raised briefly between bouts of probing. Dowitchers are distinctive as dowitchers (note white stripe up back in flight), but plumages of the two species very similar and voice is the most reliable ID feature. Long-billed favors freshwater, is darker in all plumages, and dark tail bars average wider than white bars, vs. narrower on Short-billed. Long-billed juv. has narrow chestnut edging to upperparts, lacks buff notching on tertials and coarser mottling on scapulars of juv. Short-billed; nonbr. has darker chest without dusky spotting of Short-billed; breeding Long-billed is solidly rusty below, barred on sides of breast, with white tips to fresh scapulars. Populations of Short-billed differ in breeding plumage, some populations extensively rusty below. SOUNDS: Mellow *chu-tu-tu* and variations; quality recalls Lesser Yellowlegs. STATUS: Fairly common to common Aug–May on Pacific coast, smaller numbers on Caribbean coast; a few oversummer locally, mainly Gulf of Nicoya; scarce and local migrant inland. (Breeds N America, winters to S America.)

LONG-BILLED DOWITCHER *Limnodromus scolopaceus* 25.5–29cm. Best identified by voice. Medium-size, long-billed sandpiper of freshwater wetlands and lakes, coastal lagoons, mangroves, sewage ponds, flooded fields; rarely tidal mudflats. Habits much like Short-billed Dowitcher (which see for ID criteria), and the two species sometimes occur together, mainly during migration and at roosts. Fresh (spring) breeding plumage shown here; becomes appreciably darker above and below by fall. SOUNDS: High sharp *keek!* singly or in rapid series; recalls piping call of Black-necked Stilt. STATUS: Uncommon to fairly common late Sep–Apr on Pacific slope, locally inland to 1500m; presumably occurs on Caribbean coastal slope, at least in migration, but status requires elucidation vs. very similar Short-billed Dowitcher. (Breeds N America, winters to Cen America.)

RED KNOT

juv.
(Sep–Oct)

breeding.
(Mar–Aug)

nonbr.
(Aug–Mar)

STILT SANDPIPER

juv.
(Aug–Oct)

nonbr.
(Aug–Mar)

breeding.
(Mar–Aug)

SHORT-BILLED DOWITCHER

nonbr.
(Aug–Mar)

variation

breeding
(Mar–Aug)

juv.
(Aug–Oct)

LONG-BILLED DOWITCHER

nonbr.
(Aug–Mar)

juv.
(Sep–Nov)

breeding.
(Mar–Aug)

LEAST SANDPIPER *Calidris minutilla* 13–14cm. Commonest, most wide-spread small migrant sandpiper in Costa Rica, found in varied habitats from small roadside ponds and lakeshores to tidal mudflats, coastal lagoons, sewage ponds; less often open beaches and rocky coasts, mainly when roosting. Often in flocks, locally of 100s, mixing readily with other small sandpipers but often keeps to drier and more vegetated habitats than Western Sandpiper. Feeds by picking and probing; creeps along muddy shores with flexed legs. Best identified by rather mouse-like demeanor, overall brownish plumage with white belly, medium-length decurved bill; yellowish legs often muddy. Western and Semipalmated Sandpipers are larger and whiter-breasted, walk and run with more upright gait, favor more open habitats, often wade in open water. **SOUNDS:** High, reedy, rolled *krreep* and lower *krriit*; varied low trilling. **STATUS:** Fairly common to common May–May, mainly below 1500m; more widespread in migration. (Breeds N America, winters to n. S America.)

SEMIPALMATED SANDPIPER *Calidris pusilla* 14–15cm. Small, rather com-pact migrant sandpiper with short to medium-length straightish bill, dark legs; structure suggests a mini-Sanderling. Coastal lagoons, salt ponds, mudflats, river mouths, beaches. Feeds by probing and picking. From Western Sandpiper by structure, especially shorter, blunter-tipped bill (some female Semipalmated have longer bill, overlapping short-billed male Western); juv. more uniform above (vs. grayish with rusty scapulars) than juv. Western; nonbr. slightly darker above, more brownish gray. Cf. Least and other small sandpipers. **SOUNDS:** Fairly sharp *kyip*, lower *chrit*; nasal twitters from feeding flocks. **STATUS:** Fairly common to common Aug–Oct, Mar–May on Pacific coast, smaller numbers on Caribbean coast and inland; uncommon to fairly common in winter in Gulf of Nicoya. (Breeds N America, winters Mexico to S America.)

WESTERN SANDPIPER *Calidris mauri* 15–16.5cm. Small, rather long-necked migrant sandpiper with relatively long, slightly decurved and tapered bill, black legs. Coastal lagoons, mudflats, salt ponds, river mouths, beaches, lakeshores. Feeds by probing and picking, often wading up to its belly in water. Note bright rusty tones on juv. and breeding plumages; cf. Semipalmated and Least Sandpipers. **SOUNDS:** High, scratchy, downslurred *chiit*, burry *chrrit*; wheezy twitters from feeding flocks. **STATUS:** Fairly common to common Aug–May on Pacific coast, especially Gulf of Nicoya, small numbers oversummer locally; uncommon to fairly common on Caribbean coast; rare inland during migration. (Breeds N America, winters to n. S America.)

WHITE-RUMPED SANDPIPER *Calidris fuscicollis* 17–18.5cm. Small, very long-winged transient migrant sandpiper of varied wetland habitats, from mudflats and lakeshores to river mouths, flooded fields. Singles or small groups, mixing readily with other small sandpipers. Feeds by picking, less often probing, often while wading in shallow water. Note long wings projecting past tail tip, lack of buffy plumage tones, variable pink base to mandible, voice; white uppertail coverts distinctive in flight. Cf. Baird's, Semipalmated, and Western Sandpipers. **SOUNDS:** Very high, slightly tinny, descending *jit*, easily missed or passed off as a songbird. **STATUS:** Scarce to uncommon Sep–Nov, Apr–May on both slopes, mainly in coastal lowlands. (Breeds N America, winters S America.)

BAIRD'S SANDPIPER *Calidris bairdii* 16.5–18cm. Small, very long-winged transient migrant sandpiper of inland and coastal habitats, from wetlands and volcano lakes to grassy marshes, coastal lagoons, rarely open beaches and mudflats. Singles or groups, mixing readily with other sandpipers. Feeds by picking, less often probing, regularly in fairly dry habitats away from water. Note long wings projecting past tail tip, buffy plumage, dark legs, rather fine bill, voice. Cf. White-rumped and Pectoral Sandpipers. **SOUNDS:** Dry trilled *krrih*, higher and drier than Pectoral Sandpiper. **STATUS:** Uncommon, mainly Sep–Oct, Mar–May through interior, to 3000m; scarce on Pacific coast, rare on Caribbean coast. (Breeds N America, winters S America.)

LEAST SANDPIPER

juv.
(Aug–Oct)

nonbr. (Aug–Mar)

breeding
(Mar–Aug)

**SEMIPALMATED
SANDPIPER**

juv.
(Aug–Oct)

nonbr.
(Aug–Mar)

breeding
(Mar–Aug)

**WESTERN
SANDPIPER**

juv.
(Aug–Oct)

nonbr.
(Aug–Mar)

breeding
(Mar–Aug)

WHITE-RUMPED SANDPIPER

juv.
(Sep–Nov)

breeding
(Mar–Aug)

nonbr. (Aug–Mar)

BAIRD'S SANDPIPER

juv.
(Aug–Oct)

nonbr.
(Aug–Mar)

breeding
(Mar–Aug)

PECTORAL SANDPIPER *Calidris melanotos* 19.5–23cm. Medium-size, cryptic transient migrant sandpiper of marshy wetlands, flooded fields, lakeshores, coastal lagoons; rarely on open mudflats, beaches. Singles or small groups, at times associating with other shorebirds; feeds by probing and picking, often near or within grassy vegetation. Note medium size (male appreciably larger than female), yellowish legs, clean-cut 'pectoral' demarcation between streaky brown breast and whitish belly. Little age/seasonal variation. Cf. Baird's Sandpiper. SOUNDS: Rolled *krrip*, lower and often wetter than Baird's Sandpiper. STATUS: Fairly common to common Aug–Nov, Mar–May, on both slopes, smaller numbers inland to 1500m; rare in winter. (Breeds N America, winters S America.)

BUFF-BREASTED SANDPIPER *Calidris subruficollis* 18–20.5cm. Attractive small transient migrant sandpiper of open habitats, especially fields, sod farms, lakeshores; often not near water. Singles or small groups, at times associating loosely with other shorebirds. Walks with high-stepping gait, picking for food; can be confiding. Distinctive, with blank face, beady eye, plain buffy breast, yellow legs; white underwings contrast with buff body. Little age/seasonal variation. SOUNDS: Mostly quiet; soft low clucks on occasion. STATUS: Scarce to locally uncommon late Aug–Oct on Pacific slope and inland to 1500m; rare on Caribbean slope. No spring records, but occurrence seems plausible. (Breeds N America, winters S America.)

WILSON'S PHALAROPE *Steganopus (Phalaropus) tricolor* 20.5–22cm. Elegant, medium-size migrant sandpiper of lakes, salt ponds, coastal lagoons, marshy wetlands. Feeds mainly while swimming, picking at water surface with fairly long fine bill; also feeds on land, at times with tail cocked high, chasing flies. Singles or flocks, locally of 100s, associating readily with other shorebirds. Breeding plumage distinctive (male duller); nonbr. notably pale and silvery gray overall, lacks distinct black mask of smaller Red-necked Phalarope, and in flight note white rump. Cf. Lesser Yellowlegs and Stilt Sandpiper, which swim on occasion. SOUNDS: Mostly silent; rarely utters low grunts. STATUS: Fairly common Aug–Oct, late Mar–May on Pacific slope, mainly around Gulf of Nicoya, where small numbers winter locally. (Breeds N America, winters mainly S America.)

RED-NECKED PHALAROPE *Phalaropus lobatus* 17–19cm. Small, swimming migrant sandpiper of inshore marine waters, salt ponds, coastal lagoons, river mouths. Singles or flocks, locally of 1000s on ocean. Feeds mainly while swimming; picks at water surface and sometimes spins in circles to stir up prey; ungainly on land. Breeding plumage distinctive (male duller); juv. and nonbr. told from larger and bulkier Red Phalarope by fine bill, striped back (can be fairly plain on some winter Red-necked), voice. Beware that small *Calidris* sandpipers can swim on occasion. SOUNDS: Clipped sharp *plik* and harder *tik*, lower than Red Phalarope. STATUS: Fairly common to common off and along Pacific coast Aug–Nov, very rarely inland; smaller numbers off Pacific coast Apr–May; irregularly uncommon to common in winter over inshore Pacific waters. (Breeds n. Eurasia and N America, winters in New World from Mexico to S America.)

RED (GRAY) PHALAROPE *Phalaropus fulicarius* 20–21.5cm. Small, swimming migrant sandpiper of marine waters; rarely seen on land at river mouths and coastal lagoons, usually in stormy weather. Feeds mainly while swimming; picks at water surface and sometimes spins in circles to stir up prey; ungainly on land. Often in flocks, especially in slick water along breaks between water masses. Cf. smaller, fine-billed Red-necked Phalarope. SOUNDS: High, slightly tinny *tink*, can carry surprisingly well over the ocean. STATUS: Uncommon well offshore Sep–Apr, sometimes within range of day trips; very rare on land, mainly Oct–Nov. (Breeds n. Eurasia and N America, winters in New World from Mexico to S America.)

PECTORAL SANDPIPER

juv. female
(Aug–Nov)

breeding
male

BUFF-BREASTED SANDPIPER

juv. (Aug–Nov)

adult male

**WILSON'S
PHALAROPE**

breeding female
(Mar–Aug)

nonbr.
(Aug–Mar)

breeding male
(Mar–Aug)

juv. (Aug–Oct)

RED-NECKED PHALAROPE

breeding female
(Apr–Aug)

nonbr.
(Aug–Apr)

RED PHALAROPE

nonbr. (Aug–Apr)

breeding female
(Apr–Aug)

78

HERONS (ARDEIDAE; 18+ SPECIES) Worldwide family of typically long-necked, long-legged birds with dagger-like bills; usually near water. Fly with neck retracted in bulge, unlike ibises, spoonbills, storks. Ages differ or similar, attain adult appearance in 1–3 years. Bare parts often brighten or change color strikingly for brief periods at height of breeding season. Most species nest colonially in trees and marshes, often in mixed-species aggregations. Usually quiet except when disturbed or interacting at colonies; bitterns and tiger herons, however, have 'songs.'

WESTERN CATTLE EGRET *Bubulcus ibis* 45–53cm. Fairly small, compact white heron usually found near cattle, horses, tractors, that flush up prey from fields and pastures; also flooded fields, lakeshores, but not habitually wading in wetlands like most herons and egrets. Nests in reedbeds, trees, often with other wading birds, cormorants. Social, usually in groups, locally 100s. Distinctive, with stocky shape, yellowish bill, dark legs; cinnamon-buff plumes on crown, chest, and back most extensive on breeding adult, can be absent on 1st-year. In flight note rather stocky shape without strong deep neck bulge of Snowy Egret. At height of breeding, bill and lores flush salmon, legs scarlet. Fledgling bill can be blackish, soon like adult. **SOUNDS:** Gruff clucks and grunts, mainly when nesting. **STATUS:** Fairly common to locally common in lowlands, in smaller numbers to 2000m. (Americas, Africa, and W Eurasia.)

SNOWY EGRET *Egretta thula* 49–59cm. Elegant, fairly small white egret of varied wetland habitats from beaches and river mouths to small ponds, lakeshores, mangroves. Singles or loose groups; hunts while wading or waiting, often dashing rather actively in shallows. Note slender black bill and contrasting yellow lores; adult has shaggy crest, ornate back plumes, yellow feet contrasting with blackish legs; lores flush orange at height of breeding. Fledgling bill can be yellowish, tipped black, soon like adult; 1st-year has greenish-yellow feet, hind edge to legs, cf. 1st-year Little Blue Heron. **SOUNDS:** Varied guttural rasps and croaks, averaging throatier than Little Blue Heron; higher, more nasal than American Great Egret. **STATUS:** Fairly common to locally common Sep–Apr, mainly below 1500m; smaller numbers in summer (mainly nonbr. imms.); breeds locally in nw. lowlands, perhaps elsewhere. (Americas.)

*****AMERICAN GREAT EGRET** *Ardea [alba] egretta* 84–99cm. The only large white heron in Costa Rica, found in a wide variety of wetland habitats from roadside ditches and flooded fields to coastal lagoons, estuaries, mangroves. Mostly singles or small groups, but 100s can gather at favored feeding sites with aggregations of other wading birds. Note wholly white plumage, yellow bill, blackish legs and feet; adult has long ornate back plumes. At height of breeding, lores flush bright green and maxilla is extensively black. Cf. much smaller Cattle Egret. **SOUNDS:** Varied, deep guttural calls, often with creaky quality; average less stentorian than Great Blue Heron, lower and harsher than Snowy Egret. **STATUS:** Fairly common to locally common Sep–Apr, mainly below 1500m; smaller numbers in summer (mainly nonbr. imms.); breeds locally in nw. lowlands, perhaps elsewhere. (Americas.)

White Herons in Flight (opposite, far right) are best identified by a combination of structure and coloration of bare parts; smaller species have quicker wingbeats, more often in flocks.

Western Cattle Egret is stockiest, lacking pronounced deep neck bulge of other species, always with yellow bill.
Juv. Little Blue Heron very similar to Snowy Egret but with pale, black-tipped bill, uniformly pale greenish legs and feet; wing-tips have fine dark tips visible with good view.
Snowy Egret has distinct neck bulge, black bill, contrasting yellow feet.
White morph Reddish Egret larger and rangier than Snowy and Little Blue, with very long blackish legs, slender bill.
American Great Egret is largest with relatively slow wingbeats, big yellow bill, black legs.

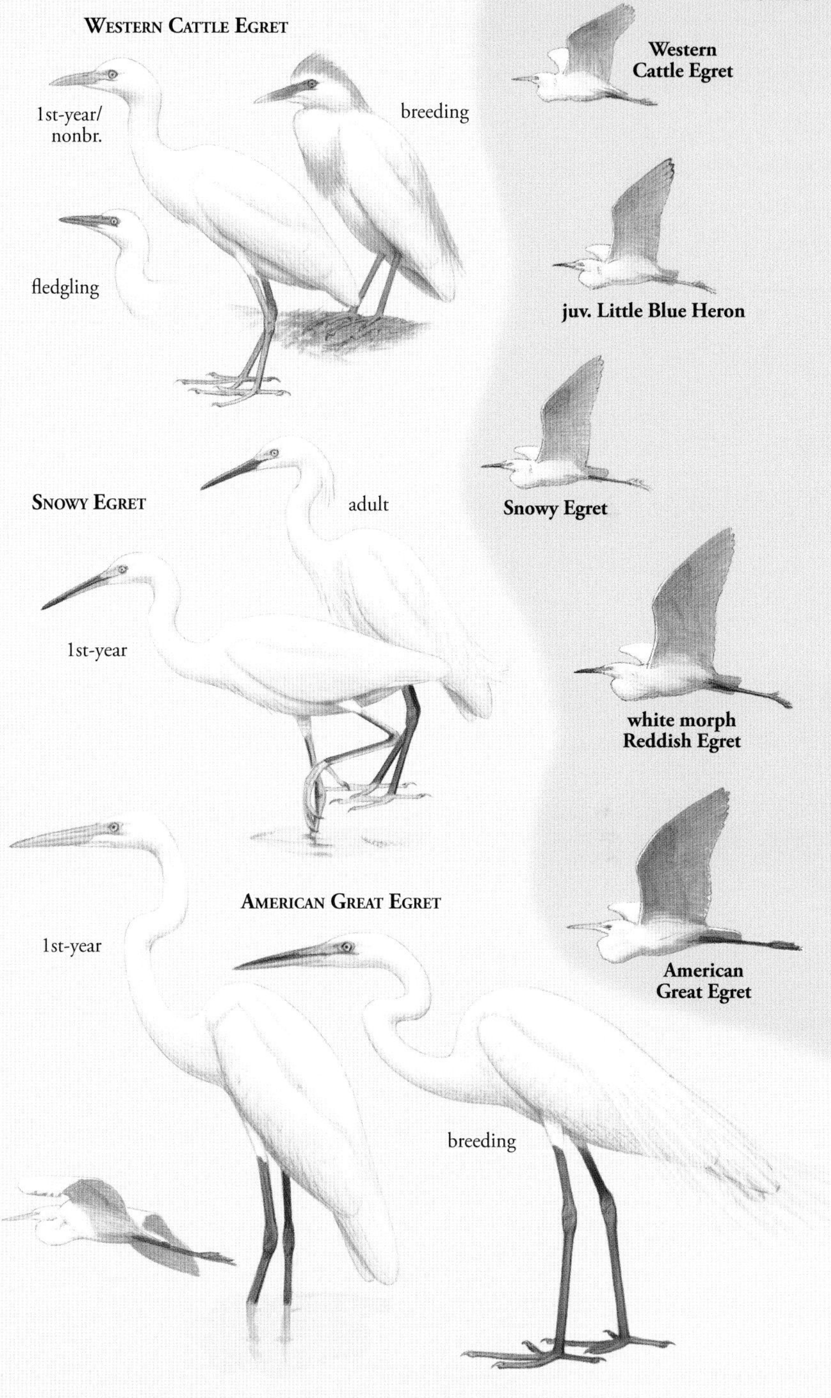

WESTERN CATTLE EGRET

1st-year/
nonbr.

breeding

fledgling

**Western
Cattle Egret**

juv. Little Blue Heron

SNOWY EGRET

adult

1st-year

Snowy Egret

1st-year

AMERICAN GREAT EGRET

**white morph
Reddish Egret**

**American
Great Egret**

breeding

LITTLE BLUE HERON *Egretta caerulea* 51–61cm. Fairly small dark heron of varied wetland habitats, from estuaries and mangroves to flooded fields, lakeshores, rocky coasts; more often at isolated small ponds and ditches than other egrets. Singles or small groups, often mixed with other wading birds. Hunts mainly by waiting, slow stalking. Adult smaller and darker than Reddish Egret, with blue-gray base to bill, yellow-green legs. At height of breeding, bill base and lores flush blue, legs and feet blackish. Wholly white 1st-year Little Blue easily passed off as Snowy Egret but slightly stockier, with bluish-gray face and black-tipped bill, yellowish-green legs and feet, fine dark tips to outer primaries. Piebald molting birds seen frequently for a few months in summer. **SOUNDS:** Much like Snowy Egret, but often slightly raspier. **STATUS:** Fairly common Sep–Apr, mainly below 1500m; smaller numbers in summer (mainly nonbr. imms.); breeds locally in nw. lowlands. (Americas.)

TRICOLORED HERON *Egretta tricolor* 56–66cm. Handsome, 'snake-necked' heron of varied wetland habitats, from river mouths and mangroves to flooded fields, coastal lagoons, lakeshores. Singles or small groups, often with other wading birds. Hunts by waiting, often coiled and hunched low in shallow water, and by active dashing. Distinctive, but perhaps better named 'bicolored' heron, with overall dark gray plumage and contrasting white belly; also note long slender bill, yellowish face. At height of breeding, bill base and lores flush violet-blue, legs and feet pinkish red. 1st-year has rusty head and neck sides, like adult in 2nd year. **SOUNDS:** Relatively high, drawn-out, squawking *aaáah*, at times in short series; also lower nasal calls. **STATUS:** Uncommon to fairly common Sep–Apr, mainly in coastal lowlands but locally to 1500m; smaller numbers in summer (mainly nonbr. imms.); breeds locally in nw. lowlands. (Americas.)

REDDISH EGRET *Egretta rufescens* 66–77cm. Rather large, dimorphic (white morph scarce) egret of coastal habitats from river mouths and lagoons to salt ponds, beaches, mangroves. Hunts by dashing actively, often raising wings; also by stalking and waiting. Note fairly large size, slender bill (with pink base most of year on adult), dark legs. Dark morph adult has shaggy rusty head and neck plumes; white morph wholly white (all ages; also see p. 78). 1st-year dark morph (representing most records in Costa Rica) dull slaty gray overall with variable rusty tinge to neck, dark bill; cf. adult Little Blue Heron. **SOUNDS:** Mostly quiet; rarely low moaning groans and grunts. **STATUS:** Rare nonbr. migrant Sep–Apr, mainly on Pacific coast, a few imms. may oversummer. (N America to Caribbean, winters to S America.)

GREAT BLUE HERON *Ardea herodias* 102–127cm. The only very large dark heron in Costa Rica, widespread in fresh and saltwater habitats, from beaches, estuaries, and mangroves to lakeshores, flooded fields, roadside ponds and ditches. Often in areas with other herons, egrets, storks, ibises. Hunts by waiting and slow stalking. Flight heavy, with slow deep wingbeats, neck retracted in a bulge like other herons but can be extended briefly after takeoff. Adult has clean white crown, shaggy neck and back plumes, clean plumage. 1st-year has black crown, duskier plumage with pale edgings to upperparts; 2nd-year like dull adult, crown partially to mostly white. **SOUNDS:** Flight call a loud, explosive *rrEK!* Other varied sounds include deep throaty croaks, often with raspy, 'complaining' quality. **STATUS:** Fairly common to uncommon nonbr. migrant Sep–Apr, mainly below 1500m, rarely higher; small numbers of imms. oversummer locally. (N America to Mexico, winters to S America.)

LITTLE BLUE HERON

juv.

breeding

adults

molting
1st-years

TRICOLORED HERON

breeding

adult

breeding

juv.

dark morphs

white
morph

1st-year

REDDISH EGRET

adults

1st-year

GREAT BLUE HERON

adult

BLACK-CROWNED NIGHT HERON *Nycticorax nycticorax* 56–64cm. Chunky, mainly nocturnal heron often seen during the day in varied fresh and brackish wetland habitats, from lakes in town parks to mangroves. Hunts along edges and in shallow water, waiting and stalking slowly for fish. Roosts mainly in trees, often not deeply hidden, at times with or near Yellow-crowned Night Herons. Rather compact in flight, with short foot projection past tail tip, cf. longer-legged, more lightly built Yellow-crowned. Adult plumage distinctive. Juv./1st-year from Yellow-crowned by shape, especially pointed bill, shorter legs, coarser pale streaks on upperparts (vs. pale spots and fringes to feathers). Cf. Boat-billed Heron. 2nd-year like duller, browner version of adult. At height of breeding, adult lores become black, legs flush bright salmon-red. **SOUNDS:** Flight call a gruff barking *worhk!* or *wahk*, with rising inflection. Other low guttural calls when nesting and disturbed. **STATUS:** Uncommon to fairly common Sep–Apr on both slopes, locally to 1500m; more local in summer, breeding mainly in nw. lowlands and Central Valley. (Worldwide except Australasia.)

YELLOW-CROWNED NIGHT HERON *Nyctanassa violacea* 51–59cm. Mainly nocturnal but often seen during the day, in varied brackish and freshwater habitats, especially mangroves, along rivers. Main food is crabs, and regularly hunts away from water, as in coconut plantations and on open beaches. Roosts mainly in trees, often not deeply hidden. More lightly built than Black-crowned Night Heron with stouter blackish bill, longer neck, longer legs; in flight, feet project well past tail tip. Adult distinctive. Cf. Juv./1st-year Black-crowned (nestling Yellow-crowned has yellow at bill base, soon darkens). 2nd-year like duller, browner version of adult. At height of breeding, adult lores become black, legs flush bright salmon-red. **SOUNDS:** Flight call a slightly grating *owhr* or *kyowh*, higher and more nasal than Black-crowned, typically with more downward inflection. Low guttural clucks when nesting and disturbed. **STATUS:** Uncommon to fairly common on both slopes, especially nw. lowlands; more widespread Sep–Apr when n. migrants present, rarely to 1400m. (Americas.)

***BOAT-BILLED HERON** *Cochlearius cochlearius* 46–53cm. Distinctive nocturnal heron of fresh and brackish marshes, lakeshores, coastal lagoons, slow-moving rivers, mangroves; spends the day roosting, well hidden in trees; tends to leave roost later than night herons. Hunts at night along shorelines and in shallow water. Flight direct with slightly stiff wingbeats emphasizing the upstroke, subtly distinct from steadier bowed wingbeats of night herons. Note very broad bill with distensible pouch, big dark eyes. Slightly smaller and more compact than Black-crowned Night Heron, with shorter toe projection in flight; adult has contrasting black underwing coverts. Juv. lacks pale spots and streaks of juv. night herons. **SOUNDS:** Usually silent in flight at dusk. At roost when disturbed, and when nesting, utters varied clucks and chatters, often with chuckling cadence, such as *kuh-kuh kuk-kuh ku-kah*. **STATUS:** Fairly common to uncommon in coastal lowlands on both slopes, locally inland to 800m. (Mexico to S America.)

BLACK-CROWNED NIGHT HERON

adults

juv.

YELLOW-CROWNED NIGHT HERON

adults

juv.

BOAT-BILLED HERON

adults

juv.

LEAST BITTERN *Ixobrychus exilis* 28–31cm. Tiny heron of fresh and brackish marshes with tall reeds and rushes, lakes with bordering reeds. Stealthy and retiring; mainly hunts from perch over water, clambering easily through reeds. Flushes from close range and usually flies a short distance before dropping back to cover; wingbeats fairly quick. Distinctive (note big buff wing panel in flight); cf. larger, overall dark Green Heron. At height of breeding, male lores flush scarlet, legs bright orange. **SOUNDS:** Common call a short series of (usually 5–9) rasping barks *kyeh-kyeh...*, slowing slightly at end, given irregularly. In breeding season, 'song' a fairly rapid series of about 3–10 muffled coos, *cuh-cuh-cuh-cuh-cuh*, often repeated steadily and can be given at night; may suggest Black-billed Cuckoo song but lower, huskier. **STATUS:** Uncommon and local breeder in nw. lowlands, likely elsewhere; more widespread Sep–Apr when n. migrants present, rarely to 1500m. (Americas.)

PINNATED BITTERN *Botaurus pinnatus* 64–76cm. Freshwater marshes with tall grassy vegetation, reedbeds, flooded rice fields. Mostly skulking; tends to crouch or freeze when alarmed, but at times flushes from close range; flight heavy, with wingbeats mainly above body plane, reminiscent of a tiger heron. Pale buffy plumage with finely barred neck sides and coarsely streaked upperparts distinctive; white tufts at chest sides usually concealed but flared in display. Cf. imm. tiger herons. **SOUNDS:** Flushed birds give gruff *owhk*, singly or in short series. 'Song' a very low-pitched, deep booming or gulping *uungh*, often preceded by a few liquid clucks and at times repeated steadily; quality recalls American Bittern. **STATUS:** Scarce to fairly common locally on both slopes, mainly in nw. lowlands, to 600m. (Mexico to S America.).

GREEN HERON *Butorides virescens* 38–43cm. Small dark heron of varied wetland habitats from mangroves and rocky coasts to small roadside ponds, extensive wetlands, lakeshores, often with wooded edges. Usually singles, often apart from other herons. Hunts by waiting or slow stalking, often hunched on low branch or other perch over water. Note small size, overall dark plumage with dark rusty neck sides, bright yellow legs. Juv. has streaked neck, much like adult by end of 1st year. At height of breeding, adult lores become black, legs flush bright salmon-orange. **SOUNDS:** Flight call a clipped, slightly explosive yap *kyah!* or *kyowh*, often in short series when flushed; hollow, low clucking series when agitated, *kuh-kuh-kuh.…*In breeding season, 'song' is a low, frog-like growl, *reeohr*, repeated. **STATUS:** Fairly common but low-density on both slopes, locally to 1800m; more widespread and numerous Sep–Apr when n. migrants present, especially on Caribbean slope and inland. (N America to Panama.)

STRIATED HERON *Butorides striata* 38–43cm. Rare but increasing visitor, the southern counterpart to Green Heron. Typical adult differs from Green Heron in gray (rarely brownish) neck sides, slightly paler plumage with contrasting black whisker mark. Juv. perhaps not safely separable from Green Heron. Habits and voice like Green Heron. **STATUS:** Very rare but increasing (records year-round), mainly on Pacific slope and in nw. lowlands since 2000s; could occur anywhere. (Panama to S America, Old World.)

AGAMI HERON *Agamia agami* 66–76cm. Rarely seen, very long-billed heron of shady forested wetlands, mangroves, quiet forest streams and ponds. Usually solitary, quiet, and stealthy; often rather shy and usually apart from other herons. Easily overlooked, as dark plumage blends well with shady habitats, but breeds locally in colonies. Note very long slender bill, rather short dull legs, habits. Adult stunning, with silvery blue-gray filigree neck plumes, chestnut neck and belly, deep oily-green upperparts; attains plush silvery-gray crest in breeding season, when lores and throat flush bright red. 1st-year distinctive, with very long bill, brown face, neck and upperparts, pale belly. **SOUNDS:** Territorial call a low, throaty, purring growl, about 1–2 secs, repeated every few secs. **STATUS:** Uncommon to scarce on Caribbean slope, locally on s. Pacific slope; to 700m. (Mexico to S America.)

LEAST BITTERN

juv.

female

male

PINNATED BITTERN

GREEN HERON

adults

juv.

STRIATED HERON

adult

AGAMI HERON

breeding

1st-year

adult

TIGER HERONS (GENUS *TIGRISOMA*) (3 species). Large, heavyset tropical herons with very long necks, relatively short legs. Usually close to wooded cover and perch readily in trees; hunt by waiting and slow stalking. Flight heavy, with stiff wingbeats emphasizing upstroke; note broad wings, very short foot projection relative to other herons. Ages differ: 1st-years of all species similar and boldly 'tiger-barred' with tawny and dark brown; 2nd-year resembles adult but with coarser barring, duller pattern; like adult in 3rd year. Deep throaty 'songs' (may suggest large owl or mammal) often given at night.

BARE-THROATED TIGER HERON *Tigrisoma mexicanum* 71–82cm. Lowland wetlands with slow-moving water, ponds, mangroves, wooded swamps, damp pastures; locally also rocky streams and rivers in foothills. See genus note. Singles or locally loose concentrations up to 10 or so birds may hunt in fairly open situations along with other herons, storks, ibises. All ages have diagnostic naked yellow throat skin, but can be difficult to see (pale yellowish on imm., orange-yellow on displaying adult). Adult distinctive: gray face contrasts with black cap, warm brownish neck has fine barring. Imm. plumages much like other tiger herons, differs from Fasciated Tiger Heron in longer bill, habitat (but both can occur in fast-flowing rocky streams); averages duller rusty than Rufescent Tiger Heron, but plumage tones and patterning of both species variable, not known to be reliable for ID; note habitat differences (Bare-throated in mangroves, semi-open habitats, Rufescent in rainforest; but can occur together in some areas). Also cf. Pinnated Bittern. **SOUNDS:** Flushed birds often give low, guttural grunts. In breeding season, especially at dusk or during night, 'song' is a far-carrying, steadily repeated, throaty grunt or roar, at times with paired cadence from dueting or countersinging birds, *rrohr, rrohr...*, 10/10–15 secs. **STATUS:** Fairly common to uncommon on both slopes, mainly below 1000m. (Mexico to nw. Colombia.)

FASCIATED TIGER HERON *Tigrisoma fasciatum* 61–66cm. Relatively small and compact tiger heron of fast-flowing rocky streams and rivers in forested foothills. See genus note. Usually singles, stalking or standing quietly along banks near cover, or out on rocks in mid-flow; relatively agile, hopping readily from rock to rock. Usually identified readily by habitat, but locally Bare-throated Tiger Heron can be in similar habitat. Note relatively short bill and legs of Fasciated; adult has overall gray neck, white median throat stripe, cf. Bare-throated Tiger Heron (some imms. similar in plumage to adult Fasciated but throat naked, yellow). Imm. very similar to imm. Rufescent Tiger Heron, note habitat, slightly shorter bill (but young juv. Rufescent has relatively short bill); plumage tones and patterning of both species variable, not known to be reliable for ID. **SOUNDS:** May give low guttural croaks when disturbed. **STATUS:** Uncommon and local on both slopes, mainly 100–1000m, locally to 2500m. (Costa Rica to S America.)

RUFESCENT TIGER HERON *Tigrisoma lineatum* 65–75cm. Humid lowland forest and adjacent second growth, along quiet streams, at small ponds, in swampy understory, sometimes in more open situations at edges of lakes and larger rivers; not in fast-flowing open situations of Fasciated Tiger Heron, or more open, often second-growth habitats of Bare-throated. See genus note. Usually rather retiring, heard more often than seen. Adult handsome and distinctive, with deep rusty head and neck; 1st-year very similar to other tiger herons, note habitat, also feathered white median throat (can be difficult to see clearly) vs. Bare-throated. **SOUNDS:** Flushed birds often give a low, guttural grunts. 'Song' mainly at night in breeding season comprises low, slightly roaring moans in varied arrangement, often fairly rapid series of 10 or more shorter notes, *whoh whoh...*, 2–3/sec, final notes longer; may suggest large owl. Also low, drawn-out moans of 2–3 secs duration, every few secs or in short series; at times with an introduction of 2–15 shorter moans, *ooah ooah ooah oooaaaahhh....* **STATUS:** Scarce on Caribbean slope, to 500m. (Honduras to S America.)

1st-year

2nd-year

1st-year

**BARE-THROATED
TIGER HERON**

adult

2nd-year

1st-year

adult

FASCIATED TIGER HERON

2nd-year

adult

1st-year

RUFESCENT TIGER HERON

88

IBISES AND SPOONBILLS (THRESKIORNITHIDAE; 4+ SPECIES)
Worldwide family of elegant wading birds; ibises have slender decurved bills, spoonbills (p. 90) have flattened bills with spatulate tips. Ages differ, sexes similar; attain adult appearance in 2–3 years. Build stick nests in trees; often nest colonially with other waterbirds.

WHITE IBIS *Eudocimus albus* 53–63cm. Mangroves, tidal flats, coastal lagoons, freshwater marshes; main food is crabs, other crustaceans. Gregarious, usually in groups; feeds by probing and picking. Flies with neck and legs outstretched, wingbeats fairly quick and shallow, interspersed with brief glides; often flies in lines and Vs, usually not mixed with other waterbirds. Distinctive, with decurved reddish-pink bill, pinkish-red legs; small black wing-tips of adult often hidden at rest. Imm. slightly bulkier than Glossy Ibis, immediately told by white underparts, pink face and bill; attains white upperparts gradually over 1st year. Cf. much larger Wood Stork. SOUNDS: Low grunts mainly when flushed and in interactions. STATUS: Fairly common to common locally in nw. lowlands and on Pacific coast; in smaller numbers elsewhere on both slopes, rarely to 1200m. (Americas.)

GLOSSY IBIS *Plegadis falcinellus* 53–63cm. Slender, long-legged, tall-standing dark ibis of varied fresh and brackish wetland habitats, from roadside ponds to extensive marshes, flooded fields, lakeshores. Locally in small flocks, also singles, associating readily with other wading birds; feeds by probing. Flies with neck outstretched and slightly drooped, legs trailing (feet project noticeably farther on male), wingbeats fairly stiff and shallow, often interspersed with brief glides on bowed wings; distant flocks in flight may suggest Neotropic Cormorant. Cf. Green Ibis, imm. White Ibis. Juv. has sooty brownish neck with variable, sparse white blotches, soon attains 1st-year plumage resembling nonbr. adult but without chestnut on shoulders. Like adult in 2nd year. SOUNDS: Mostly silent; low grunts when flushed. STATUS: Uncommon to fairly common locally in nw. lowlands and on s. Pacific slope; rare and irregular elsewhere on both slopes, mainly Sep–May. (Old World, N America, Caribbean region.)

GREEN IBIS *Mesembrinibis cayennensis* 56–63.5cm. Rather compact, short-legged, distinctive dark ibis of humid forest and edge, adjacent swamps. Found as singles and pairs, rarely small groups, along creeks, at quiet pools, and in flooded understory, locally in more open situations at wetland edges, adjacent fields, lawns; perches readily in trees. Forages by probing, sometimes nodding its head as it walks along. Often calls loudly when flushed. Note decurved bill, short legs (feet do not project in flight); nape often appears shaggy; cf. Glossy Ibis. Imm. duller overall, with little or no greenish gloss on head and neck. SOUNDS: Clucking and gobbling rhythmic short series, such as *koh'lo-hop koh'lo-hop...*, cf. wood rail songs; can be loud when flushed. Foraging and agitated calls include slow-paced, guttural growls. STATUS: Fairly common to uncommon on Caribbean slope; scarce and local but increasing on Pacific slope, since 2000s. (Honduras to S America.)

LIMPKINS (ARAMIDAE; 1 SPECIES) New World family related to cranes and rails.
Ages differ slightly, sexes similar; like adult in 1st year.

*LIMPKIN *Aramus guarauna* 58–64cm. Freshwater marshes, lakes, swampy woodland, locally mangroves. Usually near cover and can be retiring, at other times singles or locally small groups feed in the open, probing for snails; often perches in trees. Flight distinctive but usually not prolonged, with neck outstretched, stiff snappy wingbeats with emphasis on upstroke. Nothing very similar, but cf. Glossy Ibis. Note stout straight bill with black tip, white-spattered plumage, habits. Juv. has neater and smaller white markings than adult. SOUNDS: Varied loud trumpeting, screaming, and clucking calls, especially early and late in the day and at night, including a rolled *krrrreeah* and honking *krrrrowh*; also a clipped barking *owhk!* in alarm and a sharp, piercing *bihk bihk...* when agitated. STATUS: Fairly common but somewhat nomadic in nw. lowlands; smaller numbers locally elsewhere on both slopes, to 1500m. (Mexico and Caribbean region to S America.)

WHITE IBIS

juv.

adult

imm.

GLOSSY IBIS

1st-year
(nonbr. similar)

breeding

GREEN IBIS

LIMPKIN

ROSEATE SPOONBILL *Platalea ajaja* 71–79cm. Stunning pink wading bird of wetlands, coastal marshes and lagoons, mangroves. No similar species. Associates readily with other wading birds, especially White Ibis. Feeds by filtering food with its bill tip. Flies with neck and legs outstretched, wingbeats fairly quick and shallow, interspersed with brief glides; regularly soars, at times in kettles with vultures and Wood Storks. Juv. much paler pink, with fine dusky wing-tips, feathered head that changes to naked pale greenish over 1st-year; 2nd-year like duller version of adult; attains adult appearance in 3rd year. SOUNDS: Mostly quiet except when nesting; colonies produce low clucking and chuckling calls. STATUS: Uncommon to fairly common locally in nw. lowlands, irregular s. along Pacific coast and on Caribbean slope, rare inland to 1200m. (Americas.)

STORKS (CICONIIDAE; 2+ SPECIES) Mainly Old World family of large to very large wading birds with stout pointed bills, long broad wings often used for soaring. Ages differ, sexes similar; adult appearance attained in 2–3 years. Build bulky stick nests high in trees; Wood Stork usually colonial. Utter low grunts and hisses, also bill-rattling noises; mostly silent away from nest.

WOOD STORK *Mycteria americana* 89–101cm. Fresh and brackish wetlands, from flooded fields and roadside ponds (especially when drying up) to mangroves, lakes, wooded swamps. Feeds by wading and probing, often in association with other waterbirds; perches readily in trees. Often soars on mid–late morning thermals, at times high overhead, with vultures, other large birds; flocks tend to wheel in somewhat disorganized kettles, not strongly synchronized. Juv./1st-year has creamy bill, downy head feathering; head becomes naked and attains adult pattern over 2 years. STATUS: Fairly common but nomadic year-round in nw. lowlands; irregular wanderer elsewhere on both slopes, occasional inland to 1200m. (Americas.)

JABIRU *Jabiru mycteria* 130–153cm. Huge, the largest flying bird in the Americas, and difficult to misidentify. Singles or locally small groups forage in open wetland habitats, savannas, flooded rice fields, often in areas with aggregations of egrets, herons, other wading birds, when large size usually obvious; also adjacent swampy woodland and forest patches in wetlands. Nests high in emergent, often bare trees. Flight strong, with smooth wingbeats, neck outstretched; soars occasionally. Juv./1st-year has upperparts edged silvery gray-brown and mixed with blackish feathers, but looks largely white at any distance; red on neck duller than adult, often some downy whitish feathering on head. 2nd-year like dull adult, with scattered brownish feathers on upperparts. STATUS: Uncommon to locally/seasonally fairly common but nomadic in nw. lowlands, where breeds Nov–Apr; very rare wanderer elsewhere, mainly in n. lowlands. (Mexico to S America.)

ROSEATE SPOONBILL

1st-years

adults

adults

adults

JABIRU

WOOD STORK

juv.

RAILS, GALLINULES, ALLIES (RALLIDAE; 15+ SPECIES) Worldwide family of very small to medium-size marsh birds. Can be divided into more skulking rails and crakes, more conspicuous gallinules and coots, which are often seen swimming. Ages differ, sexes usually similar; precocial downy young of all species are black and fuzzy; attain adult appearance in 1st year. Flight can be surprisingly strong, but migrate at night and rarely seen in flight unless flushed.

Gray-headed

Rust-faced

WHITE-THROATED CRAKE *Laterallus albigularis* 14.5–15.5cm. Commonest small crake in Costa Rica, often heard but rarely seen. Varied grassy and marshy habitats from damp fields and roadsides ditches to extensive wetlands with taller reeds, lakeshores, mangrove edge. Mostly skulking and difficult to see; sometimes comes out at edges, when can be confiding. Distinctive, with bright ruddy neck and breast, barred flanks. Juv. duller overall, with little or no ruddy plumage, cf. Gray-breasted Crake. Comprises 2 groups that may represent species: **Gray-headed Crake** *L. [a.] cinereiceps* of Caribbean slope, with gray head; **Rusty-faced Crake** *L. [a.] albigularis* of Pacific slope, with rusty face, brownish crown. SOUNDS: **Gray-headed** contact call a slightly descending churring trill, typically preceded by hesitant piping notes audible at close range, *whiit, whiit...urrrrrrrr...*, mainly 2–6 secs; also prolonged series up to 30 secs, with vaguely rising and falling cadence, cf. Least Grebe. Song (?) a sharp, clipped *tchip!* singly or in slow pairs, every few secs, may recall Yellow Warbler. **Rusty-faced** trills average slightly faster-paced, drier, and gruffer. Song (?) a sharp smacking *tchik*, singly or in slow pairs, slightly lower, more smacking than Gray-headed, may recall Common Tody-Flycatcher. STATUS: Fairly common to common on both slopes, especially Caribbean lowlands; to 1500m. (Honduras to nw. S America.)

GRAY-BREASTED CRAKE *Laterallus exilis* 14.5–15.5cm. Varied grassy and marshy habitats from extensive wetlands with taller reeds to overgrown weedy fields, roadside ditches; often in same areas as much commoner White-throated Crake. Skulking and difficult to see; may approach within a few feet but be hidden like a mouse, even in short vegetation; rarely flies. Note lime-green base to bill, rusty hindneck contrasting with gray head and breast, barred flanks. Juv. duller with little or no rusty on hindneck. SOUNDS: Song a fairly rapid series of (usually 2–9) high piping notes, often with a soft introductory note audible at close range: *tik, dee-dee...*, every 2–5 secs; easily passed off as a frog. Churring contact trills similar to White-throated Crake but harsher, drier, more rattling, often shorter. STATUS: Scarce to locally common on both slopes, mainly below 1000m. (Mexico to S America.)

YELLOW-BREASTED CRAKE *Laterallus (Hapalocrex) flaviventer* 12.5–13.5cm. Freshwater marshes with reeds, emergent and floating vegetation, from small ponds to large wetlands. Typically retiring, but locally may feed at edges, walking on floating vegetation. Flushes silently from underfoot, legs dangling, and flies a short distance back to cover. Distinctive, with striped face, buffy breast, bold tawny back striping. SOUNDS: Song a plaintive, slightly metallic, 2-note whistled phrase, *chieh-dii*, every 1.5–5 secs, including at night; less often a single *chieh*. Quiet short rattle, *chrrrt*, when agitated may run into series of gruff rasping scold notes, *zzheh-zzheh....*STATUS: Scarce to fairly common locally on both slopes. (Mexico to S America.)

OCELLATED CRAKE *Micropygia schomburgkii* 14–15cm. Poorly known and rarely seen small crake of dense grassland and savanna with scattered shrubs; often in relatively dry areas, not marshes. Skulking and elusive; rarely flies unless virtually stepped on. Distinctive if you are lucky enough to see it, with black-edged white spots on upperparts, rich buffy face and breast; also note red eyes, dark bill, bright reddish legs. SOUNDS: Song (often at night) a drawn-out, slurred raspy buzz, about 1 sec, every 1–2 secs; sometimes varied to slightly pulsating series of shorter rasping notes; quality may suggest a low, slow-paced fishing reel unspooling. STATUS: Scarce to fairly common but local in interior valleys of s. Pacific slope, mainly around Buenos Aires. (Costa Rica to S America.)

Caribbean
(Gray-headed)

juv.

WHITE-THROATED CRAKE

Pacific
(Rusty-faced)

GRAY-BREASTED CRAKE

YELLOW-BREASTED CRAKE

OCELLATED CRAKE

SORA *Porzana carolina* 20.5–21.5cm. Fairly small migrant crake of varied marshy habitats, from roadside ditches and extensive wetlands with tall rushes to mangroves, lakeshores, rice fields. Often more conspicuous than other crakes, but dashes quickly for cover when alarmed. No similar species in Costa Rica: note short yellowish bill, black face, buffy-white wedge under tail, which is often held cocked in a point, near-vertical. Imm. browner overall, attains adult appearance over 1st winter. SOUNDS: Slurred, slightly nasal squealing *kee-ur*, bright clipped *keek*, and short rolled squeal run into a descending, slow-paced whinny, *kreeh, dee-de-du-du-du...*, 1.5–4 secs. STATUS: Fairly common to uncommon Oct–Apr on both slopes; most numerous in lowlands, locally inland to 1500m. (Breeds N America, winters to S America.)

PAINT-BILLED CRAKE *Neocrex erythrops* 18–19cm. Fairly small crake of grassy marshes, roadside ditches, rice fields, small ponds with vegetated margins. Skulking like most crakes, but sometimes in the open at edges and can flush fairly readily from close range. Note short yellow bill with intense red base, overall dark plumage with barring on rear flanks and undertail coverts (barring can be difficult to see, often mostly cloaked by wings), pinkish-red legs. Juv. duller than adult, red bill base reduced or lacking, flank barring weaker. SOUNDS: Song a semi-metallic, sharp clucking or yipping *puik-puik...*, to 10 secs or longer, 2–4 notes/sec; quality suggests Sora; at times single sharp yips. Agitated birds give low, throaty, purring trill, *urrrr...*, 3–5 secs, vaguely like a small motor; also fairly rapid pumping series of gurgling grunts, *ugh-ugh...*, up to 10 secs, about 7 notes/sec, and rhythmic whining calls. STATUS: Uncommon to fairly common locally on both slopes, to 1000m. (Costa Rica to S America.)

SPOTTED RAIL *Pardirallus maculatus* 25.5–28cm. Medium-size, strikingly patterned rail of freshwater marshes and lakes with reeds, rice fields, overgrown wet ditches. Often skulking and difficult to see, emerging mainly at dusk along marsh edges, but at other times feeds unconcerned in open situations at any time of day, as singles or even small groups. Size, striking plumage, and bright bare parts distinctive. Juv. may be dimorphic: some like duller version of adult, others dark overall, but soon attaining distinctive barring and spotting. SOUNDS: Overslurred, rough screeching *rreéah*, about 0.5 sec. Varied series of nasal pumping grunts or rough screeching clucks, often disyllabic with overall descending cadence, 2–5 notes/sec. Agitated birds give very low, hollow, stuttering or purring chatter suggesting a distant outboard motor, 12–15 notes/sec. STATUS: Uncommon and local (nomadic?), mainly in nw. lowlands, on s. Pacific slope, and in Central Valley; might be found anywhere. (Mexico to S America.)

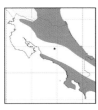

UNIFORM CRAKE *Amaurolimnas concolor* 20.5–22cm. Medium-size, rather plump-bodied crake of damp grassy thickets, *Heliconia* stands, humid forest floor. Typically skulking and rarely seen, walks and runs with fairly upright stance suggesting a tinamou; usually detected by voice. No similar species in Costa Rica, but cf. Little Tinamou. Note short yellowish bill, overall dull rusty plumage with no barring, bright pinkish-red legs. SOUNDS: 'Song' mainly early and late in day, and at night, a series of (usually 7–20 or more) easily imitated, upslurred whistles, each 0.5–1 sec, series at times intensifying then fading quickly: *tuuíh tuuíh...TOO'IH TOO'IH...too-ih*; at a distance, only loudest sections audible. Sharp clucking *plik!* when disturbed. STATUS: Uncommon to scarce on both slopes, locally to 1200m. (Mexico to S America.)

SORA

1st-year
(Sep–Dec)

PAINT-BILLED CRAKE

SPOTTED RAIL

juv.

UNIFORM CRAKE

RUSSET-NAPED [GRAY-NECKED] WOOD RAIL *Aramides [cajaneus] albiventris* 38–43cm. Very large, handsome rail of fresh and brackish wetland habitats, typically with wooded or other cover nearby, from swampy woodland and forest understory to ponds, lakes, roadside ditches; locally in mangroves. Details of distribution and extent of range overlap with Gray-cowled Wood Rail (both formerly considered conspecific as Gray-necked Wood Rail) await elucidation; note voice, head pattern. Also cf. Rufous-necked Wood Rail. Juv. has grayish belly, duller bare parts, duller and less well-defined nape patch. SOUNDS: 'Song' mainly early and late in day in spring–summer, a rollicking, clucking and shrieking phrase repeated over and over, *koh-koh KWIdi-KWIdi...*, or *koh koh-koh ki-KWIdi-KWIdi...*, at times in crazed-sounding duets; cf. wood quails. Sharp clucking shrieks when disturbed, occasional low grunts when foraging. STATUS: Fairly common in n. lowlands, locally to 1200m. (Mexico to Costa Rica.)

GRAY-COWLED [GRAY-NECKED] WOOD RAIL *Aramides cajaneus* 38–43cm. Replaces Russet-naped Wood Rail in most of Costa Rica (both formerly considered conspecific as Gray-necked Wood Rail). Habitat and habits similar to Russet-naped. Averages shorter bill and legs, longer tail than Russet-naped, best identified by song; lacks contrasting russet nape patch (nape diffusely washed brownish), but some poorly marked Russet-naped may be similar, perhaps imms., which also may have relatively short bills (study needed). Also cf. Rufous-necked Wood Rail. SOUNDS: Rhythmic shrieky honking and braying *EE-ohr EE-ohr...* or *OHR-ki-di OHR-ki-di...*, sometimes with cadence suggesting a braying donkey; at times alternated with or preceded by fairly rapid series of (up to about 10) low clucking hoots, *koh-koh..., KI-di-hohr, KI-di-hohr....* Quality similar to Russet-naped Wood Rail but rhythm different, often slightly slower-paced. Cf. wood quails. STATUS: Fairly common to common on Pacific slope (except far north), locally inland to 1500m, and on extreme s. Caribbean slope. (Costa Rica to S America.)

RUFOUS-NECKED WOOD RAIL *Aramides axillaris* 29.5–31.5cm. Gallinule-size rail of mangroves, wooded swamps, semi-deciduous forest. Tends to be skulking and elusive, but can be found feeding quietly along mangrove edge, on open mudflats near cover, on quiet forest trails. Adult distinctive, with bright rusty head, neck, and breast, blue-gray upper back, black vent and undertail coverts; juv. has dirty grayish head and neck, soon replaced with adult-like plumage. Cf. Russet-naped and Gray-cowled Wood Rails. Often in same areas as larger Mangrove Rail. SOUNDS: Mainly in spring–summer, a steady series of piercing, semi-metallic clucks repeated steadily, *kyih! kyih!*, 2–3 notes/sec, (dueting?) with faster, rhythmic cadence, such as *ki ki-ki kyi, ki ki-ki kyi...* or *ki ki-ki, ki-ki-ki, ki ki-ki, ki-ki-ki...*, 4–5 notes/sec. STATUS: Uncommon locally Sep–early May (year-round?) on n. Pacific coast; and Apr–Sep (year-round?) inland, to 1500m in Northern Mts. (Mexico to S America.)

MANGROVE [CLAPPER] RAIL *Rallus longirostris* 31–37cm. Large rail of low mangroves, adjacent mudflats and channels. Mostly seen as singles at mangrove edge, especially early and late in the day; prefers to run rather than fly. No similar species in Costa Rica. Note long, mostly orange bill, grayish upperparts with dark back striping, peachy tones to breast, barred flanks, and orange-red legs. Juv. has dusky grayish neck and underparts with little or no flank barring, duller bill and legs; like adult by fall. SOUNDS: Loud clucking chatters year-round, typically with distinctive stuttering rhythm, *keh-keh-kehrrr keh-keh keh-keh-kehrr...*, 4–6 notes/sec, mainly for 5–10 secs but can be prolonged in duet or when triggering other birds. Alarm call an overslurred rasping growl *grrehrr*, about 0.5 secs. STATUS: Fairly common to uncommon but local around Gulf of Nicoya; first found Costa Rica in 2000s and may be more widespread than shown (e.g., reports from n. Pacific coast). (Honduras to S America.)

RUSSET-NAPED WOOD RAIL

GRAY-COWLED WOOD RAIL

RUFOUS-NECKED WOOD RAIL

juv.

MANGROVE RAIL

AMERICAN COOT *Fulica americana* 35.5–40.5cm. Distinctive, chunky, rather duck-like migrant waterbird of varied fresh and brackish habitats, from lakes and coastal lagoons to wetlands with open water, mangroves, estuaries. Locally in flocks of 100s, elsewhere singles and small groups associating readily with other waterbirds. Feeds by diving and up-ending, also while walking on shore, when big lobed toes distinctive. Juv. has extensively whitish head and neck, attaining adult appearance over 1st winter. SOUNDS: Varied nasal clucks, rough quacks, and gruff chatters, mainly in interactions; typically lower and gruffer than calls of Common Gallinule; most commonly a gruff *krreh*, and nasal, slightly trumpeting *puh!* STATUS: Fairly common locally Oct–Mar on both slopes, mainly in nw. lowlands, smaller numbers to 1500m. A few may stay into summer, and exceptionally has bred in nw. lowlands. (Breeds N America to Cen America, winters to n. S America.)

COMMON GALLINULE (MOORHEN) *Gallinula galeata* 33–35.5cm. Freshwater marshes, small ponds, and lakes with reeds and other vegetation cover; flooded fields; drainage ditches. Singles or small groups, locally loose aggregations; usually near cover. Feeds mainly while walking, also swims readily. Distinctive, with white stripe along sides, big white undertail-covert wedges; attains adult appearance over 1st year. SOUNDS: Varied. Sharp, overslurred nasal *kek!* and sharp clucking *kuh*, at times repeated steadily or in short series; accelerating then slowing series of sharp clucks with laughing or cackling cadence, tailing off with disyllabic notes, 2–5 secs, *k'keh-kehkehkeh keh keh, k'eh, k'eh.…* STATUS: Uncommon to fairly common but often local, mainly in nw. lowlands and Central Valley, to 1500m. (Americas.)

PURPLE GALLINULE *Porphyrio martinicus* 30.5–33cm. Spectacular large 'rail' of vegetated freshwater habitats, especially with water hyacinth, reedbeds, overhanging bushes. Feeds in open areas, especially on floating vegetation, but often rather shy; runs or flies to cover when disturbed and climbs readily in marshy vegetation, often fairly high in bushes. Distinctive, with long, bright yellow legs and toes, large single white wedge on undertail coverts; note blue-green sheen on juv. wings; attains adult appearance over 1st year. Cf. Common Gallinule. SOUNDS: Varied sharp clucks, typically more nasal, lower than Common Gallinule and often repeated in faster series, sometimes speeding and slowing slightly; overslurred wailing or nasal trumpeting *meéah*, about 0.5 sec, often doubled or in short series, can suggest Limpkin. STATUS: Fairly common to uncommon on both slopes, to 1500m. (Americas.)

JACANAS (JACANIDAE; 2 SPECIES) Small pantropical family of rail-like shorebirds with very long toes that help them walk on floating vegetation; thus, also known as lily-trotters. Ages differ, sexes similar but female larger; male takes care of young. Attain adult appearance in about 1 year.

NORTHERN JACANA *Jacana spinosa* 21.5–24 cm. Familiar bird of varied wetland habitats with floating vegetation, from lakes and roadside pools to flooded fields and mangroves. Singles or locally aggregations of 10s. Walks with high-stepping gait, flies with quick stiff wingbeats and short glides, long legs and toes trailing; bright yellow wings flash in flight. Only similar species in Costa Rica is rare Wattled Jacana. SOUNDS: Loud screechy clicks and raucous chatters. STATUS: Fairly common to common on both slopes; increasing and expanding locally inland, to at least 1500m. (Mexico to Panama.)

WATTLED JACANA *Jacana jacana* 21.5–24 cm. Rare visitor that resembles Northern Jacana in habitat and habits. Adult distinctive, with red shield and bill wattle, blackish body; bright yellow in wings like Northern. Imm. resembles Northern but soon develops red base to bill, small wattle. Birds with Wattled bill pattern but some chestnut mixed in on body and wings are presumed hybrids with Northern. SOUNDS: Similar to Northern Jacana but lower-pitched, often more nasal, buzzier. STATUS: Very rare and irregular year-round (birds may remain for months); has occurred on both slopes and inland, mainly in s. Pacific lowlands since 2000s. (Panama to S America.)

AMERICAN COOT

imm.

COMMON GALLINULE

imm.

PURPLE GALLINULE

imm.

NORTHERN JACANA

1st-year

WATTLED JACANA

SUNBITTERNS (EURYPYGIDAE; 1 SPECIES) Striking and distinctive
neotropical species of wetland habitats; vaguely suggests a large rail, aberrant large sandpiper, or even a weird heron. Ages/sexes similar.

*NORTHERN SUNBITTERN *Eurypyga [helias] major* 44–48cm. Distinctive bird of fast-flowing streams and rivers in forested foothills, especially with rocky and stony shorelines, nearby pools; less often swampy woodland. Nothing similar in Costa Rica, but cf. larger and bulkier Fasciated Tiger Heron (p. 86). Singles or pairs forage along shorelines, out on rocks in mid-flow; runs easily and hops among rocks, where gray plumage blends in well. Flies readily; wingbeats stiff and shallow, gliding short distances on bowed wings. In display flight, climbs steeply with a few quick flaps and glides down, whistling. SOUNDS: 'Song' a plaintive, drawn-out, semi-metallic whistled scream, *wheee'eee*, 1.5–2 secs, often inflected upward partway through, repeated every few secs; may suggest a hawk. High reedy chatter when agitated, 0.5–1 sec. STATUS: Uncommon on both slopes, mainly 100–1500m. (Guatemala to S America.)

TINAMOUS (TINAMIDAE; 5 SPECIES) Neotropical family of fat-bodied,
seemingly tail-less terrestrial birds, heard far more often than seen. Most vocal early and late in day. Ages similar, sexes often differ slightly, females usually brighter than males.

GREAT TINAMOU *Tinamus major* 38–46cm. Very large, heavy-bodied tinamou of humid forest, especially shady and fairly open lowland rainforest interior. Typically wary, and runs or freezes when alarmed; flushes explosively with whistling wings. In some areas, however, has become acclimated and can be quite confiding, such as in Carara National Park and La Selva. Note large size, rather plain plumage (varies from browner to grayer overall) with sparse black bars above, narrow whitish eyering, grayish legs. Crown and face markings dark grayish on Caribbean slope, rusty on Pacific slope. SOUNDS: Haunting song mainly early and late in day, also at night: intensifying, measured series of (usually 2–6) pairs of mournful, quavering whistles with variable introduction of 1–4 shorter notes, *whi, who, who who-hooorr, who-hooorr....* More mournful than Little Tinamou, with different cadence. Flushed birds make rapid whistling twitter as they fly off. STATUS: Fairly common (where not hunted) to uncommon or scarce (where hunted) on both slopes, locally to 1700m on Pacific slope, to 1500m on Caribbean slope. (Mexico to S America.)

HIGHLAND TINAMOU *Nothocercus bonapartei* 35.5–38cm. Only tinamou in highlands, where it favors elfin forest, humid forest with dense undergrowth, versus more open habitats typically inhabited by Great Tinamou (ranges may overlap locally at mid-elevations). Usually singles and rarely seen, although not especially shy in areas away from disturbance. Note large size, dark slaty-gray head, richly colored plumage with pale buff spots on wings, sometimes on rump and back. SOUNDS: Slightly overslurred nasal crowing *whaáh*, repeated steadily about 1/sec. At close range suggests a large gull crowing; at a distance, could easily be mistaken for a frog. STATUS: Uncommon to fairly common in highlands, above 1200m in Northern Mts., mainly above 1000m elsewhere. (Costa Rica to S America.)

NORTHERN SUNBITTERN

display

GREAT TINAMOU

Pacific

Caribbean

HIGHLAND TINAMOU

102

LITTLE TINAMOU *Crypturellus soui* 20–24cm. Small tinamou of humid lowland second-growth thickets, grassy forest edge, rarely forest interior. More skulking and usually harder to see than medium-size and large tinamous, aided by its denser habitat. Note unbarred plumage, greenish-yellow legs, small size; cf. Uniform Crake (p. 94) as well as other tinamous. **SOUNDS:** Drawn-out clear whistle, 1–2 secs, often rising slightly and falling off with slight quaver, *wheee-eeeerr*, every 3–15 secs, at times in paired or tripled cadence. Less frequently, series of (usually 4–8) clear, tremulous whistles, about 1/sec; series intensifies then ends abruptly, *wheeeéh, wheeeer, wheeeer....* **STATUS:** Fairly common on both slopes, to 1500m. (Mexico to S America.)

THICKET TINAMOU *Crypturellus cinnamomeus* 25.5–29cm. Medium-size, relatively brightly marked tinamou of lowland dry forest and second-growth woodland with brushy understory, plantations. Walks quietly and often quickly on ground, but may be detected when rustling in dry leaves; prefers to run or freeze when alarmed; flushes explosively with whirring wings. The only tinamou in most or all of its range, but local overlap seems possible with Slaty-breasted Tinamou, which favors humid forest, has grayish head and breast, duller or no pale barring, very different voice. **SOUNDS:** Song a melancholy, drawn-out pure whistle, 0.5–1 sec; subtle modulation often produces 2-parted cadence, *whoo-oo*; usually 15 secs or longer between songs. **STATUS:** Fairly common on n. Pacific slope, to 1000m. (Mexico to Costa Rica.)

SLATY-BREASTED TINAMOU *Crypturellus boucardi* 25.5–28cm. Medium-size, rather dark tinamou of humid lowland forest, adjacent second growth. Walks quietly and often quickly on shady forest floor; prefers to run or freeze when alarmed. Note medium size, grayish breast, red legs. Cf. other lowland tinamous; wood quail usually in groups, have grayish legs. **SOUNDS:** Far-carrying, low, slightly tremulous, drawn-out *whoooo-oo-oooo*, about 2 secs; usually at least 15 secs between songs; rarely a shorter *hoo-oo*; quality recalls the sound made by blowing across the top of a bottle. **STATUS:** Uncommon to fairly common on n. Caribbean slope, to 700m. (Mexico to Costa Rica.)

LITTLE TINAMOU

male

female

THICKET TINAMOU

male

female

SLATY-BREASTED TINAMOU

male

female

CHACHALACAS, GUANS, CURASSOW (CRACIDAE; 5 SPECIES)
Neotropical family of large, long-tailed, frequently arboreal gamebirds known as cracids.
Ages usually similar, sexes similar or (in Great Curassow) strikingly different.

PLAIN CHACHALACA *Ortalis vetula* 48–56cm. Brushy forest and edge, second growth, overgrown clearings, plantations; no confirmed range overlap with Gray-headed Chachalaca. Usually in groups of 4–15 birds, feeding from ground to high in trees; typically calls from mid–upper levels in trees. Often seen flying across roads, rivers, and small clearings with sweeping glides, neck outstretched, tail fanned on landing to show pale tips. SOUNDS: Loud raucous calls. 'Song' a 3-syllable *kuh-kuh-ruh* or *cha-cha-lac*, male lower and burrier, female higher and screechier; characteristically in chanting duets started by male, phrases repeated several ×. Gruff purring and growling calls when agitated; other shrieking and honking chatters can suggest *Amazona* parrots. STATUS: Uncommon to fairly common locally on n. Pacific slope (mainly foothills), to 800m. (Mexico and s. Texas to Costa Rica.)

GRAY-HEADED CHACHALACA *Ortalis cinereiceps* 46–54cm. Humid forest and edge, second growth, riverside thickets, plantations; no confirmed range overlap with Plain Chachalaca. Usually in groups of 4–15 birds, feeding from ground to high in trees; typically calls from mid–upper levels in trees. Often seen flying across roads, rivers, small clearings, with sweeping glides that show off diagnostic bright rusty primaries; underwings extensively rusty. Juv. slightly browner overall than adult, including head; like adult within a few months. Tail tips vary from buffy white in drier areas to buffy cinnamon in more humid areas. SOUNDS: Loud, slightly shrieky *rriéuh* and clucking *riehohk*, at times in prolonged raucous duets and choruses that may suggest large parrots but are even worse, more discordant and unpleasant. Lacks a 'cha-cha-laca' song. Also plaintive whistled squeals. STATUS: Fairly common to common (where not hunted) on both slopes, locally to 1500m. (Honduras to nw. Colombia.)

BLACK GUAN *Chamaepetes unicolor* 58–64cm. Distinctive, rather chunky arboreal guan of cloud forest, elfin forest, adjacent second growth, especially with fruiting trees and shrubs. Found as singles, pairs, and seasonally family groups moving easily along branches in canopy; infrequently on ground, may flush with quiet low croak and rather quiet wing noise, vs. noisy wings of Crested Guan. Can be difficult to see in dense canopy amid thick branches, moss, and bromeliads, but sometimes confiding and curious. Distinctive in range and habitat: note overall blackish plumage with cobalt-blue bare face, red eyes, pinkish-red legs. Juv. duller and sootier overall, face duller, soon like adult. Crested Guan of lowlands and foothills much larger, with big red wattle, often noisy when flushed. SOUNDS: Mostly silent; disturbed birds give muffled coughing grunts. In early breeding season, male produces fairly loud, dry crackling rattle in gliding flight between trees, 1–1.5 secs, often preceded by a double snap. STATUS: Fairly common (where not hunted) to rare and local (with deforestation and hunting), from timberline down locally to about 1000m. (Costa Rica to w. Panama.)

Plain Chachalaca

Gray-headed Chachalaca

Black Guan

CRESTED GUAN *Penelope purpurascens* 81–91cm. Very large, dark, arboreal cracid of lowland and foothill forest, adjacent plantations. In pairs or small groups, usually in canopy and at fruiting trees and shrubs; rarely on the ground. Distinctive; much larger and darker than chachalacas, with big red throat wattle, gray face and bill, white streaks on neck and breast, erectile bushy crest. Often looks blackish overall in poor light, cf. much smaller Black Guan. SOUNDS: Far-carrying honking and yelping cries, often repeated tirelessly early and late in day, such as *yoink yoink...*, 2–3 calls/sec, at a distance might suggest a pygmy owl; can break into more excited screaming when disturbed. Loud rushing or crashing of wings when flushed from trees. In breeding season around dawn, muffled wing-drumming rattle produced in display flight through canopy: about 5 accelerating notes, a brief pause, then about 12 fast-paced notes, *drruh drruh-drruh-drruhdrruh, drruhdrruh...*, 2.5 secs total. 'Song' in early morning an overslurred rasping honk or nasal whistle that fades into a moan, *reówhn* or *wheéohrr*, every 2–8 secs; at a distance might suggest a frog. STATUS: Fairly common (where not hunted) to scarce and widely extirpated (by deforestation and hunting) on both slopes, to 1800m on Pacific slope, to 1200m on Caribbean slope. (Mexico to S America.)

GREAT CURASSOW *Crax rubra* 76–92cm. Distinctive, very large, mostly terrestrial cracid of lowland and lower foothill forest. Singles, pairs, or small groups feed on ground, less often in fruiting trees; males may sing from perch in canopy. Wary in most areas and runs off quickly when disturbed, but can be tame and acclimated when not hunted; rarely flies. Note very large size, curly crest, big yellow bill knob of male. Female plumage variable, rusty morph most frequent but less common barred and dark morphs are present in most populations. Juv. resembles adult of respective sex, even when only about 60% of adult size; male develops yellow bill knob over a few months. SOUNDS: 'Song' from male at any time of day, a very low-pitched, almost subliminal booming *uhmmm*, and variations. Alarm call a sharp, overslurred piping *wheep!* STATUS: Fairly common (where not hunted) to scarce and widely extirpated (by deforestation and hunting) on both slopes, to 1200m. (Mexico to S America.)

CRESTED GUAN

GREAT CURASSOW

females

male

108

NEW WORLD QUAIL (ODONTOPHORIDAE; 8 SPECIES) Handsome
'chickens' of scrubby and forested habitats, often in groups in nonbr. season; can be very
elusive, but confiding when acclimated. Ages differ; adult appearance attained within a month
or so by near-complete molt. Sexes differ or similar. Often detected by voice. Flush explosively
from close range.

SPOT-BELLIED BOBWHITE *Colinus [cristatus] leucopogon* 20–23cm. Small
quail of open brushy country, grassy fields, farmland, savanna, open woodland;
along quiet roadsides early and late in day. In pairs or groups, tending to run for
cover or flush when disturbed. Distinctive in range and habitat (no overlap with
Crested Bobwhite): note head pattern, white-spotted belly. SOUNDS: 'Song'
(mainly spring–summer) a slightly hoarse to ringing whistled *h-hoo-whuiih!* or
less often simply *hu-whiih!* ('bob-white!'), typically every 10–20 secs. Ringing,
hollow whistled clucks year-round, at times in rhythmic series, *hú-widi hú-
widi...*; varied nasal clucks and twitters. Rattling wing whirr when flushed.
STATUS: Fairly common on n. Pacific slope, locally to 1500m and likely spreading with deforestation.
(Guatemala to Costa Rica.)

CRESTED BOBWHITE *Colinus cristatus* 19–22cm. Very poorly known in
Costa Rica. Small quail of open brushy country, rice and cane fields, savanna.
Habits much like Spot-bellied Bobwhite, should be distinctive in range and
habitat (no known overlap with Spot-bellied): note striking head pattern,
erectile spiky crest. SOUNDS: Similar to Spot-bellied Bobwhite but song averages
clearer, less harsh and emphatic, with less strongly upslurred last note. Rattling
wing whirr when flushed. STATUS: Uncertain. Described by Stiles & Skutch
(1989) as "locally common … in Golfo Dulce lowlands" and expected to spread
with deforestation; very few reports in recent years, however, and inexplicably
seems at best scarce and local in Costa Rica. (Costa Rica to S America.)

TAWNY-FACED QUAIL *Rhynchortyx cinctus* 18–20cm. Elusive small quail of
humid forest in lowlands and lower foothills. Pairs or small coveys run when
alarmed or may freeze; flushes explosively from underfoot. Appreciably smaller
than wood quail; note distinctive head and breast patterns. SOUNDS: Ventriloquial,
slightly nasal sad whistles, 0.5–1 sec, often 3 longer descending notes followed
by 1–3 shorter rising notes, *wowhh wowhh wowhh owhh owhh*, series repeated
every 2–3 secs; at other times steady series of simply longer or shorter notes
every 0.5–2 secs. STATUS: Scarce to uncommon and local in hilly n. Caribbean
lowlands, mainly 150–800m. (Honduras to nw. Ecuador.)

BUFFY-CROWNED WOOD PARTRIDGE *Dendrortyx leucophrys* 28–35cm.
Long-tailed quail of humid foothill and highland forest, shade coffee
plantations, especially in brushy ravines. Typically shy and elusive, heard far
more than seen. Often walks and runs with tail cocked and slightly fanned, like
a chicken. In pairs or small groups, scratching in leaf litter; runs well and rarely
flies. Distinctive if seen: note long tail, whitish forecrown and throat, deep pink
legs. Sexes similar. SOUNDS: Rhythmic duets of repeated 2–4-syllable whistled
phrases with slightly hoarse, braying quality, such as *i'hohr…* or *whíta-horr'a...*;
about 1 phrase/sec; short nasal hoot, repeated, or at start of song series. Semi-
metallic high twitters when agitated. STATUS: Uncommon to fairly common locally on wetter slopes
surrounding Central Valley and in n. Talamanca Mts., mainly 900–3000m. (Mexico to Costa Rica.)

female
Spot-bellied Bobwhite
male

female
Crested Bobwhite
male

female
Tawny-faced Quail
male

Buffy-crowned Wood Partridge

110

WOOD QUAIL (GENUS *ODONTOPHORUS*) (4 species). Chunky, usually elusive quail of
humid forest floor, heard more often than seen; loud 'songs' often given in prolonged duets that can last
a minute or more, mainly early and late in day. Usually in coveys of 4–10 birds; roost in trees. All species
have erectile crests.

SPOTTED WOOD QUAIL *Odontophorus guttatus* 23.5–26cm. Humid foothill and highland forest, often with bamboo and other dense understory. See
genus note. Overlaps at lower elevations with smaller Black-breasted Wood
Quail; note voice. When seen, note Spotted's blackish throat, white droplets on
underparts; often raises and lowers crest while walking. Sexes similar (both have
brown and rufous morphs) but male has extensive orange base to crest.
SOUNDS: Single birds give rhythmic, steadily repeated *hu'wik!* or *hoh-woh*, 1–2
phrases/sec, that can lead into duets, typically alternated pairs of 3–4-syllable
whistled phrases, such as *hu-WA-hoo hu-widl, hu-WA-hoo hu-widl.…*Slower-
paced and more braying than duets of Black-breasted Wood Quail. **STATUS:** Fairly common to uncommon
on both slopes of Central and Talamanca Mts., mainly 1000m to timberline. (Mexico to Panama.)

BLACK-EARED WOOD QUAIL *Odontophorus melanotis* 23–25.5cm. Humid
lowland forest, adjacent taller second growth. See genus note. Distinctive in
habitat and range, note overall dark appearance with blackish throat, deep rusty
crown and breast. May overlap locally at higher elevations with Black-breasted
Wood Quail; note voice. Also cf. Tawny-faced Quail. Sexes similar but male has
more solidly black face. **SOUNDS:** Single birds give rather fast-paced, steadily
repeated, rhythmic honking *ho-wóhk…,* about 2 phrases/sec, and higher
braying *ha-wah,* sometimes combining into relatively simple, rolling duets, *ka-
wá-hu ka-wá-hu.…*Distinct from higher, shriekier, and more complex duets of
Black-breasted Wood Quail. Alarm call a slightly squeaky, rapidly rolled *kwididi kwididi...,* recalling
alarm call of Chestnut-backed Antbird. **STATUS:** Fairly common to uncommon but local (widely extirpated
by deforestation) on Caribbean slope, to 1000m. (Honduras to Panama.)

MARBLED WOOD QUAIL *Odontophorus gujanensis* 23.5–26cm. Humid
lowland forest, adjacent taller second growth. See genus note. Distinctive in
habitat and range, note broad orange eyering, plain grayish breast; short
blackish to dark brown crest sometimes raised. Possible local overlap in foothills
with Black-breasted Wood Quail; note voice. Sexes similar. **SOUNDS:** Single
birds give rhythmic, steadily repeated, low ringing *how-ah* or *hóha-woh* about 1
phrase/sec, can run into prolonged duets, *oh-wóha-hu a-woh-hu, oh-wóha-hu
a-woh-hu,...*; relatively low and gobbling, or marble-mouthed, vs. higher, jerkier
choruses of Black-breasted and Spotted Wood Quails. **STATUS:** Fairly common
to uncommon but local (widely extirpated by deforestation and hunting) on s. Pacific slope, to 900m.
(Costa Rica to S America.)

BLACK-BREASTED WOOD QUAIL *Odontophorus leucolaemus* 23–25cm.
Humid foothill forest, cloud forest. See genus note. Note overall dark appearance with white throat (can be inconspicuous), white-spotted belly; from
behind, golden-buff droplets on scapular edgings often noticeable. Overlaps
locally with Spotted Wood Quail at higher elevations, with Black-eared at
lower elevations on Caribbean slope, possibly with Marbled in s. Pacific
foothills; note voice. Sexes similar; imm. has duller throat, browner underparts.
SOUNDS: Single birds give rhythmic, steadily repeated, slightly braying *kee-ohr*
about 2 phrases/sec, can run into prolonged rhythmic duets, *ch-wí-di ch-hóh-a,*
ch-wí-di ch-hóh-a..., or *get-wídit je-hó-vah...*; faster-paced and higher than Spotted Wood Quail, with
different emphasis; may recall choruses of White-fronted Nunbird. Alarm call a squeaky rolled *kw-di.*
STATUS: Fairly common to uncommon on both slopes, mainly 700–1850m. (Costa Rica to w. Panama.)

SPOTTED WOOD QUAIL

males

brown morph

female

rusty morphs

BLACK-EARED WOOD QUAIL

male

female

MARBLED WOOD QUAIL

BLACK-BREASTED WOOD QUAIL

NEW WORLD VULTURES (CATHARTIDAE; 4 SPECIES) Small New World
family of carrion feeders. Differ from hawks and eagles in weaker bills and feet, lighter build,
naked and often colorful heads. Ages differ slightly to distinctly, sexes similar; adult appearance
attained in 1 year for smaller species, 3–4 years for King Vulture.

*NORTHERN TURKEY VULTURE *Cathartes aura* 66–76cm, WS 165–
183cm. Widespread and familiar soaring bird (often known simply as TV)
found in a wide variety of habitats from beaches and towns to mountains and
marshes; mainly in open, semi-open, and wooded country, tends to avoid heavy
forest. Roosts communally in trees, also in towns on tall pylons. Soars and
glides for long periods with little flapping, often tilting side to side; wings held
in a shallow V and wingbeats deep, elastic. Migrant flocks often mix with
Swainson's and other hawks. Distinctive in most of range, but cf. Lesser Yellow-
headed Vulture of lowland marshes and savannas. Adults on s. Pacific slope
average darker upperparts, show variable whitish markings on nape, sometimes a pale crown patch. Juv.
attains reddish head within a few months. SOUNDS: Occasional soft clucks and hisses. STATUS: Common
to fairly common, to 2000m; uncommon higher. Much of N American population migrates through
Costa Rica, mainly late Jan–Apr, late Sep–Nov. (N America to Cen America, winters to S America.)

LESSER YELLOW-HEADED VULTURE *Cathartes burrovianus* 56–62cm, WS
148–165cm. Northern Turkey Vulture look-alike of marshes, savannas, and
open country. Shape and flight manner similar to Northern Turkey Vulture but
tail slightly shorter, less graduated. Rarely flies high overhead, mainly quarters
low over marshes, other open country. Slightly smaller and blacker than
Northern Turkey, with more-contrasting whitish shafts on outer primaries.
Adult head colors gaudy and striking. Juv. has mostly grayish head with
ghosting of adult pattern, attains adult colors within a few months. Usually
silent. STATUS: Fairly common to uncommon locally in nw. lowlands and s. on
Pacific slope, mainly below 300m. (Mexico to S America.)

BLACK VULTURE *Coragyps atratus* 56–66cm, WS 140–158cm. Widespread,
familiar, and distinctive soaring bird of towns, villages, other open and semi-
open country, often near water and along rivers, at garbage dumps; tends to
avoid heavy forest. Often roosts on cliffs, pylons. Typically soars higher than
Northern Turkey Vulture, often in disorganized kettles; flies with wings less
raised than Northern Turkey, and wingbeats very different: stiff and hurried,
usually in short bursts. Commonly in groups on the ground, where hops and
ambles readily, unlike Northern Turkey, which is awkward on the ground. Juv.
has smoother head and darker bill than adult, like adult in 1–2 years.
SOUNDS: Occasional sneezy coughs. STATUS: Common to fairly common, especially near water bodies in
lowlands and foothills; less numerous above 2000m. Not migratory. (Americas.)

KING VULTURE *Sarcoramphus papa* 71–82cm, WS 176–193cm. Large spectacular vulture of forest and adjacent semi-open country. Mostly seen as singles
or pairs in flight, often high overhead; sometimes in kettles with other vultures.
Small groups may gather locally at carcasses, when dominates smaller Black
Vulture. Adult distinctive, but soaring at long range cf. Wood Stork (p. 90). Juv.
lacks white primary panels of Black Vulture and has whitish mottling on underwing coverts, broader and longer wings held flatter with tips curled up. Attains
adult plumage in about 3–4 years. Usually silent. STATUS: Uncommon to scarce
on both slopes, locally to 1500m; perhaps most numerous on Osa Peninsula.
(Mexico to S America.)

NORTHERN TURKEY VULTURE

s. Pacific slope

juv.

adults

Widespread

adults

juv.

LESSER YELLOW-HEADED
VULTURE

BLACK VULTURE

adult

juv.

adults

juv.

KING VULTURE

114

DIURNAL RAPTORS (51+ SPECIES) Popular, widespread assemblage of predatory birds, comprising 3 families: Hawks (Accipitridae; including harriers, kites, eagles), Falcons (Falconidae; including caracaras), and Ospreys (Pandionidae; sometimes merged into hawks). Range from dainty American Kestrel to huge Harpy Eagle. Genetic studies indicate that falcons share a common ancestor with parrots, but traditionally they have been grouped with hawks as birds of prey, as done here for ID purposes.

Ages differ, sexes different or similar (females larger, strikingly so in some species); adult appearance attained in 1–2 years for falcons and medium-size to large hawks, up to 4–5 years for eagles. ID of some raptors straightforward but others can be challenging, compounded by age variation and highly variable plumages. Appreciation of behavior, habitat, and structure (wing shape on flying birds, relative wing and tail lengths on perched birds, head and bill size) often more helpful than colors and patterns, although those should always be noted.

NORTHERN MIGRANT ACCIPTERS (2 species). Mostly favor forest habitats; seen infrequently except when migrating. Relatively short wings and long tails good for maneuvering among trees, where mostly hunt birds. Soar readily, mainly in mid–late morning and during migration, when may associate loosely with large movements of other raptors. Tropical forest resident accipiters are on p. 128.

SHARP-SHINNED HAWK *Accipiter striatus* 28–36cm, WS 51–64cm. Uncommon winter migrant to varied wooded and forested habitats, mainly in foothills and highlands. Flies with bursts of quick flapping and short glides; soars mainly in migration. Hunts from cover and rarely perches in open situations. Note small size, quick snappy wingbeats, relatively short rounded wings, long tail with overall squared tail tip, thin legs. Main confusion is with larger Cooper's Hawk, which has larger head, longer wings, longer and rounded tail with bolder white tip, adult often appears more capped; in flight, Cooper's holds wings out straighter, accentuating big head, not pushed forward like small-headed Sharp-shinned. Also cf. Tiny Hawk (p. 128), Double-toothed Kite (p. 132). Usually silent in winter. STATUS: Uncommon Oct–Mar on Pacific slope and in highlands, mainly 500–2500m; more widespread during migration, Oct–Nov, Mar–Apr, when rare in Caribbean lowlands. (Breeds N America to Mexico, winters to Panama.)

COOPER'S HAWK *Accipiter cooperi* 38–44cm male, 44–51cm female, WS 68–86cm. Scarce winter migrant to varied wooded, forested, and adjacent semi-open habitats, mainly in foothills and highlands. Flies with strong, fairly quick stiff wingbeats, brief glides; soars on flattish wings. Hunts mainly from cover but perches in open and semi-open situations, on fence posts, utility poles. Female appreciably bigger than male, can be mistaken for Gray or Gray-lined Hawks; male easily confused with smaller Sharp-shinned Hawk (which see). Also cf. adult Double-toothed Kite (p. 132). Usually silent in winter. STATUS: Scarce Oct–Mar on n. Pacific slope and in highlands, mainly 1000–3000m; more widespread during migration, Oct–Nov, Mar–Apr, when very rare in Caribbean lowlands. (Breeds N America to Mexico, winters to Costa Rica.)

NORTHERN HARRIER *Circus hudsonius* 46–56cm, WS 99–117cm. Scarce winter migrant to open country, especially marshes. Note white rump and broad dark trailing edge to secondaries in all plumages, rather owl-like facial discs, and habits. Often seen in flight, quartering and sailing low over marshes, grassland, other open habitats; perches on ground and fence posts. Flies with buoyant and smooth wingbeats and glides easily, wings held in a shallow V. During migration can be disconcertingly high overhead, best identified by long narrow wings and long tail, buoyant flight; cf. Swainson's Hawk. Male has gray head and upperparts, sparse rusty barring on belly, black wing-tips; female brownish overall, heavily streaked below; 1st-year has mostly unstreaked rusty underparts, often fading to buff by spring. Usually silent in winter. STATUS: Rare to uncommon Oct–Apr on both slopes to 1500m, mainly in nw. lowlands. (Breeds N America, winters to n. S America.)

SHARP-SHINNED HAWK

adult

1st-years

adult

adult

COOPER'S HAWK

1st-years

adult

adult

1st-year

NORTHERN HARRIER

females

male

ROADSIDE HAWK *Rupornis magnirostris* 33–41cm, WS 68–79cm. Small lowland hawk of open and semi-open country; often perches on roadside wires, fence posts. Flight mostly low with rapid stiff wingbeats, brief glides. Soars on flattish wings; display flight of fluttering wingbeats interspersed with glides on wings held in a strong V. Adult distinctive, with staring pale eyes, grayish head and breast, rusty-barred belly; rusty wing panels in flight; pale tail bands grayish to rusty. 1st-year has distinctive streaked breast but barred belly, broad pale tail bands, cf. Broad-winged Hawk. SOUNDS: Nasal, complaining, overall descending scream, *meeahh*, about 1 sec; 'song' (mainly in display flight, less often from perch) an often persistent, fairly rapid series of clipped nasal yaps, intensifying and fading, *heh-heh-heh...*, can suggest Lineated Woodpecker. STATUS: Fairly common to uncommon on both slopes, to 1500m. (Mexico to S America.)

GRAY HAWK *Buteo [nitidus] plagiatus* 42–46cm, WS 81–94cm. Medium-size hawk of forest and edge, semi-open habitats. Commonly perches on roadside wires, utility poles. Soars frequently, wings held flattish and tail usually slightly spread; often in mid–late morning kettles with vultures and other hawks. Adult distinctive in most of range, with pearly gray plumage barred below, brown eyes, black-and-white tail bands; cf. Gray-lined Hawk which overlaps locally on cen. Pacific slope (see under that species). 1st-year Gray from most species by size, shape, habits; whitish face with bold dark eyestripe and mustache; also note fairly long tail with pale bands typically slightly wavy and progressively wider toward tip, dusky barring on thighs. In flight, often appears uniformly pale below without distinct dark trailing edge to underwing of 1st-year Broad-winged Hawk. Cf. 1st-year Gray-lined, Common Black, and Broad-winged Hawks. SOUNDS: Adult has drawn-out, overall descending scream, *whéeeeu*, 1–1.5 secs, not as hoarse as Roadside Hawk. 'Song' a series of inflected mournful whistles, often around or before dawn, typically 3–10×, *h'wheeeu, h'wheeeu....* STATUS: Fairly common to uncommon on both slopes, to 1600m. (Mexico and sw. US to w. Panama.)

GRAY-LINED HAWK *Buteo nitidus* 41–45cm, WS 80–92cm. Habitat and habits like Gray Hawk, which Gray-lined replaces on s. Pacific slope. Adult averages paler than Gray, with more distinct dark barring above, broader white tail bands, but some very similar to Gray; in flight, note lack of dark trailing edge to wings, more distinct dark barring on underside of primaries. 1st-year from Gray Hawk by sparser dark blotching below concentrated on breast sides and flanks, plain pale buffy thighs; averages fewer and broader dark tail bars. Cf. 1st-year Common Black and Broad-winged Hawks. SOUNDS: Adult has overall descending scream, *whéeeu*, 0.5–1 secs, usually higher, more abrupt, and more sharply descending than Gray Hawk. 'Song' a series of inflected mournful whistles, up to 10× or so, *huwéoo huwéoo...*, more strongly inflected than Gray. STATUS: Uncommon to fairly common on s. Pacific slope, to 1200m. (Costa Rica to S America.)

BROAD-WINGED HAWK *Buteo platypterus* 38–43cm, WS 82–92cm. Winter migrant to forest and edge, woodland, plantations; transient migrants occur widely. often streaming overhead with Swainson's Hawks and Turkey Vultures. Wintering birds mainly in subcanopy, on roadside wires. In flight note relatively tapered wings, evenly pale flight feathers (primary panel translucent when backlit) with dark trailing edge; adult has single broad whitish tail band. At rest, note long wings extending well down tail. 1st-year has variable dark streaking below, dark spots (not bars) on thighs, cf. Gray and Gray-lined Hawks. Rare dark morph (all ages) solidly blackish brown body and underwing coverts, cf. dark Short-tailed Hawk. SOUNDS: High, thin, slightly tinny scream *ssiiiiiiu*, about 1 sec, from perch and in flight. STATUS: Common transient on both slopes and through highlands, late Sep–Nov, Mar to mid-May; fairly common to common in winter on both slopes, especially foothills and mainly below 2000m. (Breeds N America, winters Mexico to S America.)

adults

ROADSIDE HAWK

1st-year

adult

tail variation

adult

1st-years

GRAY HAWK

adult

adult

1st-years

GRAY-LINED HAWK

adult

adult

BROAD-WINGED HAWK

1st-year

adults

dark morph

adult

1st-year

SWAINSON'S HAWK *Buteo swainsoni* 48–56cm, WS 119–132cm. Fairly large but lightly built migrant buteo with relatively long tapered wings, notably variable plumage; often best identified by structure. Winters mainly in agricultural land, especially sugar cane fields, also marshes, savannas; ranges widely in migration. Best known as a spring and fall transient, when 1000s stream overhead, often with Turkey Vultures and Broad-winged Hawks. Wintering birds mainly seen soaring in mid–late morning, often with kettles of vultures, or hunting with other hawks over burning cane fields. Flight buoyant and agile, soaring with wings in a shallow V. Perches readily on ground, also on low bushes, trees, utility poles. In flight note relatively narrow, tapered wings with contrast between pale coverts and dark flight feathers; light-morph adult has dark breast band. At rest note long wings, projecting to or just beyond tail tip, small head and bill. Uncommon dark morph has dark body contrasting with pale undertail coverts, rusty underwing coverts. Juv. has buff face and underparts, fading to whitish, with dark eyestripe and mustache. Cf. larger and bulkier White-tailed and Red-tailed Hawks. Mostly silent. STATUS: Common transient on both slopes and through highlands, late Sep–Nov, late Feb–early May. Rare to uncommon and irregular in winter, mainly on Pacific slope, occasionally inland to Central Valley. (Breeds N America to Mexico, winters Mexico to S America.)

RED-TAILED HAWK *Buteo jamaicensis* 48–59cm, WS 117–137cm. Large, rather stocky hawk, mainly in highlands. Varied semi-open habitats with trees or utility poles for perches, forest edge; not in forested humid lowlands. Soars with wings slightly raised to flattish, glides on flattish wings; hunts from perches and in flight. Kites and hovers, mainly in open country when windy. Note thickset shape with broad, rather blunt-tipped wings, medium-length tail (1st-year has narrower wings, longer tail); light morph has dark leading edge to underwing. Plumage highly variable (dark morph rare in Costa Rica); migrant adult (rare) has whitish underwings, variable dark belly band. On perched birds, all except darkest morphs show distinct pale mottling on scapulars. Adult has diagnostic rusty tail. Juv. can be confusing, note size and structure, brown tail with numerous narrow dark bars, cf. Swainson's Hawk (narrower, longer wings), Short-tailed Hawk (smaller, rarely seen perched). Attains adult appearance in 2nd year. SOUNDS: Classic Hollywood hawk scream: drawn-out, rasping, overall descending *whieeéahrr*, mainly in flight; juv. has higher, shriller *wheéirr*, at times repeated persistently. STATUS: Uncommon to fairly common on both slopes, mainly 1500m to timberline, locally down to 800m. More widespread Oct–Mar, when small numbers of n. migrants (mainly imms.) occur locally in nw. lowlands, rarely elsewhere on both slopes. (N America to Panama.)

WHITE-TAILED HAWK *Geranoaetus albicaudatus* 48–59cm, WS 124–137cm. Large hawk, local in open country, especially drier areas with scattered trees and bushes; also marshes and ranchland. Perches mainly on low posts and bushes. Soars and glides with wings in distinct shallow V; at times kites and hovers, especially over fields being burned; hunts mainly in flight. Note long, broad-based, and tapered wings, short tail (1st-year has distinctly narrower wings, longer tail); at rest, wing-tips project past tail, especially on adult. Adult distinctive, with bold tail pattern, but cf. light-morph Short-tailed Hawk; 1st-year variable, most are extensively dark below, a few mostly whitish below with limited dark streaking, cf. Red-tailed Hawk; 2nd-year resembles adult but darker above, with dark hood, duller tail pattern, variable narrow dark barring on belly. Attains adult appearance in 3rd year. SOUNDS: Mostly quiet away from nest. Short, slightly hoarse screams, often couplets in short series, *whee-ah whee-ah....* STATUS: Uncommon to scarce and local in nw. lowlands, to 1500m, rare (at least formerly) inland to Central Valley and in interior valleys of s. Pacific slope; declining with increased agricultural development. (Mexico and sw. US to S America.)

SWAINSON'S HAWK

1st-year

adult

light adults

dark adult

1st-year

RED-TAILED HAWK

1st-years

adults

1st-year

dark morphs

WHITE-TAILED HAWK

1st-year

adults

1st-year

SHORT-TAILED HAWK *Buteo brachyurus* 41–46cm, WS 86–102cm. Widespread small buteo, rarely seen perched; despite the name, tail not strikingly short. Light morph and dark morph both frequent, sometimes together in pairs. Usually seen as singles or pairs soaring over semi-open and wooded habitats; also towns, mangroves. Hunts from flight, stooping on prey. Often among mid–late morning kettles of vultures and other hawks. In flight note slightly tapered wingtips, slightly pinched-in trailing edge to wings, dusky secondaries vs. whiter primaries; soars with wings flat but distinctively curled up at tips. On perched birds, note long wings reaching near tail tip, tawny wash on sides of neck. Cf. Zone-tailed Hawk, dark-morph Broad-winged Hawk. **SOUNDS:** Slightly modulated or overslurred whistled scream, *wheéeu* or *klee-ee*, usually in short series. **STATUS:** Uncommon to fairly common on both slopes, locally to 2000m. (Mexico and sw. US to S America.)

ZONE-TAILED HAWK *Buteo albonotatus* 45–53cm, WS 122–137cm. Fairly large, long-winged buteo easily passed off in flight as a Northern Turkey Vulture (TV). Occurs in varied open and wooded habitats from ranchland and towns to marshes and forest edge. Usually singles, soaring and gliding with wings in a shallow V much like TV, with which it often associates in kettles and at roosts. Smaller than TV with narrower, more even-width wings; yellow cere often stands out against feathered gray head. Appreciably larger than Short-tailed Hawk, with longer wings and tail, different flight manner. On perched birds, cf. stockier Common Black Hawk. Adult has bold white tail band below; juv. has finely barred flight feathers. **SOUNDS:** Mostly silent. Near nest may give a slightly rough to piercing scream, about 1 sec. **STATUS:** Scarce to uncommon on both slopes, to 1500m; most widespread Oct–Apr, and breeding status unclear in much of Costa Rica. (Mexico and sw. US to S America.)

CRANE HAWK *Geranospiza caerulescens* 46–54cm, WS 92–105cm. Lanky, fairly small-headed hawk of varied semi-open and forested habitats, from mangroves and ranchland to forest and plantations; often near water. Distinctive: note very long red legs, small head with red eyes, gray cere (no yellow in face), long tail with 2 white bands. In flight note variable band of white spots across primaries. Clambers around in trees, using its long double-jointed legs to reach into crevices and cavities for prey, flapping its wings for balance. Wingbeats rather loose, slow, and floppy, suggesting a larger bird; soars on flattish wings, mainly for short periods in mid-morning. In display flight, flap-flap-flap-glide progression over canopy interrupted by brief climbs with quicker loose flaps, then glides back to original level. Juv. has grizzled pale face, amber eyes, red-orange legs, variable pale mottling below; attains adult plumage in 2nd year. **SOUNDS:** Slightly plaintive, overall descending whistled scream, *WHEeooo*. **STATUS:** Uncommon and local on both slopes, mainly n. lowlands, rarely to 1000m. (Mexico to S America.)

SNAIL KITE *Rostrhamus sociabilis* 45–51cm, WS 104–119cm. Distinctive, broad-winged raptor of wetlands and lakes with large snails, virtually its sole food source. Mostly seen perched overlooking water or quartering over water in unhurried flight with measured wingbeats and buoyant glides on distinctively arched wings, dropping to snatch snails with its feet. Usually breeds and roosts communally. On perched birds note slender bill with long hook, reddish eyes, long wings projecting to or beyond tail tip, fairly short legs. On flying birds note flight manner, large white base to fairly short squared tail. Juv. has buff face and underparts, fading to whitish, duller eyes, yellowish legs; adult female and 2nd-year male have mostly dark underparts, pale face; adult male dark slaty gray overall with deep red eyes, salmon-orange legs. Attains adult plumage in 3rd year. **SOUNDS:** Stuttering, harsh creaky cackle, 1–2 secs; varied low rasping calls, including a shrieky *shiéhr*. **STATUS:** Fairly common to uncommon locally in nw. lowlands; rare and irregular wanderer elsewhere on both slopes; since 2010s, established at Angostura reservoir, near Turrialba. (Mexico and se. US to S America.)

SHORT-TAILED HAWK

1st-year

adults

light morphs

1st-year

adult

dark morphs

ZONE-TAILED HAWK

adult

with TV

1st-year

adult

CRANE HAWK

adults

1st-year

SNAIL KITE

1st-year

female

males

1st-year

122

COMMON BLACK HAWK *Buteogallus anthracinus* 46–53cm, WS 109–127cm. Fairly large, heavily built hawk of marshes, mangroves, forested and semi-open areas near water. Perches on roadside wires, bare snags overlooking water; can be very confiding. Plunges feet first to snatch fish; runs on beaches and mudflats hunting crabs. Soars regularly, mainly in mid–late morning, wings flattish, tail spread. Note broad wings, short tail (appreciably longer on juv.), long yellow legs. Adult has single white tail band, often shows whitish patch across base of outer primaries. Main confusion risk is Great Black Hawk (see that species for details). Also cf. perched adult Zone-tailed Hawk; plumage of juv. Gray and Gray-lined Hawks suggests juv. Common Black but note structure. Attains adult appearance in 2nd year. Some adults have underside of flight feathers washed rusty. SOUNDS: Often calls when soaring and in display. Varied series of loud ringing whistles, often intensifying and then fading quickly: *yih yih yih yeep Yeep YEEP YEEP yeep yih-yih-yih* and variations. STATUS: Fairly common in coastal lowlands, especially Pacific mangroves; uncommon and local inland to 750m. (Mexico and sw. US to n. S America.)

GREAT BLACK HAWK *Buteogallus urubitinga* 51–61cm, WS 120–137cm. Large, broad-winged hawk of forested and semi-open areas, marshes, mangroves. Habits much like Common Black Hawk but rarely seen on ground, less confiding. Soars with wings flattish, tail rarely spread widely, and often dangles long legs. Slightly rangier, less compact than Common, with longer neck, appreciably longer legs, and longer tail that projects noticeably past tail tip on perched birds (especially juv.); also note voice. Adult Great has less extensive, often duller yellow at base of bill, coarse white barring on thighs. In flight, wings of adult Great bulge less strongly on secondaries, feet project past white tail band; 2nd white tail band of Great hard to see from below but obvious from above, when can appear as a white tail split by a black band. Juv. Great has paler head than Common, without thick dark mustache, longer tail has numerous narrow dark bars, broad dark distal band, vs. fewer and broader dark bars of Common; uppertail coverts mostly white (mostly dark on Common). 2nd-year Great Black resembles juv. but can show dark mustache and has coarse tail bars, suggesting Common; note structural differences, mostly white uppertail coverts. Attains adult appearance in 3rd year. Also cf. Crane Hawk. SOUNDS: High, piercing, drawn-out wailing whistle, perched and in flight from both adult and juv., 2–5 secs. 'Song' given in flight carries well: short, overslurred piping whistles in prolonged rapid series, *whi' pih-pih-pih*…. STATUS: Uncommon on both slopes, locally to 1800m. (Mexico to S America.)

[SOLITARY EAGLE] *Buteogallus solitarius* 64–79cm, WS 152–188cm. No unequivocally documented record from Costa Rica, and perhaps does not occur in the country. Included here to facilitate confirmation of potential occurrence. Very large hawk of humid forest and edge, most likely in foothills. Soars mainly in mid–late morning. Adult from smaller Common Black Hawk (which can appear disconcertingly large thanks to its shape and slow wingbeats) by paler, slaty-gray plumage, relatively shorter tail, and thicker legs; in flight, toes project almost to tail tip, vs. projecting just into white tail band on Common Black. Juv. has distinctive plumage, with large dark patches at sides of breast, dark thighs, and overall plain underside to flight feathers, with no distinct tail bars. 2nd-year resembles adult but browner overall, with sparse buff streaks on head, body, underwing coverts; tail pattern like adult but broad median band pale gray, not white. Probably attains adult appearance in 3rd year. Also cf. Great Black Hawk. SOUNDS: Melancholy drawn-out whistle, 1–2 secs, lower and less piercing than Great Black Hawk. In flight, powerful whistled screams in slightly speeding and slowing series, *whieh-whieh*…, cadence reminiscent of Common Black Hawk but notes stronger, lower-pitched. STATUS: Uncertain. Has been reported from Caribbean slope and s. Pacific slope, mainly in foothills. (Mexico locally to S America.)

Common Black Hawk

1st-year

adults

dorsal

1st-year

1st-year

Great Black Hawk

adults

dorsal

1st-year

1st-year

Solitary Eagle

adults

dorsal

1st-year

HARRIS'S HAWK *Parabuteo unicinctus* 49–54cm, WS 102–120cm. Large dark hawk, local in open country, especially ranchland and marshes with scattered trees, adjacent scrubby woodland. Perches prominently on utility poles, tall bare snags; hunts from perches and in flight. Soars infrequently, with wings mostly flat; wingbeats rather floppy and loose, unlike stiffer wingbeats of buteos. Distinctive, but cf. perched dark-morph Red-tailed Hawk, imm. Savanna Hawk. Note long graduated tail with big white base above and below, long yellow legs, deep rusty shoulders and leggings. Attains adult appearance in 2nd year. **SOUNDS:** Generally quiet. Adult gives gruff rasping calls, mainly near nest. Juv. has shrill whistled *whiéih*, at times repeated steadily. **STATUS:** Uncommon to locally fairly common in nw. lowlands; scarce and local elsewhere on both slopes, rarely to 1200m. (Mexico and sw. US to S America.)

BLACK-COLLARED HAWK *Busarellus nigricollis* 46–56cm, WS 114–134cm. Distinctive, stocky, very broad-winged hawk of freshwater wetlands, lakes, slow-moving rivers. Mainly eats fish and hunts from perches. Rather sluggish; perches in trees overlooking water, on low posts, at times on ground. Wingbeats slow and fairly deep, soars on flattish wings with tips often curled up. Adult essentially unmistakable, bright orangey with whitish head; black collar not always easy to see. On juv. note habits, stocky shape with short tail, ghosting of adult plumage pattern, grayish cere, pale legs. Cf. Savanna Hawk. 2nd-year like adult but underparts flecked whitish and dark, thighs barred dusky. Attains adult plumage in 3rd year. **SOUNDS:** Usually quiet. Occasional hoarse rasps and a slightly piercing, slurred screaming *hileeee*. **STATUS:** Uncommon to fairly common locally on n. Caribbean slope, to 300m. Scarce and local on Pacific slope, at least formerly. (Mexico to S America.)

SAVANNA HAWK *Buteogallus meridionalis* 48–53cm, WS 120–140cm. Large, long-legged, and long-winged hawk of open country with scattered trees and forest patches. Perches prominently on utility poles, tall bare snags; hunts from perches and on ground, where walks confidently and may follow plows. Soars with wings mostly flat; wingbeats rather smooth, unlike stiffer wingbeats of buteos. Adult distinctive; imm. might be confused with Harris's and imm. Great Black Hawks. Note relatively short tail, with wing-tips at rest about equal with or slightly longer than tail tip (vs. long tail on Harris's and Great Black); variable rusty on upperwing coverts and thighs; variable cinnamon rusty bases to primaries and secondaries in flight. Imm. variable, 1st-year has extensively pale creamy head and underparts, 2nd-year darker overall; attains adult appearance in 3rd year. **SOUNDS:** Drawn-out, downslurred scream, 1–1.5 secs, *heeéueeee*, suggests Gray Hawk. In flight display, varied series of short nasal screams, *mehy'hr meyh'h meh-meh*, and variations. Juv. has steady series of plaintive, sometimes modulated whistles, *whiéh, whiéh....* **STATUS:** Uncommon and local but increasing in s. Pacific lowlands; first recorded Costa Rica in mid-2000s and likely to spread n. with deforestation. (Costa Rica to S America.)

HARRIS'S HAWK

1st-year

adults

1st-year

BLACK-COLLARED HAWK

1st-year

adults

1st-year

SAVANNA HAWK

1st-year

adults

1st-year

126

SEMIPLUMBEOUS HAWK *Leucopternis semiplumbeus* 34–38cm, WS 56–63cm Attractive, medium-size hawk of humid lowland forest and edge, adjacent semi-open areas and plantations with taller trees. Hunts from perches, mainly at mid-levels, and does not soar; flights usually short and low over canopy. Sometimes sits on exposed perches at forest edge, where can be confiding. Distinctive, with bright orange face and legs, clean white underparts, single narrow white tail band. 1st-year has streaky head, fine dusky streaks on breast, 2 narrow white tail bands. Like adult in 2nd year. SOUNDS: High, thin, semi-metallic, drawn-out whistle from perch, *psiiiiiih*, to 1.5 secs, rising overall or level. 'Song' comprises short series of plaintive whistles, *hu'rieeh hu'rieeh...*, with upward inflection. STATUS: Uncommon to fairly common on Caribbean slope, rarely to 800m. (Honduras to w. Ecuador.)

***NORTHERN WHITE HAWK** *Pseudastur [albicollis] ghiesbreghti* 48–56cm, WS 114–132cm. Stunning, essentially unmistakable large hawk of humid forest and edge; at a distance in flight cf. adult King Vulture. Singles and pairs soar low over forest canopy in mid–late morning, often revealing their presence by loud screaming calls. Wingbeats rather slow and floppy; soars on flattish wings. Perches mainly in subcanopy, where easily overlooked. Juv. has more extensive black on wings and tail; 2nd-year like adult but with some black mottling on bases of secondaries, more extensive black in wing-tip; like adult in 3rd year. Eye varies from dark brown to honey-colored. SOUNDS: Drawn-out, husky, slightly overslurred scream, 1–1.5 secs, typically repeated a few times; suggests a pig squealing. STATUS: Uncommon to fairly common on both slopes, locally to 1400m. (Mexico to nw. S America.)

BARRED (BLACK-CHESTED) HAWK *Morphnarchus princeps* 52–60cm, WS 117–135cm. Large, broad-winged, and short-tailed hawk of humid foothill and highland forest and edge; rarely seen perched. Hunts mainly from perches inside forest, but singles and pairs often soar in mid–late morning, calling loudly. Note shape, with very broad wings, short tail, diagnostic contrast between dark head and neck and whitish underparts (barring on body and underwing coverts visible at closer range). Juv. similar to adult but with blacker head and breast, narrow whitish edgings to upperwing coverts. Like adult in 2nd year. SOUNDS: Far-carrying, downslurred, slightly plaintive screaming whistles, such as *wh'ieeeu*, repeated in flight. In 'flight song,' calls run into series of accelerating and slowing, overslurred piping whistles, 4–7 notes/sec, *wheeu, hiu-hiu...hlieh-hlieh...*, up to 20 secs or longer. Averages slower, more screaming, and less even-paced than Great Black Hawk. STATUS: Uncommon locally on both slopes, mainly 500–2500m, rarely lower and up to 3000m; also reports from Nicoya and Osa Peninsulas. (Costa Rica to nw. Ecuador.)

SEMIPLUMBEOUS HAWK

1st-year   adult

NORTHERN WHITE HAWK

1st-year   adults

BARRED HAWK

adults

128

TROPICAL FOREST ACCIPITERS (3 species). Rarely encountered denizens of humid forest, where relatively short wings and long tails good for maneuvering among trees. Unlike North American accipiters, not known to engage in flight displays. Habits and often plumage recall forest falcons (next plate). Hunt from perches in cover, dashing out after small birds and, in the case of Tiny Hawk, large flying insects such as *Morpho* butterflies. Sometimes perch on exposed snags in early or mid-morning sun, and can be confiding when encountered perched inside forest. Northern migrant accipiters are on p. 114.

TINY HAWK *Accipiter superciliosus* 21–24cm male, 26–29cm female, WS 38–48cm. Very small, rather compact, and relatively short-tailed hawk of humid forest and edge. See genus note. Flight fast, dashing, and agile, usually in brief bursts when pursuing prey. Note small size, barred underparts on all plumages. Shorter tailed, more finely and sparsely barred below than migrant adult Sharp-shinned Hawk (p. 114). Imm. Barred Forest Falcon larger with longer tail, narrow white tail bars, darker barring below, subtly different face pattern with dark eyes. Adult female plumage similar to male but washed browner above, often tinged buff below; juvs. variable, either brown or bright rusty above. **SOUNDS:** 'Song' a fairly rapid series of high, shrill piping notes, *pieh-pieh...*, 4–5 notes/sec, in short series or prolonged for several secs. Other high whistles and chirps may suggest a songbird rather than a raptor. **STATUS:** Rare or scarce on both slopes, locally to 1200m. (Nicaragua to S America.)

BICOLORED HAWK *Accipiter bicolor* male 33–38cm, female 43–48cm, WS 61–79cm. Rarely seen but widespread hawk of humid forest and edge, adjacent semi-open areas with trees. See genus note. Flight rapid and direct with quick wingbeats, brief glides. Adult distinctive, with plain pale gray to smoky gray underparts, staring amber eyes; rusty thighs often difficult to see. 1st-year has whitish to rich buff underparts, most likely to be confused with forest falcons, which share similar habits: note staring pale yellow eyes of Bicolored, subtly different extent and pattern of bare facial skin; forest falcons have more strongly graduated tails with narrower, more contrasting whitish bars. Attains adult appearance in 2nd year. **SOUNDS:** Much like Cooper's Hawk of N America, and rarely vocal away from nest. Adult 'song' a variably-paced series of barking clucks, *keh-keh-keh...*, 4–8 notes/sec; also a downslurred, rough snarling mew. Juv. has overall descending wheezy scream. **STATUS:** Uncommon to rare on both slopes, especially foothills and locally to 2200m. (Mexico to S America.)

GRAY-BELLIED HAWK *Accipiter poliogaster* 38–41cm male, 46–51cm female, WS 64–83cm. Very rare and poorly known, medium-large accipiter of humid forest and edge. See genus note. Flight rapid and direct with quick wingbeats, brief glides; not known to soar. 1st-year distinctive, except that plumage resembles much larger and crested adult Ornate Hawk Eagle (p. 134), which has long feathered leggings. Adult larger and paler below than Bicolored Hawk, with contrasting white throat, pale (not rusty) thighs; also cf. Slaty-backed Forest Falcon, which has different face pattern with dark eyes, narrow whitish tail bars. **SOUNDS:** Usually quiet. 'Song' is a series of (usually 4–15) semi-musical, upslurred screaming whistles, *huwieh' huwieh'...*, 3–4/sec; suggests an attila or some other tyrant flycatcher as much as a raptor. **STATUS:** Very rare (overlooked?) in Caribbean slope lowlands, with a handful of records since first recorded Costa Rica in late 2000s; possibly a migrant from S America or range may be expanding north. (S America; recently s. Cen America.)

TINY HAWK

1st-years

adult

1st-years

adult

BICOLORED HAWK

GRAY-BELLIED HAWK

1st-year

adults

FOREST FALCONS (GENUS _MICRASTUR_) (3 species). Rarely seen but frequently heard denizens of humid forest. 'Sing' mainly at dawn and dusk, variations on series of crowing or barking notes, often with a vaguely laughing cadence. Habits and often plumage recall tropical forest accipiters (preceding plate), but facial skin differs and eyes not staringly pale yellow or amber like accipiters, tails strongly graduated.

BARRED FOREST FALCON _Micrastur ruficollis_ 33–38cm, WS 49–59cm. Heard far more often than seen; a retiring, fairly small raptor of humid foothill forest, cloud forest. Usually calls from concealed perch at low to mid-levels, when elusive; at other times tends to perch quietly inside forest, often fairly low, and can be confiding. Sometimes attends army ant swarms to prey on small birds. Flight fast and direct, accipiter-like; does not soar. Adult distinctive, with bright yellow face, pale eyes, finely barred underparts. 1st-year much smaller and less lanky than Collared Forest Falcon, with brighter facial skin, less strongly graduated tail. Also cf. Bicolored and Tiny Hawks. Attains adult appearance in 2nd year. **SOUNDS:** Distinctive, overslurred yapping bark, repeated steadily, _káah, káah,...,_ 10/12–18 secs, and more hesitant series mainly around dawn; also short, slightly descending series, usually 5–8 notes, with slightly laughing cadence, _kah, kaah-kaah-kaah-kah;_ cf. quieter but rather similar-sounding calls of Plain Antvireo. **STATUS:** Uncommon on both slopes to 1800m, mainly in foothills. (Mexico to S America.)

SLATY-BACKED FOREST FALCON _Micrastur mirandollei_ 41–45cm, WS 65–75cm. Rarely encountered inhabitant of humid lowland forest, adjacent plantations, taller second growth. Calls mainly from mid-levels and subcanopy, hunts mainly from perches in dense understory. Slightly more compact and relatively shorter-tailed than other forest falcons, and fairly distinctive, if you are lucky enough to see it: note head pattern with dark eyes, slaty-gray upperparts, cf. imm. Bicolored Hawk, adult Gray-bellied Hawk. **SOUNDS:** 'Song' mainly at dawn and dusk, a varied series of (usually 12–20) hollow, slightly laughing or crowing notes, usually 2–3/sec in slightly intensifying or accelerating series that sometimes run into slower-paced, longer laughing notes, _nyaáh-nyaáh...,_ or _aah aah aah... aaáaah, aaáah....._Faster-paced and often higher, more nasal than Collared Forest Falcon. Cf. Laughing Falcon. **STATUS:** Scarce on Caribbean slope, to 750m. (Honduras to S America.)

COLLARED FOREST FALCON _Micrastur semitorquatus_ male 53–56cm, female 61–64cm, WS 76–94cm. Heard far more often than seen; a spectacular, rather large and lanky raptor of varied forested and wooded habitats; also ranges into semi-open areas with hedgerows and forest patches. Usually calls from high perch in subcanopy, and can be elusive. At other times ranges low to high, mostly perching quietly inside forest; sometimes attends army ant swarms. Flight direct, with fairly quick loose wingbeats and short glides; does not soar. Note dark eyes, dark cheek crescent, very long graduated tail, long legs; overhead, note boldly barred underside to flight feathers. Cf. 1st-year of smaller Bicolored Hawk, much smaller Barred Forest Falcon. Most likely to be confused by sound with Laughing Falcon. Adults typically buff to white below; dark morph rare. Attains adult appearance in 2nd year. **SOUNDS:** Far-carrying, hollow, slightly overslurred _cowh_ or _owhh,_ in short series or repeated steadily but not hurriedly, mainly early and late in day; rarely faster than 1 note every 1.5–2 secs; at times breaks into an accelerating then slowing laugh of about 12–20 clucks, ending with a pause and final plaintive note, _hoh-hoh-hoh..., owh._ Laughing Falcon has shorter, higher, typically faster-paced notes with, dare we say it, a more laughing quality (by comparison, forest falcon sounds as though it's being hit, _owh...).._ Cf. Slaty-backed Forest Falcon. Also quiet single notes on occasion. Juv. has a more plaintive _mehow_ or _kyeow,_ and quiet reedy chippering in alarm. **STATUS:** Uncommon to fairly common on both slopes, to 1600m; most numerous on Pacific slope. (Mexico to S America.)

**BARRED
FOREST FALCON**

1st-years

adult

1st-year

**SLATY-BACKED
FOREST FALCON**

adult

**COLLARED
FOREST FALCON**

1st-years

adults

132

DOUBLE-TOOTHED KITE *Harpagus bidentatus* 32–36cm, 64–74cm. Small, rather accipiter-like kite of humid forest and edge, adjacent plantations, taller second growth. Often one of the first rainforest raptors to soar in mid-morning, as singles or pairs, at times stooping in display flights. Typical flight on distinctively bowed wings, with tail closed and puffy white undertail coverts flared; at other times soars on flattish wings, tail slightly spread, much like an accipiter. Perches quietly in subcanopy and at edges; at times accompanies bands of monkeys, which flush prey from foliage. In flight note slightly paddle-shaped wings (longer than accipiters'), whitish underwing coverts, bold dark barring on primaries; on adult, rusty underparts contrast with white underwing coverts, cf. accipiters. On perched birds note greenish-yellow facial skin, dark median throat stripe; double notch on cutting edge of bill (double 'tooth') rarely visible in field. Cf. adult Cooper's Hawk (p. 114), Broad-winged Hawk (p. 116). **SOUNDS:** High thin whistles given in flight by displaying birds and pairs, *tseéu-ip*, and *tseéu tsee-u*, faster *tsip tsí-yiip*, and variations; high, slightly shrill whistled *shiiep* from perched bird. **STATUS:** Uncommon to fairly common on both slopes, to 1500m, least numerous and more local in drier nw. lowlands. (Mexico to S America.)

HOOK-BILLED KITE *Chondrohierax uncinatus* 38–46cm, WS 81–94cm. Medium-size, broad-winged kite with large bill, bright facial skin, variable plumage. Found in varied wooded and forested habitats, from mangroves to highland oak forest; feeds mainly on land snails. Soars often, but rarely for long periods, mainly in mid–late morning, at times in small groups. Wingbeats rather loose and floppy, suggesting a larger bird. Soars with wings flattish, tail slightly to widely spread. The floppy wingbeats and paddle-shaped wings, with pinched-in bases and spread-fingered hands, separate Hook-billed Kite from superficially similar buteos, which have stiffer wingbeats, different tail patterns. Cf. larger Ornate Hawk Eagle, imm. Gray-headed Kite. On perched birds note big bill, bright facial skin, small feet. Adult male barred gray below (can appear dark against the sky, with bold white checkering in primaries), female barred rusty; 1st-year plain whitish below or with variable dark barring. Scarce dark morph (sexes similar) blackish overall with 1–2 broad pale tail bands. **SOUNDS:** Infrequently heard. From perch, a rapid, overslurred, slightly chuckling chatter of about 10–20 notes, *weh keh-eh-eh...*, 1–1.5 secs; may suggest a woodpecker. **STATUS:** Uncommon but widespread on both slopes to 1500m, rarely to 2700m. (Mexico to S America.)

GRAY-HEADED KITE *Leptodon cayanensis* 45–53cm, WS 92–107cm. Fairly large, broad-winged kite of humid lowland forest and edge, gallery woodland, taller mangroves. Soars on flattish wings, tail rarely spread wide; wingbeats typically languid and easy. In display, interrupts glides with short steep climbs powered by deep, quick, floppy wingbeats followed by a brief glide down with wings held in deep V. Adult distinctive, with soft gray head, dark eyes, blue-gray cere and feet; in flight, black underwing coverts contrast with white body. Imm. plumages variable: note long broad tail with broad pale bands, small feet, brownish eyes. Cf. Hook-billed Kite, Black-and-white Hawk-Eagle. **SOUNDS:** From perch and in flight display, a fairly rapid, steady, at times rather prolonged series of hollow laughing clucks, 4–5 notes/sec, *kyuh-kyuh...*, or *keh-keh...*, usually 5–12 secs; recalls Lineated Woodpecker but lower, less nasal, with shorter notes. Overslurred to slightly inflected wailing *meeaowh*, rather mammal-like, about 1 sec. **STATUS:** Uncommon on both slopes to 1000m, rarely to 1200m. (Mexico to S America.)

DOUBLE-TOOTHED KITE

1st-year

1st-years

adult

adults

HOOK-BILLED KITE

dark morph

males

1st-year

female

female

1st-year

GRAY-HEADED KITE

adults

1st-years

1st-year

134

HAWK-EAGLES (GENUS *SPIZAETUS*) (3 species). Fairly large crested raptors of humid forest. Most often seen in flight, especially between 10:30 a.m. and noon, when morning thermals are strongest before cloud buildup. Like many tropical raptors, juvs. seen very infrequently.

BLACK-AND-WHITE HAWK-EAGLE *Spizaetus melanoleucus* 51–64cm, WS 117–142cm. Scarce eagle of humid forest, mostly seen in flight, especially in mid–late morning. Soars and glides on flattish wings, although tips sometimes curled up; tail slightly spread when soaring. Hunts by stooping from considerable heights. Relatively long-winged and short-tailed compared to other hawk-eagles, and can suggest much smaller Short-tailed Hawk. Also note white head with black lores and striking, diagnostic white leading edge to upperwing, which shows well at long range when birds bank and wheel; short, spiky black crest apparent with good views. Cf. Short-tailed Hawk (p. 120), imm. Gray-headed Kite, imm. Ornate Hawk-Eagle (very rarely seen soaring). 1st-year similar to adult but browner above, tail bars narrower (4–5 dark bars vs. 3–4 on adult); attains adult appearance in 2nd year. SOUNDS: Calls infrequently, unlike other hawk-eagles. Piercing to piping whistles in flight suggest Ornate Hawk-Eagle in quality, but have steadier rhythm: even-paced to slightly accelerating series may end with a more emphatic, at times disyllabic whistle, *whee whi-whi-whi-whi whee-eer*, and variations. STATUS: Scarce on both slopes, especially foothills, to 1500m. (Mexico to S America.)

ORNATE HAWK-EAGLE *Spizaetus ornatus* 56–69cm, WS 117–142cm. Spectacular, fairly large eagle of humid forest. Soars often in mid–late morning, when usually detected by far-carrying whistled calls. Soars on flattish wings, tail slightly spread; wingbeats deep and powerful. In display, climbs with deep floppy wingbeats and stoops with wings closed, almost somersaulting at times. Perches mainly in subcanopy, where can be quite confiding or curious. Perched adult virtually unmistakable (cf. imm. Gray-bellied Hawk, p. 128), but often seen high overhead, when looks rather uneventful and best identified by voice: note rather plain underwings, bold tail banding, white throat contrasting with rusty head sides. 1st-year rarely seen but distinctive, with barred flanks, white head with blank face, long spiky crest; 2nd-year like adult but averages duller and messier; attains adult appearance in 3rd year. Cf. Hook-billed and Gray-headed Kites, Black-and-white Hawk-Eagle. SOUNDS: Far-carrying piping whistles, often repeated tirelessly when soaring, typically with a pause after 1st note and overall a distinctive, slightly stuttering cadence: *whi, whee-whee-wheep, wh, whi, whee-whee-wheep...*, and variations. Unlike Black Hawk-Eagle, introductory series more hurried and last note not drawn out. Perched juv. has loud clear whistle, repeated, *wheeeu*. STATUS: Uncommon to scarce on both slopes, especially in foothills; locally to 2000m. (Mexico to S America.)

BLACK HAWK-EAGLE *Spizaetus tyrannus* 61–74cm, WS 127–155cm. Spectacular, fairly large eagle of humid forest and edge, plantations; more tolerant of cut-over and second-growth forest patches than other hawk-eagles, and usually the most frequently encountered hawk-eagle. Soars often in mid–late morning, when usually detected by far-carrying whistled calls. Soars on flattish wings, tail slightly spread; wingbeats deep and powerful. In display, soars with tail closed, wing-tips quivering. Perches mainly in subcanopy and at edges. Perched adult spectacular and distinctive, with golden eyes, bushy white-based crest, boldly barred leggings, long tail. 1st-year distinctive, with bushy crest, broad black mask, heavily barred underparts; 2nd-year like adult but averages messier, with scattered whitish flecking on head and underparts; attains adult appearance in 3rd year. Cf. Hook-billed Kite, Ornate Hawk-Eagle. SOUNDS: Far-carrying piping whistles, often repeated tirelessly when soaring. Loud, clear, overslurred whistle, often preceded by 1 or more shorter whistles not always audible at a distance, *wheéoo* or *wh-wheéoo*; also *whi-whi whi-wh-wh-wheéoo* and variations. Imm. has steady ringing whistles, *whee whee...*, perched and in flight, and perched adult may give single *weeoo*. STATUS: Uncommon to fairly common on both slopes, especially in foothills; locally to 2000m. (Mexico to S America.)

BLACK-AND-WHITE HAWK-EAGLE

adults

ORNATE HAWK-EAGLE

adults

1st-year

1st-year

BLACK HAWK-EAGLE

adults

1st-year

1st-year

CRESTED EAGLE *Morphnus guianensis* 71–87cm, WS 152–185cm. This very large eagle is a very rarely encountered bird of humid forest and edge. Hunts from canopy and subcanopy perches, preying on mammals and larger birds. Rarely soars and hence overlooked easily. Most likely to be seen perched along waterways or sunning itself in early–mid morning on emergent canopy snags; can be confiding. Cf. larger, bulkier, and more powerful Harpy Eagle, which has shaggier, forked crest. Hawk-Eagles are appreciably smaller, with different plumage patterns, feathered legs, staring golden-yellow eyes (eyes brown to dull yellowish on Crested Eagle). Adult Crested variable, typically has pale rusty to blackish barring on underparts; exceptionally all-dark below. Attains adult plumage in about 3 years. **SOUNDS:** Perched adult has short series of full-bodied, slightly overslurred whistles, introduced by 1–2 shorter notes, *whi whi wheeéooo wheeéooo wheeéooo*; longer, at times persistent series of short overslurred whistles, *whi wheée wheée wheée...*; and plaintive, slightly rising, clear-toned whistle, 1–1.5 sec, higher, less mournful than Harpy Eagle. **STATUS:** Very rare and local (mostly extirpated by deforestation and hunting) on n. Caribbean slope (mainly Tortuguero area) and s. Pacific slope, to 1000m. (Mexico to S America.)

HARPY EAGLE *Harpia harpyja* 87–107cm, WS 183–224cm. This huge powerful eagle is a very rarely encountered bird of humid lowland forest and edge. Hunts from canopy and subcanopy perches, preying on mammals and larger birds. Does not soar and hence overlooked easily—in our experience, you have much more chance of seeing a jaguar. Most likely to be seen perched along waterways or sunning itself in early–mid morning on emergent canopy snags; can be confiding. Flights mainly short and low over canopy or across rivers. Only possible confusion species is slightly smaller and equally rare Crested Eagle. Crested is less heavily built (but can still appear huge), overall slimmer and longer-tailed. Crested has smaller bill, less massive legs, and erectile crest is single-pointed. In flight, Crested shows heavier dark barring across secondaries and inner primaries; adult Crested has gray hood (without Harpy's black chest patch) and unmarked whitish underwing coverts. Harpy also has broader tail banding relative to similar-age Crested, and attains adult plumage in about 4 years. **SOUNDS:** Mainly vocal around nest. Adult gives mournful, slurred wailing whistles, 1–1.5 secs; imm. has higher, shriller, drawn-out whistles. **STATUS:** Very rare and local (mostly extirpated by deforestation and hunting) on n. Caribbean slope and s. Pacific slope, to 500m. (Mexico to S America.)

1st-year

CRESTED EAGLE

adults

adult

1st-year

HARPY EAGLE

adults

1st-year

1st-year

138

SWALLOW-TAILED KITE *Elanoides forficatus* 56–61cm, WS 117–135cm. Spectacular aerial raptor with long pointed wings and very long, deeply forked tail; no similar species in Costa Rica. Breeds in humid forest, often near water. Migrants occur widely over any open and forested habitats. Flight graceful and buoyant with deep easy wingbeats and leisurely soaring, snatching insects from canopy and on the wing; soars on flattish wings with tips curled up. Often in pairs or small groups; flocks up to 50 or so during migration. 1st-year has shorter tail than adult, white tips to primaries and primary coverts. Attains adult appearance in 2nd year. SOUNDS: Shrill piping and ringing whistles, mainly in flight, at times in rapid yelping series, accelerating and slowing, *kleeh kleeh-kleeh-kleep* and variations. STATUS: Fairly common to uncommon breeder Jan–Aug locally on both slopes, mainly 100–1800m, a few to 3000m; more widespread Aug–Sep, late Nov–Mar during migration; occasional in Oct to mid-Nov, mainly on s. Pacific slope. (Breeds N America to S America, winters S America.)

WHITE-TAILED KITE *Elanus leucurus* 38–41cm, WS 89–99cm. Distinctive elegant raptor of open country with scattered trees, marshes, ranchland, even towns. Note pointed wings, fairly long whitish tail, black shoulders. No really similar species, but cf. male Northern Harrier (p. 114). Flies with easy wing-beats, wings held in a shallow V during glides and infrequent soaring. Often hovers and perches on roadside wires, like a kestrel. Attains adult appearance in 2nd year. SOUNDS: Mostly silent when not nesting. Varied low rasping notes, at times paired with rising whistles; series of short, downslurred whistles, *hüw, hüw...*, recalling Osprey. STATUS: Fairly common on both slopes, locally to 1500m. Expanding range with deforestation; first recorded Costa Rica in late 1950s. (Americas.)

MISSISSIPPI KITE *Ictinia mississippiensis* 34–38cm, WS 84–94cm. Spring and fall transient found widely in forested and semi-open country, often amid much larger movements of Broad-winged and Swainson's Hawks. Hunts in flight like Plumbeous Kite; soars on flattish wings, the tips often curled up, tail slightly spread; wingbeats languid and smooth. Confusion most likely with Plumbeous Kite, which is darker overall, has rusty primary flashes (can be hard to see); adult Plumbeous has white tail bands, lacks pale secondary panel on upperwing; juv. has sparser dark brown (not rusty) streaking below. Also cf. Peregrine Falcon. 1st-summer has mostly adult-like head and body, retains juv. wings and tail. Attains adult appearance in 2nd year. Usually silent. STATUS: Fairly common to sporadically common Sep–Oct, late Mar–early May on Caribbean slope, locally to 2700m, stragglers into Nov; uncommon on Pacific slope and inland. (Breeds N America, winters S America.)

PLUMBEOUS KITE *Ictinia plumbea* 33–37cm, 84–94cm. Dark aerial kite of humid forest and edge, often near rivers; locally in mangroves. Highly aerial, spends much time soaring and gliding; catches insects on the wing. Soars on flattish wings, the tips often curled up, tail slightly spread; wingbeats languid and smooth. Often perches high in trees adjacent to clearings and rivers. Cf. paler Mississippi Kite, a later migrant in both spring and fall. SOUNDS: Mostly quiet when not nesting. From perch and in flight, a high, plaintive, downslurred whistle, typically preceded by a short overslurred note, *si-hiiew*; short piping whistles. STATUS: Fairly common breeder Feb–Jul on both slopes, locally to 2000m; more widespread Jul–Sep, Jan–Mar during migration, rarely to 2700m, with early return migrants rarely from late Dec. (Breeds Mexico to S America, winters S America.)

SWALLOW-TAILED KITE

adults

WHITE-TAILED KITE

juv.

adult

MISSISSIPPI KITE

juvs.

adults

adult

juvs.

PLUMBEOUS KITE

adult

PEARL KITE *Gampsonyx swainsonii* 22–26cm, WS 45–55cm. Handsome, very small raptor of open and semi-open country, especially ranchland with scattered trees. Often perches on roadside wires, isolated trees; hunts from perch and in flight while soaring. Distinctive: note small size, pointed wings, dark cap contrasting with pale buffy forehead and cheeks, short dark bar at breast sides, rusty flanks. Imm. has narrow pale edgings to crown and back; like adult in 2nd year. SOUNDS: High piping whistles, often in steady series, *pieh-pieh...*; downslurred whistle followed by short rippling series, *pseeu, pi-pi-pi-pi.* STATUS: Uncommon to rare but increasing, mainly on Pacific slope, locally on Caribbean slope and inland to 2100m; first recorded Costa Rica in mid-1990s, and spreading with deforestation. (Nicaragua to S America.)

FALCONS (12+ species; forest falcons on p. 130, caracaras p. 144). Fairly diverse, worldwide family of raptors; genetic studies indicate falcons share a common ancestor with parrots, but traditionally they have been grouped with hawks as 'birds of prey,' as done here for ID purposes. Ages differ, sexes similar or different (female often noticeably larger); like adult in 2nd year.

AMERICAN KESTREL *Falco sparverius* 26–29cm, WS 61–65cm. Attractive, lightly built, small migrant falcon of varied open and semi-open habitats with trees and scattered bushes, from farmland and open woodland to wetlands and rural areas. Distinctive: all plumages have complex head pattern, long rusty tail, overall pale underwings. Often seen perched on roadside wires and utility poles. Wingbeats rather loose and floppy, not strong and purposeful like Merlin; soars on flattish wings, often hangs in wind and hovers. Juv. male has whiter breast, heavier black spotting than adult. SOUNDS: Mostly high shrill screaming *kyieh-kyieh...*, usually in short bursts, repeated. STATUS: Uncommon to fairly common Oct–Apr on both slopes, to 1800m, rarely higher; winters mainly in Pacific lowlands and interior, more widespread Sep–Oct, Mar–Apr. (Americas.)

MERLIN *Falco columbarius* 27–32cm, WS 64–70cm. Small, dashing migrant falcon of varied open and semi-open habitats, from ranchland and forest clearings to wetlands and coastal lagoons. Generally rather dark; all plumages have blackish tail with narrow whitish to pale gray bars, overall dark underwings. Cf. Bat Falcon, much larger Peregrine Falcon. Perches on fence posts, utility poles, in trees; rarely on wires, unlike kestrel. Wingbeats quick and powerful, hunting flight usually low and fast; soars on flattish wings; does not hover. Imm. brownish above, much like female. SOUNDS: Mostly quiet; high screaming *kriih-kriih...*, in interactions, with quality suggesting Killdeer. STATUS: Scarce to uncommon Oct–Apr throughout; mainly in coastal lowlands, but rarely to 3000m. (Holarctic; winters in New World to S America.)

BAT FALCON *Falco rufigularis* 23–28cm, WS 61–73cm. Handsome small falcon of lowland forest and edge, adjacent clearings and semi-open areas with taller trees; locally in towns. Distinctive: dark overall with white to buffy throat, rusty thighs, but cf. Merlin, larger Peregrine Falcon. Typically perches conspicuously on bare snags, antennas, often in pairs, when size difference between sexes readily apparent (female larger). Flight fast and powerful, chasing birds, bats, insects, and dive-bombing larger raptors; soars on flattish wings, at times high overhead, when can be mistaken for White-collared Swift (p. 234). Throat and neck variably washed buff, on some birds strongly cinnamon. Imm. washed brownish overall, with dark throat streaks, barring on thighs and undertail coverts. SOUNDS: Penetrating, at times persistent screaming often draws attention to birds perched and in flight: slower-paced *krieh krieh…*and rapid *hew-hew...*; single sharp *kik.* STATUS: Uncommon on both slopes, locally to 2200m, rarely higher. (Mexico to S America.)

PEARL KITE

adults

AMERICAN KESTREL

female

males

female

MERLIN

female

male

female

1st-year

BAT FALCON

variation

adults

cf. White-
collared Swift

PEREGRINE FALCON *Falco peregrinus* 38–51cm, WS 96–119cm. Widespread, powerful migrant falcon of varied open and semi-open habitats, especially wetlands, coastal lagoons. Soars on flattish or slightly raised wings; wingbeats smooth and powerful. Hunting flights notably swift, including steep dives; regularly hunts bats late in day, more so than Bat Falcon. Often perches on utility poles, antennas in towns; not on wires. Only large falcon regular in Costa Rica, cf. very rare, much more lightly built and long-tailed Aplomado Falcon. Note adult Peregrine's dark hood, barred underparts. Male obviously smaller than female when seen together. Attains adult appearance in 2nd year. **SOUNDS:** Mostly quiet; harsh screams and hoarse whistles in interactions. **STATUS:** Uncommon Sep–Apr on both slopes, to 2000m; more widespread and numerous Sep–Oct, Mar–Apr in migration, especially along Caribbean coast. (Almost worldwide.)

APLOMADO FALCON *Falco femoralis* 38–46cm, WS 81–93cm. Very rare. Attractive, lightly built, and long-tailed falcon of open habitats, especially ranchland and wetlands with scattered trees. Perches on trees, low shrubs, roadside wires and posts. Flight smooth and powerful, dashing after small birds, hunting over burning fields, and soaring in a leisurely manner, snatching insects in flight. Note very long tail, bold white eyebrow, black breast band, cinnamon belly; also white trailing edge to wings, narrow white tail bars. Cf. larger and stockier Peregrine Falcon. Juv. has browner upperparts, heavier dark streaking on chest, buff wash to face and breast in fresh plumage; blue-gray cere and eyering become yellow like adult over 1st year; attains adult appearance in 2nd year. **SOUNDS:** Mostly quiet; fairly high screaming calls mainly in interactions. **STATUS:** Very rare fall–winter visitor to nw. lowlands, exceptionally to Central Valley; mainly 1st-year birds, all since 2010. (Mexico and sw. US to S America.)

> **OSPREY (PANDIONIDAE; 1 SPECIES)** Small but virtually worldwide family of fish-eating raptors, sometimes subsumed into hawk family. Ages/sexes differ slightly, female larger; like adult in 2nd year.

*(WESTERN) OSPREY *Pandion haliaetus* 56–66cm, WS 149–175cm. Distinctive, long-winged, fish-eating migrant raptor found along coasts and rivers, at lakes, reservoirs, and near any water body likely to hold fish. Note white head and underparts with dark mask; grayish feet. Perches on prominent snags, utility poles. Soars easily on crooked and slightly arched wings; as likely to be mistaken in flight for a large gull as for any other raptor. Feeds from flight, splashing feet-first to snatch fish near surface. Female averages heavier dark breast streaking than male; juv. has buff wash to breast and neat pale tips to upperparts, lost through 1st winter. **SOUNDS:** Clear to slightly hoarse ringing whistles and downslurred yelps, often in slightly intensifying series. **STATUS:** Uncommon to fairly common Sep–Apr (imms. regularly remain through summer) on both slopes; smaller numbers inland to 2500m, occasionally higher, especially during migration. (Breeds N America to Mexico and Caribbean, migrant s. to S America; also Old World.)

1st-year

adults

PEREGRINE FALCON

1st-year

APLOMADO FALCON

1st-year

adults

adults

OSPREY

144

LAUGHING FALCON *Herpetotheres cachinnans* 46–56cm, WS 79–94cm. Distinctive, large-headed and long-tailed snake-eating raptor of open and semi-open country with scattered large trees, forest edge. Often perches on prominent snags, fence posts, utility poles. Does not soar; flight direct, with hurried stiff wingbeats that show off bold buff wing panels. Note creamy-buff head and underparts with broad black 'bandit mask,' boldly banded tail. Ages/sexes similar. **SOUNDS:** Far-carrying crowing and laughing calls often reveal its presence; regularly calls after sunset. Steady *hah hah*…or *haâh, haâh*..., about 1 note/sec, or a slightly slower *wáko, wáko*,...; series can be prolonged, sometimes breaking in maniacal laughing cackles. Also a softer, conversational *hah*, repeated irregularly. Cf. Collared Forest Falcon (p. 130). **STATUS:** Uncommon to fairly common on both slopes, to 1800m. (Mexico to S America.)

RED-THROATED CARACARA *Ibycter americanus* 54–64cm, WS 97–115cm. Rare in humid lowland forest, adjacent plantations and semi-open areas with taller trees; more often heard than seen. Mostly in pairs at mid–upper levels; can be very noisy. Food mainly arboreal wasp larvae, palm fruits. Flight direct with unhurried wingbeats mainly below body plane; does not soar. No visually similar species, but calls can suggest macaws. Note large size and long tail, colorful face and bill, white belly. Imm. has duller eye and facial skin. **SOUNDS:** Loud and raucous; ear-splitting when close overhead. Semi-metallic crowing *kyah-kyah-kahrr* and variations; hoarse braying screeches; deep throaty *rrah* in flight can suggest Scarlet Macaw. **STATUS:** Rare and local on both slopes, to 1200m; formerly widespread in lowlands, having largely disappeared from much of its Middle American range in past 40–50 years for reasons unknown. (Honduras to S America.)

YELLOW-HEADED CARACARA *Milvago chimachima* 41–46cm, WS 81–95cm. Open and semi-open country, towns, forest edge, often along rivers. Singles and pairs, sometimes small groups, feed mostly on ground, walking confidently. Flies directly with steady loose wingbeats, glides and soars on cupped wings. Distinctive, with pale buffy head and underparts, big pale wing panels; cf. Laughing Falcon, which has very different habits. Juv. has variable dark streaking and barring on head and underparts, like adult in 2nd year. **SOUNDS:** Varied loud screams, at times in short series, often rather hoarse and unpleasant: range from clearer wailing *heeéahr* to rasping downslurred *sheeáhrr*. **STATUS:** Fairly common to common on s. Pacific slope, uncommon to fairly common elsewhere, mainly below 1500m. Expanding range with deforestation, first recorded Costa Rica in 1970s. (Nicaragua to S America.)

CRESTED CARACARA *Caracara plancus* 48–59cm, WS 115–132cm. Large striking scavenger, widespread in fairly open country, especially ranchland and marshes with scattered trees. Note white head and breast with black cap, brightly colored face, long yellow legs. Flight pattern distinctive, with big white wing panels, white tail tipped black. Flies with steady strong wingbeats; soars occasionally. Often seen as singles and pairs in early morning on 'highway patrol,' looking for roadkill to scavenge, when associates readily with vultures and walks confidently on ground. Juv. has similar pattern to adult but browner overall with streaked (not barred) breast, duller face; 2nd-year like duller, messier version of adult. **SOUNDS:** Often silent; throaty clucks and creaky rattles given mainly in interactions, with head thrown backwards. **STATUS:** Common on n. Pacific slope; uncommon to fairly common (increasing with deforestation) elsewhere on both slopes, mainly below 1500m. (Mexico and s. US to S America.)

LAUGHING FALCON

adults

RED-THROATED CARACARA

juv.

adult

YELLOW-HEADED CARACARA

1st-year

adult

CRESTED CARACARA

1st-year

adults

146

TYPICAL OWLS (STRIGIDAE; 14+ SPECIES) Popular worldwide family of mainly nocturnal raptors, ranging from tiny pygmy owls to very large and spectacular Spectacled Owl. Plumage of many species very similar (especially screech owls), varying more with habitat than with species, reflecting a common need to be cryptic at daytime roosts. Many species distinctive, easy to ID visually, others notoriously similar but vocally distinct. In addition to songs, all owls have sundry other calls, mainly shrieks, mews, wails, and hisses given in various contexts, especially when breeding. Many species sing in duets, male song typically lower-pitched than female.

*NORTHERN MOTTLED OWL *Strix virgata* 33–38cm. Medium-size owl of varied wooded and forested habitats, from dry forest and humid forest edge to town parks, highland oak, mangroves; nocturnal. Roosts low to high, typically in dense shady foliage; hunts from perches at low to mid-levels at edges of clearings, other semi-open areas. Note rounded head, dark eyes, voice; averages darker in wetter regions. Juv. has whitish facial disks, plain buff underparts. SOUNDS: Song a measured series of (usually 3–6, rarely to 10) deep, overslurred, slightly emphatic hoots, at a distance may suggest a dog barking; often with louder notes toward the end before fading with last 1–2 notes, *whuúh, whuúh, WHUÚH, WHUÚH, wuh*; typically about 1note/sec, faster when excited. Fairly rapid bouncing-ball series of about 20 hoots suggests Spectacled Owl, *wup wup wup-wup-wupwup...*, 5–6 notes/sec. Slurred wailing scream, about 1 sec. STATUS: Fairly common on both slopes, to 1500m, locally to 2200m. (Mexico to nw. Peru.)

BLACK-AND-WHITE OWL *Strix nigrolineata* 38–41cm. Striking large owl of humid forest and edge, plantations; nocturnal. Mainly at mid–upper levels, often in canopy and subcanopy; sometime roosts in rather open situations. Visually distinctive, with bright yellow bill and feet, black face, barred whitish underparts. Juv. whitish overall with faint darker barring. SOUNDS: Typical song a slightly nasal, 2-note barking, 1st note quiet and inaudible at a distance, 2nd note loud, emphatic, *oh, WOAH!* every 15–30 secs. Longer series with quiet last note, *hoh-hoh-hoh-hoh-hoh, HWAOH, hoh*. Nasal quality distinct from gruff, resonant hoots of Northern Mottled Owl. Less often more measured short series hoots, *Hóah, Hóah,...*. Wailing scream lower, less shrieky than Northern Mottled. STATUS: Uncommon to fairly common on both slopes, to 1600m. (Mexico to nw. S America.)

CRESTED OWL *Lophostrix cristata* 38–43cm. Spectacular large owl of humid forest, adjacent taller second growth, and edge; nocturnal. Calls mainly from canopy, where can be hard to see, but roosts at low to mid-levels in rather open but shady understory, often in pairs. Remarkable long bushy crests render ID straightforward, if you are lucky enough to see this stunning bird; dark and light morphs frequent, sometimes within pairs. Juv. whitish overall with dark facial disks, short whitish ear tufts, cf. juv. Spectacled Owl. SOUNDS: Song a deep, throaty, slightly overslurred growl, with short stuttering introduction audible at closer range, *k'k'k'Króhrrrr*, about 1 sec, every 6–15 secs. STATUS: Uncommon to scarce on both slopes, to 1500m. (Mexico to S America.)

SPECTACLED OWL *Pulsatrix perspicillata* 43–48cm. Spectacular and distinctive large owl of humid lowland forest and edge, plantations; nocturnal. Calls mainly from canopy, but roosts at any level, such as in shady understory whence may be flushed during day; often hunts at edges, sometimes in adjacent semi-open habitats. Juv. whitish overall with dark facial disks, lacks whitish ear tufts of juv. Crested Owl. Some birds have variable dark barring on underparts. SOUNDS: Song a fairly rapid, pulsating series of usually 6–10 deep hoots, accelerating then fading, 1–2 secs; cadence suggests a sheet of metal being flexed quickly, *Wuup-wuup-wuupwuup....*Cf. similar but usually longer variation of Northern Mottled Owl. Deep low *whoa*, suggesting large pigeon, sometimes given from roost on dull days. STATUS: Uncommon to fairly common on both slopes, to 1600m. (Mexico to S America.)

NORTHERN MOTTLED OWL

darker
morph

paler
morph

CRESTED OWL

BLACK-AND-WHITE OWL

paler
morph

barred
variant

darker
morph

SPECTACLED OWL

juv.

148

SCREECH OWLS (GENUS *MEGASCOPS*) (5 species). Small nocturnal owls with erectile ear tufts. Roost in cavities or perched against trunks, where plumage highly cryptic. Do not screech; songs are series of hoots or purring trills. Species taxonomy vexed by plumage similarities, best resolved by voice.

PACIFIC SCREECH OWL *Megascops cooperi* 23–25cm. Lowland forest, mangrove edge, ranchland with hedgerows and taller trees, gardens. Best told by voice; lacks strong black rim to facial discs. Brownish gray overall; no rusty morph known. **SOUNDS:** Song a slightly overslurred, vaguely bouncing-ball series of gruff, slightly barking hoots, *koh-koh...*; typically 12–15 notes in 2 secs. Faster-paced, rattled purrs and whinnies when agitated, often with laughing or chuckling cadence. **STATUS:** Fairly common to common on n. Pacific slope and adjacent n. Caribbean slope, to 1500m. (Mexico to Costa Rica.)

TROPICAL SCREECH OWL *Megascops choliba* 23–24cm. Humid foothill forest and edge, plantations, suburban areas with trees, gardens. Mainly in fairly open and edge habitats; sometimes feeds under street lights. Gray-brown and rare rusty morphs occur. Note voice, distinct black rim to facial discs. **SOUNDS:** Song a short quavering trill ending with 1–2 louder hoots, *oo-oo-oo-oo-oo-oorr WOOP!* typically every 4–9 secs; at a distance, introductory trill inaudible. **STATUS:** Fairly common to common on Pacific slope, mainly 400–1500m, locally to coastal lowlands in south. (Costa Rica to S America.)

*COSTA RICAN [VERMICULATED] SCREECH OWL *Megascops [guatemalae] vermiculatus* 21–23cm. Humid lowland forest, taller second growth, plantations. Usually in fairly dense understory, not in open habitats. Gray-brown and rusty morphs occur. Note voice, habitat, face pattern, relatively weak dark streaks on underparts. **SOUNDS:** Song a purring trill, typically 4–9 secs, sometimes intensifying slightly before fading abruptly; cf. Cane Toad *Rhinella marina.* **STATUS:** Uncommon to fairly common on Caribbean slope, to 1000m; presumably (?) this taxon reported locally on Nicoya Peninsula. (Costa Rica to w. Panama; presumably s. Nicaragua.)

*SKUTCH'S [VERMICULATED] SCREECH OWL *Megascops [guatemalae]* undescribed. 21–23cm? Habitat, habits, and plumage like Costa Rican Screech Owl (no range overlap). Note voice, lack of strong black rim to facial discs, weak dark streaks below; cf. Tropical Screech Owl. **SOUNDS:** Song a short, swelling, quavering trill, about 0.5–0.7 sec, repeated every 10–18 secs. **STATUS:** Uncommon on s. Pacific Slope, to 1400m. (Costa Rica; and adjacent Panama?).

PYGMY OWLS (GENUS *GLAUCIDIUM*) (3 species). Very small owls active by day. Songs are series of toots, easily imitated. Rounded heads have 'eye-spots' on sides of nape; juvs. have plain crown or only a few pale crown markings. Little range overlap among species; note habitat, voice.

*FERRUGINOUS PYGMY OWL *Glaucidium brasilianum* 17–18cm. Tropical and subtropical forest edge, gardens, plantations, mangroves, semi-open areas with hedgerows; avoids closed forest. See genus intro. Grayish, brown, and rusty morphs occur. Note voice, long tail (often twitched side-to-side), with numerous bars, diagnostic whitish streaking on crown. **SOUNDS:** Song an often prolonged series of hollow whistles, typically rather steady and often upslurred with 'inhaled' quality, *hoo hoo...*, or *whi' whi'...*; 10/3–3.5 secs. Bursts of high yelping twitters. **STATUS:** Fairly common on n. Pacific slope, spreading to s. Pacific slope and n. Caribbean lowlands; rarely to 2000m. (Mexico to S America.)

CENTRAL AMERICAN PYGMY OWL *Glaucidium griseiceps* 14–15cm. Humid forest, mainly in hilly lowlands. See genus intro. Mainly at mid–upper levels, often in subcanopy. Note spotted crown, relatively short tail with few pale bars; cf. Ferruginous and Costa Rican Pygmy Owls. **SOUNDS:** Song a series of hollow ringing toots, usually starting with 2–4 notes, increasing to 6–9 notes (rarely up to 18); 10/2–3.5 secs. Song often preceded by soft quavering trills, also given alone and suggesting trill of Costa Rican Screech Owl. **STATUS:** Uncommon on Caribbean slope, locally to 1000m. (Mexico to nw. Ecuador.)

PACIFIC SCREECH OWL

brown
morph

**TROPICAL
SCREECH OWL**

rusty
morph

rusty
morph

brown
morph

**COSTA RICAN SCREECH OWL/
SKUTCH'S SCREECH OWL**

brown
morph

rusty
morph

FERRUGINOUS PYGMY OWL

all pygmy owls have
false 'eye-spots' on nape

**CENTRAL AMERICAN
PYGMY OWL**

COSTA RICAN PYGMY OWL *Glaucidium costaricanum* 16–17cm. Very small owl of highland oak forest and cloud forest; diurnal. See genus intro (p. 148). Often sings from subcanopy; hunts low to high, at edges and in adjacent semi-open areas. Only pygmy owl in most of its range; brown and rusty morphs both frequent. Note voice, spotted crown (spots washed out in brightest rusty morphs); cf. Ferruginous and Central American Pygmy Owls, mostly at lower elevations. SOUNDS: Rapid hollow tooting, easily imitated. Varies from steady to an irregular paired cadence (about 2 pairs/sec); typically 10 notes/3–3.5 secs. Bouts of tooting often preceded by 1 or more rapid, slightly quavering *huhuhuhu* phrases, with initial hooting bouts hesitant, shorter than later series. STATUS: Uncommon to fairly common on both slopes; from timberline down to 1200m on Pacific slope, locally down to 900m on Caribbean Slope. (Costa Rica to w. Panama).

BARE-SHANKED SCREECH OWL *Megascops clarkii* 25–27cm. Rather distinctive large screech owl of cloud forest, elfin forest, and edge; nocturnal. Calls mainly from canopy and subcanopy, but often hunts lower at edges and in adjacent semi-open areas. Plumage brown to rusty overall. No similar species in range and habitat: note large size, short ear tufts (head often looks rather rounded), yellow eyes, cinnamon face, white-scalloped underparts; cf. Tropical Screech Owl. SOUNDS: Song a short series of (usually 4–7) slow-paced low hoots with slightly overslurred cadence, *hu-ooo-ooo-ooo*, every 3–10 secs; 1st and sometimes last notes shorter and quieter. Agitated birds give wailing screams that grade into triplets of strong hoots, faster-paced than song. STATUS: Uncommon to fairly common on both slopes, above 900m in Northern Mts., above 1200m in Talamanca Mts. (Costa Rica to nw. Colombia).

UNSPOTTED SAW-WHET OWL *Aegolius ridgwayi* 20–21.5cm. Small, compact owl of highland oak forest and cloud forest; nocturnal. Sings from mid–high levels, often well hidden; hunts from lower perches, sometimes along edges of clearings. No visually similar species in Costa Rica: note big head, white brows, plain underparts. Cf. slightly faster song of Costa Rican Pygmy Owl; saw-whet toots tend to be hollower, slightly downslurred vs. overslurred in pygmy owls. SOUNDS: Whistled tooting series, easily imitated, 10 notes/3.5–5 secs; toots sometimes subtly grouped in series of 3–8 or so notes within protracted bouts of hooting. Wailing screech, about 1 sec. STATUS: Scarce to uncommon on both slopes, above 2400m. (Mexico to w. Panama.)

STRIPED OWL *Asio clamator* 33–38cm. Savanna, oil palm plantations, ranchland, open country with scattered trees and thickets; roosts on ground and in dense trees. Nocturnal; hunts from perches such as fence posts, roadside wires. Flies with fairly shallow rapid wingbeats. Cf. Barn Owl. SOUNDS: Song a low, moaning, overslurred *hoóh*, every 4–18 secs. Piercing, hawk-like, whistled scream, *keeer*, about 0.5 sec, usually downslurred, sometimes in duet with hoots. Less often (agitated?) a fairly rapid series of about 12–20 short clucks or yelping hoots, about 3/sec. STATUS: Uncommon to fairly common locally on both slopes to 1000m, rarely to 1500m; may be spreading with deforestation. (Mexico to S America.)

BARN OWLS (TYTONIDAE; 1 SPECIES) Worldwide family of owls with heart-shaped facial discs, relatively small eyes, short squared tails. Downy young molt directly into adult-like plumage.

*****BARN OWL** *Tyto alba* 36–41cm, WS 93–110cm. Widespread and distinctive 'white owl' of open and semi-open country with scattered trees, forest patches, old buildings, towns; nocturnal. Often perches on roadside fence posts and wires. Roosts in caves, buildings, tree hollows, dense palm crowns. Hunts mainly in flight, quartering over grassy areas with easy 'floating' wingbeats; often hovers. Male averages whiter below than female. Cf. Striped Owl, often in same areas. SOUNDS: Far-carrying rasping shriek, often given in flight; other shrieks and hisses, none very heart-warming. STATUS: Uncommon to fairly common on both slopes, locally to 1800m. (Worldwide.)

COSTA RICAN
PYGMY OWL

brown
morph

rusty
morph

BARE-SHANKED
SCREECH OWL

UNSPOTTED
SAW-WHET OWL

STRIPED OWL

paler
morph

BARN OWL

darker morph

POTOOS (NYCTIBIIDAE; 3 SPECIES) Small neotropical family of large-headed nocturnal birds that pass the day roosting cryptically on branches and stumps. Ages differ slightly, with paler and more loosely textured juv. plumage soon replaced by adult-like plumage; sexes similar. Readily detected at night by brilliant amber eyeshine reflected in light beams like burning coals; appreciably larger and brighter than nightjar eye reflection.

NORTHERN POTOO *Nyctibius jamaicensis* 38–43cm, WS 91–101cm. Varied forested and semi-open habitats, from dry forest and mangroves to clearings in humid forest, farmland, even villages and towns; nocturnal. Roosts at mid–upper levels in trees, often in rather exposed situations and relying on its cryptic plumage. Hunts more often from low to mid-level perches, including fence posts, branches over rivers, less often high perches such as emergent snags, radio antennae. Hunting birds perch upright and sally out for insect prey, often returning to same perch like a giant nocturnal pewee. Much larger than nightjars, and in flight as likely to be mistaken for a large hawk (much longer-tailed than owls); Common Potoo averages smaller and darker, but safely separable only by voice; little or no range overlap with Great Potoo. SOUNDS: Song (mainly spring–summer; at other seasons mostly on calm, often moonlit nights) a low, drawn-out rasp, about 1–1.5 secs, usually followed by 1–6 gulping, upslurred clucks, *WAAAAHRR, wah wah wah*, repeated every 6–22 secs. STATUS: Uncommon to fairly common on n. Pacific slope, locally to 1500m. (Mexico and Caribbean to Costa Rica.)

COMMON POTOO *Nyctibius griseus* 36–41cm, WS 88–98cm. Replaces Northern Potoo away from n. Pacific slope; habitat and habits similar. Averages smaller and darker than Northern, but safely identified only by voice. Much larger than nightjars, and in flight as likely to be mistaken for a large hawk (much longer-tailed than owls). Great Potoo appreciably larger and plainer, with vermiculated vs. streaked plumage, brown eyes (but eyeshine amber on all potoos). SOUNDS: Haunting, overall descending and slowing series of (usually 3–7) hollow mournful whistles, often just before dawn: *Huwooaah hwoah, hwoah hwah...*, repeated every 8–23 secs. STATUS: Uncommon to fairly common on both slopes, to 1200m. (Nicaragua to S America.)

GREAT POTOO *Nyctibius grandis* 49–58cm, WS 112–125cm. Humid lowland forest and edge. Roosts and hunts mainly from mid–upper levels, often in canopy or subcanopy along rivers. Like Common Potoo, hunting birds perch upright and sally out for insect prey, often returning to same perch like a giant nocturnal pewee. Common Potoo appreciably smaller with streaked vs. vermiculated plumage, dark mustache, golden-yellow eyes. SOUNDS: Song 'unpleasant,' a throat-clearing, overslurred moaning roar, *BWAAHr*, about 1 sec, occasionally followed by a quiet 2nd note, repeated about every 8–10 secs; throatier and unhappier-sounding than Northern Potoo (little or no range overlap). In flight a shorter, more emphatic *woah!* STATUS: Uncommon to fairly common on both slopes, rarely to 1200m. (Mexico to S America.)

OILBIRD (STEATORNITHIDAE; 1 SPECIES) Neotropical family comprising a single species of nocturnal, fruit-eating bird; nests colonially in caves (nesting unknown in Central America). Ages/sexes similar.

OILBIRD *Steatornis caripensis* 42–47cm. Distinctive, large nocturnal bird of humid forest, where may be found during day roosting on branches. Feeds in canopy and clearings with fruiting trees, hovering to pluck palm fruit and wild avocados from outer branches like a giant nocturnal trogon. No similar species: note long tail, rich rusty plumage spotted with white; also heavy hooked bill, cf. potoos, nightjars; eyeshine amber, not as brilliant as potoos. SOUNDS: Single birds usually silent, but multiple birds feeding at night may utter rough gasping sounds and echo-locating clicks. STATUS: Very rare presumed migrant, found May–Aug at scattered sites from lowlands to highlands on both slopes, most frequently in heavily birded Monteverde region; might be found almost anywhere in Costa Rica, perhaps especially in foothills. (S America; migrant (?) to Cen America.)

NORTHERN POTOO

juv.

roosting

COMMON POTOO

GREAT POTOO

at night, potoo
eyes reflect like
burning coals

OILBIRD

NIGHTJARS (CAPRIMULGIDAE; 10 SPECIES) Worldwide family of nocturnal, insect-eating birds that sleep by day and rely on cryptic plumage to avoid detection and predators. Ages/sexes differ slightly in most species (mainly in tail pattern, and females more often have rusty morph than males); like adult in 1 year. Typically nest on ground.

SHORT-TAILED NIGHTHAWK *Lurocalis semitorquatus* 20–21cm. Humid forest and edge, especially along rivers and streams in lowlands; roosts and nests in forest canopy. Singles or pairs emerge at dusk to feed low over forest canopy and along edges; erratic flight may suggest a large bat rather than *Chordeiles* nighthawks. Distinctive, with fairly large size, short tail, overall dark plumage (no white wing bands). Sexes similar. SOUNDS: In flight a sharp, slightly liquid cluck, singly or in short quick series, *g'wik* and *gwik whik-whik*; rougher *gwirrr* in interactions. STATUS: Uncommon to fairly common on both slopes, to 1200m. (Mexico to S America.)

LESSER NIGHTHAWK *Chordeiles acutipennis* 20.5–23cm. Open and semi-open areas with scattered trees, forest and edge, beaches, mangroves, towns; roosts on tree branches and ground, nests on ground. Mainly an aerial feeder, flight fairly erratic with bursts of quick flicking wingbeats and short glides on wings held in distinct V; flies low to high, mainly fairly low on breeding grounds, flocks often high overhead in migration. Also hunts from ground and perches, flushing off roads like typical nightjars. Post-roost flights of 100s seen locally in migration and winter. Only real ID concern is with Common Night-hawk; note that both species when perched usually show white on bend of wing, unlike other Costa Rican nightjars. Common has longer, more pointed wings, flight stronger and less fluttery with deeper, more rangy wingbeats; white wing band farther from wing-tip and slightly longer, extends across 5 primaries (only 4 primaries on Lesser); lacks bold pale barring across inner primaries. On perched Lesser, note grayish band of fine barring on breast (lacking on Common), white wing band of male Lesser lies under tip of tertials, vs. forward of tertials on Common; female Lesser has buff wing band. On both species, wing-tips can project past tail at rest, more often on Common. SOUNDS: Song (spring–summer) from ground or low perch a churring trill, swells quickly and fades abruptly, *urrrr...*, can go on for minutes, typically in bursts of 7–13 secs, with pauses of 1–3 secs; can be mistaken for Cane Toad *Rhinella marina*, which is lower-pitched, more pulsating. Bleating *whik* in flight, mainly in interactions. Flushed winter birds usually silent. STATUS: Fairly common breeder locally on Pacific slope, especially near coast; more widespread and locally numerous Sep–Apr on both slopes, mainly below 1200m. (Mexico and sw. US to S America.)

COMMON NIGHTHAWK *Chordeiles minor* 23–24cm. Breeds locally in drier open and semi-open areas of foothills, from savanna to marshes, airfields; migrants occur in any habitat; roosts mainly on tree branches, nests on ground. Habits much like Lesser Nighthawk but flight stronger, less fluttery; in breeding season often flies much higher. Only real confusion possible is with Lesser Nighthawk (which see for ID criteria); also note that Common undergoes wing molt in S America, whereas Lesser molts during late summer–fall in Costa Rica. Plumage tones more variable than Lesser, with local breeders smaller and rustier overall than boreal migrants, which vary from dark overall to relatively pale and sandy gray. SOUNDS: Call in flight (mainly breeding season, also migration) a sharp nasal *beenk* or *peehn*; in display flight, male stoops steeply and produces loud rushing boom at bottom of dive. STATUS: Fairly common breeder late Mar–Aug locally on Pacific slope, mainly 400–1000m; more widespread and sporadically fairly common to common in migration, Sep–Nov, Apr–May, mainly below 1500m. (Breeds N America to Panama, winters S America.)

SHORT-TAILED NIGHTHAWK

LESSER NIGHTHAWK

male

female

male

males

migrants

COMMON NIGHTHAWK

female

breeder

males

(COMMON) PAURAQUE *Nyctidromus albicollis* 26–30cm. Familiar and wide-spread large nightjar of varied habitats, from pastures and roadsides to humid forest edge, mangroves, plantations, dry forest. Nests and mainly roosts on ground, in leaf litter under bushes and trees, not in open habitats. Hunts mainly from ground, also low perches, whence sallies out with stiff, flicking wingbeats and flat-winged glides, often returning to or near same spot. Note very long tail at rest, cf. *Antrostomus* nightjars; also bold scapular pattern, rows of buff spots on wing coverts, pale underparts with fine dark barring. White wing and tail flashes of male striking and distinctive; note buff wing band of female; imm. male resembles female but with more white in tail, paler wing band. **SOUNDS:** Song (mainly spring–summer) a loud, slightly burry whistled *pWEER!* repeated steadily every 2–3 secs; year-round a quieter *p'weéir*, often preceded by hesitant, stuttering clucks. Nervous quiet clucks from perched birds. **STATUS:** Fairly common to common on both slopes, locally to 1700m. (Mexico s. Texas to S America.)

WHITE-TAILED NIGHTJAR *Hydropsalis cayennensis* 20.5–21.5cm. Poorly known small nightjar of savanna, grassland, and open ranchland with scattered bushes, open low scrub; roosts and nests on ground, often near or under a shady bush. Typically hunts from ground, much like appreciably larger and longer-tailed Pauraque, which is often in the same habitat; also cf. Common and Lesser Nighthawks, which have long wings reaching to around tail tip. Note small size, bright cinnamon hindcollar, buff scapular lines, tail pattern, and squared to slightly notched tail. **SOUNDS:** Song a high overslurred whistle preceded by a quiet, clipped tick, *t'seeeiu*, every 2–11 or so secs, not repeated as steadily or interminably as many nightjars; quality suggests Black Phoebe or some other songbird, not like other nightjars in Costa Rica. **STATUS:** Not well known in Costa Rica, with few documented records in recent decades Uncommon to fairly common but local on Pacific slope, to 900m; also reported from s. Caribbean slope where status unclear. (Costa Rica to S America.)

OCELLATED POORWILL *Nyctiphrynus ocellatus* 21–22cm. Small dark night-jar of humid lowland forest and edge, perhaps mainly in hilly country. Hunts mainly from mid-levels in trees, less often from ground; often sings from perch in dense cover. Note voice, rather plain face and breast with narrow white forecollar (can be concealed), dark 'eye-spots' on scapulars, white dots on upperwing coverts and belly, small white tail corners. No similar species in Costa Rica. Sexes similar but female averages rustier. **SOUNDS:** Song a strongly burry, slightly downslurred whistled *wheíurrr*, every 2–8 secs; lower, less emphatic, and more quavering than Pauraque. **STATUS:** Scarce and local in n. Caribbean lowlands. (Honduras to S America.)

female

PAURAQUE

males

rusty morph

WHITE-TAILED NIGHTJAR

males

female

OCELLATED POORWILL

rusty morph

gray morph

DUSKY NIGHTJAR *Antrostomus saturatus* 23–24cm. Medium-size, rather dark nightjar of humid highland forest and edge, páramo, overgrown pastures; local counterpart to whip-poor-wills. Hunts and sings mainly from snags and low perches in trees. Note voice, elevation, dark plumage (varies from sooty to dark rusty overall, belly usually spotted white to buff); no other nightjars likely in same range and habitat, but overlap possible at lower elevations with distinctive Pauraque. Also cf. Eastern Whip-poor-will. **SOUNDS:** Slow-paced, burry *tk, whiirr'p-wieh*, every 1–11 secs, the introductory low *tk* audible only at close range; suggests a medicated, asthmatic Eastern Whip-poor-will. Quiet low growls when agitated. **STATUS:** Fairly common in highlands, mainly above 1500m in Northern Mts., above 1800m in Central and Talamanca Mts. (Costa Rica to w. Panama.)

EASTERN WHIP-POOR-WILL *Antrostomus vociferus* 23–24cm. Poorly known in Costa Rica, apparently rare. Medium-size, nonbr. migrant of forest and edge habitats. Note relatively gray plumage with slightly paler and grayer crown sides and scapulars, blackish median crown stripe, tail pattern; cf. Chuck-will's Widow, Dusky and Rufous Nightjars. **SOUNDS:** Rarely sings in Costa Rica, but possible in spring migration, a whistled *whie-pura-weén*, every 1–1.2 secs or faster, lacks burry drawled quality of slower-paced Dusky Nightjar. Flushed birds may give hollow clucks. **STATUS:** Scarce to rare Nov–Mar on Pacific slope, to 1200m in Central Valley. (Breeds e. N America, winters s. to Costa Rica.)

RUFOUS NIGHTJAR *Antrostomus rufus* 26–28cm. Poorly known in Costa Rica. Medium-large, rusty-toned nightjar of forest edge, second growth woodland, adjacent semi-open areas and savannas with thickets. Roosts and hunts from ground or low perches, including fence posts. Slightly smaller and shorter-winged than Chuck-will's-widow, with overall more rusty plumage (can be grayed out by LED flashlights, and Chuck can be quite rusty), but silent birds not easily separated in the field; note shorter white distal tail patches of male, vs. white extending up to base of tail on Chuck. Beware that most other nightjars can be bright rusty, especially Pauraque. **SOUNDS:** Song a fairly rapid-paced, clipped whistled phrase, *chük! wit-wit-weéo* repeated steadily, every 1–2 secs. **STATUS:** Scarce and local on both slopes, to 1000m; perhaps most frequent in foothills. (Costa Rica to S America.)

CHUCK-WILL'S-WIDOW *Antrostomus carolinensis* 29–33cm. Large and big-headed nonbr. migrant nightjar of varied wooded habitats from humid forest and edge to second growth, plantations, mangroves. Roosts and hunts from ground and perches, sometimes at mid–upper levels in trees. Note large size and very long wings, overall warm brown plumage (some birds grayer) without striking contrast except male tail pattern (from above shows only on spread tail). Cf. Rufous Nightjar, Eastern Whip-poor-will. **SOUNDS:** Migrants sometimes sing briefly in spring, usually for short periods around dawn and dusk, a rapid *chk weéu-weéu*, 1st note inaudible at a distance. **STATUS:** Uncommon to scarce Oct–Apr on both slopes, to 1500m. (Breeds e. US, winters to n. S America.)

DUSKY NIGHTJAR

female

male

EASTERN WHIP-POOR-WILL

female

male

RUFOUS NIGHTJAR

female

male

male

CHUCK-WILL'S-WIDOW

female

male

PIGEONS (COLUMBIDAE; 25+ SPECIES) Worldwide family of rather plump-bodied birds with small heads, relatively short sturdy legs. Ages differ slightly, sexes similar (female often averages duller than male) or strikingly different; adult appearance attained in 1st year.

MOURNING DOVE *Zenaida macroura* 25.5–31cm. Open and semi-open areas from farmland to brushy second growth, especially in drier regions; often along roadsides. Feeds on ground, where overlooked easily until flushed; often seen early and late in day in fast direct flight. In display, climbs with slow wingbeats and glides down on bowed wings, at times in pairs, when can suggest parakeets. Locally in flocks, at times 100s during winter. Distinctive, with long pointed tail, big dark droplet spots on wing coverts. Juv. scaly and smaller than adult, might be mistaken for Inca Dove. Female slightly duller than male, without blue-gray hindneck. SOUNDS: In flight, including when flushed, makes high rapid wing whistle. Song a low mournful cooing, 1st note longest and slightly broken, with 2nd part higher, followed by 1–4 (typically 3) coos fading away, *whoo'oo ooo ooo ooo*. STATUS: Fairly common locally on n. Pacific slope, to 3000m on slopes of Irazú; more numerous and widespread Oct–Mar, when n. migrants present. (N America to Panama.)

WHITE-WINGED DOVE *Zenaida asiatica* 27–30.5cm. Semi-open areas from dry forest and ranchland to brushy woodland, towns, villages. Feeds mainly on ground but often perches on roadside wires and can be confiding where not hunted; winter flocks locally number 100s. Flight fast and direct but slower and usually higher overhead than Mourning Dove, more like larger pigeons. Distinctive, with bold white wing band, white tail corners; cf. larger and paler Eurasian Collared Dove. SOUNDS: Short song a mournful, slightly hoarse cooing *wh-koó ku-kooo* ('who cooks for you'); long song lower, slightly chanting, a 3-note then 4-note phrase and a varied ending of 1–4 notes, such as *h-hoo-coo, h-hoo coo-oo, oo oóo oo*. STATUS: Common in nw. lowlands and Central Valley, to 1500m; uncommon to locally fairly common and spreading on n. Caribbean slope and s. along Pacific slope. More widespread in north Oct–Apr, when n. migrants occur. (Mexico and sw. US to w. Panama.)

EURASIAN COLLARED DOVE *Streptopelia decaocto* 31–34cm. Open and semi-open areas from towns and villages to ranchland. Often perches on road-side wires and utility poles, locally in small flocks. Flight direct, with slightly clipped wingbeats, not as fast as Mourning Dove and often higher overhead. Plumage tones variable, some notably pale and milky, others rather dark, but note plain upperparts with narrow black hindcollar, big white tail corners. SOUNDS: Song a mournful 3-syllable cooing *wh'Huuu hu*, about 1 sec, often repeated several times in tedious succession. Flight call a slightly overslurred, burry *réhhr*. STATUS: Scarce and local but increasing on Pacific slope; first recorded Costa Rica in 2000s. (Native to Eurasia.)

FERAL PIGEON (ROCK DOVE) *Columba 'livia'* 30.5–35cm. Widespread, bastardized human commensal of towns, villages, city parks; rarely far from habitation. Often in flocks, perching on roadside wires, buildings, around animal feed lots; infrequently perches in trees. Plumage highly variable, an annoying source of potential confusion with native pigeons, but note habitat and habits; in flight, underwing coverts often white (dark on native pigeons). SOUNDS: Low muffled cooing audible at close range. STATUS: Fairly common to common locally almost throughout, to 3000m. (Native to Eurasia.)

MOURNING DOVE

juv.

male

WHITE-WINGED DOVE

**EURASIAN
COLLARED DOVE**

FERAL PIGEON

PALE-VENTED PIGEON *Patagioenas cayennensis* 30–34cm. Lowland savanna with wetlands and forest patches, forest edge along rivers, plantations, mangroves. Mainly at mid–upper levels, often perched in canopy, on roadside wires. In display flight, climbs with exaggerated slow wingbeats, glides down with wings in V. Note blue-gray head with red eye, dark bill; white undertail coverts contrasting with grayish tail. Cf. Red-billed and Scaled Pigeons. Juv. duller overall with narrow pale edgings to upperparts. SOUNDS: Song a drawn-out coo followed by a repeated 3-syllable phrase (usually 3–4 ×): *whoooo, oo-k-hoooo, oo-k-hoooo...*, cf. Red-billed Pigeon song; also a deep purring *whoorr*. STATUS: Fairly common to common on both slopes, especially near coast; mainly below 600m. (Mexico to S America.)

RED-BILLED PIGEON *Patagioenas flavirostris* 31–35cm. Forest edge, plantations, semi-open areas with taller trees and forest patches, wooded gardens; often in drier areas, not typically in rainforest. Mainly at mid–upper levels, often perched on bare snags in canopy and clearings. Commonly looks simply dark overall; 'red' bill is mostly pale yellowish with small reddish area at base often hard to see. Note pinkish head and neck, slaty blue-gray belly contrasting with black tail. Cf. Pale-vented, Short-billed, and Scaled Pigeons. Juv. has dark bill, rustier tone to chest and back. SOUNDS: Song a drawn-out coo followed by a repeated 4-syllable phrase (usually 2–5 ×): *whooooo, óo k-hoo-oo, óo k-hoo-oo...*, cf. Pale-vented Pigeon song; also a single swelling *whoo*, often repeated several times. STATUS: Fairly common in nw. lowlands, less numerous and more local s. on both slopes, especially foothills, locally to 2100m. (Mexico to Costa Rica.)

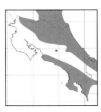

SHORT-BILLED PIGEON *Patagioenas nigrirostris* 27–29cm. Fairly small dark pigeon of humid lowland and foothill forest and edge, locally in tree-scattered farmland. Often heard but infrequently seen. Mainly at mid–upper levels in canopy; most often seen as singles or pairs in flight over canopy or across small openings, not in flocks; sometimes found at fruiting trees or on quiet roadsides taking grit. Dark overall and rather nondescript; note small black bill, brownish upperparts, voice. Beware that juv. Red-billed Pigeon has dark bill. Limited overlap in foothills with Ruddy Pigeon, best separated by voice. SOUNDS: Song a far-carrying, relatively high 4-syllable cooing, *ooh HOO-ku-koo*, with slightly jerky cadence, repeated every few secs, emphasis on 2nd syllable; lacks introductory notes of larger pigeons; also a purring *urrrrr*, at times repeated steadily. STATUS: Fairly common on both slopes, locally to 1500m. (Mexico to nw. Colombia.)

RUDDY PIGEON *Patagioenas subvinacea* 28–30cm. Fairly small dark pigeon of humid highland and upper foothill forest and edge. Habits much like Short-billed Pigeon (limited overlap in foothills), and these species often not separable given typical field views, although Ruddy averages slightly ruddier upperparts (especially male); safely identified by song. SOUNDS: Song a far-carrying, relatively high 4-syllable cooing, *WOOka hoo'hoo*, every few secs; emphases on 1st (and 3rd) syllables vs. 2nd (and 4th) in Short-billed Pigeon; lacks introductory notes of larger pigeons; also a purring *urrrrr*, at times repeated steadily. STATUS: Uncommon to fairly common on both slopes, mainly above 1500m in Central Mts. and Talamancas, above 600m in Northern Mts., with local downslope movement in winter, mainly on Caribbean slope. (Costa Rica to S America.)

PALE-VENTED PIGEON

RED-BILLED PIGEON

SHORT-BILLED PIGEON

RUDDY PIGEON

164

*SOUTHERN BAND-TAILED PIGEON *Patagioenas [fasciata] albilinea* 32–37cm. Large pigeon of highland oak forest and edge, adjacent clearings and semi-open areas with taller trees; often in small flocks. Mainly at mid–upper levels in trees, but feeds on ground at times; like most large pigeons, mainly seen in flight, at times fairly high overhead. Only large pigeon in most of the highlands (local overlap with Red-billed Pigeon and smaller Ruddy Pigeon); note yellow bill (tipped dusky on imm) and feet, white hindcollar, broad pale tail tip set off by dark median tail band. Juv. duller overall, lacks white hindcollar. **SOUNDS:** Deep, slightly overslurred and swelling single coo, repeated (usually 7–13×) in steady series, *whoóh, whoóh...*, about 1/sec. Deep purring *whuuhrr*. **STATUS:** Fairly common to common on both slopes, mainly above 1500m in Central Mts. and Talamancas, above 1000m in Northern Mts., occasionally wandering lower. (Costa Rica to S America.)

SCALED PIGEON *Patagioenas speciosa* 30.5–35cm. Humid forest and edge, adjacent clearings with tall trees. Mainly at mid–upper levels in canopy; overlooked easily but sometimes perches on bare snags in canopy and clearings. Mostly seen in flight as singles or small groups: note white undertail coverts contrasting with black tail; flight slightly 'looser' and floppier than other pigeons. Boldly scaled neck and breast distinctive; cf. Red-billed and Pale-vented Pigeons. Juv. duller overall with indistinct scaling. **SOUNDS:** Song a deep, slightly moaning single note followed by a repeated 2–3-syllable phrase (usually 2–4×): *whoooo huh-woóhr, huh-woóhr…*and variations; overall more sonorous, slower-paced than other lowland *Patagioenas*. **STATUS:** Uncommon to fairly common on nw. Caribbean slope and in interior valleys of s. Pacific slope; scarce and local (nomadic?) elsewhere, to 1600m; may undergo seasonal movements. (Mexico to S America.)

FOREST GROUND DOVES (2 species). Small doves of humid forest edge and adjacent habitats. Appreciably larger and bulkier than *Columbina* ground doves (on next plate). Often rather nomadic, frequently seen in flight. Formerly both placed in genus *Claravis*.

BLUE GROUND DOVE *Claravis pretiosa* 20–21.5cm. Humid forest edge and clearings, second growth. Feeds on ground as singles, pairs, small groups; most often seen in flight, crossing roads or clearings. Sings from mid–upper levels in trees, often well concealed. Powder-blue male stunning and distinctive, even with a brief flight view. Female in flight shows contrasting rusty rump and tail, broad chestnut wingbars, grayish underwings, cf. smaller Ruddy Ground Dove, scarce Maroon-chested Ground Dove at higher elevations. **SOUNDS:** Song a far-carrying, clear hooting *booop* or *ooop* every 1.5–2 secs; usually 2–10× in unhurried, measured series; typically 3–15 sec pauses between series. **STATUS:** Uncommon to fairly common on both slopes, to 1200m; more local in drier nw. lowlands. (Mexico to S America.)

MAROON-CHESTED GROUND DOVE *Paraclaravis mondetoura* 20.5–22cm. Rare but distinctive small dove of humid highland forest edge, adjacent clearings, mainly in areas with seeding bamboo. Often rather shy and elusive, mostly detected when vocal: sings from mid-levels in trees and bamboo thickets. Flight fast and direct, like Blue Ground Dove of lowlands. Note deep purplish breast, bold white tail sides of male, which can flash in flight; female has broad purplish wingbars, pale tail corners, brownish underwings. **SOUNDS:** Song lower than Blue Ground Dove, often more prolonged and disyllabic: a far-carrying low *woop* or *t'hwoop* with 2nd syllable rising, every 1–1.5 secs up to 40× or so. **STATUS:** Scarce and nomadic on both slopes, mainly 900–3000m. (Mexico to S America.)

female

juv.

male

**SOUTHERN
BAND-TAILED PIGEON**

male

SCALED PIGEON

female

BLUE GROUND DOVE

female

male

female

males

MAROON-CHESTED GROUND DOVE

GENUS *COLUMBINA* (4 species). Very small, easily overlooked ground doves of open habitats, often along roadsides; perch readily on fences and in low trees. Flush explosively from ground with variable wing whirr; all species have rusty wing flashes. Frequently form flocks, and species mix readily.

INCA DOVE *Columbina inca* 20–22cm. Open and semi-open areas, from town streets and brushy woodland to ranchland, beaches, especially in drier regions. Mainly in pairs or small groups. Feeds on ground where mixes readily with Common and Ruddy Ground Doves; often perches on roadside wires. Distinctive, with overall scaly plumage, long squared tail with white sides; bright rusty wing patches flash in flight. Cf. juv. Mourning Dove. SOUNDS: Wings make whirring rattle when flushed. Song a pair of hollow, slightly burry, overslurred coos, *whooh pooh*, every 1–2 secs, often repeated steadily; less often a faster, burry *h'p'wuurrr….* STATUS: Common to fairly common on n. Pacific slope, inland to 1500m in Central Valley; uncommon and local but range expanding s. along Pacific slope and into Caribbean lowlands. (Mexico and sw. US to w. Panama.)

COMMON GROUND DOVE *Columbina passerina* 16–17cm. Open and semi-open areas, from towns to ranchland, especially in drier regions. Feeds on ground, mainly as pairs or small groups, where inconspicuous until flushed; mixes readily with Inca Dove and Ruddy Ground Dove. Note scaly neck and breast (old name of Scaly-breasted Ground Dove much more appropriate), orange to pinkish bill base; dark marks on upperwing coverts more extensive than Ruddy and Plain-breasted Ground Doves. Flight quicker, slightly more bounding than Ruddy Ground Dove, when appears overall paler and grayer, with pale band across upperwing coverts, dark secondaries; lacks black axillars. SOUNDS: Song a low hooting *whuuh*' or slightly disyllabic *h'wooh*, repeated steadily every 1–1.5 secs. Flushes with quiet wing whirr. STATUS: Common to fairly common on n. Pacific slope; in smaller numbers to 1500m in Central Valley and spills over locally to n. Caribbean slope. (Mexico and s. US to S America.)

PLAIN-BREASTED GROUND DOVE *Columbina minuta* 14.5–15.5cm. Lowland savanna and ranchland with scattered bushes and trees. Feeds on ground, mainly as pairs or small groups, when sometimes mixes with other ground doves. Mostly inconspicuous and overlooked easily, but sings from low perch such as fence or shrub. Note small size, plain neck and breast, purple sheen to dark upperpart markings; bill base of Plain-breasted can be dull pinkish, cf. Common Ground Dove. Appreciably smaller and shorter-tailed than female Ruddy Ground Dove, grayer overall with dark secondaries, lacks black axillars. SOUNDS: Song a low hooting *wüp* or *w'üp* repeated steadily every 0.5–1 secs; notes much shorter and song faster-paced than Common Ground Dove. STATUS: Uncommon and local on Pacific slope and in adjacent n. Caribbean lowlands, disjunctly near Turrialba; to 800m. (Mexico to S America.)

RUDDY GROUND DOVE *Columbina talpacoti* 17–18cm. Open and semi-open areas, from towns to ranchland, especially in humid regions. Commonest ground dove in many areas, locally in flocks. Feeds on ground, mainly as pairs or small groups, and mixes readily with other ground doves. Male distinctive, with bright ruddy plumage, contrasting blue-gray head. Female best told by relatively large size, plain neck and breast, relatively warm plumage tones, mostly rusty secondaries; also note diagnostic black axillars, sometimes visible in flight; cf. Common and Plain-breasted Ground Doves, female Blue Ground Dove. SOUNDS: Song a 2-syllable hooting *per-woop* or *h'woop*, repeated steadily every 0.5–1 secs, quieter 1st note not always audible at a distance, when cf. Plain-breasted Ground Dove; at times varied to 3-syllable *h'i'woop*. STATUS: Fairly common to common on both slopes, to 1500m; less numerous in drier nw. lowlands. (Mexico to S America.)

INCA DOVE

COMMON GROUND DOVE

female

male

PLAIN-BREASTED GROUND DOVE

female

male

RUDDY GROUND DOVE

female

male

168

GENUS *LEPTOTILA* (3+ species). Rather plain, fairly plump doves of forest floor; mostly detected by voice. Typical view is a bird flushing into forest understory or flying low across a road or trail. All species have white tail corners ('white tips'), cf. plain, shorter tails of quail-doves. Often best seen early and late in day on quiet roadsides and at edges. Flush with higher, more whistling wing whirr than quail-doves; sometimes land on low branch after being flushed. Sing from ground and low perches.

*VERREAUX'S [WHITE-TIPPED] DOVE *Leptotila verreauxi* 26–29cm. Wide variety of forested and edge habitats, from dry forest to humid plantations, second growth, gardens; in rainforest areas occurs at edges and in second growth, not inside heavy forest. See genus intro. Note voice, overall rather plain pinkish head and breast, bluish eyering (sky-blue on breeding adult, blue-gray on imm.); cf. other *Leptotila*. Juv. duller overall, upperparts and breast with pale edgings. SOUNDS: Song a low, mournful, hollow 2–3-syllable cooing, *ooh-wooooo*, 2nd note sometimes inflected, or *ooh'h-woooo*, every 3–10 secs; 1st note often inaudible at a distance. STATUS: Common to fairly common on Pacific slope, locally to 2500m; uncommon and local but increasing with deforestation on Caribbean slope. (Nicaragua to S America.)

GRAY-HEADED DOVE *Leptotila plumbeiceps* 25.5–27.5cm. Humid lowland forest and edge, adjacent plantations, second growth. See genus intro. Note voice, blue-gray crown and nape, dusky pinkish breast; white tail corners smaller than White-tipped Dove. Gray-chested Dove darker overall with warm brown crown and nape. Juv. duller overall, upperparts edged cinnamon, breast narrowly scalloped buff. SOUNDS: Short, mournful, slightly overslurred cooing *whooo* or *huuu*, about 0.5 sec duration, repeated steadily every 2–3 secs, cf. lower, more fading away, and often longer song of Ruddy Quail-Dove. STATUS: Uncommon to locally fairly common in nw. lowlands, to 1000m. (Mexico to w. Colombia.)

GRAY-CHESTED DOVE *Leptotila cassinii* 25–27cm. Humid forest and edge, adjacent plantations, second growth, *Heliconia* thickets. See genus intro. Distinctive, rather small *Leptotila* with warm brown crown and nape, dusky grayish breast, small white tail corners. Occurs locally alongside White-tipped and Gray-headed Doves. Also cf. female Ruddy Quail-Dove. Juv. duller and darker overall with variable cinnamon feather edgings. Comprises 2 groups that may represent species: darker **Cassin's Dove** *L. [c.] cassinii* of Caribbean slope, paler **Rufous-naped Dove** *L. [c.] rufinucha* of Pacific slope, with larger white tail tips. SOUNDS: Song a low, mournful, drawn-out *whoooo* or *whoóóoo*, fading away, about 1.5 secs duration, every 4.5–6.5 secs; averages shorter, more overslurred in Rufous-naped than Cassin's. Cf. shorter, faster-paced song of Ruddy Quail-Dove. STATUS: Fairly common on both slopes, locally to 1200m. (Mexico to nw. Colombia.)

QUAIL-DOVES (6 species). Rather chunky, compact, and generally elusive forest doves which, as their name suggests, can appear intermediate between doves and quail. Mostly detected by voice. Singles or pairs walk on forest floor, where may be located by rustling in leaf litter. Run quickly when alarmed; also may freeze and flush explosively from close range with wing whirr, like quail. Sing from ground and low to mid-level perches. Formerly all placed in genus *Geotrygon*.

VIOLACEOUS QUAIL-DOVE *Geotrygon violacea* 22–24cm. Local and poorly known dove of humid forest with shady understory. See quail-dove intro; perhaps more arboreal than other quail-doves. Plain face and overall plumage pattern suggest *Leptotila*, but note bright red bill, ruddy upperparts of male, contrasting ruddy rump and tail of female; lacks white tail corners. Violet mantle can be striking in good light, but often not apparent in typical field views. Juv. has rusty tipping to upperparts and breast, dark bill tip. SOUNDS: Short hollow *whoóoo*, 0.5 sec, every 2.5–4 secs; slightly higher, more nasal than Ruddy Quail-Dove. STATUS: Scarce to uncommon and local on both slopes; perhaps most frequent in Guanacaste Cordillera, mainly 500–1200m. (Nicaragua to S America.)

VERREAUX'S DOVE

GRAY-HEADED DOVE

Pacific
(Rufous-naped)

juv.

Caribbean
(Cassin's)

GRAY-CHESTED DOVE

VIOLACEOUS QUAIL-DOVE

female

male

RUDDY QUAIL-DOVE *Geotrygon montana* 23–25cm. Humid forest, shady plantations. See quail-dove intro (p. 168). Sometimes seen in flight, low and fast along a quiet road or across clearings, when bright ruddy male is readily identified. Female/juv. slightly smaller, stockier, and shorter-tailed than *Leptotila* doves, with no white on tail corners; also note striped face, vertical pale bar at breast sides, red bill. SOUNDS: Song a low, mournful, slightly moaning *whoooo*, fading away slightly, every 2–5 secs. Cf. Chiriqui Quail-Dove, Gray-chested Dove. STATUS: Fairly common on Pacific slope, locally to 1200m; less numerous on Caribbean slope, especially in foothills, to 1000m. (Mexico to S America.)

OLIVE-BACKED QUAIL-DOVE *Leptotrygon veraguensis* 21–24cm. Rather small dark quail-dove of humid lowland forest, adjacent taller second growth, usually with dense understory. See quail-dove intro (p. 168). Distinctive in range, with bold white cheek stripe in all plumages; female darker overall than male, with buffy vs. white forehead; juv. browner overall with cinnamon wing bands. SOUNDS: Low, slightly downslurred, and twangy gulping *owhh*, every 1–3 secs; could easily be passed off as a frog. STATUS: Fairly common on Caribbean slope, locally to 1500m. (Nicaragua to nw. Ecuador.)

PURPLISH-BACKED QUAIL-DOVE *Zentrygon lawrencei* 25–27cm. Handsome, medium-size quail-dove of humid foothill forest with dense understory. See quail-dove intro (p. 168). Note boldly striped face with whitish forehead, grayish head and breast; purple gloss to mantle apparent with good view. Cf. Buff-fronted Quail-Dove, which may overlap locally. Sexes similar. Juv. duller overall, upperparts edged pale cinnamon, breast barred buff. SOUNDS: Song a 3-syllable, slightly twangy cooing *huh-w'hohw*, every 2–3 secs; 1st part underslurred, last note loudest, slightly downslurred. At a distance, only last *hohw* audible, cf. shorter, higher, and faster-paced song of Buff-fronted Quail-Dove. STATUS: Uncommon to fairly common but local on Caribbean slope, 400–1000m. (Costa Rica to w. Panama.)

BUFF-FRONTED QUAIL-DOVE *Zentrygon costaricensis* 25–28cm. Handsome, medium-size quail-dove of humid foothill and highland forest. See quail-dove intro (p. 168). Note boldly striped face, bright ruddy upperparts; also buff forehead contrasting with blue-gray crown, glossy green hindneck. Cf. Purplish-backed Quail-Dove, which may overlap locally. Juv. duller overall, with whitish forehead, diffusely barred above and below. SOUNDS: Relatively high, slightly overslurred *wowh*, every 1–1.5 secs, often repeated steadily; could be passed off as a frog; higher and more nasal, not gulping like Olive-backed Quail-Dove. STATUS: Uncommon to fairly common on both slopes, 1000–3000m; mainly 2000–2500m on Pacific slope, mainly 1500–2000m on Caribbean slope. (Costa Rica to w. Panama.)

CHIRIQUI QUAIL-DOVE *Zentrygon chiriquensis* 28–31cm. Large, heavily built quail-dove of humid highland and foothill forest. See quail-dove intro (p. 168). Distinctive, with overall pinkish-ruddy plumage, contrasting blue-gray head, faint dark face stripes. Juv. lacks blue-gray cap, duller and browner overall with variable dark scalloping. SOUNDS: Low mournful *whooOOoo*, about 1 sec, every 3–5 secs; at a distance, only the loudest middle section audible. Suggests Ruddy Quail-Dove but slightly longer and deeper, intensifies slightly, and ends more abruptly. STATUS: Uncommon on both slopes, mainly 1000–2500m on Pacific slope, 600–2000m on Caribbean slope. (Costa Rica to w. Panama.)

RUDDY QUAIL-DOVE

female

juv.

male

OLIVE-BACKED
QUAIL-DOVE

female

juv.

male

PURPLISH-BACKED QUAIL-DOVE

BUFF-FRONTED QUAIL-DOVE

CHIRIQUI
QUAIL-DOVE

CUCKOOS (CUCULIDAE; 10+ SPECIES) Worldwide, notably diverse family found mainly in warmer climates; most species rather long-tailed, all have 2 toes pointing forward, 2 backward. Ages similar or different, attaining adult appearance in 1st year; sexes similar.

YELLOW-BILLED CUCKOO *Coccyzus americanus* 28–30.5cm. Nonbr. migrant to varied wooded, forested, and scrubby habitats, including hedgerows, coastal scrub, humid forest edge, mangroves. Forages low to high: hops and peers about in foliage for caterpillars, other invertebrates; often sluggish and easily overlooked. Flight fast and direct, often slipping into cover and vanishing. Note clean white underparts, big white tail spots, bright rusty flash in wings, bright yellow on bill; cf. Black-billed and Mangrove Cuckoos. Juv. has less contrasting tail pattern than adult. Typically silent in Costa Rica. STATUS: Fairly common to uncommon Sep–Nov, Apr–May, mainly in lowlands and foothills; rare in winter, mainly on Pacific slope. (Breeds N America and Mexico, winters S America.)

BLACK-BILLED CUCKOO *Coccyzus erythropthalmus* 27.5–30cm. Transient migrant in varied wooded and forested habitats from humid forest to coastal scrub, mangroves. Habits like Yellow-billed Cuckoo, and thus easily overlooked and infrequently encountered. Note dingy whitish underparts, weak pattern on underside of tail, dark bill. Cf. Yellow-billed and Mangrove Cuckoos. Typically silent in Costa Rica. STATUS: Uncommon Sep–Nov, Apr–May, mainly in lowlands and foothills. (Breeds N America, winters S America.)

MANGROVE CUCKOO *Coccyzus minor* 30.5–33cm. Handsome cuckoo of dry forest and edge, gallery forest, second growth, semi-open areas with taller trees, mangroves. Habits much like Yellow-billed Cuckoo. Like most cuckoos, often suns itself in early morning, at times on exposed branches. Note buff underparts, dark mask, big white tail spots, bright yellow on bill; cf. Yellow-billed Cuckoo. Juv. has less contrasting tail pattern. SOUNDS: Mostly silent unless breeding. Song a typically accelerating series of harsh croaks, 6–9 secs, ending with an abrupt switch to a quieter short series of lower coos, *AHRR, AHRR, AHRR-AAHR-AAHR...owh-owh...*; sometimes preceded by quiet dry rattle of 1–2 secs. STATUS: Uncommon Nov–May on Pacific slope, scarce on Caribbean slope, to 1500m; scarce and local Jun–Oct, and may breed along Pacific coast. (Mexico to n. S America.)

GROOVE-BILLED ANI *Crotophaga sulcirostris* 30.5–34.5cm. The common and widespread ani in most of Costa Rica, found in open and semi-open habitats, from ranchland to forest edge, often around livestock. Social, usually in small groups. Perches on wires, hops readily on ground, clambers in foliage, long tail often loosely flopped about. Flight distinctive: rapid flaps interspersed with flat-winged glides, one bird following another across a field or road; often crash-lands into foliage. Bill shape and habits distinctive, except for very local overlap with slightly larger Smooth-billed Ani (which see), often best separated by voice. SOUNDS: Common call a squeaky *pí-chwiep* or *pí-weérp*, emphasis on 1st note, often in short series. Other varied piping, squealing, and growling noises. STATUS: Fairly common to common on both slopes to 1500m, locally inland to 2000m; absent from s. Pacific lowlands, where replaced by Smooth-billed Ani. (Mexico to S America.)

SMOOTH-BILLED ANI *Crotophaga ani* 33–37cm. Replaces Groove-billed Ani on s. Pacific slope. Habits much like Groove-billed but flight a little stronger. Slightly larger than Groove-billed (noticeable in direct comparison), but often best detected and identified by voice. Also note more raised culmen of Smooth-billed (especially male), smooth bill sides (can be hard to see, and juv. Groove-billed has smooth bill, lacking grooves for a few months after fledging). SOUNDS: Slurred squealing whistles, distinct from Groove-billed Ani, typically *reeéah* or *wheeéreh*, can suggest a hawk. Other squealing, mewing, and clucking sounds. STATUS: Fairly common to common on s. Pacific slope, to 1200m; may be spreading north. (Caribbean region to S America.)

YELLOW-BILLED CUCKOO

juv.

BLACK-BILLED CUCKOO

MANGROVE CUCKOO

variation

GROOVE-BILLED ANI

SMOOTH-BILLED ANI

male

174

*COMMON SQUIRREL CUCKOO *Piaya cayana* 40–47cm. Striking cuckoo of varied forested and wooded habitats, semi-open areas with hedgerows, scrubby thickets with taller trees, mangroves. Mainly at mid–upper levels, where can be surprisingly difficult to see; hops and runs along branches and amid foliage a little like a squirrel. Flights usually short, bursts of wingbeats alternated with sweeping glides. No similar species in Costa Rica. Juv. has duller bill and eyes, less white on tail tips. SOUNDS: Sharp, woodpecker-like *chik!* sometimes doubled, often followed by overslurred low scream, *chik! reowh* gruff, slightly raspy stuttering *ehk'ehr-rrer*. Song (mainly spring–summer) usually fairly steady-paced, often prolonged series of overslurred sharp whistles, *wheep wheep...*, typically 10 notes/5.5–8 secs. STATUS: Fairly common on both slopes, rarely to 2400m. (Mexico to S America.)

STRIPED CUCKOO *Tapera naevia* 28–30.5cm. Open and semi-open areas with brushy thickets, second growth, overgrown grassy fields, forest edge; brood parasite of various species with domed nests. Rarely seen unless singing, when often perches on fence post, roadside wires, in trees; otherwise on or near ground in cover. Distinctive, with striped upperparts, erectile spiky crest (raised and lowered when singing), plain pale underparts; black 'wrist flags' rarely visible, flashed in display. SOUNDS: Song (spring–summer) far-carrying, a clear, deliberate double whistle, easily imitated, *whee whee*, 2nd note slightly higher; less often longer series, *whee' whee' whee' whee'buh*, and variations. STATUS: Uncommon to fairly common on both slopes, locally to 1500m; spreading with deforestation. (Mexico to S America.)

PHEASANT CUCKOO *Dromococcyx phasianellus* 35.5–37cm. Rarely seen, distinctive cuckoo of lowland forest and edge, adjacent taller second growth; brood parasite, mainly of flycatchers with enclosed nests. Usually goes un-detected unless singing, when often perches high in trees; otherwise usually on or near ground, where elusive. Flight direct, wingbeats mostly below body plane. Distinctive, with small head, slender bill, pointed crest, long expansive tail. Cf. juv. with juv. Striped Cuckoo. SOUNDS: Song (spring–summer) far-carrying, typically 3 deliberate, haunting whistles with tinamou-like quality, the last variably quavering, *whee whee wheerr*; less often longer series, accelerating overall and rising slightly, *whee whee whee'whee-bee*, and variations. STATUS: Scarce and local on Pacific slope, to 1400m. (Mexico to S America.)

LESSER GROUND CUCKOO *Morococcyx erythropygus* 25–27cm. Small, retiring, terrestrial cuckoo of dry forest, plantations, adjacent brushy thickets. Heard far more often than seen. Forages on ground, walking at times with agonizingly slow, deliberate gait, and often freezes when alarmed. Sings from ground or low perch in bush. Distinctive, with colorful face and rich buffy-cinnamon underparts. Juv. duller overall, outer tail feathers tipped buff. SOUNDS: Song an arresting series of (usually about 20–35) loud burry whistles that starts slowly, builds into a fairly rapid series, and tails off with increasingly slower-spaced whistles, *preee, preee, prreee, prree-prree..., preee, prreee, prree*. Also a single, mournful, slightly burry *whieeuh* and bill snapping when agitated. STATUS: Fairly common on n. Pacific slope, locally to 1200m in w. Central Valley. (Mexico to Costa Rica.)

RUFOUS-VENTED GROUND CUCKOO *Neomorphus geoffroyi* 46–51cm. Spectacular but rarely seen inhabitant of humid forest, where walks and runs stealthily on ground; rarely perches in low understory. Attends army ant swarms to hunt prey flushed by ants, where sometimes juv. accompanies adults. Despite its size, can be frustratingly shy and elusive. Unmistakable, if you're lucky enough to see it, with bushy erectile crest, stout pale yellowish bill, black breast band, long tail glossed purple to green. Juv. dark overall, with muted adult pattern. SOUNDS: Song a low moaning coo that swells and ends abruptly, *whooooOOo*, 1.5–2 secs, repeated every few secs; could be passed over as a dove. Loud bill snaps and rattles often given. STATUS: Scarce on Caribbean slope, mainly 400–1600m; spills over to adjacent n. Pacific foothills. (Honduras to S America.)

COMMON
SQUIRREL CUCKOO

juv.

STRIPED CUCKOO

PHEASANT CUCKOO

juv.

LESSER GROUND CUCKOO

RUFOUS-VENTED
GROUND CUCKOO

juv.

NEW WORLD PARROTS (PSITTACIDAE; 18 SPECIES) Familiar group of brightly colored, often noisy birds associated with the tropics. Ages/sexes similar or slightly different; attain mostly adult appearance in 1st year. Several species wiped out from large areas of Costa Rica by deforestation and trapping for pet trade. Often seen in flight, when pairs tend to segregate within flocks. Beware that escaped cage birds might be seen anywhere, especially in the Central Valley and near other population centers; in some areas, feral populations may become established.

ORANGE-CHINNED PARAKEET *Brotogeris jugularis* 18–19cm. Small para-keet of open and semi-open country with scattered trees, forest patches, plantations, forest edge. Usually in pairs or small groups in canopy, sometimes alongside larger and longer-tailed *Eupsittula* parakeets. Distinctive, with bronzy shoulders, yellow underwing coverts; orange chin patch small, usually difficult to see. Flight distinctly bounding, several quick wingbeats interspersed with short, undulating glides, quite different from larger *Eupsittula*. SOUNDS: Shrill, often slightly buzzy phrases, typically short and clipped, *ch-chi-chit* and *chree-ee chi-chit*, etc. STATUS: Common to fairly common on both slopes, locally to 1200m; has spread with deforestation. (Mexico to nw. S America.)

CRIMSON-FRONTED PARAKEET *Psittacara finschi* 27–29cm. Largest Costa Rican parakeet, found in open and semi-open country with scattered trees and forest patches, plantations, hedgerows in farmland, gardens. Typically in flocks, locally of 100s. Flight often higher overhead than smaller *Eupsittula* parakeets, with which it usually doesn't mix. Distinctive, with diagnostic bright red-and-yellow underwing pattern in flight. Adult has red forecrown, reduced or lacking on imm. SOUNDS: Loud raucous screaming, somewhat similar to *Eupsittula* parakeets but lower pitched, more nasal or laughing, and less rapid-paced. STATUS: Fairly common to common, to 1800m; somewhat nomadic in nonbr. season and range likely still expanding with deforestation. (Nicaragua to w. Panama.)

ORANGE-FRONTED PARAKEET *Eupsittula canicularis* 23–25cm. Forest and edge, ranchland and other semi-open areas with trees, plantations, mangroves. In pairs or small flocks; flight fast and direct to twisting, mainly at treetop height. Note distinctive head and breast patterns. Cf. Crimson-fronted Para-keet, which often flies higher overhead in larger flocks. Orange-chinned Parakeet smaller, with distinctive bounding flight. SOUNDS: Screechy, slightly burry *krrieh* and *kreeíh*, often doubled and in screaming series; also lower burry calls when perched, *rreh* and *krreh*. Higher and shriller than Crimson-fronted Parakeet. STATUS: Fairly common to common on Pacific slope, locally to 1200m in Central Valley. (Mexico to Costa Rica.)

*AZTEC [OLIVE-THROATED] PARAKEET *Eupsittula [nana] astec* 23–25cm. Lowland forest and edge, ranchland and other semi-open areas with trees, plantations, mangroves. In pairs or small flocks, locally to 30 or so birds; flight fast and direct to twisting, mainly at treetop height. Cf. larger Crimson-fronted Parakeet. SOUNDS: Varied screeching, slightly burry calls, similar to Orange-fronted Parakeet; higher, shriller, and faster-paced than Crimson-fronted Parakeet. STATUS: Fairly common to common on Caribbean slope, mainly below 700m. (Mexico to w. Panama.)

*VERAGUAS [BROWN-THROATED[PARAKEET *Eupsittula [pertinax] ocularis* 23–25cm. Ranchland, savanna, other open and semi-open areas with trees, wooded patches, plantations. Distinctive in its limited Costa Rican range, where no other *Eupsittula* species occurs: note brownish face and upper breast with contrasting yellow-orange patch below eyes, dark bill. Cf. larger Crimson-fronted Parakeet, smaller Orange-chinned Parakeet. SOUNDS: Varied screechy and shrieking calls, relatively low and scratchy or gravelly, distinctly more grating than relatively mellow calls of Crimson-fronted Parakeet. STATUS: Fairly common in s. Pacific lowlands, where has spread from Panama in 2000s, following deforestation. (Costa Rica to Panama.)

ORANGE-CHINNED PARAKEET

CRIMSON-FRONTED
PARAKEET

ORANGE-FRONTED PARAKEET

AZTEC PARAKEET

VERAGUAS PARAKEET

178

SCARLET MACAW *Ara macao* 81–96cm. Spectacular, essentially unmistakable large parrot of humid lowland forest and edge, ranchland with forest patches; often near rivers where larger trees persist. No similar species in Costa Rica; however, when colors not discernible at long range or against bright cloudy skies, note appreciably longer tail than Great Green Macaw. In pairs or small groups, ranging widely for food; mainly seen in flight early to mid-morning and late in day, commuting to and from feeding areas or near roosting and nesting sites. At other times can sit quietly in canopy, where easily overlooked. In some areas, associates loosely with Great Green Macaws. Flight direct and relatively unhurried, with strong steady wingbeats, tail flowing out behind. **SOUNDS:** Far-carrying, deep raucous cries in flight, *rrah*, and *rrrahk*; quieter calls sometimes when perched. Not as crowing and drawn-out as calls of Great Green Macaw. **STATUS:** Uncommon to fairly common but very local in n. lowlands, fairly common (and noisy!) on s. Pacific slope; formerly common on both slopes, but widely extirpated by deforestation and hunting for pet trade. (Mexico to S America.)

GREAT GREEN MACAW *Ara ambiguus* 71–79cm. Spectacular large parrot of humid lowland forest and edge, ranchland with forest patches. No similar species in Costa Rica; when colors may not be discernible at long range or against bright cloudy skies, note appreciably longer, more flowing tail of Scarlet Macaw. In pairs or small groups, locally flocks up to 20 or so birds, ranging widely for food; mainly seen in flight early to mid-morning and late in day commuting to and from feeding areas or near roosting and nesting sites. At other times can sit quietly in canopy, where easily overlooked. Flight direct and relatively unhurried, with strong steady wingbeats. **SOUNDS:** Far-carrying, raucous, slightly crowing calls, *rraah*, and *ráahh*, average higher, less throaty than Scarlet Macaw; quieter and lower calls sometimes when perched. **STATUS:** Uncommon to scarce and local on Caribbean slope, mainly below 600m; widely extirpated by deforestation and hunting for pet trade. (Honduras to S America.)

SULPHUR-WINGED PARAKEET *Pyrrhura hoffmanni* 23–25cm. Distinctive, medium-size parakeet of foothill and highland forest and edge, adjacent second growth and semi-open areas with taller trees. Usually in small flocks, locally up to 50 or so birds. Mostly seen in flight, shrieking by quickly above the treetops in compact groups: note voice, extensive yellow underwing flashes, reddish underside to tail. Feeds quietly low to high in bushes and trees, especially alders, when can be confiding; perched birds easily identified by red cheek patch, yellow scalloping on head and neck. Juv. has less yellow in wing, duller head pattern. **SOUNDS:** High, semi-metallic, often upslurred screeches, typically higher and simpler than other medium-size and larger parakeets in Costa Rica, sometimes with strongly buzzy quality. **STATUS:** Fairly common on both slopes of Talamanca Mts., mainly 1500–3000m; descends locally to 700m, mainly in wet season. (Costa Rica to w. Panama.)

SCARLET MACAW

GREAT GREEN MACAW

SULPHUR-WINGED PARAKEET

180

BARRED PARAKEET *Bolborhynchus lineola* 16.5–18cm. Small parakeet of humid highland forest, adjacent second growth with seeding bamboo. In pairs or small groups, seasonally larger flocks to 50 or so birds. Often seen overhead in flight (or simply heard from within low clouds and fog), rarely perched. Flight rapid and slightly bounding. Note small size, pointed tail, voice. Dark barring variable, strongest on adult male. SOUNDS: Shrill, short screeching and chirping calls, *krrieh* and *krieh-kriet*, etc.; can carry well and be difficult to locate; lower, more chirping than Sulphur-winged Parakeet, lack metallic whining quality of Red-fronted Parrotlet. STATUS: Uncommon to fairly common and somewhat nomadic on both slopes, mainly 1000–3000m, lower locally. (Mexico to S America.)

RED-FRONTED PARROTLET *Touit costaricensis* 15–16cm. Small, rather chunky, scarce parrot of humid foothill forest and edge. Usually seen in flight, often fairly high overhead, in pairs or small groups. Note small size and squared tail, voice. With good views, note yellow underwing coverts; male has diagnostic, big red forewing patches. Juv. has little or no red on head. SOUNDS: High whistled calls with distinctive, semi-metallic whining quality, *sriieh* and clipped, slightly lower *si-si-chirh*; lacks screechy quality of Barred Parakeet, not buzzy like Sulphur-winged Parakeet. STATUS: Uncommon to scarce on Caribbean slope, mainly 500–1500m, occasionally to 3000m; also locally on s. Pacific slope of Talamanca Mts. (Costa Rica to w. Panama.)

BROWN-HOODED PARROT *Pyrilia haematotis* 20.5–23cm. Small, rather compact parrot of humid lowland forest and edge, plantations, and taller second growth; not in open country. In pairs or small groups, typically seen briefly in flight at canopy level. Flight fast and direct with quick deep wingbeats, more hurried than slightly larger White-crowned and Blue-headed Parrots, which have slower deep wingbeats, often fly higher. Feeds at mid–upper levels in fruiting trees, where quiet and overlooked easily. Note voice, dark head, bright red axillar flashes in flight; also pale spectacles in dark brown head, variable red ear spot. Juv. has paler brown hood, duller ear spot, greener chest. SOUNDS: Shrill, slightly metallic screeches in flight, *kreéik* or *kreeíh'* and short series, *kreiik krríik*; higher, more metallic than White-crowned Parrot. STATUS: Fairly common on both slopes, to 1600m. (Mexico to nw. Colombia.)

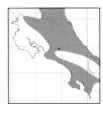

WHITE-CROWNED PARROT *Pionus senilis* 23–25.5cm. Medium-size, rather compact parrot of humid forest and edge, plantations, adjacent semi-open areas with forest patches. Often in small flocks, at times of 50 or so birds. Flies with deep wingbeats, unlike shallow flapping of amazons. Feeds mainly in canopy, at times perching on exposed snags. Distinctive, with overall deep blue-green plumage, big white crown patch, pale bill, red undertail coverts but no red in wings. Juv. duller and greener overall, with smaller white crown patch. SOUNDS: Raucous screeches in flight, *rreéahk* and rolled *rriéah*, higher and screechier than amazons, deeper and less metallic than Brown-hooded Parrot. STATUS: Fairly common on both slopes, locally to 1800m; sporadic visitor to Central Valley. (Mexico to w. Panama.)

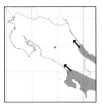

BLUE-HEADED PARROT *Pionus menstruus* 23–25cm. Medium-size, rather compact parrot of humid lowland forest and edge, plantations, adjacent semi-open areas with forest patches. Habits much like White-crowned Parrot; similarly flies with deep wingbeats, unlike shallow flapping of amazons and hurried flight of Brown-hooded Parrot. Distinctive, with overall deep green plumage, blue head and breast, dark bill, red undertail coverts but no red in wings. Juv. duller overall, with limited blue on head. SOUNDS: Raucous shrieks and screeches, recalling White-crowned Parrot but averaging mellower, slightly higher, and faster-paced. STATUS: Fairly common on both slopes and spreading north; rarely to 1200m and typically at lower elevations than White-crowned Parrot where ranges overlap. (Costa Rica to S America.)

BARRED PARAKEET

females

males

RED-FRONTED PARROTLET

male

BROWN-HOODED PARROT

adult variation

WHITE-CROWNED PARROT

juv.

adults

juv.

adults

BLUE-HEADED PARROT

AMAZON PARROTS (GENUS *AMAZONA*) (4 species). Relatively large New World parrots, with broad rounded wings, relatively short squared tails, red upperwing patches; fly with distinctive shallow stiff wingbeats. For species ID note head patterns, voice, habitat. Heavily affected by illegal capture for pet trade.

WHITE-FRONTED AMAZON (PARROT) *Amazona albifrons* 25.5–27cm. Only small amazon in Costa Rica, mainly in drier forest and edge, open areas with scattered trees, mangroves, but also ranges up to clearings in cloud forest. In pairs and loose flocks; often flies lower than large amazons, at or below canopy height, but roost flights can be high overhead. Wingbeats relatively quick, flight looks hurried relative to large amazons. Note distinctive head pattern, red on forewing of male but no red on secondaries. **SOUNDS:** Raucous screaming and yapping, typically faster-paced than large amazons, including sharp *kyi kyeh-kyeh...*, and rapid, often paired yapping *kyak-yak-yak-yak, yak-yak*. Mellower, rolled and screeching calls especially when perched. **STATUS:** Fairly common to common on n. Pacific slope; spreading to n. Caribbean slope and Central Valley, to 1500m. (Mexico to Costa Rica.)

YELLOW-NAPED AMAZON (PARROT) *Amazona [ochrocephala] auropalliata* 35.5–38cm. Large amazon of ranchland, other semi-open country with forest patches, taller trees, mangroves. In pairs and loose flocks, like other large amazons. Often detected by voice, which carries well. Distinctive in range (where only other widespread amazon is much smaller White-fronted), with large size, yellow nape, dusky bill, voice. Juv. lacks yellow on head or can show a few yellow flecks, crown tinged greenish blue; cf. Northern Mealy Amazon. **SOUNDS:** Raucous but relatively deep and mellow calls have vaguely human quality, including gruff rolled *rrowh* or *grrrowh*, repeated; flight calls include rolled *chrr'rrr uhrr'rr*, etc. **STATUS:** Uncommon to fairly common locally on n. Pacific slope, mainly below 600m; widely extirpated by capture for pet trade. (Mexico to Costa Rica.)

YELLOW-CROWNED AMAZON *Amazona ochrocephala* (not shown) occurs in open country of Pacific lowlands in w. Panama; with forest clearing, might expand into adjacent s. Costa Rica (one record to date), although potential population expansion countered by capture for pet trade. Similar to Yellow-naped Parrot in habits and voice; adult has yellow forecrown patch on green head.

RED-LORED AMAZON (PARROT) *Amazona autumnalis* 32–35.5cm. Large amazon of humid forest and edge habitats, open and semi-open areas with forest patches, taller trees; more tolerant of forest clearing than Northern Mealy Amazon. In pairs and loose flocks; typically flies high overhead, feeds mainly in canopy. Commonest and most conspicuous large amazon in much of range, often seen perched on high open snags. Note red forehead, trace of yellow on cheeks, voice. **SOUNDS:** Varied raucous screams, often with fairly shrill, slightly shrieking quality, *zeek churrik churrik* and *ch-reek ch-reek...*; quieter and mellower calls mainly when perched. Typically slightly higher, shriekier than Northern Mealy Amazon. **STATUS:** Fairly common to common on both slopes, mainly below 1200m. (Mexico to nw. S America.)

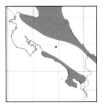

NORTHERN MEALY AMAZON (PARROT) *Amazona [farinosa] guatemalae* 38–43cm. Large, rather plain amazon of humid lowland forest and edge, adjacent taller second growth; locally in tree-scattered farmland with forest patches. In pairs and loose flocks; heard more often than seen in forested habitat, where feeds mainly in canopy. Broad pale eyering often more noticeable than bluish crown (beware Red-lored Parrot facing away, when face colors may not be visible, also has contrasting pale eyering); hindneck has pale, 'mealy' scalloping. Overlaps mainly with Red-lored Amazon, which favors edge and more-open habitats; also cf. imm. Yellow-naped Amazon. **SOUNDS:** Loud and raucous, but lower, less shrieky than Red-lored Amazon, including *chíuk chíuk...*, and *chriuk chriuk churh....* Often silent in flight. **STATUS:** Fairly common to uncommon on both slopes, mainly below 600m; widely extirpated by forest clearing. (Mexico to w. Panama.)

AMAZONS

WHITE-FRONTED AMAZON

females

males

imm.

YELLOW-NAPED AMAZON

imm.

adult

RED-LORED AMAZON

adult

adult

NORTHERN
MEALY AMAZON

184

TROGONS (TROGONIDAE; 9 SPECIES) Pantropical family of fairly large, colorful, mostly forest-based birds. Ages/sexes differ; attain adult plumage in 1 year. Nest in cavities.

BLACK-HEADED TROGON *Trogon melanocephalus* 26.5–28cm. Medium-size, rather long-tailed trogon of lowland forest and edge, gallery forest, semi-open areas with scattered trees, plantations, mangroves; nests in occupied termitaries. Mainly at mid–upper levels, sometimes on roadside wires; birds gather at fruiting trees, where can be confiding. Often occurs alongside appreciably smaller, more compact Gartered Trogon, which has bold barring under tail (1st-year Black-headed has some dark bars at edges of tail); male Gartered also has yellow eyering, pale gray wing panel; female has white eye-crescents, barred wing coverts. Cf. smaller Northern Black-throated Trogon, typically in forest interior. SOUNDS: Song a series of hollow nasal clucks that accelerate into a rattle and end fairly abruptly, *kuh kuh-kuh...keh-keh...*, 2–4 secs; may suggest an antshrike but lacks snarl at end of song. Hollow, thrush-like clucks. STATUS: Fairly common to common on n. Pacific slope, to 800m; uncommon to scarce and local on n. Caribbean slope. (Mexico to Costa Rica.)

BAIRD'S TROGON *Trogon bairdii* 27–29cm. Fairly large, rather long-tailed trogon of humid lowland forest and edge. Mainly at mid–upper levels, often rather high in subcanopy. Distinctive in range, with orange-red underparts, blue eyering; from behind, cf. Black-headed Trogon (little range overlap). Imm. male tail resembles female but with broader white tips. SOUNDS: Fairly rapid series of hollow, overslurred clucks, accelerating partway through and often with slightly laughing quality, *kyowh, kyowh, kowh-kowh...kuh-kuh...*, mostly 4–8 secs duration and can suggest an antshrike; starts at 4–5 notes/sec, increasing to 7–8 notes/sec, often slowing again slightly at end. Calls include rippling nasal chatters, mostly 1–2 secs, often with vaguely laughing cadence. STATUS: Fairly common on Pacific slope, to 1200m. (Costa Rica to w. Panama.)

GARTERED [VIOLACEOUS] TROGON *Trogon caligatus* 24–25.5cm. Small, rather compact, yellow-bellied trogon of humid forest and edge, gallery forest, plantations; often nests in arboreal wasp nests. Mainly at mid–upper levels; sings from subcanopy, at times on exposed perches. Often occurs alongside appreciably larger, longer-tailed Black-headed Trogon; readily separated by structure, plumage, voice. Northern Black-throated Trogon favors shady understory; male told by green head and breast with blue eyering, female has brown head and breast. SOUNDS: Song a fairly rapid, steady series (usually 4–9 secs) of overslurred nasal hoots, *kyow-kyow...*or *kuh-kuh...*, 3–4 notes/sec; easily mistaken at a distance for Ferruginous Pygmy Owl. Slightly overslurred dry growl, and series of nasal clucks, often with slightly laughing cadence. STATUS: Fairly common on both slopes, to 1500m; uncommon and more local in drier nw. lowlands. (Mexico to nw. S America.)

*NORTHERN BLACK-THROATED TROGON *Trogon [rufus] tenellus* 25–26cm. Fairly small trogon of humid forest, plantations, adjacent taller second growth. Favors shady forest interior at low to mid-levels, where singles or pairs often sit quietly and can be confiding. Distinctive, with yellow belly, barred tail pattern, habits; also note male's combination of green head and breast with pale bluish eyering, cf. Gartered Trogon. Female's brown head and breast and rusty tail suggest female Northern Collared Trogon, which has dark face, red belly, distinct tail pattern. SOUNDS: Song an unhurried series of (2–5, usually 3) plaintive, downslurred whistles, *hyowh hyowh hyowh*, typically at least 10 secs between series; suggests Northern Collared Trogon but slightly slower, more evenly paced. Call a slightly descending nasal growl, *ehrrrrr*. STATUS: Fairly common to uncommon on both slopes to 1000m, rarely to 1500m. (Honduras to nw. Colombia.)

BLACK-HEADED TROGON

female

males

BAIRD'S TROGON

female

males

imm. male

female

GARTERED TROGON

males

NORTHERN BLACK-THROATED TROGON

males

females

*ELEGANT TROGON *Trogon elegans* 28–30.5cm. Medium-size red-bellied trogon of lowland dry forest, gallery forest, humid forest in foothills, especially on hillsides and in gullies. Feeds low to high, calls mainly from subcanopy; often wary. Note red belly, undertail pattern, voice; male has finely vermiculated, silvery-gray upperwing panel, red eyering; female has diagnostic long white teardrop, yellow bill; in foothills, cf. locally overlapping orange-bellied form of Northern Collared Trogon. **SOUNDS:** Song a series of (2–9, usually 3–4) steadily repeated, hoarse, slightly disyllabic phrases, *kwa'h kwa'h...*, or *ah'rr ah'rr...*, about 2 notes/sec, faster when excited. Gruff, slow-paced clucks in short series, *krruh krruh...*; drawn-out, slurred low growl when agitated. **STATUS:** Fairly common to uncommon on n. Pacific slope, to 800m. (Guatemala to Costa Rica.)

*NORTHERN COLLARED TROGON *Trogon [collaris] puella* 26.5–28.5cm. Relatively small red-bellied trogon of humid foothill and highland forest. Feeds and perches low to high, calls mainly from mid-levels in shady understory where can be fairly confiding. Distinctive in range: note undertail pattern, white breast band, voice, cf. Elegant Trogon, which overlaps very locally in Northwest; in Caribbean foothills, cf. larger, pale-eyed Lattice-tailed Trogon. Populations in Northern Mts., and some individuals in Central and Talamanca Mts., have orange vs. red belly, formerly treated as a separate species, Orange-bellied Trogon *T. aurantiiventris*. **SOUNDS:** Song 2–3 plaintive, downslurred whistles with measured cadence, *kyow kyow*, easily imitated, often rather quiet; less often *kyow kyow-kow* and rarely single notes or short series with slightly descending, laughing cadence. Call a slightly descending nasal growl, *ahrrrrr*, often repeated steadily as tail is raised and lowered. **STATUS:** Fairly common on both slopes, mainly 700–2500m, rarely higher; some post-breeding dispersal to lower elevations in summer–fall. (Mexico to Panama.)

SLATY-TAILED TROGON *Trogon massena* 33–35cm. Large, stout-billed, red-bellied trogon of humid forest and edge, sometimes adjacent tree-scattered farmland with forest patches; often nests in termitaries. Mostly at mid–upper levels; sings mainly from subcanopy, often confiding. Distinctive, with stout orange bill, lack of white breast band, dark slaty undertail (narrowly barred white at edges on imm.). Cf. female Baird's Trogon, which has blue eyering, grayish bill, barred wing coverts. **SOUNDS:** Song a steady, often prolonged series of hard, overslurred clucks, *koh-koh...*, or *ka-ka...*, 3–4 notes/sec up to 30 secs or longer. Quiet clucking chatters, at times with laughing cadence. **STATUS:** Fairly common to common on both slopes, rarely to 1200m. (Mexico to nw. Ecuador.)

LATTICE-TAILED TROGON *Trogon clathratus* 30–32cm. Rather large red-bellied trogon of humid lower foothill forest. Mostly at mid–upper levels; sings mainly from subcanopy; sometimes nests in termitaries. Distinctive in range: note pale eyes, stout yellowish bill, voice, undertail pattern, lack of white breast band; cf. larger Slaty-tailed Trogon. Juv. has duller eyes, male has brownish breast. **SOUNDS:** Song a fairly rapid, slightly overslurred laughing series of (usually 7–20) hollow nasal clucks, 1st and last notes quieter, *ha-hah-hah...*; 1–4 secs duration. Call a rapid purring rattle, about 1 sec. **STATUS:** Uncommon to fairly common locally on Caribbean slope, mainly 100–1100m. (Costa Rica to w. Panama.)

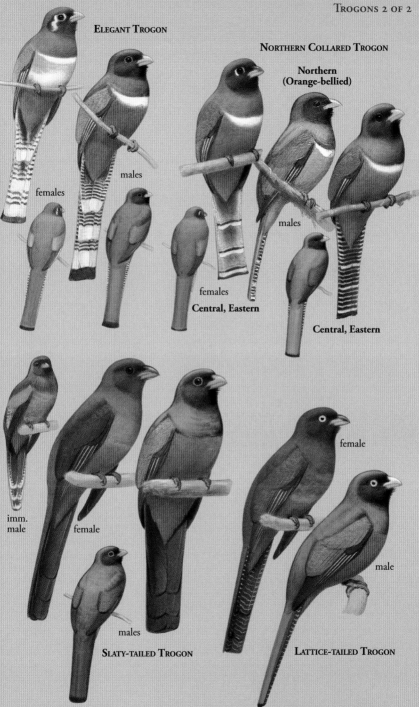

ELEGANT TROGON

females

males

NORTHERN COLLARED TROGON

**Northern
(Orange-bellied)**

males

females

Central, Eastern

males

Central, Eastern

imm.
male

female

female

males

male

SLATY-TAILED TROGON

LATTICE-TAILED TROGON

RESPLENDENT QUETZAL *Pharomachrus mocinno* 36–39cm + male plumes. Spectacular and distinctive large trogon of mossy cloud forest and humid highland oak forest, adjacent clearings with fruiting trees. Mainly at mid–upper levels, where easily overlooked unless vocal. Note broad but slightly tapered tail, small head, lack of white breast band, gray bill of female. Long plumes of male blow in breeze and blend well with hanging mosses, ferns; plumes molted in summer–fall. Imm. male resembles imm. female (bill dark), but with mostly white underside to tail. **SOUNDS:** Song (spring–summer) an unhurried series of (usually 6–15) plaintive, hollow nasal whistles, about 1/sec in subtly paired cadence, *k'yiow k-yowh, k'yiow k-yowh....* In courtship, male gives series of intensifying and fading, 2–3-syllable nasal barks, *k-weh k-weh K'Wéh-ka K'WÉH-ka...*, including in display flight over and through canopy; female has a wailing moan, *waówhh*, 1–1.5 secs. **STATUS:** Fairly common to uncommon on both slopes, above 1200m in Northern Mts., above 1500m in Central and Talamanca Mts. Moves locally to lower elevations in fall, rarely to 500m. (Mexico to w. Panama.)

JACAMARS (GALBULIDAE; 2 SPECIES) Neotropical family of forest and forest edge birds. Ages similar, sexes differ slightly in Costa Rica; attain adult appearance in 1st year. Nest in burrows in banks.

RUFOUS-TAILED JACAMAR *Galbula ruficauda* 22–23.5cm. Distinctive, slender, long-billed bird of humid forest and edge, adjacent clearings and openings, especially with looping vines. Found as singles or pairs, typically perched at mid-levels on vines or slender branches, bill raised above horizontal. Sallies for flying insects and often returns to the same perch, where makes about-face leaps to switch the angle of its prey-seeking vigils. Male has white throat, female buff. **SOUNDS:** Loud, shrieking whistled calls often draw attention. High, shrieking, sharply overslurred *wheéuk*, often repeated steadily; may suggest Northern Royal Flycatcher. Faster, ringing series of whistles can end with a quick chortling trill, *whee-whee-whee....* Song (?) a slightly rising then falling series of drawn-out whistles that accelerate into a short trill. **STATUS:** Fairly common on both slopes, to 1200m. (Mexico to S America.)

GREAT JACAMAR *Jacamerops aureus* 29–32cm. Large robust jacamar of humid lowland forest, adjacent taller second growth. Mainly at mid–upper levels, especially in subcanopy; often at light gaps or other semi-open areas within forest, but overlooked easily unless vocal. Singles or pairs perch quietly for long periods then sally for prey. Note long stout bill, dark underside to tail; male has white throat band. **SOUNDS:** Song a high, descending, whistled scream, *siiieeeeer*, 2–4 secs, at times with inflection near start, *siii'eeeeeer*. Plaintive wailing quality can suggest a hawk; cf. scream of Great Black Hawk. **STATUS:** Rare and local on Caribbean slope, to 500m. (Honduras to S America.)

females

imm.
female

RESPLENDENT QUETZAL

male

RUFOUS-TAILED JACAMAR

female

male

female

male

GREAT JACAMAR

190

KINGFISHERS (ALCEDINIDAE; 6 SPECIES) Worldwide family of small to fairly large birds with big heads, long pointed beaks. Ages differ slightly, like adult in 1st year; sexes differ. Nest in burrows in banks.

BELTED KINGFISHER *Megaceryle alcyon* 31–33cm. Widespread winter migrant to varied habitats with water, from rocky coasts and mangroves to lakes, rivers, roadside ditches. Hunts from perches and from hovering fairly high over open water; often perches conspicuously on wires. Distinctive; cf. appreciably larger Tropical Ringed Kingfisher, which has rusty underparts. Slightly larger than Amazon Kingfisher but with smaller bill, distinct plumage, including large white wing panels obvious in flight. SOUNDS: Rapid-paced, dry, 'machine-gun' rattle, 1–5 secs, often in flight. STATUS: Fairly common mid-Sep to Apr, rarely into May; commonest in lowlands, in smaller numbers to 1500m. (Breeds N America, winters to nw. S America.)

*TROPICAL RINGED KINGFISHER *Megaceryle torquata* 38–41cm. Mainly lowland freshwater habitats, especially lakes, slow-moving rivers, less often mangroves, estuaries, foothill streams. Hunts from perches and from hovering fairly high over open water; often perches conspicuously on wires. Flies with fairly slow deep wingbeats; regularly seen flying high overhead, sometimes well away from water. Distinctive, with solidly rusty underbody, large size, massive bill; large white wing panels on primaries much like Belted Kingfisher. Juv. resembles female but breast band darker, mottled cinnamon. SOUNDS: Deep *chrek!* in flight; powerful chattering rattles, deeper, slower-paced, and often more prolonged than Belted Kingfisher. STATUS: Fairly common on both slopes, locally to 1500m. (Mexico and s. Texas to tropical S America.)

AMAZON KINGFISHER *Chloroceryle amazona* 28–29cm. Mainly freshwater lowland habitats, from coastal lagoons and large rivers to small streams and ponds, locally in mangroves. Hunts mainly from perches, at times on wires, but tends to be less conspicuous than larger kingfishers. Flight usually low over water; sometimes hovers, usually fairly high like Belted Kingfisher. Distinctive, with massive bill, dark oily-green upperparts; lacks bold white wing spotting of appreciably smaller Green Kingfisher and large white wing panel of Belted Kingfisher. Juv. resembles female but male upper breast washed buffy. SOUNDS: Gruff to low rasping *chruk* or *zzrk*, mainly in flight, at times run into short rattling and screechy chatters. STATUS: Fairly common to common on both slopes, locally to 1200m, rarely higher. (Mexico to S America.)

GREEN KINGFISHER *Chloroceryle americana* 19–21cm. Small darting sprite of lowland fresh and brackish habitats, from small pools and streams to mangroves, larger rivers, reservoirs. Hunts from perches, usually fairly concealed and low over water, rarely high on open wires; does not hover. Flight typically low and fast, flashing white outer tail feathers as it brakes to land. Distinctive, with small size, contrasting white neck sides, distinct white wing spotting. Juv. resembles female but male upper breast washed buffy. SOUNDS: Dry rasping clicks, often run into short rattles; gruff buzzy *zzher* mainly in flight; short buzzy and squeaky chatters. STATUS: Fairly common on both slopes, mainly in lowlands but locally to 1500m. (Mexico and sw. US to S America.)

LARGER KINGFISHERS

BELTED KINGFISHER

female

male

TROPICAL
RINGED KINGFISHER

female

male

AMAZON KINGFISHER

male

female

GREEN KINGFISHER

male

female

AMERICAN PYGMY KINGFISHER *Chloroceryle aenea* 13–14cm. Tiny darting sprite of lowland fresh and brackish habitats, from forest pools and streams to small channels in mangroves; usually in wooded and forested areas, where overlooked easily. Hunts from shady perches low over water; at times catches insects. Distinctive, with very small size, buffy neck sides, rusty underparts. Larger Green Kingfisher has bright white neck sides. SOUNDS: Dry ticking notes and short rattles, slightly higher and often softer than Green Kingfisher; high, slightly metallic burry *zzrieh*; downslurred, slightly squeaky to shrill short chatters. STATUS: Uncommon on both slopes, to 600m. (Mexico to S America.)

GREEN-AND-RUFOUS KINGFISHER *Chloroceryle inda* 22–24cm. Medium-size kingfisher of quiet shady streams, channels, and pools in swampy lowland forest. Typically hunts from low branches over water, in shady cover, where difficult to see well. Flies low and quickly over water and darts back into cover. Distinctive, with overall dark appearance, medium size, and habits; plumage resembles much smaller American Pygmy Kingfisher. Larger than Green Kingfisher, which has bright white neck sides. SOUNDS: Hard dry clicks, lower and more gravelly than Green Kingfisher; short buzzy rasps and squeaky chatters similar to Amazon Kingfisher. STATUS: Uncommon to scarce and local on Caribbean slope, to 600m. (Honduras to S America.)

MOTMOTS (MOMOTIDAE; 6 SPECIES) Small neotropical family of large-headed, long-tailed forest birds, presumed of Central American origin. Colorful plumage cryptic within shady forest. Ages differ slightly; juvs. duller overall but soon resemble adults; sexes similar. Newly molted tails are fully feathered but larger species have intrinsically weakened sections soon removed by preening to produce 'racket tips.' Nest in burrows in banks.

TODY MOTMOT *Hylomanes momotula* 16.5–18cm. Small, unobtrusive motmot of humid foothill forest, especially shady gullies. Perches quietly at low to mid-levels, and flushes with low whirr of wings. Slowly flicks tail up and down, not side-to-side like larger motmots. Distinctive, no similar species in range. SOUNDS: Song mainly in early morning, often before first light, a nasal, slightly rising or overslurred hoot, *wah* or *woah*, usually in prolonged series, 10 notes/10–12 secs; can suggest Gartered Trogon but more nasal, usually slower-paced. Excited birds give faster series of burrier notes, 10/2.5–6 secs, at times in pulsating duets, *wah'awah'awah....* STATUS: Uncommon and local on n. Pacific slope, spilling over locally to adjacent Caribbean foothills; mainly 500–1000m. (Mexico to nw. Colombia.)

TURQUOISE-BROWED MOTMOT *Eumomota superciliosa* 33–38cm. Very fancy, medium-size motmot of lowland dry forest and edge, semi-open areas with larger trees, hedgerows, gardens; favors more open areas than Lesson's Motmot, but the two species occur alongside each other in places. Perches low to high, at times on roadside wires; switches tail side-to-side like a jerky pendulum. Distinctive, with silvery-turquoise brow, rusty back, contrasting turquoise-blue wings and tail, very long naked tail shafts, and big racket tips to tail. Juv. duller, with reduced blue brow and throat markings, little or no rusty on back; soon like adult. SOUNDS: Song a hollow, slightly nasal or crowing *owhh* every 2–6 secs. Calls include slightly hoarse, excited clucks and duets, including a rhythmic *k-wok k-wok'...* and *k'wok t'k'wok t'k'wok....* STATUS: Fairly common to common on n. Pacific slope, mainly below 900m. (Mexico to Costa Rica.)

AMERICAN PYGMY KINGFISHER

male

female

GREEN KINGFISHER
FOR COMPARISON (p. 190)

GREEN-AND-RUFOUS KINGFISHER

male

female

TODY MOTMOT

TURQUOISE-BROWED MOTMOT

LESSON'S [BLUE-CROWNED] MOTMOT *Momotus [momota] lessonii* 38–43cm. Large motmot of humid forest and edge, gallery forest, plantations, adjacent taller second growth; semi-open areas with larger trees. Forages low to high, often in subcanopy, and regular at army swarms; also visits feeders. Often sits quietly and overlooked easily if not vocal; switches tail side-to-side like a jerky pendulum. Distinctive if seen well, but in northwest cf. Turquoise-browed Motmot. **SOUNDS:** Song typically a low double hoot, *whoop woop*, less often short series or single notes; often given pre-dawn and easily mistaken for an owl. Calls include harsh low clucks and chatters, and a soft, bouncing-ball hooting series suggesting Spectacled Owl. **STATUS:** Fairly common in humid Pacific lowlands, Central Valley, and on adjacent Caribbean slope, locally to 2000m; less numerous and more local in drier nw. lowlands. (Mexico to Panama.)

KEEL-BILLED MOTMOT *Electron carinatum* 31–33cm. Scarce, medium-size motmot of humid foothill forest, especially hilly country near streams. Feeds low to high, but mainly at mid–upper levels inside shady forest, less often at edges. Calls mainly from subcanopy. Combination of turquoise-blue brow, black mask, and rusty forehead distinctive; also note relatively broad bill from below, cf. Lesson's Motmot, and overall greenish underparts, cf. structurally and vocally similar Broad-billed Motmot. Has paired with Broad-billed Motmot, and taxonomic status unclear; the 2 species may simply be color morphs. **SOUNDS:** Song a far-carrying, ringing nasal *kwaah* or *ownhh* every 3–6 secs; not readily told from Broad-billed Motmot. Varied rhythmic clucking series when excited, such as *owhn k-k-owhng k-k-k-owhng...*, all much like Broad-billed. **STATUS:** Scarce and local on n. Caribbean slope, mainly 300–1000m. (Mexico to Costa Rica.)

BROAD-BILLED MOTMOT *Electron platyrhynchum* 31–33cm. Medium-size motmot of humid lowland and foothill forest and edge, taller second growth, overgrown plantations. Feeds low to high, but mainly at mid–upper levels inside shady forest, less often at edges. Calls mainly from subcanopy. Appreciably smaller than large and bulky Rufous Motmot, with narrower black mask, turquoise chin, and less extensive rusty on underparts; also note broad bill, best seen from below. Juv. reportedly duller overall, with greenish underparts, greenish-tinged crown, short blue streak above eye (Stiles & Skutch 1989), thus resembling Keel-billed Motmot. Has paired with Keel-billed Momtot, and the 2 species may simply be color morphs. **SOUNDS:** Ringing nasal *kwaah*, repeated, and hard, hollow honking clucks when agitated; much like Keel-billed Motmot. **STATUS:** Fairly common on Caribbean slope, to 1500m; spills over locally to adjacent n. Pacific slope foothills. (Guatemala to S America.)

RUFOUS MOTMOT *Baryphthengus martii* 45–50cm. Very large, rather bulky motmot of humid forest and edge, taller second growth, overgrown plantations; often in same areas as Broad-billed Motmot. Feeds low to high, mainly at mid–upper levels. Told from smaller Broad-billed Motmot by size, broader black mask, extensively rusty underparts, and voice. Juv. paler and duller overall, without black chest spots; soon like adult. **SOUNDS:** Song a resonant, rapid-paced (usually 3–7-note) low hooting *whu-du-du*, and higher 2–3-note *whuu-whuup*, often in overlapping choruses at and before dawn; might be mistaken for large owl. Harsh chatter when agitated. **STATUS:** Uncommon to fairly common on Caribbean slope to 1000m, locally to 1400m in south. (Honduras to S America.)

LESSON'S MOTMOT

variation

KEEL-BILLED MOTMOT

BROAD-BILLED
MOTMOT

RUFOUS MOTMOT

PUFFBIRDS (BUCCONIDAE; 5 SPECIES) Neotropical family of forest and forest edge birds. Ages/sexes similar or slightly different; attain adult appearance in 1st year. Nest in burrows in ground and termitaries. Often perch quietly for long periods; overlooked easily unless vocal.

WHITE-WHISKERED PUFFBIRD *Malacoptila panamensis* 19–20cm. Inconspicuous, small plump puffbird of humid forest and edge. Singles or pairs perch quietly at low to mid-levels in shady understory where can be quite confiding, seeming almost sleepy at times. No similar species in Costa Rica. Male rusty overall, female colder brown; extent of streaking below and pale spotting above highly variable. **SOUNDS:** Song a very high, penetrating, slightly descending reedy whistle, *tsssiiiiiir*, about 1 sec, every 5–10 secs. Calls include very high, short, downslurred whistles and burry clucks. **STATUS:** Uncommon to fairly common on both slopes, to 1200m. (Mexico to w. Ecuador.)

*LESSER PIED PUFFBIRD *Notharchus [tectus] subtectus* 14–15.5cm. Attractive small puffbird of humid lowland forest and edge, adjacent clearings and second growth with taller trees. In pairs or small groups, usually in canopy where heard far more easily than seen. Perches upright and sometimes dips tail; sallies for insects. No similar species in Costa Rica. Juv. browner above with buffy-white wing edgings, buff wash to face. **SOUNDS:** Song a rather complex series of high piping whistles, 8–12 secs duration; initial notes may suggest Rufous-tailed Jacamar but higher, thinner. Typically a series of ascending notes interspersed with 2–3-syllable phrases, *whieh whieh...whieh'didit whieeh whie'di-di dieh dieh...ch-dieh ch-dieh*, intensifying and then slowing to end with slightly lower, often disyllabic notes. **STATUS:** Uncommon on Caribbean slope, to 1000m. (Nicaragua to w. Ecuador.)

LANCEOLATED MONKLET *Micromonacha lanceolata* 13–13.5cm. Very small, cute puffbird of humid foothill forest and edge, adjacent second growth. Feeds and calls low to high, from roadside shrubs to forest canopy. Easily overlooked unless vocal, but can be quite confiding. Singly or in pairs, at times associated loosely with mixed flocks. No similar species in Costa Rica: note white spectacles, bold black droplet streaks on whitish underparts. **SOUNDS:** Song a slightly ascending series of (usually 4–15 or so) upslurred, high penetrating whistles, easily imitated, *sssiiih, sssiiih...*, 7–9 secs; increases in tempo and volume, with notes becoming shorter; repeated every few secs. **STATUS:** Scarce on Caribbean slope, 400–1500m. (Costa Rica to S America.)

WHITE-NECKED PUFFBIRD *Notharchus hyperrhynchus* 24–25.5cm. Distinctive, big-billed inhabitant of lowland forest canopy, from dry forest and gallery forest to rainforest, plantations; nests in arboreal termitaries. Seen mainly from edges or overlooks of canopy, as singles or pairs perched on high and often rather exposed branches of large, emergent trees. Sits still and often quietly for long periods. No similar species in Costa Rica. **SOUNDS:** Song a high, slightly bubbling, slow trill *wui-wui...*, 3–8 secs; suggests flight song of Great Black Hawk; at times ends with a few inflected nasal whistles, *k'wik k'wik...*or *wiki wiki....***STATUS:** Uncommon on both slopes, locally to 800m. (Mexico to S America.)

WHITE-FRONTED NUNBIRD *Monasa morphoeus* 28–30.5cm. Distinctive large puffbird of humid lowland forest canopy and edge, adjacent clearings with trees. Usually in small groups, often associating with mixed flocks that include caciques, woodcreepers; at times follows groups of monkeys, hoping for prey to be flushed. Can be loud and conspicuous, at other times perches quietly more like classic puffbird and overlooked easily. Nothing similar in Costa Rica: note large size, long tail, bright pinkish-red bill, and bushy white face. **SOUNDS:** Loud mellow and rolled whistles, at times in rhythmic duets and 'gobbling' choruses that can go on for minutes. **STATUS:** Fairly common to uncommon locally on Caribbean slope, to 800m. (Honduras to S America.)

WHITE-WHISKERED
PUFFBIRD

males

female

LESSER PIED
PUFFBIRD

LANCEOLATED
MONKLET

WHITE-NECKED
PUFFBIRD

WHITE-FRONTED
NUNBIRD

198

TOUCANS (RAMPHASTIDAE; 6 SPECIES) Neotropical family of spectacular, big-billed, forest and forest edge birds most diverse in South America. Ages differ slightly (juvs. duller overall, with duller-patterned bills), attaining adult appearance in 1st year; sexes similar, but males average bigger, longer bills. Nest in tree cavities.

BLUE-THROATED [EMERALD] TOUCANET *Aulacorhynchus [prasinus] caeruleogularis* 28–32cm. Small green toucan of humid highland forest and edge, adjacent clearings with trees. Usually in pairs or small groups, often at fruiting trees and shrubs, but easily overlooked given its green coloration. Flight fairly fast and direct with whirring wingbeats. No similar species, the only bright green toucan in Costa Rica. Juv. has paler throat, lacks neat pale line around base of bill. SOUNDS: 'Song' a nasal clucking to slightly rasping grunt repeated steadily *rruhk rruhk...*, 2–3 notes/sec; may suggest a frog. Other grunts and creaky barks in interactions. At a distance could suggest Keel-billed Toucan, which has higher, slightly longer, and creakier notes. STATUS: Fairly common to common on both slopes, mainly 800–2700m, occasionally lower in winter. (Costa Rica to Panama.)

YELLOW-EARED TOUCANET *Selenidera spectabilis* 37–41cm. Stunning but rarely seen small toucan of humid foothill forest. Usually in pairs or small groups at mid–upper levels where easily overlooked unless vocal; occasionally lower at edges and fruiting trees. Distinctive if you are lucky enough to see it, with colorful face, black throat and underparts, golden-yellow flank tufts, bright red undertail coverts. Only Costa Rican toucan in which sexes differ in plumage. SOUNDS: Dry, slightly rasping or clicking 2-syllable croak, usually in short series, *k'rrehk k'rrehk....* STATUS: Uncommon to scarce on Caribbean slope, mainly 300–1200m; rarely to lowlands, mainly in winter; spills over locally to adjacent n. Pacific slope foothills. (Honduras to nw. Colombia.)

COLLARED ARACARI *Pteroglossus torquatus* 38–43cm. Distinctive small toucan of varied wooded and forested habitats, adjacent clearings with larger trees, gardens. Typically in small loose groups, moving through canopy or flying across clearings one at a time, with rather direct flight and rapid whirring wingbeats, short glides. Limited range overlap with Fiery-billed Aracari, and hybridization may occur locally. Juv. has smaller and duller bill without strong black-edged serrations, yellowish facial skin soon becomes grayish, then red. SOUNDS: Sharp, squeaky, slightly metallic *píchi* or *skweí-zi*, sometimes repeated steadily; may suggest Groove-billed Ani. STATUS: Fairly common to common on both slopes, locally to 1500m. (Mexico to w. Ecuador.)

FIERY-BILLED ARACARI *Pteroglossus frantzii* 38–43cm. Replaces Collared Aracari on s. Pacific slope (limited range overlap), where found in humid forest, plantations, adjacent semi-open areas with trees and fruiting shrubs. Habits much like Collared Aracari. Identified by fiery bill coloration, broad red belly band, but may hybridize locally with Collared Aracari. Juv. duller overall and paler below; facial skin yellowish, soon becoming grayish and red. SOUNDS: Much like Collared Aracari, although *pí-chi* averages less compressed; also may suggest Groove-billed Ani. STATUS: Fairly common to common on s. Pacific slope, to 1500m; appears to be spreading north into range of Collared Aracari. (Costa Rica to w. Panama.)

BLUE-THROATED TOUCANET

YELLOW-EARED TOUCANET

female

male

COLLARED ARACARI

juv.

FIERY-BILLED ARACARI

KEEL-BILLED TOUCAN *Ramphastos sulfuratus* 45–52cm. Spectacular big toucan of humid forest, adjacent second growth, tree-scattered farmland with forest patches, gallery forest, plantations. Essentially unmistakable, with big, rainbow-colored bill; cf. Yellow-throated Toucan, with which it sometimes associates. More often heard than seen, but can be conspicuous, especially in early to mid-morning, perched on emergent bare snags in canopy or along forest edge; typically in pairs or small groups. Flight often high and deeply undulating, bursts of wingbeats interspersed with long swooping glides. Male has longer bill than female, noticeable within pairs. SOUNDS: Loud throaty croak, typically repeated steadily *rrek-rrek...*, 10 notes/4.5–7 secs; at a distance sounds like frogs (and cf. Blue-throated Toucanet), up close has an ear-splitting, shrieking quality. STATUS: Fairly common to common on both slopes, to 1600m and expanding upslope; uncommon to rare in drier nw. lowlands. Like other toucans, may wander rarely outside mapped range if fruit is scarce. (Mexico to nw. S America.)

YELLOW-THROATED (CHESTNUT-MANDIBLED) TOUCAN *Ramphastos ambiguus* 51–59cm. Spectacular big toucan of humid forest, adjacent tree-scattered farmland with forest patches, plantations. Essentially unmistakable, with big, bicolored 'banana bill'; cf. slightly smaller Keel-billed Toucan. Habits much like Keel-billed, which Yellow-throated dominates at fruiting trees; voice very different. In good light, bill deep maroon but often looks blackish in the field. Male has longer bill than female, noticeable within pairs. SOUNDS: Loud, downslurred yelping scream followed by (usually 1–3) paired yelps, *EERik, ki-di ki-di*, with distinctive rhythm, repeated steadily and often tirelessly; at a distance, only 1st part audible, but ear-splitting up close. STATUS: Fairly common to common on both slopes, locally to 1800m. (Honduras to S America.)

NEW WORLD BARBETS (CAPITONIDAE; 1 SPECIES) Small family of chunky, medium-size, often colorful birds related to toucans. Ages differ slightly, sexes differ; like adult in 1st year.

RED-HEADED BARBET *Eubucco bourcierii* 14.5–15.5cm. Colorful, thickset bird of humid foothill forest and edge, adjacent second growth and semi-open areas with fruiting trees and shrubs. Feeds low to high, often in canopy; visits feeders. Singles and pairs join mixed flocks, moving slowly and deliberately, poking in leaf clusters, at times hanging like a titmouse. No similar species in Costa Rica; stunning male particularly eye-catching; on female note stout yellowish bill, complex head pattern. SOUNDS: Rather quiet. Song a low purring trill, *urrrrr...*, 1–2 secs, every 5–15 secs; suggests Scaled Antpitta, but more even in pace and pitch. Varied grating and scratchy calls in interactions. STATUS: Uncommon to fairly common on both slopes, mainly 300–1800m. (Costa Rica to S America.)

TOUCAN BARBETS (SEMNORNITHIDAE; 1 SPECIES) Small family of chunky, medium-size birds formerly merged with barbets. Ages/sexes differ slightly; like adult in 1st year.

PRONG-BILLED BARBET *Semnornis frantzii* 17–18.5cm. Vocally arresting but drab-plumaged bird of mossy cloud forest and edge, adjacent semi-open areas, gardens. Most often detected by voice. In pairs or small groups, mainly moving sluggishly at mid–upper levels in fruiting trees; sometimes joins mixed flocks. Nothing especially similar in Costa Rica, but cf. Southern Black-faced Grosbeak (p. 400): note ochre-brown plumage with black mask, stout silvery-gray bill with black tip; male has blue-black pointed crest, usually held flat. SOUNDS: Loud nasal honking and braying calls often in pulsating duets that can last 30 secs or more, *ohng-ohng…*or *waah-waah...*, 4–5 notes/sec. Harsh clucks in alarm. STATUS: Fairly common on both slopes, mainly 700–2500m; occasionally wanders lower. (Costa Rica to w. Panama.)

Keel-billed Toucan

Yellow-throated Toucan

Red-headed Barbet

female

male

Prong-billed Barbet

juv.

female

male

WOODPECKERS (PICIDAE; 16 SPECIES) Widespread family, absent Australasia.
Ages/sexes differ slightly to distinctly; usually attain adult appearance in 1–2 months after fledging. Male usually has more red on head than female. Calls often useful for ID. 'Song' is mechanical drumming of bill on wood, distinguishable with practice, only described here if obviously distinct.

OLIVACEOUS PICULET *Picumnus olivaceus* 9–10cm. Can be puzzling when first encountered—doesn't really look like a woodpecker. Inhabits forest edge, open woodland, second growth, plantations, semi-open areas with scattered trees. Very small and easily overlooked, but taps persistently when foraging, which may draw attention. Mainly on outer branches and twigs, often hanging and clambering like a titmouse, not hitching on trunks. No similar species in Costa Rica, but cf. larger and longer-tailed Plain Xenops, which has similar habits. **SOUNDS:** High, thin, downslurred *ssip* and high sharp *tk*; very high, overall descending, rippling trill, 1–2 secs; may suggest song of Yellow-faced Grassquit but thinner, with subtly rippling cadence, higher and faster-paced than White-faced Gnatcatcher song. **STATUS:** Uncommon to fairly common on s. Pacific slope, to 1500m, uncommon locally on n. Caribbean slope. (Guatemala to w. Ecuador.)

RED-RUMPED WOODPECKER *Veniliornis kirkii* 14.5–15.5cm. Small brown woodpecker of humid lowland forest, adjacent semi-open areas with taller trees, second growth, mangroves. Mainly at mid–upper levels, often in canopy, sometimes lower at edges and in semi-open habitats. Hops actively on smaller trunks and branches. Note small size, barred underparts, yellowish nape, paler eyering; red rump often cloaked by wings and not obvious. Cf. Smoky-brown Woodpecker, larger Golden-olive and Rufous-winged Woodpeckers. **SOUNDS:** Nasal squeaky *eihk*, and sharply inflected *ih'dihk*, can be repeated steadily, 1–2 phrases/sec, at times run into a slightly descending, rapid chortling rattle similar to Smoky-brown Woodpecker but usually shorter, about 1 sec. Drum relatively high and rapid, about 1 sec, *dirrrr....* **STATUS:** Uncommon on both slopes, to 200m. (Costa Rica to w. Ecuador.)

SMOKY-BROWN WOODPECKER *Dryobates (Veniliornis) fumigatus* 15–16cm. Small brown woodpecker of humid foothill forest and edge, second growth, plantations, adjacent clearings with taller trees. Low to high, often in vine tangles or other thick vegetation. Note overall plain plumage (no barring), slightly paler face. Cf. Red-rumped Woodpecker; also Golden-olive Woodpecker, especially in shady understory. **SOUNDS:** Sharp *chik!* and rough shrieky rattle, 2–3 secs; squeaky rhythmic *chwíka chwíka…* in interactions. Drum rapid and rather low, *durrrr...*, <1 sec, lower than Red-rumped Woodpecker. **STATUS:** Fairly common on both slopes, especially foothills, to 1800m. (Mexico to S America.)

RUFOUS-WINGED WOODPECKER *Piculus simplex* 18–19cm. Medium-size green woodpecker of humid forest, especially canopy, where easily overlooked. Note olive face, pale-spotted breast, slightly bushy nape; cinnamon barring on remiges best seen in flight. Distinctive when seen clearly but cf. Red-rumped and Golden-olive Woodpeckers. **SOUNDS:** Loud, screaming, overall slightly descending *kéeeah*, at times in steady series, about 2 notes/sec; suggests Red-shouldered Hawk *Buteo lineatus* of N America. Drum distinctive, relatively high and slow-paced, *ahr-r-r...*, 1–1.2 secs. **STATUS:** Uncommon to fairly common on both slopes, locally to 1200m. (Honduras to w. Panama.)

GOLDEN-OLIVE WOODPECKER *Colaptes (Piculus) rubiginosus* 21–22.5cm. Medium-size green woodpecker of humid foothill forest and edge, adjacent clearings with taller trees, plantations. Mainly at mid–upper levels in taller trees, where can remain still and quiet for long periods; easily overlooked unless vocal. Juv. resembles adult but male mustache mottled gray. **SOUNDS:** Rapid-paced, shrill churring rattle, 2–3.5 secs. Sharp, slightly explosive *keéah* or *kyaah*, recalling a North American flicker. Drum relatively low, moderate-paced, *urrrr...*, 1–2 secs. **STATUS:** Fairly common on both slopes, mainly 400–2100m; scarce and local in Caribbean lowlands. (Mexico to S America.)

OLIVACEOUS PICULET

male

female

RED-RUMPED
WOODPECKER

male

male

SMOKY-BROWN
WOODPECKER

female

female

male

RUFOUS-WINGED
WOODPECKER

male

female

female

GOLDEN-OLIVE
WOODPECKER

CENTURUS WOODPECKERS (4 species). Widespread New World group, often in edge and fairly open habitats with larger trees and hedgerows. Most species have black-and-white barring on back. Churring and rattled calls can be similar between species. Often merged into genus *Melanerpes*.

hybrid zone

HOFFMANN'S WOODPECKER *Centurus (Melanerpes) hoffmannii* 18–19.5cm. Medium-size 'ladder-backed' woodpecker of forest and edge, plantations, semi-open areas with trees, hedgerows, gardens. Distinctive in most of range, with boldly barred back, white rump showing in flight. Hybridizes with Red-crowned Woodpecker on cen. Pacific slope, where many birds resemble Hoffmann's but have orange hindneck and belly patch. SOUNDS: Hard chattering or churring rattles, 1–10 secs, at times repeated in pulsating bursts; can suggest a large kingfisher rattle but more nasal. Rapidly rolled burry *cheh'eh'eh'ehrt*, often in short, fairly rapid-fire series. STATUS: Common on n. Pacific slope and into Central Valley, locally to 2800m; uncommon to locally fairly common on Caribbean slope, where spreading with deforestation. (Honduras to Costa Rica.)

RED-CROWNED WOODPECKER *Centurus (Melanerpes) rubricapillus* 16.5–18cm. Fairly small 'ladder-backed' woodpecker that replaces Hoffmann's Woodpecker on s. Pacific slope, where found in varied wooded and semi-open habitats, plantations, mangroves, gardens, hedgerows. Distinctive in most of range, with boldly barred back, white rump showing in flight. Note zone of hybridization with Hoffmann's Woodpecker on cen. Pacific slope, where many birds intermediate in plumage. SOUNDS: Very similar to Hoffmann's Woodpecker; rattles average higher pitched, rolled burry *chihr'ihr'ihr* averages higher, faster-paced. STATUS: Common to fairly common on s. Pacific slope to 1600m, locally to 2500m; range may be expanding with deforestation. (Costa Rica to n. S America.)

GOLDEN-NAPED WOODPECKER *Centurus (Melanerpes) chrysauchen* 17–18.5cm. Fairly small woodpecker of humid lowland forest and edge, adjacent clearings and second growth with taller trees. Feeds low to high on trunks, branches, and at fruiting and flowering trees. No range overlap with Black-cheeked Woodpecker, which has red nape, different back pattern. SOUNDS: Rapidly rolled, slightly nasal *chu'huh'huh'uhr* or *eh'eh'ehr*, typically in short, fairly rapid-fire series; averages higher and faster-paced than similar call of Black-cheeked Woodpecker. Low, short gravelly rattle, can be repeated steadily. STATUS: Fairly common to uncommon on s. Pacific slope, to 1500m; declining with deforestation. (Costa Rica to w. Panama.)

BLACK-CHEEKED WOODPECKER *Centurus (Melanerpes) pucherani* 18–19cm. Fairly small woodpecker of humid forest and edge, adjacent clearings and tree-scattered farmland with forest patches. Feeds low to high on trunks, branches, and at fruiting and flowering trees. No range overlap with Golden-naped Woodpecker, which has yellow nape, different back pattern. SOUNDS: Slightly nasal rolled *huh'duh'duh*, often in short, fairly rapid-fire series. Short churring rattle, can be repeated steadily. STATUS: Fairly common to common on Caribbean slope, to 1200m; spills over locally to humid n. Pacific slope foothills. (Mexico to w. Ecuador.)

HOFFMANN'S WOODPECKER

female

male

HYBRID HOFFMANN'S × RED-CROWNED

male

female

male

RED-CROWNED WOODPECKER

GOLDEN-NAPED WOODPECKER

male

female

BLACK-CHEEKED WOODPECKER

male

female

206

YELLOW-BELLIED SAPSUCKER *Sphyrapicus varius* 19–20.5cm. Long-winged, winter migrant woodpecker found in highland forest and semi-open areas with taller trees, hedgerows, gardens. Feeds low to high on trunks and larger branches, where maintains winter territories; typically rather sluggish and overlooked easily, but presence often revealed by 'sapsicles'—neat rows of holes drilled on trunks to access sap. Distinctive: note big white patch on wing coverts, white barring on back and wings. Adult male (rarely seen in Costa Rica) has red throat, female white; some females have black crown, cf. Hairy Woodpecker. Retains much juv. plumage into winter, and these imms. are the most frequently encountered plumage in Costa Rica; resembles adult by spring. **SOUNDS:** Mostly quiet. Mewing downslurred *meeah* mainly in interactions. **STATUS:** Uncommon Nov–Mar, mainly above 1000m; rare in lowlands, mainly during migration. (Breeds N America, winters s. US to Panama.)

HAIRY WOODPECKER *Dryobates (Picoides) villosus* 18–20cm. Medium-size woodpecker of highland oak forest, cloud forest, adjacent semi-open areas with taller trees, second growth, gardens. Feeds mainly at mid–upper levels, but sometimes on ground or fallen logs; joins mixed flocks. No similar species in Costa Rica (cf. scarce black-crowned female Yellow-bellied Sapsucker), but looks quite different from larger and whiter North American birds: note broad white back stripe, dirty buff-brown underparts, head pattern. Juv. (both sexes) has variable red crown patch. **SOUNDS:** Sharp *chriek!* or *chik*; rapid chattering rattle, 1–2.5 secs; rhythmic *chree'ka chree'ka* and varied shrieks in interactions. Drum rapid and even-paced, *drrrr...*, about 1 sec. **STATUS:** Fairly common, from 1500m to timberline. (N America to w. Panama.)

ACORN WOODPECKER *Melanerpes formicivorus* 21–23.5cm. Distinctive, social, 'clown-faced' woodpecker of highland oak forest, adjacent clearings and pastures with scattered trees, forest patches. Often conspicuous and noisy, in pairs or small groups, perched on exposed snags, fence posts. Feeds from ground to canopy and often sallies for flying insects, sailing easily on broad wings, when big white wing patches conspicuous. Male lacks black forehead band. **SOUNDS:** Varied nasal laughing and crowing calls, including rhythmic *yáka yáka...*; rolled churring *prrreh* and *krreh'eh*. Drum relatively slow-paced, about 1 sec, often slightly slower at start and end. **STATUS:** Common to fairly common, from 1500m to timberline; rarely wanders lower, to about 900m. (N America to n. Colombia.)

YELLOW-BELLIED SAPSUCKER

imm.

female

male

HIGHLAND WOODPECKERS

juv.

female

male

ACORN WOODPECKER

male

female

HAIRY WOODPECKER

CINNAMON WOODPECKER *Celeus loricatus* 18.5–21cm. Stunning but often rather inconspicuous, cinnamon-brown crested woodpecker of humid lowland forest and edge. Feeds mainly at mid–upper levels; often in canopy, where easily overlooked unless vocal. Smaller than Chestnut-colored Woodpecker, with cinnamon-brown head, paler underparts boldly scalloped blackish. SOUNDS: 'Song' a far-carrying, slightly descending series of (3–5, usually 4) loud ringing notes, last 1–2 abruptly lower and shorter, *keeu keeu keu ku.* Agitated call a rapid chittering rattle, 1–3 secs, often ending with an emphatic cluck, *k-k-k-k-k-kyu!* STATUS: Uncommon to fairly common on Caribbean slope, to 900m. (Nicaragua to w. Ecuador.)

CHESTNUT-COLORED WOODPECKER *Celeus castaneus* 21.5–24cm. Stunning but often rather inconspicuous, crested woodpecker of humid lowland forest and edge. Feeds mainly at mid–upper levels, including at fruiting and flowering trees. Distinctive, with rather wobbly blond to cinnamon crest; cf. slightly smaller Cinnamon Woodpecker. SOUNDS: Slightly explosive, overslurred hollow *whéow*, at times followed by a short cluck, *kéyow hik*, or by laughing series of nasal notes; sharp, nasal, slightly squeaky *wí-chk!* Drum relatively high and hollow, often rather soft, *ohrrrr...*, 1–1.5 secs. STATUS: Uncommon to fairly common on Caribbean slope, to 750m. (Mexico to w. Panama.)

LINEATED WOODPECKER *Dryocopus lineatus* 31.5–34cm. Large 'Woody Woodpecker' of varied wooded habitats, mangroves, plantations, hedgerows; often in semi-open country. Feeds low to high, often perches conspicuously on bare snags. Pale-billed Woodpecker slightly larger with blockier red head, pale bill (Lineated in northwest has pale bill), white lines on back more closely spaced into broken V, not parallel lines of Lineated; beware juv. Pale-billed, which has black face and white cheek stripe suggesting Lineated. SOUNDS: Fairly rapid, overall steady laughing series of yelping clucks, *yeh-yeh...*, often gets louder and then fades abruptly at end, 3–6 secs duration; may suggest Roadside Hawk and also recalls N American flickers. Sharp *chik* notes, often repeated steadily or run into a low growl, *puik! errrr*, recalling Common Squirrel Cuckoo. Drum powerful and resonant, fairly slow-paced, *durrrr...*, 1–2 secs. STATUS: Fairly common on both slopes, to 1200m. (Mexico to S America.)

PALE-BILLED WOODPECKER *Campephilus guatemalensis* 35.5–38cm. Largest woodpecker in Costa Rica, favoring woodland and forest with large trees, adjacent semi-open areas, plantations. Habits much like Lineated Woodpecker, but Pale-billed is more of a forest-based bird. In deeply undulating flight, wings make louder rush than Lineated. Note close-spaced white back stripes forming a V. Adult male has red head, female has black forehead and throat. Juv. very different, with black face and broad white cheek stripe, cf. Lineated; attains adult appearance in 1–2 months. SOUNDS: Sharp nasal clucks, often repeated persistently with hesitant cadence; recalls a squirrel scolding. Classic drum a distinctive, loud, rapid double-rap. STATUS: Fairly common on both slopes, to 1500m. (Mexico to w. Panama.)

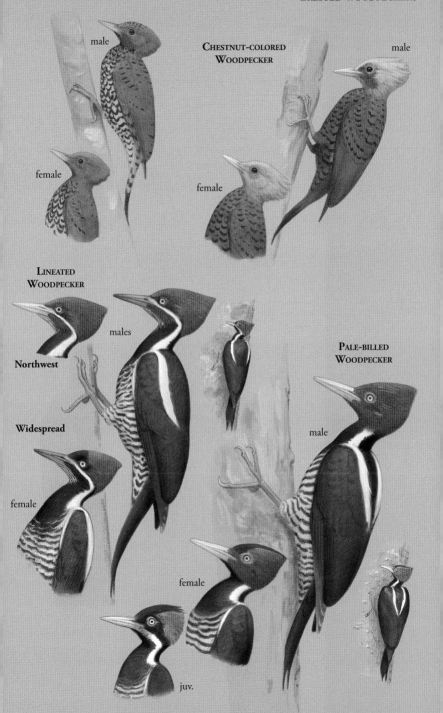

CINNAMON WOODPECKER

male

female

CRESTED WOODPECKERS

CHESTNUT-COLORED WOODPECKER

male

female

LINEATED WOODPECKER

males

Northwest

Widespread

female

PALE-BILLED WOODPECKER

male

female

juv.

JAYS (CORVIDAE; 5 SPECIES) Worldwide family of social, intelligent, and often noisy birds found mainly in wooded and forested habitats. Ages differ slightly; attain adult appearance in 1st year, although Brown Jay retains patches of imm. bill color into 2nd year; sexes similar.

WHITE-THROATED MAGPIE-JAY *Calocitta formosa* 43–56cm. Spectacular large jay of woodland and edge, gallery forest, open and semi-open areas with hedgerows, taller trees, gardens. In pairs or small groups, foraging low to high; flight rather slow and measured. Like many jays, can be loud and obnoxious, at other times relatively quiet and inconspicuous. No similar species in Costa Rica. Juv. has reduced black on face, weaker necklace, shorter crest. SOUNDS: Varied; often loud and noisy. Calls range from harsh and raucous to mellow and squeaky, can suggest large parrots. Most commonly a harsh *rrah*, often in series; mellow rolled *chowh*; loud *whee-wheep*; and sharp *whuit!* STATUS: Common to fairly common on n. Pacific slope, locally to 1200m; range expanding, rarely s. to Osa Peninsula since 2000s. (Mexico to Costa Rica.)

BROWN JAY *Psilorhinus morio* 38–43cm. Distinctive, very large jay of forest edge, open and semi-open areas with hedgerows and taller trees. Usually in loose groups of 5–15 birds; forages low to high, from forest canopy to open grassy fields. Flight rather slow and fairly direct; flying across open areas at a distance may suggest Montezuma Oropendola. Note overall dark plumage, bold white tail tip. 1st-year has yellow bill and eyering, becoming dark in 2nd-year. SOUNDS: Notably limited vocabulary. Monotonous and all-too-soon familiar, a loud screaming *KYEEAH!* or *KYAAH!* often repeated mercilessly; accompanied by quiet explosive pop, audible at close range. More mewing *reyaah* mainly in breeding season, may be repeated steadily. STATUS: Fairly common on both slopes, especially at mid-elevations, locally to 2400m; spreading with deforestation. (Mexico to w. Panama.)

BLACK-CHESTED JAY *Cyanocorax affinis* 35–38cm. Large handsome jay of humid forest and edge, plantations, semi-open areas with taller trees. In pairs or small groups, mainly at mid–upper levels in trees, but forages from ground to canopy. Often rather shy, heard more often than seen. Distinctive, with contrasting black face and chest, pale yellow eyes, bluish upperparts, bold white tail tip. Juv. duller overall, with dingier eyes. SOUNDS: Downslurred, abrupt rich *chuup!* and yelping *kyuuh*, both often doubled or in short series, repeated; slightly nasal short rattles and chatters, *cheh-cheh-chehr*; varied other calls including rough mews and scolds. STATUS: Uncommon to fairly common on s. Caribbean slope, to 1200m; scarce and local (sporadic?) on s. Pacific slope since 2000s. (Costa Rica to nw. S America.)

*AZURE-HOODED JAY *Cyanolyca cucullata* 28–30cm. Small jay of humid foothill and highland oak forest, cloud forest. Forages low to high, usually in pairs or small groups, sometimes with mixed flocks. Distinctive, but azure hood can be hard to see from below. Juv. duller and sootier overall, duller hood lacks white frontal border. SOUNDS: Bright, ringing, upslurred *eihnk...*, usually doubled or in short series; upslurred, inflected nasal rasp, *zzeh'k*, often repeated steadily. STATUS: Uncommon to fairly common on both slopes, mainly 800–2100m. (Mexico to w. Panama.)

SILVERY-THROATED JAY *Cyanolyca argentigula* 26–27cm. Handsome small jay of humid highland oak forest and edge, adjacent second growth and bamboo thickets. In pairs or small groups, at times to 20 or so birds, foraging low to high, at times joining loosely with mixed flocks. Often rather quiet and inconspicuous, but distinctive when seen. Juv. duller and sootier overall, with dirty whitish brow and throat. Eyebrow and throat silvery white in Central Mts., tinged lilac in Talamanca Mts. SOUNDS: Varied nasal and rasping calls include an upslurred rasping *zzhéhr*, sometimes doubled; rough nasal *zheihn*, often doubled or in short, overall descending series; mewing *rreihr*, often in short series. STATUS: Uncommon on both slopes, mainly 2000–3200m. (Costa Rica to w. Panama.)

BROWN JAY

WHITE-THROATED MAGPIE-JAY

imm.

BLACK-CHESTED JAY

Talamanca
Mts.

AZURE-HOODED JAY

Central Mts.

SILVERY-THROATED JAY

HUMMINGBIRDS (Trochilidae; 49+ species) 'Hummers' are a distinctive New World family best known for their small size, spectacular flight powers, and brilliant colors. Ages differ slightly to strongly; sexes similar or different; adult appearance attained in 1st year. ID can be challenging, but feeders may allow prolonged good views rarely possible 'in the wild,' when views are often brief and many birds get away as unidentified. Voice often useful for ID and detection.
  Many 'resident' hummers (especially those in the subtropical zone) are prone to wander seasonally, but details tend to be poorly known; the proliferation of feeders at many places will undoubtedly help clarify seasonal movements as well as revealing individuals out of range.

HERMITS (6 species). Mainly forest-based hummers with long arched bills, striped faces, and graduated tails that on some species have long white central feathers. Ages/sexes mostly similar. Mainly feed low and often 'trap-line,' making predictable circuits to isolated single flowers or groups of flowers (like a hunter checking traps); sometimes defend flower patches in *Heliconia* thickets. Will visit feeders.

STRIPE-THROATED HERMIT *Phaethornis striigularis* 9–9.5cm. Tiny, distinctive hummer of humid forest and edge, *Heliconia* thickets, gallery forest. Note small size, striped face, rusty rump. Feeds low to high, zipping quickly among and between flowers, often low along edges. Males gather to sing, usually a few birds 5–10m apart, perched low in dense understory, often within 1m of the forest floor; tail wagged constantly while singing. Ages/sexes similar. SOUNDS: Call a high sharp *siip!* suggesting Long-billed Hermit but weaker. Song a high, squeaky, prolonged jerky warble with slightly tinny quality, often frustratingly difficult to pinpoint; suggests song of northern Orange-billed Sparrow but slightly slower-paced, more hesitant. STATUS: Fairly common on both slopes, to 1500m; uncommon and local in drier nw. lowlands. (Mexico to nw. S America.)

BRONZY HERMIT *Glaucis aeneus* 10–11cm. Humid lowland forest edge and second growth, streamsides, swampy areas, especially with *Heliconia* thickets. Mainly low and often difficult to see well, zipping among *Heliconia* patches; males sing alone, not in leks, in dense understory. Note rusty underparts, weakly striped face, bronzy-green upperparts, and diagnostic tail pattern with bright rufous base. Sexes similar; juv. duller overall, especially on underparts. SOUNDS: Thin downslurred *tsiew*, often in short series. Varied song alternates high, mostly downslurred whistles with squeaky descending twitters and short trills, up to 6 secs. STATUS: Uncommon to fairly common on both slopes, locally to 750m on s. Pacific slope. (Honduras to w. Ecuador.)

BAND-TAILED BARBTHROAT *Threnetes ruckeri* 11–12cm. Humid forest and edge, *Heliconia* thickets. Mainly low and often difficult to see well, zipping about quickly in shady understory; males sing alone or in small leks, from low perch in understory. Note distinctive face and breast pattern, white base to tail. Sexes similar; juv. duller overall. SOUNDS: High, sharp, downslurred *ziik*, often doubled, shriller than other hermit calls. Song recalls Bronzy Hermit, alternates descending squeaky trills and high downslurred notes, with overall slightly jerky cadence, up to 7 secs. STATUS: Uncommon to fairly common on both slopes, rarely to 1200m. (Guatemala to nw. S America.)

LONG-BILLED HERMIT *Phaethornis longirostris* 16–17cm. Most frequently seen hermit in most areas. A spectacular if dull-plumaged hummer of humid forest understory, adjacent second growth, *Heliconia* thickets, gallery forest. Note long white tail streamers, long arched bill, striped face, pale grayish underparts. Typical views brief, as birds zip between flowering patches to feed, often hovering briefly with white tail streamers near vertical and quivered. Singing males gather seasonally in leks, perching 1–4m up and often 10–15m apart in shady understory; tail wagged constantly while singing. Ages/sexes similar. SOUNDS: Call a high, lisping, emphatic *sweik!* often given in flight as birds zip past. Song a monotonously repeated, slightly buzzy *zzreih, zzreih...*, about 2 notes/sec. STATUS: Fairly common to common on both slopes, locally to 1200m; uncommon and local in drier nw. lowlands. (Mexico to Colombia.)

Many colors on hummingbirds are iridescent, and lighting plays a huge role in how these appear in life. The plate illustrations show how colors would ideally look if perfectly lit, but this is rarely the case. Compare the 'field guide' male Blue-throated Goldentail at right with a more 'real-life' view at far right, and bear this in mind when viewing hummers in the field. The main problems lie with throat patches (known as gorgets) and crown patches, which often appear dark or colorless, and with tail coloration, which can change greatly with only a slight change in light angle.

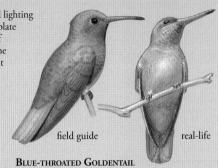

field guide

real-life

BLUE-THROATED GOLDENTAIL

LOWLAND HERMITS

variation

STRIPE-THROATED HERMIT

BRONZY HERMIT

juv.

BAND-TAILED BARBTHROAT

LONG-BILLED HERMIT

214

WHITE-TIPPED SICKLEBILL *Eutoxeres aquila* 12.5–13.5cm. Spectacular, if dull-plumaged, rather thickset hermit of humid lower foothill forest understory and edge, adjacent plantations, *Heliconia* thickets. Habits much like hermits, but usually clings to flowers (rather than hovers) when feeding. Singing males gather in small leks in dense understory and *Heliconia* patches. Note unique striped underparts, strongly arched bill, white tail tip. Sexes similar; juv. has buff tinge to pale underpart streaks. **SOUNDS:** High *tsit* in flight, at times in short rapid series. Song a varied, often prolonged series of high squeaky chips with slightly jerky, unhurried cadence, sometimes for a min or longer. **STATUS:** Uncommon to scarce on both slopes, mainly 300–1200m. (Costa Rica to Peru.)

GREEN HERMIT *Phaethornis guy* Male 14–15cm; female 15.5–16.5cm. Spectacular large hummer of humid foothill forest and edge, adjacent second growth. Feeds mostly at low to mid-levels, at times up to subcanopy; singing males gather at leks in dense understory. Distinctive, with long arched bill, overall dark plumage, and deep green upperparts; limited overlap with much paler Long-billed Hermit of lowlands. Female has long white tail streamers. **SOUNDS:** High sharp *sriek*, slightly higher and tinnier than Long-billed Hermit. Song a monotonously repeated, twangy, and slightly metallic *jriek, jriek...*, 1–2 notes/sec; lower, more metallic than Long-billed Hermit. **STATUS:** Fairly common on both slopes, mainly 500–2000m. (Costa Rica to nw. S America.)

GREEN-FRONTED LANCEBILL *Doryfera ludovicae* 11–12cm. Dark, very long-billed hummer of humid foothill forest, typically near streams and waterfalls. Feeds low to high, often in canopy and at edges, especially on long-tubed hanging flowers; also hawks insects. Note habits, long and slightly upswept bill, overall dark plumage with white eyespot, bronzy crown and nape. Cf. larger and bulkier male Talamanca Hummingbird. **SOUNDS:** High, thin, downslurred *ssip*, perched and in flight; hard smacking *tsik* when feeding, at times run into short rattles. **STATUS:** Uncommon on both slopes, mainly 750–2500m; rarely below 1500m on Pacific slope. (Costa Rica to S America.)

PLAIN-CAPPED STARTHROAT *Heliomaster constantii* 12–13cm. Large, long-billed hummer of drier forest edge, second growth, hedgerows, often near streams. Zips quickly between flower patches; also spends time flycatching with jerky hovering flight and often perches on prominent bare twigs or wires over streams. Note very long straight bill, broad white mustache bordering dark throat, white back patch; local overlap with Long-billed Starthroat, which favors more-humid habitats, is darker overall with whitish eyespot (vs. whitish stripe on Plain-capped), lacks dark notches in white tail corners. Sexes similar; juv. has little or no reddish on throat. **SOUNDS:** High sharp *peek!* recalls Black Phoebe. Song (?) a persistent high chipping from perch. **STATUS:** Uncommon on n. Pacific slope and into Central Valley, mainly below 1500m, rarely to 2200m; scarce and local in s. Pacific foothills. (Mexico to Costa Rica.)

LONG-BILLED STARTHROAT *Heliomaster longirostris* 11.5–12.5cm. Large, long-billed hummer of humid forest edge, adjacent clearings and gardens with flowering bushes. Habits much like Plain-capped Starthroat, but tends to perch less conspicuously. Note face pattern, very long straight bill, white back patch; cf. drabber and usually paler Plain-capped Starthroat. Male has iridescent turquoise-blue crown (varying to blue-green in north); female crown duller blue-green. Juv. has little or no reddish on throat. **SOUNDS:** Sharp *chiup* while feeding and hovering, quite distinct from Plain-capped Starthroat. **STATUS:** Uncommon to fairly common on s. Pacific slope, uncommon to scarce on Caribbean slope, rarely to 1500m. (Mexico to S America.)

**WHITE-TIPPED
SICKLEBILL**

female

male

GREEN HERMIT

female

**GREEN-FRONTED
LANCEBILL**

male

imm.

adults

female

male

**PLAIN-CAPPED
STARTHROAT**

**LONG-BILLED
STARTHROAT**

216

WHITE-NECKED JACOBIN *Florisuga mellivora* 11–12cm. Large stocky hummer of forest edge, adjacent semi-open habitats. Often conspicuous and aggressive at feeders. Mainly at mid–upper levels, hovering in fairly horizontal plane with tail slightly cocked, at times flashed open. Male (some females similar) striking and distinctive, with blue hood, extensively white tail; other females best identified by chunky shape, thick black bill, scalloped bib and white belly, cf. Scaly-breasted Hummingbird, which has big white tail corners. Imm. male has variable buffy on face and throat. SOUNDS: Rather quiet; high, slightly wiry chips and twitters on occasion. STATUS: Fairly common to uncommon on both slopes to 1500m, rarely 2000m. (Mexico to S America.)

SCALY-BREASTED HUMMINGBIRD *Phaeochroa cuvierii* 11.5–12.5cm. Large hummer of forest edge, adjacent clearings and gardens with taller trees, plantations, mangroves. Feeds low to high; mostly sings from high, rather open perches. Note drab plumage with bold white tail corners, medium-length bill, white eyespot, dingy buff belly; 'scaly breast' rarely apparent. Cf. female White-necked Jacobin; from below, female Rufous-tailed Hummingbird often looks scaly-breasted but has brighter reddish mandible, lacks big white tail corners. Ages/sexes similar. Comprises 2 groups that may intergrade in n. Costa Rica (study needed): northern **Robert's Hummingbird** *P. [c.] roberti* on n. Caribbean slope and perhaps in adjacent n. Pacific foothills, with black mandible, duskier bases to outer tail feathers; southern **Cuvier's Hummingbird** *P. [c.] cuvierii* of Pacific slope and adjacent n. Caribbean slope, with pinkish base to mandible, bronzy-green bases to outer tail feathers. SOUNDS: Song a variably paced chanting of varied chips, squeaks, and thin whistles with slightly jerky cadence, at times for 30 secs or longer; may suggest a euphonia. Sharp chip calls can suggest Yellow Warbler. STATUS: Fairly common to uncommon, to 1200m. (Mexico to Colombia.)

PURPLE-CROWNED FAIRY *Heliothryx barroti* 11.5–13cm. Striking hummer of humid forest and edge, adjacent taller second growth; does not usually visit feeders. Mainly at mid–upper levels where feeds actively, dashing from flower to flower or darting for insects; rarely seen perched. Distinctive, with gleaming white underparts, short pointed bill, black mask, white-sided tail (much longer on female). Male has violet crown; juv. has sparse dark spotting on breast, cinnamon edgings to upperparts. SOUNDS: Mostly quiet; high, thin *tsik*, at times run into twitters. STATUS: Uncommon to fairly common on both slopes, locally to 1600m. (Mexico to w. Ecuador.)

GREEN-BREASTED MANGO *Anthracothorax prevostii* 11–11.5cm. Large stocky hummer of open and semi-open areas with taller trees and hedgerows, gardens, plantations, mangroves, forest edge. Often perches (and nests) conspicuously on tall bare branches and twigs. Feeds low to high at flowers and sometimes defends feeding territories; flashes tail open when hovering. Distinctive in most of range, with rather thick, arched black bill, bright purple to coppery purple in tail, dark median stripe on female/imm. underparts; some females resemble adult male. Cf. very similar Veraguas Mango. SOUNDS: Often quiet. High sharp chips and twitters on occasion. STATUS: Fairly common in nw. lowlands, uncommon to fairly common elsewhere but spreading with deforestation; to 1500m. Status of mangos in areas of overlap with Veraguas Mango awaits elucidation. (Mexico to w. Panama.)

VERAGUAS MANGO *Anthracothorax [prevostii] veraguensis* 10.5–11cm. Counterpart to Green-breasted Mango on s. Pacific slope, in open and semi-open lowland habitats. Habits like Green-breasted and has been considered conspecific. All plumages resemble Green-breasted but differ in blue-green to green median throat and breast (vs. blackish on Green-breasted, but color often difficult to discern in the field). SOUNDS: High sharp chips, perhaps averaging harder, more smacking than Green-breasted. STATUS: Uncommon, but spreading with deforestation on s. Pacific slope, to 1500m; first recorded Costa Rica in late 1990s. (Costa Rica to w. Panama.)

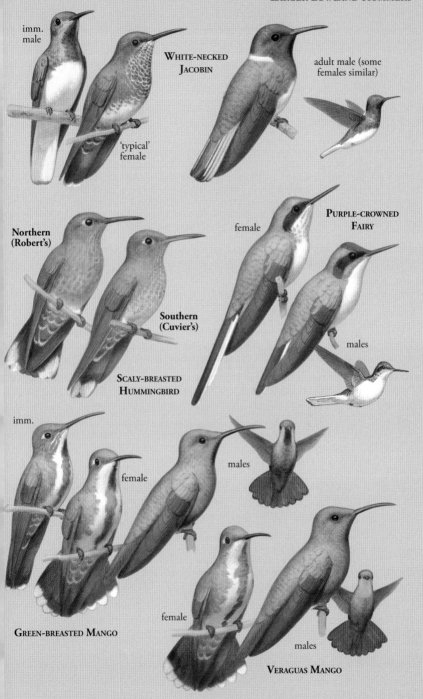

imm. male

WHITE-NECKED JACOBIN

'typical' female

adult male (some females similar)

PURPLE-CROWNED FAIRY

female

Northern (Robert's)

Southern (Cuvier's)

males

SCALY-BREASTED HUMMINGBIRD

imm.

female

males

GREEN-BREASTED MANGO

female

males

VERAGUAS MANGO

BROWN VIOLET-EAR *Colibri delphinae* 10.5–11.5cm. Drab but subtly attractive hummer of humid foothill forest edge, adjacent second growth and semi-open areas in foothills. Mainly at mid–upper levels, often in fairly open canopy; singing males form loose groups. No similar species in Costa Rica: note brownish plumage, broad whitish mustache, short bill, cinnamon rump. SOUNDS: Song from perch a series of (usually 3–8) strong, slightly metallic downslurred chips, *tchik tchik...*, repeated after short pause. Rattling chatters in interactions. STATUS: Uncommon on both slopes, mainly 400–1600m; ranges seasonally to adjacent lowlands. (Guatemala to S America.)

LESSER VIOLET-EAR *Colibri cyanotus* 11–11.5cm. Medium-size, overall green hummer of humid foothill and highland forest edge, clearings with flower banks, second growth. Mainly feeds low in flower patches, when can be hard to see, but sings persistently from exposed bare twig, mainly at mid-level in trees at forest edge or in clearings. Distinctive in highland habitat, with overall deep green plumage, medium-length slightly decurved black bill, bluish-violet cheeks, dark tail band. Female slightly duller than male; imm. duller overall, with duskier underparts, scattered glittering green feathers. SOUNDS: Song a fairly steady series of varied semi-metallic chips, about 3/sec, can be continued tirelessly at any time of day: *tik tsik tik tik chik tsik...*, often with repetitive paired phasing, *tsi chik tsi chik....* Short, rapid-paced dry rattles in flight, while feeding. STATUS: Fairly common to common, mainly 1500–3300m; some range down to 900m, mainly Apr–Sep. (Costa Rica to S America.)

GREEN-CROWNED BRILLIANT *Heliodoxa jacula* 12–13.5cm, male>female. Large hummer of humid foothill and highland forest and edge, ranging to adjacent second growth and semi-open areas. Mainly at mid–upper levels where flight quick and darting; often perches to feed rather than hovering. Distinctive male deep green overall with long, forked blue-black tail; female best told by large size, short white whisker stripe, spotted underparts. Imm. has variable cinnamon patch on throat sides. SOUNDS: High, sharp, downslurred *chip*, suggests Yellow Warbler; squeaky, relatively low nasal *kyew*, at times in chattering series. Song a rapid, rhythmic, squeaky warble, 2–3 secs. STATUS: Fairly common to uncommon on both slopes, mainly 700–2200m, rarely to lower foothills. (Costa Rica to w. Ecuador.)

VIOLET SABREWING *Campylopterus hemileucurus* 14–15cm. Striking large hummer of humid foothill and highland forest and edge, second growth, adjacent semi-open areas. Mainly at low to mid-levels; singing males form groups in shady understory. Distinctive, with thick arched bill, white eyespot, big white tail corners often flashed in flight. Male can look simply dark overall, but violet tones spectacular in good light. SOUNDS: Hard sharp chips at times run into rattles. Song a steady, often prolonged series of sharp, slightly metallic chips interspersed with lower squeaks, about 2 notes/sec. STATUS: Fairly common on both slopes, mainly 1000–2400m; often descends to foothills, rarely to coastal lowlands. (Mexico to w. Panama.)

BROWN VIOLET-EAR

LESSER VIOLET-EAR

imm. female

imm. male

GREEN-CROWNED BRILLIANT

females

female

males

imm. female

female

males

VIOLET SABREWING

FIERY-THROATED HUMMINGBIRD *Panterpe insignis* 10–11cm. Fairly large, stocky, and rather short-billed hummer of humid highland forest, shrubby edges, adjacent second growth. Feeds low to high and often rather aggressive at flower patches. Note stocky build, short bill (pinkish below), and overall dark plumage with sapphire rump and blue tail, small white eyespot; fiery throat can be frustratingly difficult to see (most extensive in Guanacaste Mts.). Sexes similar. **SOUNDS:** Distinctive. Nasal and twangy downslurred squeaks when feeding; burry squeaky twitters and harder chatters in interactions. **STATUS:** Common to fairly common, mainly 1500m to timberline, locally down to 750m (mainly Feb–Jul). (Costa Rica to w. Panama.)

TALAMANCA [MAGNIFICENT] HUMMINGBIRD *Eugenes [fulgens] spectabilis* 12.5–13.5cm. Large, long-billed hummer of humid highland forest and edge, adjacent clearings, gardens. Feeds low to high, often aggressive at flowering trees and feeders. Male often looks dark overall: note long bill, white eyespot, greenish tail, cf. Fiery-throated Hummingbird. Female best told by long bill, dingy grayish underparts. **SOUNDS:** Low, buzzy rasping *zzrt* in flight; varied chattering series with similar, rough buzzy quality. Squeaky chatters in chases. **STATUS:** Common to fairly common, mainly 2000m to timberline, locally down to 1800m. (Costa Rica to w. Panama.)

WHITE-BELLIED MOUNTAIN-GEM *Lampornis hemileucus* 9.5–11cm. Distinctive, fairly large hummer of humid foothill forest and edge, adjacent second growth. Feeds low to high. Note distinctive combination of large size, white underparts, and white eyestripe, also bronzy-green tail; male has purple gorget that often looks dark. Imm. has buffy fringes to upperparts, male throat dull bronzy. **SOUNDS:** High, slightly tinny, downslurred *tssi*; slightly metallic, sharp squeaky *tsieh!* steadily from perch, 1–2 notes/sec. **STATUS:** Uncommon to fairly common on Caribbean slope, mainly 700–1500m. (Costa Rica to w. Panama.)

*****GRAY-TAILED (WHITE-THROATED) [VARIABLE] MOUNTAIN-GEM** *Lampornis [castaneoventris] cinereicauda* 9.5–11cm. Also known as White-throated Mountain-gem. Striking, fairly large hummer of humid highland forest and edge, especially with oaks; ranges to adjacent second growth, semi-open areas. Feeds low to high, often in canopy. Male distinctive, with striking face pattern, pale ashy-gray tail (often flashed open in flight); white throat often has a few purplish feathers, mainly at edges. Female very similar to female Purple-throated Mountain-gem but tail duller, bronzy green, duller than uppertail coverts; in areas where both occur, Gray-tailed favors higher elevations. **SOUNDS:** Low rough *zzirt*; short, dry rattled trills in chases. **STATUS:** Endemic to Talamanca Mts. of Costa Rica: fairly common to common, mainly 1800–3000m, with some post-breeding movement down to 1500m, mainly May–Sep.

*****PURPLE-THROATED [VARIABLE] MOUNTAIN-GEM** *Lampornis [castaneoventris] calolaemus* 9.5–10.5cm. Striking, fairly large hummer of humid foothill and highland forest and edge, ranging to adjacent second growth, semi-open areas. Feeds low to high, often in canopy. Male distinctive, with striking face pattern (throat often looks simply dark), dark blue tail. Female very similar to female Gray-tailed Mountain-gem but tail brighter greenish, not duller than uppertail coverts; in areas where both occur, Gray-tailed favors higher elevations. **SOUNDS:** Slightly liquid, rolled buzzy *zrit* and lower, rougher, buzzy *zzirt*. Song a rapid-paced, complex, buzzy gurgling warble, mostly 4–7 secs. **STATUS:** Common to fairly common on both slopes, mainly 800–2500m, s. to n. Talamanca Mts.; some post-breeding movement down to 300m, mainly May–Sep. (Nicaragua to w. Panama.)

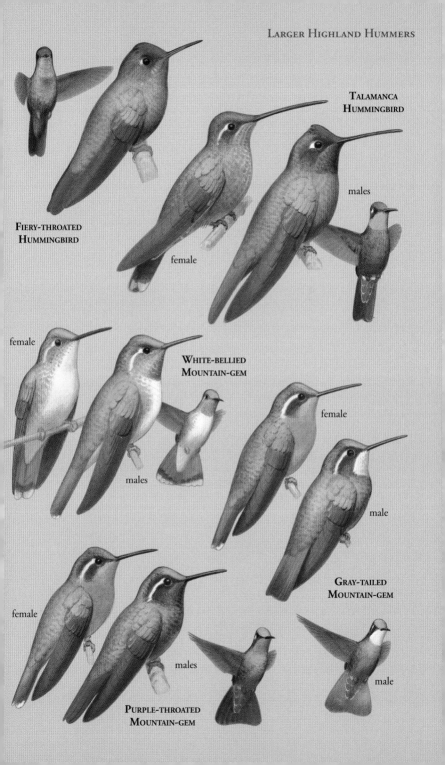

TALAMANCA
HUMMINGBIRD

males

FIERY-THROATED
HUMMINGBIRD

female

female

WHITE-BELLIED
MOUNTAIN-GEM

males

female

male

males

GRAY-TAILED
MOUNTAIN-GEM

female

males

PURPLE-THROATED
MOUNTAIN-GEM

male

222

THORNTAIL AND COQUETTES (3+ species). Very small and easily overlooked hummers with bold white rump band, ornate male plumage. Typically hover with tail cocked above back, when can be mistaken for a large bee or sphinx moth, and vice versa. Feed low to high, often in canopy of flowering trees where easily overlooked; rarely visit feeders, but—like many smaller hummers—often found at ornamental verbena bushes (see photo on p. 15). Usually rather quiet; males perch on thin bare twigs in canopy or subcanopy, from which they may sing quietly or make display flights.

GREEN THORNTAIL *Discosura conversii* Male 9.5–11cm, female 7–7.5cm. Distinctive, very small hummer of humid foothill forest and edge, adjacent second growth. Feeds low to high, often in low ornamental bushes. See intro note. Note small size, overall dark plumage with white rump band; male has long, wire-like tail feathers, female and imm. have broad white mustache and big white flank patch. Imm. male variably intermediate between female and adult male. SOUNDS: Mostly quiet. High soft chips in interactions. STATUS: Uncommon on Caribbean slope, mainly 700–1500m; ranges mainly Jun–Aug to adjacent lowlands. (Costa Rica to w. Ecuador.)

BLACK-CRESTED COQUETTE *Lophornis helenae* 6.5–7cm. Tiny hummer of humid forest and edge, adjacent clearings and second growth with flowering trees, mainly in foothills. See intro note. Distinctive, with broad white rump band, coarse bronzy spotting on underparts, short reddish bill. Imm. male variably intermediate between female and adult male. SOUNDS: Mostly quiet. Quiet chips and high twitters sometimes when feeding. Song from perch a clear, upslurred *tsuwee*, repeated. STATUS: Locally/seasonally uncommon to scarce on Caribbean slope, mainly 300–1200m; wanders to adjacent lowlands, rarely to Pacific slope in Central Valley. (Mexico to Costa Rica.)

WHITE-CRESTED COQUETTE *Lophornis adorabilis* 6.5–7cm. Tiny hummer of humid forest and edge, adjacent clearings and second growth with flowering trees, mainly in foothills. See intro note. Distinctive, with broad white rump band (tinged cinnamon on juv.), rusty belly; fully adult males with white crest seen much less frequently than female/imm. plumages. Imm. male variably intermediate between female and adult male. SOUNDS: Mostly quiet. High sharp chips sometimes when feeding. STATUS: Locally/seasonally uncommon to scarce on s. Pacific slope, mainly 300–1800m; rare but apparently regular (mainly Jun–Nov) in cen. Caribbean foothills, mostly around 1000m. (Costa Rica to w. Panama.)

VIOLET-HEADED HUMMINGBIRD *Klais guimeti* 7.5–8cm. Small, very short-billed hummer of humid foothill forest and edge, adjacent second growth. Feeds low to high, often in canopy and at ornamental verbena bushes. Singing males gather at edges or gaps in forest, perching on bare twigs in open subcanopy. Flight notably quick and darting. Distinctive, although violet-blue on head can be hard to see: note small size and short straight bill, bold white eyespot. Imm. male resembles female but crown duller, greenish blue, throat often with some violet feathers. SOUNDS: High, slightly liquid rolled chips, at times run into rattled trills. Song a high, thin twittering phrase, repeated insistently, *tsi-s-sii tsi-s-sii...*, or *tiz-i-zit tiz-i-zit....* STATUS: Uncommon to fairly common; mainly 300–1600m on Pacific slope (very rarely wandering to 3000m), 50–1200m on Caribbean slope. (Honduras to S America.)

beware of large sphinx moths, which
are easily mistaken for coquettes

GREEN THORNTAIL

female

males

BLACK-CRESTED COQUETTE

females

males

female

WHITE-CRESTED COQUETTE

males

VIOLET-HEADED
HUMMINGBIRD

female

males

MAGENTA-THROATED WOODSTAR *Philodice (Calliphlox) bryantae)* Male 8.5–9.5cm, female 7.5–8cm. Attractive small hummer of humid foothill forest and edge, adjacent second growth and clearings. Feed low to high, and can be territorial at flower patches. Hovering flight rather slow and deliberate, typically with tail cocked above back, when could be mistaken for a large bee or sphinx moth. Distinctive, with bold whitish patches at sides of rump, insect-like flight. Cf. smaller Scintillant Hummingbird, which has 'typical' quick flight. SOUNDS: Low *cht*, sometimes doubled or in short series, and longer rolled *chrrrt*. Wings make rather strong low humming in flight. STATUS: Uncommon to fairly common on Pacific slope, mainly 700–1800m; spills over locally to adjacent Caribbean slope foothills. (Costa Rica to w. Panama.)

RUBY-THROATED HUMMINGBIRD *Archilochus colubris* 8–9cm. Small migrant hummer of varied open and semi-open habitats, from coastal scrub to humid forest edge, hedgerows, plantations, weedy fields with flowers. Feeds and perches low to high, often rather inconspicuously. Adult male distinctive (gorget often looks dark), note forked blackish tail; female rather plain, but note white tail tips, white eyespot, black bill, whitish underparts. Imm. male in fall resembles female, attains adult plumage over winter. SOUNDS: High twangy *tchi*, at times doubled; varied twitters in interactions. STATUS: Uncommon to fairly common Nov–Mar on n. Pacific slope, uncommon to scarce elsewhere, locally to 1800m; more widespread in migration, Sep–Oct, Feb–Apr. (Breeds N America, winters Mexico to w. Panama.)

SCINTILLANT HUMMINGBIRD *Selasphorus scintilla* 6–7cm. Tiny highland hummer of second growth, overgrown pastures, forest edge, gardens, hedgerows. Feeding flight quick, often clinging and piercing flower bases; territorial males perch atop shrubs adjacent to open areas with flowers. Note male gorget color, mostly orangey tail, cf. slightly larger Volcano Hummingbird. Imm. female has central pair of tail feathers mostly green, margined rusty; other tail feathers bright rusty with black subterminal band, cinnamon to whitish tips to outer 3 pairs. In display, male zigzags to 15–20m and swoops in U trajectory, less steep than Volcano Hummingbird dives. SOUNDS: High, rather soft downslurred chips when feeding; twitters in interactions. Male wings produce high shrill trill in flight. In dive, male makes pulsating wing trills plus a stuttering 7–8-syllable clicking at bottom of dive. STATUS: Uncommon to locally common in highlands, mainly 900–2100m on Pacific slope, ranging and wandering locally to Caribbean slope; post-breeding movements rarely up to 2500m, mainly Apr–Aug. (Costa Rica to w. Panama.)

VOLCANO HUMMINGBIRD *Selasphorus flammula* 6.5–7.5cm. Very small highland hummer of shrubby clearings, second growth, páramo, cloud forest edge, gardens. Habits similar to Scintillant Hummingbird, which occurs alongside locally. Scintillant has mostly orangey tail, whereas female/imm. Volcano has central pair of tail feathers green, adjacent pair mostly green, not rusty; white to buffy tips to outer 3 pairs; male Scintillant has flame gorget. In display, male Volcano climbs to 20–25m and dives in steep J or U trajectory. Complex variation, with 3 populations that have been considered species: **Cerise-throated Hummingbird** *S. [f.] simoni* breeding on Poás and Barva volcanoes; **Heliotrope-throated Hummingbird** *S. [f.] torridus* on Irazú and Turrialba volcanoes; **Purple-throated Hummingbird** *S. [f.] flammula* in Talamanca Mts. SOUNDS: Mostly rather quiet. High thin chips when foraging; high squeaky chippering in interactions. Male song from perch a high, downslurred whining whistle, *tssiiiiiiiiu*, about 2.5 secs, repeated. In dive, male produces wing whistle plus a stuttering 3–4-syllable low clicking at bottom of dive. STATUS: Fairly common to common, above 1800m in Central Mts., above 2000m in Talamanca Mts. Post-breeding movements rarely down to 1200m, mainly Mar–Jul, when different taxa can occur together, with *torridus* ranging nw. to Poás volcano. (Costa Rica to w. Panama.)

MAGENTA-THROATED WOODSTAR

males

female

RUBY-THROATED HUMMINGBIRD

females

males

SCINTILLANT HUMMINGBIRD

females

males

imm. female

VOLCANO HUMMINGBIRD

variation (mainly Poás)

females

males

Poás

Irazú

male

Talamancas

COPPERY-HEADED EMERALD *Elvira cupreiceps* 7.5–8cm. Small white-tailed hummer of humid foothill forest and edge, adjacent second growth. Feeds low to high, males often in canopy; singing males gather at mid-levels in trees at forest edge. Distinctive in range, with fairly short, slightly decurved bill; male has coppery crown and upperparts, female has mostly white tail (central feathers bronzy green), whitish underparts; cf. female Black-bellied Hummingbird. **SOUNDS:** High liquid *puit*, often doubled or run into short rolled twitters. **STATUS:** Uncommon to fairly common locally on Caribbean slope, mainly 700–1500m; ranges to adjacent lowlands (mainly Apr–Sep) and spills over locally to humid n. Pacific slope. (Endemic to Costa Rica.)

WHITE-TAILED EMERALD *Elvira chionura* 7.5–8cm. Small white-tailed hummer of humid foothill forest and edge, adjacent second growth. Feeds low to high, often at ornamental verbena; small groups of singing males gather at mid-levels in forest edge. Distinctive in range (no overlap with Coppery-headed Emerald), with fairly short, slightly decurved bill; male green overall with no rusty wing patch, female has mostly white tail (central feathers green), whitish underparts; cf. female Black-bellied Hummingbird, which has straighter bill, rusty wing patch, dingier underparts, lacks black subterminal tail band. **SOUNDS:** High liquid *puit* and short rolled twitters, much like Coppery-headed Emerald. Song a high, wiry, twittering warble. **STATUS:** Uncommon to fairly common locally on s. Pacific slope, mainly 800–2000m. (Costa Rica to w. Panama.)

SNOWCAP *Microchera albocoronata* 6.5–7cm. Tiny, rather short-tailed hummer of humid foothill forest and edge, adjacent second growth. Feeds low to high, often at ornamental verbena; flight typically quick and darting. Singing males gather at mid-levels in forest edge. Male stunning and distinctive; on female note small size, short straight bill, bronzy central tail feathers; extensive white shows in spread tail. Imm. male has variable purplish patches, typically a broad dark median stripe on underparts. **SOUNDS:** High liquid *puit* and short twitters in flight; recalls White-tailed Emerald. Song a squeaky chippering warble, at times alternated with high buzzy trills, up to several secs. **STATUS:** Uncommon to fairly common locally on Caribbean slope, mainly 300–1200m; ranges to adjacent lowlands (mainly Jun–Sep) and spills over locally to humid n. Pacific slope. (Honduras to w. Panama.)

*STRIPE-TAILED HUMMINGBIRD *Eupherusa eximia* 9.5–10cm. Medium-size hummer of humid foothill forest and edge, adjacent semi-open areas. Feeds low to high. Feeding flight often quick and darting. White tail flashes often striking when hovering, but concealed from above with tail closed. Male underparts can appear black in poor light, cf. smaller Black-bellied Hummingbird, which has more white in tail; female Back-bellied has 3 vs. 2 white outer tail feathers. **SOUNDS:** High, springy, slightly rolled *tzzit*, with variable metallic or buzzy quality, often doubled or run into short chatters; lower, buzzier, and slower-paced than White-tailed Emerald. Song a high, squeaky, rather fast-paced chippering warble, at times with sputtering trills and squeaks, up to several secs. **STATUS:** Uncommon to fairly common on both slopes, mainly 800–2100m. (Mexico to w. Panama.)

BLACK-BELLIED HUMMINGBIRD *Eupherusa nigriventris* 7.5–8.5cm. Small white-tailed hummer of humid foothill forest and edge. Feeds low to high, often at mid–upper levels in forest, lower along edges. Feeding flight often quick and darting. White tail flashes often striking when hovering, concealed from above with tail closed. Male black face and underparts distinctive, but cf. larger Stripe-tailed Hummingbird, which has more extensive rufous in wings, less white in tail. Female Stripe-tailed larger and longer-billed with only 2 white outer tail feathers. **SOUNDS:** High sharp *tsiet* when feeding, very different from rolled chips of Stripe-tailed. **STATUS:** Uncommon to fairly common on Caribbean slope, mainly 900–2000m; ranges down to 500m (mainly Apr–Jul). (Costa Rica to w. Panama.)

female

males

COPPERY-HEADED EMERALD

female

males

WHITE-TAILED EMERALD

SNOWCAP

imm.
male

female

male

males

**STRIPE-TAILED
HUMMINGBIRD**

females

males

female

females

**BLACK-BELLIED
HUMMINGBIRD**

*SALVIN'S [CANIVET'S] EMERALD *Cynanthus (Chlorostilbon) [canivetii] salvini* 7.5–8.5cm. Very small hummer of second growth, woodland and edge, gardens, overgrown clearings, especially in drier areas. Mainly at low to mid-levels; tail often fanned slightly while hovering. Distinctive in most of range, but potential overlap with Garden Emerald unclear; birds with intermediate characters have been reported from cen. Pacific slope. Male Salvin's averages longer, more deeply forked tail than Garden and has reddish bill tipped black. Female from Garden by reddish base to mandible (can be difficult to see), diffuse whitish median band on outer tail feathers. SOUNDS: Fairly quiet, gruff dry *cht*, often doubled or run into short staccato chatters. STATUS: Uncommon to fairly common on n. Pacific Slope, to 1500m in Central Valley; spills over locally to adjacent n. Caribbean slope; status on cen. Pacific slope unclear cf. Garden Emerald. (Guatemala to Costa Rica.)

GARDEN EMERALD *Chlorostilbon [canivetii] assimilis* 7–8cm. Replaces Salvin's Emerald on s. Pacific slope, and similar in habits and habitat, although favoring more humid areas. Distinctive in most of range, but potential overlap with Salvin's Emerald unclear; birds with intermediate characters have been reported from cen. Pacific slope. Note wholly black bill. Male Salvin's averages longer, more deeply forked tail and has reddish bill tipped black; female has reddish base to mandible, whitish median band on outer tail feathers. SOUNDS: Fairly quiet dry *cht* and dry staccato chatters, much like Salvin's Emerald. STATUS: Uncommon to fairly common on s. Pacific Slope, locally to 2000m; spills over locally to cen. Caribbean slope; status on cen. Pacific slope unclear cf. Salvin's Emerald. (Costa Rica to Panama.)

CROWNED WOODNYMPH *Thalurania colombica* 10–11cm. Medium-size hummer of humid forest, adjacent second growth. Feeds low to high, often in shady understory, but regularly visits feeders in more open situations. Male distinctive, stunning when colors catch the light, with glittering emerald and purple plumage, forked blue-black tail. Female distinctive, with bicolored underparts, small white corners to blue-black tail. Imm. male resembles female but with emerald patches on breast, tail lacks pale corners. SOUNDS: Fairly hard, ticking rattled chips, at times run into rapid chatters. STATUS: Fairly common on both slopes, locally to 1400m. (Guatemala to nw. S America.)

BRONZE-TAILED (RED-FOOTED) PLUMELETEER *Chalybura urochrysia* 11.5–12.5cm. Medium-large lowland hummer of humid second growth, *Heliconia* thickets, forest edge, and shady understory. Mainly at low levels, where often aggressive, chasing off other hummers and perching in shady thickets where can be difficult to see well. Note bright pinkish-red feet, rather long and overall dark tail. Male often looks dark overall; on female note pale gray tail corners. SOUNDS: Loud, slightly squeaky to low rolled chips, at times in short rattling or spluttering series; flight call a distinctive sharp *pit pit*.... Song a varied short medley of nasal rattles and sharp chips. STATUS: Uncommon to locally fairly common on Caribbean slope, to 900m. (Honduras to w. Ecuador.)

EMERALDS, WOODNYMPH, PLUMELETEER

female

males

SALVIN'S EMERALD

female

GARDEN EMERALD

males

female

males

CROWNED
WOODNYMPH

female

males

BRONZE-TAILED PLUMELETEER

CHARMING (BERYL-CROWNED) HUMMINGBIRD *Amazilia decora* 8.5–9cm. Fairly small hummer of open forest and edge, taller second growth, adjacent gardens. Pacific-slope counterpart to Blue-chested Hummingbird (no range overlap). Feeds low to high, often at verbena bushes; flight typically quick and rather darting. Singing males form loose groups, perching at low to mid-levels along edges. From Blue-chested by range, also dorsal tail color (more bronzy green, less purplish than Blue-chested), more extensively glittering crown of male (extending to nape, unlike Blue-chested), brighter green crown of female. Cf. Blue-throated Goldentail, which has bright red bill, green-gold tail. SOUNDS: Call from perch a high sharp *chik*, at times repeated steadily; hard rolled *tik* in flight, often run into short rattles. Song a high, slightly tinny and squeaky rhythmic chant, 1–6 secs. STATUS: Uncommon to fairly common on s. Pacific slope, to 1200m. (Costa Rica to w. Panama.)

BLUE-CHESTED (LOVELY) HUMMINGBIRD *Amazilia amabilis* 8.5–9cm. Fairly small lowland hummer of open forest and edge, taller second growth, adjacent gardens. Caribbean-slope counterpart to Charming Hummingbird (no range overlap) and habits similar. Often looks rather dull and uninteresting, purplish-blue chest rarely catching the light. From Charming by range, also note coppery uppertail coverts (beware, worn tail can look dark overall). Cf. Blue-throated Goldentail, which has bright red bill, green-gold tail. SOUNDS: Call from perch a high sharp *tsik*, at times in short series; hard rolled *tik* in flight, often doubled in short rattles. Song a high, slightly lisping, squeaky rhythmic chant, 1–2 secs, slower-paced, less tinny, often simpler than Charming Hummingbird. STATUS: Uncommon to fairly common on Caribbean slope, locally to 700m. (Honduras to w. Ecuador.)

SAPPHIRE-THROATED HUMMINGBIRD *Lepidopyga coeruleogularis* 8.5–9.5cm. Fairly small hummer of open and semi-open lowland areas with hedgerows, forest patches and edge, second growth. Feeds low to high, often at mid–upper levels in canopy. No similar species in range and habitat: note long forked tail; male often looks dark overall, but violet-blue gorget striking in good light; female best told by strongly forked tail with white tips, plain head sides. SOUNDS: Fairly high slow trill, repeated in pulses from perch; in flight a low rasping *tzk*, at times run into short rattles; chase call a high rattling twitter. STATUS: Scarce, but expanding with deforestation, on s. Pacific slope, to 200m; first recorded Costa Rica in late 2000s. (Costa Rica to n. Colombia.)

MANGROVE HUMMINGBIRD *Amazilia boucardi* 9–10cm. Medium-size hummer of Pacific coast mangroves, ranging to adjacent woodland and second growth. Only white-bellied hummer likely in its specialized habitat, but cf. female of migrant Ruby-throated Hummingbird, which is smaller, with different face and neck pattern, lacks red on bill. Male has green gorget, notched dark tail; female has clean white throat and underparts. SOUNDS: Low rasping or crackling *zzirt* in flight; series of fairly hard sharp, downslurred chips from perch; rapid, slightly squeaky twitters when agitated. STATUS: Fairly common locally in mangroves along Pacific coast. (Endemic to Costa Rica.)

SNOWY-BELLIED HUMMINGBIRD *Amazilia edward* 8.5–9.5cm. Distinctive medium-size hummer of foothill second growth, brushy savanna, scrubby woodland, hedgerows. Feeds low to high; males sing alone from inconspicuous perches. Note sharp contrast between green breast and snowy-white belly; from above note coppery back and rump, blue-black tail (no range overlap with Blue-vented Hummingbird). Sexes similar. SOUNDS: Downslurred, rather burry or gravelly *zrrih* and sharper *zrip* when feeding; downslurred chipping chatter when agitated. Song a short, plaintive, slightly squeaky *bieh-ti-bieh* and variations, repeated. STATUS: Uncommon to locally fairly common on s. Pacific slope, mainly 300–1800m. (Costa Rica to Panama.)

female

male

CHARMING HUMMINGBIRD

males

female

males

female

BLUE-CHESTED HUMMINGBIRD

males

female

SAPPHIRE-THROATED HUMMINGBIRD

female

males

adults

MANGROVE HUMMINGBIRD

SNOWY-BELLIED HUMMINGBIRD

RUFOUS-TAILED HUMMINGBIRD *Amazilia tzacatl* 9.5–10.5cm. Most common and widespread Costa Rican hummer of lowlands and foothills. Favors humid forest edge, gardens and other semi-open areas, gallery forest. Feeds low to high; often fairly aggressive at flower patches. Males sing alone or in loose gatherings, mainly in early morning. Only medium-size, green-breasted, and rusty-tailed hummer in Costa Rica. Male has red bill, iridescent throat and chest, buffy-gray belly; female has dark maxilla, duller throat and chest, pale grayish belly. Chest can look scaly, cf. larger Scaly-breasted Hummingbird (p. 216), and often rather blue-toned, cf. smaller Blue-chested and Charming Humminbirds. **SOUNDS:** Hard to sharp staccato chips from perch and when feeding, typically a higher nasal *tük tük...*on Pacific slope, and noticeably different, harder clicking chips on Caribbean slope; downslurred rattled trill when agitated, 1–2 secs. High rapid twitters in chases. Varied song an unhurried short medley of high, thin, slightly squeaky to lisping notes, 2–3 secs. **STATUS:** Common to fairly common on both slopes, locally to 1800m, least numerous in drier nw. lowlands. (Mexico to n. S America.)

BLUE-VENTED [STEELY-VENTED] HUMMINGBIRD *Saucerrotia (Amazilia) [saucerottei] hoffmanni* 9–9.5cm. Medium-size hummer of lowland and foothill woodland and edge, plantations, gardens. Feeds low to high, from roadside flower banks to canopy; males sing alone from low to mid-level perches. Distinctive if seen well, with diagnostic deep blue tail (often looks simply dark when closed). Male has glittering green underparts with white thigh tufts, deep blue undertail coverts; female duller green below, undertail coverts edged dusky buff. **SOUNDS:** Hard, ticking, downslurred *tsik*, distinct from Pacific Rufous-tailed Hummingbird, often repeated steadily when feeding; dry rattled trills when agitated. Song a short, rather simple, high squeaky phrase, repeated, such as *tsirr seen seen*. **STATUS:** Fairly common on both slopes, rarely to 1800m. (Costa Rica to w. Panama.)

BLUE-THROATED GOLDENTAIL (SAPPHIRE) *Chlorestes (Hylocharis) eliciae* 8.5–9cm. Small hummer of humid lowland forest and woodland, gallery forest, second growth, gardens. Feeds low to high, from canopy to low in ornamental verbena plantings; males often gather to sing throughout day from perches at mid–upper levels in fairly open but shady subcanopy. Note small size (smaller than Rufous-tailed Hummingbird), bright red bill, greenish-gold tail. Despite the colorful name, can appear rather dull unless seen in the right light (see p. 213). Cf. Rufous-tailed Hummingbird. **SOUNDS:** High sharp *sik* in flight. Varied song a high, lisping, short rhythmic twitter, typically 1–2 secs, repeated. **STATUS:** Uncommon to fairly common locally in nw. lowlands and on s. Pacific slope, scarce elsewhere, to 1000m. (Mexico to n. Colombia.)

CINNAMON HUMMINGBIRD *Amazilia rutila* 9.5–10cm. Distinctive, medium-size hummer of lowland deciduous forest and edge, semi-open areas with hedgerows, gardens; mainly in drier regions. Feeds low to high, often fairly aggressive; singing males sometimes in small loose gatherings at low to mid-levels. No similar species in Costa Rica: note wholly cinnamon underparts, rusty tail. Viewed from behind, cf. Rufous-tailed Hummingbird, which prefers humid areas. Sexes similar; imm. has mostly dark maxilla. **SOUNDS:** Fairly rough dry chips and rattling chatters. Varied song a short medley of high, thin, slightly squeaky notes. **STATUS:** Fairly common to common on n. Pacific slope, locally to 1200m in Central Valley. (Mexico to Costa Rica.)

female

males

RUFOUS-TAILED HUMMINGBIRD

BLUE-VENTED HUMMINGBIRD

adults

BLUE-THROATED GOLDENTAIL

female

males

CINNAMON HUMMINGBIRD

adults

SWIFTS (APODIDAE; 10 SPECIES) Worldwide family of supreme aerialists, only seen perched at roosts and nests, which tend to be in caves, behind waterfalls, other inaccessible places. Ages/sexes similar in most species, different in a few; adult appearance attained in about 1 year.

CHESTNUT-COLLARED SWIFT *Streptoprocne rutile* 12.5–14cm; WS 30.5–33cm. Mainly foothills and highlands; nests in caves and rocky gorges. Usually in groups of 10–100 birds, associating readily with *Chaetura* and other swifts. Flight recalls *Chaetura* but stronger, less fluttery, with more frequent gliding; note longer tail (distinctly notched on male) than *Chaetura*, more scimitar-like wings, voice; chestnut collar diagnostic when present (lacking on 1st-year and some females). SOUNDS: Dry buzzy crackling notes and chatters; suggests electricity crackling in power lines; occasional screechy notes thrown in. STATUS: Fairly common, mainly 1000–2500m but ranges locally to coastal lowlands. (Mexico to S America.)

WHITE-COLLARED SWIFT *Streptoprocne zonaris* 20–21.5cm; WS 48.5–53cm. Wide-ranging, spectacular large swift; nests colonially in caves, often near waterfalls. Feeds low to high, at times sweeping past at head height when wings make strong rushing sound; soars frequently, wings spread in paddle-like bulges. Usually in groups, locally 100s, from dispersed feeding bands to tightly synchronized screaming squadrons that wheel high overhead. Note large size, broad white collar, forked tail. 1st-year has white hindcollar, weak whitish scaling across upper neck. In poor light, cf. Black Swift, Bat Falcon. SOUNDS: Loud screaming and screeching chatters can suggest parakeets. STATUS: Fairly common to common; breeds locally in mountains, ranges widely to lowlands. (Mexico to S America.)

GENUS *CYPSELOIDES* (3 species). 'Terrestrial' equivalent to storm petrels, breeding at scattered colony sites and ranging widely to feed; thus could be encountered anywhere in the country. Black and White-chinned routinely commute long distances daily, as from mountains to coastal lowlands. *Cypseloides* often feed much higher overhead than *Chaetura* and are easily overlooked unless flying lower near roost sites, or brought low by rainy weather. ID challenging, and many birds often best left unidentified to species.

BLACK SWIFT *Cypseloides niger* 14–18cm; WS 36–42cm. Breeds in highlands, often behind waterfalls; ranges over varied habitats, at times in flocks; associates with other swifts when feeding. Wingbeats strong, not hurried; often soars and glides. Note size (bigger than Chestnut-collared Swift, smaller than White-collared), broad-based, sickle-like wings; in some lights shows striking frosty whitish forehead. Male has forked tail. N American migrants average larger than Costa Rican breeding birds. SOUNDS: Fairly hard dry chips, usually in short series, *chi-chi-chi-chit*, not harsh or buzzy. STATUS: Local breeder Apr–Sep in highlands, ranging to foothills and lowlands; winter status in Costa Rica unclear. Uncommon migrant Sep–Oct, Apr–May, mainly on Pacific slope. (Breeds w. N America to Panama, winters S America.)

*****WHITE-CHINNED SWIFT** *Cypseloides cryptus* 14–15cm; WS 33–35.5cm. Breeds in highlands, often around waterfalls; ranges over varied habitats, at times in flocks, and associates with other swifts when feeding. Slightly larger, chunkier than Chestnut-collared Swift, with bigger head, squared tail. Stockier, less sickle-winged than Black Swift, but longer-winged and longer-tailed, less compact than Spot-fronted Swift. Wingbeats rapid, direct flight heavy-bodied, but soars readily. White chin can be distinct when throat is full of food, but cf. Black Swift, which also can show whitish chin when throat is full. Some birds (imms.? females?) have whitish mottling on belly or whitish vent band. SOUNDS: Sharp buzzy chips and chatters; slightly more shrieking, less 'electric' than Chestnut-collared Swift. STATUS: Uncommon to scarce resident; potentially wide-ranging. (Honduras to S America.)

SPOT-FRONTED SWIFT *Cypseloides cherriei* 12.5–13.5cm, WS 30.5–32.5cm. Breeds in highlands and foothills, often around waterfalls; ranges over varied habitats, often in small groups. Associates with other swifts, especially Chestnut-collared. Similar size to Chestnut-collared Swift but chunkier, with bigger head, shorter squared tail. Wingbeats rapid, direct flight heavy-bodied, but soars readily, at least for short periods. In good light, white 'headlight' spots can be striking, postocular spot usually less so. SOUNDS: High sharp chips often accelerate into rhythmic, slightly buzzy phrases, *tchip, tchip chípi-chípi-chirr-chirr, chípi-chípi-chirr-chirr.…* STATUS: Uncommon to scarce resident; perhaps mainly in Pacific slope foothills. (Costa Rica to S America.)

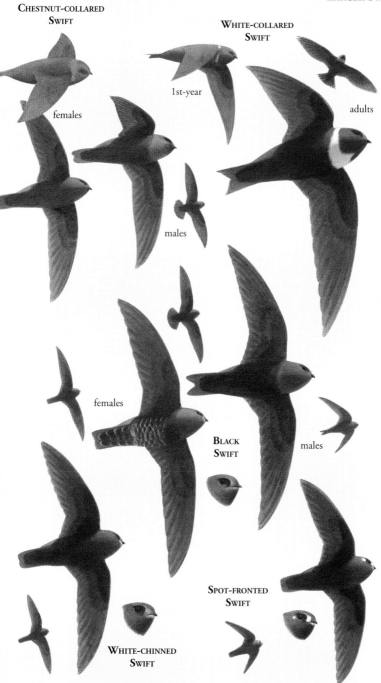

CHESTNUT-COLLARED SWIFT

WHITE-COLLARED SWIFT

1st-year

females

adults

males

females

BLACK SWIFT

males

SPOT-FRONTED SWIFT

WHITE-CHINNED SWIFT

GENUS *CHAETURA* (4 species). Widespread, taxonomically vexed New World genus of small swifts with stiff shaft spines projecting on tail tip (visible with good views); throat and rump variably paler than rest of dark sooty plumage. Often in small groups, typically flying lower than *Cypseloides* swifts, often not much higher than treetops; associate readily with swallows. Rapid, at times almost fluttering wingbeats interspersed with brief glides; soar less often than *Cypseloides*. Nest in hollow trees, buildings.

CHIMNEY SWIFT *Chaetura pelagica* 12–12.5cm; WS 30–32.5cm. Transient migrant over Caribbean lowlands and adjacent foothills, especially near the coast. Often in loose groups, typically with a focused heading: southeast in fall, northwest in spring. Flight strong and fast with rapid wingbeats and only brief gliding; soars only occasionally, unlike larger swifts. Mixes with feeding groups of Hellmayr's Swift, when larger size and slower, stronger wingbeats of Chimney can be appreciated, but plumage rather similar. **SOUNDS:** Usually silent; high sharp chips and short twitters rarely in interactions, fuller and mellower than Hellmayr's and Richmond's Swifts. **STATUS:** Sporadically fairly common to common Oct–early Nov, mid-Mar to Apr on Caribbean slope, especially near coast; rarely to 1500m. (Breeds e. N America, winters S America.)

*RICHMOND'S [VAUX'S] SWIFT *Chaetura [vauxi] richmondi* 10.5–11cm; WS 25–27.5cm. Common small swift of highlands and foothills, foraging over varied habitats from forest and towns to pastures and lakes. See genus note. Not easily told from Hellmayr's Swift of Caribbean lowlands but throat typically paler and more contrasting whereas rump typically duller and browner. Lacks contrasting pale rump patch of Costa Rican Swift. Cf. larger, longer-winged Chimney Swift. Wing molt mainly May–Sep? **SOUNDS:** High thin chips and twitters, including an accelerating, overall descending *tsi-tsi-si-sirr*; higher and shriller than Chimney Swift. **STATUS:** Fairly common locally on both slopes, mainly 700–2000m, at times to 3000m and (mainly in rainy weather) down to coastal lowlands. (Mexico to Panama.)

*HELLMAYR'S [GRAY-RUMPED] SWIFT *Chaetura [cinereiventris] phaeopygos* 10.5–11cm, WS 25–27cm. Common small swift of humid Caribbean lowlands, where replaces Richmond's Swift of higher elevations; ranges over forested and open habitats, rivers. See genus note. From Richmond's Swift by duller throat, grayer and more contrastingly pale rump. Cf. Chimney Swift, which is larger and longer winged, evident in direct comparison. Costa Rican Swift does not overlap in range, differs in smaller and brighter rump patch. Wing molt mainly Jun–Oct? **SOUNDS:** High single sharp chips and twitters, relatively shrill and thin. **STATUS:** Fairly common locally on Caribbean slope, to 1000m. (Honduras to Panama.)

COSTA RICAN [BAND-RUMPED] SWIFT *Chaetura [spinicauda] fumosa* 10.5–11cm, WS 25–27.5cm. Distinctive small swift of humid Pacific lowlands, ranging over forested and open habitats, rivers. See genus note. From below difficult to distinguish from Richmond's Swift, but has more restricted pale throat area; from above note distinctive, strongly contrasting pale rump patch. Wing molt mainly Mar–Jul? **SOUNDS:** High sharp chips and twitters, lower and richer than Richmond's (and Hellmayr's). **STATUS:** Fairly common locally on s. Pacific slope, to 1500m. (Costa Rica to w. Panama.)

LESSER SWALLOW-TAILED SWIFT *Panyptila cayennensis* 12.5–14cm; WS 29–31cm. Distinctive and handsome small swift of humid lowlands, over forest, adjacent semi-open areas, water bodies. Singles or small groups associate readily with flocks of *Chaetura* but also fly higher and separate. Flight very fast with flickering wingbeats, short glides, tail usually closed in a point. No similar species in Costa Rica. Nest a long funnel (up to 1m long) of plant down and spider webs attached to side of large trunk or rock face, entrance at bottom. **SOUNDS:** Thin reedy chips and twitters; short, slightly explosive *speeez*, fading abruptly. **STATUS:** Uncommon to fairly common locally on both slopes, to 1000m; rarely to Central Valley. (Mexico to S America.)

CHIMNEY SWIFT

RICHMOND'S SWIFT

HELLMAYR'S SWIFT

COSTA RICAN SWIFT

LESSER SWALLOW-TAILED SWIFT

SWALLOWS (HIRUNDINIDAE; 13 SPECIES) Worldwide family of aerial insectivores recalling swifts, but the families not closely related. Wingbeats less stiff than swifts, perch readily on wires, buildings; migrant roosts in reedbeds and towns can number 1000s. Ages differ, sexes similar or different; adult appearance attained 1st year in most species, 2nd year in Purple Martin.

MARTINS (3 species). Large swallows with forked tails; often nest in small colonies in cavities of dead trees, buildings. Flight powerful, with strong wingbeats, frequent gliding and soaring; often range more widely and higher than other swallows; migrant roosts locally of 1000s, often on buildings.

PURPLE MARTIN *Progne subis* 18–19.5cm. Transient migrant over varied open and wooded habitats, mainly coastal lowlands. Mixes readily with other swallows; large flocks and roosts on Caribbean slope during migration. Blue-black adult male distinctive, wholly dark. Female/imm. variable: note contrasting paler forehead and hindcollar. Also note deeper tail fork of Purple vs. Gray-breasted, large dark centers to undertail coverts and distinct dark streaks below on adult female Purple. Juv. whiter below than female, with only faint dark streaks; juv. male bluish above, juv. female brownish above, more similar to Gray-breasted Martin; note deeper tail fork, paler hindcollar of Purple. 1st-summer male resembles female but with scattered blue-black feathers on breast. **SOUNDS:** Downslurred, relatively low-pitched, rich twangy *chreu*; higher, slightly burry nasal *chrrih*. **STATUS:** Sporadically fairly common to common late Jul–early Nov, mid-Jan to May on Caribbean slope; small numbers occur inland and on Pacific slope, mainly in fall. (Breeds N America to Mexico, winters mainly S America.)

GRAY-BREASTED MARTIN *Progne chalybea* 16.5–18cm. Widespread in open and semi-open country of lowlands in towns, forest clearings, on coastal cliffs and rocky islets. Ranges widely over open and wooded habitats, mixing readily with other swallows. Both sexes resemble female Purple Martin but slightly smaller with less strongly forked tail, cleaner white underparts (fine dusky streaks rarely visible in field); lack pale hindcollar but forehead can be paler. Adult male blue-black above, female has dull blue gloss above; juv. dark sooty brownish above, paler throat and chest contrast less strongly with belly than adult. Cf. smaller rough-winged swallows. **SOUNDS:** Chirps slightly higher, burrier, more twittering than Purple Martin, may equally suggest Tree Swallow. Song a chirping, slightly jerky slow-paced warble. **STATUS:** Common to fairly common breeder Feb–Aug on both slopes, to 1700m. Wanders more widely Sep–Jan, when absent from many breeding areas, uncommon to fairly common locally on Pacific slope; more widespread and numerous Aug–Oct, Jan–Feb, when n. migrants may occur. (Mexico to S America.)

***BROWN-BANDED [BROWN-CHESTED] MARTIN** *Phaeoprogne (Progne) [tapera] fusca* 16–18cm. Rare nonbr. migrant to open habitats, especially near water. Like other martins, often perches on wires, feeds over open country, lakes, rivers. Flight strong, with snappier wingbeats than Gray-breasted Martin, and glides on stiff bowed wings. Distinctive, suggests a giant Bank Swallow: note brown upperparts, brown breast band contrasting with whitish throat and neck sides; median stripe of dark spots on breast variable, can be hard to see. Wing molt mainly May–Sep vs. Jul–Dec in Gray-breasted. **SOUNDS:** Burry *chirr* and raspy nasal *jihr*, often doubled or in short series; lower and distinctly burrier than Gray-breasted Martin. **STATUS:** Very rare and irregular nonbr. migrant, mainly Feb–early May, Aug to mid-Dec; most records from Pacific coastal lowlands but could occur anywhere. (Breeds s. S America, winters cen. S America to s. Cen America.)

PURPLE MARTIN

1st-summer male

juv.

females

male

GRAY-BREASTED MARTIN

female

male

BROWN-BANDED MARTIN

NORTHERN ROUGH-WINGED SWALLOW *Stelgidopteryx serripennis* 12–13.5cm. Fairly chunky, rather plain swallow of open and semi-open country, lightly wooded regions, often near water; nests in holes in banks, road cuts, buildings. Tail slightly notched, appears rounded when spread. Flight distinctly swooping, wingbeats smooth and floppy, not snappy; rarely soars and glides for prolonged periods, cf. martins. Nests in scattered pairs or small groups. Note brown upperparts, dingy brownish breast (throat variably tinged cinnamon in fresh plumage), notched tail, white undertail coverts (can have 1–2 dark subterminal spots). Southern Rough-winged Swallow has contrasting pale rump, black distal undertail coverts. **SOUNDS:** Slightly wet buzzy *zzurt* and *zzrih*, harsher calls when alarmed, often in rapid series; typically drier and rougher than Southern Rough-winged. **STATUS:** Uncommon to fairly common but local breeder Mar–Aug, mainly 300–1800m. Uncommon to fairly common migrant, Aug–early May, mainly in lowlands. (Breeds N America to Costa Rica, winters Mexico to Panama.)

SOUTHERN ROUGH-WINGED SWALLOW *Stelgidopteryx ruficollis* 12–13cm. Replaces Northern Rough-winged Swallow as a breeding bird in humid lowlands, but the species occur together, especially in fall–winter. Habits similar to Northern Rough-winged but all plumages of Southern have contrasting pale rump; also note black distal undertail coverts. Juv. rump washed cinnamon, cf. Cliff Swallow. **SOUNDS:** Rolled, slightly burry *chrih* or *chirrih*, averaging mellower, less gruff than Northern Rough-winged; higher *chrieh-chrieh* in alarm. **STATUS:** Fairly common to uncommon, to 1800m; more widespread in fall–winter, when small numbers range to nw. lowlands, but status vs. Northern Rough-winged in many areas awaits elucidation. (Honduras to S America.)

(AMERICAN) CLIFF SWALLOW *Petrochelidon pyrrhonota* 12–13.5cm. Chunky, rather square-tailed transient migrant swallow of open and semi-open areas, often near water. Regularly mixes with other swallows, feeding and perched on wires. Note dark throat contrasting strongly with pale underparts; whitish forehead of n. breeders distinctive (Mexican breeders have rusty forehead), and rump often paler than Cave Swallow; wing molt in winter, vs. late summer–fall in Cave. Juv. has weaker head pattern, browner back, like adult by spring. **SOUNDS:** Burry *chrreh* and variations; alarm call a downslurred, twangy nasal *chiehr*. **STATUS:** Common to fairly common Aug–early Nov, Feb to mid-May, mainly in coastal lowlands; scarce and local in winter, mainly on Pacific slope. (Breeds N America to Mexico, winters S America.)

*CAVE SWALLOW** *Petrochelidon fulva* 12–13.5cm. Chunky, rather square-tailed migrant swallow found in varied open habitats, often near water; regularly with other swallows feeding and perched on wires, as singles or small flocks. Note pale rusty face and throat, contrasting poorly with pale underparts, cf. Cliff Swallow. **SOUNDS:** Nasal *zweih* and *chrieh*, suggesting Barn Swallow, less burry than Cliff Swallow. **STATUS:** Scarce and irregular Nov–Feb in nw. lowlands; first detected Costa Rica in 2000s. (Breeds Mexico and sw. US, to Greater Antilles, winters to Cen America.)

BARN SWALLOW *Hirundo rustica* 12.5–14.5cm + streamers. Slender, fork-tailed migrant swallow widespread in open and semi-open habitats, often near human habitation and water. Roosts can number 1000s, sometimes on wires in towns. Adult has dark rusty throat, diagnostic long tail streamers, variable rusty to buff wash below (can fade to whitish in winter). Juv. has shorter tail, throat and forehead can fade to whitish; note white subterminal tail spots. Winter birds often in wing molt. **SOUNDS:** Upslurred squeaky *chiet* or *zwieh*, often run into twittering series; agitated call a clipped *pi-chiip*. **STATUS:** Common to fairly common Aug–Nov, Feb–May, mainly in coastal lowlands; smaller numbers inland, rarely to 3000m; uncommon to locally common in winter, especially on Pacific slope. (Breeds Holarctic; winters Mexico to S America.)

juv.

Northern migrant

NORTHERN ROUGH-WINGED SWALLOW

Resident

SOUTHERN ROUGH-WINGED SWALLOW

juv.

Mexican

CLIFF SWALLOW

CAVE SWALLOW

Northern

faded juv.

BARN SWALLOW

fresh adult

*BLUE-AND-WHITE SWALLOW *Pygochelidon cyanoleuca* 11.5–13.5cm. Common and widespread swallow of highlands and foothills; ranges from cities and farmland to páramo and forest; nests in holes in banks, buildings, hollow trees. Locally in flocks, regularly gathering on wires with other swallows. Flight quick and 'twinkling' with brief glides, at times soaring high overhead. Note black undertail coverts, deeply forked tail. Juv. brownish above with variable dusky wash across breast, shallower tail fork. Comprises 2 groups that may represent species: smaller resident **Mountain Swallow** *P. [c.] cyanoleuca* (11.5–12.5cm) with blackish underwing coverts, more extensive black on undertail coverts, Jun–Oct wing molt; and larger austral migrant **Patagonian Swallow** *P. [c.] patagonica* (12.5–13.5cm) with dusky whitish underwing coverts, slightly deeper tail fork, Mar–Jul wing molt. SOUNDS: **Mountain** has downslurred, high burry *tzzih* and *tssiu*; varied, high and often rather buzzy chipping and twittering; **Patagonian** a lower buzzy *dzzzhir* and *zzhie*. STATUS: **Mountain** is common to fairly common resident, mainly above 500m, rarely lower. **Patagonian** is austral nonbr. migrant Apr–Aug n. regularly to Panama, likely overlooked in Costa Rica; any birds in lowlands should be checked. (Costa Rica to S America.)

VIOLET-GREEN SWALLOW *Tachycineta thalassina* 11.5–12.5cm. Rather compact, short-tailed migrant swallow found as singles or small flocks that associate with other swallows. Flight rather quick and 'twinkling,' often fairly high overhead. Note white 'saddlebags' (rarely can appear white-rumped), short tail (at rest, wing-tips project past tail tip; cf. larger, longer-tailed Tree Swallow), face pattern. SOUNDS: High chipping *chi-chit* and variations, higher and drier than Tree Swallow, less burry than Mangrove Swallow. STATUS: Scarce and irregular Oct–Mar, mainly in nw. lowlands, also rarely in highlands. (Breeds w. N America and Mexico, winters Mexico to Costa Rica.)

TREE SWALLOW *Tachycineta bicolor* 13.5–14.5cm. Rather chunky migrant swallow of varied open habitats, often near water; singles or small groups often with other swallows. Flight fairly powerful, often direct, recalling martins rather than smaller, more 'twinkling' Violet-green and Mangrove Swallows. Note notched tail, white underparts, face pattern. 1st-year female dusky gray-brown above with dingy breast band; male and adult female metallic greenish blue above. SOUNDS: Chirping *chrit* and *chri-chii*, lower, more liquid than Mangrove Swallow. STATUS: Scarce and irregular Nov–Apr in nw. lowlands; could occur anywhere, mainly below 1500m. (Breeds N America, winters s. US to Panama.)

MANGROVE SWALLOW *Tachycineta albilinea* 11–12cm. Small spritely swallow never far from water, from mangroves and coastal lagoons to larger rivers well inland; nests in cavities in dead trees, rocks, buildings. Flight fast and twinkling, often low over water; perches on sticks and rocks in water, and with other swallows on wires. White rump diagnostic; also note white underwing coverts (dark on Tree and Violet-green Swallows), small white forehead chevron. Juv. dusky gray-brown above, attains adult plumage by winter. SOUNDS: High chipping *chrrit* and *chiri-chrit*, at times buzzier notes. Song a varied series of chirps and burry chips. STATUS: Fairly common to common on both slopes, locally to 1000m. (Mexico to Panama.)

BANK SWALLOW (SAND MARTIN) *Riparia riparia* 11.5–12.5cm. Small, rather compact migrant swallow of varied open habitats, commonly near water; often with other swallows feeding over water, resting on wires. Distinctive: note small size, cleft tail, white throat and neck sides offset by brown breast band. Cf. imm. Tree Swallow, rough-winged swallows. SOUNDS: Rolled gravelly *zzzr*, often doubled; drier and buzzier than rough-winged swallows. STATUS: Sporadically common mid-Aug to Nov, Mar to mid-May, in lowlands, locally to 1500m; uncommon to scarce and local in winter. (Breeds Holarctic; winters Mexico to S America.)

**Migrant
(Patagonian)**

BLUE-AND-WHITE SWALLOW

juv.

**Resident
(Mountain)**

adult

**VIOLET-GREEN
SWALLOW**

female

males

TREE SWALLOW

imm.
female

adult male

MANGROVE SWALLOW

BANK SWALLOW

adult

244

OVENBIRDS (FURNARIIDAE; 35 SPECIES) Large New World family most diverse in South America. Plumage mainly shades of brown, many species with a pale wingstripe visible in flight. Ages similar or slightly different, sexes similar. Voice and behavior helpful for ID.

WOODCREEPERS (16 species). Formerly considered a separate family and, as name suggests, typically creep and hitch on trunks and branches, like woodpeckers. For ID note overall size, habitat, behavior, bill size and shape, extent of any paler streaks and spots, voice (sing mostly very early and at dusk).

*NORTHERN WEDGE-BILLED WOODCREEPER *Glyphorynchus [spirurus] pectoralis* 14–15cm. Very small, short-billed woodcreeper of humid forest, taller second growth, plantations. Low to high on trunks of trees all sizes; often fairly active. Joins mixed flocks. Often looks rather dark: note small size, wedge-shaped bill, pale eyebrow, spotted chest. SOUNDS: Song a high, squeaky, twittering crescendo, overall slightly ascending, ends abruptly, 1–2.5 secs. Sharp, high chipping *chrrik*, often doubled, and longer series of chips that may suggest a scolding squirrel. STATUS: Fairly common to common on both slopes, to 1500m. (Mexico to S America.)

*GRAYISH [OLIVACEOUS] WOODCREEPER *Sittasomus [griseicapillus] griseus* 15–16cm. Small plain woodcreeper of humid forest, taller second growth, gallery forest. Low to high on trunks of trees all sizes; often fairly active, spirals up one tree before dropping to base of nearby tree and starting again. Joins mixed flocks. Note small size, lack of streaking, small slender bill. SOUNDS: Song a fast-paced, overslurred, liquid trill, usually about 1 sec; cf. Plain Xenops. Also quiet churring trills that can last 2–3 mins, and a short, dry, rattling trill that suggests Long-billed Gnatwren. STATUS: Fairly common on both slopes, mainly 500–1700m; uncommon and local in drier nw. lowlands. (Mexico to n. S America.)

TAWNY-WINGED WOODCREEPER *Dendrocincla anabatina* 18–19cm. Rather chunky woodcreeper of humid lowland forest, mangroves. Mainly at low to mid-levels, often on thin trunks at ant swarms where overlooked easily. Note pale eyebrow, bicolored wings, whitish throat; often raises slightly bushy crest. SOUNDS: Plaintive, sometimes sharp slurred whistle, *tcheu!* or *tchee-u*, at times re-peated steadily. Song (?) an insistent, prolonged staccato rattle of rough nasal chips almost slow enough to count, *chri-chri...*, sometimes to over a min. STATUS: Fairly common (at ant swarms, otherwise seen infrequently), mainly on s. Pacific slope; rarely to 1500m. (Mexico to w. Panama.)

PLAIN-BROWN WOODCREEPER *Dendrocincla fuliginosa* 20–21.5cm. Rather chunky, notably plain but distinctive woodcreeper of humid lowland forest, adja-cent second growth. Habits much like Tawny-winged Woodcreeper. Note dark mustache offsetting paler gray face. SOUNDS: Slightly explosive tinny, underslurred *p'SIEK*, at times with rough, snarling quality. Song an overslurred or slightly de-scending nasal rattle, 1.5–3 secs, slowing into a few laughing notes at the end. Also fairly rapid, prolonged chipping rattles, notes too fast to count, *dirr-irr...*, often pulsating and sometimes to over a min. STATUS: Fairly common (at ant swarms, otherwise seen infrequently) on Caribbean slope, locally to 1000m. (Honduras to S America.)

RUDDY WOODCREEPER *Dendrocincla homochroa* 19–20cm. Rather chunky, bright ruddy woodcreeper of humid lowland and foothill forest, adjacent second growth. Habits much like Tawny-winged Woodcreeper. Note bushy face, paler eyering. SOUNDS: High, reedy, slightly plaintive slurred *sreeah* and more drawn-out *tleeeoo*. Song a slightly descending, churring rattle, 3–4 secs; slower, slightly harsher than Plain-brown, without laughing quality. Also a prolonged, churring rattle of harsh wooden chips, up to a min or longer, slowing slightly at end; faster-paced than Tawny-winged, notes too fast to count. STATUS: Uncommon (at ant swarms, otherwise seen infrequently) on Pacific slope, to 1500m; scarce on Caribbean slope, mainly 500–1000m. (Mexico to nw. S America.)

**NORTHERN
WEDGE-BILLED
WOODCREEPER**

**GRAYISH
WOODCREEPER**

**TAWNY-WINGED
WOODCREEPER**

**PLAIN-BROWN
WOODCREEPER**

**RUDDY
WOODCREEPER**

246

STRONG-BILLED WOODCREEPER *Xiphocolaptes promeropirhynchus* 30–32cm. Very large, stout-billed woodcreeper of mature, humid foothill forest, especially with large bromeliads. Feeds low to high, often in bromeliads and sometimes on ground; joins mixed flocks of larger birds. Note overall size, long and stout pale grayish bill, whitish throat bordered by broad dark mustache. Cf. Costa Rican Woodcreeper. SOUNDS: Song a loud, often slightly descending series of (usually 4–10) paired whistles, with jerky, ratcheting cadence: higher 1st part slurred, 2nd part short, fairly abrupt, *chooh'ih chooh'ih...*, mostly 6–10 secs. Calls infrequently, a muffled, drawn-out snarl slurred into a short emphatic cluck, *ryehhr chk!* STATUS: Scarce on both slopes, mainly 500–1700m. (Mexico to S America.)

*COSTA RICAN [BLACK-BANDED] WOODCREEPER *Dendrocolaptes [picumnus] costaricensis* 26–27.5cm. Poorly known large woodcreeper of humid foothill and highland forest. Mainly at mid–upper levels; often sluggish and overlooked easily. Distinctive if seen well, with rather straight bill, streaked head and chest in contrast to plain back, barred belly. Cf. larger, much stouter-billed Strong-billed Woodcreeper. SOUNDS: Song a laughing, descending, slightly accelerating series of slightly nasal whistles, starts fairly abruptly and fades quickly at end, *Whii-whii-whii-whiihuihhuihuih*, 3–4 secs. STATUS: Scarce on Caribbean slope and locally on cen. Pacific slope, mainly 900–2000m. (Costa Rica to w. Panama.)

NORTHERN BARRED WOODCREEPER *Dendrocolaptes sanctithomae* 26–28 cm. Distinctive large woodcreeper of humid lowland forest; often at army ant swarms, where sits quietly and overlooked easily. Barring can be difficult to see in shady forest, often looks rather dark and plain overall; note dark lores, stout blackish bill with pinkish base. SOUNDS: Song a slightly ascending and intensifying series of (usually 2–8) upslurred, 2-syllable, twangy whistles that ending with a sharp upward inflection, *duuwih' duuwih'...*; sometimes breaks into quicker, shorter notes and agitated clucking. Infrequent call a downslurred, fairly quiet nasal *che'eh*. STATUS: Uncommon to fairly common on both slopes, locally to 1500m; uncommon and local in drier nw. lowlands. (Mexico to nw. Ecuador.)

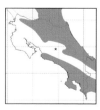

BLACK-STRIPED WOODCREEPER *Xiphorhynchus lachrymosus* 23.5–25cm. Fairly large, distinctive, and boldly marked woodcreeper of humid forest and edge, adjacent second growth woodland, plantations. Mainly at mid–upper levels, often with mixed flocks. No similar species in Costa Rica: note bold whitish to pale buff spotting on back and underparts. SOUNDS: Calls include a rich underslurred whistle, *tchooih* and a slightly descending, laughing series of (usually 3–5) quick whistled notes *whee-wee-weep*, or *whir'wee-wee-weep*. Song an overall slightly descending or overslurred, fairy rapid laughing series of notes, *hui-hui...*, mostly 2–4 secs, with 8–9 notes/sec; more prolonged and harsher when agitated; faster-paced, more laughing than Cocoa Woodcreeper. STATUS: Uncommon to fairly common on both slopes, to 1200m. (Nicaragua to nw. Ecuador.)

STRONG-BILLED
WOODCREEPER

COSTA RICAN
WOODCREEPER

BLACK-STRIPED
WOODCREEPER

NORTHERN BARRED
WOODCREEPER

248

IVORY-BILLED WOODCREEPER *Xiphorhynchus flavigaster* 22.5–25cm. Fairly large woodcreeper of lowland forest, gallery forest, adjacent plantations, mangroves. Forages low to high on trunks and larger branches, in bromeliads, and regular at army ant swarms; sometimes with mixed flocks; often rather sluggish. Note relatively large size, long stout bill (not strikingly ivory-colored, often dusky pale pinkish overall, sometimes with mostly dark maxilla), bold pale droplet-streaks on back, and voice. Cocoa Woodcreeper (limited overlap) has dark maxilla, reduced back streaking, distinct voice; cf. smaller, finer-billed Streak-headed Woodcreeper. SOUNDS: Common call a fairly abrupt slurred whistle, *tcheu!* or *tchoo*. Song an overall descending or overslurred, fairly fast-paced laughing series of clear whistles, often slowing and slurring slightly at end, mostly 2–6 secs with 8–9 notes/sec; sometimes longer series, rising and falling. Laughing series at times start hesitantly, other times preceded by a quick whistled roll or followed by an abrupt, upslurred *whee whee-wheep!* that is also given separately. STATUS: Uncommon to fairly common on n. Pacific slope, most numerous 400–900m, scarce in adjacent n. Caribbean lowlands. (Mexico to nw. Costa Rica.)

COCOA [BUFF-THROATED] WOODCREEPER *Xiphorhynchus susurrans* 21.5–23cm. Fairly large woodcreeper of humid forest, adjacent second-growth woodland, plantations, mangroves, gallery forest. Forages low to high, poking in crevices and bromeliads; sometimes with mixed feeding flocks; often rather sluggish. Cf. Ivory-billed Woodcreeper, smaller and finer-billed Streak-headed Woodcreeper. SOUNDS: Song a steady, slightly laughing series of rich upslurred whistles, at times rising and falling slightly overall, *weet-weet...*, mainly 3–6 secs with 3–5 notes/sec, rarely to 15 secs or longer; slower-paced, less laughing than Black-striped Woodcreeper song. Calls include a downslurred rolled *chirrr*, singly or in short series, may suggest Boat-billed Flycatcher; and a descending, inflected nasal *tch'eu*. STATUS: Fairly common to common on both slopes, locally to 1000m; scarce and local in drier nw. lowlands. (Guatemala to nw. S America.)

***SOUTHERN SPOTTED WOODCREEPER** *Xiphorhynchus [erythropygius] aequatorialis* 22–23.5cm. Medium-large woodcreeper of humid foothill forest, cloud forest. Forages low to high on trunks and larger branches, often at bromeliads. Distinctive, with pale buff goggles, spotted underparts; fairly stout straight bill extensively dark above. Cf. Southern Spot-crowned, Ivory-billed, and Cherrie's Woodcreepers. SOUNDS: Song a descending, unhurried series of 2–6 drawn-out, melancholy, slightly downslurred whistles, *tcheeeeu cheeeeu, cheeeeu...*, about 1/sec, often with a slightly quavering quality at the start of each note; 1st note often strongest and falls most strongly. Call a short, descending, strongly rolled *whier'r'r'ru* with quality similar to start of song notes. STATUS: Fairly common on both slopes, mainly 500–1700m. (Costa Rica to w. Ecuador.)

***CHERRIE'S [LONG-TAILED] WOODCREEPER** *Deconychura [longicauda] typica* 18–20cm. Medium-size, rather slender, long-tailed woodcreeper of humid foothill forest. Note slender, medium-length bill, variable pale spectacles, spotted breast, and often a slightly shaggy nape; male appreciably larger and longer-tailed than female. Often rather quick and active, mainly at low to mid-levels on trunks and larger branches; joins mixed flocks. SOUNDS: Song a fairly rapid, ringing or vaguely laughing and overall descending series of piping chips, slightly hesitant at start and slowing at end, *chii-chii...*, 10–17 secs. STATUS: Uncommon to rare on both slopes, mainly 400–1300m; also to near sea level on s. Pacific slope. (Honduras to n. Colombia.)

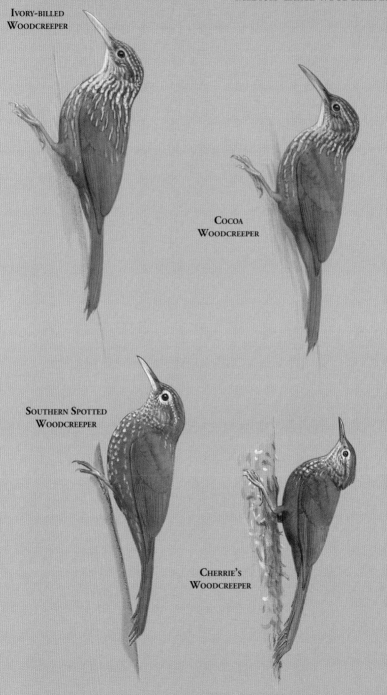

IVORY-BILLED
WOODCREEPER

COCOA
WOODCREEPER

SOUTHERN SPOTTED
WOODCREEPER

CHERRIE'S
WOODCREEPER

250

STREAK-HEADED WOODCREEPER *Lepidocolaptes souleyetii* 19–20.5cm. Medium-size, slender-billed woodcreeper of forest edge, woodland, semi-open areas with hedgerows and taller trees, plantations. Mainly at mid–upper levels on trunks and branches; often fairly quick and active, much more so than Ivory-billed Woodcreeper. Note fine, mostly pale bill, streaked crown. Cf. Ivory-billed and Southern Spot-crowned Woodcreepers (limited elevational overlap with latter). SOUNDS: Song a descending, rapid rolled trill or rattle, suggesting Grayish Woodcreeper but lower, less liquid, slower-paced, 1.5–2 secs. Call a short trilled *eeihrrr* or *chirrr*, with similar quality. STATUS: Fairly common to common on both slopes to 1000m; in smaller numbers locally to 1600m. (Mexico to nw. S America.)

*SOUTHERN SPOT-CROWNED WOODCREEPER *Lepidocolaptes [affinis] neglectus* 20.5–21.5cm. Medium-size, slender-billed woodcreeper of humid highland forest, adjacent clearings with taller trees. Mainly at mid–upper levels on mossy trunks and branches; joins mixed flocks. No similar species in most of range: note spotted crown, slender pale bill, mostly plain back, bold pale streaking on underparts, cf. larger Southern Spotted Woodcreeper, lowland Streak-headed Woodcreeper. SOUNDS: Overslurred, slightly squeaky *skwieh*, at times in short series, such as *skwieh kwieh kwieh*. Song an overall descending, slightly squeaky, chippering rattle, 2–3 secs, often introduced with a single call. STATUS: Fairly common to uncommon, mainly above 1000m in Northern Mts., above 1200m in Central and Talamanca Mts., very rarely down to 500m on Caribbean slope. (Costa Rica to w. Panama.)

BROWN-BILLED SCYTHEBILL *Campylorhamphus pusillus* 22–24cm. Medium-size woodcreeper with strongly arched bill, found in humid forest, especially mossy foothill forest. Mainly at mid–upper levels on trunks and branches, probing in crevices, palm fronds, bromeliads. Joins mixed flock but can be wary and difficult to see well. Distinctive, with long, sickle-shaped bill (which is pinkish, not brown), distinct pale streaking and spotting on head. SOUNDS: Song a varied, overall rather stuttering and descending series of short melancholy whistles, often alternated with bursts of chippering, such as *ti-ti ti-ti-ti-chwee chwee chwee ti-ti-tchi-wheer t-t-chi-wheer*, mainly 3–6 secs; at times a simpler short series of plaintive slurred whistles, the 1st longer, *tcheeeeuee tchwee twee twee twee*, quality recalling Southern Spotted Woodcreeper and at times ending with a short descending whinny. STATUS: Uncommon to scarce on both slopes, mainly 300–1500m, and in s. Pacific lowlands. (Costa Rica to nw. S America.)

BUFFY TUFTEDCHEEK *Pseudocolaptes lawrencii* 19.5–21cm. Large, bulky, distinctive ovenbird of humid highland forest and adjacent clearings with taller trees, especially with mossy vine tangles, bromeliads. Mainly at mid–upper levels, often feeding in bromeliads and moving with mixed flocks. Note contrasting whitish throat and big buff cheek patches, bright rusty tail. SOUNDS: Sharp, abrupt metallic *tching!* at times repeated steadily. Song a rippling slow trill, faster and drier at first, then rising and slowing into bright squeaky chips before fading away, 3–6 secs. STATUS: Uncommon, mainly 1600m to timberline, rarely down to 1200m. (Costa Rica to w. Panama.)

STREAK-HEADED
WOODCREEPER

SOUTHERN SPOT-CROWNED
WOODCREEPER

BROWN-BILLED
SCYTHEBILL

BUFFY TUFTEDCHEEK

RUDDY TREERUNNER *Margarornis rubiginosus* 15–16cm. Small, bright rusty ovenbird of humid highland forest, adjacent second growth and clearings with trees and shrubs. Forages low to high, as singles or small groups, climbing along trunks and mossy branches, clambering among twigs, bamboo stalks, dead-leaf clusters; often with mixed flocks including bush tanagers. Could suggest a small woodcreeper but has short pinkish bill, brighter plumage, pale eyebrow (weaker on juv.). SOUNDS: High thin *sip* and varied high thin twitters, at times in prolonged rising and falling series. Song a high, thin, descending or slightly overslurred, rapid sibilant trill, about 1 sec. STATUS: Fairly common to common, from timberline down to 1400m in Northern Mts., down to 1800m in Central and Talamanca Mts. (Costa Rica to w. Panama.)

*NORTHERN SPOTTED BARBTAIL** *Premnoplex [brunnescens] brunneicauda* 13.5–14.5cm. Small dark ovenbird of humid mossy forest, adjacent second growth. Forages mainly at low to mid-levels, as singles or pairs, clambering in tangles and bromeliads, hitching along branches and trunks, cf. woodcreepers; often with mixed flocks of antwrens, *Basileuterus* warblers. Note dark brown plumage, bold buff spotting on underparts, pale eyebrow. SOUNDS: High, thin, overslurred *ssip*, at times doubled or in short series. Song a rapid-paced, rather insect-like, dry ticking trill, *tirrrrrrrrr*, 0.7–1.5 secs; could suggest a wren. STATUS: Fairly common on both slopes, mainly 600–2500m. (Costa Rica to w. Panama.)

STREAKED XENOPS *Xenops rutilans* 12–13cm. Small arboreal ovenbird of humid foothill and highland forest, adjacent taller second growth, plantations. Forages mainly at mid–upper levels on twigs and smaller branches, among vine tangles; rather agile, climbing and often hanging upside-down like a chickadee, hammering at twigs; does not use its tail for support. Ones and twos often with mixed flocks, which at lower elevations can also include Plain Xenops. Note distinct pale streaking on crown, back, and underparts, wedge-shaped bill, habits; white whisker often less striking than on Plain. SOUNDS: Poorly known in Costa Rica. Song a slightly descending, unhurried series of (6–8) high, slightly sibilant chips, *tsip tsip...*, 2–3 secs, 1st 1–2 notes often hesitant. STATUS: Uncommon to scarce on both slopes, 800–2500m. (Costa Rica to S America.)

*PLAIN XENOPS** *Xenops [minutus] genibarbis* 11–12.5cm. Small arboreal ovenbird of humid forest, adjacent taller second growth, gallery forest. Mainly at mid-levels in fairly open subcanopy on twigs and smaller branches, among vine tangles; habits much like Streaked Xenops, and often with mixed flocks. Note contrasting white whisker, lack of pale streaking on crown, back, and underparts, wedge-shaped bill, habits. SOUNDS: Song a high, fast-paced, rippling trill, overslurred and slowing at the end, 1–2 secs; typically starts with 1 or more high *tsip* or *pip* notes; suggests Grayish Woodcreeper but higher, thinner, more rippling. Calls a high thin *tseep* and hissing *psssi*. STATUS: Fairly common on both slopes, locally to 1500m; scarce and local in drier nw. lowlands. (Mexico to S America.)

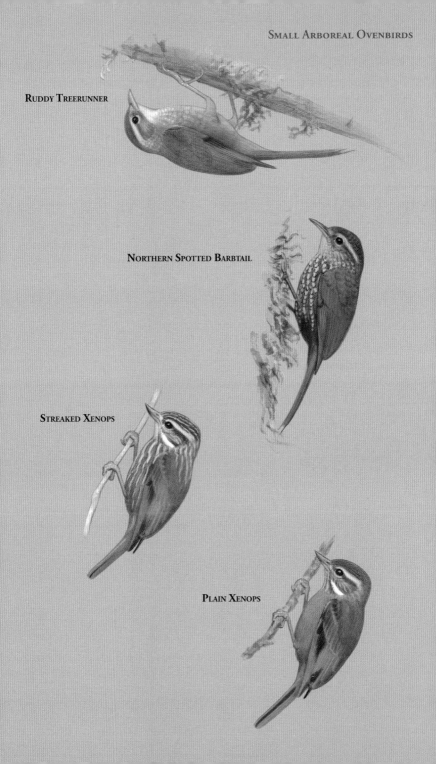

SMALL ARBOREAL OVENBIRDS

RUDDY TREERUNNER

NORTHERN SPOTTED BARBTAIL

STREAKED XENOPS

PLAIN XENOPS

254

FOLIAGE-GLEANERS AND ALLIES (8 species). Medium-size, overall brown and rusty ovenbirds that can be difficult to see well; often best detected (and identified) by voice. Also note feeding habits and height in forest, head and breast patterns, extent of any pale streaking, bill size and shape. Nest in burrows in banks.

STREAK-BREASTED TREEHUNTER *Thripadectes rufobrunneus* 20–22cm. Large, dark, rather thickset 'foliage-gleaner' of humid mossy forest and edge, adjacent dense second growth, especially in shady gullies and tangles. Forages mainly at low to mid-levels in dense understory amid vine tangles, bromeliads, dead-leaf masses, where tends to be skulking and difficult to see well; joins mixed flocks. Note stout dark bill, dark hood contrasting with bright cinnamon throat and neck sides. Cf. juv. Lineated Foliage-gleaner. **SOUNDS:** Sharp, rather low nasal clucking *chiuk*, can be repeated slowly when foraging, and a sharp, slightly nasal *chihk*, often in short series or run into slightly overslurred, slow shrieky chatters. Song (?) a harsh, sneezy, 2-note phrase, 1st note clipped, 2nd burry and overslurred, *ki'rrrih* or *ch'rreh*, often repeated steadily as fast as 2–3 phrases/sec; at times in pulses of 2–4 phrases, may suggest Boat-billed Flycatcher; songs can be alternated with longer shrieky chatters when excited. **STATUS:** Uncommon on both slopes, mainly 800–2500m, rarely to 3000m. (Costa Rica to w. Panama.)

SCALY-THROATED (SPECTACLED) FOLIAGE-GLEANER *Anabacerthia variegaticeps* 16–17cm. Arboreal, relatively conspicuous foliage-gleaner of humid foothill forest. Forages acrobatically, low to high in trees and bushes, probing in mossy vine tangles, dead-leaf clusters, epiphytes. Singles or pairs often with mixed flocks. Note bold spectacles, grayish crown, habits; cf. larger and bulkier Middle American and Chiriqui foliage-gleaners. **SOUNDS:** Common call a slightly harsh, emphatic *skweer!* or *squeezk!* Song a steady to accelerating series of sharp, high, slightly metallic to squeaky chips, mostly 5–11 secs; at times intensifying toward the end and including paired notes, *chiih! chiih! chiih! chii-chiih! chii-chiih!...*, 3–7 notes/sec. **STATUS:** Scarce and local on both slopes, mainly 800–2000m. (Mexico to w. Ecuador.)

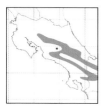

LINEATED FOLIAGE-GLEANER *Syndactyla subalaris* 18–19cm. Medium-size, streaky foliage-gleaner of humid foothill and highland forest, especially at treefalls and along streams. Forages in thickets, vine tangles, and other shady areas where can be difficult to see clearly; often with mixed flocks. Note fine buff streaking on head and breast, contrasting buff throat, relatively short bill, voice; cf. Western Woodhaunter of lower elevations. Juv. plumage (held briefly) suggests larger Streak-breasted Treehunter, but note foliage-gleaner's smaller bill, cinnamon eyebrow, paler upperparts. **SOUNDS:** Low, slightly hollow, abrupt gruff *tchek*, at times doubled and repeated steadily. Song an accelerating, intensifying, rather rapid-paced, gruff nasal chatter, 2–6 secs, sometimes descending at the end; up to 15 notes/sec. **STATUS:** Uncommon to fairly common on both slopes, mainly 1200–2400m, rarely down to 800m. (Costa Rica to S America.)

WESTERN [STRIPED] WOODHAUNTER *Automolus [subulatus] virgatus* 16.5–18cm. Medium-size, streaky foliage-gleaner of humid lowland and lower foothill forest, adjacent taller second growth, mainly at mid-levels in shady understory. Forages in dense vine tangles, bromeliads, dead-leaf clusters, and can be difficult to see clearly; often with mixed flocks of antwrens, greenlets, woodcreepers. Note fine buff streaking on head, upper back, and breast, relatively long slender bill, voice; throat and eyebrow less contrasting than Lineated Foliage-gleaner of higher elevations. **SOUNDS:** Fairly loud, abrupt, slightly burry *rrieh!* or *brrih* at times doubled and repeated steadily. Song an unhurried staccato series of sharp, downslurred nasal chips, *chiih-chiih...*, 1–7 secs; longer series often slightly rising and falling, 3–5 notes/sec. **STATUS:** Uncommon on both slopes, mainly 200–1000m. (Nicaragua to w. Ecuador.)

STREAK-BREASTED TREENHUNTER

SCALY-THROATED FOLIAGE-GLEANER

juv.

LINEATED FOLIAGE-GLEANER

WESTERN WOODHAUNTER

*MIDDLE AMERICAN [BUFF-THROATED] FOLIAGE-GLEANER *Automolus [ochrolaemus] cervinigularis* 19–20cm. Fairly bulky foliage-gleaner of humid forest, adjacent taller second growth. Mainly skulks at low to mid-levels in shady tangles, probing in dead-leaf clusters, but at times ranges into subcanopy with mixed flocks, and also digs in leaf litter. Sings from low perch, shivering its tail with each song. Note bold buff spectacles, rich buffy throat, stout bill, habits; cf. smaller, arboreal Scaly-throated Foliage-gleaner of foothills. **SOUNDS:** Low gruff *chuk*, sharp nasal *pe-duk*, and hard scolding *tchehrr*. Song a downslurred, chortling rattle, often repeated steadily early and late in the day; 1–1.5 secs. **STATUS:** Fairly common on Caribbean slope, to 1200m; spills over locally to humid n. Pacific slope. (Mexico to nw. Panama.)

CHIRIQUI [BUFF-THROATED] FOLIAGE-GLEANER *Automolus [ochrolaemus] exsertus* 19–20 cm. Pacific-slope counterpart to Middle American Foliage-gleaner (no range overlap), and until recently considered conspecific. Habitat and habits like Middle American Foliage-gleaner, from which differs in voice, also in paler throat, lack of dusky scalloping on upper breast; cf. smaller, arboreal Scaly-throated Foliage-gleaner of foothills. **SOUNDS:** Short, nasal, downslurred *nyeh*. Song a fairly slow-paced, descending, hollow nasal rattle, 0.75–1 sec, slowing slightly at the end; slower-paced than Middle American. **STATUS:** Fairly common on s. Pacific slope, to 1200m. (Costa Rica to w. Panama.)

*NORTHERN RUDDY FOLIAGE-GLEANER *Clibanornis rubiginosus* 20–21.5cm. Fairly bulky, unstreaked foliage-gleaner of humid foothill forest understory, adjacent second growth tangles, especially in shady gullies. Skulks and forages in shady tangles, dead-leaf clusters, where difficult to see clearly; most often detected by voice. Note tawny-rufous throat and upper breast, subtle paler grayish eyering, long rusty tail, cf. Tawny-throated Leaftosser. **SOUNDS:** Short hard rattle, and slowly repeated *chak*. Song a distinctive, 2-syllable nasal phrase, the 2nd part upslurred, *eh'rek'* typically 2–3×, repeated after a short pause. **STATUS:** Uncommon and local in hills surrounding Coto Brus Valley, mainly 1000–1500m. (Mexico to w. Ecuador.)

BUFF-FRONTED FOLIAGE-GLEANER *Philydor rufus* 18.5–20cm. Handsome, often relatively conspicuous, arboreal foliage-gleaner of humid foothill forest and edge, taller second growth. Mainly at mid–upper levels on branches and amid foliage, hopping and clambering easily, at times hanging upside down to poke into leaf clusters; travels with mixed flocks. Distinctive, with bright buff face and breast, dusky eyestripe, contrasting bright rusty wings and tail; cf. much smaller juv. Red-faced Spinetail. **SOUNDS:** Sharp, dry metallic *chik* or *tzik*, more resonant than somewhat similar White-throated Spadebill. Song a squeaky woodpecker-like *woika-woika…*(Stiles & Skutch 1989). **STATUS:** Scarce and local on both slopes, mainly 800–2500m. (Costa Rica to S America.)

RED-FACED SPINETAIL *Cranioleuca erythrops* 14.5–15.5cm. Small, active, arboreal ovenbird of humid foothill and highland forest and edge, adjacent second growth, plantations. Mainly at mid–upper levels on branches, twigs, amid foliage, hopping and clambering easily, at times hanging upside down to poke into dead-leaf clusters; often with mixed flocks. Adult distinctive, with contrasting rusty head, wings, tail. Juv. plumage (summer–fall) quite different, cf. larger and much brighter Buff-fronted Foliage-gleaner. **SOUNDS:** High nasal *chieh* and high sharp *tsip*, at times in excited series. Song a fairly fast-paced, accelerating series of high, thin to slightly sibilant chips, 1–2 secs, rising overall and often ending in a rapid twittering trill; also longer series, to 5 secs or more, often with an overall rather rippling cadence. **STATUS:** Fairly common on both slopes, mainly 700–2300m. (Costa Rica to w. Ecuador.)

MIDDLE AMERICAN
FOLIAGE-GLEANER

CHIRIQUI FOLIAGE-GLEANER

NORTHERN RUDDY
FOLIAGE-GLEANER

juv.

BUFF-FRONTED
FOLIAGE-GLEANER

RED-FACED SPINETAIL

juv.

258

GENUS *SYNALLAXIS* (SPINETAILS) (2 species). Skulking, long-tailed, rather wren-like ovenbirds of scrubby and grassy habitats; heard far more often than seen. Singles and pairs creep slowly and inconspicuously; sometimes sing from atop grass clump or small bush. Flight low and direct but rather weak, tail held loosely; usually soon crash back into cover. Nests are bulky globular masses of grasses and twigs.

PALE-BREASTED SPINETAIL *Synallaxis albescens* 14–15cm. Skulks in weedy fields, grassy thickets, shrubby second growth. See genus note. Distinctive when seen, with rusty cap and wings, black neck patch below whitish throat; juv. plumage (held briefly) quite different, much duller and browner overall but not much like other species in Costa Rica; cf. House Wren (p. 344). SOUNDS: Bright clucking *kuip*, and excited burry rattle. Song a sneezy, slightly harsh *whi'cheu!* often repeated steadily every 1–2 secs, faster when agitated. STATUS: Fairly common to uncommon on s. Pacific slope, locally to 1200m; spreading with deforestation. (Costa Rica to S America.)

SLATY SPINETAIL *Synallaxis brachyura* 15–16.5cm. Skulks in weedy fields, grassy thickets, shrubby second growth, roadsides. See genus note. Distinctive when seen, with dark slaty plumage, contrasting bright rusty cap and wings; juv. plumage (held briefly) duller and browner overall, without rusty cap. SOUNDS: Sharp nasal *chk* and gruffer *chrek*, at times repeated steadily. Song a short, overall slightly descending, gruff chattering rattle, *chk-k-k-k-krr* that slows and fades slightly at the end, about 0.5 sec. STATUS: Fairly common to common on both slopes, to 1250m on Pacific slope, to 1500m on Caribbean slope. (Honduras to S America.)

LEAFTOSSERS (GENUS *SCLERURUS*) (3 species). Stocky, mostly terrestrial ovenbirds with rather long slender bills, relatively short tails. Forage in leaf litter, eponymously tossing leaves with bill. Most often detected by voice, especially call notes as birds flush from forest floor with a quiet whirr of wings, when they may perch briefly on a low branch. Often sing from low perch; nest in burrows in banks.

TAWNY-THROATED (MIDDLE AMERICAN) LEAFTOSSER *Sclerurus mexicanus* 16–17cm. Shady floor of humid foothill forest, favoring tangled gullies, overgrown banks. Note long slender bill, ruddy throat and breast (can be quite dull), short dark tail. Cf. Gray-hooded Leaftosser. SOUNDS: Sharp explosive *sweek!* Song a slightly descending, unhurried series of (usually 2–7) high, thin, overslurred whistles, *Squeeih squeeih...*, 2–3 secs, sometimes run into a short rippling trill. STATUS: Uncommon on both slopes, 1000–1800m on Pacific slope, 700–1500m on Caribbean slope. (Mexico to Panama.)

*GRAY-HOODED [GRAY-THROATED] LEAFTOSSER *Sclerurus [albigularis] canigularis* 17–18cm. Shady floor of humid foothill forest, often with fairly open understory. Slightly larger and stouter-billed than Tawny-throated Leaftosser, with grayer head, plain grayish throat contrasting with dark rusty breast. SOUNDS: Sharp metallic *chik*, lower, more smacking than Tawny-throated Leaftosser. Song a fairly rapid, descending series of (usually 5–8) short squeaky whistles slowing at the end and often run into 1–3 rising squeaky chips, *swee-swee-swee-sweee-sweee weik weik*, 1–2 secs; repeated over and over when agitated. STATUS: Scarce to uncommon on n. Caribbean slope, 600–1600m; spills over locally to humid Pacific slope. (Costa Rica to w. Panama.)

SCALY-THROATED LEAFTOSSER *Sclerurus guatemalensis* 17–18cm. Shady floor of humid lowland forest, often in rather open areas with abundant leaf litter. Often flicks its wings as it hops and shuffles; sings from ground or low perch. Other leaftossers mainly at higher elevations; Scaly-throated often looks simply dark brown overall, pale mottling on breast more evident than scaly throat. SOUNDS: Sharp explosive *sweeik!* Song a fairly rapid, slowing and speeding series of bright whistles, 2–5 secs, at times ending with a short twittering trill; when excited, songs repeated steadily with flowing rhythm, barely a pause between them. STATUS: Uncommon on Caribbean slope, to 1000m. (Mexico to nw. Ecuador.)

PALE-BREASTED SPINETAIL

juv.

SLATY SPINETAIL

juv.

TAWNY-THROATED
LEAFTOSSER

GRAY-HOODED
LEAFTOSSER

SCALY-THROATED
LEAFTOSSER

TYPICAL ANTBIRDS (THAMNOPHILIDAE; 22 SPECIES) Large neotropical family most diverse in South America; named for the habits of some species that attend army ant swarms to snatch prey flushed by ants. Plumage predominantly shades of black, white, grays, and browns. Ages/sexes different or similar; adult appearance attained in 1st year. Voice and behavior can be very helpful for ID.

ANTSHRIKES (6 species). Varied assemblage of medium-size to large antbirds with stout hooked bills (suggesting shrikes). Usually in pairs and often rather skulking, best detected by voice.

BARRED ANTSHRIKE *Thamnophilus doliatus* 16–17cm. Most widespread and familiar antbird, a poster child for the family. Favors second-growth thickets, forest edge, gallery woodland; rarely forest interior. Fairly skulking, usually in pairs foraging methodically at low to mid-levels in tangles. Male unmistakable; female might suggest a wren but note staring pale eyes, stout hooked bill, spiky erectile crest, unbarred wings and tail. Juv. male barred blackish and creamy buff, soon attains adult-like plumage. Pacific-slope males average more extensive white in crown. SOUNDS: Song a fairly rapid, laughing series of (about 20–40) nasal notes, accelerating into a roll before ending abruptly with an emphatic yap, *ah-ah…anh!*; 2–3 secs; both sexes sing, female higher. Common call a gruff slurred growl, *ahrrrr*. STATUS: Fairly common to common on both slopes, to 1500m; less numerous in humid areas, commonest in drier nw. lowlands. (Mexico to S America.)

FASCIATED ANTSHRIKE *Cymbilaimus lineatus* 17–18cm. Large, heavy-billed antshrike of vine tangles and thickets in humid forest and edge, gaps inside forest and along streams, adjacent taller second growth. Rather sluggish and deliberate, skulking at low to mid-levels and usually difficult to see well, but often heard. Note finely barred plumage, very stout bill, reddish eyes, bushy crest. Distinctive, but cf. male Barred Antshrike. SOUNDS: Song a measured series of (usually 5–8) hollow, slightly rising or overslurred nasal whistles, *whiéuh whiéuh…*, 2–3 notes/sec; both sexes sing. Calls include a hard, slightly gruff, slow chattering scold that may suggest a wren. STATUS: Uncommon to fairly common on Caribbean slope, to 1200m. (Honduras to S America.)

GREAT ANTSHRIKE *Taraba major* 19–21cm. Easily heard but rarely seen, a skulking denizen of second-growth thickets, leafy vine tangles, canebrakes, and forest edge in humid lowlands. Usually in pairs, foraging at low to mid-levels in shady tangles. Distinctive if seen, with very heavy hooked bill, staring red eyes, clean white underparts. Juv. has duller eyes, soft dusky scalloping on underparts, cinnamon tips to wing coverts. SOUNDS: Song a bouncing-ball series of (about 15–30) hollow whistles accelerating toward the end and fading quickly; often ends with a quiet snarl, hard to hear at a distance, *koh, koh…*, 3–4 secs; both sexes sing. Cf. song of Black-headed Trogon. Calls include hard *chak* notes and growls, and a gruff rattle. STATUS: Fairly common on both slopes, to 1000m. (Mexico to S America.)

female

Caribbean

BARRED ANTSHRIKE

males

Pacific

female

male

FASCIATED ANTSHRIKE

GREAT ANTSHRIKE

female

male

BLACK-CROWNED [SLATY] ANTSHRIKE *Thamnophilus atrinucha* 14–15cm. Medium-size antshike of humid lowland forest understory and edge, second growth thickets, plantations. Fairly skulking, mainly at low to mid-levels in thickets and tangles; usually in pairs that sometimes associate with mixed flocks. Male distinctive, with bold white spots on wings and tail, black cap, stout bill. Female usually with male; note bold wing and tail spotting; cf. antvireos. Both sexes have white back patch usually concealed, flared in display. Imm. male resembles adult male but has brownish wings. SOUNDS: Song a rapid series of (about 15–30) nasal *cah* or *aah* notes ending with a more emphatic *ahk*, 1.5–2.5 secs; suggests Barred Antshrike but more even-paced, averages slightly lower, often ends less emphatically; both sexes sing. Calls include a nasal cawing *aáanh*, overall descending and sometimes doubled; and a low purring growl, *ah'rrrrrrrrr*, about 1.5 secs. STATUS: Fairly common on Caribbean slope to 1000m, local on n. Pacific slope. (Guatemala to w. Ecuador.)

BLACK-HOODED ANTSHRIKE *Thamnophilus bridgesi* 16–17cm. Poorly named but distinctive and relatively conspicuous antshrike of humid forest understory and tangles, second growth, mangroves; pairs often associate with mixed flocks and can be quite confiding. Male blackish overall: note white wing dots; female very different, with distinctively streaked head and breast. SOUNDS: Song a fairly rapid, accelerating series of (about 15–20) nasal *ah* notes ending with an emphatic downslurred or overslurred *eáah*; 2–3 secs; both sexes sing, female higher; cf. song of Barred Antshrike. Calls include series of (usually 6–12) sharply overslurred, slightly wooden clucks, *ahk-ahk...*, 5 notes/sec, can suggest a *Turdus* thrush. STATUS: Fairly common to common on Pacific slope, to 1200m. (Costa Rica to w. Panama.)

RUSSET ANTSHRIKE *Thamnistes anabatinus* 14.5–15.5cm. Rather plain, medium-size arboreal antshrike of humid foothill forest, adjacent taller second growth. Inconspicuous, sluggish, and easily overlooked, mainly at mid–upper levels, foraging in vine tangles, dead-leaf clusters; often joins mixed flocks of antwrens, greenlets, tanagers. Distinctive but uneventful, with stout hooked bill, broad pale eyebrow; sexes similar, but male has concealed pale tawny patch on back, flared in interactions. Most likely to be mistaken for an ovenbird, cf. larger and brighter Buff-fronted Foliage-gleaner, juv. Red-faced Spinetail (p. 256). SOUNDS: Song a high slurred whistle followed by an unhurried series of (usually 4–6) high whistled notes, *tssieur, tsiu-tsiu-tsiu-tsiu-tsiu*, 2–2.5 secs. Calls include a high, thin, slightly sibilant *tsip-si*, and upslurred *sweek*. STATUS: Uncommon to fairly common (most numerous on s. Pacific slope), to 1500m, mainly in foothills. (Mexico to n. Peru.)

BLACK-CROWNED ANTSHRIKE

female

male

BLACK-HOODED ANTSHRIKE

female

male

RUSSET ANTSHRIKE

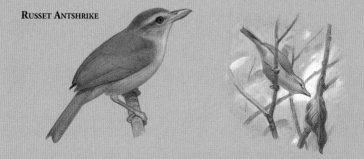

264

ANTVIREOS (GENUS *DYSITHAMNUS*) (3 species). Medium-size, rather chunky arboreal antbirds with fairly stout bills (recalling vireos). Usually in pairs, often with mixed flocks.

PLAIN ANTVIREO *Dysithamnus mentalis* 11–12cm. Humid foothill forest, arboreal. Often in pairs, foraging methodically at low to mid-levels in shady understory; joins mixed feeding flocks. Distinctive, with heavy bill, shortish tail, narrow pale wingbars; note dark cheeks of male, rusty cap and white eyering of female; cf. Tawny-crowned Greenlet (p. 368), sometimes in same flocks. Streak-crowned and Spot-crowned Antvireos occur in lowlands, have pale eyes, streaked chest. SOUNDS: Song an accelerating, laughing, and overall descending series of (usually 14–28) hollow, slightly nasal whistles, *hyu-hyu-hyu-hyuhyu...*, 2–3 secs; recalls Barred Antshrike but higher, more laughing, lacks final snarl. Calls include a low nasal *nyeu-nyeut*; and nasal barking *kah*, often repeated fairly steadily (suggests quiet Barred Forest Falcon). STATUS: Fairly common to uncommon on both slopes, mainly 700–1500m, rarely lower and locally up to 2500m. (Mexico to S America.)

STREAK-CROWNED ANTVIREO *Dysithamnus striaticeps* 10.5–11.5cm. Humid lowland and foothill forest, adjacent taller second growth; arboreal. Often in pairs, foraging methodically at low to mid-levels in shady understory; joins mixed feeding flocks. Told from slightly larger Spot-crowned Antvireo (limited overlap) by voice, stronger dusky streaking on breast, crown pattern. SOUNDS: Song a slightly overslurred series of (usually 12–21) slightly whining nasal whistles accelerating strongly at the end, *whi hiu-hiu...*, 2.5–3.5 secs. Calls include a mellow, descending whistled *wheu heu* and *heu*. STATUS: Fairly common on n. Caribbean slope, to 800m, less numerous in s. Caribbean lowlands around Limón. (Honduras to Costa Rica.)

SPOT-CROWNED ANTVIREO *Dysithamnus puncticeps* 11–12cm. Humid lowland forest and adjacent taller second growth; arboreal. Often in pairs, foraging methodically at low to mid-levels in shady understory; joins mixed feeding flocks. Told from slightly smaller Streak-crowned Antvireo (limited overlap) by voice, weaker dusky streaking on breast, crown pattern. SOUNDS: Song a fairly rapid, slightly overslurred, laughing series of (usually 21–34) high piping whistles accelerating slightly at the end, *whii pii-pii...*, 2.5–3.5 secs; distinctly higher and faster paced than Streak-crowned Antvireo song. Calls include quiet, mellow piping notes, soft twittering trills, and a lower frog-like *chirrrr*. STATUS: Fairly common on s. Caribbean slope near Panama border, to 800m; in smaller numbers n. to vicinity of Limón. (Costa Rica to w. Ecuador.)

RUFOUS-RUMPED ANTWREN *Euchrepomis callinota* 11–12cm. Handsome, arboreal, very small and rather warbler-like antwren of humid foothill forest and edge. Singles and pairs forage actively at mid–upper levels, mainly on smaller twigs and in foliage, at times hanging upside down; does not hover or sally as do many warblers and flycatchers. Often with mixed flocks including tanagers, ovenbirds, warblers. Distinctive, but rusty rump often covered by wings. Note small size, habits, pale lemon belly contrasting with ashy-gray breast, distinct lemon to buff wingbars. SOUNDS: Inconspicuous, easily missed. Song an overslurred, accelerating, chippering trill of high thin notes, *tsi-si-si...*, 1–2 secs; recalls a warbler. Calls include a high lisping *siik* and short high twitters. STATUS: Uncommon on Caribbean slope, mainly 700–1200m. (Costa Rica to S America.)

PLAIN ANTVIREO

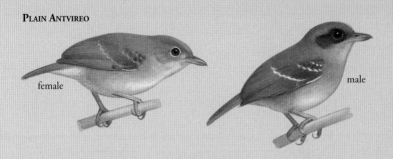

female

male

STREAK-CROWNED ANTVIREO

female

male

SPOT-CROWNED ANTVIREO

female

male

RUFOUS-RUMPED ANTWREN

female

male

ANTWRENS (4 species). Diverse group of small, mostly arboreal antbirds with slender bills (recalling wrens); feed low to high, mainly at mid-levels in understory and edge, often with mixed flocks.

CHECKER-THROATED ANTWREN (STIPPLETHROAT) *Epinecrophylla fulviventris* 10–11cm. Understory of humid forest, adjacent taller second growth. In pairs or family groups, foraging actively at low to mid-levels in leafy foliage, dead-leaf clusters, vine tangles; often with mixed flocks of other antwrens, antvireos, greenlets, tanagers. Note distinct buff-spotted wingbars, relatively stout bill, pale eyes; male has bold black throat spotting. Cf. female White-flanked Antwren, which has duller wingbars, gray cast to head, dark eyes. SOUNDS: Song an overall slightly descending series of (usually 4–11) high, sharp, slightly lisping chips, *tsip tsip...*, 4–5 notes/sec. Calls include single high lisping chips. STATUS: Fairly common on Caribbean slope, locally to 1000m. (Honduras to w. Ecuador.)

***WESTERN WHITE-FLANKED ANTWREN** *Myrmotherula [axillaris] melaena* 9–10cm. Understory of humid forest, adjacent taller second growth. Mainly in pairs, foraging at mid-levels in leafy foliage, vine tangles; often with mixed flocks. White flank tufts of male typically conspicuous and distinctive; female usually near male, has buff-spotted wingbars, grayish head, warm buffy underparts. Cf. female Checker-throated Antwren. SOUNDS: Calls include a downslurred nasal *chew*, typically doubled or trebled, *chew teu*, and a quick churring chatter. Song an overall descending, steady series of (usually 10–19) slightly plaintive, often overslurred whistles, *péeu péeu...*, 3–4/sec. STATUS: Fairly common to uncommon on Caribbean slope, to 900m. (Honduras to nw. Amazonia.)

SLATY ANTWREN *Myrmotherula schisticolor* 10–11cm. Understory of humid foothill forest, adjacent taller second growth. Typically in pairs, foraging at low to mid-levels in foliage, mossy tangles; often with mixed flocks. Note white-dotted wingbars and blackish throat of male (white shoulder tufts usually concealed); female plain overall, with rather blank face, buffy underparts. Cf. imm. male White-flanked Antwren (mainly lower elevation). Cf. larger, long-tailed Dusky Antbird, which differs in behavior and voice. SOUNDS: Common call a short, nasal, downslurred mewing *meah* or *nyieh*. Infrequently heard song a short, measured series of (usually 2–9) rising, slightly nasal whistles, *wiep, wiep...*, about 2/sec. STATUS: Fairly common on both slopes, mainly 700–2000m on Pacific slope (uncommon in s. lowlands), 700–1700m on Caribbean slope. (Mexico to S America.)

DOT-WINGED ANTWREN *Microrhopias quixensis* 11–12cm. Attractive, long-tailed antwren of humid lowland forest and edge, adjacent second growth. Usually in pairs or small groups moving actively at low to mid-levels in leafy foliage and vine tangles; often independent of mixed flocks. Note bold white wing spots, long graduated tail tipped white; concealed white back patch flared in display. SOUNDS: Song a fairly rapid, overslurred bouncing-ball series of (usually 9–17) high, thin, slightly squeaky or lisping chips, *pii, pii, pii-pii-pii...*, 1.5–3 secs; cadence can suggest Dusky Antbird, but notes much higher, thinner. Varied calls are mostly chipping and piping whistles, including loud clear *tchip teeoo*, a sharp liquid *tew*, and a harsh mew. STATUS: Fairly common on both slopes, to 1000m. (Mexico to S America.)

CHECKER-THROATED
ANTWREN

female

male

imm. male

female

WESTERN
WHITE-FLANKED ANTWREN

male

imm. male

female

SLATY ANTWREN

male

DOT-WINGED ANTWREN

males

female

white back patch
flared in display

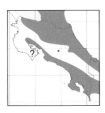

DUSKY ANTBIRD *Cercomacroides tyrannina* 13–14cm. Notably skulking, heard far more often than seen. Humid forest edge, dense second growth, gallery forest understory and tangles. Usually in pairs, moving low and furtively in thickets; does not join mixed flocks. Distinctive, if plain: note narrow whitish wingbars of male, blank face and rusty underparts of female; male has concealed white back patch flared in display. SOUNDS: Song a rapid series of (usually 9–18) bright piping whistles, accelerating and then fading abruptly, *pyi-pyi...*, 2–2.5 secs; at times pairs duet, female giving higher, slightly rising song. Calls include a harsh rasping *brreeea* (cf. White-collared Manakin) and hard churring *kehrrr*. STATUS: Fairly common to uncommon on both slopes, to 1400m on Pacific slope, 1200m on Caribbean slope; uncommon and more local in drier nw. lowlands. (Mexico to S America.)

'PROFESSIONAL' ANTBIRDS (3 species). Boldly patterned antbirds that habitually attend army ant swarms and are infrequently seen away from them. Often perch low on slender vertical saplings and twigs, whence they drop on or dash after prey flushed by the ants. Can be quite confiding and unconcerned by a quiet human observer.

BICOLORED ANTBIRD *Gymnopithys bicolor* 14–15cm. Striking medium-size antbird of humid forest understory, ranging into adjacent second growth; usually at ant swarms. See group intro. No similar species in Costa Rica: note pale blue facial skin offset by dark cheeks, clean white underparts. Juv. plumage (held briefly) duller above with rusty wingbars, sooty-brown underparts, dull facial skin. SOUNDS: Song a slightly overslurred series of (usually 7–14) slightly breathy whistled notes, starting as longer, upslurred whistles and accelerating then fading into lower, sometimes huskier notes, *whieeh whieh whieh-whi-whi-ih-ih-ih-ieh*, 2–2.5 secs; also single rising whistled notes and attenuated songs at ant swarms. Call a burry snarling *whéeeir*, often downslurred. STATUS: Fairly common on both slopes, to 1700m on Pacific slope, 1500m on Caribbean slope. (Honduras to w. Ecuador.)

OCELLATED ANTBIRD *Phaenostictus mcleannani* 20–21cm. Spectacular large antbird of humid forest understory, sometimes ranging into adjacent second growth; usually at ant swarms. See group intro. No similar species in Costa Rica: note blue facial skin offset by black throat, rusty collar and underparts, bold black scallops ('ocellations') on upperparts. Juv. plumage (held briefly) duller overall with weaker pattern above, darker underparts. SOUNDS: Song an ascending, slightly accelerating series of slurred piping whistles run into a quicker roll or trill and usually ending with a few slower, downslurred notes, 3.5–5.5 secs; may suggest Bicolored Antbird but higher and faster, more prolonged and varied. Also single piping whistles and attenuated songs at ant swarms. Call a burry, downslurred, semi-metallic *srrrieu*, much higher than Bicolored Antbird, not snarling. STATUS: Uncommon on Caribbean slope, to 1200m; spills over locally to humid n. Pacific foothills. (Honduras to nw. Ecuador.)

SPOTTED ANTBIRD *Hylophylax naevioides* 11–12cm. Attractive small antbird of humid forest understory, ranging into adjacent second growth; often at ant swarms. See group intro. No similar species in Costa Rica: note short tail, bold cinnamon wingbars, breast band of coarse dark spots; male has concealed white back patch flared in display. Juv. plumage (held briefly) resembles female but head grayer, underparts mostly brownish. SOUNDS: Song a pulsating or ratcheting series of (usually 6–10) paired wheezy whistles, accelerating then fading and overslurred or descending overall, *whiéz'i whiéz'i...*; 3–4.5 secs. Call a burry trilled or rattled *tssirrr*, shorter and less whiny than more strongly downslurred call of Ocellated Antbird. STATUS: Fairly common on Caribbean slope, to 1000m; spills over locally to humid n. Pacific foothills. (Honduras to w. Ecuador.)

DUSKY ANTBIRD

female

male

BICOLORED ANTBIRD

OCELLATED ANTBIRD

SPOTTED ANTBIRD

female

male

DULL-MANTLED ANTBIRD *Sipia laemosticta* 14–15cm. Shady dense understory of humid foothill forest, especially tangled gullies and ravines. Pairs forage unobtrusively on or near ground, usually well hidden. Note ruby-red eyes with no blue facial skin, fine white dots on wing coverts; concealed white back patch flared is display. Cf. Chestnut-backed Antbird of lowlands. Juv. (plumage held briefly) has brownish eyes, brown wash to head, faint buff mottling on throat. SOUNDS: Song a slightly rising or overslurred series of (usually 8–11) high piping to slightly wheezy whistles, typically with a break in pitch about midway through, *pii-pii-pii-piu-piu-piu-piu-piu*, 1.5–2 secs. Call a burry, slightly clipped, downslurred *béeu* or *chreu*, singly or in short series. STATUS: Uncommon to fairly common on Caribbean slope, mainly 300–1000m. (Costa Rica to w. Panama.)

CHESTNUT-BACKED ANTBIRD *Poliocrania (Myrmeciza) exsul* 14.5–15.5cm. Handsome, medium-size antbird of humid forest understory, especially thickets along streams and at light gaps, adjacent second growth, canebrakes. Usually in pairs, occasionally attending ant swarms; often dips tail persistently. Note short tail, gray hood with pale blue facial skin, relatively bright rusty-brown upperparts; very rarely shows a few pale spots on wing coverts. Juv. plumage (held briefly) smudgy dull blackish overall. Pacific-slope females brighter rusty overall. SOUNDS: Song imitated easily, a whistled 2–3-note *whi heu* or *pih peu peu*, recalls Hoffmann's Antthrush but more lethargic, notes higher, longer, more downslurred. Calls include a gruff, overslurred *reáahh*, and in alarm an excited, rippling, slightly nasal *whi-di-dit* and chatters to 1 sec or longer, cf. Zeledon's Antbird. STATUS: Fairly common to common on both slopes, to 1000m. (Honduras to w. Ecuador.)

ZELEDON'S [IMMACULATE] ANTBIRD *Hafferia (Myrmeciza) zeledoni* 18.5–19.5cm. Large, rather long-tailed antbird of humid foothill forest understory and edge, adjacent second growth. Usually in pairs, foraging low in dense understory, at times with army ant swarms; often dips tail persistently. Note size and shape, dark unmarked plumage with conspicuous pale blue facial skin, voice; white wing bend of male flashes in display, also can be striking in flight. SOUNDS: Song a slightly descending, steady ringing chant of (usually 8–12) overslurred whistled notes, *heu heu...*, 4–5 notes/sec; female song slightly higher and often shorter. Calls include an emphatic sharp *week!* suggesting a leaftosser, and an excited, slightly squeaky or nasal rippling *chirr-irr-irrt*, and longer chatters, mainly 1–2.5 secs; slightly gruffer, less squeaky than chatters of Chestnut-backed Antbird. STATUS: Uncommon to fairly common on both slopes, mainly 700–1700m on Pacific slope, 500–1700m on Caribbean slope. (Honduras to w. Ecuador.)

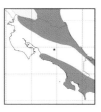

BARE-CROWNED ANTBIRD *Gymnocichla nudiceps* 15–16cm. Distinctive, medium-size antbird of humid lowland forest edge and second growth, especially swampy *Heliconia* thickets. Usually in pairs on or near ground, often attending army ant swarms. Note stocky build, bright blue facial skin (and crown on adult male); male has distinct white wingbars (cf. larger, long-tailed Zeledon's Antbird), white back usually concealed, flared in display; female rusty brown overall with paler wingbars (indistinct on Pacific-slope birds). SOUNDS: Song a chant of (usually 8–16) downslurred, slightly nasal whistles, *tcheu tcheu...*, often accelerates slightly at the end, 3–4 notes/sec. Calls include a harsh mewing *meéahr*, and an abrupt *sweik!* suggesting a leaftosser. STATUS: Uncommon to scarce and local on both slopes, to 1200m on Pacific slope, 700m on Caribbean slope. (Guatemala to n. Colombia.)

female

DULL-MANTLED ANTBIRD

male

Pacific

females

Caribbean

CHESTNUT-BACKED ANTBIRD

male

ZELEDON'S ANTBIRD

female

male

imm. male

male

Pacific

females

BARE-CROWNED ANTBIRD

Caribbean

ANTTHRUSHES (FORMICARIIDAE; 3 SPECIES) Small neotropical family of
terrestrial antbirds. Ages differ slightly; juv. plumage soon replaced by adult-like plumage; sexes similar. Heard much more often than seen. Walk like crakes on the floor of humid forest, tail cocked, tossing leaves aside with their bill. Sing from ground while walking, also from low perches. Flush strongly, usually accompanied by sharp call and wing whirr.

*HOFFMANN'S [BLACK-FACED] ANTTHRUSH *Formicarius [analis] hoffmanni* 18–19.5cm. Humid lowland and foothill forest; see family intro. Limited overlap in foothills with other antthrushes, from which told by rusty neck sides, grayish breast, voice. SOUNDS: Measured song easily imitated, a sharp mellow whistle followed by (usually 1–2, rarely up to 10) often slightly lower whistles, *pee, piu piu*; recalls song of Chestnut-backed Antbird but faster-paced, more strident, notes not distinctly downslurred. Call a clipped, hollow *p'rik* much like Rufous-breasted Antthrush, at times run into rapid clucking series. STATUS: Fairly common on s. Pacific slope, locally to 1500m; on Caribbean slope to 500m in north, to 1200m in south. (Honduras to nw. Venezuela).

*BLACK-HOODED [BLACK-HEADED] ANTTHRUSH *Formicarius nigricapillus* 17.5–18.5cm. Humid foothill forest; see family intro. Limited overlap with other antthrushes (Hoffmann's lower, Rufous-breasted higher), from which told by blackish head and breast, voice. Juv. duller overall, head and breast sootier. SOUNDS: Song easily imitated, a fairly rapid series of tooting, hollow to nasal whistles, initially intensifying and then fading abruptly at the end, *huihui...*, 2.5–6 secs at 5–6 notes/sec. STATUS: Fairly common to uncommon locally on Caribbean slope, mainly 400–800m in Northern and Central Mts., 600–1200m in Talamanca Mts. (Costa Rica to Panama.)

RUFOUS-BREASTED ANTTHRUSH *Formicarius rufipectus* 19–20cm. Humid foothill forest; see family intro. Limited overlap with other antthrushes, from which told by rusty crown, neck sides, and breast framing black face; also voice. Juv. duller overall, with lower breast mostly grayish. SOUNDS: Song easily imitated, a hollow, plaintive whistled *whiu whiu*, repeated after several secs; notes on same pitch or 2nd slightly higher. Call a rolled *p'rik*, much like Hoffmann's Anthrush, at times run into short rapid series. STATUS: Uncommon on Caribbean slope, mainly 800–1500m in Northern and Central Mts., 1200–1800m in Talamanca Mts. (Costa Rica to Peru.)

GNATEATERS (CONOPOPHAGIDAE; 1 SPECIES) Small neotropical family,
occurring mainly in South America. Ages differ slightly; weak juv. plumage soon replaced by adult-like plumage; sexes differ.

BLACK-CROWNED ANTPITTA *Pittasoma michleri* 18–19.5cm. Spectacular but elusive and rarely seen, on and near floor of humid foothill forest, adjacent taller second growth. Hops on ground with springy bounds, digging in leaf litter and attending army ant swarms; sings from low perch in understory. No similar species in Costa Rica: note long pale bill, boldly scalloped underparts, rusty upperparts with spotted wingbars. Male has solid black hood, female has rusty cheeks, variably mottled throat. Juv. plumage (held briefly, rarely seen) duller, less strongly patterned overall. SOUNDS: Song a prolonged series of semi-metallic plaintive whistles, often intensifying for 20–30 secs at up to 6–7 notes/sec before slowing into longer notes that may continue more or less steadily for another 1–2 mins at 2–3 notes/sec, *pui-pui-puipui...puii puii...*; also simply steady-paced series at 2–3 notes/sec for a min or longer, *puii puii...*, that might suggest a high-pitched pygmy owl or even a truck backing up. Call a rapid, gruff clucking chatter, starting abruptly and slowing slightly at the end, 1.5–2 secs; suggests a rapid, gruff Wood Thrush clucking. STATUS: Scarce to rare on Caribbean slope, mainly 300–1000m. (Costa Rica to nw. Colombia.)

juv.

HOFFMANN'S ANTTHRUSH

BLACK-HOODED ANTTHRUSH

RUFOUS-BREASTED ANTTHRUSH

BLACK-CROWNED ANTPITTA

female

male

ANTPITTAS (GRALLARIIDAE; 5 SPECIES) Neotropical family most diverse in South America. Ages differ; weak juv. plumage soon replaced by adult-like plumage; sexes similar.

*SPECTACLED [STREAK-CHESTED] ANTPITTA *Hylopezus perspicillatus* 13.5–14.5cm. Floor of humid forest, often in fairly open but shady areas with leaf litter; relatively easy to see, for an antpitta. Hops quickly and at times runs like a thrush; can be confiding to a quiet observer. Sings from low perch or ground, and may fly to low perch when flushed. No overlap with Tawny-flanked or Thicket Antpittas. SOUNDS: Song easily imitated, a relatively unhurried, slightly overslurred series of 6–9 mournful whistles, 1st note often short and softer, easily missed, *wh heu heu heu heu heu*, every few secs; 7–9 notes/2.5–3 secs. Call a slightly descending nasal chatter of about 15 or so downslurred notes, *hew hiu-hiu...*, 12–15 notes/1.5 secs. STATUS: Fairly common on s. Pacific slope, locally to 1600m. (Costa Rica to nw. Ecuador.)

*TAWNY-FLANKED [STREAK-CHESTED] ANTPITTA *Hylopezus [perspicillatus] intermedius* 13.5–14.5cm. Floor of humid forest, often along streams. Hops on or near ground, usually well hidden; sings from low perch. Note bold pale eyering, strong dark whisker and breast streaking, distinct wingbars, cf. Thicket Antpitta, which is usually harder to see. SOUNDS: Song higher, more plaintive than Spectacled Antpitta, descending overall: 1st note highest, 2nd lower, then 3–4 slightly higher notes run into 2–4 longer notes, *hiew huu hu-hu-hu hoo hoo hoo*; 7–10 notes/2.5–3 secs. STATUS: Uncommon to fairly common on Caribbean slope, locally to 1400m. (Honduras to w. Panama.)

THICKET (FULVOUS-BELLIED) ANTPITTA *Hylopezus fulviventris* 13.5–14.5cm. Dense understory thickets of humid forest, adjacent second growth, especially along streams and at light gaps. Often heard but rarely seen. Hops on or near ground, usually well hidden in tangled cover; sings from perch in understory. Like a duller version of Tawny-flanked Antpitta: note face pattern, plainer wings, diffuse dusky streaks below. SOUNDS: Song a fairly rapid, intensifying and overall ascending series of (typically 12–14) short mellow whistles, *tü-tü...*ending abruptly, 1.5–2 secs. Call a slightly descending, short nasal chatter or rattle. STATUS: Fairly common on Caribbean slope, locally to 1100m. (Honduras to nw. Ecuador).

OCHRE-BREASTED ANTPITTA *Grallaricula flavirostris* 10–11cm. Tiny cute antpitta of humid foothill forest, especially tangled understory in ravines and around light gaps. Hops easily and stealthily on smaller branches and vines, also on ground, often swaying its rear end slowly side-to-side; sings from low perch in understory. Note very small size, ochre-buff face and breast with paler eyering, diffuse dusky streaking below, small bill; cf. larger, more terrestrial *Hylopezus* antpittas. SOUNDS: Inconspicuous, easily missed. Song (?) a short, overslurred, slightly descending plaintive whistle, *hieéu*, usually every 6–20 or so secs. STATUS: Uncommon on both slopes, mainly 900–1800m on Pacific slope, 700–1300m on Caribbean slope. (Costa Rica to S America.)

SCALED ANTPITTA *Grallaria guatimalensis* 18–19cm. Elusive terrestrial denizen of shady understory and tangled thickets in humid foothill forest. Hops like a kangaroo, often surprisingly quickly, rarely runs; flushes with a whirr of wings but without calling, and sometimes perches briefly on a low branch before dropping to vanish like a ghost. Sings from well-hidden perch near ground. Note broad pale mustache, rusty underparts; dark scaling often hard to see in the field. SOUNDS: Song (heard infrequently, mainly around dawn) a quavering, accelerating crescendo of resonant hoots that rises in pitch, slows slightly at end, and fades abruptly, 2–3 secs. Low grunt when disturbed. STATUS: Scarce (overlooked?) on both slopes, 800–1700m. (Mexico to S America.)

SPECTACLED ANTPITTA

TAWNY-FLANKED ANTPITTA

THICKET ANTPITTA

OCHRE-BREASTED ANTPITTA

juv.

SCALED ANTPITTA

TAPACULOS (RHINOCRYPTIDAE; 1 SPECIES) Neotropical family occurring mainly in South America. Ages differ, with juv. plumage soon replaced by adult-like plumage; sexes differ slightly.

SILVERY-FRONTED TAPACULO *Scytalopus argentifrons* 11–12cm. Very small, skulking denizen of humid highland forest edge and understory, second growth, especially bamboo thickets. Heard far more often than seen. Typically on or near the ground in tangles, moving like a mouse through dense vegetation; tail often cocked. No truly similar species, but seen poorly may suggest a small wren. SOUNDS: Song a staccato, slightly ringing series of hard chips, *chi-chi...*, 6–7/sec, mainly 2.5–7 secs duration; typically starts slightly faster and quieter before quickly settling to a steady pace. Common call a ringing slow rattle, sometimes loud, of (usually 6–11) semi-metallic to nasal downslurred notes; shorter series often descending overall and slowing slightly, longer series faster-paced and may suggest a wren, *chih-chih*. Quiet, downslurred nasal *chieh* when foraging. STATUS: Fairly common, from timberline locally down to 1200m on Pacific slope, to 800m on Caribbean slope. (Costa Rica to w. Panama.)

SHARPBILLS (1 species) Enigmatic, small neotropical group; has been included with cotingas, now usually merged with tityra family or treated as its own family (Oxyruncidae). Ages/sexes differ slightly; like adult in 1st year.

*CENTRAL AMERICAN SHARPBILL *Oxyruncus [cristatus] frater* 16–17cm. Distinctive but often unobtrusive species of humid foothill forest. Mainly in canopy, as singles, probing in mossy tangles and dead-leaf clusters, hanging acrobatically at times; joins mixed flocks. Can be sluggish and quiet for long periods, when overlooked easily. Singing males may gather in small groups high in canopy. Nothing really similar in Costa Rica: note spotted underparts, head pattern, greenish upperparts. Female lacks serrated outer primary of male, crest shorter with central scarlet area reduced to a line. SOUNDS: Song a descending, semi-metallic, burry whistle, 2–2.5 secs, *whieeeurrr*. STATUS: Scarce to uncommon and local on Caribbean slope, mainly 500–1500m. (Costa Rica to nw. Colombia.)

COTINGAS (COTINGIDAE; 8 SPECIES) Neotropical family, occurring mainly in South America (includes Rufous Piha, p. 284). Ages/sexes differ strikingly or similar. Immature plumage progression of some strongly dimorphic species poorly known.

LOVELY COTINGA *Cotinga amabilis* 18–19cm. Stunning and sought-after species of humid forest and edge, adjacent second growth and clearings with taller fruiting trees. No overlap with Turquoise Cotinga. Mainly in canopy, where small numbers may gather at fruiting trees; plucks berries by brief sallying flutters. Often sits quietly for long periods and males especially can perch on exposed snags and be seen from long distance. 'Electric-blue' male unmistakable; female distinctive but can be puzzling: note plump shape with rounded head, spotted underparts, scalloped upperparts. Imm. like female with buffier wing edgings, more spotted vs. scaly upperparts; males can show patches of adult color. SOUNDS: Mostly quiet. Abrupt, slightly squeaky high *piic!* easily passed off as a frog. In flight, male makes soft, dry, ticking wing rattle, easily passed over as an insect. STATUS: Uncommon to scarce and local on Caribbean slope, mainly in lower foothills but locally to 1700m. (Mexico to w. Panama.)

TURQUOISE COTINGA *Cotinga ridgwayi* 17.5–18.5cm. Stunning Pacific-slope counterpart to Lovely Cotinga, inhabiting humid forest and edge, adjacent clearings with taller trees. Habits much like Lovely Cotinga (no range overlap). Male differs from Lovely in dark-dappled back, black eyering; female warmer and buffier than Lovely. SOUNDS: Mostly quiet. In flight, male makes soft, dry, rippling wing rattle, rather insect-like. STATUS: Uncommon to scarce and local on s. Pacific slope, locally to 1800m. (Costa Rica to w. Panama.)

juv.

**SILVERY-FRONTED
TAPACULO**

female

male

**CENTRAL AMERICAN
SHARPBILL**

LOVELY COTINGA

males

female

TURQUOISE COTINGA

male

female

278

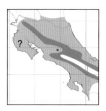

THREE-WATTLED BELLBIRD *Procnias tricarunculatus* Male 30–33 cm, female 25–26cm. Spectacular large cotinga breeding in humid highland forest, especially mossy cloud forest; ranges to adjacent semi-open areas, especially with fruiting wild avocado trees, and elevational migrant to lowland forest. Mainly at mid–upper levels, where easily overlooked if not vocal; male sings from exposed snag in canopy. Adult male unmistakable, female and imm. very different but no similar species in Costa Rica. Imm. male resembles female but larger, with shorter bill wattles, some have chestnut patches on underparts; plumage sequences remain poorly known. SOUNDS: Male song (mainly Feb–Jul, sporadically year-round) a far-carrying, resonant, often slightly wooden *bohng!* or *oihng!* usually preceded by and alternated with 1 or more piercing whistles and low burry twangs at irregular intervals; details vary regionally. Imm. males may practice in fall–winter, with varied discordant clangs. STATUS: Fairly common breeder Feb–Aug on both slopes, mainly 1200–2300m, locally down to 900m in Northwest. Post-breeding birds may wander to 3000m and most descend Sep/Nov–Jan/early Apr to lowlands and lower foothills; formerly may have bred in higher mountains of Nicoya Peninsula. (Honduras to w. Panama.)

PURPLE-THROATED FRUITCROW *Querula purpurata* 26–29cm, male> female. Fairly large, distinctive black cotinga of humid lowland forest and edge, adjacent clearings with fruiting trees. Typically in small, often noisy groups roaming in forest canopy; sometimes joins mixed flocks with larger species such as White-fronted Nunbirds, oropendolas. Flight buoyantly undulating, with deep sweeping wingbeats. Often quivers tail upon landing and when calling. Nothing very similar in Costa Rica, but cf. much larger Bare-necked Umbrellabird. Deep purple gorget of male stunning in good light. SOUNDS: Far-carrying, twangy and mellow whistled calls *ów-ah ow-ah, ahh*, or *ow'ah owaaáh*, and variations. STATUS: Fairly common to uncommon on Caribbean slope, locally to 600m. (Nicaragua to S America.)

BARE-NECKED UMBRELLABIRD *Cephalopterus glabricollis* Male 41–45cm, female 36–38cm. Distinctive, heavily built, large-headed, and rather short-tailed black cotinga of humid forest and edge, adjacent taller second growth with fruiting trees. Perches mainly at mid–upper levels, where often still and quiet, easily overlooked. Away from display sites, singles or small groups may be found at fruiting trees, shuffling along branches and sallying for fruit with noisy wingbeats. Flight rather direct but unhurried, suggesting a large jay. Small loose groups of males display mainly around dawn, from perches in subcanopy. Nothing very similar in Costa Rica, but cf. much smaller Purple-throated Fruit-crow. Male throat pouch inflated like balloon in display. Juv. male resembles female but plumage sootier grayish, crest shorter than adult male. SOUNDS: Song a deep, almost subliminal boom with pouch inflated, then a quiet cluck and a 2nd boom as pouch deflates: *üüm, hk, üüm*, the whole sequence about 3 secs; often 30 secs or longer between songs. Calls include low coughs and grunts. STATUS: Scarce to uncommon and local on Caribbean slope: breeds Mar–Jul, mainly 800–2000m, descends Aug–Jan (some birds year-round) to lower foothills and adjacent lowlands. (Costa Rica to w. Panama.)

THREE-WATTLED BELLBIRD

female

male

PURPLE-THROATED
FRUITCROW

female

males

BARE-NECKED UMBRELLABIRD

female

male

SNOWY COTINGA *Carpodectes nitidus* 20–23cm, male>female. Stunning, fairly large cotinga of humid lowland forest and edge, adjacent second growth and tree-scattered farmland with forest patches. No overlap with Yellow-billed Cotinga. Mainly in canopy, where small numbers may gather at fruiting trees; plucks berries by brief sallying flutters. Flight rather direct but unhurried, and male stands out as starkly snow white against green canopy. Often sits quietly for long periods and males especially can perch on exposed snags and atop trees, visible from long distances. Gleaming adult male unmistakable (smoky-gray blush to upperparts usually washed out in bright light); female distinctive but can be puzzling: note shape, white eyering, white wing edgings. Imm. male resembles female but whitish above with dusky scalloping. SOUNDS: Typically quiet. STATUS: Uncommon to scarce on Caribbean slope, locally to 750m. (Honduras to w. Panama.)

YELLOW-BILLED COTINGA *Carpodectes antoniae* 20–22.5cm, male>female. Pacific-slope counterpart to Snowy Cotinga (no range overlap), inhabiting taller mangroves, humid lowland forest and edge, adjacent tree-scattered farmland with forest patches. Habits much like Snowy Cotinga; differs visually from Snowy in mostly yellow bill. SOUNDS: Typically quiet. STATUS: Uncommon to scarce on s. Pacific slope, locally to 750m. (Costa Rica to w. Panama.)

BECARDS, TITYRAS, AND ALLIES (TITYRIDAE; 9+ SPECIES) Recently recognized neotropical family, many members of which were formerly treated as cotingas; includes Speckled and Northern Mourners (p. 284), and perhaps Sharpbills (p. 276). Ages/sexes differ strikingly or similar; attain adult appearance in 1st year.

BLACK-CROWNED TITYRA *Tityra inquisitor* 18.5–19.5cm. Humid forest and edge, plantations, semi-open areas with fruiting trees. Often in pairs, mainly at mid–upper levels and at fruiting trees; associates readily with Masked Tityra. Flight slightly undulating, suggesting a compact woodpecker; note translucent primary panels, lacking on Masked Tityra, which also differs in head pattern, voice. SOUNDS: Gruff, slightly rasping *shehk*, singly or in short, at times chattering series; lacks nasal, burrier quality of Masked Tityra. STATUS: Uncommon to fairly common on both slopes, locally to 1200m. (Mexico to S America.)

MASKED TITYRA *Tityra semifasciata* 20–22cm. Widespread and often conspicuous in humid forest and edge, plantations, semi-open areas with fruiting trees. Often in pairs, mainly at mid–upper levels where frequently perches on prominent snags. Flight slightly undulating, suggesting a compact woodpecker. Distinctive, with naked reddish-pink face, but cf. Black-crowned Tityra, which often occurs alongside Masked. SOUNDS: Short croaking and rasping nasal notes, often doubled or in rhythmic series, *rehk* and *reh-rehk*, or *reh-rehk reh-reh-rehk...*, and variations; could be passed off as a frog. STATUS: Fairly common on both slopes, locally to 1800m on Pacific slope, to 1500m on Caribbean slope; rarely to 2400m. (Mexico to S America.)

SNOWY COTINGA

female

male

YELLOW-BILLED COTINGA

female

male

juv.

BLACK-CROWNED TITYRA

female

male

female

male

MASKED TITYRA

282

BECARDS (GENUS *PACHYRAMPHUS*) (5 species). Chunky, rather large-headed, often sluggish, and mostly arboreal birds. Usually found as singles and pairs, often at mid–upper levels in forest and edge. Ages/sexes usually differ; 1st-year male looks variably intermediate between adult male and female.

ROSE-THROATED BECARD *Pachyramphus aglaiae* 16–17cm. Lowland woodland and edge, gallery forest, plantations, second growth. Forages low to high, sometimes ranging into overgrown fields. Tail not graduated as on other Costa Rican becards. Distinctive male dark overall, with little or no rose-pink on throat. Female told by dark sooty cap, cf. smaller Cinnamon Becard. **SOUNDS:** Plaintive downslurred *tseeu*, often run into a reedy, spluttering chatter or trill, or a squeaky chatter may slur into a downslurred *tew*. Dawn song a high, slightly reedy, plaintive *si-tchew, wii-chew* or simply *si-tchew*, repeated every 2–6 secs. **STATUS:** Uncommon to fairly common on Pacific slope, locally to 1200m, most numerous in nw. lowlands; scarce Nov–Mar (locally resident?) in n. Caribbean lowlands. (Mexico and sw. US to w. Panama.)

CINNAMON BECARD *Pachyramphus cinnamomeus* 14–15cm. Humid forest edge, gardens, plantations, especially along streams; also mangroves on Pacific slope. Sexes alike. At mid–upper levels, sometimes with mixed flocks. Note subtle face pattern with dark lores, short paler brow, dark rusty cap, cf. female Rose-throated Becard. **SOUNDS:** Song comprises 1–2 drawn-out, plaintive high whistles followed by a faster, slightly descending series of (usually 3–9) shorter notes, *teeeu dee-dee...*, or *cheei deu-deu-deu*. Calls are varied series of high reedy whistles, at times rapid twittering series, and a plaintive *seeeeiu*. **STATUS:** Fairly common to uncommon on both slopes, locally to 1500m. (Mexico to w. Ecuador.)

WHITE-WINGED BECARD *Pachyramphus polychopterus* 14–15cm. Humid lowland forest edge, woodland, plantations, gallery forest, mangroves. Mainly at mid–upper levels, often in canopy of fruiting trees. Attractive male is distinctive, cf. Northern Black-and-white Becard of foothills. Female distinctive but can be puzzling, note broken pale eyering, cinnamon wing edgings. **SOUNDS:** Songs comprise variations on 2 themes: series of (usually 4–9) mellow, downslurred whistles, the 1st typically longest, then speeding and slowing at end, *tcheu chu chu...*, about 6 notes/sec; also 1–2 mellow notes followed by a rapid series of (usually 8–20) descending chips that slow at end, *chiu chi-chi...*, about 10 notes/sec. Varied, twangy whistled phrases when agitated. **STATUS:** Fairly common to uncommon on both slopes in humid areas, locally to 1200m on Pacific slope, to 1000m on Caribbean slope; uncommon and local in drier nw. lowlands. (Mexico to S America.)

*NORTHERN BLACK-AND-WHITE BECARD *Pachyramphus albogriseus* 14–15cm. Humid foothill forest and edge. Mainly at mid–upper levels, often with mixed flocks. Male much paler below than White-winged Becard of lowlands, female has distinctive black head band. **SOUNDS:** Song a short, varied arrangement of plaintive, slightly squeaky or reedy notes with rhythmic 2–3-syllable sequence, such as *teu teu whee'ti-chu whee'ti-chu whee ti* and *ch'wi-chee wh-chee wi-chee wi-chee*. **STATUS:** Uncommon to scarce on Caribbean slope, locally on cen. Pacific slope, mainly 800–1800m; some wander to lower Caribbean foothills in fall. (Costa Rica to ne. Peru.)

BARRED BECARD *Pachyramphus versicolor* 12–13cm. Rather cute and distinctive small becard of highland forest and edge, adjacent second growth. Mainly at mid-levels, often with mixed flocks. Note black cap, big beady eyes in blank face; barring soft, can be difficult to see. Imm. male duller, more greenish overall than adult. **SOUNDS:** Song a fairly rapid, often slightly rising or overslurred series of (usually 8–17) high, slightly squeaky to husky, overslurred whistles, *twieh-twieh...*, 6–7 notes/sec. Also an accelerating, slightly overslurred series of (usually 9–12) slightly piping or squeaky whistles, *fieeeh fieeh fee fi-fi-fi....* **STATUS:** Fairly common to uncommon in Central and Talamanca Mts., mainly 1500–3000m; scarce in Northern Mts., mainly above 1500m. (Costa Rica to S America.)

ROSE-THROATED BECARD

female

male

CINNAMON BECARD

male

female

WHITE-WINGED BECARD

female

male

NORTHERN BLACK-AND-WHITE BECARD

female

male

BARRED BECARD

*MIDDLE AMERICAN [BRIGHT-RUMPED] ATTILA *Attila [spadiceus] flammulatus* 19–21cm. Distinctive tyrant flycatcher of lowland and foothill forest, adjacent second growth, plantations. Forages low to high, at times with mixed flocks and at ant swarms; often wags and flicks tail. Sings, often tirelessly at dawn, from subcanopy. Plumage variable; note stout hooked bill, staring amber eyes, streaked breast, bright rump. Juv. has brownish eyes, broad cinnamon tertial edges. SOUNDS: Far-carrying, strident whistled series. Dawn song an unhurried, often prolonged series of paired whistles, about 2 pairs/sec, typically ending with a single overslurred note and sometimes a terminal chip, *whie-dii whie-dii...wheéu chu*, or *knee-deep knee-deep...whóh*; at times faster-paced, with 3-syllable phrases, *whie-di-di whie-di-di...* 'Day song' a rapid, slightly overslurred series of (usually 4–10) bright upslurred whistles, about 6/sec, such as *wh-wheéu-wheéu...*, often slowing and followed by *whee-dee-deu*, and variations. Call a sharp nasal *kí-di-dik* and *ki-di-dik*. STATUS: Fairly common to uncommon on both slopes, to 1800m. (Mexico to w. Ecuador.)

RUFOUS MOURNER *Rhytipterna holerythra* 19.5–21cm. Plain rusty tyrant flycatcher of humid forest. Mainly at mid–upper levels; sometimes joins mixed flocks; sings from subcanopy. Perches quietly when not singing; flutters after invertebrate prey. Notoriously similar Rufous Piha, often in same areas, has stouter bill with less extensive pale pinkish below, paler eyering and chin; note voice. SOUNDS: Distinctive leisurely wolf whistle, *wheeeeu-heeu*, rising then falling, 1.5–2 secs, rarely with short introductory whistle; also mournful descending *wheeeu*. Song a steady series of (usually 5–20) plaintive whistles, *wheéu wheéu...*, 10/7–8 secs, at times with a longer introductory *whi'heeeu*; at dawn also a simple *teeuu te-du*, repeated. STATUS: Fairly common to uncommon on both slopes, to 1200m. (Mexico to nw. Ecuador.)

RUFOUS PIHA *Lipaugus unirufus* 23–26cm. Plain rusty cotinga of humid forest; heard more often than seen. Cf. very similar Rufous Mourner. Mainly at mid–upper levels; sings from open midstory and subcanopy. Feeds on fruit and invertebrates plucked from foliage; sallies more deliberately, with heavier fluttering, than slimmer, more lightly built Rufous Mourner. SOUNDS: Loud ringing whistles given irregularly, often in response to an abrupt loud noise: *p'wEE-oo!* and *cheEOo! p-wee'oo!* Often simply *pweEOO!* suggesting Pauraque. Hard squirrel-like clucks, often in short 'machine-gun' bursts when agitated. STATUS: Uncommon to fairly common on both slopes, locally to 1200m. (Mexico to nw. Ecuador.)

SPECKLED MOURNER *Laniocera rufescens* 20–21cm. Rarely encountered inhabitant of humid lowland forest; overlooked easily unless singing. At mid–upper levels, perching upright and still for long periods, fluttering after invertebrate prey in foliage; sings from open midstory and subcanopy. Slightly chunkier than Rufous Mourner, with patterned wing coverts, blockier head with pale eyering; cf. larger and plainer Rufous Piha. Yellow breast tufts flared when singing. SOUNDS: Distinctive song a plaintive, slightly tinny, slurred whistle, *tew-i-tieh*, usually 2–7×, sometimes introduced by a longer note. Call a plaintive, slightly overslurred *wheeeeeu*, about 1 sec, ending fairly abruptly. STATUS: Scarce and local on both slopes, to 700m. (Mexico to nw. Ecuador.)

NORTHERN [THRUSHLIKE] MOURNER (SCHIFFORNIS) *Schiffornis [turdina] veraepacis* 16.5–17.5cm. Unobtrusive denizen of humid forest; overlooked easily unless singing. Mainly at low levels in fairly open to dense understory; often perches on thin vertical twigs and stalks. Distinctive but rather nondescript: note earth-brown plumage with paler eyering, habits, voice. SOUNDS: Haunting whistled song repeated at irregular intervals, 1st note long and overslurred before a sharp upward inflection and abrupt ending, *tjeeeuuu-i wi-chi*, 1.5–2 secs; less often a shorter *tjeeuu wi-chi*. Short low rattle when agitated. STATUS: Uncommon to fairly common on Pacific slope, locally to 1700m; uncommon to scarce on Caribbean slope, to 1000m; most numerous in lower foothills. (Mexico to nw. Peru.)

MIDDLE AMERICAN
ATTILA

variation

RUFOUS MOURNER

RUFOUS PIHA

juv.

SPECKLED MOURNER

NORTHERN MOURNER

MANAKINS (PIPRIDAE; 8 SPECIES) Neotropical family of small fruit-eating birds; males often colorful and noted for complex displays. Ages/sexes differ; adult appearance attained in 1–3 years. Tend to sit quietly in shady understory and mid-story, sallying briefly to pluck berries, when wings can make distinctive strong whirr. Easily overlooked if not vocal or displaying.

LONG-TAILED MANAKIN *Chiroxiphia linearis* 11–12cm + male tail streamers. Distinctive manakin of drier forest and adjacent second growth, gallery forest, locally mangrove edge. No overlap with Lance-tailed Manakin. Mainly at low to mid-levels in shady understory. In display, 2–3 males leap up, hover briefly, and sometimes reverse leapfrog each other along a low thin branch. Adult male unmistakable; female relatively large and pale-bellied with long tail, bright orange legs, black bill; cf. White-collared Manakin. 1st-year male like female but with red crown patch, sometimes blackish in face; 2nd-year has head and underparts variably mottled black, long tail streamers, sometimes some blue on back; 3rd-year male mostly like adult but messier, mottled with some olive. **SOUNDS:** Varied calls include rich whistled *téeeu-hu*, quieter *wheu*, clipped *pic!* and slurred, semi-metallic burry *u'yeeaah*. Hollow whistled *to-lee-doh* in male duet; burry frog-like *jeh-rréuh* repeated steadily in leaping display, superimposed with low burry bleating of wings. **STATUS:** Fairly common to common on n. Pacific slope, to 1500m; spills over locally to adjacent Caribbean slope. (Mexico to Costa Rica.)

LANCE-TAILED MANAKIN *Chiroxiphia lanceolata* 11–12cm + male tail streamers. Counterpart to Long-tailed Manakin on extreme s. Pacific slope, in humid forest and woodland, taller second growth. Favors shady understory, and habits much like Long-tailed; in display, 2 males leap up, hover briefly, and sometimes reverse leapfrog each other along a low thin branch. Female larger and paler than other manakins in range, with long tail. 1st-year male has red crown patch, older 1st-years have blackish face; 2nd-year male has blue back, body mottled black and olive. **SOUNDS:** Varied calls include clipped downslurred *téu*, downslurred nasal *brreeah*. Hollow whistled *te-wee-hu* in male duet, higher and quicker than Long-tailed Manakin; burry, low pulsating display in leaping display, often interjected with nasal *breéh* calls; could be passed off as insects or frogs. **STATUS:** Fairly common to common locally on s. Pacific slope, mainly 1000–1500m. (Costa Rica to n. Venezuela.)

ORANGE-COLLARED MANAKIN *Manacus aurantiacus* 9.5–10cm. Stunning little manakin of humid forest understory and edge, adjacent taller second growth, plantations. Mainly at low levels in shady understory. Displays much like White collared Manakin, but clears smaller area of forest floor. Distinctive in range, cf. local overlap with larger female Long-tailed Manakin. Imm. male resembles female but throat and upper breast tinged golden yellow. **SOUNDS:** Downslurred, slightly explosive whistled *ts-reéu* and downslurred, burry to slightly rattled *chierrr*. In display, male makes loud wing snaps and rattles recalling White-collared Manakin, often alternated with burry whistles; wings make papery rustling in flight. **STATUS:** Fairly common locally on s. Pacific slope, to 1100m. (Costa Rica to w. Panama.)

WHITE-COLLARED MANAKIN *Manacus candei* 11.5–12cm. Striking manakin of humid lowland forest edge, second growth thickets such as *Heliconia*, overgrown plantations. Mainly at low levels in shady thickets, where males often detected by wing whirr during sallies for fruit; less often at mid–upper levels in fruiting trees. Displaying males clear a circle of forest floor and make snapping display leaps between slender saplings either side of the cleared area. Male unmistakable; female told by yellow belly, orange legs, black bill, cf. female Red-capped and Long-tailed Manakins. Imm. male resembles female but throat and median upper breast pale gray. **SOUNDS:** Downslurred, burry whistled *brréu*, and lower burry *rrreu*. In display, males make remarkably loud 'firecracker' wing snaps and mechanical wing rattles, often alternated with burry whistles; wings make papery rustling in flight. **STATUS:** Fairly common on Caribbean slope, to 800m; spills over locally to adjacent n. Pacific slope. (Mexico to w. Panama.)

imm. males

male

LONG-TAILED MANAKIN

female

imm. male

LANCE-TAILED MANAKIN

female

male

ORANGE-COLLARED MANAKIN

female

male

WHITE-COLLARED MANAKIN

display

female

male

RED-CAPPED MANAKIN *Ceratopipra mentalis* 9.5–10.5cm. Humid forest, adjacent shady clearings and second growth. Low to high, mainly at mid- levels in shady understory, at times with mixed flocks. Displaying male 'dance' includes various slides, pivots, and leaps along mid-level horizontal branches, accompanied by wing snaps and buzzes. Male unmistakable; female very drab, note pinkish bill and legs. Imm. male like female but often some red flecks on head (as is true of some older adult females), and eye becomes whitish in 1st year (rarely white on adult female). SOUNDS: Calls include high sharp *píp* and thin, drawn-out whistle, about 1 sec, often followed by sharp chip, *tsssiuu chk!* In display, varied arrangements of sharp, often slightly liquid chips in short series; high overslurred whistles tailing off, often followed by a rasping mechanical buzz or sharp *chk*; plus wing snaps, buzzes, and rattles. STATUS: Fairly common on both slopes, locally to 1100m. (Mexico to w. Ecuador.)

BLUE-CROWNED MANAKIN *Lepidothrix coronata* 8.5–9cm. Humid forest and taller second growth, mainly at low to mid-levels in shady understory. In display, males dart between branches of low trees while singing but with no wing sound. Male often appears wholly black inside forest, blue crown best seen when head turned. Female distinctive: grass-green overall (a color unlike other female manakins) with grayish face. Imm. male like female but often has some blue crown feathers. SOUNDS: Calls include an upward-inflected, extremely frog-like croaking *ch'reih* and a slightly overslurred slow ringing trill, 0.5–1.5 secs. In display, male alternates twitters with frog calls, sometimes adds down-slurred churring *chirrr*. STATUS: Fairly common on s. Pacific slope, uncommon on extreme s. Caribbean slope; locally to 1400m. (Costa Rica to S America.)

WHITE-RUFFED MANAKIN *Corapipo altera* 9.5–10cm. Humid lower foothill forest, adjacent shady clearings and second growth. Mainly at low–mid levels in understory, at times in loose small groups; sometimes joins mixed flocks. Display centers on a mossy log on forest floor, where males fly around in slow-motion bounding and hovering flights and alight briefly to flare their ruffs. Male distinctive (ruff more restricted on Pacific slope); female told by dull plumage, dark bill and legs. SOUNDS: Calls include a downslurred, high wiry *tssieu*, and an abrupt high *sssi*. Short rippling twitters (in display?) and an abrupt 2-syllable snap-buzz in display. STATUS: Fairly common, mainly 500–1500m on Pacific slope, 400–900m on Caribbean slope; descends to adjacent lowlands mainly Jul–Jan. (Honduras to nw. Colombia.)

*WHITE-CROWNED MANAKIN** *Pseudopipra pipra* 9–10cm. Humid foothill forest and adjacent second growth, mainly in dense shady understory. In display, male flies between horizontal branches in mid-story, often with slow deep wingbeats, showing off gleaming crown; flicks wings while perched. Striking male unmistakable; female told by grayish head (variable, some have mostly olive head with little gray, mainly on crown, perhaps imm. males?), reddish eyes, grayish legs; cf. female Red-capped Manakin. Imm. like female, with brownish to amber eyes. SOUNDS: Song from perch a harsh, upslurred, buzzy *jzzrieh*, usually about every 20–60 secs; also quiet *pip* calls. STATUS: Uncommon on Caribbean slope, mainly 700–1500m, rarely lower. (Costa Rica to S America.)

male

RED-CAPPED MANAKIN

female

display

male

BLUE-CROWNED MANAKIN

female

Caribbean

imm. male

males

**WHITE-RUFFED
MANAKIN**

juv. male

female

Pacific

**WHITE-CROWNED
MANAKIN**

male

female

WHISKERED FLYCATCHERS

(4 species) Small, enigmatic New World assemblage formerly subsumed within tyrant flycatchers, now variously treated as a separate family or merged with tityras and allies. Ages/sexes similar overall; all have notably long rictal bristles, or 'whiskers.'

RUDDY-TAILED FLYCATCHER *Terenotriccus erythrurus* 9–9.5cm. Tiny, rather cute inhabitant of humid forest, adjacent taller second growth. Singles and pairs perch in fairly open midstory and subcanopy, often on thin vines; sometimes joins mixed flocks. Distinctive, with small size, cinnamon underparts, rusty wings and tail. SOUNDS: Fairly quiet, high, 2-part whistle, 1st note lisping and reedy, 2nd emphatic, *pssii pit*; less often simply *speeu*. STATUS: Uncommon to fairly common on both slopes, locally to 1200m. (Mexico to S America.)

SULPHUR-RUMPED FLYCATCHER *Myiobius sulphureipygius* 11.5–12.5cm. Attractive and active little bird of humid forest, adjacent shady second growth, gallery forest. Usually at low to mid-levels in shady understory, often near water; joins mixed feeding flocks. Fairly active, flitting with tail fanned and wings drooped to show off bright yellow rump, which can 'glow' in shady understory. Yellow crown patch usually concealed, reduced or absent on female and juv. Cf. Black-tailed Flycatcher on s. Pacific slope. SOUNDS: Rather quiet. Soft clipped *tlik* given on occasion. STATUS: Fairly common to uncommon on both slopes, locally to 1200m in south. (Mexico to w. Ecuador.)

BLACK-TAILED FLYCATCHER *Myiobius atricaudus* 11.5–12.5cm. Humid lowland woodland, second growth, especially in low dense tangles along small streams. Less of a forest bird than Sulphur-rumped Flycatcher, but enters humid forest in areas where Sulphur-rumped is absent. Habits much like Sulphur-rumped, and the two species can be difficult to distinguish in shady understory. Note dingy, dusky buff breast of Black-tailed (vs. rich cinnamon-buff of Sulphur-rumped), slightly plainer, more olive-tinged head with narrow pale eyering (vs. grayer face, richer brown neck of Sulphur-rumped). Black-tailed often looks relatively small-headed and long-tailed, vs. more compact Sulphur-rumped. Yellow crown patch usually concealed, reduced or absent on female and juv. SOUNDS: Rather quiet. Slightly emphatic high *tsik*! is higher, less wet than Sulphur-rumped Flycatcher. STATUS: Uncommon on s. Pacific slope, to 900m. (Costa Rica to S America.)

NORTHERN ROYAL FLYCATCHER *Onychorhynchus mexicanus* 16.5–18cm. Humid lowland forest and taller second growth; gallery forest in drier nw. lowlands. Singles or pairs range in mid-levels of shady understory, often near streams. Long, scraggly nest structure hanging over streams or other openings such as quiet roads can be a good clue to presence. Often active, sallying and fluttering after prey in leafy foliage; joins mixed flocks. Distinctive, with hammerhead crest, pale cinnamon rump and tail. Crest raised mainly in alarm, very rarely seen spread unless birds are held in-hand; male crest fiery red, female crest yellow-orange. Juv. upperparts and chest scalloped dusky, soon like adult. SOUNDS: Slightly hollow, plaintive *whee-uk*, suggests a muffled Rufous-tailed Jacamar. Song a descending, slowing series of (usually 5–8) plaintive whistles with short intro note, *whi'peeu, peeu....* STATUS: Uncommon to fairly common on Pacific slope, to 900m; uncommon to rare on Caribbean slope, locally to 800m. (Mexico to nw. Venezuela.)

RUDDY-TAILED
FLYCATCHER

male

SULPHUR-RUMPED
FLYCATCHER

female

BLACK-TAILED
FLYCATCHER

males

nest

female

NORTHERN
ROYAL FLYCATCHER

TYRANT FLYCATCHERS (TYRANNIDAE; 77+ SPECIES) Large, diverse, and taxonomically vexed New World assemblage of insectivorous and frugivorous birds, ranging from tiny tyrannulets to large and conspicuous kingbirds; also see whiskered flycatchers (p. 290). Ages usually differ slightly, sexes similar; like adult within 1st year. Many species visually similar, voice often very important for ID, as is an appreciation of genus characters. Most forest species best detected by voice and can seem rare or even absent until vocalizations are learned.

GRAY-HEADED PIPRITES (MANAKIN) *Piprites griseiceps* 11–12cm. Enigmatic small bird of humid lower foothill forest; once considered a manakin, now usually treated as a tyrant flycatcher. Typically found as singles at mid–upper levels in shady understory and subcanopy; joins mixed flocks of antwrens, greenlets, flycatchers, tanagers. Sings from subcanopy, where can be hard to spot. No truly similar species: note upright pose, striking white eyering on gray head giving big-eyed look, contrasting pale lemon tertial edges, yellowish underparts. Imm. has head tinged olive. SOUNDS: Song a variably jerky or initially hesitant series of mellow, overslurred *whip* notes run into a short stutter and ending with an emphatic note, 1.5–3 secs: *wip, wip wi-wi-wip wirr-rr-rrip whuip!* and variations. Up to a min or so between songs, or songs follow on rapidly when excited. STATUS: Scarce to uncommon and local on Caribbean slope, 100–1000m. (Guatemala to nw. Panama.)

SPADEBILLS (GENUS *PLATYRINCHUS*) (3 species). Very small, compact, short-tailed forest flycatchers with big eyes, strong face patterns, and broad flat bills. Easily overlooked if not vocal. Found as singles or loose pairs in shady understory, where often sit still for long periods then make a short sally to pluck food from underside of leaf or twig and move to new perch, often leading an observer to spot the empty moving twig of the former perch and still not see the bird!

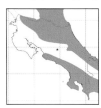

GOLDEN-CROWNED SPADEBILL *Platyrinchus coronatus* 8.5–9.5cm. Humid forest, adjacent taller second growth. See genus note. Sometimes flicks wings open on alighting and when calling. Note strikingly patterned pale yellowish face with blank lores, orange crown stripe; cf. White-throated Spadebill, mainly at higher elevations. SOUNDS: Varied, high sibilant to rapid ticking trills, 0.5–2.5 secs, easily passed off as an insect, *ssssiirrrr*, and variations; shorter trills often descending overall, longer versions often descend then rise, sometimes with a quiet introductory *tsi*. STATUS: Uncommon to fairly common, to 1200m on Pacific slope, to 700m on Caribbean slope. (Honduras to S America.)

STUB-TAILED SPADEBILL *Platyrinchus cancrominus* 9–10cm. Humid forest, including gallery forest. See genus note. Distinctive in most of range, but limited overlap at mid-elevations in n. Pacific foothills with White-throated Spadebill, which is slightly larger, darker, and colder-toned, with dark mandible tipped pale; easily told by voice. Male has yellow crown patch, usually concealed. SOUNDS: Slightly descending, high, abrupt nasal or squeaky *ki-di-dik* and *kidik*, repeated irregularly. Dawn song an excited, rolled nasal trill alternated with sharp nasal chips. STATUS: Uncommon and local in nw. lowlands, to 1300m. (Mexico to w. Panama.)

*WESTERN WHITE-THROATED SPADEBILL *Platyrinchus [mystaceus] albogularis* 9.5–10.5cm. Humid foothill and highland forest, adjacent taller second growth. See genus note. Distinctive in most of range, but limited overlap at mid-elevations in n. Pacific foothills with Stub-tailed Spadebill, which is slightly smaller, paler, and warmer-toned, with mostly pale pinkish mandible; easily told by voice. Male has yellow crown patch (more extensive than Stub-tailed), usually concealed. SOUNDS: Sharply overslurred, slightly emphatic *piik!* or *whiik!* occasionally doubled; recalls a small woodpecker, such as Smoky-brown. Dawn song a rippling, high nasal trill, 1–1.5 secs, typically an ascending crescendo ending with an abrupt *eek!* Also varied rising and falling trills, slowing slightly and fading at the end; lower and harsher than trills of Golden-crowned Spadebill. STATUS: Fairly common to uncommon on both slopes, 700–2100m. (Costa Rica to w. S America.)

GRAY-HEADED PIPRITES

male

GOLDEN-CROWNED SPADEBILL

STUB-TAILED SPADEBILL

male

WESTERN WHITE-THROATED SPADEBILL

294

SCALE-CRESTED PYGMY TYRANT *Lophotriccus pileatus* 9.5–10cm. Very small but distinctive flycatcher of humid foothill forest and shrubby edges, adjacent second-growth thickets. Mainly at low to mid-levels in shady cover; feeds by short sallies to pluck from foliage. Crest usually held flat to produce bushy nape; also note fine dark streaking below, amber eyes, cf. Northern Bentbill. Female has slightly smaller crest; juv. duller overall with pale cinnamon crown, no crest. SOUNDS: Rather loud voice easily passed off as an insect or frog. Ascending reedy *prríep*, often repeated steadily, and clipped, slightly nasal, hollow rolled *prrik*. Song (?) a series of (usually 3–10) *prrik* calls, often slightly descending, accelerating, or slowing overall, 4–5 notes/sec; at times repeated steadily; faster-paced, more prolonged when agitated. STATUS: Fairly common on both slopes, mainly 300–1700m, locally down to 100m on Osa Peninsula. (Costa Rica to S America.)

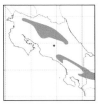

SEPIA-CAPPED FLYCATCHER *Leptopogon amaurocephalus* 12.5–13.5cm. Humid forest and edge, taller second growth. Mainly at mid-levels in shady understory; sallies for insects and also eats berries. Frequently flicks open one wing at a time. Note brown crown, pale cinnamon wingbars and tertial edgings, voice; cf. Slaty-capped Flycatcher of foothills. Juv. has brighter, buffier wingbars. SOUNDS: Infrequently heard. Rapid, rattling or spluttering trill, slightly overslurred or descending overall, 1.5–2 secs; at times preceded by 1–2 sharp clucking chips, *whik, whik, prrrrrrrrrru*. STATUS: Uncommon to scarce on n. Caribbean slope and in interior valleys of s. Pacific slope, mainly in lower foothills, locally to 1300m. (Mexico to S America.)

*WESTERN SLATY-CAPPED FLYCATCHER *Leptopogon [superciliaris] transandinus* 13–14cm. Humid foothill forest and edge, adjacent second growth. Mainly at mid-levels; habits much like Sepia-capped Flycatcher but often more active, frequently with mixed flocks. Note slaty-gray crown, pale yellowish to pale cinnamon wingbars and tertial edgings, voice. Juv. has cinnamon wingbars, crown tinged olive. SOUNDS: High, sharp, slightly sibilant *siík*, at times doubled or repeated steadily; prolonged, slightly squeaky rippling chatter, 2–4 secs. Song a slightly squeaky *sík! chiíirr*, 2nd note trilled and descending, repeated steadily. STATUS: Uncommon to fairly common on both slopes, mainly 600–1600m. (Costa Rica to nw. S America.)

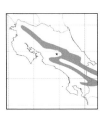

*OLIVE-STREAKED [OLIVE-STRIPED] FLYCATCHER *Mionectes olivaceus* 12.5–13.5cm. Distinctive, overall rather dark flycatcher of humid foothill and highland forest and edge, adjacent second growth and shrubby clearings, especially with fruiting trees and bushes. Perches low to high, slowly jerking its head back and forth, quickly lifting one wing at a time; often at fruiting trees and shrubs, sometimes with mixed flocks. Sings from perch in shady mid-story. Note whitish teardrop, slender bill, finely streaked breast. Juv. duller overall with fainter breast streaking, faint pale teardrop, buffy wing edgings; soon like adult. SOUNDS: Mostly quiet. Song a very high, thin, whining or sibilant trilled whistle that rises and falls gently, 2–7 secs overall with about 1 oscillation/sec; beyond the range of hearing for many people. STATUS: Fairly common on both slopes, 600–2400m; some post-br. movement Aug–Jan to adjacent Caribbean lowlands. (Costa Rica to w. Panama.)

*NORTHERN OCHRE-BELLIED FLYCATCHER *Mionectes [oleagineus] assimilis* 12–13cm. Distinctive but rather plain flycatcher of humid forest and edge, adjacent second growth, gallery forest. Habits much like Olive-streaked Flycatcher, with distinctive slow head jerking. Sings from perch in shady, fairly open mid-story, usually 2–3 males in a loose 'lek.' Note rounded head, slender bill, ochre belly. SOUNDS: Song a repetition of sharply overslurred, bright nasal clucks, every 1–2 secs, alternated with typically slightly faster bursts of downslurred nasal yaps, *whík whik...kyeh-kyeh-kyeh whík whik....*Infrequent calls include plaintive *cheu* and sharp *plik*. STATUS: Fairly common on both slopes, locally to 1200m; uncommon and local in drier nw. lowlands. (Mexico to n. S America.)

SCALE-CRESTED PYGMY TYRANT

SEPIA-CAPPED FLYCATCHER

variation

WESTERN SLATY-CAPPED FLYCATCHER

OLIVE-STREAKED FLYCATCHER

NORTHERN OCHRE-BELLIED FLYCATCHER

BLACK-HEADED TODY-FLYCATCHER *Todirostrum nigriceps* 7.5–8.5cm. Tiny, rather short-tailed flycatcher of humid forest and edge, adjacent second growth, plantations. Typically in canopy and easily overlooked if not vocal; makes short sallies for prey snatched from foliage. Distinctive, with black head, dark eyes, white throat, cf. Common Tody-Flycatcher, mainly in more open, second-growth habitats but occurs alongside Black-headed at forest edge. Juv. duller overall, soon like adult. SOUNDS: Measured series of (usually 5–15) high, sharp, downslurred metallic chips, *tchik tchik...*, or *chink chink...*, about 2/sec. STATUS: Fairly common on Caribbean slope to 1000m, rarely 1500m; spills over locally to n. Pacific foothills. (Honduras to nw. S America.)

COMMON TODY-FLYCATCHER *Todirostrum cinereum* 9–10cm. Handsome and rather distinctive little flycatcher of varied open and semi-open habitats, from farmland with hedgerows and scattered trees to mangroves, rainforest edge, second growth. Forages low to high, mainly at low to mid-levels. Often in pairs, turning its head slowly and staring about curiously, loosely swinging its cocked tail, and darting quickly after prey. Note fairly long cocked tail with graduated white tips, staring pale eyes in blackish hood. Juv. has duller eyes, dingier plumage. SOUNDS: Hard smacking *chk* suggests a warbler, often repeated steadily; short, high twittering trill often repeated quickly 2–6×, *till-ill-ill*, recalls Middle American Kingbird. STATUS: Common to fairly common on both slopes, mostly below 1500m. (Mexico to S America.)

SLATE-HEADED TODY-FLYCATCHER *Poecilotriccus sylvia* 9–10cm. Skulking and easily overlooked in thickets and tangles at lowland forest edge, in second growth, sometimes with bamboo. Hops inconspicuously in dense tangles, rarely in open at edges. Told from Northern Bentbill by habits, white spectacles, longer and straight bill; voice can suggest some bentbill calls. Juv. has duller eyes, olive head. SOUNDS: Abrupt, frog-like cluck and short growling churr, often combined, *pc prrrrr*. STATUS: Uncommon to fairly common on s. Pacific slope, uncommon to scarce and local in nw. lowlands and on Caribbean slope; locally to 1500m. (Mexico to S America.)

BLACK-CAPPED PYGMY TYRANT *Myiornis atricapillus* 6–7 cm. Tiny, 'tailless' flycatcher of lowland forest, adjacent taller second growth; resides mainly in canopy, but nests in understory. Forages by quick darting sallies to pluck insects and such from foliage. Difficult to spot when it sits still in canopy, given its tiny size, but distinctive when seen: note very short tail, cute face with whitish spectacles, habits. Juv. has crown washed brownish, upperparts duller with buffy wingbars. SOUNDS: Underwhelming, high-pitched calls easily passed over as an insect or frog. Upslurred, high burry *tssiirr* and abrupt, high rising *tsiik!* often repeated or alternated every 1–5 secs. STATUS: Uncommon on Caribbean slope, to 700m. (Costa Rica to nw. Ecuador.)

NORTHERN BENTBILL *Oncostoma cinereigulare* 9.5–10.5cm. Forest understory and edge, second-growth thickets. At low to mid-levels, often in fairly open understory with thin branches and vines. Perches fairly upright, often leaning forward slightly; sallies in foliage. Tiny size, pale eyes, thin pinkish legs, and eponymous bent bill distinctive; cf. Slate-headed Tody-Flycatcher. Juv. has duller eyes, olive head, buffy wingbars. SOUNDS: Varied low churrs and clucks, most often a drawn-out, frog-like *urrrrrrr*, 1–1.5 secs. Song (?) a slightly stuttering *pirrrip pirrrip p-p-prrrr*, 1st note 1–3×. STATUS: Fairly common to uncommon on both slopes, to 1200m on Pacific slope, to 1000m on Caribbean slope. (Mexico to w. Panama.)

**BLACK-HEADED
TODY-FLYCATCHER**

COMMON TODY-FLYCATCHER

**SLATE-HEADED
TODY-FLYCATCHER**

BLACK-CAPPED PYGMY TYRANT

NORTHERN BENTBILL

YELLOW-BELLIED TYRANNULET *Ornithion semiflavum* 8–9cm. Tiny, short-tailed flycatcher of humid lowland forest, taller second growth. Mainly in canopy and subcanopy, where overlooked easily. Gleans in foliage, dead-leaf clusters; does not usually sally or hover. Told from Brown-capped Tyrannulet by slaty gray vs. brown cap, voice. SOUNDS: Strident, overslurred or rising *sweéh*, at times doubled or in short series; nasal chips and clucks when agitated. Song repeated steadily, a slightly descending series of (usually 3–5) plaintive whistles, *deee-dee-dee-di*, last note sometimes upslurred. STATUS: Uncommon to fairly common on both slopes, to 600m. (Mexico to w. Panama.)

BROWN-CAPPED TYRANNULET *Ornithion brunneicapillus* 8–9cm. Tiny, short-tailed flycatcher of humid lowland forest, taller second growth. Habits like Yellow-bellied Tyrannulet; best told by voice in small area of overlap; also note brown crown. SOUNDS: High, upslurred plaintive *sweeih*; nasal chips and clucks when agitated. Song repeated steadily, a slightly descending series of (usually 3–5) plaintive whistles, last 1–2 notes sometimes upslurred; unlike Yellow-bellied Tyrannulet, typically preceded by, or interspersed with, rising call: *sweeeh, deee-dee-dee-di...*. STATUS: Uncommon to fairly common on Caribbean slope, to 900m. (Nicaragua to nw. S America.)

NORTHERN BEARDLESS TYRANNULET *Camptostoma imberbe* 9.5–10.5cm. Open woodland, second growth, semi-open areas with trees, especially in drier areas. Low to high, mainly at mid–upper levels; hops and flutters, plucking food from foliage. Posture often fairly upright, tail held below body plane and loosely wagged. Note bushy crest (rarely held flat), small bill with bright orange base, habitual tail pumping; fresh plumage has broad cinnamon wingbars, fading to whitish. Central American Beardless Tyrannulet tends to perch more horizontally, with tail cocked, plumage more contrasting, with yellowish belly, whitish wingbars; note voice. SOUNDS: Slightly overslurred *peért* and softer, drawn-out *peeeu*; slightly descending, measured series of (usually 3–8) downslurred notes, *dee dee dee...*; short bubbling *deedl-idl-it*. Song a varied short series of piping reedy whistles, typically including 1–2 louder notes, at times repeated over and over, such as *pi pii pii pee PEE pii-pi*. STATUS: Fairly common in nw. lowlands, locally to 1600m around Central Valley. (Mexico to Costa Rica.)

***CENTRAL AMERICAN [SOUTHERN] BEARDLESS TYRANNULET** *Camptostoma [obsoletum] flaviventre* 9.5–10.5cm. Open woodland, second growth, semi-open areas and scrub with taller trees, plantations. Habits much like Northern Beardless Tyrannulet but often holds tail cocked, posture less vertical. Note bushy crest (rarely held flat), yellowish belly, whitish wingbars, voice; cf. Northern Beardless Tyrannulet. Juv. duller and browner above, with buffy wingbars. SOUNDS: Calls average stronger, less plaintive than Northern Beardless. Downslurred, slightly emphatic *peéur* and overslurred *peeéu*, sometimes followed by short rolled squeak; slightly descending series of (usually 3–7) plaintive whistles, *pwee pwee...*. Song a varied, often prolonged repetition of piercing, slightly overslurred to descending whistles, singly or in series of 2–3 notes every 1–2 secs: *peeéu, peeéu, peeh-peeh, peeéu, peeéu-peeh-peeh, peeéu, peeéu...*. STATUS: Fairly common to uncommon on s. Pacific slope, locally to 1000m. (Costa Rica to Panama.)

***MOUSE-COLORED TYRANNULET** *Phaeomyias murina* 11–12cm. Distinctively drab small flycatcher of lowland second growth, scrubby thickets, forest edge, plantations. Typically inconspicuous at low to mid-levels in shrubs and smaller trees, where gleans for insects. Note dull buffy wingbars, broad pale eyebrow; cf. appreciably smaller beardless tyrannulets. SOUNDS: Overslurred, nasal to slightly squeaky chatter, *chi-chi-chi-chi-chi-chi*, about 0.5 sec, sometimes repeated steadily. Song a slightly rising, nasal to burry chattering crescendo, *ch-ch-ch-ch-chichichichir*, about 1 sec, repeated steadily. STATUS: Scarce and local in interior valleys of s. Pacific slope; scattered reports elsewhere; first recorded Costa Rica in 1996; likely spreading with deforestation. (Costa Rica to S America.)

YELLOW-BELLIED
TYRANNULET

BROWN-CAPPED
TYRANNULET

crest rarely
held flat

NORTHERN
BEARDLESS TYRANNULET

CENTRAL AMERICAN
BEARDLESS TYRANNULET

MOUSE-COLORED TYRANNULET

Northern

Southern

MISTLETOE [PALTRY] TYRANNULET *Zimmerius [vilissimus] parvus* 9.5–10.5cm. Widespread in humid forest edge, semi-open areas with scattered trees, hedgerows, open woodland, gardens; especially with mistletoe. Low to high, regularly in canopy; often perches with tail slightly cocked. Plucks berries and snatches insects with short flits. Best detected (and identified) by call; also note yellow wing edgings (not wingbars), stubby dark bill, whitish eyebrow. Cf. appreciably larger Sclater's Flatbill, Colombian Elaenia. Comprises 2 vocal groups that may represent species: **Northern Mistletoe Tyrannulet** *Z. [p.]* undescribed in north (to 1200m); **Southern Mistletoe Tyrannulet** *Z. [p.] parvus* in south (to 3000m). SOUNDS: **Northern:** overslurred, relatively loud whistled *peeéu*, often repeated steadily. Song a relatively quick, slightly rolled *chew'dl-it*, or *tyeeu chi-ti*, with a flourish. **Southern**: slightly plaintive *peeyíp*, sharply rising and overslurred at the end. Song a slower, more measured, mellow *teuw tew tew tew* or *dyew di-di-dit*. STATUS: Fairly common to common. Details of distribution for the 2 vocal types await elucidation. (Belize to nw. Colombia.)

YELLOW-CROWNED TYRANNULET *Tyrannulus elatus* 10–10.5cm. Second growth, hedgerows, semi-open areas with taller trees and forest patches. Singles or pairs, typically perching rather upright at mid–upper levels; makes short sallies for berries and insects. Note stubby bill, flattish head with blackish crown and yellow median stripe (usually visible), distinct whitish wingbars, voice. Juv. duller overall, lacks yellow crown stripe, wingbars buffy; soon like adult. SOUNDS: Distinctive, measured, mellow double whistle given throughout day, *wheéh peeu*, 2nd note slightly higher, overslurred. STATUS: Uncommon on s. Pacific slope, to 1200m; spreading n. with deforestation. (Costa Rica to S America.)

COLOMBIAN [GREENISH] ELAENIA *Myiopagis [viridicata] accola* 13–14cm. Humid woodland and edge, second growth; usually not in denser humid forest. Mainly at mid–upper levels where perches fairly vertically and quietly for long periods. Forages with short sallies, plucking insects and berries. Distinctive but relatively plain, with short whitish brow, weak wing markings, narrow bill; yellow crown patch usually concealed. Juv. duller, with dull buffy wingbars, lacks crown patch. SOUNDS: Downslurred, high burry *tsiéuhr* and overslurred variants. Dawn song comprises upslurred and downslurred burry whistles, repeated and alternated every 1–5 secs, *t'seéu, seeyu, t'seéu, t'seéu, seeyu, t'seéu, seeyu....* STATUS: Uncommon to scarce on Pacific slope, locally on Caribbean slope, to 1500m. (Nicaragua to nw. S America.)

RUFOUS-BROWED TYRANNULET *Phylloscartes superciliaris* 10.5–11.5cm. Attractive, rather perky little flycatcher of humid foothill forest canopy and subcanopy. Hops and sallies rather like a warbler, often cocks tail or lifts one wing at a time; joins mixed flocks. Face pattern distinctive, although rufous brow can be difficult to see; also note yellowish wing edgings (no distinct wingbars), long tail. Juv. has olive crown, little or no rufous in face. SOUNDS: Slightly squeaky, nasal to sibilant *sweik*, singly or in short series. Song a descending, slightly sibilant rippling twitter, about 1 sec, sometimes preceded by *sweik!* calls. STATUS: Uncommon to locally fairly common on Caribbean slope, mainly 600–1200m. (Costa Rica to nw. S America.)

WHITE-FRONTED (ROUGH-LEGGED) TYRANNULET *Phyllomyias zeledoni* 11–12cm. Scarce small flycatcher of humid highland forest. Mainly at mid–upper levels, sallying actively in outer foliage; often flicks wings between sallies. Cf. much commoner Mistletoe Tyrannulet, which differs in posture, dark bill, wing pattern, voice. Juv. browner above with little gray on head, belly tinged buff. SOUNDS: High, slightly piercing or sibilant whistles. High, shrill, overslurred *sseeíh*, can be repeated steadily; also slightly descending series of 4–10 *sseeíh* notes, 2–3/sec. Song (?) comprises drawn-out overslurred *pssiéeh* and *siéh-sieh* phrases repeated and alternated. STATUS: Scarce to uncommon and local on both slopes, mainly 1500–3200m, locally down to 600m in north. (Costa Rica to nw. S America.)

MISTLETOE
TYRANNULET

YELLOW-CROWNED
TYRANNULET

COLOMBIAN ELAENIA

RUFOUS-BROWED
TYRANNULET

WHITE-FRONTED
TYRANNULET

EYE-RINGED FLATBILL *Rhynchocyclus brevirostris* 15–16.5cm. Humid lowland and foothill forest, taller second growth. Mainly at mid-levels; often quiet, overlooked easily; joins mixed flocks. Distinctive, with big head, contrasting white eyering, overall olive head and upperparts with yellowish wing edgings. SOUNDS: Easily passed off as an insect. Song a series of (usually 2–5) high, lisping, slightly rough upslurred notes, 1st note(s) often longer, such as *zzzzíh zzzi-zzzi-zzi*; notes longer, closer-spaced than Sclater's Flatbill. Also single *ssshirrrr*, harsher, more steeply rising than Sclater's, and short harsh *zhhih*. STATUS: Uncommon on both slopes, to 2100m on s. Pacific slope, to 1700m on Caribbean slope. (Mexico to nw. Colombia.)

*SCLATER'S [YELLOW-OLIVE] FLATBILL *Tolmomyias [sulphurescens] cinereiceps* 12.5–13.5cm. Humid forest and edge, gallery forest, second growth, plantations; where Yellow-margined Flatbill also occurs, Sclater's typically around clearings and in second growth vs. forest canopy. Mainly at mid-levels. Sallies to snatch insects from foliage; often holds tail slightly cocked. Best told from Yellow-margined by voice; also note pale eyes (darker on imm.), wholly pale mandible (often extensively dark-tipped on Yellow-margined, but can be mostly pale), pinkish legs, less contrasting yellowish edges to wing coverts. SOUNDS: Easily passed off as an insect. Song a series of (usually 2–5) high, lisping, slightly shrill upslurred notes in measured, often slightly intensifying series, 1–1.5 secs between notes, such as *sssih sssih sssih sssih*. Call a quiet lisping *ssi*. STATUS: Fairly common on Pacific slope, uncommon to fairly common on Caribbean slope, to 1600m. (Mexico to w. Panama.)

*PANAMA [YELLOW-OLIVE] FLATBILL *Tolmomyias [sulphurescens] flavoolivaceus* occurs in Pacific lowlands of w. Panama; may be overlooked in adjacent Costa Rica. Told from Sclater's Flatbill by voice, olive tinge to head, pale brownish eyes, more-distinct wingbars. SOUNDS: High, sharp, downslurred *chiik* in measured series, usually 3–4×, and single high sharp *chik!*

YELLOW-MARGINED FLATBILL *Tolmomyias [assimilis] flavotectus* 12–13cm. Humid forest, adjacent taller second growth. Mainly at mid–upper levels, often in canopy; joins mixed flocks. Habits like Sclater's Flatbill, which see for differences. Juv. has broader, less distinct wing edgings tinged buffy. SOUNDS: Song a series of (usually 4–7) slightly shrill, emphatic, sharply overslurred whistled notes in slightly intensifying series, 1st note lower, slightly quieter: *tsii ssíeh ssíeh ssíeh ssíeh*, 2–3 notes/sec; quality suggests slurred Yellow-bellied Flycatcher. Call an emphatic single *psiéh*. STATUS: Uncommon to fairly common on Caribbean slope, to 1000m. (Honduras to nw. Ecuador.)

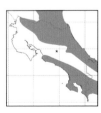

YELLOW TYRANNULET *Capsiempis flaveola* 10–11cm. Small, slender, long-tailed flycatcher of humid second growth, overgrown pastures with shrubs, bamboo, small trees, hedgerows. Often in pairs; forages with hops and short fluttering sallies, plucking from foliage. Distinctive: note shape and habits, yellowish brow and underparts, pale wingbars. Juv. duller overall, wingbars buffier. SOUNDS: Bright nasal *piic* and upslurred *puic*, can be given singly, repeated steadily, or run into fairly rapid series with slightly excited, pulsating cadence, 4–5 notes/sec. Also more-complex, rhythmic bickering chatters, *p-pidic pid-i pid-i pidik….* STATUS: Fairly common on both slopes, to 1200m on s. Pacific slope, to 800m on Caribbean slope. (Nicaragua to S America.)

TAWNY-CHESTED FLYCATCHER *Aphanotriccus capitalis* 11.5–12.5cm. Rather retiring small flycatcher of humid forest, adjacent second-growth thickets, often along streams in shady understory; forages by short sallies to snatch food from vegetation. No similar species in Costa Rica: note narrow whitish spectacles on gray head, cinnamon wingbars, tawny breast (duller on juv.); plus habits, voice. SOUNDS: Slightly explosive *tchéu!* suggesting burry Yellow-bellied Flycatcher call; chirping clipped *chet*, sometimes doubled. Song a slightly accelerating and often stuttering series of (usually 3–7) chips, ascending slightly and ending emphatically with a burry note, 0.5–1.5 secs, such as *chp chp-chp chp chp-chupeéuh*. STATUS: Uncommon to fairly common locally on n. Caribbean slope, to 1000m. (Honduras to Costa Rica.)

EYE-RINGED FLATBILL

juv.

SCLATER'S FLATBILL

PANAMA FLATBILL

YELLOW-MARGINED
FLATBILL

YELLOW
TYRANNULET

TAWNY-CHESTED
FLYCATCHER

chest can be quite dull,
and muted in shade

ELAENIAS (GENUS *ELAENIA*) (3 species). Neotropical genus of often notoriously similar species, with species limits still poorly known. Often crested, with pale eyering or spectacles, pale wingbars. Dawn songs repeated over and over, tirelessly. Elaenias mainly glean from foliage and often eat berries.

YELLOW-BELLIED ELAENIA *Elaenia flavogaster* 15–16.5cm. Bushy-crested flycatcher of varied open and semi-open habitats, from overgrown grassy fields to forest edge, often with fruiting shrubs. Can be inconspicuous, but at other times perches atop bushes calling noisily; crest typically raised and conspicuous, but can be held flattened. Gleans from foliage by short sallies, often eats berries. Larger and bulkier than Lesser Elaenia with more conspicuous, white-based spiky crest, showier habits; note voice. Juv. has shorter crest with little or no pale base, buffy wingbars. **SOUNDS:** Burry, overslurred drawling *breéuh*; hoarse rhythmic bickering *rreeahr-ch'reer…*or *bríka-weehr...*, usually 3–5× in duets. Dawn song a burry *frrí-diyu* or *prri di-di-eu* and variations, over and over. **STATUS:** Fairly common to common on both slopes to 1800m, locally to 2200m; spreading with deforestation. (Mexico to S America.)

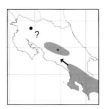

LESSER ELAENIA *Elaenia chiriquensis* 13–14.5cm. Varied open and semi-open habitats, from overgrown grassy fields and marshes to scrubby savanna, forest edge, often with fruiting shrubs. Mainly at low to mid-levels, often perched inconspicuously; gleans from foliage and often eats berries. Crest short and relatively inconspicuous, with small whitish base; cf. larger and bulkier Yellow-bellied Elaenia. Juv. duller overall, lacks crown patch, wingbars buffy. **SOUNDS:** Sharply overslurred, slightly plaintive whistled *wheéh*, less often a burry *rreéu*, shorter than drawl of Yellow-bellied. Dawn song a slightly burry *ch'wee* or *p'rieh* repeated steadily and interspersed with short chatters, *ch'wee ch'wee ch'wee-chchchur ch'wee….***STATUS:** Fairly common to uncommon in interior valleys of s. Pacific slope, locally n. to Central Valley, to 1500m; spreading with deforestation. (Costa Rica to S America.)

MOUNTAIN ELAENIA *Elaenia frantzii* 14–15cm. Humid highland forest and edge, adjacent clearings with fruiting shrubs. Low to high, often sluggish and inconspicuous; gleans from foliage and often eats berries. Notably drab: note rounded to slightly bushy crown (not strongly crested), pale eyering, broad whitish tertial edges. **SOUNDS:** Slightly burry whistled *péeuh*, falling away, and strongly burry, overslurred *bhíerr*, occasionally doubled; burry bickering chatters in interactions. Dawn song a slightly burry, overall rising *chíliéh*, repeated steadily; might suggest a musical House Sparrow. **STATUS:** Common to fairly common throughout in highlands, breeds mainly above 1200m in Northern Mts., above 1800m in Central and Talamanca Mts.; variable Sep–Jan downslope movement to Pacific foothills, when usually scarce or absent at highest elevations. (Mexico to nw. S America.)

NORTHERN SCRUB FLYCATCHER *Sublegatus arenarum* 14–15cm. Medium-size, small-billed flycatcher of mangroves; ranges to adjacent scrubby habitats. Usually solitary and rather low, sometimes on mangrove roots. Sallies for insects and fruit, and often pumps tail once or twice on landing. Distinctive but unremarkable: note small black bill, bushy crest, elaenia-like plumage, habitat; cf. much larger, longer-billed Panama Flycatcher (p. 322) of same habitat. Juv. has pale fringes to head and upperparts, soon like adult. **SOUNDS:** Slightly squeaky whistled *huweép*; varied, squeaky nasal chatters when agitated. Dawn song a steady alternation of simple whistled phrases, *ch'weép feéu ch'weép feéu...*, 1 phrase/1.5–3 secs. **STATUS:** Uncommon locally on n. Pacific coast. (Costa Rica to nw. S America.)

YELLOW-BELLIED ELAENIA

juv.

LESSER ELAENIA

MOUNTAIN ELAENIA

NORTHERN SCRUB FLYCATCHER

BRAN-COLORED FLYCATCHER *Myiophobus fasciatus* 11.5–12.5cm. Unobtrusive small flycatcher of brushy second growth, overgrown weedy fields, scrubby savanna. Perches low, often along fences; sallies for insects. Note brownish plumage, dusky-streaked breast, short pale eyebrow, buffy wingbars. **SOUNDS:** Slightly emphatic, mellow twittering chatters, such as *whee-chchchchchi*, 0.5 secs, may be repeated steadily. Dawn song a mostly downslurred, mellow chirping *chi'li*, every 1–2 secs, interspersed with overslurred *h'wiép* phrases. **STATUS:** Uncommon to fairly common locally on s. Pacific slope, to 1500m; spreading with deforestation. (Costa Rica to S America.)

*COSTA RICAN TUFTED FLYCATCHER *Mitrephanes [phaeocercus] aurantiiventris* 11.5–12.5cm. Distinctive, small crested flycatcher of humid foothill and highland forest edge, adjacent second growth and clearings with shrubs, trees. Perches low to high, often on prominent twigs; fluttering sallies for insects often followed by return to same perch, shivering tail upon landing, like a pewee. **SOUNDS:** Slightly ringing slow twitter of (usually 3–10) rising chip notes, *pyi-pyi...*, 6–7 notes/sec; slightly emphatic, overslurred whistle, *pséeih*, and quiet overslurred *pip*, which may precede twitters and whistle. Dawn song a short, slightly stuttering series of bright chips run into a high whistle, *pip pi-pih pih seéuh*, and variations, repeated over and over with slow rippling cadence. **STATUS:** Fairly common to common on both slopes, 500–3000m, most numerous 1200–2100m. (Costa Rica to Panama.)

PEWEES (GENUS *CONTOPUS*) (6+ species). Rather drab flycatchers with slightly peaked or crested crowns, paler wingbars; lack distinct pale eyerings. Perch rather upright on exposed twigs or prominent high snags and sally out for insects, often returning repeatedly to the same perch and quivering tail upon landing. Unlike empids (pp. 308–312), pewees do not habitually flick tails and wings.

OCHRACEOUS PEWEE *Contopus ochraceus* 16–17cm. Scarce, medium-size, crested flycatcher of highland oak forest, adjacent second growth with taller trees. See genus note. Mainly at mid–upper levels, at breaks in canopy or within open midstory. Cf. much smaller Costa Rican Tufted Flycatcher. Juv. has brighter ochre-buff wingbars. **SOUNDS:** Short series of (usually 5–6, more when agitated) ringing, slightly metallic ascending to overslurred chips, *pying pying...*, 5–6/sec; suggests Costa Rican Tufted Flycatcher but lower, more metallic, and slower-paced. Song a high, piping, overall rising *wi-seíh* every 3–6 secs. **STATUS:** Scarce and local in Central and Talamanca Mts., mainly 2200–3000m. (Costa Rica to w. Panama.)

DARK PEWEE *Contopus lugubris* 16–17cm. Humid foothill and highland forest edge; adjacent clearings with taller trees. See genus note. Mainly at mid–upper levels, often on exposed snags. Note tufted crest, overall slaty-gray plumage; appreciably larger than migrant Western Pewee. Juv. has dull buffy wingbars. **SOUNDS:** Overslurred bright *piic* or *pwic*, at times in short, measured series of (usually 2–7) notes, slower-paced and higher-pitched than Olive-sided Flycatcher. Dawn song repeated over and over, *fred-rick-fear, rick* ascending, *fear* lower (Stiles & Skutch 1989). **STATUS:** Fairly common to uncommon on both slopes, mainly 1200–2300m. (Costa Rica to w. Panama.)

OLIVE-SIDED FLYCATCHER *Contopus cooperi* 17–18.5cm. Large, rather bulky migrant pewee of foothill and highland forest and edge; migrants also in lowlands. Perches atop taller trees, rarely lower at edges of clearings. Note relatively short tail, peaked head (not crested, cf. longer-tailed Dark Pewee), white throat with dark-vested underparts; from behind, sometimes shows white flank tufts. Two song types may represent cryptic species, not visually separable: **Northern Olive-sided Pewee** *C. [c.] cooperi* (breeds n. N America); **Western Olive-sided Pewee** *C. [c.]* undescribed? (breeds w. N America). **SOUNDS:** Call of both types a clipped, overslurred *bihk*, typically in series of 2–4 notes; songs sometimes heard in spring, rarely fall–winter, a 3-note *wot! peeves you* (Western) or *whit free beeh* (Northern). **STATUS:** Uncommon but widespread transient, late Aug–Oct, mid-Mar to early Jun, to 3000m; rare in winter on both slopes, mainly 600–2300m. Status of the 2 types in Costa Rica awaits elucidation; wintering birds most likely Western.

BRAN-COLORED FLYCATCHER

juv.

COSTA RICAN
TUFTED FLYCATCHER

juv.

OCHRACEOUS
PEWEE

DARK PEWEE

OLIVE-SIDED
FLYCATCHER

*NORTHERN TROPICAL PEWEE *Contopus [cinereus] bogotensis* 13–14.5cm. Woodland and edge, adjacent second growth, pastures with hedgerows, scattered trees; mainly mangroves in northwest. See genus note (p. 306). Low to high, often on fences. Slightly more compact and richly colored than Eastern and Western Pewees; note shorter primaries, darker crown, voice. Also cf. migrant Willow and Alder Flycatchers, readily told by habits, voice. SOUNDS: Short, slightly overslurred ringing trill, suggesting Middle American Kingbird; high, sharply overslurred *pyeép*. Song a high, vaguely disyllabic, upslurred *pseep* or *p'seíh*, every 1–3 secs; at longer intervals after dawn. STATUS: Fairly common to uncommon in humid lowlands, to 1500m; scarce and local on drier n. Pacific slope. (Mexico to n. South America.)

WESTERN PEWEE (WOOD PEWEE) *Contopus sordidulus* 13.5–15cm. Wooded and semi-open foothill and highland habitats with hedges, scattered trees, fences. See genus note (p. 306). Averages duskier and grayer than Eastern Pewee, with more strongly vested underparts, but ID best by voice. Note long wings vs. Northern Tropical Pewee, also voice. Cf. shorter-winged Willow and Alder Flycatchers, readily identified by habits. Imm. has fresher plumage, buff wingbars. SOUNDS: Overslurred, burry drawled *brréeu* or *bzzhiu*, distinct from Eastern Pewee; less often a plaintive, slightly upslurred *peéur*, suggesting Eastern but slightly lower, shorter, less inflected. STATUS: Fairly common to common Aug to mid-Nov, late Mar–May, on both slopes, mainly above 700m; rare in winter, mainly on Pacific slope. (Breeds w. N America to Mexico, winters S America.)

EASTERN PEWEE (WOOD PEWEE) *Contopus virens* 13.5–15cm. Wooded and semi-open lowland and foothill habitats with hedges, scattered trees, fences. See genus note (p. 306). Very similar to Western Pewee, and often not separable in field unless heard. Note long wings vs. Northern Tropical Pewee, also voice. Cf. Willow and Alder Flycatchers, readily identified by habits, voice. Imm. has fresher plumage, buff wingbars. SOUNDS: Plaintive upslurred *p'weée* or *du-weée*, clearer and higher than Western Pewee; rarely a clipped *puik*. STATUS: Fairly common to common mid-Aug to mid-Nov, Mar–May, on both slopes to 1500m, in smaller numbers to 2500m; rare in winter, mainly below 1200m. (Breeds e. N America, winters S America.)

EMPIDS (GENUS *EMPIDONAX*) (8 species). Small flycatchers with pale wingbars and usually pale eyerings; crown often slightly peaked but not distinctly crested. Unlike pewees, empids do not return repeatedly to the same prominent perches and they tend to perch more inconspicuously, several species inside forest or woodland. Habitually flick tails up and twitch wings, unlike pewees. Best identified by voice and structure; also note habitat, overall plumage tones (grayish and whitish vs. greenish and yellowish).

WILLOW FLYCATCHER *Empidonax traillii* 12.5–14cm. Nonbreeding migrant in open and semi-open habitats with hedgerows, scattered trees, second growth, marshes. See genus note. Weak eyering (often appears plain-faced, cf. pewees), whitish throat, and relatively dull wingbars separate Willow and Alder Flycatchers from other migrant empids. Some Willows (from w. N America) duller and browner than Alder, with duller wingbars; others (from e. N America) only safely told from Alder by voice. SOUNDS: Sharply upslurred, mellow *whit* or more liquid *whuit*, similar to Least Flycatcher. STATUS: Fairly common mid-Aug to Oct, mid-Mar to May on both slopes, to 1500m; uncommon locally in winter in nw. lowlands and on Pacific slope. (Breeds N America, winters Mexico to S America.)

ALDER FLYCATCHER *Empidonax alnorum* 12.5–14cm. Transient migrant in open and semi-open habitats with hedgerows, scattered trees, second growth. See genus note and under Willow Flycatcher. Averages brighter, more contrasting than eastern Willow, but reliably separated in field only by voice; also cf. Least Flycatcher. SOUNDS: High, sharply overslurred *piic* or *peek*, unlike other Costa Rican empids. STATUS: Fairly common late Aug–early Nov on Caribbean slope, uncommon on Pacific slope, rarely to 2000m; uncommon to fairly common on both slopes, Mar–May. (Breeds n. N America, winters S America.)

NORTHERN
TROPICAL PEWEE

juv.

WESTERN
PEWEE

EASTERN PEWEE

imm.
(Sep–Dec)

WILLOW
FLYCATCHER

ALDER
FLYCATCHER

imm.
(Sep–Dec)

Eastern

Western

310

WHITE-THROATED FLYCATCHER *Empidonax albigularis* 12–13cm. Local in semi-open and open areas with hedgerows, shrubby growth, marshes, damp pastures; often near water. See genus note (p. 308). Typically low and inconspicuous, often perches on fences, grass stalks; sallies for insects. Best located and identified by voice. Appearance similar to migrant Willow and Alder Flycatchers but slightly smaller and more compact, with browner upperparts, buff wingbars, ochre tinge to flanks; whitish throat not an especially good ID feature. SOUNDS: Call quite unlike other empids: relatively low, burry, over-slurred *rréah* or *brriéh*. Song a short burry snarl run into an emphatic ending, *brr-rreeuh'* repeated steadily. STATUS: Uncommon to fairly common but local, mainly 1000–2000m around Central Valley; in winter, some range to n. Caribbean lowlands. (Mexico to w. Panama.)

LEAST FLYCATCHER *Empidonax minimus* 11.5–12.5cm. Small migrant empid of open woodland and edge, shrubby second growth; usually at edges and in fairly open situations, not inside forest. See genus note (p. 308). Mainly at low to mid-levels, often fairly active; tail flicks often loose and slightly wobbly, not discrete. Note voice, relatively compact shape, dirty whitish throat, bold wingbars and eyering; relatively small bill typically has dusky or dark tip to mandible. Cf. Alder and eastern Willow Flycatchers, which have longer wings, less striking eyerings. SOUNDS: Sharply upslurred *swik* or *whit*, similar to Willow Flycatcher but slightly higher. STATUS: Scarce Oct–Apr on both slopes, mainly Pacific slope; to 1200m. (Breeds n. N America, winters Mexico to Costa Rica.)

YELLOW-BELLIED FLYCATCHER *Empidonax flaviventris* 12.5–13.5cm. Migrant empid of humid forest, taller second-growth woodland, plantations, gallery forest. See genus note (p. 308). Low to high, mainly at mid-levels in shady understory and edge; rarely in open situations during migration. Fairly compact shape recalls slightly smaller Least Flycatcher; note pale yellowish wash to throat and underparts (belly not especially yellow), contrasting wingbars (with broad dark band across base of secondaries), voice (but call very similar to Acadian Flycatcher), pale orangey-pink mandible. Often in obvious wing molt over the winter, unlike Acadian. SOUNDS: Sharply overslurred, slightly explosive *speéik* (much like Acadian); mainly in spring, a more leisurely downslurred *pyeeh* and plaintive slurred *tch'wee*, suggesting Eastern Pewee but shorter. Song (mainly fall, when establishing winter territories) an abrupt, burry *ch'bik*. STATUS: Fairly common to common Sep–Apr on both slopes, to 1500m; more widespread in migration, late Aug–Oct, Mar to mid-May. (Breeds n. N America, winters Mexico to w. Panama.)

ACADIAN FLYCATCHER *Empidonax virescens* 13–14cm. Relatively large, big-billed, and long-winged migrant empid of humid lowland and foothill forest, plantations. See genus note (p. 308). Low to high, mainly from mid-levels in shady understory to subcanopy; rarely in open situations during migration. Note big bill with pale orangey-pink mandible, buff wingbars, dingy whitish throat; call very similar to Yellow-bellied Flycatcher. All ages are fresh in fall–winter (not undergoing wing molt as are Yellow-bellied); also note weaker dark band across base of secondaries than Yellow-bellied. SOUNDS: Sharply overslurred, slightly explosive *speéip*, averages higher and more explosive than Yellow-bellied call. STATUS: Uncommon to fairly common Sep–Nov, Mar to mid-May, mainly on Caribbean slope and inland to 1800m. Rare in winter on both slopes (but many winter reports refer to Yellow-bellied Flycatcher). (Breeds e. N America, winters s. Cen America to nw. S America.)

WHITE-THROATED FLYCATCHER

juv.

LEAST FLYCATCHER

imm.
(Sep–Dec)

YELLOW-BELLIED FLYCATCHER

imm.
(Sep–Dec)

ACADIAN FLYCATCHER

imm.
(Sep–Dec)

BLACK-CAPPED FLYCATCHER *Empidonax atriceps* 11.5–12cm. Small, perky, rather dark resident empid of highland oak forest, adjacent shrubby clearings, pastures, second growth. See genus note (p. 308). Forages from low shrubs to high in canopy, often on exposed perches and can be confiding; sallies for insects. Distinctive for an empid, overall dark with darker crown, contrasting whitish eyering, dull pale wingbars. Juv. has buffier wingbars. **SOUNDS:** Sharp, clipped, slightly liquid *pik*. Dawn song a progression of clipped, semi-metallic, short rolled phrases, such as *pridiree didi-ree pidiree pipipirree...*, repeated steadily, 1 phrase/1–2 secs. **STATUS:** Fairly common in Central and Talamanca Mts., mainly 1900–3300m. (Costa Rica to w. Panama.)

*****SOUTHERN YELLOWISH FLYCATCHER** *Empidonax flavescens* 12–13cm. Resident empid of humid highland and foothill forest and edge. See genus note (p. 308). Mostly low to high in shady understory; sallies for insects and plucks from foliage. Relatively distinctive, best told from migrant Yellow-bellied and Acadian Flycatchers by strongly contrasting, pale teardrop-shaped eyering, peaked hindcrown; also note ochre breast, dull buffy-olive wingbars. Juv washed browner overall. **SOUNDS:** High, slightly lisping, underslurred *tssi* and upslurred *seéin*. Song a measured 3-part chant, repeated steadily at dawn, *ssi sii ch'li*, about 2 secs; 1st 2 notes high and lisping, 3rd lower, slightly clipped. **STATUS:** Fairly common to common, mainly 1200–2500m on Pacific slope, 700–2100m on Caribbean slope. (Costa Rica to w. Panama.)

TORRENT TYRANNULET *Serpophaga cinerea* 9.5–10.5cm. Distinctive tiny flycatcher of rushing streams and rivers, where pairs hold territories year-round; ranges to nearby wet roads and pastures. Perches mainly on rocks in and beside rushing water, often loosely flipping its tail; less often in adjacent vegetation. Sallies for insects. Male averages blacker head, with concealed white crown patch; female has sootier head, crown patch reduced or lacking. Juv. duller overall, washed brownish, with buffy wingbars. **SOUNDS:** High, sharp, overslurred *psíp*, at times run into excited rapid chipping series. Song a high sharp *ti-siíp*, every 2–6 secs. **STATUS:** Fairly common on both slopes, mainly 600–2000m on Pacific slope, 300–1800m on Caribbean slope. (Costa Rica to S America.)

LONG-TAILED TYRANT *Colonia colonus* 12.5–13.5cm, + 8–12cm tail streamers. Distinctive flycatcher of humid lowland forest and edge, adjacent open areas and clearings with tall bare trees, plantations. Pairs and singles perch conspicuously atop trees and on bare branches, sallying for insects. No similar species in Costa Rica. Female averages paler belly, duskier crown and back stripe than male. **SOUNDS:** High upslurred *pweet*; stronger, upslurred, and abruptly ending *pweeíh?* Song one or more rising whistles run into descending rolled chipper, *wheee p-p-peu*. **STATUS:** Uncommon to fairly common on Caribbean slope, to 1000m. (Honduras to S America.)

*****BLACK PHOEBE** *Sayornis nigricans* 15–16cm. Distinctive, medium-size fly-catcher of foothills and highlands, usually near water, especially rocky rivers and streams, around bridges, buildings; also towns, villages. Singles or pairs perch on rocks in streams, sallying out for insects; often sings in fairly high fluttering flight. Note size, habits, tail-flicking; white belly can be hard to see. Juv. has duller plumage, cinnamon wingbars. **SOUNDS:** High, sharp, downslurred *siik!* Song high, short piping phrases repeated and alternated *si-ii, s-si-sii, si-ii, s-si-sii...*every 1–2 secs, from perch or in high fluttering flight. **STATUS:** Fairly common on both slopes, mainly 600–2000m; post-breeding birds wander lower. (Mexico and w. US to S America.)

SOUTHERN YELLOWISH
FLYCATCHER

BLACK-CAPPED
FLYCATCHER

juv.

TORRENT TYRANNULET

juv.

LONG-TAILED TYRANT

BLACK PHOEBE

KISKADEE-LIKE FLYCATCHERS (7 species). A group of medium-size and large flycatchers, not always closely related, share the kiskadee pattern of a boldly striped head and bright yellow underparts (also cf. Golden-bellied Flycatcher, p. 318). Often noisy and conspicuous, yet generally avoided by predators, these flycatchers may represent examples of mimicry, reinforcing or imitating the pattern of the bad-tasting Great Kiskadee. Multiple species can associate together, especially at fruiting trees. For ID note bill size and shape, details of head pattern, habitat, and especially voice. Like many tyrant flycatchers, adults have a yellow to red crown patch, usually concealed but flared in interactions.

GREAT KISKADEE *Pitangus sulphuratus* 23–25cm. Large, conspicuous, and often noisy flycatcher of varied semi-open and open habitats, often near water; not typically in forest. Forages low to high, often at fruiting trees with other large flycatchers, thrushes, etc. Note stout pointed bill, bright rusty wings and tail, voice; yellow crown patch often concealed. Cf. Boat-billed and social flycatchers. Juv. has even more extensive rusty on wings and tail, lacks yellow crown patch. **SOUNDS:** Loud. Raucous overslurred *reéah*, and *híh-reéah*, plus longer variations, including *kíh káh-réah* ('Kis ka-dee'). Dawn song a steady series of short, overslurred raucous screeches alternated with short burry chatters, *h-rríeah h-rríeah rríeah kihr-rr-rr, h'rríeh...*, and variations. **STATUS:** Common to fairly common on both slopes, locally to 2200m, rarely higher. Increasing and spreading with deforestation. (Mexico to S America.)

BOAT-BILLED FLYCATCHER *Megarynchus pitangua* 23–24cm. Large, stout-billed flycatcher of forest and edge, plantations, adjacent semi-open areas with larger trees, gallery forest. Mainly at mid–upper levels in canopy, in pairs or family groups. Note very stout black bill, lack of bright rusty in wings and tail, voice; cf. Great Kiskadee, smaller White-ringed and social flycatchers. Orange-yellow crown patch of adult usually concealed. Juv. has cinnamon wing and tail edgings, lacks colored crown patch. **SOUNDS:** Grating, harsh, drawn-out *eihrrrrr*, often upslurred at end, and screechy, rhythmic bickering chatters, with cadence suggesting Northern Social Flycatcher. Dawn song a simple, burry, downslurred *prrriu*, every 1–2 secs. **STATUS:** Fairly common to common on both slopes, locally to 2200m, rarely higher. (Mexico to S America.)

WHITE-RINGED FLYCATCHER *Conopias albovittatus* 15–16cm. Medium-size flycatcher of humid lowland forest canopy and edge, often along rivers; not usually in open and semi-open habitats like *Myiozetetes* flycatchers (next plate). Looks like a mini Boat-billed Flycatcher, longer-billed than social flycatchers of more open habitats. Usually in pairs or small groups in and atop canopy, sallying to pluck insects and fruit from foliage; often detected by ringing calls. Note medium size, bold white head stripes, habits, voice; cf. social flycatchers, Boat-billed Flycatcher. Yellow crown patch usually concealed. Juv. has cinnamon wing edgings, lacks crown patch. **SOUNDS:** Shrill, rattled, staccato trills, mostly 0.5–1 sec, usually introduced by a faster, overslurred *brreéhr* and often given persistently. Dawn song (?) a short version of call, *wheéih dr-drit* or *wheéih dr-dr-drit*, repeated about every 1 sec. **STATUS:** Uncommon to fairly common on Caribbean slope, locally to 700m. (Honduras to nw. Ecuador.)

with Middle American Kingbird,
Northern Social Flycatcher

GREAT KISKADEE

BOAT-BILLED FLYCATCHER

WHITE-RINGED FLYCATCHER

GENUS *MYIOZETETES* (4 species). Medium-size, kiskadee-like flycatchers of scrubby and second-growth habitats; build bulky domed nests of grasses, other vegetation. Appreciably smaller than Great Kiskadee, with small bills. Plumage often similar among species, and ID easiest by voice. Also note head pattern, prominence of pale wingbars, extent of rusty edgings on wings (varies with age).

*NORTHERN SOCIAL FLYCATCHER *Myiozetetes [similis] texensis* 17–18cm. Conspicuous, often noisy, in varied edge and semi-open habitats, second growth, plantations, gardens; often near water. In pairs or small groups ('social') on wires, at fruiting trees with kiskadees, other larger flycatchers. On s. Pacific slope cf. Colombian Social Flycatcher, Rusty-margined Flycatcher; ID often best made by voice. Also cf. larger Great Kiskadee, Boat-billed Flycatcher. Flame crown patch of adult often concealed. Juv. has cinnamon wing and tail edgings, lacks crown patch. **SOUNDS:** Downslurred, slightly piercing *tseéyh*; at times followed by shrieky series that can suggest parakeets, *seéya tortéeya tortéeya...*; other varied burry calls and bickering chatters. Dawn song a varied alternation of downslurred whistles and short burry phrases, *tséu, tséu chirríeu...*, on and on. **STATUS:** Common to fairly common on both slopes, locally to 2100m, rarely higher. (Mexico to w. Panama.)

species uncertain

*COLOMBIAN SOCIAL FLYCATCHER *Myiozetetes [similis] columbianus* 16–17cm. Replaces Northern Social Flycatcher on s. Pacific slope; best identified by voice. Also averages more-distinct wingbars, slightly paler grayish crown than slightly larger Northern Social. Rusty-margined Flycatcher most easily separated by voice, has duller wings with rusty edgings to primaries (beware, juv. social flycatchers also have rusty wing edgings), blacker crown. Also cf. larger Great Kiskadee, Boat-billed Flycatcher. Flame crown patch of adult often concealed.

Juv. has cinnamon wing and tail edgings. **SOUNDS:** Overslurred, slightly piercing *chréeu* or *tcheéu*, burrier and quicker-paced than Northern Social; other varied burry calls and bickering chatters. Dawn song appears to be varied repetition of calls alternated with rapid, gruff burry chatters, *chréeu, cheu, chí-chírri-chi....* **STATUS:** Common to fairly common on s. Pacific slope, but details of distribution vs. Northern Social Flycatcher await elucidation. (Costa Rica to nw. S America.)

RUSTY-MARGINED FLYCATCHER *Myiozetetes cayanensis* 15.5–16.5cm. Second growth, semi-open lowland areas with scattered trees, scrub, plantations, often alongside social flycatchers. Best told from social flycatchers by voice; also note blacker crown sides (yellow, not flame-colored, crown patch of adult usually concealed), browner upperparts, rusty edgings to primaries (but. juv. and perhaps some 1st-year social flycatchers have rusty wing edgings). Also cf. larger Great Kiskadee, Boat-billed Flycatcher. Juv. has cinnamon wing and tail edgings, lacks crown patch. **SOUNDS:** Common call a plaintive screaming whistle, typically overslurred to slightly descending, *peeééeu*, suggesting Dusky-capped Flycatcher but more drawn-out; vaguely hawk-like, and very different from social flycatchers. Variably pulsating series of downslurred, slightly nasal squeaky whistles *tchieh-tchieh...*, up to 5 secs or longer, 5–6 notes/sec, at times preceded by upslurred scream, *wheeeih chieh-chieh....* **STATUS:** Uncommon locally on s. Pacific slope, to 200m; first reported Costa Rica in 2004. (Costa Rica to S America.)

GRAY-CAPPED FLYCATCHER *Myiozetetes granadensis* 15–16.5cm. Second growth and semi-open areas with scattered trees and forest patches, forest edge, plantations; often near water. Typically conspicuous, in pairs or small groups feeding low to high on insects, fruit. Distinctive, with overall gray head lacking bold stripes; flame crown patch of adult often concealed. Juv. has cinnamon wing and tail edgings, duller crown. **SOUNDS:** Sharply overslurred nasal *bík* or *bek!* suggesting Western Kingbird; sharp, overslurred nasal *kyew,* at times in short series; short burry chatters. Dawn song 2–3 calls run into a short sneezy phrase, vaguely kiskadee-like, repeated steadily about every 1–3 secs, *bik, bik, bíchi-biehrr....* **STATUS:** Fairly common to common on both slopes to 1000m, in smaller numbers locally to 1700m. (Honduras to S America.)

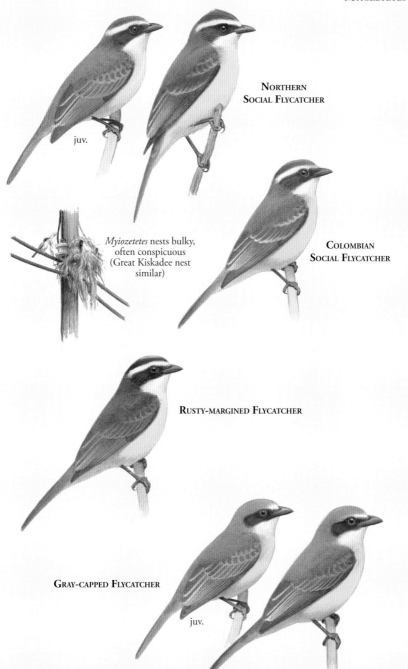

NORTHERN SOCIAL FLYCATCHER

juv.

Myiozetetes nests bulky, often conspicuous (Great Kiskadee nest similar)

COLOMBIAN SOCIAL FLYCATCHER

RUSTY-MARGINED FLYCATCHER

GRAY-CAPPED FLYCATCHER

juv.

PIRATIC FLYCATCHER *Legatus leucophaius* 15–17cm. Medium-size, small-billed flycatcher of semi-open country and clearings with taller trees, forest edge, gallery forest, plantations, Steals and uses the nests of other species, especially becards and oropendolas, hence 'piratic.' Perches conspicuously in canopy, where may vocalize tirelessly. Distinctive, with stubby bill, dark mask, blurry streaking below; yellow crown patch usually concealed. Juv. has cinnamon wing and tail edgings. SOUNDS: Loud ringing whistle, often followed by 1 or more short twitters, often over and over, *Sweée, di-di-dit,...* STATUS: Fairly common to uncommon breeding migrant on both slopes, locally to 1800m; arrives Jan–Feb, departs Sep, with stragglers into Oct. (Breeds Mexico to S America, winters S America.)

GENUS *MYIODYNASTES* (3 species). Large, heavy-billed flycatchers with bold head patterns, dark whisker marks; nest in tree cavities, crannies amid epiphytes. Often at fruiting trees, especially in migration.

GOLDEN-BELLIED FLYCATCHER *Myiodynastes hemichrysus* 19–21cm. Humid foothill and highland forest and edge, especially at light gaps and along streams. Mainly at mid–upper levels, often perched on mossy snags, sometimes on power lines. Note large size, boldly striped head with diagnostic dark whisker, yellow underparts; cf. kiskadees and similar species. Juv. has browner upperparts, cinnamon wing and tail edgings. SOUNDS: Variably explosive, overslurred nasal *skweéh!* often repeated steadily; rarely short excited series, *skweizih-skwei-izih...*; quality recalls Sulphur-bellied Flycatcher. Dawn song a clear, melodious *tree-le-loo*, repeated steadily (Stiles & Skutch 1989). STATUS: Fairly common to uncommon on Caribbean slope, 700–1800m, locally on cen. Pacific slope, 1400–2300m. (Costa Rica to w. Panama.)

SULPHUR-BELLIED FLYCATCHER *Myiodynastes luteiventris* 19–21cm. Lowland and foothill forest and edge, gallery forest, semi-open country with taller trees, forest patches. Mainly at mid–upper levels, often hidden in leafy canopy. Note broad black mustaches meeting under bill, coarse breast streaking, whitish face stripes vs. yellowish belly, voice; yellow crown patch usually concealed. Juv. has pinkish bill base, cinnamon wing and tail edgings, cf. Northern Streaked Flycatcher. SOUNDS: High, piercing *skweeízik*, suggesting a child's squeezy toy; excited sneezy chatters. Song a fairly quick, rolled *tcheu-wheézilit,...* about every 2 secs. STATUS: Uncommon to fairly common breeding migrant Mar–Sep on both slopes, locally to 2100m; widespread transient, mid-Feb to Apr, late Aug–Oct, stragglers into Nov. (Breeds Mexico to Costa Rica, winters S America.)

***NORTHERN STREAKED FLYCATCHER** *Myiodynastes maculatus* 20–22cm. Lowland forest, adjacent clearings with taller trees, gallery forest, mangroves; more widely in migration, when rarely in small loose groups. Mainly at mid–upper levels. Slightly bulkier and bigger-billed than Sulphur-bellied Flycatcher, with pale bill base, pale chin, finer streaking below extending to undertail coverts (cf. Sulphur-bellied), yellow-tinged face but whiter belly; also note voice. Yellow crown patch usually concealed. Juv. has pinkish bill base, cinnamon wing and tail edgings. SOUNDS: Sharp clucking *bihk!* and full-bodied, downslurred *h'chew*; both can be repeated steadily and run into excited chatters. Dawn song a rich, whistled, rippling *wheé-didl-i-eu,...* every 2–3 secs. STATUS: Fairly common on Pacific slope, locally to 1500m; less numerous in winter, especially in nw. lowlands. More widespread in migration, mainly Feb–Apr, Aug–Sep, when scarce on Caribbean slope. (Breeds Mexico to n. S America, winters Costa Rica to S America.)

PIRATIC FLYCATCHER

watching nest of
Rose-throated Becard

GOLDEN-BELLIED
FLYCATCHER

SULPHUR-BELLIED
FLYCATCHER

NORTHERN STREAKED
FLYCATCHER

GENUS *MYIARCHUS* (6 species). Medium-size to rather large flycatchers of wooded and scrubby habitats; nest in tree cavities. Raise bushy crest and puff out throat when agitated or curious (as in response to pygmy owls), slowly jerking head back and forth. Often at fruiting trees, especially in winter. ID often best made by voice (a cryptic species was recognized from Middle America as recently as the 2000s). Also note bill size, face pattern, prominence of pale wingbars, extent of rusty edgings on wings.

*NUTTING'S FLYCATCHER *Myiarchus nuttingi* 18–19cm. Lowland dry forest and edge, gallery woodland, second growth. May occur alongside Brown-crested and Salvadoran Flycatchers; best identified by voice. Note brownish face and blended rusty edgings to secondaries vs. grayer face and abrupt rusty/whitish break on primary/secondary edgings of Brown-crested. Nutting's lacks distinct dark stripe on underside of outer tail feathers of Salvadoran, but tail pattern similar to Brown-crested. Juv. has extensive rusty wing and tail edgings. SOUNDS: Overslurred, slightly emphatic whistled *wheéh* or *wheér*, less often *wheéh dee*; a clipped *whiep* suggesting Brown-crested but clearer, less emphatic; a querulous twittering *kwirri* repeated or run into series; and varied burry chatters. Dawn song a repetition of bright, whistled phrases, each phrase every 1–2 secs: *whiek, wie-dieh, whiek, wie-dih...*, and variations. STATUS: Uncommon to fairly common, to 1200m. (Mexico to nw. Costa Rica.)

*SALVADORAN [NUTTING'S] FLYCATCHER *Myiarchus [nuttingi] flavidior* 18–19cm. Status uncertain in Costa Rica. Favors brushy open woodland, semi-open areas with hedgerows. Note distinct dark stripe on underside of outer tail feathers, brighter yellow belly than Nutting's and Brown-crested; best identified by voice. Juv. has extensive rusty wing and tail edgings. SOUNDS: Overslurred, slightly plaintive *wheeéu*, suggesting a clipped Dusky-capped Flycatcher, not as emphatic as Nutting's and at times with short introductory note, *wh'wheeéu*; an overall slightly descending, piping twitter, 1.5–2 secs, *whii, pii-pii-....*Dawn song a measured repetition of whistles and short chips, each phrase every 1.5–2.5 secs: *w'wheeéu, wip, wídit, wheeéu, wídit....* STATUS: May occur in nw. lowlands, as reported by Lanyon (1961), but presence in Costa Rica considered unconfirmed by Slud (1964) and we have found no unequivocal record. (Mexico to Nicaragua; and nw. Costa Rica?)

BROWN-CRESTED FLYCATCHER *Myiarchus tyrannulus* 19–20.5cm. A relatively small race of this widespread *Myiarchus* inhabits semi-open and open country with hedgerows, scrubby woodland, mangroves. Notoriously similar to Nutting's Flycatcher (at one time considered conspecific), but note voice; contrast between rusty and whitish primary/secondary edgings of Brown-crested (beware, imms. of all *Myiarchus* have rusty edgings to all flight feathers); relatively big bill; and grayish face. Also cf. migrant Great Crested Flycatcher, which prefers more-humid habitats. Juv. has more extensive rusty wing and tail edgings. SOUNDS: Sharply overslurred, clipped *wuík!* and overslurred burry *weéhrr*, latter sometimes in steady series; varied, rhythmic bickering chatters in interactions. Dawn song a measured, varied repetition of quiet 'whip' notes, burry whistles, and short burry chatters, each phrase every 1–2 secs: *whiep, whi'pi-pi-reer, whip, whip, whee-b-beeihr, rreihr....* STATUS: Fairly common to uncommon, locally to 1200m; spills over to adjacent n. Caribbean slope. (Mexico and sw. US to S America.)

GREAT CRESTED FLYCATCHER *Myiarchus crinitus* 20–21.5cm. Large, relatively brightly colored migrant *Myiarchus* of forested habitats, taller second growth, plantations. Mainly at mid–upper levels, often well hidden in leafy canopy. From other *Myiarchus* by richer coloration, especially dusky gray breast contrasting with bright yellow belly; also note sharply defined, relatively broad whitish edging to shortest tertial, dull pinkish base to mandible, voice. SOUNDS: Upslurred, rich whistled *wheeép*, ending abruptly with slight downward inflection; often repeated steadily. STATUS: Fairly common to common Oct–Mar on Pacific slope, uncommon to fairly common on Caribbean slope, to 1500m; more widespread in migration, late Sep–Oct, late Mar–Apr, to 1800m. (Breeds e. N America, winters Mexico to nw. S America.)

NUTTING'S
FLYCATCHER

SALVADORAN
FLYCATCHER

BROWN-CRESTED
FLYCATCHER

GREAT CRESTED
FLYCATCHER

DUSKY-CAPPED FLYCATCHER *Myiarchus tuberculifer* 16–17cm. Smallest *Myiarchus*, widespread in varied wooded, forested, and semi-open habitats, from mangroves to foothill forest. Ranges low to high, from overgrown weedy fields to forest canopy. Best identified by size, dark head (especially crown), dull wingbars but bright rusty wing edgings, little rusty in tail, voice. Juv. paler below, tail broadly edged rusty. SOUNDS: Common call a plaintive overslurred *wheeeeu*, varied to shorter, more screaming *reeeu* and burrier *wheeer*; also a shorter note followed by rolled whistle, *whee peeerrrrr*, about 1.5 secs. Dawn song a measured, varied repetition of overslurred whistles and upslurred *wuik* notes, each phrase every 1.5–3 secs: *wheeéu, wheeéu, wuik! wheébeeu, wuik! wheeéu....* STATUS: Fairly common on both slopes, locally to 1200m, in smaller numbers to 1800m. (Mexico and sw. US to S America.)

PANAMA FLYCATCHER *Myiarchus panamensis* 18.5–19.5cm. Medium-size, rather plain *Myiarchus* of mangroves, ranging rarely to adjacent wooded and scrubby habitats. Mainly at low to mid-levels inside and at edges of mangroves. Note lack of rusty in wings and tail, dull wingbars, overall grayish head and breast, voice. Cf. smaller Northern Scrub Flycatcher (p. 304), often in same habitat, which has small bill, more distinct wingbars. Juv. plumage (held briefly) has wings and tail edged bright rusty; mandible can be pale pinkish at base. SOUNDS: Common call a rolled, slightly nasal, clipped *whiéduh*; also a more plaintive *whee-diheu*; in agitation, a fairly rapid, slightly ringing series of (usually 11–17) loud, slightly shrieky, overslurred whistles, 1st note longer, more emphatic, *whieh-dee-dee...*, 1.5–2 secs, at times preceded by 1–2 burry downslurred notes; varied, low gruff notes and short chatters. Dawn song *kweea-hurr, kwiheer, kweeahurr* repeated in various combinations, the *hurr* with a rolling burry quality (Stiles & Skutch 1989). STATUS: Fairly common along Pacific coast n. to Gulf of Nicoya. (Costa Rica to nw. S America.)

KINGBIRDS (GENUS *TYRANNUS*) (6+ species). Large conspicuous flycatchers of open and semi-open country. Ages/sexes differ slightly, like adult in 1st year. Juvs. lack concealed yellow or flame crown patches, wing coverts fringed pale cinnamon, fading to whitish. Main sex difference is shape of outer primaries: adult males have narrower, more strongly tapered tips. Many species roost communally in winter.

*MIDDLE AMERICAN [TROPICAL] KINGBIRD *Tyrannus [melancholicus] satrapa* 21–23cm. Large conspicuous flycatcher of open and semi-open areas, ranchland, towns, parks, lighter woodland, beach scrub, forest clearings and edge; often perches on roadside wires, fences. Note big bill, bright yellow belly, notched tail, cf. migrant Western Kingbird. SOUNDS: Varied twittering trills, mainly a short *till-ill-ill-it*, and longer rippling trills that start hesitantly, upslur, then fall at end. Dawn song a series of hesitant tiks run into 2–4-part twittering trills, with overall rippling cadence, *tk tk tk tk widdle-íwiddli,...* and variations STATUS: Common to fairly common on both slopes to 1800m, in smaller numbers locally to 2400m. (Mexico and s. Texas to nw. S America.)

WESTERN KINGBIRD *Tyrannus verticalis* 19.5–21cm. Winter migrant to open and semi-open areas with taller trees, hedges, orchards, scrub, gallery forest, especially with fruiting trees where may associate with other large flycatchers. Note relatively small bill, long wings, short black tail with white sides, cf. larger and brighter Middle American Kingbird. SOUNDS: Clipped, sharply overslurred *bek* and querulous chatters, suggesting Scissor-tailed Flycatcher. STATUS: Irregular Oct–Apr on Pacific slope and inland to Central Valley, to 1200m; fairly common some years, scarce in others; very rare and sporadic on s. Pacific slope. (Breeds w. N America to Mexico, winters Mexico to Costa Rica.)

DUSKY-CAPPED FLYCATCHER

PANAMA FLYCATCHER

MIDDLE AMERICAN KINGBIRD

WESTERN KINGBIRD

EASTERN KINGBIRD *Tyrannus tyrannus* 19.5–21cm. Transient migrant in open and semi-open areas, forest and woodland edge, fruiting canopy. Migrant flocks of 100s stream overhead all day. Distinctive, with fairly small bill, blackish head, bold white tail tip; flame crown patch usually concealed. Faded juv. notably duller, white tail tip can be virtually worn away. SOUNDS: High, shrill, slightly tinny, downslurred *tseih*; high buzzy twitters. STATUS: Fairly common to very common Sep–Oct, late Mar to mid-May (small numbers from late Aug and into Nov), in Caribbean coastal lowlands, uncommon to sporadically fairly common elsewhere, locally to 1800m. (Breeds N America, winters S America.)

GRAY KINGBIRD *Tyrannus dominicensis* 21–23cm. Rare migrant to open coastal areas, towns; often on roadside wires. Associates with Eastern and Middle American Kingbirds, especially at roosts. Note long heavy bill, relatively long cleft tail, gray upperparts with black mask, whitish underparts; yellow-orange crown patch usually concealed. SOUNDS: Twittering trills similar to Middle American Kingbird but average lower, rougher, slower-paced. STATUS: Rare transient on and near Caribbean coast, Sep–early Nov, Mar; exceptional in winter. (Breeds Caribbean region, winters se. Caribbean to n. S America.)

SCISSOR-TAILED FLYCATCHER *Tyrannus forficatus* 19–35.5cm. Spectacular migrant kingbird of open brushy habitats, ranchland with hedgerows and fences. Perches low to high, often on roadside wires; migrants mix readily with other kingbirds. Flocks of 100s can stream overhead all day during migration. Distinctive, with pale head and upperparts, variable salmon-pink flush below (deepest on adult male, palest on imm. female); red crown patch usually concealed. Tail longest on adult male. SOUNDS: Clipped, sharply overslurred *pic* and bickering chatters similar to Western Kingbird. STATUS: Fairly common to common Nov–Mar on n. Pacific slope, in smaller numbers to s. Pacific slope and in Central Valley, to 1500m; more widespread in migration, Oct–Nov, Mar–Apr. (Breeds sw. US and Mexico, winters Mexico to Panama.)

*FORK-TAILED FLYCATCHER *Tyrannus savana* 19–40.5cm. Spectacular kingbird of savanna, marshy areas, ranchland. Perches on ground, low bushes and fences, less often on roadside wires; usually in pairs or small groups, locally to 50+ birds. Long tail fans in a lyre shape, unlike diverging fork of Scissor-tailed Flycatcher. Distinctive, with dark head, long black tail (longest on adult male); yellow crown patch usually concealed. Austral migrants from South America are regular vagrants to North America (mainly Aug–Nov), and may be overlooked in Costa Rica. Differ from resident birds in duskier gray upperparts not contrasting as strongly with wings, slightly lower-pitched call, details of wing-tip structure. Any birds away from normal range should be checked carefully. SOUNDS: High sharp, slightly metallic *tik* and crackling twitters; song a few *tik* notes accelerating into a short, downslurred gurgle. STATUS: Fairly common locally on s. Pacific slope and in nw. lowlands, to 1200m; irregular occurrences elsewhere throughout the country suggest nomadic movements. (Mexico to S America.)

EASTERN KINGBIRD

GRAY KINGBIRD

SCISSOR-TAILED FLYCATCHER

imm.
(Sep–Dec)

juv.

FORK-TAILED FLYCATCHER

326

MOCKINGBIRDS AND ALLIES (MIMIDAE; 2 SPECIES) New World family of slender, long-tailed birds noted for varied songs. Ages differ slightly, adult appearance attained within a month or so of fledging; sexes similar.

GRAY CATBIRD *Dumetella carolinensis* 20–21.5cm. Distinctive winter migrant favoring humid thickets, forest edge, and second growth with fruiting shrubs. Mainly singles, skulking at low to mid-levels in cover, but sometimes ventures into more open canopy, and at times birds gather at fruiting bushes. No similar species in Costa Rica. SOUNDS: Complaining nasal mew, may suggest a cat, *meéah*, and rougher *nyaah*; abrupt mewing cluck, *myeh!*; short hard rattle in alarm, mainly in flight. STATUS: Fairly common mid-Oct to mid-Apr on Caribbean slope, to 1500m, a few from Sep and into early May; rare or very rare on Pacific slope. (Breeds N America, winters Mexico to Panama.)

*VIEILLOT'S [TROPICAL] MOCKINGBIRD *Mimus gilvus* 24–26cm. Distinctive mimid of varied semi-open and open habitats, with trees, hedgerows, fruiting shrubs, especially residential areas, gardens, playing fields. Runs well on ground, often stopping with tail cocked; also feeds on fruit in bushes and trees, often on roadside wires and atop utility poles. No similar species in Costa Rica: note overall pale gray plumage, dark mask, slender black bill, broad white tail tip, habits. Juv. has variable dark spotting on underparts. SOUNDS: Calls include a gruff *chek!* and downslurred *cheuh*. Song notably varied, may suggest a *Turdus* thrush: typically prolonged but variably disjointed, an unhurried medley of rich and burry whistles and clucks with frequent repetition of notes or phrases; often pauses of 2–5 secs between sets of phrases. STATUS: Uncommon to fairly common locally and increasing on Pacific slope, to 2200m; less numerous but also increasing on Caribbean slope. First reported Costa Rica in 2000, having spread nw. from Panama. (Cen America to S America.)

THRUSHES (TURDIDAE; 15 SPECIES) Worldwide family of small to medium-size songbirds with slender bills, often pleasing songs. Ages differ, adult appearance attained within a month or so of fledging; sexes similar or different.

MOUNTAIN THRUSH *Turdus plebejus* 22.5–25cm. Drab gray-brown thrush of humid highland forest and edge, adjacent clearings and second growth with fruiting shrubs; forms small flocks in winter. Feeds in trees and shrubs, also on ground in damp pastures. Note black bill, dark legs, overall plain cold-toned plumage with paler edgings to undertail coverts; cf. Pale-vented and Clay-colored Thrushes. Juv. warmer-toned overall, upperparts flecked cinnamon-buff, breast mottled and spotted dark brown and buff; soon like adult. SOUNDS: Song a singularly underwhelming, tedious, rather fast-paced and tuneless chirping, *chu-chu-chi-chrih-chrih-chi-chu...*, about 3 notes/sec with the same note often repeated several times; can last a min or longer. Call a low wooden cluck, at times in short series; high thin *siip* mainly in flight. STATUS: Fairly common to common, mainly from 1300m to timberline; in winter ranges lower, locally down to 900m. (Mexico to w. Panama.)

SOOTY THRUSH *Turdus nigrescens* 24.5–27cm. Large, distinctive dark thrush of highlands, favoring more-open areas such as páramo, forest clearings, second growth; ranges locally into oak forest. Feeds mainly on ground, also in fruiting shrubs and trees. Distinctive, with bright yellow-orange bill, yellow legs, pale eyes; female averages duller overall. SOUNDS: Song an unhurried, rather 'boring' chant of variably rich, squeaky, and burry chirps, *chirih chirih tchih tchih tchih...*, at most 1–2 notes/sec with notes often repeated several times; on occasion, short warbling phrases inserted to relieve the cadence. Call a low burry or gravelly *chehrr*, at times in short series and repeated rapidly. STATUS: Fairly common to common, mainly above 2400m; locally down to 2100m in fall–winter. (Costa Rica to w. Panama.)

Gray Catbird

Vieillot's Mockingbird

juv.

Mountain Thrush

juv.

Sooty Thrush

328

CLAY-COLORED THRUSH *Turdus grayi* 22–25cm. National bird of Costa Rica, found widely in wooded and semi-open habitats, from highland pastures to suburban gardens, plantations to humid forest edge. Often feeds on the ground, also in fruiting trees and shrubs. Note warm brown plumage tones (darkest in more humid areas), yellowish bill, amber eyes; cf. Pale-vented and Mountain Thrushes, both of which can occur alongside Clay-colored. **SOUNDS:** Song a rich caroling of mellow whistles, often with slightly lilting or jerky cadence and irregular repetition of phrases; song of Pale-vented Thrush averages steadier, richer, overall slower-paced, and less jerky. Calls include a slurred mewing *iyeuuh* or *uíreeh*, often rising overall; and a short soft cluck, often in fairly rapid, slightly laughing series, *kuh-kuh...*, mainly 1–2 secs; high thin *siip* mainly in flight. **STATUS:** Common to fairly common and widespread, especially in lowlands; locally to 2700m, occasionally higher. (Mexico and s. Texas to n. Colombia.)

PALE-VENTED THRUSH *Turdus obsoletus* 22–24cm. Humid foothill forest and edge, adjacent second growth and clearings with fruiting trees and shrubs. Mainly arboreal, but also feeds on ground, usually in shady cover; often forms small post-breeding flocks. Note black bill and dark legs, contrasting whitish undertail coverts. Cf. Clay-colored, White-throated, and Mountain Thrushes. **SOUNDS:** Song a rich, rather steady-paced caroling of mellow whistles, lower and less varied than White-throated Thrush, with less-frequent repetition of phrases; averages slower-paced, more melodic, and less jerky than Clay-colored Thrush. Call a nasal upslurred *whiéh*, at times in short series. **STATUS:** Fairly common to uncommon on Caribbean slope, mainly 700–1600m; some fall–early winter movement to adjacent lowlands. (Costa Rica to w. Ecuador.)

*****WHITE-THROATED THRUSH** *Turdus assimilis* 22–24cm. Humid foothill forest and edge, adjacent second growth with fruiting trees and shrubs. Mainly arboreal, but also feeds on ground, usually in shady cover; often forms small post-breeding flocks. Plumage tones variable, but note rich yellow bill and eyering, blackish-streaked throat, white foreneck collar (may be hard to see when birds are overhead or fluffed up). Adult male on n. Caribbean slope slaty gray above with blacker head, yellowish legs; s. male brownish gray above, legs often more pinkish yellow; female browner overall; imm. often has duller bill, dull pinkish legs, especially in south. Juv. browner overall with duller bare parts, variable dark spotting on breast, ghosting of adult throat pattern. **SOUNDS:** Song a prolonged, often varied, rich caroling series of mellow whistles, high trills, and fluty notes with frequent 2–3× repetition of phrases, typically fairly leisurely in pace. Calls include a nasal upslurred *rriéh* and *hoo-rieh*; and a low, burry or twangy *urrh*, easily passed off as a frog; high thin *ssi* mainly in flight. **STATUS:** Fairly common to uncommon on Pacific slope, uncommon on Caribbean slope; mainly 800–1800m, locally higher; some fall–early winter movement to adjacent lowlands. (Mexico to Panama.)

LOWLAND AND FOOTHILL *Turdus*

CLAY-COLORED THRUSH

juv.

PALE-VENTED THRUSH

juv.

WHITE-THROATED THRUSH

adult male
Northern

juv.

female

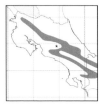

BLACK-FACED SOLITAIRE *Myadestes melanops* 17–18cm. Retiring arboreal thrush of humid highland and foothill forest, adjacent second growth and pastures with fruiting shrubs. Mainly at low to mid-levels in shady understory, bamboo thickets, but ventures to canopy in fruiting trees. Perches rather upright and still for long periods; easily overlooked unless singing. Distinctive, with bright orange bill, black face, habits. SOUNDS: Song a varied phrase of fluty to burry semi-metallic whistles; sometimes bouts of 2–4 phrases, often in alternating high-low sequence, with up to 30 secs or longer between bouts; other times a more continuous sequence with phrases every 2–3 secs. Call a rough, semi-metallic upslurred or overslurred *rrreíeh.* STATUS: Fairly common on both slopes, mainly 900–2700m; some descend in fall–winter to adjacent Caribbean lowlands; reduced or extirpated locally by capture for cagebird trade. (Costa Rica to w. Panama.)

GENUS *CATHARUS* (8 species). Small forest thrushes, 4 spot-breasted migrants (this plate) and 5 more brightly marked residents known as nightingale-thrushes (next plate). Ages differ, with spotted juv. plumage held briefly; sexes mostly similar. Favor shady forest floor and often elusive; also range at mid–upper levels in fruiting trees; migrants may sing in spring (mainly Apr to mid-May).

*****SWAINSON'S THRUSH** *Catharus ustulatus* 16.5–18cm. Varied wooded and forested habitats, shade coffee plantations; mainly in humid foothills and lowlands. Note pale buff spectacles, distinct buff wash to face and breast, olive-gray upperparts. Cf. Gray-cheeked Thrush. SOUNDS: Call a sharp, slightly metallic *wuit.* Song often heard in spring migration, a fluty, rich, upward-spiraling warble, 1.5–2 secs. STATUS: Common transient late Sep–Nov, late Mar to mid-May, with smaller numbers from mid-Sep and into late May; fall migration mainly on Caribbean slope, spring migration on both slopes; commonest in foothills, locally to 3300m. Uncommon to scarce and local in winter on both slopes, to 1500m. (Breeds N America, winters Mexico to S America.)

VEERY *Catharus fuscescens* 16.5–18cm. Transient migrant on Caribbean Slope. Rather shy and elusive. Note rusty upperparts, weak breast spotting, gray face with weak pale eyering showing mainly as a postocular crescent, smoky-gray flanks, voice. Some birds appreciably duller above, cf. Gray-cheeked Thrush. SOUNDS: Downslurred, slightly burry *vheeu.* STATUS: Uncommon to fairly common late Sep–Oct on Caribbean slope, to 1500m, a few from mid-Sep and into Nov; scarce late Mar–early May, mainly on Caribbean slope. (Breeds N America, winters S America.)

GRAY-CHEEKED THRUSH *Catharus minimus* 16.5–18cm. Transient migrant on Caribbean slope. Rather shy and elusive, rarely seen. From Swainson's Thrush by dull grayish face with poorly defined pale eyering, colder tones to breast, voice; both have variably extensive dark spotting below. SOUNDS: Overslurred, slightly nasal *veeu,* similar to Veery. STATUS: Uncommon to scarce late Sep to mid-Nov on Caribbean slope, to 1500m; very rare Dec–Apr in humid lowlands on both slopes. (Breeds n. N America, winters mainly S America.)

WOOD THRUSH *Hylocichla mustelina* 19–20.5cm. Handsome small thrush favoring humid lowland forest with fairly open understory. Habits like *Catharus* thrushes, but can be more confiding in areas where acclimated to people. Distinctive, with bright rusty upperparts (brightest on head), bold black spotting on white underparts; larger and bulkier than *Catharus.* SOUNDS: Mainly early and late in day, a fairly quick series of (usually 3–6) slightly liquid clucks, *whuit-whuit...,* and lower *wheh-wheh....* STATUS: Uncommon to fairly common Oct–Apr on both slopes, locally to 1700m; more widespread in migration, late Sep–Oct, Apr–early May. (Breeds e. N America, winters Mexico to Panama.)

BLACK-FACED SOLITAIRE

juv.

SWAINSON'S THRUSH

VEERY

GRAY-CHEEKED THRUSH

WOOD THRUSH

NIGHTINGALE-THRUSHES (5 species). Mostly rather retiring, heard far more often than seen and may even appear absent from an area when not singing. Usually seen at edges and on quiet trails early and late in day. Feed mainly on ground, where hop strongly, but regularly ascend to fruiting trees and shrubs, even at times in canopy; mostly sing from concealed perches at low to mid-levels.

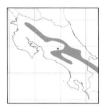

SLATY-BACKED NIGHTINGALE-THRUSH *Catharus fuscater* 16.5–17.5cm. Humid foothill forest, where mostly retiring in shady understory and on forest floor. Distinctive, relatively large and overall dark nightingale-thrush with bright orange bill (culmen sometimes dark) and legs, pale eyes. SOUNDS: Rising, slightly burry or hollow quavering *whiéh*. Song a rather simple, short fluty warble, 0.5–1 sec, every 2–6 secs; same phrase often repeated several ×, or 2 phrases alternated. Songs simpler, more plaintive than Ruddy-capped Nightingale-Thrush. STATUS: Fairly common on Caribbean slope, locally on cen. Pacific slope, mainly 800–2500m. (Costa Rica to S America.)

BLACK-HEADED NIGHTINGALE-THRUSH *Catharus mexicanus* 15–16.5cm. Humid foothill forest, where mostly retiring in dense understory and on shady forest floor; raises crown feathers when agitated. Note diagnostic black cap with deep orange bill and eyering; cf. Orange-billed Nightingale-Thrush if seen poorly in shady understory. Juv. duller overall with buff-spotted upperparts, dull buffy underparts mottled and scalloped blackish. SOUNDS: Rising to slightly overslurred, rough burry mew, *meahh*. Song a rather complex, slightly tinny warble with trilled components, 1–2 secs, every 1–6 secs; repeats or alternates songs. STATUS: Fairly common on Caribbean slope, 300–1000m; locally on adjacent n. Pacific slope, 700–1500m. (Mexico to w. Panama.)

ORANGE-BILLED NIGHTINGALE-THRUSH *Catharus aurantiirostris* 15.5–16.5cm. Humid foothill forest edge, plantations, adjacent second growth thickets; often in scrubbier, slightly drier habitats than other nightingale-thrushes. Often cocks tail briefly before slowly lowering it. Note bright orange bill (culmen sometimes dark) and legs, plain gray underparts. Juv. bill mostly orange by 1st winter, cf. juv. Ruddy-capped Nightingale-Thrush. Comprises 2 groups in Costa Rica that have been considered species: northern **Brown-headed** (*melpomene*) group and southern **Gray-headed** (*griseiceps*) group. SOUNDS: Slightly overslurred, nasal mew, *meéahr*; may suggest Gray Catbird.
Song a rather jerky, short tinny warble, 0.5–1.5 secs, every 2–5 secs; same phrase typically repeated over and over. STATUS: Fairly common on Pacific slope: Brown-headed s. to nw. Talamanca Mts., 600–2300m, Gray-headed on s. Pacific slope, 400–1500m. (Mexico to nw. S America.)

RUDDY-CAPPED NIGHTINGALE-THRUSH *Catharus frantzii* 16–17cm. Humid highland forest and edge, adjacent second growth, where mainly in dense shady understory, bamboo thickets. Told from Orange-billed Nightingale-Thrush by dark maxilla, duller legs, lack of orange eyering; crown often slightly brighter than back. Juv. duller overall with dark mottling on breast, not easily told from juv. Orange-billed but legs may be duller. SOUNDS: Rising, burry to quavering *rrríeh* and longer *churriehr*. Song a varied, short, rich fluty warble with semi-metallic tones, 0.5–1 sec, every 1–6 secs; alternating songs often on slightly different pitches. STATUS: Fairly common, mainly 1500–2500m. (Mexico to w. Panama.)

BLACK-BILLED NIGHTINGALE-THRUSH *Catharus gracilirostris* 14–15cm. Small, often confiding thrush of humid highland forest, adjacent second growth, páramo, overgrown clearings, gardens. Hops on ground like other *Catharus*, and often cocks tail briefly before slowly lowering it. Distinctive, with black bill, grayish head, diffuse rusty breast band. Juv. duller, more olive-toned overall, underparts with dark smudging and mottling. SOUNDS: Clear rising whistle, *whieeeh*; short rough mew run into burry chatter, *mehr-chchch...*, 1–2 secs. Song a varied, thin fluty warble, often with terminal trill, 1–1.5 secs, every 2–6 secs; alternating songs typically on different pitches. STATUS: Fairly common to common in Central and Talamanca Mts., mainly 1900–3500m. (Costa Rica to w. Panama.)

SLATY-BACKED
NIGHTINGALE-THRUSH

juv.

BLACK-HEADED
NIGHTINGALE-THRUSH

female

male

juv.

ORANGE-BILLED
NIGHTINGALE-THRUSH

Northern

Southern

RUDDY-CAPPED
NIGHTINGALE-THRUSH

BLACK-BILLED
NIGHTINGALE-THRUSH

334

DIPPERS (CINCLIDAE; 1 SPECIES) Small family of plump, heavy-bodied, aquatic songbirds found in Eurasia and the Americas. Ages differ slightly, sexes similar; like adult in 1st year.

AMERICAN DIPPER *Cinclus mexicanus* 15–17cm. Distinctive plump gray bird of clear running water in foothills and mountains, typically with rocky and stony banks, from larger rivers to small streams in cloud forest. Never far from water: singles and pairs forage in and beside rushing water, at times fully submerging; often perches on rocks in streams, when bobs almost constantly. Flight fast and direct, typically low over water. Juv. has pinkish bill, paler underparts, like adult by late fall. SOUNDS: Rasping to shrill, slightly metallic calls carry over the sound of rushing water, *zzeip* and *zrreip*; also longer ringing series, *zzi-zi zi-zi-zit*, etc. Song an often prolonged series of rich to metallic chips, warbles, buzzes, and trills with repetition suggesting a mockingbird. STATUS: Fairly common but local on Caribbean slope, mainly 700–2500m; on Pacific slope n. to Central Mts., where mainly above 1700m. (N America to Panama, Venezuela.)

WAXWINGS (BOMBYCILLIDAE; 1 SPECIES) Small Northern Hemisphere family of elegant, rather plump, crested birds. Ages differ, like adult in 1st year; sexes differ slightly.

CEDAR WAXWING *Bombycilla cedrorum* 16–17cm. Distinctive winter migrant found in varied semi-open and wooded habitats, mainly in highlands. Usually in flocks of 5–25 birds, occasionally singles; often perches high on prominent branches. Flocks fly with slightly undulating motion, often wheel and circle before alighting in fruiting trees. No similar species in Costa Rica. Male has bolder black throat patch than female, broader yellow tail tips. Juv. has blurry dark streaking on underparts; resembles adult by mid-winter. SOUNDS: High, thin, sibilant whistled *sssir*, perched and in flight. STATUS: Irregular, rare to uncommon Jan–Apr, sometimes from Dec and into May; mainly 500–2000m, but could occur anywhere. (Breeds N America, winters irregularly s. to Panama.)

SILKIES (PTILIOGONATIDAE; 2 SPECIES) Small Middle American family of elegant and typically crested fruit-eating birds with notably sleek plumage. Ages/sexes differ, like adult in 1st year.

LONG-TAILED SILKY (SILKY-FLYCATCHER) *Ptiliogonys caudatus* 20.5–24.5cm, male>female. Handsome and distinctive bird of highlands; no similar species in Costa Rica. Typically in roving groups in forest canopy and edge, also at fruiting shrubs in adjacent clearings and second growth; frequently near mistletoe. Often perches conspicuously in tall trees, and sometimes sallies for insects; flight high and slightly bounding, with long sailing glides; white tail flashes often eye-catching in flight. Juv. duller overall, with shorter crest and tail; soon like adult. SOUNDS: Varied, slightly nasal high chirps and short twitters or rattles, such as rolled staccato *chi-ri-rit*, easily passed off as a cricket. Song a prolonged, slightly jerky series of semi-metallic, squeaky and high nasal chirps and short rolls, 3–4 phrases/sec. STATUS: Fairly common to common, mainly 1800m to timberline; wanders locally down to 1200m. (Costa Rica to w. Panama.)

BLACK-AND-YELLOW SILKY (SILKY-FLYCATCHER) *Phainoptila melanoxantha* 20–22cm Distinctive, heavy-bodied, often rather sluggish inhabitant of highland forest and edge, adjacent second growth and clearings with fruiting trees and shrubs; mainly elfin forest in Northern Mts. Usually in pairs or small groups, foraging inconspicuously in fruiting foliage; at times sallies for insects. Note stocky shape, bold colors of male, black cap and yellow flanks of female. Juv. resembles dull version of female, soon like adult. Birds in Northern Mts. brighter overall, male yellow-bellied. SOUNDS: Rather quiet. High, thin, sharp *tsit*, perched and in flight, easily overlooked or passed over as a bush-tanager or some smaller bird. STATUS: Fairly common to uncommon; mainly above 1200m in Northern Mts., above 1800m in Central and Talamanca Mts. (Costa Rica to w. Panama.)

AMERICAN DIPPER

juv.

CEDAR WAXWING

LONG-TAILED SILKY

male

female

males

females

Northern Mts.

BLACK-AND-YELLOW SILKY

Central, Talamanca Mts.

WRENS (TROGLODYTIDAE; 22+ SPECIES) Mainly New World family of small (most species) to medium-size (genus *Campylorhynchus*) songbirds known for loud, frequently complex songs but visually elusive habits. Heard much more than seen, and many species best detected (and identified) by voice; several species perform duets where members of a pair contribute distinct elements to what sounds like a seamless song that could be thought to come from one bird. All species have slender bills, barred wings and tail. Ages similar in some species, different in others; attain adult appearance in 1st fall; sexes similar. Most species territorial, paired year-round.

*COSTA RICAN [BAND-BACKED] WREN *Campylorhynchus [zonatus] costaricensis* 16–18cm. Large noisy wren of humid forest and edge, adjacent semi-open areas with taller trees, forest patches. No similar species in Costa Rica; note boldly banded upperparts, spotted breast, bright cinnamon flanks and belly. Pairs or small groups forage mainly at mid–upper levels in trees, clambering with agility along mossy branches, probing in bromeliads and under loose bark. **SOUNDS:** Rather fast-paced, rasping chatters, often with excited or rollicking cadence; single gruff *cheh* and fast doubled *cheh-heh*. **STATUS:** Uncommon to fairly common on Caribbean slope, locally to 1700m. (S. Nicaragua to nw. Panama.)

RUFOUS-BACKED [RUFOUS-NAPED] WREN *Campylorhynchus [rufinucha] capistratus* 16–18cm. Large, social, noisy, and typically conspicuous wren of scrubby woodland and edge, ranchland with hedges. No similar species in Costa Rica. In pairs or small groups, hopping and clambering low to high in bushes and trees; often around buildings and in yards. Juv. duller overall, less sharply marked than adult. **SOUNDS:** Varied chortling rhythmic songs of rich 3–6-syllable phrases, such as *whie-tee ti-ti-whi-chur, whie-tee ti-ti-whi-chur...*, about 1 phrase/1–2 secs, typically repeated 3–8×. Nasal downslurred rasps, often in fairly rapid series; low, grunting, overslurred *rruh*. **STATUS:** Fairly common to common on n. Pacific Slope, to 1200m; range expanding s. and inland. (Mexico to Costa Rica.)

BANDED WREN *Thryophilus pleurostictus* 13–14cm. Handsome wren of lowland dry forest and edge, locally in mangroves. Mainly at low to mid-levels, often in fairly open situations. Adult distinctive, with white face and eyebrow, bold blackish barring on sides and flanks. Juv. can be similar to well-marked juv. Rufous-and-white Wren, but note weaker dark whisker, distinct dark flank barring. **SOUNDS:** Song unhurried, varied series of rich whistled phrases and trills, often arresting and resonant, typically including a rapid staccato series, such as *teeeeu, ti, hoorrrr, whit-whit-whit-whit-whit-whit, wheet,* 2–4 secs. Short, dry staccato rattles, higher and quicker than Rufous-and-white Wren; low gruff *churh*, at times alternated with low clipped *whieh*; nasal, raspy scolding *chrih-chrih....* **STATUS:** Fairly common to common on n. Pacific slope, to 900m. (Mexico to Costa Rica.)

RUFOUS-AND-WHITE WREN *Thryophilus rufalbus* 14.5–15.5cm. Gallery forest, open woodland, plantations, especially in more-humid areas; locally in mangroves. Mainly at low to mid-levels in shady understory, often along streams. Adult distinctive, a rather large and bulky 'small wren' with rusty upperparts, striped face; best located by song. Juv. less strongly marked below than juv. Banded Wren, with dark whisker. **SOUNDS:** Song haunting, varied series of mellow whistles and hollow quavers, starting or ending with 1 or more discrete whistles, such as *whu heee, hoohoohoohoohoohoohoohoo, hürrrr,* 1.5–3 secs. Hard, dry staccato rattles and chatters, at times given steadily, lower and slower than Banded Wren; hollow moaning *ooah*; hard dry *tek*, often in short series. **STATUS:** Fairly common on n. Pacific slope and locally in interior valleys of s. Pacific slope, to 1400m. (Mexico to n. S America.)

juv.

Costa Rican Wren

Rufous-backed Wren

juv.

Banded Wren

Rufous-and-white Wren

juv.

Cabanis's

Isthmian

Canebrake

PLAIN WREN *Cantorchilus modestus* 12.5–14.5cm. Attractive wren of overgrown weedy fields, second growth, forest edge, especially with bamboo, grassy tangles. Mostly skulking at low to mid-levels, often in dense grassy vegetation, but at times ranges up into more open subcanopy. Note bold white eyebrow, plain pale grayish face and breast, bright buffy-cinnamon to buffy-brown flanks, unbarred undertail coverts. Comprises 3 groups often treated as 2 or 3 species: **Cabanis's Wren** *C. [m.] modestus* (12.5–13.5cm) on n. Pacific slope, averages darker, less rusty-toned, and with weaker dark tail barring than slightly paler **Isthmian Wren** *C. [m.] elutus* (12.5–13.5cm) of s. Pacific slope. **Canebrake Wren** *C. [m.] zeledoni* (13.5–14.5cm) of Caribbean slope averages largest and darkest, with grayer upperparts, duller flanks, stronger dark tail barring than Cabanis's. Juv. Cabanis's and Isthmian duller overall than adults; juv. Canebrake averages brighter, with buffier flanks suggesting Cabanis's. SOUNDS: Varied song of short, rich whistled phrases usually repeated quickly a few times, often with a lisping introductory note, such as *ss ti-been ti-been...*; longer and more complex in duets. Also much higher, thin whistled phrases with rippling cadence, such as *tsi-pii-siip* every few secs. Song of Isthmian may average mellower, slower-paced, than Cabanis's but not separable; song of Canebrake averages lower-pitched. Calls include a dry, slightly scratchy *cht*, often doubled and repeated steadily when scolding. Isthmian scold of accelerating staccato tiks run into dry trill, *tik-tik-t-trrrrrr* perhaps distinct from Cabanis's. Canebrake scold a dry staccato chatter, slowing toward the end. STATUS: Fairly common to common, but distribution details of the 3 groups in need of elucidation, especially on the cen. Pacific slope and n. Caribbean slope: **Cabanis's** occurs on n. Pacific Slope, to 2000m, locally on adjacent n. Caribbean slope (Mexico to Costa Rica); **Isthmian** on s. Pacific slope (Costa Rica to Panama); **Canebrake** on Caribbean slope, to 1700m, where reportedly hybridizes in foothills with Cabanis's (Nicaragua to nw. Panama).

RIVERSIDE WREN *Cantorchilus semibadius* 12.5–13.5cm. Handsome wren of dense vegetation bordering streams and swampy areas in humid forest, second-growth thickets. Mainly low in tangles, probing in dead-leaf clusters and vines. No similar species in range: note barred underparts, strong barring on wings and tail. Juv. duller, less distinctly patterned overall; soon like adult. SOUNDS: Song of (usually 2–3) rich ringing whistles, 0.5–1 sec, often repeated 2–10× in rapid series, such as *seé-chu-we, seé-chu-we...*, less often single songs every few secs; longer and more complex in duets. Songs of Isthmian Wren less rich, typically higher, quicker-paced, often with more notes. Calls include rich abrupt *h'weet*; sharply overslurred, ringing *ch'lieh*, and quiet, nasal whistled *pee'tee'chih*, all may be repeated steadily; harsh clicks and low rasping chatter, *zzzeh-zzzeh...*when scolding. STATUS: Fairly common to common on s. Pacific slope, to 1200m. (Costa Rica to w. Panama.)

BLACK-BELLIED WREN *Pheugopedius fasciatoventris* 14.5–15.5cm. Relatively large, bulky, and distinctive wren of *Heliconia* and other second-growth thickets at lowland forest edge, streamsides, overgrown plantations. At low to mid-levels, often in large-leaved plants, hanging dead leaves. Note bold white bib, blackish cheeks and belly; cf. Bicolored Antbird (p. 268). Juv. duller overall with dingier throat and breast; soon like adult. SOUNDS: Song of (usually 4–7) rich, slightly hollow, often slurred whistles, such as *to-wee hu-tchu-hu*, 1–1.5 secs, often relatively long pauses between songs, which are usually given singly, not in rapid series; longer and more complex in duets. Calls include distinctive clipped rasp paired with mellow whistle, *zhhk-whéu*, can be repeated steadily; varied short hollow whistles; and low rasping churrs. STATUS: Fairly common on s. Pacific slope, to 500m. (Costa Rica to w. Colombia.)

North Pacific (Cabanis's)

PLAIN WREN

South Pacific (Isthmian)

Caribbean (Canebrake)

RIVERSIDE WREN

BLACK-BELLIED WREN

RUFOUS-BREASTED WREN *Pheugopedius rutilus* 12–13cm. Handsome, distinctive wren of humid foothill forest edge, second growth, bamboo thickets, especially with vine tangles. Forages low to high in tangles. Note spotted and streaked face and throat contrasting with rusty breast, bright rusty crown. Juv. duller overall, especially crown, face less distinctly marked. SOUNDS: Similar to congeneric Spot-breasted Wren. Song of (usually 4–6) rich slurred whistles, *seee'ch-úwhee...*, or *see'wee si-wee-ch'wee...*, 1–1.2 secs, every few secs; longer and more complex in duets. Springy rising trill, more musical than Spot-breasted; bursts of staccato churring. STATUS: Fairly common on Pacific slope, mainly 300–1800m, locally lower. (Costa Rica to nw. S America.)

SPOT-BREASTED WREN *Pheugopedius maculipectus* 12.5–13.5cm. Humid lowland thickets and second growth, forest edge with leafy and viny tangles. Tends to be rather skulking, low to high. Distinctive, with striped face and dense black spotting on underparts. Juv. has dusky face and underparts, traces of adult pattern. SOUNDS: Similar to congeneric Rufous-breasted Wren. Song a bright series of (usually 4–6) slurred rich whistles, such as *swee chur-tili-wheechu*, 1.2–1.5 secs, every few secs; longer and more complex in duets. Springy, drawn-out rising trill; dry, gruff rapid chatters. STATUS: Fairly common locally in n. Caribbean lowlands; disjunct population found late 2010s in Río Chirripo drainage, 600–1200m. (Mexico to Costa Rica.)

STRIPE-BREASTED WREN *Cantorchilus thoracicus* 11–12cm. Fairly small, distinctive, rather short-tailed wren of humid forest and edge, streamside thickets, second growth. Forages at all levels in tangles, dead-leaf clusters, along branches. Note boldly striped face and breast, barred wings, relatively short tail. Juv. has more-muted striping, soon like adult. SOUNDS: Song a fairly simple chant of rich loud whistles, usually 4–13× in almost continuous flow, such as *to-wee-te-chur, to-wee-te-chur...*; more complex in duet, but typically less variation in pitch than Spot-breasted Wren. Clipped *cheuk* and low, gruff, slightly rolled *chert*, often in short bursts; slightly plaintive whistle repeated steadily, *peeh, peeh...*, 10 notes/8 secs; might suggest a slow pygmy owl. STATUS: Fairly common to common on Caribbean slope, to 1000m; spills over locally to adjacent n. Pacific slope. (Honduras to Panama.)

BAY WREN *Cantorchilus nigricapillus* 14–15cm. Distinctive, boldly patterned wren of humid thickets, second growth, especially streamsides and around lagoons, also roadsides, forest edge. Note striking head pattern, bright rusty body. Juv. duller overall, with less distinct whitish head markings; soon like adult. SOUNDS: Song notably rich, powerful, and varied. Short phrases, 0.5–1 sec, every few secs, such as a quick, rich *pee-chu-churree*, a slower *whuh chee'huhrr*, sometimes ending with rapid staccato rolls; duets typically involve rapid 4–12× repetition of short, often complex phrases, *whee-chwíchiti whee-chwíchiti...*, can include staccato rolls. Calls include rough, low rasping *zzzeh* often repeated steadily; spluttering raspy chatters; burry *beeihr*; and rich rolled *chehrrr*. STATUS: Fairly common to common on Caribbean slope, to 1200m. (Honduras to w. Ecuador.)

BLACK-THROATED WREN *Pheugopedius atrogularis* 14.5–15.5cm. Relatively large, dark chestnut-brown wren of dense second growth at forest edge, along streams, in adjacent overgrown plantations. At low to mid-levels in thickets, vine tangles. Note black face and breast, vestigial white face streaks, barred undertail coverts but relatively plain wings and tail; could suggest an antbird. Juv. duller overall with olive-brown upperparts, dusky face and breast. SOUNDS: Song rich and powerful, typically a few slurred rich whistles run into a staccato roll or mellow trill, such as *wheeu cheu'whee'h'h'huhuhu*, 1.5–2.5 secs, every few secs; less hurried and vigorous than shorter songs of Bay Wren; longer and more complex in overlapping duets. Calls include a slowing dry *churr*, 1 sec, faster-paced than Canebrake Wren. STATUS: Fairly common on Caribbean slope, to 1100m; spills over locally to adjacent n. Pacific slope. (Honduras to nw. Panama.)

Rufous-breasted Wren

Spot-breasted Wren

juv.

Stripe-breasted Wren

Bay Wren

Black-throated Wren

GRAY-BREASTED WOOD WREN *Henicorhina leucophrys* 10–11.5cm. Humid highland forest, adjacent second growth, especially with bamboo. Singles or pairs hop on and near forest floor, usually hidden in dense foliage. Cf. juv. Middle American Wood Wren (local overlap in foothills). Juv. Gray-breasted has grayish throat, weaker face pattern than adult. SOUNDS: Songs varied, often involving duets: loud rich whistled phrases, typically richer, fuller, more varied than Middle American Wood Wren, such as *wheer heer chee-dee-hu-weedee,...* Hard dry *chak* and varied chatters, more rattling than Middle American; low gruff *chuk* run into chatters; hollow ringing *cheuh*. STATUS: Fairly common to common, from timberline down to 1100m on Pacific slope, to 800m on Caribbean slope. (Mexico to S America.)

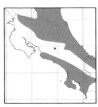

*MIDDLE AMERICAN [WHITE-BREASTED] WOOD WREN *Henicorhina [leucosticta] prostheleuca* 10–11.5cm. Humid forest understory. Singles or pairs hop on and near forest floor, often hidden in tangles, foliage. Gray-breasted Wood Wren (local overlap in foothills) has streaked throat, gray breast; told readily by voice. Juv. Middle American has grayish breast and sides, like adult by fall. SOUNDS: Songs varied: rich to slightly plaintive, short whistled phrases, repeated, *ss chee ree-eu,...* or *hoo-ee hoo'ee-ee,...*, longer and more complex in duets; often introduced by a quiet lisp. Less rich and forceful than songs of Gray-breasted. Bright, ringing, burry *breeh!* notably ventriloquial, could be passed off as a frog; dry scolding *chek*; dry rattling chatters. STATUS: Fairly common to common, to 1800m on Pacific slope (mainly foothills), to 1200m on Caribbean slope. (Mexico to Colombia.)

(NORTHERN) NIGHTINGALE WREN *Microcerculus philomela* 10–11cm. Distinctive but elusive dark wren of humid forest understory, especially ravines in foothills; no range overlap with Whistling Wren. On or near shady forest floor, where rarely seen unless located by song. Walks with almost constant bobbing motion; sings from ground or low perch. SOUNDS: Song unmistakable and haunting, a seemingly random, confident to hesitant rising and falling series of plaintive short whistles interspersed with high lisps, such as *hee hoo, hee hoo, hoo hoo hee hoo, ss hoo hee...*, 2–3 notes/sec. Calls include sharp *chek*. STATUS: Uncommon locally on n. Caribbean slope, to 1400m, mainly in foothills; spills over locally to adjacent Pacific slope. (Mexico to Costa Rica.)

*WHISTLING [SOUTHERN NIGHTINGALE-] WREN *Microcerculus [marginatus] luscinia* 10–11cm. Habits like Nightingale Wren, but no range overlap. Note overall plain plumage with whitish throat, song. SOUNDS: Song starts with rapid short twitter of rising whistles and runs into a variably prolonged series of well-spaced, high, thin piercing whistles that become progressively longer (from 0.5 sec to 1 sec) and slightly lower, with longer pauses between them (up to 10 secs with later notes, which are sometimes doubled), a whole song sometimes taking 3 mins or longer: *sisisi-sii sii siiii, siiii....* Calls include slightly wooden, abrupt *chek*. STATUS: Uncommon locally, to 1700m on Pacific slope, to 1100m on s. Caribbean slope. (Costa Rica to Panama.)

SONG WREN *Cyphorhinus phaeocephalus* 11.5–12.5cm. Chunky, distinctive dark wren of humid lowland forest understory, adjacent taller second growth. Often in pairs or small groups, hopping on and near forest floor, tossing leaves, probing in tangles; sometimes joins mixed flocks and attends ant swarms. No similar species, but blue-gray orbital skin and rusty breast could suggest an antbird. Juv. has dark barring above, pale rear margin to rusty face and breast. SOUNDS: Gruff, slightly spluttering short rasping chatter, *grr rreh-reh-rrehk*, and variations, may suggest a frog; also guttural but vaguely musical, frog-like chuttering or gurgling, typically in short bursts. Song a series of (usually 2–6) alternating short–long and often high–low melodic whistles, which can combine with bursts of chuttering to produce distinctive, slightly haunting effect. STATUS: Uncommon to fairly common on Caribbean slope, to 1100m; spills over locally to adjacent n. Pacific slope. (Honduras to w. Ecuador.)

GRAY-BREASTED WOOD WREN

MIDDLE AMERICAN
WOOD WREN

juv.

NIGHTINGALE WREN

juv.

WHISTLING WREN

juv.

SONG WREN

*HOUSE WREN *Troglodytes aedon* 10.5–11.5cm. Widespread in a variety of semi-open and wooded habitats, often around human habitation, from ranch buildings and brush piles in gardens to humid forest edge, second growth, weedy pastures. Often skulking and mouse-like, but sings from prominent perch. Distinctive but rather plain: often has pale eyering but no strong eyebrow or face striping; cf. shorter-tailed and mostly arboreal Ochraceous Wren of highland forests. Juv. has soft dusky scalloping on underparts, soon attains adult appearance. SOUNDS: Song a variably complex, fast-paced, ebullient chortling medley, 2–3 secs; often starts with a few gruff rasps, ends with 2–4 rapid staccato notes or motifs; repeated every few secs. Calls are varied chucks, mews, and rasps; commonly a gruff *chet* and rolled *cherr*, often in hesitant, fairly slow-paced chatters. STATUS: Common to fairly common to 2700m, locally (increasing?) to 3000m. (Americas.)

OCHRACEOUS WREN *Troglodytes ochraceus* 9–10cm. Attractive small wren of humid highland forest and edge, adjacent overgrown pastures with scattered taller trees. Forages low to high, often at mid-levels on trunks and branches, amid epiphytes and tangles; joins mixed flocks. Distinctive, with bright buffy face and broad pale eyebrow, rather short tail; cf. longer-tailed and duller House Wren. Juv. duller overall, with dusky scalloping on underparts. SOUNDS: Song a high, fairly rapid, tinkling and jumbled warble, 2–2.5 secs, every 2–8 secs. High, springy, downslurred trill, *t'sirrrrr*, fading and slowing slightly at end, about 0.5 sec. STATUS: Fairly common to common, mainly 900–2400m, locally to 3000m. (Costa Rica to Panama.)

TIMBERLINE WREN *Thryorchilus browni* 10–11cm. Small but chunky, short-tailed wren of thickets and tangles at humid highland forest edge and in páramo, especially with bamboo. Singles and pairs creep through tangles and along mossy branches, tail often cocked; can be inquisitive. Distinctive, with bold white eyebrow, silvery-white wing patch. SOUNDS: Song a high, rambling, often rather unhurried warble, mostly 6–20 secs, often with slightly tinny or scratchy quality but nonetheless musical; typically involves multiple repetitions of a rather complex chanting phrase. Low rasping *zzheh*, repeated; overslurred to downslurred, bright ringing *tchiih* or *psiih*, often repeated steadily; varied raspy and squeaky chatters. STATUS: Fairly common to common in Central and Talamanca Mts., mainly 2400–3600m, locally down to 2000m. (Costa Rica to w. Panama.)

*GRASS [SEDGE] WREN *Cistothorus [platensis] elegans* 11–11.5cm. Small streaky wren of tall-grass marshes and wet pastures with taller sedges, rushes. Skulking; moves like a mouse through vegetation, but often sings from prominent perch, tail cocked and dipped loosely. Note streaked upperparts, plain buffy underparts. Juv. plainer overall (cf. House Wren), crown unstreaked but wings boldy barred, tail shorter than adult. SOUNDS: Song a medley of buzzes, trills, chatters, and chips; song bursts usually 1–2 secs, with pauses of 2–7 secs; same song often repeated several times before changing to another variant. Low rasping *cherr* and gruff *cheht*, often repeated steadily. STATUS: Uncommon and local (declining) around Central Valley, mainly 1250–1800m. (Mexico to w. Panama.)

*ROCK WREN *Salpinctes obsoletus* 13.5–14.5cm. Distinctive open country wren, around and above timberline in rocky habitats, grassy slopes and ravines with rocks and boulders. On or near ground, perching conspicuously on rocks; often bobs as it calls. Flight low and slightly bounding. Distinctive in habitat, with variable dark barring on underparts, buff tail corners. Juv. less distinctly patterned than adult. SOUNDS: Song often prolonged: varied series of trills, gruff rattles, bright chips, and springy buzzes, each usually repeated 2–8× in bouts, with 1–10 secs between bouts. Fairly high, springy, rolled trill, *trir'rr'rr*, often repeated steadily; downslurred, gruff burry *jihrr*. STATUS: Uncommon and local on n. Pacific slope, 500–1600m. (Mexico and w. US to nw. Costa Rica.)

HOUSE WREN

OCHRACEOUS WREN

TIMBERLINE WREN

juv.

GRASS WREN

juv.

ROCK WREN

346

GNATWRENS AND GNATCATCHERS (POLIOPTILIDAE; 4 SPECIES)

New World family of very small, fine-billed, thin-legged, and relatively long-tailed birds. Ages differ slightly (weak juv. plumage soon replaced by adult-like plumage); gnatcatcher sexes differ in head pattern.

*NORTHERN [LONG-BILLED] GNATWREN *Ramphocaenus [melanurus] rufiventris* 12–12.5cm. Active but easily overlooked inhabitant of humid forest edge, overgrown plantations, taller second growth, especially with vine tangles. Forages actively, low to high in tangles and leafy foliage, often in pairs; tail typically cocked and swung loosely around; sometimes associates with mixed flocks. Distinctive, but cf. Tawny-faced Gnatwren. Juv. duller overall than adult. SOUNDS: Song a dry to vaguely musical ringing trill, often rising and falling (quality can suggest Northern Tropical Pewee), at times preceded by a quiet *tik* or chortle, 1.5–3 secs; lower and harsher trills and chatters when agitated. Calls rather wren-like: short dry *tcherr* and nasal scolding *cheut*, both can be repeated steadily. STATUS: Fairly common on both slopes, to 1200m; more local in drier nw. lowlands. (Mexico to nw. Peru.)

TAWNY-FACED GNATWREN *Microbates cinereiventris* 9.5–10.5cm. Inconspicuous inhabitant of humid forest, typically in shady understory. Forages on and near forest floor, where hops and clambers actively, probing into leaf litter and foliage; joins mixed flocks of antwrens. Distinctive, with tawny face offset by black whisker, shorter bill and tail than Long-billed Gnatwren. Juv. darker and duller overall than adult. SOUNDS: Downslurred, burry nasal *nyeeah* and staccato, short dry chatters, often alternated; slightly plaintive, downslurred whistled *peeee*, about 0.5 sec, repeated every few secs. Song (?) a prolonged medley of mews, chatters, and rasping notes, at times interspersed with plaintive whistles. STATUS: Fairly common to uncommon on Caribbean slope, locally to 1200m. (Nicaragua to S America.)

*CENTRAL AMERICAN [WHITE-LORED] GNATCATCHER *Polioptila albiloris* 11–12cm. Forest edge, scrubby woodland, and second growth; not usually inside taller and more-humid forest. Forages actively, low to high, often in pairs; long tail often cocked and swung loosely. Confusion possible with White-browed Gnatcatcher, which favors more-humid habitats, often in forest canopy. White-browed has broad white eyebrow extending well behind eye and imparting distinctive 'open-faced' expression, never has solid black cap. Breeding male Central American attains solid black cap; juv. resembles female but face pattern softer, upperparts tinged brownish. SOUNDS: Relatively low, slightly downslurred burry *zhheh*, and a more hissing *zzzh*, at times doubled; lower and rougher than mews of White-browed Gnatcatcher. Song an unhurried medley of mews, chips, and buzzes. STATUS: Fairly common on n. Pacific slope, locally to 800m. (Guatemala to Costa Rica.)

WHITE-BROWED [TROPICAL] GNATCATCHER *Polioptila [plumbea] bilineata* 10–11cm. Humid forest and edge, gallery forest. Singly or in pairs, mostly flitting actively in canopy; comes lower at edges. Joins mixed flocks of warblers, greenlets, honeycreepers. Note open white face on both sexes; cf. Central American Gnatcatcher (occurs side-by-side locally in Northwest); no seasonal change in appearance. Juv. resembles female but face pattern softer, upperparts tinged brownish. SOUNDS: Overslurred, nasal mewing *meéah* and clipped nasal *meeh*; distinctly higher than rough rasping calls of Central American. Song a high, overall descending, silvery slow trill, 2–3 secs. STATUS: Fairly common to common on both slopes, to 1500m; uncommon and more local in drier nw. lowlands (Mexico to w. Peru.)

346

NORTHERN GNATWREN

TAWNY-FACED GNATWREN

CENTRAL AMERICAN GNATCATCHER

female

nonbr. (Aug–Feb)

males

breeding (Feb–Aug)

WHITE-BROWED GNATCATCHER

female

male

VIREOS (VIREONIDAE; 15+ SPECIES) Mainly New World family of small songbirds. Typical vireos resemble heavily built warblers but are, in fact, more closely related to jays and crows. Ages similar or different, soon attain adult appearance; sexes usually similar. Often sluggish, best detected by tirelessly repeated songs; calls mainly scolding mews and chatters.

LESSER GREENLET *Pachysylvia decurtata* 10.5–11.5cm. Rather plain little bird of humid forest canopy, adjacent taller second growth, occasionally coming lower at edges. In pairs or small groups, foraging in leafy canopy; often with mixed flocks of tanagers, warblers, other vireos. Note small size, rather short tail, gray head with 'soft' face and whitish eyering. SOUNDS: Nasal, often persistent scolding *yiih yiih....* Song an unhurried repetition of simple, 2–4-syllable, slightly plaintive whistled phrases, 2nd part lower than 1st, *sípi-chee* or *wíchil-i-wee*, every 2–8 secs. STATUS: Fairly common to common on both slopes, to 1500m. (Mexico to w. Ecuador.)

TAWNY-CROWNED GREENLET *Tunchiornis ochraceiceps* 11.5–12.5cm. Odd little bird of shady lower and mid-levels in humid forest, often in areas with understory palms. Regularly travels with mixed flocks including antwrens, Stripe-crowned Warblers. Note bushy tawny cap, pale eyes in gray face, ochre breast, pinkish legs; cf. female Plain Antvireo (p. 264). SOUNDS: Short series of nasal, overslurred notes, *dwoi-dwoi-dwoi...* and variations. Song a high, plaintive, whining, insect-like whistle, *whiiii*, about 0.5 sec, every 2–3 secs; may be preceded by a short liquid trill or chortling chatter. STATUS: Fairly common on both slopes, to 1200m. (Mexico to S America.)

*YELLOW-GREEN [SCRUB] GREENLET *Hylophilus [flavipes] viridiflavus* 11–12cm. Distinctive but often inconspicuous little bird of low scrub, overgrown pastures, dense second growth. Singles or pairs move sluggishly in foliage, plucking fruit and insects; usually independent of flocks. Note pale eyes, sharply pointed pinkish bill. SOUNDS: Low rasping churr, at times in short series. Song a series of (usually 3–20) rich, slurred, disyllabic whistles *ch'wee ch'wee...* or *d'wee d'wee...*, at times speeding slightly toward the end, 2–3 phrases/sec; repeated after pauses. STATUS: Uncommon to fairly common on Pacific slope, to 900m. (Costa Rica to Panama.)

RUFOUS-BROWED PEPPERSHRIKE *Cyclarhis gujanensis* 14–15cm. Distinctive bulky vireo of varied wooded and forested habitats from oak forest and mangroves to gardens, scrubby thickets. Sluggish at mid–upper levels, often with mixed flocks or at fruiting trees. No similar species; note staring amber eye, rusty brow on gray head, stout pale bill. SOUNDS: Song a varied, short warbled phrase of loud rich whistles, such as *chikee wheer peeripee pee-oo*, or *weer cheery-choo*, every 5–15 secs. Also (female only?) a slightly descending series of (usually 5–12) sad rich whistles, given irregularly, often difficult to trace: *treéu treéu....* STATUS: Fairly common to uncommon on both slopes, mainly 700–2400m, and locally in nw. lowlands. (Mexico to S America.)

GREEN SHRIKE-VIREO *Vireolanius pulchellus* 13.5–14.5cm. Chunky bright green bird of humid lowland forest canopy; heard far more often than seen. At upper and mid-levels in taller trees, at times with mixed flocks. Sings from perch in subcanopy. Distinctive, but cf. Golden-browed Chlorophonia (p. 388), which has stubby bill, yellow belly. Comprises 2 groups: **Northern** *V. [p.] pulchellus* on Caribbean slope, with blue on forecrown, face, and nape of male (female has less blue); **Southern** *V. [p.] viridiceps* on s. Pacific slope, with blue on both sexes limited to nape. Juv. duller with diffuse yellow face stripes, soon like adult. SOUNDS: Far-carrying song a chant of (typically 3–5) rich whistled notes, every 1–4 secs. Song of **Northern** averages slower-paced with notes more strongly downslurred, often distinctly disyllabic, *chewee chewee chewee*. **Southern** song averages quicker, lower-pitched, notes downslurred or overslurred, *héu héu héu*. Hard, rasping scold, *djehr djehr...* and squeaky rippling chatters. STATUS: Fairly common to uncommon on both slopes, especially in lower foothills, to 1200m. (Mexico to Panama.)

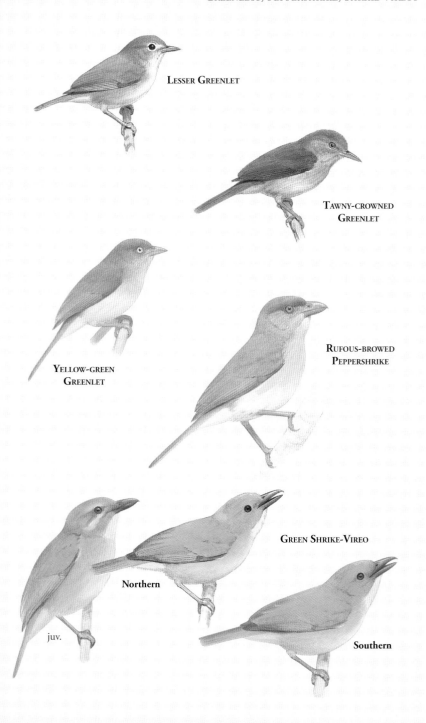

LESSER GREENLET

TAWNY-CROWNED
GREENLET

YELLOW-GREEN
GREENLET

RUFOUS-BROWED
PEPPERSHRIKE

GREEN SHRIKE-VIREO

Northern

juv.

Southern

350

YELLOW-WINGED VIREO *Vireo carmioli* 11–12cm Attractive small vireo of humid highland forest, adjacent clearings and second growth with taller trees. Mainly at mid–upper levels, often in canopy; lower at edges and in shrubby second growth with fruiting trees, bushes; joins mixed flocks. Distinctive, with broad pale eyebrow and crescent below eye, broad pale wingbars, pale tertial edges. Juv. duller, less distinctly marked overall. SOUNDS: Song comprises varied, slightly burry, rich short phrases (usually 2–3 syllables) alternated steadily, or sometimes the same phrase repeated a few times: *chreu ch'iliet chríeh…*or *b'zzhiu, b'zzhiu, zzhlíeh...*, 1 phrase/1.5–8 secs. Calls include rapid buzzy chatter, 0.5–1 sec, rather wren-like. STATUS: Fairly common, mainly 2000m to timberline; some descend locally to 1500m in fall–winter. (Costa Rica to w. Panama.)

*MANGROVE VIREO** *Vireo pallens* 11.5–12.2cm. Local in mangroves along Pacific coast, favoring denser red mangroves. Ranges low to high, singly or in pairs; at times with mixed flocks of warblers, especially when mobbing pygmy owls. Distinctive in range and habitat, with overall dingy plumage, pale yellow loral stripe, pale grayish eyes. Juv. browner above, buffier below. SOUNDS: Rough rasping scold, *zzheh-zzheh.…*Song comprises varied series of (usually 3–11) twangy or buzzy notes, *jwieh-jwieh...*, or *ch'wih ch'wih...*, 0.5–2 secs, repeated every few secs; pace varies, but often slow enough to count notes. STATUS: Fairly common but often rather local on n. Pacific coast. (Mexico to Costa Rica.)

YELLOW-THROATED VIREO *Vireo flavifrons* 13–14cm. Distinctive large migrant vireo of varied wooded and forested habitats, from rainforest and hedgerows to dry forest, gardens, plantations. Note bright yellow spectacles, contrasting white belly, blue-gray shoulders and rump. Mainly at mid–upper levels, often with mixed flocks and at fruiting trees. SOUNDS: Gruff, slow-paced, steady chatter and slightly descending, slowing chatter with longer 1st note, *sheh ch-ch-ch-ch-ch-ch-ch.* STATUS: Fairly common Oct–Apr on both slopes, to 1800m; more widespread in migration, Sep–Oct, late Mar–Apr, a few into early May. (Breeds e. N America, winters Mexico to nw. S America.)

WHITE-EYED VIREO *Vireo griseus* 11–12cm. Rare winter migrant to brushy woodland, forest edge, semi-open areas with thickets and scrub. Forages low to high, often at fruiting trees and shrubs; associates with mixed flocks of warblers, other vireos. Distinctive, with gray neck sides, yellow spectacles, staring white eyes (dusky into 1st-winter). SOUNDS: Nasal scolding *sheh-sheh...*, often repeated insistently. STATUS: Very rare mid-Oct to Mar; has been found in lowlands of both slopes and in Central Valley. (Breeds e. US to Mexico, winters Mexico to Honduras, rarely to Costa Rica.)

BLUE-HEADED VIREO *Vireo solitarius* 12.5–13.5cm. Rare winter migrant to varied wooded and forested habitats, mainly in highlands and foothills. Forages sluggishly, mainly at mid–upper levels, often in association with mixed flocks of warblers, other vireos. No similar species in Costa Rica: note blue-gray hood with sharply defined white spectacles, contrasting silky-white throat, greenish back, bold white wingbars, yellow flanks. SOUNDS: Gruff, scolding, staccato chatter, 1st note often longer and followed by a slightly slowing, descending series: *jehh jeh-jeh.…*STATUS: Very rare to rare Nov–Mar; most records from n. highlands but also reported from Pacific lowlands. (Breeds e. N America, winters to Nicaragua, rarely to Costa Rica.)

YELLOW-WINGED
VIREO

MANGROVE VIREO

YELLOW-THROATED VIREO

WHITE-EYED VIREO

imm.
(Oct–Dec)

BLUE-HEADED VIREO

YELLOW-GREEN VIREO *Vireo flavoviridis* 14–15cm. Common summer migrant to varied forested and wooded habitats from gallery forest and plantations to dry forest, gardens, mangroves; generally not in dense and wetter forests. Mainly at upper levels in leafy foliage, coming lower to feed at edges and in fruiting shrubs. Sings tirelessly from canopy; often cocks tail, and raises crown when agitated. Fairly distinctive, with more diffuse face pattern than Red-eyed Vireo, bright yellowish neck sides and flanks, bigger bill. Juv. has dark eyes, duller overall. SOUNDS: Gruff downslurred mewing *miehh* and soft dry chatter. Song of varied, burry to slightly nasal chirps given in leisurely, often hesitant manner, *ch-ree, chree, swi ch-ree, chree...*, repeated tirelessly; suggests a House Sparrow that's taken singing lessons. STATUS: Common to fairly common Feb–Sep on Pacific slope, uncommon on Caribbean slope, to 1500m; more widespread in migration, late Jan–Mar, Sep–Oct. (Breeds Mexico to S America, winters S America.)

RED-EYED VIREO *Vireo olivaceus* 14–15cm. Transient migrant in varied wooded and forested habitats, second growth, scrub. Forages low to high, mainly in canopy and at fruiting trees and shrubs. Note distinctive face pattern, with neat, thin dark line between broad whitish eyebrow and blue-gray crown; underparts silky whitish overall, with pale yellowish undertail coverts; flanks rarely tinged pale yellow on some fall birds. Cf. Yellow-green Vireo. Imm. has brown eyes. SOUNDS: Mostly silent in migration; rough, downslurred mewing *rrieh*, averages more drawn-out, rougher than Yellow-green Vireo. STATUS: Fairly common to common mid-Aug to Nov, Mar–May; commonest in lowlands and foothills. (Breeds N America, winters S America.)

*SOUTHERN BROWN-CAPPED VIREO *Vireo leucophrys* 11–12cm. Humid highland forest, adjacent second growth and pastures with taller trees. Mainly at mid–upper levels, often probing in leafy foliage and at fruiting trees; joins mixed flocks of warblers, other vireos, bush-tanagers. Note broad pale eyebrow, contrast between whitish throat and pale yellow underparts, brown crown and back. Cf. migrant Philadelphia Vireo. Juv. has duller face pattern, paler underparts, soon like adult. SOUNDS: High, shrill, slightly hissing, overslurred *ssiih*, recalling a *Tolmomyias* flatbill. Song a rambling, rather even-paced short warble, 1.5–2 secs, every 6–15 or so secs; slower-paced and mellower than North American warbling vireos. STATUS: Fairly common on both slopes, 1500–2400m; lower locally in fall after breeding, to 1200m. (Costa Rica to S America.)

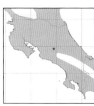

PHILADELPHIA VIREO *Vireo philadelphicus* 11–12cm. Rather small, compact migrant vireo of varied wooded and forested habitats, plantations, second growth. Mainly at mid–upper levels; often joins mixed flocks and visits fruiting trees. Note variable yellow wash to throat and breast (some birds extensively yellowish below), relatively small bill, dark lores (prominence of which varies with angle of viewing). Cf. Tennessee Warbler. SOUNDS: Low gruff *cheh*, often in short series or repeated steadily. STATUS: Uncommon to fairly common Oct–Apr on both slopes, locally to 2100m; more widespread in migration, Sep–Oct, Apr– early May. (Breeds N America, winters Mexico to Panama.)

*EASTERN WARBLING VIREO *Vireo gilvus* 12–13cm. Rare winter migrant to wooded and forested habitats, hedgerows, second growth. Forages low to high, often with mixed flocks of warblers, other vireos, and at fruiting trees. Note broad pale eyebrow, overall drab plumage. Faded Philadelphia Vireo often mistaken for Eastern Warbling but smaller and more compact, with rounder head, smaller bill, brighter yellow wash on throat and breast, darker lores; also cf. Red-eyed Vireo, which has stronger face pattern, bigger bill, longer wings, shorter tail. SOUNDS: Slurred nasal *nyeih*, at times repeated insistently when scolding, buzzier and less mewing than Red-eyed Vireo. STATUS: Very rare Oct–Apr; reported on both slopes but not annual, should be documented carefully. (Breeds N America, winters Mexico to Nicaragua, rarely to Costa Rica.)

YELLOW-GREEN VIREO

RED-EYED VIREO

SOUTHERN
BROWN-CAPPED VIREO

PHILADELPHIA VIREO

EASTERN WARBLING
VIREO

354

NEW WORLD WARBLERS (PARULIDAE; 47+ SPECIES) Large New World
family of small, mainly insect- and nectar-eating birds, ranging from arboreal to terrestrial,
colorful to rather drab. Ages/sexes similar in some species, different in others; attain adult
appearance in 1st year. A few North American migrants have marked seasonal plumage
changes; among species with complex age/sex plumages, adult males generally brightest,
imm. females dullest, with adult female and imm. male falling between these extremes.

Many migrants may sing in spring, mainly Apr–May, as they move north; some also sing in
fall when establishing winter territories. These songs mainly heard briefly in Costa Rica, not
described in species accounts. Chip call notes shorter, more stereotyped, and easier to learn,
often heard in winter; all species also give contact calls ('flight calls'), mostly high-pitched and
often buzzy, more challenging to distinguish and mostly not described in species accounts.

AMERICAN REDSTART *Setophaga ruticilla* 12–13cm. Winter migrant to varied lowland wooded and forested habitats, mangroves. Forages low to high, often actively fluttering and conspicuous; tail typically fanned to show off big orange (male) to yellow (female/imm.) patches at base. No similar species if seen well. Imm. male resembles female but has orangey breast patches, and by spring often some black spots on head and breast. **SOUNDS:** High sharp *tsip!* similar to Yellow Warbler but slightly higher, sweeter. **STATUS:** Uncommon to fairly common Sep–Apr on both slopes, to 1500m, rarely higher in migration; smaller numbers from mid-Aug and into early May. (Breeds N America, winters Mexico to S America.)

(AMERICAN) YELLOW WARBLER *Setophaga [petechia] aestiva* 11–12cm. Winter migrant to varied open and semi-open habitats with trees, hedgerows, gardens, mangroves, forest edge and clearings. Forages low to high, mainly at mid–upper levels; territorial. Plumage tones variable (some imm. females almost colorless), but always rather compact, with pale eyering on open face, pale wing edgings (no wingbars), yellow undertail patches. Cf. Mangrove Warbler. **SOUNDS:** High, sharp, 'generic' warbler *chip!* good to learn for comparison with other species. **STATUS:** Fairly common to common Sep–Apr on both slopes, to 1500m; smaller numbers from Aug and into mid-May, rarely to 2100m. (Breeds N America to Mexico, winters Mexico to nw. S America.)

MANGROVE [YELLOW] WARBLER *Setophaga petechia* 11.5–12.5cm. Resident in mangroves, rarely adjacent habitats. Note shorter primary projection and different voice than migrant Yellow Warbler, which occurs alongside in winter. Adult male Mangrove distinctive, with chestnut head, fine rusty streaking below; imm. and female like Yellow Warbler but often with some rusty markings on face. **SOUNDS:** Sharp *chuip*, lower and fuller than Yellow Warbler, can suggest Ovenbird. Song a bright, fairly fast, warbled series of sweet chips, 1.5–2 secs; averages richer, lower, and more varied than Yellow Warbler song. **STATUS:** Common to fairly common on Pacific coast, rather local on Caribbean coast (from Moín to Matina). (Mexico to nw. S America.)

PROTHONOTARY WARBLER *Protonotaria citrea* 13–14cm. Winter migrant mainly to mangroves, swampy woodland; in migration also forest and edge, second growth, usually near water. Mainly low in bushes and trees over water, but migrants can be at mid–upper levels in fruiting trees and shrubs. Distinctive, with stout pointed bill, yellow head and breast, plain blue-gray wings, white undertail patches. **SOUNDS:** High tinny *tchín*, less emphatic than Northern Waterthrush. **STATUS:** Fairly common to common Sep–Mar on Pacific slope, rare on Caribbean slope, mainly coastal but locally to 1200m; more widespread in migration, Aug–Oct, Mar–Apr, when common on Caribbean slope and rarely to 2500m. (Breeds e. N America, winters Mexico to nw. S America.)

AMERICAN REDSTART

imm. female

male

female
(imm. male similar)

YELLOW WARBLER

drab imm. female
(Sep–Mar)

female

males

MANGROVE WARBLER

imm. female

female

male

PROTHONOTARY WARBLER

imm. female

male

BLUE-WINGED WARBLER *Vermivora cyanoptera (pinus)* 11.5–12cm. Winter migrant to humid forest and edge, second growth; more varied habitats in migration. Low to high, often in dead-leaf clusters and vine tangles; joins mixed flocks. Distinctive, with dark lores, white wingbars on blue-gray wings, white tail flashes. Hybrids with Golden-winged Warbler rarely reported, show intermediate characters. SOUNDS: High, slightly buzzy *tssi*, often doubled. STATUS: Uncommon Sep–Apr on Caribbean slope, mainly below 1500m; rare in winter on Pacific slope. (Breeds e. N America, winters Mexico to Panama.)

GOLDEN-WINGED WARBLER *Vermivora chrysoptera* 11.5–12cm. Winter migrant to humid forest and edge; more varied habitats in migration, from beach scrub to semi-open areas with taller trees. Mainly at mid–upper levels, in dead-leaf clusters and vine tangles; joins mixed flocks. Distinctive, with dark mask and throat, yellow wingbars; cf. hybrids with Blue-winged Warbler. SOUNDS: High, slightly buzzy *tssi*, often doubled; not readily told from Blue-winged call. STATUS: Fairly common to uncommon Sep–Apr on both slopes, locally to 2400m, most numerous in foothills; more widespread in migration but rare in nw. Pacific lowlands. (Breeds e. N America, winters Mexico to nw. S America.)

NORTHERN PARULA *Setophaga americana* 10–11cm. Rare winter migrant to varied wooded habitats, semi-open areas with hedgerows and taller trees, mangroves. Mainly at mid–upper levels, often holds tail cocked. Told from Tropical Parula by more extensive gray-blue hood with distinct white eye-arcs, less extensive yellow on underparts; adult male has slaty breast band. Imm. male and adult female resemble strongly marked imm. female, sometimes with partial breast band. SOUNDS: Sharp *stik*. STATUS: Rare late Oct–Apr on both slopes and in Central Valley; mainly below 1200m, with most records from Caribbean slope. (Breeds e. N America, winters mainly Mexico and Caribbean.)

TROPICAL PARULA *Setophaga pitiayumi* 10–11cm. Humid foothill and highland forest, adjacent semi-open areas with taller trees; especially in areas with Spanish moss (*Tillandsia* spp.). Mainly at mid–upper levels; at times joins mixed flocks. Distinctive, with mostly deep blue upperparts, rich yellow underparts, weak white wingbar; lacks white eye-arcs of drabber Northern Parula. Male has more extensive black mask than female, richer orange suffusion to breast. SOUNDS: Sharp *stik*, like Northern Parula. Song a variable, high rapid twittering and chipping, at times ending with 1–2 short trills, 1.5–3 secs. STATUS: Fairly common to common on both slopes, mainly 900–2400m on Pacific slope, 600–1800m on Caribbean slope; rarely descends lower in winter. (Mexico to S America.)

FLAME-THROATED WARBLER *Oreothlypis gutturalis* 11.5–12.5cm. Stunning resident of highland oak forest, adjacent semi-open areas. Mainly at mid–upper levels, often foraging actively in canopy; joins mixed flocks. Adult male has flame-orange throat; also note lack of white wingbars; female and imm. average duller, often with yellowish throat but same unique plumage pattern; juv. plumage held briefly, much duller. SOUNDS: Song a rough, slurred, rather insect-like buzz, ending emphatically, 1–1.5 secs, *zzzzzhhh'* every 1–3 secs, at times preceded by a rapid ringing twitter, *chi-chi-chi-chi-chi-zzzzzhhee*, and variations, 1.5–2 secs. Call a high thin *sik*, at times in short series. STATUS: Fairly common to common, mainly 1800m to timberline; occasionally wanders down to 1400m. (Costa Rica to w. Panama.)

males

female

hybrid Blue-winged ×
Golden-winged Warblers

male

**BLUE-WINGED
WARBLER**

**GOLDEN-WINGED
WARBLER**

female

male

NORTHERN PARULA

imm. female

male

TROPICAL PARULA

FLAME-THROATED WARBLER

juv.

adults

358

TENNESSEE WARBLER *Leiothlypis (Oreothlypis) peregrina* 11–12cm. Winter migrant to varied forest and woodland habitats, especially foothill forest, shade coffee plantations. Mostly in canopy, often in small flocks at flowering trees. Face can stain pink from pollen. Note sharp bill, dark eyestripe, whitish undertail coverts. Fall/winter birds bright greenish above, washed yellow on breast, often have narrow pale wingbar, adult male crown grayish, tinged olive; spring adults whiter below, adult male crown blue-gray. SOUNDS: Sharp, high, slightly smacking *chik*. STATUS: Fairly common to common Oct–Apr on both slopes, especially foothills; more widespread in migration, mid-Sep to Nov, Apr–early May. (Breeds n. N America, winters Mexico to nw. S America.)

BLACK-AND-WHITE WARBLER *Mniotilta varia* 11.5–12.5cm. Winter migrant to varied woodland and forest habitats, from mangroves to highland oak forest. Creeps along trunks and branches like a nuthatch; joins mixed flocks. Behavior distinctive, plus boldly black-and-white striped back, dark centers to undertail coverts. Ad. male has black cheeks, attains black throat Mar–Apr; imm. and female have pale cheeks, variably washed buff on flanks. SOUNDS: High, slightly liquid *spik*, at times in fairly rapid spluttering series. STATUS: Fairly common to uncommon Sep–Mar on both slopes, locally to 2500m; more widespread in migration, late Jul–Oct, Mar–early May. (Breeds N America, winters Mexico to nw. S America.)

YELLOW-THROATED WARBLER *Setophaga dominica* 12–13cm. Rare winter migrant to open and semi-open areas with taller trees (especially coconut palms in coastal lowlands, pines in highlands), woodland edge; often creeps around balconies and lights, seeking insects. Usually solitary, independent of flocks. Distinctive, with broad black sideburns, white eyebrow and neck patch, long pointed bill. Ages/sexes similar but imm. female averages dullest, adult male brightest. SOUNDS: Sharp *chik*, suggests Yellow Warbler but averages higher, sharper. STATUS: Rare Aug–Mar on both slopes, mainly on Caribbean slope and in Central Valley, below 1500m. (Breeds e. N America, winters Mexico to Panama.)

MYRTLE [YELLOW-RUMPED] WARBLER *Setophaga coronata* 12.5–13.5cm. Winter migrant to varied open and lightly wooded habitats from scrub and pastures to dry forest edge, fruiting shrubs. Mainly forages low, often on ground, but also ranges to canopy; usually independent of mixed flocks. Often makes fluttering sallies for insects. Note relatively large size, habits, face pattern, yellow rump (often covered by wings) and variable yellowish patches at sides of breast; breeding plumage seen rarely in Costa Rica. SOUNDS: Fairly strong sharp *tchek*; high *sit*, mainly in flight. STATUS: Irregular, uncommon to rare Nov–Mar on both slopes to 1800m; more widespread in migration, Oct–Nov, Mar–early Apr. (Breeds n. N America, winters US to Cen America.)

TENNESSEE WARBLER

imm.
(Sep–Mar)

face or whole head can
be stained by pollen

male breeding
(Mar–Aug)

**BLACK-AND-WHITE
WARBLER**

males

imm. female
(Sep–Mar)

nonbr.
(Sep–Mar)

breeding
(Mar–Aug)

**YELLOW-THROATED
WARBLER**

MYRTLE WARBLER

nonbr. female

male breeding
(Mar–Aug)

BLACKBURNIAN WARBLER *Setophaga fusca* 11.5–12.5cm. Winter migrant to varied forest and woodland habitats, second growth. Mainly at mid–upper levels, often with mixed flocks. Male stunning and unmistakable, female/imm. have same pattern, with pale back stripes, triangular dark cheek patch; yellow throat and breast usually have warm orangey tone, unlike lemon-yellow of superficially similar Townsend's Warbler. SOUNDS: High sharp *tsik*, at times with vaguely tinny quality. STATUS: Fairly common to common Sep–Apr on both slopes, mainly 500–1600m, in smaller numbers to lowlands, rarely to 2500m; more widespread in migration, mid-Aug to Oct, Apr to mid-May. (Breeds e. N America, winters Costa Rica to S America.)

TOWNSEND'S WARBLER *Setophaga townsendi* 11.5–12.5cm. Winter migrant to highland oak and cloud forest, shade coffee plantations, adjacent second growth. Mainly at mid–upper levels; often with mixed flocks. Distinctive, with dark cheek mask, yellow breast, streaked flanks; cf. imm. Hermit Warbler. Hybrid Townsend's × Hermit show variable mixed features, often with Hermit-like face but streaked flanks. SOUNDS: High, sharp, rather abrupt *tik*, much like Black-throated Green Warbler. STATUS: Uncommon to rare Oct–Mar on both slopes, 1200–3000m, with a few from late Sep and into early Apr. Hybrids with Hermit Warbler not reported from Costa Rica but likely occur. (Breeds w. N America, winters w. US to w. Panama.)

BLACK-THROATED GREEN WARBLER *Setophaga virens* 11.5–12.5cm. Winter migrant to varied woodland and forest habitats, shade coffee plantations, adjacent thickets and second growth. Mainly at mid–upper levels; often with mixed flocks. Note yellow face with weak olive frame to cheeks, greenish back; cf. Townsend's Warbler. SOUNDS: High, sharp *tik* like Townsend's Warbler. STATUS: Fairly common to common Oct–Apr on both slopes, mainly 1000–3000m; more widespread in migration, Sep–early Nov, Apr to mid-May, when uncommon in Caribbean lowlands, scarce in Pacific lowlands. (Breeds N America, winters Mexico to nw. S America.)

HERMIT WARBLER *Setophaga occidentalis* 12–13cm. Rare winter migrant to highland forest, adjacent second growth and semi-open areas with non-native cypress and pine trees. Mainly at mid–upper levels, sometimes with mixed flocks. Distinctive, with yellow face, whitish breast, unstreaked flanks; imm. female has dusky cheek patch suggesting Townsend's Warbler, and beware Hermit × Townsend's hybrids, which overall resemble Hermit but have dark streaks on sides and flanks. SOUNDS: High sharp *tik* like Townsend's Warbler. STATUS: Rare mid-Sep to Mar on both slopes, mainly 800–2200m s. to n. Talamanca Mts. Hybrids with Townsend's Warbler not reported from Costa Rica but likely occur. (Breeds w. N America, winters Mexico to Costa Rica.)

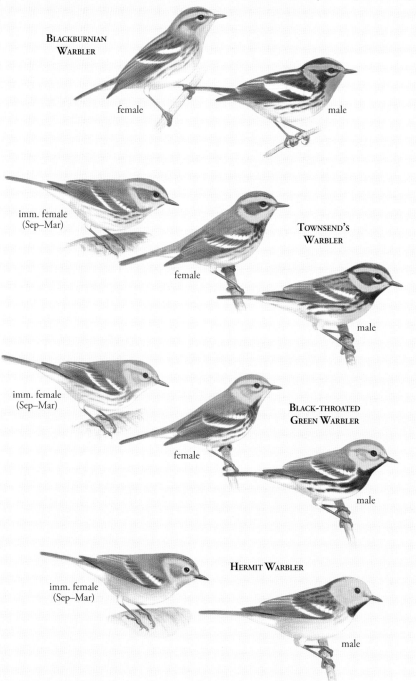

BLACKBURNIAN WARBLER

female

male

imm. female (Sep–Mar)

TOWNSEND'S WARBLER

female

male

imm. female (Sep–Mar)

BLACK-THROATED GREEN WARBLER

female

male

imm. female (Sep–Mar)

HERMIT WARBLER

male

MAGNOLIA WARBLER *Setophaga magnolia* 11.5–12.5cm. Winter migrant to lowland forest and woodland, second growth, plantations. Forages low to high; often with mixed flocks. Fairly active, fluttering in foliage, tail often slightly fanned to show diagnostic pattern on underside: white base with broad black tip. Distinctive: note tail pattern, call note, striking difference between nonbr. and breeding plumages. SOUNDS: High, nasal, slightly burry *iehh*, distinct from any other warbler. STATUS: Uncommon to scarce Oct–Apr on both slopes, locally to 1500m; a few from mid-Sep and into mid-May; rare on s. Pacific slope. (Breeds N America, winters Mexico to Panama.)

CAPE MAY WARBLER *Setophaga tigrina* 11.5–12.5cm. Rare winter migrant to woodland and edge, ornamental gardens, coconut groves. Forages low to high; often around flowering trees and bushes, where territorial. In all plumages note sharply pointed bill, rather compact shape, very fine dark streaking below. Male distinctive (duller in winter), with variable rusty cheek patch, white wing panel; female notably drab, note yellowish neck sides and rump. SOUNDS: Very high, thin, slightly wiry *ti* or *tsi*; lacks a strong chip call. STATUS: Very rare to rare Oct–Apr; scattered records from both slopes and Central Valley, mainly below 1500m. (Breeds n. N America, winters Caribbean region.)

CANADA WARBLER *Cardellina canadensis* 12–13cm. Transient migrant in varied forest and woodland habitats. At low to mid-levels, often in shady understory where hops and flutters, tail frequently held cocked. Distinctive, with yellow spectacles, dark necklace, plain gray upperparts, no white undertail patches. SOUNDS: Relatively low, slightly smacking *tchik*. STATUS: Fairly common to uncommon transient Sep–Oct on both slopes, locally to 1800m, and rare locally through winter; uncommon late Mar to mid-May, mainly on Caribbean slope. (Breeds N America, winters S America, rarely n. to Costa Rica.)

PRAIRIE WARBLER *Setophaga discolor* 11–12cm. Rare winter migrant to second growth, gardens, overgrown fields with shrubby bushes, beach scrub. At low to mid-levels; frequently dips tail while hopping around. All plumages have distinctive face pattern, strongest on adult male, with broad dark crescent under eye setting off wide yellow eye-arcs; also note weak pale wingbars, tail-dipping behavior. SOUNDS: High, sharp, slightly smacking *tchik*. STATUS: Very rare Oct to mid-Apr; scattered records mainly in lowlands on both slopes. (Breeds e. N America, winters Caribbean region.)

PALM WARBLER *Setophaga palmarum* 11.5–12.5cm. Rare winter migrant to open beach scrub, gardens, lawns, adjacent scrubby woodland. On or near ground, sometimes associating with Myrtle Warbler and seedeaters; hops with near-constant pumping of tail and might better be called 'Pipit Warbler.' Distinctive, with bold pale eyebrow, streaky underparts, yellow undertail coverts, dull yellowish rump, distal white undertail patches. Nonbr. adult often has some rusty in cap. SOUNDS: High sharp *chik* with slight metallic ring. STATUS: Rare and sporadic mid-Oct to early Apr on both slopes, mainly below 1200m; most regular in Caribbean coastal lowlands. (Breeds n. N America, winters se. US to Caribbean region.)

MAGNOLIA WARBLER

imm. (Sep–Mar)
(nonbr. similar)

breeding
(Mar–Aug)

male

female

CAPE MAY WARBLER

imm. female
(Sep–Mar)

male breeding
(Mar–Aug)

CANADA WARBLER

female

male

PRAIRIE WARBLER

female

male

PALM WARBLER

nonbr.
(Sep–Apr)

breeding
(Apr–Aug)

CHESTNUT-SIDED WARBLER *Setophaga pennsylvanica* 11.5–12.5cm. Common winter migrant to humid forest and edge, shade coffee plantations, second growth. Mainly at mid–upper levels in canopy; joins mixed flocks. Distinctive, with cocked tail and white eyering often recalling a gnatcatcher; note lime-green upperparts and yellow wingbars; nonbr. ad. male has some chestnut on flanks. Breeding female averages duller than male. SOUNDS: High sharp (descending) *chik*, similar to Yellow Warbler. STATUS: Common Oct–Apr on both slopes, mainly below 2100m, least numerous in drier nw. lowlands; more widespread in migration, mainly Sep–Oct, Apr to mid-May. (Breeds e. N America, winters Mexico to nw. S America.)

BAY-BREASTED WARBLER *Setophaga castanea* 12–13cm. Transient migrant in forest and woodland, second growth. Mainly at mid–upper levels in forest canopy; joins mixed flocks. Rather large and stocky warbler, distinctive in breeding plumage. Fall plumages can resemble Blackpoll Warbler, but Bay-breasted has more spectacled expression (vs. pale eyebrow and dark eyestripe of Blackpoll); plainer underparts with little or no dusky streaking and often tinged buff on flanks; brighter greenish upperparts with thicker white wingbars; and dark feet (yellowish on Blackpoll). SOUNDS: High sharp *chik*, slightly lower and sweeter than Blackpoll. STATUS: Fairly common to common late Sep–Nov on Caribbean slope, to 1800m, and scarce locally through winter on both slopes; uncommon Apr–early May, mainly on Caribbean slope. (Breeds n. N America, winters Panama to nw. S America.)

BLACKPOLL WARBLER *Setophaga striata* 12–13cm. Rare transient migrant in forest and woodland, second growth. Mainly at mid–upper levels in canopy; joins mixed flocks. Rather large, thickset warbler with long wings. Spring male distinctive; on spring female note narrow dark streaking above and below, yellowish feet. Fall plumages all similar: olive above, tinged yellow below with diffuse dusky breast streaking; note yellowish feet; cf. fall Bay-breasted Warbler. SOUNDS: High, sharp *chik*, slightly higher than Yellow Warbler. STATUS: Rare to very rare mid-Oct to Nov, exceptional through winter and in spring; most records from Caribbean slope and Central Valley, but possible anywhere. (Breeds n. N America, winters S America.)

CERULEAN WARBLER *Setophaga cerulea* 11–12cm. Transient migrant in forest and woodland, second growth. Mainly at mid–upper levels in canopy; joins mixed flocks. Distinctive, rather compact warbler with short tail mostly white below, often held slightly cocked. On imm. and female note bold pale eyebrow, unstreaked blue-green upperparts with bold white wingbars. SOUNDS: High sharp *tsik*, slightly higher than American Redstart. STATUS: Uncommon to rare late Aug–Oct, mid-Mar to early May on Caribbean slope, rare on Pacific slope, to 1500m. (Breeds e. N America, winters S America.)

BLACK-THROATED BLUE WARBLER *Setophaga caerulescens* 11.5–12.5cm. Rare winter migrant to forest and woodland, second growth, gardens. Mainly at low to mid-levels, often sallying and fluttering in shady lower growth; usually independent of mixed flocks. Male stunning and unmistakable; female rather drab but distinctive, with narrow whitish eyebrow and lower eye-arc set off by dark cheeks, olive upperparts with small white check at base of primaries (all but absent on some imms.); note call. SOUNDS: Rather low smacking *tchk*, suggests muted Lincoln's Sparrow. STATUS: Very rare Oct–Apr; scattered records mainly from Caribbean lowlands, also foothills on both slopes. (Breeds e. N America, winters Caribbean region.)

imm.
(Sep–Mar)

CHESTNUT-SIDED
WARBLER

nonbr.
(Sep–Mar)

males

breeding
(Mar–Aug)

breeding
(Mar–Aug)

imm.
(Sep–Mar)

BAY-BREASTED
WARBLER

female

males

nonbr.
(Sep–Mar)

breeding
(Mar–Aug)

imm.
(Sep–Mar)

BLACKPOLL WARBLER

female

males

nonbr.
(Sep–Mar)

imm. female

CERULEAN
WARBLER

female

male

male

female

BLACK-THROATED BLUE
WARBLER

WILSON'S WARBLER *Cardellina pusilla* 11–12cm. Winter migrant to foothill and highland forest, woodland, second growth. Mainly at low to mid-levels in shady understory. Active, sallying frequently for insects, tail often cocked and flipped loosely; joins mixed flocks. Note beady black eye, habits; often has a black cap. Tail lacks white flashes, cf. female Hooded Warbler. Comprises 2 groups, perhaps cryptic species: **Western Wilson's Warbler** *C. [p.] pileolata* (from w. N America) brighter overall, often with orangey lores; both sexes have glossy black cap. **Eastern Wilson's Warbler** *C. [p.] pusilla* (from n. N America) duller, more greenish overall, female lacks black cap. SOUNDS: Fairly dry *chep*, rather flat. STATUS: Fairly common to common Oct–Apr on both slopes, wintering mainly above 900m; more widespread in migration, Sep–Oct, Apr to mid-May, when regular in lowlands. Relative status of Western (common, widespread) and Eastern (uncommon?) needs study. (Breeds N America, winters Mexico to Panama.)

HOODED WARBLER *Setophaga citrina* 12–13cm. Winter migrant to humid lowland forest and edge, taller second growth, plantations. At low to mid-levels, often on forest floor; hops around, frequently flashing white tail patches. Male striking and distinctive; plainer females told by open yellow face, habits, white tail flashes, voice, cf. Wilson's Warbler. SOUNDS: High tinny *tink*, not as emphatic as waterthrushes. STATUS: Uncommon to scarce Oct–Apr on both slopes to 1200m, rarely higher; more widespread in migration, Sep–Oct, late Mar to mid-May. (Breeds e. US, winters Mexico to Panama.)

KENTUCKY WARBLER *Geothlypis formosa* 12.5–13.5cm. Winter migrant to humid lowland forest, taller second growth, gallery forest, plantations. On or near shady forest floor, where hops around and usually rather retiring. Yellow spectacles and broad dark 'sideburns' distinctive; adult male face blackest, often with blue-gray edging on crown. SOUNDS: Full deep *tchuk*, richer and deeper than Ovenbird. STATUS: Fairly common to uncommon Sep–Apr on both slopes, locally to 1800m; scarce and local in drier nw. lowlands. (Breeds e. US, winters Mexico to nw. S America.)

MACGILLIVRAY'S WARBLER *Geothlypis tolmiei* 12–13cm. Winter migrant to brushy woodland and edge, thickets, second growth. Fairly skulking, at low to mid-levels in understory and thickets; hops like a yellowthroat. Gray hood with thick white eye-arcs distinctive; also note voice, behavior; cf. imm. Mourning Warbler. SOUNDS: Slightly wet smacking *tchik*, similar to some variations of Common Yellowthroat but usually higher, sharper. STATUS: Uncommon to rare Oct–Apr on both slopes, wintering mainly 1000–2000m; more widespread in migration, mid-Sep to Oct, Apr to mid-May; rare s. of mapped range. (Breeds w. N America, winters Mexico to w. Panama.)

MOURNING WARBLER *Geothlypis philadelphia* 12–13cm. Winter migrant to lowland forest and woodland, plantations, second growth. Skulking, at low to mid-levels in understory and thickets; hops like a yellowthroat. Imm. told from MacGillivray's Warbler by call, lack of bold white eye-arcs (Mourning has narrower, broken eyering or pale yellowish spectacles), and yellowish wash to throat. SOUNDS: Slightly liquid *tchet*. STATUS: Fairly common to uncommon Oct–Apr on both slopes, to 1500m; more widespread in migration, mid-Sep to early Nov, Apr to mid-May. (Breeds n. N America, winters Nicaragua to nw. S America.)

WILSON'S WARBLER

female
Eastern

adult
Western

HOODED WARBLER

females

male

KENTUCKY WARBLER

imm. female

male

MACGILLIVRAY'S
WARBLER

imm.

female

male

MOURNING WARBLER

imm.

female

male

GRAY-CROWNED YELLOWTHROAT *Geothlypis poliocephala* 13–14cm. Distinctive, fairly bulky warbler of ranchland with rough grass and low bushes, canefields, savanna; mainly in drier grassy habitats, not marshes. Mostly skulking, but can be curious, perching up on grass stalk or fence, twitching tail side to side and raising bushy crown; sings from low perch. Note stout pinkish bill, dark lores, plus habitat and voice. Male averages brighter than female, imm. dullest. SOUNDS: Bright nasal *cheédl-ih* or simply *cheédl*; lacks gruff *chek* call of other yellowthroats. Song an unhurried, slightly burry sweet warble, suggesting a *Passerina* bunting, 1.5–3.5 secs; shorter, sweeter, often less hurried than Baird's and Chiriqui Yellowthroats. Also a descending, slowing series of slightly nasal whistles, 2–3.5 secs. STATUS: Fairly common on both slopes, to 1500m; spreading with deforestation. (Mexico to w. Panama.)

*BAIRD'S [OLIVE-CROWNED] YELLOWTHROAT *Geothlypis [semiflava] bairdi* 12.5–13cm. Grassy fields and pastures, marshes, second growth thickets, mainly in wetter areas. No overlap with Chiriqui Yellowthroat. Typically skulking in low dense vegetation but sings from taller grass stalk, low bush, fence, at times in flight. Note brighter olive upperparts, more extensive yellow underparts than smaller, finer-billed Common Yellowthroat. Cf. Gray-crowned Yellowthroat song. SOUNDS: Gruff, slighty downslurred *chrreh*. When agitated, a prolonged, overall downslurred chippering trill, 5–8 secs. Song a slightly rambling or chanting rich warble, relatively even compared to Chiriqui Yellowthroat, and often including short rattled trills, 4–10 secs. STATUS: Fairly common on Caribbean slope, mainly in lowlands but locally to 1200m; spills over to adjacent n. Pacific slope. (Honduras to Panama.)

*CHIRIQUI (MASKED) YELLOWTHROAT *Geothlypis [aequinoctialis] chiriquensis* 12.5–13.5cm. Grassy marshes, wet pastures, reedbeds, second-growth thickets in wetter areas. No overlap with Baird's Yellowthroat. Typically skulking in low dense vegetation but sings from taller grass stalk, low bush, fence, at times in flight. Note grayish face of female, diffuse grayish border to black mask of male, more extensive yellow underparts than smaller, finer-billed Common Yellowthroat. SOUNDS: Slightly burry nasal *chrrieh*. When agitated, a prolonged, overall downslurred, chippering trill, 4–9 secs. Song a rambling, slightly jerky, chanting rich warble, often relatively fast-paced, complex, and jumbled relative to Baird's Yellowthroat, 4–9 secs. STATUS: Uncommon to fairly common but local in interior valleys of s. Pacific slope, 900–1200m. (Costa Rica to w. Panama.)

COMMON YELLOWTHROAT *Geothlypis trichas* 11.5–12.5cm. Winter migrant widely to fresh and brackish marshes with reeds, taller grass, wet fields, mangroves, second growth, scrub; usually near water. Occurs alongside Baird's and Chiriqui Yellowthroats. Mostly skulking in low dense vegetation, but often responds well to pishing. Male's black mask contrastingly bordered pale bluish gray, cf. other yellowthroats; imm. male has partial black mask in 1st winter. Female relatively dull, with reduced yellow on throat and chest. SOUNDS: Gruff, slightly clipped low *tchek* or *chrek*. STATUS: Uncommon to fairly common Oct–Apr on both slopes, mainly to 1500m; more widespread in migration, late Sep–Oct, Apr–early May. (Breeds N America to Mexico, winters s. US to Panama.)

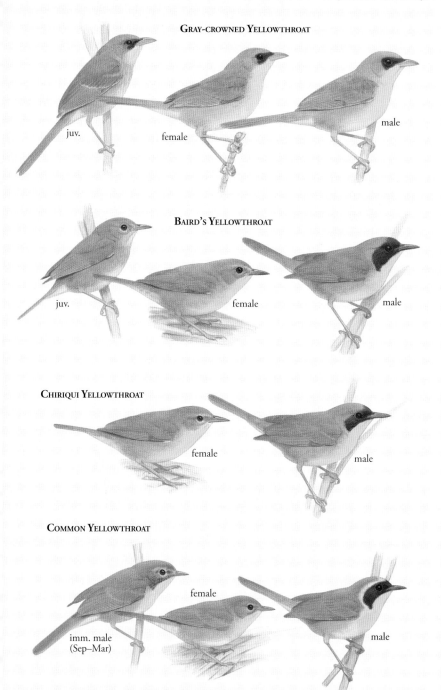

GRAY-CROWNED YELLOWTHROAT

juv.

female

male

BAIRD'S YELLOWTHROAT

juv.

female

male

CHIRIQUI YELLOWTHROAT

female

male

COMMON YELLOWTHROAT

female

imm. male
(Sep–Mar)

male

GENUS *BASILEUTERUS* (4 species). Widespread neotropical warbler genus of forested and scrubby habitats. Sexes similar, often paired year-round; juv. plumage held briefly, like adult within a week or two.

CHESTNUT-CAPPED [RUFOUS-CAPPED] WARBLER *Basileuterus delattrii* 12–13cm. Woodland understory and edge, plantations, taller second growth, brushy hedgerows. At low to mid-levels in fairly open understory, foraging in foliage, often hopping with tail slightly cocked. Distinctive, with yellow underparts, rusty cap and cheeks, bold white eyebrow. No similar species in Costa Rica. **SOUNDS:** High tinny *chiin* or *chik*, sometimes doubled or in short series. Song a pleasant, fairly rapid chipping and jangling warble, 2–3 secs. **STATUS:** Fairly common on n. Pacific slope, locally to 2000m around Central Valley; mainly 600–1600m in interior valleys of s. Pacific slope. (Mexico to nw. S America.)

*STRIPE-CROWNED [GOLDEN-CROWNED] WARBLER *Basileuterus culicivorus* 12–13cm. Humid foothill forest, adjacent taller second growth. In pairs or small groups at low to mid-levels in shady understory, hopping actively and often noisily, tail slightly cocked; joins mixed flocks. Distinctive, with yellow underparts, striped crown (central crown stripe varies, yellow to orange); upperparts vary from grayish in Northern Mts. to olive on s. Pacific slope. **SOUNDS:** Song a short, slurred sweet warble, 1–1.5 secs, ending with strongly upslurred note. Call a dry *chk* or rattled *trrk*, at times run into chatters suggesting a wren. **STATUS:** Fairly common on both slopes, mainly 900–2100m on Pacific slope, 300–1500m on Caribbean slope. (Mexico to Panama.)

BLACK-EARED (COSTA RICAN) WARBLER *Basileuterus [tristriatus] melanotis* 12–13cm. Formerly known as Three-striped Warbler. Humid highland forest and edge, adjacent taller second growth. Mainly at low to mid-levels in shady understory; small groups forage actively in foliage, flipping and twitching tail; often with mixed flocks. Strong head pattern distinctive—suggests Worm-eating Warbler with a facial makeover. Juv. duller overall with diffuse head pattern, faint paler wingbars. **SOUNDS:** High *tik* and rolled *tsirr*, often given when foraging. Song a high, fairly fast-paced jangling twitter, at times prolonged to 15 secs or more in duets, and short songs may run into each other. **STATUS:** Fairly common on Caribbean slope, 1000–2200m; spills over locally to Pacific slope. (Costa Rica to w. Panama.)

BLACK-CHEEKED WARBLER *Basileuterus melanogenys* 12.5–13.5cm. Humid highland forest edge and understory, adjacent second growth and bamboo thickets. Mainly at low to mid-levels, in pairs or small groups, foraging actively and twitching tail; sometimes with mixed flocks. Distinctive, with contrasting white eyebrow, rusty cap, blackish face. Juv. head sooty brown with weak pale eyebrow. **SOUNDS:** Calls include high, lisping, downslurred *tssi* and short high twitters. Song a high, thin, slightly tinny or squeaky jangling twitter, 1–2 secs, at times run into longer duets; thinner and tinnier than Black-eared Warbler. **STATUS:** Fairly common from timberline down to 1600m. (Costa Rica to w. Panama.)

WRENTHRUSH (ZELEDONIIDAE; 1 SPECIES) Enigmatic single-species family formerly merged into New World warblers. Sexes similar.

WRENTHRUSH *Zeledonia coronata* 11–11.5cm. Distinctive but retiring, a small plump bird of bamboo thickets and second growth at edges of humid highland forest, damp ravines, adjacent páramo. Best detected by voice. Singles hop, often rather quickly, on and near ground in dense tangles and bamboo; often flicks wings. Habits, plus plump shape and dark plumage with bright orange crown patch distinctive. Juv. plumage held briefly, duller overall than adult with weak crown pattern. **SOUNDS:** Song a very high, thin, slightly piercing warbled series of (usually 2–5) notes, 0.5–1 sec, such as *tsi-si-síin*, every 2–6 secs. Call louder, a piercing, slightly ascending, very high thin *siiii*, about 0.5 sec, at times given steadily in short series. **STATUS:** Fairly common from timberline down to 1500m in Northern Mts., down to 1800m in Central and Talamanca Mts. (Costa Rica to w. Panama.)

CHESTNUT-CAPPED WARBLER

Northwest

STRIPE-CROWNED WARBLER

South

BLACK-EARED WARBLER

BLACK-CHEEKED WARBLER

WRENTHRUSH

WORM-EATING WARBLER *Helmitheros vermivorum* 12–13cm. Winter migrant to forest, woodland, second growth. Forages mainly from mid-levels to subcanopy, typically poking into vine tangles and dead-leaf clusters; joins mixed flocks. Distinctive, with boldly striped head, buffy underparts; cf. Black-eared Warbler. **SOUNDS:** Rich sharp *tchik* and high, slightly buzzy *tssi*, often doubled, cf. Golden-winged Warbler. **STATUS:** Uncommon to scarce Sep–Mar on both slopes, to 1500m; more widespread in migration, late Aug–Oct, Apr. (Breeds e. US, winters Mexico to Panama.)

OVENBIRD *Seiurus aurocapilla* 13.5–14.5cm. Winter migrant to forest, woodland, plantations, typically with abundant leaf litter. Walks purposefully on forest floor (unlike thrushes, which hop), often with tail held cocked, foraging in leaf litter; agitated birds perch low to high, walking along branches. Distinctive, but cf. migrant *Catharus* thrushes (p. 330). **SOUNDS:** Full, slightly smacking *tchip* or *chiuk*, often repeated steadily when agitated. **STATUS:** Uncommon to fairly common Oct–Apr on both slopes, to 1500m; more widespread in migration, Sep–Oct, Apr to mid-May. (Breeds N America, winters Mexico to Panama.)

NORTHERN WATERTHRUSH *Parkesia noveboracensis* 13.5–14.5cm. Winter migrant to varied wetland habitats, from mangroves to small ponds, lakeshores, slow-moving streams; usually in areas of sluggish or stagnant water. Often rather retiring; walks on ground, pumping its rear end. Little habitat overlap with Louisiana Waterthrush, which favors flowing water. Louisiana has bolder whiter eyebrow and peachy-buff flanks (eyebrow and flanks same tone on Northern); sparser, less dense dark streaking below; deeper bobbing motion of shorter tail; note voice. **SOUNDS:** Bright metallic *chink*, higher and brighter than Louisiana. **STATUS:** Common (especially in mangroves) to fairly common Sep–Apr on both slopes, mainly below 1500m; more widespread in migration, late Aug–Oct, Apr to mid-May, ranging to 2200m. (Breeds n. N America, winters Mexico to nw. S America.)

LOUISIANA WATERTHRUSH *Parkesia motacilla* 14–15cm. Winter migrant to streams and rivers, especially in foothills, less often lake margins, humid forest floor; other habitats in migration, but rarely if ever in mangroves. Walks on ground with deep bobbing of rear end, often swung slightly side-to-side; pokes in leaf litter and shallow water. Cf. slightly smaller-billed, dingier, and more densely streaked Northern Waterthrush. **SOUNDS:** Full metallic *chink*, deeper and less tinny than Northern. **STATUS:** Uncommon to fairly common but low-density, Sep–Mar on both slopes to 2500m; more widespread in migration, late Jul–Sep, Mar to mid-Apr. (Breeds e. N America, winters Mexico to nw. S America.)

BUFF-RUMPED WARBLER *Myiothlypis fulvicauda* 12–13cm. Attractive and distinctive resident of streams, riverbanks, and other waterside habitats in forested and semi-open areas of humid lowlands and foothills. Pairs territorial year-round, hopping along shorelines and among rocks to forage, at times out on damp dirt roads and in pastures; tail fanned and dipped to continually show off contrasting pale buff tail coverts and tail base, which glows in forest shade and is striking in flight. **SOUNDS:** Song carries over rushing water: a measured, staccato series of chips, typically starts with a few slower-paced, higher notes and runs into an overall descending, increasingly loud, and often slightly slowing series of rich whistled notes, the ending often arrestingly powerful: *see see see chu-chu-chu-chu... CHU-CHU CHU*, 3–4.5 secs, repeated every few secs. Call a sharp gravelly *chit*, often doubled. **STATUS:** Fairly common on both slopes, locally to 1500m. (Honduras to S America.)

WORM-EATING
WARBLER

OVENBIRD

NORTHERN WATERTHRUSH

LOUISIANA WATERTHRUSH

BUFF-RUMPED WARBLER

juv.

374

SLATE-THROATED WHITESTART (REDSTART) *Myioborus miniatus* 12.5–13.5cm. Handsome warbler of foothill and highland forest and edge, adjacent second growth with hedgerows, brushy clearings, flower banks. Forages actively, mainly at low to mid-levels, fanning tail side-to-side; often in pairs and with mixed flocks. Distinctive, with slaty head and upperparts, yellow belly, white tail sides. Belly golden-yellow in Northern Mts., lemon-yellow in Central and Talamanca Mts. Juv. has messier pattern, with sooty head and breast, paler belly. **SOUNDS:** High thin *tsit*. Song a variable, often rather slow and simple pleasing warble, sometimes rising at the end, 1.5–2.5 secs, such as *see see swee swee swee-see swee-see swee sii*, every few secs. **STATUS:** Fairly common to common on both slopes, mainly 1100–2100m on Pacific slope, 750–1300m on Caribbean slope. (Mexico to S America.)

COLLARED WHITESTART (REDSTART) *Myioborus torquatus* 12.5–13.5cm. Attractive, distinctive, and often confiding warbler of highland forest and edge, adjacent second growth and overgrown weedy pastures. Forages actively low to high, at times on ground, fanning tail side-to-side; often with mixed flocks. Juv. has head and breast sooty dark grayish, paler yellow belly, much like juv. Slate-throated Whitestart, which is typically at lower elevations. **SOUNDS:** High, sharp, slightly smacking *tik*. Song a prolonged, pleasant, rambling high warble, 3.5–8.5 secs; longer, more varied than Slate-throated Whitestart, at times in duet. **STATUS:** Fairly common to common from timberline down to about 1600m. (Costa Rica to w. Panama.)

YELLOW-BREASTED CHAT (ICTERIIDAE; 1 SPECIES) Enigmatic songbird long placed within New World warblers, now treated in its own family. Ages/sexes differ slightly.

YELLOW-BREASTED CHAT *Icteria virens* 16.5–18cm. Scarce winter migrant to second-growth thickets, forest and woodland edge, scrubby tangles. Distinctive but mostly rather skulking, hopping at low to mid-levels in cover; rarely ranges higher into fruiting trees and at times on ground near cover. Note bulky build with long tail often cocked, white spectacles, bright yellow bib; lores black on adult male, dark grayish on female and imm., which in fall has stronger olive tinge to head, pinkish tinge to mandible. **SOUNDS:** Hard gruff *chrek* and *tek-tek*; low rasping *tcherr*. **STATUS:** Scarce to rare Oct–Mar on both slopes, locally to 1500m; occasionally from mid-Sep and into Apr. (Breeds N America to Mexico, winters Mexico to Costa Rica.)

THRUSH-TANAGERS (RHODINOCICHLIDAE; 1 SPECIES) Enigmatic terrestrial birds now treated in their own family, formerly as tanagers. Ages/sexes differ; soon attain adult appearance.

*PANAMA [ROSY] THRUSH-TANAGER *Rhodinocichla [rosea] eximia* 18.5–20cm. Distinctive but secretive bird of woodland and thickets with brushy understory, canebrakes; usually shy and difficult to see. Singles and pairs feed on ground in leaf litter, tossing leaves with their bill; sings from low perch, usually well hidden. Can appear dark in shady understory but distinctive given size, habits, long slender bill, white eyebrow; male colors brilliant, female colors muted but equally distinctive. Juv. resembles female but with messier head pattern, duller underparts. **SOUNDS:** Downslurred rich *tcheu*, and *tcheu-eu*, at times repeated steadily. Varied song comprises fairly short, rhythmic, rich whistled phrases, such as *wheeichu h'whee-chu*, or *cheu-i heu tu-weet*, repeated or alternated, typically every 3–5 secs. Songs more variable, prolonged, and can be rapidly repeated in duets. Powerful rich quality of notes may suggest some wrens. **STATUS:** Scarce to uncommon and local in interior valleys of s. Pacific slope, mainly 200–1000m. (Costa Rica to Panama.)

SLATE-THROATED WHITESTART

COLLARED WHITESTART

YELLOW-BREASTED CHAT

imm.
(Sep–Dec)

PANAMA THRUSH-TANAGER

female

male

NEW WORLD SPARROWS AND ALLIES (PASSERELLIDAE; 21+ SPECIES)
Large New World family formerly merged with Emberizid buntings of the Old World. Ages differ, attain adult appearance within a few weeks; sexes alike in Costa Rican species. Numerous species formerly placed in this family are now considered to be tanagers. Species of shady understory often best detected by voice.

LARGE-FOOTED FINCH *Pezopetes capitalis* 19–20.5cm. Large, drab, rather chunky 'finch' of humid highland forest, bamboo thickets, second growth, overgrown pastures, gardens. Hops and bounds quickly on ground, and 'jump-kicks' with both feet to dig in leaf litter; also ranges into fruiting bushes and low trees. Sings from low perch or ground, at times in duet. Note large size, olive body, black face and crown stripes—and it does have big feet. Cf. smaller, less bulky brushfinches. **SOUNDS:** Varied, often strikingly noisy. Very high, thin *sit* and *t'sit*; slightly grating, downslurred squeaky *tsiin*; high, thin, buzzy *tszir* can be run into excited, squeaky gobbling chatters. Full song remarkable, an unhurried but varied medley of rich chirps, whistles, gurgles, short trills, with phrases often repeated a few times; varies from 1–3 secs between phrases to a more continuous stream; can include mimicry. Also a simple, slightly tinny chirping *chíliu* or *chi-i-lu*, repeated or alternated every few secs. **STATUS:** Fairly common to common in Central and Talamanca Mts., 2100–3300m. (Costa Rica to w. Panama.)

YELLOW-THIGHED BRUSHFINCH (FINCH) *Atlapetes (Pselliophorus) tibialis* 17.5–18.5cm. Overall dark 'finch' of humid highland forest, bamboo thickets, second growth, overgrown pastures. Usually in pairs or small groups, foraging from ground to tree canopy, often relatively conspicuous at mid-levels; at times with mixed flocks. Loosely flips long tail while hopping around. No similar species in Costa Rica: puffy yellow thighs typically conspicuous, otherwise dark slaty gray overall with variably contrasting blackish head. Imm. duller overall, thighs pale olive and not striking. **SOUNDS:** Sharp, relatively low, slightly metallic clucking *tchek*, may be repeated steadily; slightly gruff, sharp metallic *tink!* Song a fairly rapid, chipping jangle, 1–2 secs, every few secs; longer, higher, and squeakier jumbled chatters in duets, up to about 10 secs. **STATUS:** Fairly common to common, from timberline down to 1500m in Northern Mts., down to 1700m in Central and Talamanca Mts., occasionally lower on Caribbean slope. (Costa Rica to w. Panama.)

*YELLOW-THROATED [WHITE-NAPED] BRUSHFINCH *Atlapetes [albinucha] gutturalis* 17–18.5cm. Handsome 'finch' of brushy highland pastures, second growth, forest edge, hedgerows, gardens. Often in pairs or small groups, mainly at low to mid-levels, at times hopping on ground. **SOUNDS:** High, thin, slightly sibilant *tssi*, and downslurred *t-ssi*; excited bursts of fairly rapid, squeaky chortling in duets, to 4 secs or longer. Song an unhurried series of varied, high, slurred to slightly piercing short whistled phrases, such as *tsiíu tsieh tsi tseíiu si-i tsiu...*, 1 phrase/0.5–1.5 secs; songs can be in groups of 2–3 phrases every few secs or a steadier flow prolonged a min or longer, especially around dawn. **STATUS:** Fairly common, mainly 900–2800m. (Mexico to S America.)

Large-footed Finch

Yellow-thighed Brushfinch

Yellow-throated Brushfinch

juv.

*ORANGE-BILLED SPARROW *Arremon aurantiirostris* 14.5–16.5cm. Humid forest, taller second growth, plantations. Pairs or singles hop on ground in shady understory; rarely perches in low vegetation except when singing. Distinctive, but mostly retiring: orange bill often gleams like a beacon in shadowed forest. Mostly dark bill of imm. can be retained into mid-winter. Comprises 2 groups in Costa Rica that may represent species: **Northern Orange-billed Sparrow** *A. [a.] rufidorsalis* on Caribbean slope, averages broader and bolder white eyebrow, plumage darker and richer overall; **Western Orange-billed Sparrow** *A. [a.] aurantiirostris* on s. Pacific slope averages duller eyebrow, usually tinged grayish at rear. SOUNDS: **Northern** call a slightly rough smacking *tchik!* Song a very high, squeaky, often slightly jerky warble, 1–4 secs. **Western** call a high, thin, slightly tinny clipped *tsit*. Song higher, thinner, faster-paced than Northern, with variably tinny, tinkling quality, 1.5–3.5 secs. STATUS: Fairly common on both slopes, to 1200m on Pacific slope, to 800m on Caribbean slope. (Mexico to S America.)

SOOTY-FACED FINCH *Arremon crassirostris* 15.5–17cm. Humid foothill forest and edge, especially ravines and streamside thickets. Pairs or singles forage on or near ground in shady understory, hopping over ground, at times ranging into low fruiting shrubs; sings from low perches. Distinctive but mostly retiring: note bushy whitish mustache, rusty crown; also bright yellow belly at some angles. Juv. duller and browner overall, without rusty cap; note trace of paler mustache, dark throat; cf. juv. Chestnut-capped Brushfinch, which has pale throat. SOUNDS: High, piercing to slightly metallic sibilant *tsii tsiih*, 2nd note stronger; sometimes short series of high notes, 1st slightly lower but stronger. Song a high, squeaky, slightly jerky chanting warble, can be prolonged to a min or longer; averages slower-paced, more piercing than Costa Rican Brushfinch. STATUS: Fairly common to uncommon on Caribbean slope, mainly 600–1800m; uncommon on cen. Pacific slope. (Costa Rica to w. Panama.)

CHESTNUT-CAPPED BRUSHFINCH *Arremon brunneinucha* 17–19.5cm. Humid highland forest and edge, adjacent second growth and brushy thickets. Pairs or singles forage in shady understory, hopping over ground and tossing leaves with bill; at times ranges into fruiting shrubs and low trees. Distinctive but retiring: puffy white throat often gleams in shady understory, bordered by black collar; also note bright rusty cap with variable buff margin (weak in Northwest, distinct in Talamanca Mts.). Cf. Costa Rican Brushfinch of s. Pacific slope (mainly lower elevations). SOUNDS: High thin *ssi* and *sii*. Song a short medley of thin, slurred, sibilant whistles, 1–2 secs; also longer series up to 30 secs or more, including thin wiry trills; overall slower-paced, less varied, and more sibilant than Costa Rican Brushfinch. STATUS: Fairly common on both slopes, mainly 1200–2500m on Pacific slope, 900–2500m on Caribbean slope. (Mexico to S America.)

COSTA RICAN [STRIPE-HEADED] BRUSHFINCH *Arremon costaricensis* 18–19.5cm. Humid foothill forest edge, second growth thickets, plantations. Pairs or singles forage in shady understory, hopping over ground and tossing leaves with bill; at times ranges into fruiting shrubs and low trees. Distinctive but retiring: puffy white throat often gleams in shady understory; also note broad gray eyebrow on black head, lack of black collar. Cf. Chestnut-capped Brushfinch, mainly of higher elevations. Juv. duller overall with olive head, trace of adult head pattern. SOUNDS: High, thin, slightly piercing *tsit* ot *tsiit*, may run into short twitters. Song a high, thin, jerky, slightly tinny twitter in bursts of 1–2 secs every few secs; also faster-paced prolonged twittering to 30 secs or more; overall faster-paced, more twittering and varied than thinner, sibilant songs of Chestnut-capped Brushfinch. STATUS: Fairly common, mainly 300–1200m. (Costa Rica to w. Panama.)

ORANGE-BILLED SPARROW

ARREMON

imm.

Caribbean
(Northern)

juv.

Pacific
(Western)

SOOTY-FACED FINCH

Talamanca Mts.

juv.

Northwest

CHESTNUT-CAPPED
BRUSHFINCH

COSTA RICAN
BRUSHFINCH

*OLIVE SPARROW *Arremonops rufivirgatus* 13.5–14.5cm. Rather drab sparrow of dry lowland forest, adjacent thickets, gallery forest. In pairs or family groups scratching in leaf litter, rarely ranging into fruiting bushes; sings from concealed perch at low to mid-levels in shady understory. No similar species in Costa Rican range: note drab, overall rather plain plumage with distinct dark stripes on buffy head. Juv. duller overall with dark streaking above and below, weak head pattern; soon like adult. **SOUNDS:** High, sharp, slightly smacking *tsik*, can be repeated steadily. Song a variably accelerating series of twangy to ringing chips, mostly 4–6 secs; starts with 2–5 slower-paced notes often different in quality from main song series, such as *tk, siu, s'wee tseu tseu-tseutseu…* or *tk, tik seeu, si sweeu chi-chi-chichi.…* **STATUS:** Fairly common on n. Pacific slope, locally to 900m in w. Central Valley. (Mexico and s. Texas to Costa Rica.)

BLACK-STRIPED SPARROW *Arremonops conirostris* 16–17.5cm. Fairly large and bulky sparrow of humid lowland forest edge, second growth thickets, overgrown fields, hedgerows, gardens. In pairs or family groups, mostly on or near ground, but ranges into fruiting bushes and trees, at times into subcanopy; sings mainly from low to mid-levels in shady understory. Distinctive in range, with bold black stripes on gray head, olive upperparts. **SOUNDS:** Downslurred mellow *cheu* and slightly gruff *cheuh*, both often repeated steadily. High lisping notes and twangy nasal duets when excited. Song prolonged, up to 45 secs or more: begins with hesitant rich twangy chirps and burry whistles every 1–2 secs then runs into an accelerating series of nasal *chuh* and *choo* notes that fade out or run into a roll, such as *h'uit, cheuhr, húit, cheuk, cheu...choo choo choo choo-choo-choochoo...*; sometimes ends with abrupt nasal *cheúh*. **STATUS:** Fairly common on both slopes, to 1500m. (Honduras to S America.)

CABANIS'S GROUND SPARROW *Melozone cabanisi* 15–16.5cm. Attractive and distinctively patterned sparrow of humid foothill woodland and plantations, adjacent second growth, brushy hedgerows, overgrown fields. Mostly retiring, in shady understory; pairs forage on ground in leaf litter, ranging to adjacent open edges mainly early and late in day. No similar species in Costa Rica: note bright rusty cap, complex head and breast pattern. **SOUNDS:** Rather quiet, high thin *ti* and stronger, harder *tik*. Song a short medley of 2–4 downslurred, often inflected whistled notes preceded by 1–3 short chips, such as *tik-tik ssiu p'ssiuu* or *tk ssiu ti'p'ssiu*, and variations, 1–1.5 secs. **STATUS:** Uncommon to fairly common but local, mainly in hills around Central Valley, 600–1600m. (Endemic to Costa Rica.)

*WHITE-EARED GROUND SPARROW *Melozone leucotis* 17.5–18.5cm. Fairly large, attractively patterned sparrow of humid foothill woodland and plantations, adjacent second growth. Mostly retiring, in shady understory; pairs forage on ground, often scratching noisily in leaf litter. No similar species in Costa Rica: note bold head pattern, with white face patches, yellow collar. **SOUNDS:** High thin *ti*; high sibilant twitters in pulsating duet, up to about 5 secs. Song a staccato series of (usually 5–11) slightly sibilant ringing chips, often accelerating slightly, and preceded by 2–3 high slurred chips, such as *ti siu si chi-chi-chi-chi-chichi*, 2–2.5 secs. **STATUS:** Fairly common to uncommon from n. Pacific slope s. to Central Valley, 500–2000m; spills over locally to adjacent Caribbean slope. (Mexico to Costa Rica.)

OLIVE SPARROW

BLACK-STRIPED SPARROW

juv.

CABANIS'S GROUND SPARROW

juv.

WHITE-EARED GROUND SPARROW

juv.

*STRIPE-HEADED SPARROW *Peucaea ruficauda* 17.5–19cm. Distinctive, relatively conspicuous large sparrow of brushy fields, dry scrubby woodland, ranchland with hedgerows. Often in small flocks; feeds on ground but perches readily on fence posts, in low bushes and trees. No similar species in Costa Rica: note bold head stripes, mottled breast. Juv. streaked overall with ghosting of adult pattern, soon like adult. SOUNDS: Varied, slightly nasal to smacking chips, at times repeated fairly persistently; also high thin *ssi*. High, squeaky to slightly nasal, rhythmic twittering and high rapid tinkling duets, mostly 3–12 secs. Song variable, ranges from a few sharp high chips run into a chipping trill, 2.5–3.5 secs, to a rapid, rhythmic, slightly squeaky chatter, 1–3 secs, repeated every few secs. STATUS: Fairly common to common on n. Pacific slope, in smaller numbers s. into w. Central Valley, to 1000m. (Mexico to nw. Costa Rica.)

RUSTY SPARROW *Aimophila rufescens* 17.5–19cm. Large bulky sparrow of grassy areas with scattered bushes and shrubby thickets. Mostly on or near ground, where can be skulking, but sings from low perch; flies heavily if flushed. No similar species in Costa Rica: note bold black mustache, bright rusty cap and wings, stout bicolored bill. SOUNDS: Low gruff *chehr*, may suggest a wren and can be repeated steadily; runs into squeakier chatters in excitement. Song a short emphatic medley of (usually 4–5) bright rich chips, such as *sip sip chi-chi-chi*, or *chip chip chi-cheu*, every few secs. STATUS: Uncommon and local on n. and cen. Pacific slope, 500–1100m. (Mexico to nw. Costa Rica.)

BOTTERI'S SPARROW *Peucaea botterii* 14–15cm. Rather plain, long-tailed sparrow of grassland with rocky outcrops and scattered bushes. Rarely seen unless singing: generally skulks on or near ground in grasses, but sings from low perch. Plumage rather nondescript, with weak head stripes, plain buffy breast; note long, slightly graduated tail, cf. stockier, brighter, and short-tailed Grasshopper Sparrow. Juv. has streaky breast, ghosting of adult pattern; soon like adult. SOUNDS: High, thin, slightly metallic *sik*, at times in short series. Song comprises a varied introduction of a few high tinny chips and burry chirps run into a pleasant, accelerating trill, 4–7 secs; also prolonged, slightly jerky, unhurried series of varied high chips, chirps, and short trills, about 2/sec, up to 30 secs or longer. STATUS: Scarce and local on n. Pacific slope, 400–1100m. (Mexico and sw. US to Costa Rica.)

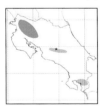

GRASSHOPPER SPARROW *Ammodramus savannarum* 12–12.5cm. Small, stocky, rather short-tailed sparrow of dry grassland, often with scattered bushes and boulders; migrants also in wetter pastures, brushy fields. Skulks on or near ground in grasses and weeds; sings from low perch. Flushed birds typically fly a short distance, silently, and drop back to cover; often difficult to relocate. Note large head, rather short tail, plain buffy breast, whitish wingbars; cf. longer-tailed and plainer Botteri's Sparrow. SOUNDS: Calls insect-like, a high, soft *tik* and short dry rattle. Song a high, thin, wiry, insect-like buzz, 1–2 secs, usually 1 or more introductory notes audible at close range. STATUS: Uncommon and local on n. Pacific slope, 100–800m; scarce in winter s. to Central Valley and s. Pacific slope. (N America to Cen America.)

*NORTHERN [WEDGE-TAILED] GRASSFINCH *Emberizoides [herbicola] sphenurus* 16.5–19cm. Now classified as a tanager, this distinctive streaky 'finch' inhabits taller grassland and savanna with scattered bushes and trees. In pairs or family groups, foraging on ground or buried in grasses; flushes abruptly and flies with pumping tail before dropping back to cover. Perches up on grass stalks and fences to sing; when curious or alarmed, often twitches tail side-to-side. No similar species in Costa Rica: note very long tail, streaky upperparts, mostly pinkish-orange bill. SOUNDS: Calls include high thin *tk*. Song a short, dry chipping phrase or trill every few secs, typically introduced by 1–2 discrete notes, such as *chi-chi chi-li-li*. STATUS: Uncommon and local in interior valleys of s. Pacific slope, 150–900m. (Costa Rica to n. S America.)

STRIPE-HEADED SPARROW

RUSTY SPARROW

juv.

BOTTERI'S SPARROW

GRASSHOPPER SPARROW

juv.

resident

northern migrant

NORTHERN GRASSFINCH

juv.

RUFOUS-COLLARED SPARROW *onotrichia capensis* 13.5–14.5cm. Distinctive and familiar bird of open and semi-open habitats in interior and highlands, from cities to forest clearings. Feeds mainly on ground but sings from rooftops, fence posts, other prominent perches. Nonbreeding flocks form locally in fall–winter. Note peaked crown, boldly patterned head with rusty collar, muted on streaky juv. SOUNDS: Slightly metallic hard *chik*, may be repeated steadily. Song a short, notably varied arrangement of (usually 4–6) sweet slurred whistles, such as *ti heuu sii tcheu*, sometimes preceded or followed by short chipping series of 2–6 notes, such as *swi heeuu chee ch-ch-ch-ch-ch-ch*. STATUS: Common to fairly common, mainly 600m to above timberline; locally down to 400m on Caribbean slope; exceptional wanderer to lowlands. (Mexico to S America.)

VOLCANO JUNCO *Junco vulcani* 15.5–16.5cm. Rather large sparrow of open grassy areas and roadsides in páramo, adjacent brushy thickets, weedy pastures; historically in areas cleared by volcanic activity. Pairs, less often singles and family groups, forage on ground, hopping strongly; also clambers in shrubs. Distinctive, with pink bill, staring golden eyes. SOUNDS: Twangy smacking *chip*, slightly squeakier than Rufous-collared Sparrow; high lisping *ssip*; greeting duet a slightly burry nasal slow chatter. Song a short, slightly jerky phrase of burry chirps, such as *chípi-chur-chieh*, 1–2 secs. STATUS: Fairly common around and above timberline, mainly above 3000m; spreading downslope with deforestation, locally to 2500m. (Costa Rica to w. Panama.)

BUSH-TANAGERS (GENUS *CHLOROSPINGUS*) (3 species). Taxonomically vexed group of social, arboreal small birds of humid foothill and highland forest; note distinctive head patterns. Ages differ slightly, soon like adult; sexes similar. Formerly considered as tanagers, now as New World sparrows.

*****MIDDLE AMERICAN [COMMON] BUSH-TANAGER** *Chlorospingus [flavopectus] ophthalmicus* 13.5–14.5cm. Humid foothill and highland forest and edge, adjacent second growth with fruiting shrubs. Mainly at low to mid-levels, where active and often noisy in shady understory and edge; usually in small groups, often a core species of mixed flocks. Dawn song can be from high perch, difficult to trace. Distinctive, with white postocular spot, yellowish breast, habits. SOUNDS: High sharp *sik*, at times in rapid twittering rattles; ascending, high lisping *ssih*. 'Song' a rather rapid, accelerating, slightly squeaky warble or chippering trill, overall rising or slightly overslurred, 1–2 secs. Dawn song a high, sibilant, slightly emphatic, overslurred *tssih*, on and on, every 1–2 secs; easily passed off as a hummingbird. STATUS: Common to fairly common on both slopes; mainly 1100–2300m on Pacific slope, 500–2300m on Caribbean slope. (Mexico to w. Panama.)

*****ASHY-THROATED BUSH-TANAGER** *Chlorospingus canigularis* 12.5–13.5cm. Humid foothill forest and edge. In pairs or small groups, mainly at mid–upper levels with mixed flocks; often forages hidden in leafy tangles. Notably drab; note contrast between yellowish breast band and pale throat with subtle but distinctive dusky whisker. Juv. more extensively yellowish below. SOUNDS: High, downslurred *chih* and smacking *tchik!* Song (S America) a fairly rapid, sharp ticking trill, often with spluttering cadence, 3–6 secs. STATUS: Scarce to uncommon on cen. Caribbean slope, 400–1200m. (Costa Rica to Peru.)

SOOTY-CAPPED BUSH-TANAGER *Chlorospingus pileatus* 14–15cm. Humid highland forest and edge, cloud forest, adjacent second growth and páramo. Usually in small groups ranging low to high, creeping along mossy branches, swarming in fruiting shrubs; often a core species of mixed flocks. Bold head pattern distinctive, cf. Middle American Bush-Tanager. Juv. duller overall but with same basic pattern as adult. SOUNDS: Varied, high thin chips, often with slightly squeaky or sibilant quality. Song a slightly jerky, fairly rapid, high squeaky warble, at times incorporating short chippering trills, 1.5–3 secs; more prolonged when excited. STATUS: Common to fairly common from timberline down to 1600m in Northern Mts., down to 2000m in Central and Talamanca Mts. (Costa Rica to w. Panama.)

RUFOUS-COLLARED
SPARROW

juv.

VOLCANO JUNCO

juv.

MIDDLE AMERICAN
BUSH-TANAGER

ASHY-THROATED
BUSH-TANAGER

SOOTY-CAPPED
BUSH-TANAGER

variation

OLD WORLD SPARROWS (PASSERIDAE; 1 SPECIES) Old World family, one species introduced to New York in 1850 and has spread widely in North and Central America. Ages/sexes differ; resembles adult within 1–2 months, following complete molt.

HOUSE SPARROW *Passer domesticus* 14–15cm. Human commensal found in urban areas, adjacent farmland, along highways at truck stops, gas stations. In pairs or small flocks, sometimes mixing with other birds but usually apart. Feeds mainly on ground, often perches on buildings, utility poles; groups roost in dense shrubbery. Handsome male distinctive; head and breast pattern veiled with paler edgings in fresh plumage, bill mostly pale in nonbr. condition. Female rather plain but no similar species in Costa Rica. Juv. resembles female, soon attains adult appearance. SOUNDS: Varied, mostly rather tuneless chirps and chips, dry chatters, churring calls. STATUS: Fairly common and widespread, especially in drier areas, least numerous in humid tropical lowlands; mainly below 1500m. (Worldwide; native to Eurasia.)

MUNIAS (ESTRILDIDAE; 1 SPECIES) Small seed-eating 'finches' of Old World origin. Populations derived from escaped cagebirds or releases are becoming established locally in New World. Ages differ, sexes similar; attain adult appearance within a few months.

TRICOLORED MUNIA *Lonchura malacca* 10–11cm. Small handsome 'finch' of seeding grassy fields, rice fields, irrigation ditches, edges of cane fields. Often in groups, in same areas as native seedeaters and migrant buntings, although flocks often keep apart from other species; rather direct 'barreling' flight suggests small compact House Sparrow. Adult (sexes similar) distinctive, with bold plumage pattern, small size; juv. rather plain but note large pale bill, rather short and graduated tail, voice. SOUNDS: Usually rather quiet; flight call a burry to twangy overslurred nasal *byehh*, singly or in short series. STATUS: Uncommon to fairly common but local on Pacific slope and nw. lowlands, to 1500m in Central Valley; first recorded Costa Rica in 1999 and range still expanding. (Native to India.)

FINCHES (FRINGILLIDAE; 12 SPECIES) Fairly large, almost worldwide family of small, often colorful seed- and fruit-eating birds. Ages/sexes usually differ, juv. often like female; attain adult appearance within 1st year. Calls and songs notably varied, sometimes including mimicry.

YELLOW-BELLIED SISKIN *Spinus xanthogastrus* 10–11cm. Highland oak forest and edge, adjacent clearings and second growth, weedy pastures with scattered trees, hedgerows. Singles, pairs, or small groups feed from low in seeding grasses to high in tree canopy. Note big yellow wing patch, cf. Lesser Goldfinch. SOUNDS: Short metallic whistled notes, such as *kleéih*; low gruff *cheh*, at times in short series. Song a rapid jangling medley, often with repetition of notes and phrases; in bursts of 2–10 secs strung together with short breaks, or prolonged to 20 secs or more; averages higher, more metallic, but also more melodic, less buzzy than Lesser Goldfinch. STATUS: Uncommon and nomadic in Central and Talamanca Mts. especially Pacific slope, mainly 800–2100m, locally to 3000m. Widely reduced in numbers by trapping for cagebird trade. (Costa Rica to S America.)

LESSER GOLDFINCH *Spinus psaltria* 9.5–10.5cm. Open and semi-open country with scattered trees, hedgerows, gardens, weedy fields. Usually in small flocks, feeding from low in seeding grasses to high in tree canopy. Note white wing patch, cf. Yellow-bellied Siskin, lack of yellow forehead patch cf. male euphonias, which favor humid lowlands. Juv. resembles female, with buffy wingbars, soon like adult. SOUNDS: High, slightly whiny whistles, often downslurred or overslurred, such as *teeuu*, about 0.5 secs; nasal *chíeh*. Song a varied, rapid jangling and burbling warble, can include buzzy trills, occasional wheezy phrases, 2–20 or more secs; averages buzzier, less jangling than Yellow-bellied Siskin. STATUS: Uncommon to fairly common in Central and Talamanca Mts., adjacent Central Valley, mainly 1200–3000m; since 2010s, scarce and local in s. Pacific and nw. lowlands. (Mexico and w. US to nw. S America.)

House Sparrow

female

breeding
male

Tricolored Munia

juv.

Yellow-bellied Siskin

juv.

female

male

Lesser Goldfinch

female

male

EUPHONIAS (GENUS *EUPHONIA*) (10 species). Small, rather stocky, colorful neotropical finches, formerly considered as tanagers. Typically in pairs or small groups at mid–upper levels, but regularly come low at fruiting shrubs, especially mistletoe, and visit feeders. Sometimes with mixed flocks. Ages/sexes differ; adult appearance attained in 1st year. Calls and songs amazingly varied; try to learn quality and pattern of one or two distinctive phrases.

GOLDEN-BROWED CHLOROPHONIA *Euphonia (Chlorophonia) callophrys* 12.5–13.5cm. Chunky emerald gem of cloud forest and edge, adjacent second growth with scattered trees, fruiting shrubs. No similar species in Costa Rica but cf. Green Shrike-Vireo (p. 348). Often in canopy and easily overlooked; forms small flocks in nonbr. season. Juv. like female but duller, 1st-year male like bright version of female with variable golden sheen to brows. SOUNDS: Hollow, mournful, slightly descending whistled *heuuu*, about 0.5 sec, repeated every 2–3 secs; short twangy clucks and grunts, rather frog-like, every 1–3 secs, *ehk, oóik, ehk, oóik, oóik, ehk...*, at times with mournful whistles thrown in. Song a jerky gurgling warble with high, slightly nasal *whui* notes thrown in, sometimes prolonged. STATUS: Fairly common from timberline down to 1500m on Pacific slope, to 900m on Caribbean slope; wanders to lower elevations in winter, mainly on Caribbean slope. (Costa Rica to w. Panama.)

ELEGANT EUPHONIA *Euphonia (Chlorophonia) elegantissima* 10–11cm. Foothill and highland forest, semi-open areas with trees and shrubs bearing mistletoe. See genus note. Distinctive, with turquoise hood. Juv. might be confusing but little or no overlap with olive-plumaged females of other euphonias; soon attains blue on crown. SOUNDS: Clipped, descending *teu*, nasal *cheh*, and varied low clucks. Song a pleasant, fast-paced, burbling liquid warble, often prolonged. STATUS: Uncommon and local on both slopes, mainly 1300–2000m; wanders rarely to coastal lowlands. (Mexico to Panama.)

TAWNY-CAPPED EUPHONIA *Euphonia anneae* 10.5–11.5cm. Canopy and edge of humid foothill forest, adjacent clearings with fruiting shrubs. See genus note. Male distinctive, with extensive rusty cap, white undertail coverts; female drabber but note rusty forehead, grayish median underparts, pale undertail coverts. Juv. resembles female. SOUNDS: Varied nasal and twangy clucks, chirps, whistles, burry squeaks, at times doubled or trebled; quality relatively squeaky, slightly mechanical. Song relatively slow-paced, prolonged, phrases often repeated a few times. STATUS: Fairly common in Caribbean foothills, mainly 500–1700m in north, 800–2000m in south. (Costa Rica to nw. Colombia.)

SPOT-CROWNED EUPHONIA *Euphonia imitans* 10–10.5cm. Humid lowland forest and edge, adjacent clearings with fruiting shrubs. See genus note. Dark spotting at rear of male's yellow crown patch often hard to see; note dark throat and plain dark underside to tail, cf. Scrub and Yellow-crowned Euphonias. Female distinctive in range; no overlap with Olive-backed Euphonia. Juv. resembles female but with little or no rusty, soon like adult. SOUNDS: Varied short bubbly, wheezy, gurgling, and bright chirping phrases, chips, and burry rolled trills, often repeated every few secs or mixed into a prolonged song. Quality relatively rich, burry overall; common call a burry rolled *trr-rr-rrit*, similar to Olive-backed Euphonia. STATUS: Fairly common on s. Pacific slope, to 1400m. (Costa Rica to w. Panama.)

OLIVE-BACKED EUPHONIA *Euphonia gouldi* 10–10.5cm. Humid lowland forest canopy and edge, adjacent clearings and semi-open areas with fruiting trees and bushes. See genus note. Distinctive: both sexes greenish overall with rusty undertail coverts; no range overlap with Spot-crowned Euphonia. Juv. resembles duller version of adult. SOUNDS: Varied burry, nasal, squeaky, and slightly bubbly short phrases, chips, burry rolled trills, often repeated every few secs or mixed into a prolonged song. Quality relatively rich and burry, including burry rolled *drrr-rr-rrt*. STATUS: Fairly common on Caribbean slope, to 1000m; spills over locally to adjacent n. Pacific foothills. (Mexico to w. Panama.)

GOLDEN-BROWED CHLOROPHONIA

female

male

ELEGANT EUPHONIA

juv.

female

male

TAWNY-CAPPED EUPHONIA

male

female

SPOT-CROWNED EUPHONIA

female

male

female

male

OLIVE-BACKED EUPHONIA

THICK-BILLED EUPHONIA *Euphonia laniirostris* 10.5–11.5cm. Relatively large, bulky, stout-billed euphonia of woodland, gardens, hedgerows, forest edge, clearings with scattered trees; not a forest-based bird. See genus note (p. 388). Male has more extensive yellow crown patch than Yellow-throated Euphonia. Female rather plain yellowish green overall, cf. slightly smaller, smaller-billed female Yellow-crowned Euphonia. Juv. resembles female; imm. male like female with mostly male head pattern. SOUNDS: Varied nasal and gurgling chirps, plaintive whistles, squeaks, short wheezy phrases, and rolled trills, often repeated every few secs or mixed into a prolonged song. Relatively bright, often slightly plaintive whistled quality averages wheezier than Yellow-throated Euphonia, including twangy whistled *dwieh dwieh.* STATUS: Fairly common on s. Pacific slope, to 1100m. (Costa Rica to S America.)

YELLOW-THROATED EUPHONIA *Euphonia hirundinacea* 10–11cm. Forest edge, gallery woodland, plantations, gardens, hedgerows. See genus note (p. 388). Male shares yellow throat only with Thick-billed Euphonia, which see for differences. Female told by pale grayish throat and median underparts. Juv. resembles female. SOUNDS: Varied chips, squeaks, short gurgles and warbles, some burry, often repeated every few secs or mixed into a prolonged song. Relatively bright, often slightly plaintive whistled quality averages richer than Thick-billed Euphonia, including slightly nasal *jieh-jieh-jieh.* STATUS: Fairly common from nw. lowlands s. into Central Valley, to 1400m; scarce to locally uncommon (increasing?) on Caribbean slope and s. Pacific slope. (Mexico to w. Panama.)

YELLOW-CROWNED EUPHONIA *Euphonia luteicapilla* 9.5–10cm. Forest edge, woodland, gardens, clearings with scattered trees, hedgerows. See genus note (p. 388). Male best told by extensive yellow crown patch, also note lack of white in tail, voice; cf. Spot-crowned and Scrub Euphonias. Female rather plain yellowish green overall, cf. larger and slightly larger-billed female Thick-billed Euphonia. SOUNDS: Varied, short wheezy whistled phrases, gurgles, tinkles, burry rolls, nasal twangy whistles. Quality relatively plaintive or slightly wheezy; common call a plaintive rising whistle in relatively slow-paced sets of 2 or 3, *wheein wheein wheein.* STATUS: Fairly common to common on both slopes, locally to 1800m. (Honduras to Panama.)

SCRUB EUPHONIA *Euphonia affinis* 9.5–10cm. Fairly small euphonia of drier forest and edge, semi-open and open areas with fruiting trees, hedgerows, gardens. See genus note (p. 388). Little or no overlap with potentially similar species. Male White-vented favors humid forest, has richer yellow underparts with white undertail coverts; larger Spot-crowned and Yellow-crowned Euphonias lack white tail spots, have larger black bib. Female rather drab but distinctive, with grayish crown, brighter yellow undertail coverts. SOUNDS: Varied short squeaky, tinkling, and bubbling phrases, often fairly fast-paced; repeated every few secs or mixed into a prolonged warbling song. Quality relatively high-pitched, often slightly plaintive; common call a high, plaintive whistled *dee-dee-dee.* STATUS: Fairly common on n. Pacific slope, locally to 1100m in w. Central Valley. (Mexico to Costa Rica.)

WHITE-VENTED EUPHONIA *Euphonia minuta* 9–9.5cm. Very small euphonia of humid forest canopy and edge, adjacent clearings with fruiting trees. See genus note (p. 388). Small size evident when seen with other species; also note relatively shallow pointed bill, white median belly and undertail coverts. Male has richer yellow underparts than other black-throated euphonias; female distinctive, with pale gray throat contrasting with yellow breast. SOUNDS: Varied chips, twangy warbles, plaintive whistles, and gurgles, repeated every few secs or mixed into a chippering and warbling song. Quality relatively low-pitched and twangy; calls include sharp, slightly smacking warbler-like *chik!* and bright, rising *whítzi-chik* phrase often incorporated into songs. STATUS: Uncommon to scarce on both slopes, rarely to 1500m. (Mexico to S America.)

THICK-BILLED EUPHONIA

female

male

YELLOW-THROATED EUPHONIA

imm. male

female

male

female

male

YELLOW-CROWNED EUPHONIA

female

male

SCRUB EUPHONIA

WHITE-VENTED EUPHONIA

female

male

GENUS *SPOROPHILA* (SEEDEATERS, SEEDFINCHES) (8+ species): Small, stubby- and stout-billed tanagers formerly considered as New World sparrows. Species often flock together, along with other seed-eating birds such as grassquits, *Passerina* buntings. Several species nomadic.

MORELET'S [WHITE-COLLARED] SEEDEATER *Sporophila [torqueola] morelleti* 10–11cm. Open grassy and weedy areas, roadsides, second growth, marshes, seeding crop fields. Sings from fence, small bush or tree. Only seedeater in Costa Rica with bold pale wingbars, but cf. Northern Ruddy-breasted Seedeater. Male rump can fade whitish and wingbars wear away, cf. male Hick's Seedeater, which has black throat. SOUNDS: Downslurred, slightly plaintive *chieh*, burrier nasal *chreh*. Song a varied medley of slurred whistles and rapid sweet chips, often ends with slurred buzzes; mainly 2–10 secs. STATUS: Fairly common to common on both slopes, to 1500m. (Mexico to w. Panama.)

*HICK'S [VARIABLE] SEEDEATER *Sporophila [corvina] ophthalmica* 11–11.5cm. Second growth, forest edge, weedy thickets, roadsides; at times in adjacent seeding fields. Usually in pairs or small groups, sometimes with other seedeaters. Male distinctive, with black head and throat, cf. Morelet's Seedeater. Female duskier, more olive-toned than other female seedeaters. SOUNDS: Downslurred nasal *chyeh* and variations. Song a fairly rapid-paced, jangling warble, at times vaguely siskin-like; mainly 2–10 secs. STATUS: Fairly common to common on Pacific slope, to 1500m. (Costa Rica to nw. Peru.)

SLATE-COLORED SEEDEATER *Sporophila schistacea* 11–11.5cm. Rare, stout-billed seedeater of forest edge and clearings, swampy wooded thickets, especially in areas with bamboo; also mature rice fields. In pairs or small groups, sometimes with other seedeaters. Sings from mid-level perches, also in flight. Male distinctive, with stout yellowish bill, slaty plumage; female from other seedeaters by stout bill with some pale at base. SOUNDS: Buzzy nasal *shih*, sometimes doubled; very high, slightly lisping *siik*. Song a varied, high, slightly buzzy and tinny twittering warble, often starts with an upslurred whistle, includes chipping trills; mainly 1–6 secs. STATUS: Scarce, local, and sporadic on both slopes, especially Pacific; to 1200m. (Belize to S America.)

YELLOW-BELLIED SEEDEATER *Sporophila nigricollis* 10.5–11cm. Open grassy and weedy areas, roadsides, second growth, marshes, seeding crop fields. Sings from fence, small shrub or tree. Male distinctive, with black face and breast, pale bill. Female notably plain, slightly smaller-billed and buffier than female Hick's Seedeater; Ruddy-breasted Seedeater has orange-pink bill. SOUNDS: Downslurred, nasal to slightly squeaky *chíeh*. Song a pleasant sweet warble, fairly fast-paced and usually short, 1.5–2 secs. STATUS: Uncommon on s. Pacific slope, spreading n. to Central Valley and locally to adjacent Caribbean slope; to 1800m. (Costa Rica to S America.)

RUDDY-BREASTED SEEDEATER *Sporophila minuta* 9.5–10cm. Open grassy and weedy areas, especially marshes, wetlands. Sings from taller grass stalk, fence, small shrub. Male distinctive, other plumages told by small size, distinct pale wing edgings, mostly orange-pink bill. Comprises 2 groups that may represent species: **Northern Ruddy-breasted Seedeater** *S. [m.] parva* breeding male blue-gray above, nonbr. male (Sep–Mar) like female but with white wing patch, rustier rump, often some rusty blotches below. Female/imm. relatively pale, buffy-toned, with distinct pale wing edgings. **Southern Ruddy-breasted Seedeater** *S. [m.] minuta* male bright year-round, browner above than breeding male Northern, especially in fresh plumage. Female/imm. more uniform overall than Northern. SOUNDS: **Northern:** quiet nasal *chih*; song an unhurried, slightly jerky warble of nasal and sweet chips, 3–17 secs. **Southern:** downslurred nasal *chieh*; song a variable, rather slow-paced warble, typically starts with unhurried sweet whistles, 2–4 secs; averages richer, slower-paced than jerkier, more chipping song of Northern. STATUS: Uncommon to locally fairly common: **Northern** in nw. lowlands, **Southern** on s. Pacific slope, mainly interior valleys, to 1200m. (Mexico to S America.)

MORELET'S SEEDEATER

female

males

HICK'S SEEDEATER

male

variation

female

male

SLATE-COLORED SEEDEATER

imm. male

female

male

YELLOW-BELLIED SEEDEATER

imm. male

female

male

RUDDY-BREASTED SEEDEATER

breeding male (Mar–Sep)

female

nonbr. male (Sep–Mar)
Northern

Southern

nonbr. male (Sep–Mar)

YELLOW-FACED GRASSQUIT *Tiaris olivaceus* 10–11cm. Small olive bird of weedy grassland and second growth, forest edge. Often in flocks with other small seed-eating birds in areas with seeding grasses. Sings from perch at low to mid-levels. Adult male striking and distinctive, female and imm. rather drab but note ghosting of male face pattern, pointed bill. **SOUNDS:** High, thin, slightly sharp *sik*. Song a fairly rapid, high, ticking trill, 0.5–1 sec, at times in short series with alternating trills of different length, pace, and pitch; easily passed off as an insect, and may suggest Olivaceous Piculet. **STATUS:** Fairly common to common on both slopes, especially at mid-elevations, to 2000m. (Mexico to nw. S America.)

BLUE-BLACK GRASSQUIT *Volatinia jacarina* 10–11cm. Open grassy and weedy areas, crop fields, marshes. Often in flocks with other small seed-eating birds in areas with seeding grasses. Sings from low perch such as fence, weed stalk; makes short leap up with each song to show off white shoulder tufts. Breeding male distinctive (can be seen year-round, depending on local conditions), other plumages told by small size, pointed bill, dusky streaking on chest (can suggest small version of female Indigo Bunting). Imm. male and nonbr. male have blue-black wings, variable dark blotching below. **SOUNDS:** High, sharp to slightly liquid *tsik*. Song a buzzy, slightly metallic or lisping *tzzzzz'u* or *tzssii'u*, 0.3–0.5 secs, repeated every few secs, often as male makes short leaps from perch. **STATUS:** Fairly common to common on both slopes, locally to 1800m. (Mexico to S America.)

*BLACK [VARIABLE] SEEDEATER *Sporophila corvina* 11–11.5cm. Second growth, forest edge, weedy thickets, roadsides; at times in adjacent seeding fields. Usually in pairs or small groups, often with other small seed-eating birds. Male told from Thick-billed Seedfinch by smaller, stubbier bill. Female duskier, more olive-toned than other female seedeaters. **SOUNDS:** Nasal *chiyh* and down-slurred *chieu*. Song a pleasant, slightly chanting warble, 2–8 secs; averages slower-paced, sweeter than Hick's Seedeater. **STATUS:** Fairly common to common on Caribbean slope, to 1500m; spills over locally to n. Pacific slope and spreading into Central Valley. (Mexico to w. Panama.)

THICK-BILLED SEEDFINCH *Sporophila funerea* 11.5–12.5cm Humid second growth, forest edge, marshes, adjacent seeding fields. In pairs, rarely small groups; sometimes with seedeater flocks but more often separate. Feeds inconspicuously in seeding grasses; sings from mid–upper levels in shrub or small tree. Male from Black Seedeater by deeper 'grosbeak' bill; female smaller and smaller-billed than female Nicaraguan Seedfinch. **SOUNDS:** Quiet nasal *chiyh*. Song a rich, slightly rambling, pleasant warble, at times with faster buzzy sections or run into a buzzy ending, mainly 5–25 secs; typically richer, more rambling, less jerky, and often more prolonged than seedeater songs. **STATUS:** Fairly common to uncommon on both slopes, to 1200m. (Mexico to nw. S America.)

NICARAGUAN (PINK-BILLED) SEEDFINCH *Sporophila nuttingi* 14–15cm. Wet grassy areas, marshes, humid second growth, adjacent seeding fields. In pairs or small groups, sometimes associating with seedeater flocks but more often separate. Feeds inconspicuously in seeding grasses; sings from mid–upper levels in shrub or small tree, from roadside wires. Adult male distinctive, with very large pale pinkish bill; female appreciably larger and larger-billed than female Thick-billed Seedfinch, with slightly raised ridge at culmen base. Also cf. female Blue-black Grosbeak, a bird of humid second growth and forest edge, not open grassy areas and marshes. **SOUNDS:** Nasal *chih*, slightly lower than Thick-billed Seedfinch. Song an unhurried series of mellow chirps and slurred chips, overall slower, lower, and richer than Thick-billed, mainly 4–7 secs, often with short breaks between songs; also longer songs including faster, more jangling sections. **STATUS:** Uncommon to scarce and local in Caribbean slope lowlands, rarely to 900m. (Nicaragua to Panama.)

YELLOW-FACED GRASSQUIT

imm. female

female

male

BLUE-BLACK GRASSQUIT

imm. male

female

breeding male

BLACK SEEDEATER

female

male

THICK-BILLED SEEDFINCH

female

male

NICARAGUAN SEEDFINCH

female

male

SLATY FLOWERPIERCER *Diglossa plumbea* 10.5–11.5cm. Highland forest and edge, flower banks, second growth, shrubby páramo. Mainly singles and pairs, not with mixed flocks. Flits actively among foliage, piercing flower bases with its distinctive 'can-opener' bill to obtain nectar. Sings from low to high, often concealed. Distinctive, given habits and bill shape, but cf. appreciably bulkier Peg-billed Finch. **SOUNDS:** Rather weak, high thin *tsit*. Song a high, pleasant, slightly squeaky twittering warble, 1–2 secs; overall descending slightly. **STATUS:** Fairly common to common from timberline down to 1200m in Northern Mts., to 1400m in Central Mts., and to 1800m in Talamanca Mts. (Costa Rica to w. Panama.)

PEG-BILLED FINCH *Acanthidops bairdi* 13–14cm. Rarely encountered denizen of highland forest edge, pastures, second growth, páramo, especially with stands of bamboo. Mainly at low to mid-levels, feeding in fruiting and flowering shrubs, seeding grasses; sometimes joins mixed flocks. Mainly singles or small groups, but 10s or even 100+ may gather at seeding bamboo. Note rather fine pointed bill with contrasting pale mandible, cf. smaller and darker, more bluish male Slaty Flowerpiercer, darker-billed Slaty Finch. **SOUNDS:** High, slightly piercing, overall downslurred *tsiii*; high, burry upslurred *zzrip*, may be repeated steadily; high, buzzy downslurred *zzri*. Song a short, rapid-paced, slightly metallic buzzy jangle, such as *tzz-zzi zzi-zzzi-zzi-zzi*, about 1 sec; also slightly longer, jerkier and squeakier versions. **STATUS:** Scarce and nomadic on both slopes, 1500m to timberline; sporadically numerous in areas with seeding bamboo. (Costa Rica to w. Panama.)

SLATY FINCH *Haplospiza (Spodiornis) rustica* 12–13cm. Rarely encountered denizen of highland forest edge, pastures, second growth, especially stands of bamboo. Feeds in seeding grasses and bamboo; sings from shrub or low tree. Mainly singles or small groups, but 10s or even 100+ may gather at seeding bamboo patches. Distinctive if undistinguished, with pointed grayish bill, fairly compact shape. Cf. Peg-billed Finch, female of appreciably smaller Blue-black Grassquit. **SOUNDS:** High, thin, slightly tinny *tsi*. Song a rapid-paced, high, slurred and buzzy metallic jangle or gurgling warble, about 2–3 secs. **STATUS:** Sporadic and nomadic on both slopes, 1500m to timberline; appears rare or absent most of the time, but swarms can appear and remain months at patches of seeding bamboo. (Mexico to S America.)

NEW WORLD GROSBEAKS AND BUNTINGS (CARDINALIDAE; 19 SPECIES) New World family of stout-billed, often colorful, seed- and fruit-eating birds; several formerly considered (and still named as) tanagers. Ages/sexes differ in most species; males of some have distinctive 1st-year plumage. A few northern migrants have seasonal plumage changes.

*BLUE SEEDEATER *Amaurospiza concolor* 11.5–12.5cm. Scarce denizen of foothill and highland forest edge, gullies with bamboo. Singles or pairs forage in seeding bamboo, mainly at mid-levels. Rather plain but habits distinctive, and often in pairs; male fairly uniform dark slaty blue overall, female rich brown, cf. much stouter-billed female Thick-billed Seedfinch and larger Blue-black Grosbeak of humid lowlands. **SOUNDS:** High, sharp, slightly metallic *tswik* or *sik*. Song a high, fairly rapid pleasant warble with slightly rambling cadence, 1–2 secs; may suggest Southern Brown-capped Vireo. **STATUS:** Scarce and local on both slopes, mainly 1000–2200m. (Mexico to S America.)

BLUE-BLACK GROSBEAK *Cyanoloxia (Cyanocompsa) cyanoides* 17–18.5cm. Humid lowland forest and edge, second-growth thickets, plantations, gallery forest. Often in pairs, mainly at low to mid-levels in leafy foliage and shady understory; usually apart from mixed flocks. Relatively large size and massive bill distinctive, along with habitat and habits; cf. female Nicaraguan Seedfinch of open grassy and marshy habitats. Juv. dusky brownish overall. **SOUNDS:** Sharp, slightly nasal to squeaky *plik* and *pli-dik!* Song fairly loud, an unhurried, rich, slightly sad descending warble, 1–2 secs; sometimes fades into soft squeaky ending. **STATUS:** Fairly common on both slopes to 1200m; less numerous and more local in drier nw. lowlands. (Mexico to nw. Peru.)

FINCH-LIKE TANAGERS, CARDINALIDS

SLATY FLOWERPIERCER

female

male

PEG-BILLED FINCH

female

male

SLATY FINCH

female

male

female

BLUE SEEDEATER

male

BLUE-BLACK GROSBEAK

female

male

PAINTED BUNTING *Passerina ciris* 12–13cm. Winter migrant to weedy fields and roadsides, second growth, brushy woodland, riversides. Singles or small groups feed in seeding grasses, associating readily with other weed-eating birds; at times ranges to fruiting canopy. Like other *Passerina*, often twitches tail side to side. Adult male unmistakable; female and imm. notably plain greenish (some imms. in fall almost colorless dirty buff with traces of green) with paler eyering, but nothing really similar in Costa Rica. SOUNDS: Clipped *tlik* and soft buzz, similar to Indigo Bunting. STATUS: Uncommon to scarce and often local late Oct–Apr on Pacific slope, scarce on n. Caribbean slope, to 1300m. (Breeds s. US and Mexico, winters Mexico to Panama.)

INDIGO BUNTING *Passerina cyanea* 12–13cm. Winter migrant to weedy fields, grassland, second growth, brushy woodland, riversides. Singles or often small flocks feed in seeding grasses, associating readily with other weed-eating birds. Larger than seedeaters and grassquits with longer bill, warm brown plumage tones; female has streaked breast, cf. female Blue-black Grassquit. Winter adult male and late winter imm. male variably blotched blue, attain mostly brilliant blue plumage by Apr. SOUNDS: Strong, slightly sharp *tlik* and buzzy *zzzrt*. STATUS: Fairly common to uncommon Oct–Apr on both slopes, to 1500m; a few from Sep and into early May; most numerous in nw. lowlands. (Breeds N America, winters Mexico to Panama.)

BLUE GROSBEAK *Passerina caerulea* 16.5–17.5cm. Breeds in ranchland with scattered trees, hedgerows, often along streams; males sing from fence or small tree. More widespread in winter, in open and semi-open areas with grassland, brushy second growth, marshes; singles or small groups feed in seeding grasses, associating readily with other weed-eating birds. Note very stout bill, cinnamon wingbars; hindcrown often distinctly blotched, even vaguely crested. Cf. appreciably smaller and smaller-billed Indigo Bunting. Adult male in fresh plumage (Aug–Feb) has blue variably veiled with cinnamon-brown edgings, wearing off to reveal waxy deep blue by spring. SOUNDS: Strong metallic *chink* and wet buzzy *zzzir*. Song a rich, slightly scratchy rambling warble, 2–2.5 secs. STATUS: Uncommon and local on n. Pacific slope, mainly foothills, to 1100m in Central Valley; more widespread Oct–Apr, when migrants scarce to uncommon locally on both slopes. (Breeds US to nw. Costa Rica, winters Mexico to Panama.)

DICKCISSEL *Spiza americana* 14.5–16cm. Rather sparrow-like cardinalid found in crop and weedy fields, damp grassy areas with shrubby bushes; singles often associate with other seed-eating birds. Flocks can number 1000s, flying overhead in undulating swarms that suggest blackbird flocks. Adult male distinctive (pattern veiled with paler feather tips in fresh plumage, Sep–Dec), with yellow face and breast, black bib; female and imm. have ghosting of male pattern, stout bill, streaked flanks. Cf. female House Sparrow (p. 386). SOUNDS: Wet buzzy *zzzrt* often given in flight, suggests emphatic rough-winged swallow; full, slightly liquid *fwit*. Spring males sometimes sing, jangling choruses including a bright buzzy *dik-cizz-l*. STATUS: Sporadically common transient on both slopes to 1500m, Sep–Oct and Apr, smaller numbers into mid-May. Irregularly uncommon to common through winter in nw. lowlands, sporadic and usually scarce elsewhere in winter. (Breeds N America, winters Mexico to n. S America.)

PAINTED BUNTING

imm. female

female
(imm. male similar,
Nov–Aug)

male

INDIGO BUNTING

female

male
(Sep–Apr)

male
(Apr–Sep)

BLUE GROSBEAK

imm. male
(Feb–Aug)

female
(imm. male similar,
Aug–Feb)

male
(Feb–Aug)

DICKCISSEL

imm.
female

male

ROSE-BREASTED GROSBEAK *Pheucticus ludovicianus* 18–20cm. Winter migrant to varied wooded and forested habitats, brushy second growth, hedgerows, gardens. Singly or small flocks, latter especially during migration, feeding on fruits mainly at mid–upper levels, where often sits quietly and is overlooked easily. Adult male striking, with big white wing patches, reddish breast (plumage heavily veiled brownish in fall–early winter); female distinctive, with stout pale bill, streaked breast. SOUNDS: High, squeaky nasal *iihk*, given infrequently. STATUS: Fairly common mid-Oct to mid-Apr, a few from Sep and into early May; mainly below 2000m. (Breeds N America, winters Mexico to nw. S America.)

*SOUTHERN BLACK-FACED GROSBEAK *Caryothraustes [poliogaster] scapularis* 17–18cm. Humid lowland forest canopy and edge, adjacent tree-scattered pastureland and second growth. Typically in small flocks (up to 20 or so birds), roving noisily at mid–upper levels, usually independent of mixed flocks. Nothing especially similar in Costa Rica, but cf. Prong-billed Barbet (p. 200): note contrasting black face, stout bill, gray belly. Juv. duller overall, pattern less sharply defined. SOUNDS: Short buzzy rasps, at times run into short series of (usually 2–4) downslurred squeaky whsitles, *d'zzzr kwee kwee kwee*. Song an unhurried, short, pleasing whistled phrase of 3–7 rich slurred notes, such as *see si-wee chu*, 1–2 secs, every few secs. STATUS: Fairly common on Caribbean slope, to 1000m. (Honduras to Panama.)

BLACK-THIGHED GROSBEAK *Pheucticus tibialis* 19–21cm. Highland forest and edge, pastures with scattered trees, second growth, gardens. Singles or pairs forage low to high, mainly in canopy; not usually with mixed flocks and easily overlooked if quiet. No similar species in Costa Rica: note stout bill, black-and-yellow plumage; white wing patch striking in flight. Sexes similar; juv. duller overall with messier plumage pattern. SOUNDS: Squeaky nasal *iihk*, similar to Rose-breasted Grosbeak. Song a short, unhurried medley of rich slurred whistles, mostly 2–3.5 secs, such as *ti hee ti'whie-chu wieh*, at times ending with a short slow trill. STATUS: Uncommon to fairly common on both slopes, mainly 1500–2500m, locally down to 100m on Caribbean slope in late wet season. (Costa Rica to w. Panama.)

SUMMER TANAGER *Piranga rubra* 17–19.5cm. Winter migrant to varied wooded and forested habitats, hedgerows, gardens. Typically singles, feeding on fruit at mid–upper levels, where sits quietly and is overlooked easily, or sallying for wasps from prominent perches; often holds tail cocked, hindcrown feathers raised. Tooth-billed Tanager has different calls; darker, grayish bill with distinct notch on cutting edge. Adult male Summer brighter red than Tooth-billed, with plainer face; female/imm. more mustard-toned, not so greenish. Cf. smaller and smaller-billed female Scarlet Tanager. SOUNDS: Rolled, slightly wet, soft chattering *pí-tuh-ruk*, or *pí-tuh-t-ruk*, typically 2–4-syllables, rarely run into a rattle; not as staccato as Western Tanager. STATUS: Fairly common to common mid-Sep to Apr on both slopes to 1500m, in smaller numbers to 2700m. (Breeds N America and Mexico, winters Mexico to S America.)

TOOTH-BILLED (HIGHLAND HEPATIC) TANAGER *Piranga lutea* 17.5–19.5cm. Humid foothill forest, adjacent clearings and second growth. Mainly singles and pairs at mid–upper levels, often in canopy; readily joins mixed flocks. Cf. migrant Summer Tanager. Juv. (plumage held briefly) paler than female, with dark streaking below; 1st-year male like bright female, some with reddish wash and patches on head and breast. SOUNDS: Clipped, slightly wooden short chip, often in fairly rapid rolled series of (mostly 2–4) notes, such as *ch-ti-tih*, lower and less insect-like than Long-tailed Silky; at times longer, slightly rippling series. Song a fairly steady, unhurried, slightly chanting series of rich whistled notes, *whee chúi wh whie chúi...*, at times for 30 secs or longer; about 2 notes/sec. STATUS: Uncommon to fairly common on both slopes, mainly 1000–1800m on Pacific slope, 600–1700m on Caribbean slope. (Costa Rica to S America.)

ROSE-BREASTED GROSBEAK

imm. male
(Sep–Mar)

female

male
(Sep–Mar)

male
(Mar–Aug)

**SOUTHERN
BLACK-FACED
GROSBEAK**

**BLACK-THIGHED
GROSBEAK**

**SUMMER
TANAGER**

imm. male
(Dec–Aug)

female

male

TOOTH-BILLED TANAGER

female

male

402

WHITE-WINGED TANAGER *Spermagra (Piranga) leucoptera* 13.5–14.5cm. Humid foothill forest, adjacent clearings and second growth with taller trees. Pairs and small groups glean in foliage at mid–upper levels, often with mixed flocks. Smaller than *Piranga* with clean white wingbars on black (male) to dark (female) wings, distinct voice. Cf. appreciably larger Flame-colored Tanager. Juv. resembles female, male soon attains red to orange-red head and body plumage. SOUNDS: Short series of (usually 1–5) high, slightly tinny upslurred whistles preceded by quiet chip, *t'sieh sieh*, and variations. High, slightly liquid chipping *tik*, may be repeated steadily; high spluttering twitter in flight. Song a high, slightly squeaky short warble, 1.5–3 secs, such as *si si-see-see chu*. STATUS: Uncommon on both slopes, mainly 1100–1800m, rarely to 2200m. (Mexico to S America.)

GENUS *PIRANGA* (5 species; also see p. 400) Arboreal, boldly colored and patterned cardinalids favoring forest canopy, where easily overlooked if not vocal. For ID note overall plumage patterns and colors, bill size and color, voice. Formerly treated as tanagers and sometimes considered to include genus *Spermagra*, which differs in structure, habits, voice, juvenile plumage pattern, molts.

FLAME-COLORED TANAGER *Piranga bidentata* 18–19cm. Foothill and highland forest, especially with oaks; adjacent pastures and second growth with taller trees. Singles and pairs forage quietly in canopy, at times with mixed flocks. Distinctive, with dusky cheeks, whitish wingbars, dusky streaking on back; also note relatively big grayish bill, cf. Western Tanager. Juv. (plumage held briefly) paler than female, with dark streaking below; 1st-year male like bright female, some with variable reddish wash and patches on head and breast. SOUNDS: Hard rolled *ch-t-ruk* and *p-terruk*, much like Western Tanager but slightly drier, sharper. Song comprises 3–5 burry phrases with unhurried, slightly jerky cadence, such as *chik churree chuwee*, and variations. STATUS: Fairly common to uncommon on Pacific slope, from timberline down to 1000m, on Caribbean slope mainly 1800–3000m. (Mexico to Panama.)

WESTERN TANAGER *Piranga ludoviciana* 16.5–18cm. Winter migrant to varied wooded and forested habitats, hedgerows, gardens. Singles and small groups forage mainly in canopy, often at fruiting trees; sometimes joins mixed flocks. Note pale bill, bold pale wingbars, unstreaked back, cf. larger Flame-colored Tanager. Some imms. very drab overall, others bright yellow below. SOUNDS: Often quiet. Rolled *ch-t-ruk*, more staccato than spluttering call of Summer Tanager, not as dry and sharp as Flame-colored Tanager. STATUS: Uncommon to sporadically fairly common on n. Pacific slope Nov–Mar, a few from Oct and into Apr; smaller numbers s. to Central Valley and rarely s. along Pacific slope, to 2200m; very rare on Caribbean slope. (Breeds w. N America, winters Mexico to Costa Rica.)

SCARLET TANAGER *Piranga olivacea* 16.5–18cm. Transient migrant in varied wooded and forested habitats, hedgerows, gardens. Singles and small groups forage mainly in canopy, often at fruiting trees. Male distinctive, with contrasting blackish wings; female smaller and smaller-billed than Summer Tanager, with greenish-yellow vs. mustard-yellow plumage tones, blank lores. Rarely shows narrow pale wingbars, cf. Western Tanager. SOUNDS: Often silent. Low clipped *chk*, can be followed by burry whistled *vrirr*. STATUS: Uncommon to fairly common late Sep–Nov, especially on Caribbean slope; more widespread late Mar–early May, mainly below 1800m; very rare in winter. (Breeds e. N America, winters S America.)

White-winged Tanager

female

male

imm. male
(Dec–Aug)

**Flame-colored
Tanager**

female

male

Western Tanager

female

male
(Sep–Feb)

male
(Mar–Aug)

Scarlet Tanager

female

male
(Sep–Feb)

male
(Mar–Aug)

GENUS *HABIA* (4 species). Rather plain cardinalids (formerly considered as tanagers), typically found in small groups foraging in lower and middle levels of shady forest understory. Often rather vocal.

CARMIOL'S [OLIVE] TANAGER *Habia (Chlorothraupis) carmioli* 17–18cm. Humid forest and adjacent shady second growth. Typically in noisy groups at low to mid-levels, roving through leafy understory, often with Tawny-crested Tanagers, ovenbirds, other species. Rather featureless olive-green plumage is a good field mark, plus stout bill, voice, and habits. Ages/sexes similar. Cf. female Red-throated Ant-Tanager, which has pinkish legs and feet, contrasting pale throat. SOUNDS: Common call a series of (typically 3–9) harsh, piercing to grating whistled notes, vaguely parakeet-like, *skeíer skeíer...*, 3–4 notes/sec, at times alternated with squeaky and metallic conversational notes. Song a rapid-paced medley of shrill and squeaky whistles, chips, trills, each usually repeated 2–6x; song can flow as a continuous stream for over a minute. STATUS: Fairly common to common on Caribbean slope, mainly 300–1000m; in smaller numbers to lowlands and locally to 1400m; a few spill over to n. Pacific slope. (Nicaragua to nw. Colombia.)

*RED-THROATED ANT-TANAGER *Habia fuscicauda* 18.5–20.5cm. Humid lowland forest edge, adjacent second growth, overgrown plantations, streamside thickets; not typically well inside primary forest. In pairs or small groups foraging in shady thickets, rarely at mid-levels; attends army ant swarms. No range overlap with Middle American Ant-Tanager; cf. Carmiol's Tanager. Juv. (plumage held briefly) overall sooty cinnamon-brown; 1st-year male resembles female. SOUNDS: Low rasping *shehh-shehh...*; hard, dry rattled *ch-ch-cht*. Song comprises rich whistled phrases (mainly 4–6 notes) repeated a few times with distinctly jerky rhythm, such as *chur-uh wee chur-uh choo, chur-uh wee chur-uh choo...*or simply *huh ch-wee-choo h-ch-wee-choo...*; mostly 3–4 notes/sec. STATUS: Fairly common on Caribbean slope, locally to 1000m. (Mexico to n. Colombia.)

*MIDDLE AMERICAN [RED-CROWNED] ANT-TANAGER *Habia [rubica] rubicoides* 17–19cm. Humid forest and adjacent taller second growth, plantations. In pairs or small groups foraging in shady understory, often with Tawny-crowned Greenlet and other species; sometimes attends army ant swarms. No range overlap with Red-throated Ant-Tanager. Erectile crown stripe not always visible. Juv. (plumage held briefly) overall sooty brown; 1st-year male resembles female. SOUNDS: Groups often utter squeaky and spluttering conversational chips and staccato chatters. Song a rather simple, slightly chanting repetition of (usually 5–10) plaintive to slightly ringing whistled notes, such as *chiéh-chiéh...*, or *chiew chiew...*, series often slightly descending overall, 4–5 notes/sec. STATUS: Uncommon to fairly common locally on Pacific slope, to 1200m; mainly humid foothills, scarce and local in drier areas. (Mexico to Panama.)

BLACK-CHEEKED ANT-TANAGER *Habia atrimaxillaris* 18–20cm. Humid lowland forest, adjacent taller second growth. In pairs or small groups foraging in shady understory, often with mixed flocks including greenlets, tanagers, ovenbirds, antwrens; sometimes attends army ant swarms. No similar species in Costa Rica: note blackish face blending into slaty upperparts, rosy throat and breast; male has erectile crown stripe. Juv. duller and browner overall. SOUNDS: Low rasping *shehh-shehh*, similar to allopatric Red-throated Ant-Tanager and harder, drier *cheht*, at times in rattling and stuttering series; might suggest a wren. Song a pleasant, varied short medley of (usually 4–10) rich whistles with warbling cadence, such as *cheh-ree-chu reh ch-ree-chuh*, 1.5–2 secs. STATUS: Fairly common in remaining forest on s. Pacific slope, mainly Corcovado National Park. (Endemic to Costa Rica.)

CARMIOL'S TANAGER

RED-THROATED ANT-TANAGER

female

male

MIDDLE AMERICAN ANT-TANAGER

females

Widespread

Northwest

female

BLACK-CHEEKED ANT-TANAGER

female

male

TANAGERS (THRAUPIDAE; 45+ SPECIES) Very large, diverse neotropical family. Molecular studies have found, however, that many species formerly treated in other families are tanagers that have diversified to fill many niches. Meanwhile, numerous former 'tanagers' are now placed in other families. Tanagers now include seedeaters and grassquits (pp. 392–395), flowerpiercers and some 'finches' (p. 396), plus saltators, honeycreepers. Ages/sexes differ or similar, attain adult appearance within 1st year, often within a few weeks.

GENUS *SALTATOR* (5 species). Large, stout-billed tanagers, formerly considered as cardinalids. Ages differ, sexes mostly similar. Often unobtrusive, quietly eating leaves, flowers, fruit; best detected by voice.

BLACK-HEADED SALTATOR *Saltator atriceps* 25–27 cm. Large saltator of humid forest edge, second growth, overgrown clearing with trees and shrubs, gardens. Typically in small groups, roving at mid–upper levels; behavior ranges from quiet and shy to loud and obnoxious. Distinctive, with big white bib, large size, loud calls. Black on head and throat variable, averages more extensive in north. Juv. has messier head pattern, bib mottled dusky. **SOUNDS:** Often rather noisy. Sharp smacking barks and chuckling chatters, often run together. **STATUS:** Fairly common to uncommon on Caribbean slope, to 1300m; may be spreading to Pacific slope. (Mexico to w. Panama.)

BUFF-THROATED SALTATOR *Saltator maximus* 20.5–22.5cm. Humid lowland forest edge, leafy second growth, overgrown plantations, gardens. Often in pairs and rather unobtrusive, low to high; feeds quietly on flowers and in fruiting trees. Juv. head mostly olive with messy whitish throat patch, paler bill. **SOUNDS:** High, slightly tinny or sibilant *tsii*. Song a short, pleasant, slightly tinny, overall down-slurred warble, mostly 1–1.5 secs. **STATUS:** Fairly common to common on both slopes, to 1800m, rarely higher; less numerous in drier nw. lowlands. (Mexico to S America.)

CINNAMON-BELLIED [GRAYISH] SALTATOR *Saltator [coerulescens] grandis* 21–23.5cm. Varied wooded and edge habitats from humid forest to dry brushy woodland, hedgerows, second growth, gardens, especially with flowering vines. Low to high, from leafy vine tangles to fruiting canopy; often rather sluggish, sitting quietly and munching flowers. Distinctive, with stout black bill, white eyebrow, grayish upperparts; 1st-year strongly suffused yellowish. **SOUNDS:** High, slightly squeaky *ssii*, more tinny than *ssip* calls of *Turdus* thrushes. Varied arrangements of rich whistles, chips, and warbles, at times prolonged; often a drawn-out, strongly upslurred whistle *teu-whieeeeeh* and a quavering trill *chur-r-r-r-r*. **STATUS:** Fairly common to uncommon in north, scarce and local but spreading in south; to 1800m. (Mexico to w. Panama.)

STREAKED SALTATOR *Saltator striatipectus* 18–20cm. Small saltator of second growth, scrubby thickets, woodland edge, overgrown gardens. Tends to be rather skulking, usually in pairs. Distinctive, with olive upperparts, streaked underparts, and weak face pattern; many birds have yellow bill tip and gape. Juv. duller, browner overall. **SOUNDS:** Fairly loud, metallic *spik!* Song an unhurried chant of (usually 5–9) slurred whistles, 1.5–3 secs; dawn song a slightly jerky slow chant of rich slurred whistles and mellow chirps, such as *chihr ch chu chiu chi chihr chih chu...*, 1–2 notes/sec, for up to 30 secs or more. **STATUS:** Fairly common in interior valleys of s. Pacific slope, to 1600m; scarce and local but spreading n. to Central Valley. (Costa Rica to Peru.)

SLATE-COLORED GROSBEAK *Saltator grossus* 19–21cm. Humid lowland forest and edge, adjacent plantations, taller second growth. Distinctive but easily overlooked; big bright red bill diagnostic. Mainly rather sluggish at mid–upper levels inside forest; sometimes joins mixed flocks. Juv. duller, sooty gray overall; bill dusky, becoming red over 1st winter. **SOUNDS:** Nasal, rough mewing *eéahr*; sharp metallic *plik*. Rich warbled song about 1 sec, often repeated monotonously at short intervals, less often alternates variations. **STATUS:** Uncommon on Caribbean slope, to 1200m. (Honduras to S America.)

SALTATORS

BLACK-HEADED SALTATOR

variation

BUFF-THROATED
SALTATOR

CINNAMON-BELLIED
SALTATOR

1st-year

STREAKED
SALTATOR

variation

SLATE-COLORED GROSBEAK

female

male

DACNISES AND HONEYCREEPERS (5 species). Small colorful tanagers, often in pairs with mixed flocks, roving in forest canopy at fruiting and flowering trees; honeycreepers also often visit fruit feeders. Calls are mainly high thin chips; songs rarely heard. Ages/sexes differ; one species has marked seasonal changes in male plumage.

SCARLET-THIGHED DACNIS *Dacnis venusta* 12–12.5cm. Humid foothill forest, adjacent semi-open areas with taller trees, fruiting shrubs. See group intro. No similar species in Costa Rica: on male note black underparts (scarlet thighs can be hard to see), blue hood; female often with male, told by blue hood and rump, sharp bill, pale underparts. Juv. resembles female but duller overall; 1st-year male soon develops some adult plumage. SOUNDS: High thin *ssip* and twitters; short, twangy upslurred *dwoih*. STATUS: Uncommon to fairly common on both slopes, mainly 900–1500m on Pacific slope, 500–1200m on Caribbean slope; variable movement to lowlands in fall–winter. (Costa Rica to nw. Ecuador.)

BLUE DACNIS *Dacnis cayana* 12–12.5cm. Humid lowland forest, adjacent second growth and semi-open areas with taller trees, fruiting shrubs, gardens. See group intro. Note sharp straight bill, pinkish legs; distinctive blue tones of male (paler, more turquoise on Pacific slope), green body and blue head of female. Juv. resembles female; 1st-year male like adult male but with greener wing edgings. Cf. honeycreepers, which all have decurved bills. SOUNDS: High, thin wiry *tsit* and high twitters. STATUS: Uncommon to fairly common on both slopes, to 1200m on Pacific slope, to 900m on Caribbean slope. (Honduras to S America.)

GREEN HONEYCREEPER *Chlorophanes spiza* 13–14cm. Rather large, bulky honeycreeper of humid forest, plantations, adjacent second growth and semi-open areas with taller trees, fruiting shrubs, gardens. See group intro. Appreciably larger than dacnises and other honeycreepers; male distinctive, with black hood, banana-yellow bill; on female note yellowish bill, grayish legs. Juv. resembles female; male attains adult plumage over 1st year. SOUNDS: High sharp *tchiip*, rather warbler-like, may be repeated persistently; thin sharp *siip* mainly in flight. STATUS: Fairly common on both slopes, to 1200m on Pacific slope, to 1000m on Caribbean slope. (Mexico to S America.)

RED-LEGGED HONEYCREEPER *Cyanerpes cyaneus* 11–12cm. Forest canopy and edge, adjacent open areas and second growth with taller trees, hedgerows, gardens. See group intro. Unlike other honeycreepers, often in small flocks. Note decurved bill, red legs (bright coral-red on male, pinkish red on female); in flight, male underwings flash bright sulphur-yellow. Breeding male distinctive, can look blackish high against bright light; female has dark eyestripe, weakly streaked underparts, cf. Green and Shining Honeycreepers. Nonbr. male like female but with black wings and tail. Juv. like female with duller pinkish legs; male has complete molt into plumage like adult nonbr. by early winter. SOUNDS: Buzzy, slightly overslurred mewing *meeah* or *meéihr*, suggesting a gnatcatcher; high, slightly nasal, rolled *srrip*; high thin *ssit* in flight. STATUS: Fairly common to common in n. lowlands; in smaller numbers s. on both slopes, locally to 1500m. (Mexico to S America.)

SHINING HONEYCREEPER *Cyanerpes lucidus* 10–10.5cm. Small, rather short-tailed honeycreeper of humid forest, adjacent second growth with taller trees, fruiting shrubs. See group intro. Yellow legs usually conspicuous; also note more strongly arched bill, shorter tail than slightly larger Red-legged Honeycreeper. Male has black throat (cf. male Blue Dacnis), female strongly streaked below. Juv. resembles female but breast streaking greenish vs. blue, lacks distinct blue whisker; male attains adult plumage over 1st year. SOUNDS: High, thin, fairly sharp *chit* and high, thin, at times slightly liquid twittering. STATUS: Uncommon to fairly common on both slopes, to 1200m. (Mexico to nw. Colombia.)

female

male

SCARLET-THIGHED DACNIS

Caribbean

BLUE DACNIS

female

males

Pacific

female

GREEN HONEYCREEPER

male

male nonbr.
(Jun–Dec)

female

RED-LEGGED HONEYCREEPER

breeding male
(Oct–Jul)

female

male

SHINING HONEYCREEPER

*COMMON BANANAQUIT *Coereba [flaveola] luteola* 9.5–10cm. Small, rather warbler-like tanager of humid forest, adjacent second growth, plantations, gardens. Singles and pairs forage low to high in flowering trees, probing and piercing flowers for nectar; also eats fruit, forages for insects, visits feeders, and sometimes joins mixed flocks. Nothing particularly similar in Costa Rica: note bold white eyebrow, pale grayish throat contrasting with yellow body, decurved bill, small white wing spot. Juv. duller overall with eyebrow and throat tinged pale yellowish. SOUNDS: High, thin sharp *seiit*, and thin, slightly lisping twitters. Song notably variable, a high, thin, fairly rapid, buzzy to sibilant warble, might be mistaken for a hummingbird, 1–2.5 secs. STATUS: Fairly common to common on both slopes, to 1600m. (Mexico to S America.)

*BLUE-GRAY TANAGER *Tangara (Thraupis) episcopus* 15.5–17.5cm. Familiar, often conspicuous tanager of open and semi-open areas with trees and bushes, towns, gardens, forest edge. In pairs or small groups, often in fruiting trees and visits feeders; at times perches on high bare twigs and phone wires. Overall powder-blue plumage with brighter wings and dark beady eye distinctive; cf. smaller and duller Plain-colored Tanager. SOUNDS: Varied chips and lisping whistles, including high, slightly piercing, downslurred *ssiiu* and more nasal *sywee*, both of which may be given in flight. Song a high, slightly lisping to squeaky twittering warble, mostly 2–5 secs; averages faster-paced, more lisping, and higher than Palm Tanager. STATUS: Common to fairly common on both slopes, to 2000m, rarely higher; more local and less numerous in drier nw. lowlands. (Mexico to S America.)

PALM TANAGER *Tangara (Thraupis) palmarum* 16–18cm. Open and semi-open areas with taller trees, especially palms; forest edge, hedgerows, gardens. Habits much like Blue-gray Tanager, and the two species readily occur together. Grayish plumage of male has variable olive or violet tones depending on light, female more yellowish overall, but contrasting dark wings distinctive; cf. Yellow-winged Tanager. Juv. resembles duller version of female plumage. SOUNDS: Various short, high whistled notes, including slightly nasal upslurred *sweih*; short squeaky chatters. Song a varied high twittering and squeaky warble, mostly 2–5 secs; averages slower-paced, less high and lisping than Blue-gray Tanager, often with more varied structure. STATUS: Fairly common to common on both slopes, to 1800m, rarely higher; more local and scarce in drier nw. lowlands. (Nicaragua to S America.)

YELLOW-WINGED TANAGER *Tangara (Thraupis) abbas* 17–19cm. Humid lowland forest edge, semi-open areas with taller trees, gardens. Habits much like Blue-gray Tanager, with which it may associate at fruiting trees. Beautiful purplish and lilac tones on head and breast often look drab grayish unless seen in good light, but note contrasting blackish wings with big yellow wing patch; cf. Palm Tanager. SOUNDS: High, thin overslurred or upslurred *ssiu* or *tsíu* and high *sweek*, both of which may be given in flight. Song a high, rapid, slightly spluttering or pulsating trill, often with 1–2 intro notes, *shee iiiiiiiiiiiiir*, 2–3 secs; faster-paced, less dry and staccato than Golden-hooded Tanager song. STATUS: Scarce and local in n. lowlands, first reported Costa Rica in mid-1980s. (Mexico to Costa Rica.)

COMMON BANANAQUIT

juv.

BLUE-GRAY TANAGER

juv.

PALM TANAGER

male

female

YELLOW-WINGED
TANAGER

juv.

CRIMSON-COLLARED TANAGER *Ramphocelus sanguinolentus* 19–20cm. Handsome and distinctive tanager of humid forest edge, adjacent second growth. Mostly in pairs ranging low to high, mainly at mid-levels; usually independent of mixed flocks. No similar species in Costa Rica. Juv. duller overall, crimson areas of adult orange-red. **SOUNDS:** Piercing whistled *ssiiew*, and high thin *ssiip*, also in flight. Song a slightly jerky, unhurried medley of high, thin, sweet to slightly squeaky whistled notes, 1–2 notes/sec. **STATUS:** Uncommon to fairly common on Caribbean slope, locally to 1500m; spills over locally to humid foothills of n. Pacific slope. (Mexico to w. Panama.)

SCARLET-RUMPED TANAGER *Ramphocelus passerinii* 17–18cm. Humid second growth, forest edge, overgrown clearings, gardens. In pairs or small groups, mainly at low to mid-levels in leafy foliage, at times with other tanagers; often visits fruit feeders. Male unmistakable, velvet-black with flame-red rump often puffed out. Female distinctive, with silver-gray bill, grayish head; Pacific slope birds have variable orange on breast and rump. Juv. resembles female but bill duller; adult male appearance attained over a few months in summer, when patchy birds are commonly seen. Comprises 2 groups that have been treated as species: **Passerini's Tanager** *R. [p.] passerinii* of Caribbean slope; **Cherrie's Tanager** *R. [p.] costaricensis* of s. Pacific slope, not separable in adult male plumage. **SOUNDS:** Slightly nasal *cheht* or *chay*, often repeated in excited chatters; rough *shih* and lisping chatters, such as *ssi-ssi cheh-chéh*, at times repeated every few secs; and high buzzy *zzrit*. Song a variable short medley of (usually 2–5) slightly nasal whistled chirps, about 2 notes/sec, at times repeated steadily, such as *chiéh'i-wieh chiieh-wieh...*, or simply *chíeh-lii...*; might suggest a musical House Sparrow. **STATUS:** Fairly common to common on both slopes to 1200m, rarely 1900m; both groups may be spreading and range overlap seems likely in w. Central Valley. (Mexico to w. Panama.)

GENUS *TANGARA* (11 species). Classic *Tangara* are rather small, 'crown jewel' tanagers most diverse in lower foothills; recent molecular work, however, shows that most tanagers traditionally placed in genus *Thraupis* (Blue-gray Tanager, etc., p. 410) are embedded within *Tangara*. Usually in pairs or small groups in forest canopy, often at fruiting trees with mixed flocks. Voices typically underwhelming: mostly high thin chips and twitters, more than compensated for by stunning plumages.

GOLDEN-HOODED TANAGER *Tangara (Stilpnia) larvata* 12.5–13cm. Humid forest, adjacent clearings, gardens, second growth with taller trees. In small groups or pairs, mainly at mid–upper levels; often with mixed flocks. Distinctive adult stunning in good light, with black body, golden hood, violet and turquoise highlights. Juv. usually with adult, shows ghosting of adult pattern. **SOUNDS:** Sharp, fairly hard chipping *chik* and gruff clipped *cheht*, which may be repeated steadily. Song a rapid dry trill, often preceded by a few sharp chips or *cheht* notes, *cheht cheht ch ssiiiiiiiiir*, 1–3 secs. **STATUS:** Fairly common to common on both slopes, to 1500m. (Mexico to nw. Ecuador.)

PLAIN-COLORED TANAGER *Tangara inornata* 12–12.5cm. Humid lowland forest, adjacent second growth with taller trees, gardens. In small groups or pairs mainly at mid–upper levels; often apart from mixed flocks. Small size and rather drab plumage distinctive, blue shoulders often concealed; cf. much larger Palm and Blue-gray Tanagers. Juv. duller and more buffy, lacks blue shoulder patch. **SOUNDS:** High thin *sip* notes and twitters, at times (song?) in prolonged series mixed with short trills. **STATUS:** Uncommon to fairly common on Caribbean slope, locally to 1000m. (Costa Rica to Colombia.)

CRIMSON-COLLARED TANAGER

SCARLET-RUMPED TANAGER

Caribbean

females

male

Pacific

molting imm. male

juv.

GOLDEN-HOODED TANAGER

PLAIN-COLORED TANAGER

SILVER-THROATED TANAGER *Tangara icterocephala* 13–13.5cm. Humid foothill forest, adjacent clearings, gardens, second growth with taller trees. In small groups or pairs, mainly at mid–upper levels; often with mixed flocks. No similar species in Costa Rica; note overall yellow plumage with pale gray throat, dark whisker, striped back. Juv. duller, greener overall, but still has dark whisker, lacks cheek patch of Emerald Tanager. SOUNDS: High, often distinctly buzzy and insect-like chips, including wiry *tssir* and high, short, cicada-like buzz. STATUS: Fairly common to common on both slopes, mainly 600–2100m; some descend to lowlands in fall rainy season. (Costa Rica to w. Ecuador.)

EMERALD TANAGER *Tangara florida* 12–12.5cm. Humid foothill forest, adjacent clearings, second growth with taller trees. In pairs or small groups, mainly at mid–upper levels; usually with mixed flocks. No similar species in Costa Rica; note overall green plumage with dark cheek patch, striped back. Juv. duller and more olive overall, but with same basic pattern as adult. SOUNDS: High, fairly sharp, downslurred or overslurred *tsip* or *chik!*, at times run into twitters. STATUS: Uncommon to fairly common on Caribbean slope, mainly 350–1100m. (Costa Rica to nw. Ecuador.)

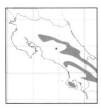

SPECKLED TANAGER *Tangara (Ixothraupis) guttata* 12.5–13cm. Humid foothill forest, adjacent clearings, second growth with taller trees. In pairs or small groups, mainly at mid–upper levels; often with mixed flocks. No similar species in Costa Rica; note dense dark spotting below, dark lores and yellow spectacles. Juv. duller and messier overall but with same basic pattern as adult. SOUNDS: High sharp *sik*, at times in short twittering series; song a few high tiks run into rapid, dry, downslurred trill, overall about 2 secs. STATUS: Uncommon to fairly common on both slopes, mainly 400–1400m. (Costa Rica to n. S America.)

BAY-HEADED TANAGER *Tangara gyrola* 13–13.5cm. Humid foothill forest, adjacent clearings, second growth with taller trees. In pairs or small groups, mainly at mid–upper levels; often with mixed flocks. One of the more familiar and striking *Tangara* tanagers, with blue underparts, dark rusty head, cf. smaller and generally scarce Rufous-winged Tanager. SOUNDS: High, downslurred, slightly metallic and relatively loud ringing *tsíer*; high lisping *tssi*, and fairly hard smacking *tik*, at times in short series. Song a slow warble of high thin lisping chips, 2–3 secs. STATUS: Fairly common on both slopes, to 1800m on Pacific slope, mainly 500–1500m on Caribbean slope, with some moving to adjacent lowlands in fall rainy season. (Nicaragua to S America.)

RUFOUS-WINGED TANAGER *Tangara lavinia* 12.5–13cm. Scarce tanager of humid foothill forest, adjacent clearings, second growth with taller trees. In pairs or small groups, mainly at mid–upper levels; often with mixed flocks that include antwrens and flycatchers, rather than with classic tanager-dominated flocks. Male told from slightly larger Bay-headed Tanager by overall green body, golden-yellow shawl, rufous wings (rufous on wings can be hard to see from below, may simply look dull, or dark, but note contrast with flanks); female from juv. Bay-headed by overall green body (turquoise belly can be striking when overhead), dull bronzy wings. Juv. resembles female but duller overall. SOUNDS: High, downslurred *tsi*, and squeaky overslurred *tsíi*; rapid, high sharp chatters. STATUS: Scarce to uncommon locally on Caribbean slope, mainly 250–800m. (Honduras to nw. Ecuador.)

SILVER-THROATED TANAGER

male

EMERALD TANAGER

female

SPECKLED TANAGER

female

male

juv.

BAY-HEADED TANAGER

female

male

RUFOUS-WINGED TANAGER

SPANGLE-CHEEKED TANAGER *Tangara dowii* 12.5–13cm. Humid highland and foothill forest, adjacent clearings, second growth with taller trees. In pairs or small groups, mainly at mid–upper levels; often with mixed flocks. Plumage distinctive among Costa Rican tanagers, with cinnamon belly, black face, boldly patterned neck sides. Juv. duller and messier overall but with same basic pattern as adult. SOUNDS: High, thin, sharp *tik* and *t'sik*, at times in short series; song a high, thin, slightly jerky twittering, 2–3 secs. STATUS: Fairly common on both slopes, mainly 1200–3000m, locally down to 800m. (Costa Rica to w. Panama.)

BLACK-AND-YELLOW TANAGER *Chrysothlypis chrysomelas* 12–12.5cm. Small, rather warbler-like tanager of humid lower foothill forest and edge, adjacent taller second growth. In small groups or pairs at mid–upper levels, often with mixed flocks; forages mainly in leafy outer foliage. Note size and shape, with slender dark bill; male striking and unmistakable; female can be puzzling (cf. Tennessee Warbler, p. 358) but often with male. Juv. resembles female but male brighter overall. SOUNDS: High, slightly tinny or wiry downslurred *tsyih* and high sharp chips, at times combined into short sharp twitters and chatters. STATUS: Fairly common locally on Caribbean slope, mainly 400–1200m. (Costa Rica to nw. Colombia.)

BLUE-AND-GOLD TANAGER *Bangsia arcaei* 15–16cm. Chunky, medium-size tanager of humid lower foothill forest, adjacent second growth with taller trees and fruiting shrubs. In pairs or small groups, mainly at mid–upper levels. Often with mixed flocks; forages sluggishly along mossy trunks and at epiphytes, also in fruiting trees. Nothing really similar in Costa Rica, but cf. much smaller euphonias (pp. 388–391). Juv. duller overall with brownish eyes. SOUNDS: High, thin, under- then overslurred wiry *t'siíuu*, about 0.5 sec; high, shrill, downslurred *tsiih*. Song a slightly jerky phrase of (usually 3) high, slightly metallic, squeaky or wheezy notes, *whí-chi-píih*, at times repeated steadily in pulses of 2–3 phrases. STATUS: Uncommon to fairly common on n. Caribbean slope, mainly 400–1200m. (Costa Rica to w. Panama.)

SULPHUR-RUMPED TANAGER *Heterospingus rubrifrons* 16–17cm. Medium-large tanager of humid lowland forest, adjacent taller second growth and overgrown clearings. In pairs or small groups, mainly at mid–upper levels of foliage; often with mixed flocks. No similar species in Costa Rica, but bright yellow rump difficult to see from below; note long stout bill, white chest tufts. Juv. duller and sootier overall, but with same basic pattern as adult. SOUNDS: High, thin, slightly buzzy to squeaky downslurred *tzziih* and other high thin chips, at times doubled or in short series. STATUS: Uncommon on s. Caribbean slope, to 700m. (Costa Rica to Panama.)

SPANGLE-CHEEKED TANAGER

female

male

BLACK-AND-YELLOW TANAGER

BLUE-AND-GOLD TANAGER

SULPHUR-RUMPED TANAGER

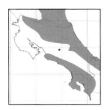

BLACK-BODIED TANAGERS (3+ species). Medium-size to fairly large tanagers, formerly all placed in genus *Tachyphonus*, now in multiple genera. Males mostly black overall, some with colored crest stripe or white wing patch; females notably plain and drab, best identified by overall plumage tones, bill shape, habits, and presence of more-distinctive males.

*WHITE-SHOULDERED TANAGER *Loriotus (Tachyphonus) luctuosus* 13.5–15cm. Fairly small tanager of humid forest and edge, adjacent taller second growth and overgrown clearings. Pairs or small groups forage mainly in leafy foliage at mid–upper levels, usually with mixed flocks. Male distinctive, with obvious white shoulder patch; female notably drab olive overall but nothing especially similar in Costa Rica given size, bill shape, habits, and usually with male. Juv. resembles female but duller and browner; male attains adult plumage within a few months. Comprises 2 groups in Costa Rica that may represent species: **Chiriqui Tanager** *L. [l.] nitidissimus* (14–15cm) of s. Pacific slope, in which male has (usually concealed) tawny crown stripe, bright silvery mandible, female has grayish tinge to face and throat; slightly smaller **Costa Rican Tanager** *L. [l.] axillaris* (13.5–14.5cm) of Caribbean slope, in which male lacks tawny crown patch, female olive overall. SOUNDS: **Chiriqui** has short, slightly smacking chatter or slow rattle, might suggest a wren, often preceded by 1–2 high sip notes, *si chi-chi-chi-chi-chit*, and variations; breaks into squeaky chatters when excited; also high rising *ssip*. **Costa Rican** gives short rapid chatter, perhaps less smacking than Chiriqui. STATUS: Fairly common on both slopes, **Chiriqui** to 800m, **Costa Rican** locally to 1200m. (Honduras to S. America.)

TAWNY-CRESTED TANAGER *Tachyphonus delatrii* 15–16cm. Humid lowland and foothill forest, adjacent taller second growth. Small, often noisy groups forage actively in leafy foliage at low to mid-levels, at times in association with Carmiol's Tanagers, ovenbirds, and other species. Male's crest usually striking and distinctive, even when not flared; female notably drab, dark olive-brown, best told by fairly stout bill, habits, and often with male. Juv. resembles female but duller and sootier; male attains adult plumage within a few months. SOUNDS: Sharp to slightly metallic high chips, sometimes doubled, and higher, slightly wiry or lisping notes; roving groups often call steadily. STATUS: Fairly common to common on Caribbean slope, mainly in lower foothills, to 1200m. (Nicaragua to Ecuador.)

WHITE-LINED TANAGER *Tachyphonus rufus* 17–18.5cm. Rather large and uniformly colored tanager of scrubby second growth, forest edge, gardens; not inside humid forest. In pairs year-round, mainly foraging at low levels, not usually with mixed flocks; visits feeders. Male flashes white underwing coverts in flight, often drawing attention; female can be puzzling, best told by stout dark bill, habits, often with male. Juv. resembles female but duller, somewhat mottled overall; male attains adult plumage within a few months. SOUNDS: Clipped, nasal to semi-metallic *chieh*, often rather quiet. Song a steady, tedious chant of underslurred or downslurred rich chirps, 2–3/sec, *cheuh cheuh...*, can be prolonged for 30 secs or more; downslurred and overslurred chirps can be alternated, *chur chieh chur chieh....* STATUS: Uncommon to fairly common on both slopes, locally to 1500m; range expanding with deforestation. (Costa Rica to S America.)

BLACK-BODIED TANAGERS

Pacific
(Chiriqui)

tawny crown stripe
usually concealed

WHITE-SHOULDERED
TANAGER

males

females

Caribbean
(Costa Rican)

female

TAWNY-CRESTED
TANAGER

male

female

male

WHITE-LINED TANAGER

*WHITE-THROATED SHRIKE-TANAGER *Lanio leucothorax* 20–21.5cm. Rather large arboreal tanager of humid forest, especially in hilly terrain. Pairs and singles range mainly at mid–upper levels inside forest, usually with diverse mixed flocks for which the shrike-tanager often acts as a core member and sentinel. Perches upright and often still for long periods, watching for invertebrate prey before sallying out to snatch it; at times sounds an alarm call to distract other birds and pirate prey items. Relatively large size and behavior distinctive, and male plumage striking, but cf. orioles. Female best told by size, habits, stout hooked bill, also note tawny rump. Juv. resembles female but rustier-toned overall, mandible paler, grayish. Comprises 2 groups that may represent species: **White-throated Shrike-Tanager** *L. [l.] leucothorax* of Caribbean slope, in which male has yellow rump and tail coverts, female has paler tawny rump; and **Black-rumped Shrike-Tanager** *L. [l.] melanopygius* of Pacific slope, in which male has black rump and tail coverts, female has concolor back and rump. SOUNDS: Varied. Common calls a downslurred whistled *chew* and *si'chew*, can be repeated steadily or given in fairly rapid short series; average higher, more piercing in Black-rumped. Also rapid, slightly squeaky descending twitter run into prolonged series of *chu* and *ch'tu* notes may be alarm call; short clucking chatters may recall Summer Tanager or (in Black-rumped) a thrush clucking, often preceded by *si chu* or *si chu-chu-chu* phrases. Song infrequently given, a prolonged, slightly disjointed medley of squeaks, whistles, chips, splutters, and short warbled phrases. STATUS: Uncommon on both slopes, to 800m on Pacific slope, mainly 100–900m on Caribbean slope. (Honduras to w. Panama.)

*GRAY-HEADED TANAGER *Eucometis penicillata* 16.5–18cm. Medium-size tanager of humid lowland forest, adjacent taller second growth. Pairs or small groups forage mainly at low to mid-levels in understory; often at army ant swarms, where can be shy and overlooked easily. Nothing really similar in Costa Rica: note bright yellow underparts, sharply demarcated gray head that often has bushy crest, habits. Juv. duller overall with olive head; soon attains adult plumage. SOUNDS: Hard, low clipped *tuk*; high sharp *siip*, at times run into lisping twitters. Song a varied, usually rather fast-paced, rich sharp warble, which might suggest a euphonia; also a slightly jerky series of high, sharp, lisping chips. STATUS: Uncommon to fairly common on humid s. Pacific slope, locally to 1600m; more local on drier n. Pacific slope and in n. Caribbean lowlands. (Mexico to S America.)

MITROSPINGIDS (MITROSPINGIDAE; 1 SPECIES) Small assemblage of neotropical songbirds, formerly subsumed within tanagers. Ages differ slightly, sexes similar.

DUSKY-FACED TANAGER *Mitrospingus cassinii* 18–19cm. Humid lowland forest understory and edge, adjacent second growth, streamside and marshy thickets, overgrown plantations. Usually in small noisy groups, often twitching wings and foraging restlessly in dense shady understory, rummaging in foliage, visiting fruiting shrubs and sometimes ranging into subcanopy. Tends to be wary and difficult to see clearly, but locally visits fruit feeders. Nothing similar in Costa Rica: note habits, voice, staring pale eyes in dark face, bright olive cap. Juv. duller and messier overall but with same basic pattern as adult, eyes duller. SOUNDS: Sharp, slightly metallic to rolled chips repeated, *chrrit, chrrit chrrit...*, at times with slow spluttering cadence. Dawn song a slightly jerky slow warble of high, vaguely tinny sharp chips, 3–8 secs, repeated every few secs. STATUS: Uncommon to fairly common on Caribbean slope, to 600m. (Nicaragua to w. Ecuador.)

Lanio, Eucometis, Mitrospingus

Caribbean

males

Pacific

females

WHITE-THROATED SHRIKE-TANAGER

GRAY-HEADED TANAGER

juv.

DUSKY-FACED TANAGER

NEW WORLD ORIOLES AND BLACKBIRDS (ICTERIDAE; 21+ SPECIES)

Medium-size to large songbirds with pointed bills, strong legs and feet. Include arboreal, fruit-eating orioles, oropendolas, and caciques, and largely terrestrial, seed-eating blackbirds, grackles, cowbirds. Ages/sexes similar or different, with males larger than females, sometimes strikingly so; attain adult appearance within 1st year.

ORIOLES (GENUS *ICTERUS*) (6 species). Colorful arboreal 'blackbirds,' often with complex age/sex plumage differences. For ID note overall size and structure, especially bill size and shape, plus wing patterns.

STREAK-BACKED ORIOLE *Icterus pustulatus* 18–21cm. Drier woodland, gallery forest, scrub, semi-open country with hedgerows, gardens, forest patches. Mainly at flowering and fruiting trees, often in pairs. Streaked back distinctive, but can be poorly marked on juv. Also note relatively extensive white on wings, straight pointed bill, cf. Spot-breasted Oriole. Bulkier than Baltimore Oriole, with dark tip to mandible, usually a distinct white flash at base of primaries. Sexes similar, adult male averages brightest, 1st-year female dullest. SOUNDS: Varied, short nasal and squeaky chirps, often repeated steadily; upslurred nasal *yehh* and *ehn*; fairly rapid dry chatters and rattles, up to 2 secs, rarely more prolonged; faster and drier than Spot-breasted Oriole. Song a hesitant, slightly jerky series of slurred squeaky whistles, nasal chirps, and short dry rattles. STATUS: Fairly common on n. Pacific slope, to 500m. (Mexico to Costa Rica.)

SPOT-BREASTED ORIOLE *Icterus pectoralis* 21–23cm. Woodland, gallery forest, scrub, semi-open country with hedgerows, gardens, forest patches. Mainly at flowering and fruiting trees, often in pairs. Adult distinctive, with black back, variable spotted breast sides (spots can be small and mostly worn away by late summer), white panel on wing. Also note slightly decurved bill, lack of white wingbars, cf. Streak-backed Oriole. SOUNDS: Nasal *nyeh*, often repeated; clipped squeaky *tchiu*; harsh staccato chatter, *cheh-cheh...*, relatively slow-paced, often fairly soft. Song a pleasing, unhurried warble or slow chant of rich slurred whistles, often some phrases repeated with rhythmic caroling cadence, at times in duet. STATUS: Uncommon on n. Pacific slope; mainly below 500m, but spreading higher into Central Valley. (Mexico to Costa Rica.)

BALTIMORE ORIOLE *Icterus galbula* 18–20.5cm. Widespread winter migrant to forest and edge, semi-open areas with hedgerows, gardens, plantations, second growth. Often in small groups, moving in canopy of flowering and fruiting trees, at times lower in scrub. Adult male striking and distinctive, with black head and back, orange body; female and imm. variable, but always with straight pointed bill, orange plumage tones, bold white wingbars; some adult females and imm. males have extensive black mottling on head and back. SOUNDS: Gruff staccato chatter, slower-paced than Streak-backed Oriole. Occasional mellow whistles, mainly in spring. STATUS: Fairly common to common Oct–early Apr on both slopes to 1800m, in smaller numbers to 2700m; more widespread in migration, Sep–Oct, Apr–early May. (Breeds N America, winters Mexico to nw. S America.)

ORCHARD ORIOLE *Icterus spurius* 15–17cm. Small migrant oriole of hedgerows, gardens, second growth, plantations, scrub. Often in small groups, feeding low to high in flowering trees and bushes. Small size and small, slightly decurved bill distinctive. Chestnut body plumage of adult male unique among orioles; female and imm. greenish yellow with distinct white wingbars. SOUNDS: Low gruff *chuk* and gruff chattering *chuh-chuh...*, lower and more spluttering, less dry and staccato than Baltimore Oriole. STATUS: Uncommon to fairly common Oct–Feb on both slopes, to 1500m, mainly Pacific slope; more widespread in migration, late Jul–Sep, Mar–Apr. (Breeds N America to Mexico, winters Mexico to nw. S America.)

STREAK-BACKED ORIOLE

juv.
(Jul–Sep)

imm.
female

adult

nest

SPOT-BREASTED ORIOLE

imm.

juv.
(Jul–Sep)

adult

BALTIMORE ORIOLE

imm.

female

male

ORCHARD ORIOLE

imm. male

female

male

424

BLACK-COWLED ORIOLE *Icterus prosthemelas* 18.5–21cm. Attractive black-and-yellow oriole of humid forest edge, plantations, taller second growth, semi-open areas with hedgerows, forest patches. Typically in pairs, feeding at mid–upper levels in flowering and fruiting trees, often perching atop leafy trees in early morning; regularly visits feeders. Sexes similar, but female has little or no rusty border to black chest bib. Imm. plumage variable (some much like adult), but no similar orioles in Costa Rica; note extensive black mask, variable black mottling on back. **SOUNDS:** Not a particularly vocal species. Plaintive nasal *tchieh* and downslurred nasal *nyeh*; both may be repeated steadily. Song a pleasant, slightly jerky rich warble, 1–2 secs. **STATUS:** Fairly common on Caribbean slope to 1200m, occasionally higher; scarce to locally uncommon but increasing on Pacific slope, since 2000s. (Mexico to w. Panama.)

YELLOW-TAILED ORIOLE *Icterus mesomelas* 20.5–23.5cm. Rare. Fairly large, handsome black-and-yellow oriole of humid lowland second-growth thickets and forest edge, canebrakes, often along rivers and in damp areas. Usually in pairs or small groups, often rather skulking at low to mid-levels in tangles; at times in more open flowering trees and shrubs. Adult (sexes alike) stunning and flashy; imm. duller but also distinctive, note stout, slightly decurved bill. Yellow tail sides often striking as birds dive into cover. **SOUNDS:** Call a rich twangy *cheuk* and downslurred *cheu*, at times repeated steadily. Song a varied, rhythmic to slightly rollicking (usually 4–20×) repetition of rich, 2–7-note whistled phrases, such as *tch wee-choo weeep, tch wee-choo weeep...*; sometimes in duet and may recall a wren. **STATUS:** Scarce and local on Caribbean slope, to 300m; formerly common and widespread, but decimated by capture for cagebird trade (Stiles & Skutch 1989). (Mexico to nw. Peru.)

*SCARLET-RUMPED CACIQUE *Cacicus microrhynchus* 20–24cm, male> female. Humid forest, locally in adjacent tree-scattered pastureland with forest patches. Mainly at mid–upper levels where often hidden in leafy foliage; heard more often than seen, but visits feeders in some places. Roams widely in pairs or small, often noisy groups in search of fruiting trees; at times associates with other canopy species such as oropendolas, Purple-throated Fruitcrows, White-fronted Nunbirds. Pendulous woven nest resembles oropendola's but isolated, not colonial. Distinctive, but beware imm. Yellow-billed Cacique has pale grayish eyes. Note Scarlet-rumped's habits, ivory bill, staring blue eyes; red rump often difficult to see when overhead. Juv. has rusty-brown rump, duller eyes, soon like adult. **SOUNDS:** Varied; often loud and strident. Calls include loud rich *chrÉEu* and *chírriHEU*, a downslurred squealing *HEUW*, usually in short series, at times repeated rapidly. Song appears to be varied, fairly rapid series of ringing to slightly screaming and piercing whistles and screeches, often alternated and combined. **STATUS:** Fairly common on both slopes, to 1200m. (Honduras to Panama.)

BLACK-COWLED ORIOLE

juv. (May–Aug)

imm.

adult

nest pouch slung under palm frond

YELLOW-TAILED ORIOLE

imm.

juv. (May–Aug)

adult

SCARLET-RUMPED CACIQUE

OROPENDOLAS (GENUS *PSAROCOLIUS*) (3 species). Large, social, arboreal 'blackbirds' with stout pointed bills, bright yellow tail sides. Ages differ slightly, soon attain adult appearance; sexes similar in plumage but males much larger than females. Colonies of woven pendulous nests conspicuous, often attended by brood-parasite Giant Cowbirds (p. 430).

CHESTNUT-HEADED OROPENDOLA *Psarocolius wagleri* Male 34–38cm, female 25–29cm. Medium-size dark oropendola of humid forest and edge; colonies typically at edges, often in isolated trees. Flight rather quick with deep swooping wingbeats that make hollow rushing sound, quite different from measured flight of large oropendolas. Usually in small groups, feeding in fruiting and flowering trees where clambers actively; visits feeders. Juv. has duller eyes and bill, back and wings lack sheen of adult. SOUNDS: Varied throaty clucks and low chatters, often more guttural than Montezuma Oropendola. Low, slightly gurgling *chuk-uk-luk*; nasal *kyah*; slightly nasal clucking *chéuh*. Song a deep gurgled *w'shLOK*, and variations, repeated. STATUS: Uncommon to fairly common on Caribbean slope to 1700m, especially foothills; scarce locally in interior valleys of s. Pacific slope. (Mexico to w. Ecuador.)

MONTEZUMA OROPENDOLA *Psarocolius montezuma* Male 45–51cm, female 37–41cm. Distinctive, very large (male much larger than female) and colorful inhabitant of lowland forest edge, woodland, semi-open country with hedgerows, scattered trees; colonies typically in isolated trees. Flight unhurried and steady with measured rowing wingbeats, usually at treetop height and often across open areas in well-spaced flocks. Mainly at mid–upper levels in fruiting and flowering trees, singly or in small groups; visits feeders. In display, male swings upside-down on perch, spreading wings and fanning tail. Juv. duller overall, underparts sooty blackish. SOUNDS: Varied. Low *chuk* often given in flight; squeaky *woik*; sneezy *rrúh-rrúh*; and varied gruff hollow clucking series. Song memorable: a bizarre, hollow gurgling and gobbling crescendo, ending abruptly, 1–1.5 secs; likened to pouring wine from an upended bottle and sometimes followed by a thin upslurred whistle; raspy wing rattles in display. STATUS: Fairly common to common on Caribbean slope; uncommon to fairly common locally on Pacific slope, where range is expanding; locally to 1800m. (Mexico to Panama.)

CRESTED OROPENDOLA *Psarocolius decumanus* Male 42–46cm, female 32–36cm. Recent arrival (from adjacent Panama) on s. Pacific slope, where found in semi-open country with hedgerows, forest patches, plantations, open woodland. Mainly in small groups moving through canopy, flying across clearings with steady flight and slightly rowing wingbeats unlike faster, sweeping flight of smaller Chestnut-headed Oropendola, which is more of a forest-based bird. Also note Crested's blackish head, concolorous with body; crest is wispy, inconspicuous (Chestnut-headed has similar crest). SOUNDS: Varied gruff clucks and a quiet nasal *whoih*. Song a downslurred wheezy whistle overlain by a clucking mechanical rattle, about 1.5 secs, at times ending with an emphatic note; also an accelerating, short clucking or popping series ending with a slightly explosive whistle and pop. STATUS: Uncommon and local, but increasing, on s. Pacific slope, especially around San Vito, 100–1500m; first recorded Costa Rica in 1999. (Costa Rica to S America.)

CHESTNUT-HEADED OROPENDOLA

MONTEZUMA OROPENDOLA

CRESTED OROPENDOLA

*YELLOW-BILLED CACIQUE *Amblycercus holosericeus* 21–26cm, male> female. Skulking and furtive in second growth and bamboo thickets, forest edge. Usually in pairs, moving deliberatively at low to mid-levels hidden in cover; often seen flying low across roads and trails; sometimes attends army ant swarms. Note habits, pale ivory bill, staring pale yellow eyes. Juv. has dark eyes, sootier plumage, soon like adult, but imm. eyes pale grayish for a few months (mainly Aug–Oct), cf. Scarlet-rumped Cacique if rump not seen. **SOUNDS:** Calls include short series of (usually 3–7) slightly gruff, crowing notes, often with slightly laughing cadence, *yeh-yeh…* or *shehr shehr...*, 4–5 notes/sec; a gruff nasal *yahnk* or *ah'nk ah'nk*. Song a measured chant of (usually 2–8) rich, whistled, 2–3-syllable phrases, 1 phrase/1–1.5 secs, such as *heeu hih, heeu hih…* or *hoóee-hwee, hoóee-hwee...*, often overlapped by a slightly descending chattering rattle from mate, *hew chrrrrrrrrr*, 4–5 secs. **STATUS:** Fairly common, locally to 3000m. (Mexico to S America.)

MELODIOUS BLACKBIRD *Dives dives* 23–28cm, male>female. Often conspicuous in varied open and semi-open habitats, especially tree-scattered pastures. In pairs or small groups, feeding mainly on ground where walks confidently; associates readily with grackles. Often flicks tail up sharply, at times accompanied by whistles. Flight slightly hesitant or jerky, not steady and direct. Best identified by shape, habits, voice. Note medium size, sharply pointed bill; 'velvet' plumage of face and neck apparent at close range. Cf. Shiny Cowbird. Juv. duller overall, soon like adult. **SOUNDS:** Varied, often 2-note piercing whistles, including *wh'chieuh* or *whi'chieh*, 2nd part downslurred; and clipped, clear whistled *wh'dieeh*, both often in short series; sharp *weet!* or *piik!* sometimes repeated persistently when agitated. **STATUS:** Uncommon to fairly common on both slopes, locally to 2400m; first recorded Costa Rica in 1987 and has spread rapidly with deforestation. (Mexico to w. Panama.)

GREAT-TAILED GRACKLE *Quiscalus mexicanus* Male 40–47cm, female 29–34cm. Conspicuous and noisy in ranchland, agricultural land, open country with scattered trees, hedgerows, towns and urban areas, mangroves, lakeshores; often near water. Feeds mainly on ground, at times in flocks of 100s; roosts communally and noisily in trees, often in town parks where 1000s may gather. Distinctive in most of range, but in flight cf. Giant Cowbird, and around Lake Nicaragua cf. smaller Nicaraguan Grackle. Juv. appreciably paler below than female, soon attains adult-like plumage. **SOUNDS:** Varied and noisy. Loud shrieks, whistles, clacks, and chatters, including a bright, piercing, ascending whistled *wheeeeu* often ending emphatically. Flight call a gruff dry *chek*, especially from females. **STATUS:** Common to fairly common on both slopes to 1500m, in smaller numbers locally to 2800m. (Mexico and sw. US to nw. S America.)

NICARAGUAN GRACKLE *Quiscalus nicaraguensis* Male 28–31cm, female 23–25cm. Very local in fresh lagoon and river edge vegetation, from low bushes to taller trees; adjacent pastures. Clearly smaller and shorter-tailed than Great-tailed Grackle with straighter, more slender bill, domed head, less brutish mien. Rarely in groups of more than 30 or so birds. Males sing and display singly and in small groups from bushes and hidden in trees; in display, male droops wings and raises tail in deep V. Feeds on ground, often around cattle, where associates readily with Red-winged Blackbirds, Bronzed Cowbirds, less often with Great-tailed Grackles. Male's strongly keeled tail often held as a diagnostic deep fan in flight; also note muted blue gloss. Female paler below than Great-tailed with pale eyebrow, variable dark eyestripe; but cf. juv. Great-tailed, which is also pale below. **SOUNDS:** Songs higher, thinner, more whining than Great-tailed. Song phrases include ascending, high nasal whistle, about 1 sec; series of (usually 5–8) short, tinny to whining downslurred whistles, *kyieh-kyieh...*; and more varied short series of discordant whining and semi-metallic notes. Call a low gruff *chek!* averages higher, weaker than Great-tailed. **STATUS:** Uncommon to fairly common but very local in lowlands s. of Lake Nicaragua, especially around Caño Negro. (Nicaragua to Costa Rica.)

juv.

YELLOW-BILLED CACIQUE

MELODIOUS
BLACKBIRD

juv.

females

male

GREAT-TAILED GRACKLE

female

males

NICARAGUAN GRACKLE

COWBIRDS (GENUS *MOLOTHRUS*)
(3 species). Medium-size to large blackbirds of open and semi-open country, often found around livestock. Ages/sexes differ slightly to distinctly, attain adult appearance in a few months; males slightly to distinctly larger than females. Brood parasites of various species; hence begging young cowbirds are found singly, being fed by sundry species but not by cowbirds.

BRONZED COWBIRD *Molothrus aeneus* 19–22cm, male>female. Ranchland (often around livestock), open country with scattered trees, hedgerows, parks in towns and urban areas; more often woodland and forest edge in breeding season. Singles and small groups in breeding season; flocks locally to 100s at other times. Feeds on ground, tail often slightly cocked; roosts communally in trees, often with grackles. Perches readily in trees and on phone wires; male in display expands neck ruff and hovers in front of female, singing. Flight strong and direct, often in fairly tight, slightly undulating flocks. Best identified by stout, deep-based bill, reddish eyes (fiery-red on male, duller on female and imm.); adult male wings have glossy bluish sheen. Juv dark sooty brown to dull blackish overall, sometimes with fine pale wingbars, faint pale streaking on belly, like duller version of adult by winter. Cf. Shiny Cowbird. **SOUNDS:** High, thin, tinny whining trills and wheezy squeaks, at times suggesting European Starling *Sturnus vulgaris*. Spluttering, chattering rattle, 1–2 secs (mainly female). Song a varied series of high whining whistles, at times mixed with short quiet gurgles. **STATUS:** Uncommon to fairly common on both slopes, locally to 1800m; least numerous in drier Northwest. (Mexico and sw. US to Panama.)

SHINY COWBIRD *Molothrus bonariensis* Male 23–24cm, female 20–21.5cm. Ranchland (often around livestock), open country with scattered trees, parks in towns and urban areas, feeders. Habits much like Bronzed Cowbird, and at times can be found together with that species. Shiny is slightly larger than Bronzed, with shallower, more pointed bill. Male has glossy purplish-blue head and body, dark eyes; also cf. Melodious Blackbird. Female distinctive, with plain pale gray-brown underparts. Juv. warmer-toned than female with dark streaking above and below (unlike plain, dark juv. Bronzed Cowbird), like duller version of adult by winter. **SOUNDS:** Male gives high thin *seeíh*; both sexes (mainly female) give clucking or bubbling rattle, 1–2 secs, averaging lower than Bronzed Cowbird. Song a high, slightly metallic to fairly sweet warble, usually overall descending, 1.5–4 secs, often preceded by series of (usually 4–8) low, wet gulping grunts that can be given separately. **STATUS:** Uncommon and local on s. Pacific slope, rare to uncommon locally but spreading to n. Pacific slope and on Caribbean slope; mainly below 1500m, rarely wanders to 2400m. First recorded Costa Rica in 2004. (Caribbean and S America.)

GIANT COWBIRD *Molothrus oryzivorus* Male 32–36 cm, female 28–30.5cm. Semi-open country and ranchland with taller trees, hedgerows, forest edge and clearings; brood parasite of oropendolas and caciques. Mostly seen in flight, often fairly high overhead, as singles or small loose groups: note distinctive, strong, flap-flap-flap-glide progression, unlike steadier wingbeats of Great-tailed Grackle. Feeds on ground around livestock, along riverbanks, but arboreal at oropendola colonies. Much larger than other cowbirds; note thick neck that contributes to rather small-headed look; in flight note pointed wings, thick neck, squared-off tail; cf. grackles. Juv. has pale bill, pale to brownish eye; soon resembles duller version of adult. **SOUNDS:** Sharp clucks and chatters mainly in interactions. Song a short, slightly jerky or discordant series of harsh, semi-metallic whistles. **STATUS:** Uncommon to fairly common on Caribbean slope and s. Pacific slope, less numerous and more local on n. Pacific slope; locally to 1800m. (Mexico to S America.)

BRONZED COWBIRD

juv.

female

male

juv. with Rufous-collared Sparrow host

SHINY COWBIRD

juv.

female

male

cf. Great-tailed Grackle

GIANT COWBIRD

juv.

female

male

432

EASTERN MEADOWLARK *Sturnella magna* 18–22cm, male>female. Distinctive inhabitant of grassland and savanna, often with scattered shrubs, also marshes, weedy fields. No similar species in Costa Rica. Sings from ground or low perch; feeds on ground where walks and clambers strongly. Flushes explosively and flies with bursts of stiff wingbeats alternated with brief glides; usually spreads tail on landing, to show off white sides. Female averages duller than male; juv. duller and paler than adult. Fresh plumage heavily veiled buff on underparts, wearing away to reveal golden yellow. SOUNDS: Raspy *zzzrt* and spluttering chatter, about 0.5–1.5 secs; high nasal *sweink* in flight. Song a simple arrangement of (usually 4–5) downslurred plaintive whistles, such as *see syee teu-eh* or *seei chu-e-leu*, about 1 sec. STATUS: Fairly common but often local, to 2500m; range has expanded rapidly in past 50 or so years with deforestation. (N America to Panama.)

RED-BREASTED BLACKBIRD (MEADOWLARK) *Leistes militaris* 16–18cm, male>female. Freshwater marshes, grasslands, crop fields, adjacent damp scrub. Sings from low perch and in flight; forages mainly on or near ground, at times in flocks. Adult male striking and distinctive; on female and imm. note bill shape (shorter and stouter than Red-winged Blackbird); adult female has variably rosy to red patches on breast. SOUNDS: Ringing, slightly metallic *tling* and *ziehk* and low nasal *jert*. Song 1–4 tinny chips followed by slightly hissing nasal buzz, such as *tk tik si-zhhhrrrr*, 1.5–2 secs. STATUS: Fairly common locally on s. Pacific slope; scarce to uncommon and local but spreading on n. Pacific slope and Caribbean slope, to 1500m. (Nicaragua to S America.)

RED-WINGED BLACKBIRD *Agelaius phoeniceus* Male 20–22cm, female 17–18cm. Fresh and brackish marshes with reedbeds, weedy growth along rivers, irrigation channels, adjacent farmland. Sings from perch on low bush or roadside wires, also in short display flight. Feeds mainly on ground, often in large flocks outside breeding season. Adult male distinctive, with bright red shoulder patch bordered creamy (red often concealed at rest); female has striped head, variable rusty tones on back, relatively long pointed bill, cf. female Red-breasted Blackbird. Juv. resembles female; 1st-year male intermediate between adult male and female, with variable red on shoulder. SOUNDS: Gruff *chek*, often given in flight overhead. Song a short, slightly metallic, strangled scream run into a short gruff rattle. STATUS: Locally common breeder in nw. lowlands, ranging more widely in fall–winter; uncommon to fairly common locally but spreading on Caribbean slope; mainly below 600m but wanders higher. (N America to Costa Rica.)

BOBOLINK *Dolichonyx oryzivorus* 15–17cm. Rare transient migrant found in weedy grasslands, crop fields, marshes. Typically feeds in grasses and rarely seen unless flushed, when may perch atop a bush, calling. Usually found as singles, sometimes with other blackbirds, but can occur in small flocks; flight strong and direct. Imm. and nonbr. adults similar, with unstreaked rich buffy breast, bold head stripes, stout pointed bill, spiky tail; cf. juv. Red-breasted and female Red-winged Blackbirds. Breeding male in spring distinctive, with black face and underparts, buff cowl; fresh plumage veiled buff; breeding female like nonbr. plumages. SOUNDS: Semi-metallic, clipped nasal *iihnk* mainly in flight; gruff clipped *chuhk!* STATUS: Rare transient mid-Sep to Oct, mainly on Caribbean slope, but also recorded inland and on Pacific slope; very rare on Caribbean coast in spring, late Apr–early May. (Breeds N America, winters S America.)

juv.

male

EASTERN MEADOWLARK

male

RED-BREASTED BLACKBIRD

juv.

female

RED-WINGED BLACKBIRD

female

male

imm. male

red on adult male can be concealed at rest

BOBOLINK

female (imm./ nonbr. male similar)

breeding male (Apr–May)

APPENDIX A: COCOS ISLAND

Cocos Island is a rarely visited, uninhabited volcanic island claimed by Costa Rica; it lies at 5°32'N 87°04'W, about 520km southwest of mainland Costa Rica and 720km north of the Galapagos Islands. Some 25km² in extent and rising steeply to about 600m, the island is cloaked in dense brushy woodland. Cocos is home to 4 breeding landbirds, 3 of them endemic and one shared with the Galapagos Islands, plus 7 widespread tropical breeding seabirds. In addition, numerous species of migrant waterbirds and landbirds have been found on the island, including several new records for Costa Rica—hardly surprising for such a remote outpost that acts as a magnet for birds lost out over the ocean.

Those Cocos breeding seabirds not included on the main plates are shown on the next plate. The resident landbirds comprise a cuckoo, flycatcher, warbler, and tanager, shown opposite and discussed below.

COCOS CUCKOO *Coccyzus ferrugineus* 32–34cm. Uncommon resident in wooded habitats. Like other *Coccyzus*, mostly sluggish and easily overlooked, foraging methodically at all levels. No similar species on the island, although vagrants of other cuckoos could occur. Note bright rusty wings, bold tail pattern (subdued on juv.).

COCOS FLYCATCHER *Nesotriccus ridgwayi* 12.5–13.5cm. Common resident in all wooded and shrubby habitats, hopping, sallying, and gleaning for food. No similar species on the island; note long slender bill, soft facial expression, buffy wingbars.

***MANGROVE WARBLER** *Setophaga petechia* 11.5–12.5cm. Common, active, and confiding resident in all wooded and shrubby habitats, often hopping on ground, on beaches, and unconcerned by people. Male has rusty cap, moderate rusty streaking below; female much like mainland female Mangrove Warbler (p. 354). No similar species occur regularly on the island, but numerous North American migrant warblers have shown up as vagrants.

COCOS FINCH *Pinaroloxias inornata* 11.5–12.5cm. Common, confiding resident found in all habitats. No similar species on the island; most closely related to iconic Galapagos finches and, like them, now considered to be a tanager. Male black overall, female and juv. brown and streaky; note sharply pointed bill, short tail.

juv.

COCOS CUCKOO

COCOS FLYCATCHER

MANGROVE WARBLER

male

female   **COCOS FINCH**   male

In addition to the Cocos Island breeding seabirds shown opposite, Red-footed Booby (p. 48), Brewster's Brown Booby (p. 46), Sooty Tern (p. 58), and Common Brown Noddy (p. 58) also breed on the island.

Adventurous birders making the trip out to Cocos can also expect to see various other oceanic birds on the transit to/from the island. As well as species shown on the main plates (pp. 40–48), other offshore possibilities include Darwin's [Band-rumped] Storm Petrel, Galapagos [Wedge-rumped] Storm Petrel, Markham's Storm Petrel, Leach's Storm Petrel, and Swallow-tailed Gull.

GREAT FRIGATEBIRD *Fregata minor* 82–100cm, WS 190–225cm. Local breeder on Cocos I., where much commoner than Magnificent Frigatebird, which is a scarce nonbreeding visitor. Juv. and imm. have variable rusty on head, rounded white belly patch; adult female has gray throat; adult male has pale axillar scallops, pale upperwing bar, green sheen to back. Cf. Magnificent Frigatebird (p. 44). Ranges widely at sea. (Tropical Oceans.)

PACIFIC BLACK NODDY *Anous minutus* 31–34cm. Common seasonal breeding species on Cocos Island, ranging over adjacent waters. Smaller and darker than Common Brown Noddy (p. 58) with much finer bill, more contrasting white cap. Juv. also has contrasting white cap vs. reduced whitish forehead patch or narrow bridle of juv. Common Brown. (Tropical Pacific.)

INDO-PACIFIC WHITE NODDY *Gygis [alba] candida* 32–34cm. Common breeding species on Cocos Island, mainly Mar–Sep, ranging over adjacent and offshore waters. Unmistakable, ethereal white tern that nests in trees, laying its single egg in a slight notch on an open branch, or in a fork. Juv. has variable cinnamon barring and tinge to plumage. (Tropical Indian and Pacific Oceans.)

Figure 28. *The lushly forested slopes of Cocos Island rise steeply from sunny tropical Pacific waters; April 2009.* © *James R. Zook.*

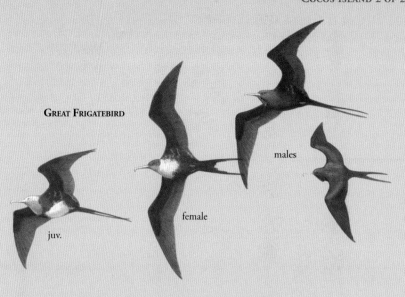

Great Frigatebird

males

female

juv.

Pacific Black Noddy

juv.

Indo-Pacific White Noddy

juv.

APPENDIX B: OFFSHORE VISITORS, RARE MIGRANTS, AND VAGRANTS

Here we list 103 species reported from Costa Rica as offshore pelagic migrants, rare visitors, and vagrants, plus potential residents overlooked or unconfirmed in Costa Rica. Some are likely of more regular occurrence than presently known, especially offshore pelagic species. If encountered, any of these species should be documented carefully. In a few cases, plate layout allowed some rare species to be incorporated in the main body of the book; these are mainly species that appear similar to more common and regularly occurring species (such as Eastern Warbling Vireo vs. Philadelphia Vireo) or species that might be found by anyone in the field and for which inclusion in the plates may help clarify status (such as Solitary Eagle, Gray-bellied Hawk).

Two 'official' checklists of the birds of Costa Rica may be found online, although details for rare species in each list do not agree: one compiled by the Unión de Ornitólogos de Costa Rica (Sandoval & Sánchez 2019) and the other by the Comité de Especies Raras y Registros Ornitológicos de Costa Rica (Garrigues et al. 2018). Our reference to these and other sources was supplemented by review from James R. Zook and online searches, but we take responsibility for any errors perceived in the following list. Also see Appendix A for some species that breed on Cocos Island.

[P] Regular visitor to offshore waters, some rarely ranging nearer shore and encountered on pelagic day trips from mainland, such as Leach's Storm Petrel, Swallow-tailed Gull;
[V] Very rare, sporadic, or potentially overlooked; not usually recorded annually but could be encountered on occasion, such as Dunlin, Lark Sparrow;
[X] Exceptional, species with at most 3 records, such as Catesby's Tropicbird, Maguari Stork;
(Parentheses indicate no substantiated records or reports of presumed wild birds since 2000, such as Orange-breasted Falcon, White-bellied Emerald);
[Brackets indicate species reported in the literature or eBird, but unconfirmed or without convincing documentation; here considered hypothetical, such as Short-tailed Shearwater, Golden-crowned Flycatcher, Pine Warbler];
(Cocos) indicates species recorded only from Cocos Island.

[X](Greater) White-fronted Goose *Anser albifrons*
[X]Orinoco Goose *Neochen jubata*
[V](White-faced Whistling Duck *Dendrocygna viduata*)
[X]Comb Duck *Sarkidiornis sylvicola*
(Mallard *Anas platyrhynchos*)
[V]White-cheeked Pintail *Anas bahamensis*
[X]Canvasback *Aythya valisineria*
[V]Redhead *Aythya americana*
[Greater Scaup *Aythya marila*]
[X]Hooded Merganser *Lophodytes cucullatus*
[X]Red-breasted Merganser *Mergus merganser*
[V]Ruddy Duck *Oxyura jamaicensis*
[X]Eared Grebe *Podiceps [nigricollis] californicus*

[V]Galapagos (Waved) Albatross *Phoebastria irrorata*
[X]Atlantic Yellow-nosed Albatross *Thalassarche chlororhynchos*
[X]Black-capped Petrel *Pterodroma hasitata*
[X]Cory's Shearwater *Calonectris [diomedea] borealis*
[X]Scopoli's Shearwater *Calonectris [d.] diomedea*
[X]Great Shearwater *Ardenna gravis*
[V]Sooty Shearwater *Ardenna grisea*

[Short-tailed Shearwater *Ardenna tenuirostris*]
[X]Manx Shearwater *Puffinus puffinus*
[V]Black-vented Shearwater *Puffinus opisthomelas*
[V][Wilson's Storm Petrel *Oceanites oceanicus*]
[V](Latham's [White-faced] Storm Petrel *Pelagodroma marina*)
[P]Darwin's [Band-rumped] Storm Petrel *Thalobata [castro] bangsi*
[P]Galapagos [Wedge-rumped] Storm Petrel *Halocyptena tethys*
[P]Markham's Storm Petrel *Hydrobates markhami.*
[P]Leach's Storm Petrel *Hybdrobates leucorhous*
[X]Red-tailed Tropicbird *Phaethon rubricauda* (Cocos)
[X]Yellow-billed Tropicbird *Phaethon lepturus* (Cocos)
[X]Catesby's Tropicbird *Phaethon [lepturus] catesbyi*
[X]Peruvian Booby *Sula variegata*
[V][South Polar Skua *Catharacta maccormicki*]
[V]Bonaparte's Gull *Chroicocephalus philadelphia*
[X]Brown-hooded Gull *Chroicocephalus cirrocephalus*
[X]Gray Gull *Leucophaeus modestus* (Cocos)
[X]Black-legged Kittiwake *Rissa tridactyla*

[X]Great Black-backed Gull *Larus marinus*
[P]Swallow-tailed Gull *Creagrus furcatus*
[X]California Gull *Larus californicus*
[X]Western Gull *Larus occidentalis*
[V]Kelp Gull *Larus dominicanus*
[V]Inca Tern *Larosterna inca*
[X]Large-billed Tern *Phaetusa simplex*
[X]Yellow-billed Tern *Sternula superciliaris*
[X]Roseate Tern *Sterna dougallii*

[X]Pacific Golden Plover *Pluvialis fulva*
[X]Piping Plover *Charadrius melodus*
[X]Curlew Sandpiper *Calidris ferruginea*
[V]Dunlin *Calidris alpina*
[V]Hudsonian Godwit *Limosa haemastica*
[V]Ruff *Calidris pugnax*
[X]Whistling Heron *Syrigma sibilatrix*
[V]American Bittern *Botaurus lentiginosus*
[V]White-faced Ibis *Plegadis chihi*
[X]Bare-faced Ibis *Phimosus infuscatus*
[X]Maguari Stork *Ciconia maguari*
[(Northern Black Rail *Laterallus jamaicensis*)]
[Ruddy Crake *Laterallus ruber*]

[Solitary Eagle *Buteogallus solitarius*]
(Orange-breasted Falcon *Falco deiroleucus*)
(Great Horned Owl *Bubo virginianus*)
(Short-eared Owl *Asio flammeus*)
Burrowing Owl *Athene cunicularia*

[X]Eared Dove *Zenaida auriculata* (Cocos)
[V]White-crowned Pigeon *Patagioenas leucocephala*
[X]Greater Ani *Crotophaga major*
[X]Yellow-crowned Amazon *Amazona ochrocephala*

[X]Rufous-crested Coquette *Lophornis delattrei*
(White-bellied Emerald *Chlorestes (Amazilia) candida*)
[Blue-tailed Hummingbird *Saucerottia (Amazilia) cyanura*]

[Great Swallow-tailed Swift *Panyptila sanctihieronymi*]

[X]Eastern Phoebe *Sayornis phoebe* (Cocos)
[X]Vermilion/Scarlet Flycatcher *Pyrocephalus obscurus/rubinus*
[V]Ash-throated Flycatcher *Myiarchus cinerascens*
[Golden-crowned Flycatcher *Myiodynastes chrysocephalus*]
[X]Couch's Kingbird *Tyrannus couchii*
[X]Northern Mockingbird *Mimus polyglottos*
[Bicknell's [Gray-cheeked] Thrush *Catharus [minimus] bicknelli*]
[V]White-eyed Vireo *Vireo griseus*
[V]Black-whiskered Vireo *Vireo altiloquus*
[X]Eastern Warbling Vireo *Vireo gilvus*
[V]Orange-crowned Warbler *Leiothlypis celata*
[V]Nashville Warbler *Leiothlypis ruficapilla*
[Connecticut Warbler *Oporornis agilis*]
[V]Golden-cheeked Warbler *Setophaga chrysoparia*
[V]Audubon's Warbler *Setophaga [coronata] auduboni*
[Pine Warbler *Setophaga pinus*]
[V]American Pipit *Anthus rubescens*
(Grassland Yellow-finch *Sicalis luteola*)
[X]Lined Seedeater *Sporophila lineola*
[Black-headed Grosbeak *Pheucticus melanocephala*]
[V]Clay-colored Sparrow *Spizella pallida*
[V]Chipping Sparrow *Spizella passerina*
[V]Lark Sparrow *Chondestes grammacus*
[V]Savannah Sparrow *Passerculus sandwichensis*
[V]Lincoln's Sparrow *Melospiza lincolnii*
[X]White-crowned Sparrow *Zonotrichia leucophrys*
[X]Crimson-backed Tanager *Ramphocelus dimidiatus*
[X]Flame-rumped Tanager *Ramphocelus flammigerus*
[V]Bullock's Oriole *Icterus bullockii*
[V]Yellow-headed Blackbird *Xanthocephalus xanthocephalus*

APPENDIX C: TAXONOMIC NOTES

Here we summarize reasons for treating various taxa as potentially separate species and mention alternative taxonomic options for some species; these are marked in the species accounts by an asterisk (*) preceding the English name and by use of brackets, for example, American Great Egret *Ardea [alba] egretta* or Veraguas [Brown-throated] Parakeet *Eupsittula [pertinax] ocularis*, as explained on p. 30. The term 'group' is used for one or more subspecies that form a potential species; group names refer to the chronologically first-named taxon in a group. Further explanation of this subject was provided by Howell & Dyer (2022).

In some cases, differences (as in plumage, morphology, vocalizations, ecology) are so clear that there is no question different species are involved (e.g., Cayenne Lapwing, Salvadoran Flycatcher); in other cases more work is needed, and our treatment is intended to draw attention to such cases in the hope of promoting careful study. Our baseline taxonomy is that of IOC (Gill et al. 2021), except for oceanic birds, for which we follow Howell & Zufelt (2019), namely for the Wedge-rumped Storm Petrel, Brown Booby, White-tailed Tropicbird, Bridled Tern, and Brown Noddy complexes. In cases where our opinions differ from or expand upon IOC (there are several IOC splits we find unconvincing), the following notes summarize our reasons.

We have attempted to consider taxonomy within Middle America and between Central America and at least adjacent South America. Taxonomy across all of South America, however, is beyond our purview, although in some cases it is clear that Central American taxa are distinct. Thus we may break species into Central American or Middle American taxa and 'all the rest,' including potentially multiple species in South America that we have not had the resources to investigate, although groups or English names may be suggested for some South American taxa.

Potential species-level differences for species in which all groups occur in Costa Rica are summarized in the species accounts and not expanded upon below, namely for Black Skimmer (p. 58), White-throated Crake (p. 92), Gray-chested Dove (p. 168), Scaly-breasted Hummingbird (p. 216), Volcano Hummingbird (p. 224), Olive-sided Flycatcher (p. 306), Green Shrike-Vireo (p. 348), Wilson's Warbler (p. 366), and Ruddy-breasted Seedeater (p. 392).

Depending on available data and philosophy, our opinions vary for different taxa, grading from "suggest that A and B may represent separate species" to "indicate that A and B are separate species." Probably every one of these cases represents a phylogenetic 'species' or lineage, according to some species concept (Howell 2021), as do others not mentioned here. We only include taxa for which we have biological support for possible species status (rather than simply uninformed molecular data), but undoubtedly we have still underestimated the number of candidates.

BLACK-BELLIED WHISTLING DUCK *Dendrocygna autumnalis* (p. 34). Differences in plumage and voice suggest that the *fulgens* group (N America to w. Panama; Northern Black-bellied Whistling Duck) and *autumnalis* group (Panama to S America, Southern Black-bellied Whistling Duck) may represent separate species. Plumage appears to intergrade from s. Costa Rica to cen. Panama, but study is needed.

SMITHSONIAN GULL *Larus [argentatus] smithsonianus* (p. 52). Molecular work and juvenile plumages indicate that N American populations of 'Herring Gull' are distinct from European populations and are more closely related to N Pacific taxa such as Glaucous-winged Gull *L. glaucescens*, as summarized by Olson & Banks (2007). As proposed by those authors, the English name 'Smithsonian Gull' removes misleading association with 'the Herring Gull' of Europe and we prefer this option over American Herring Gull, used by other authors such as IOC.

SANDWICH TERN *Thalasseus sandvicensis* (p. 54). Molecular work suggests that 'American Sandwich Tern' is more closely related to Elegant Tern than to 'European Sandwich Tern,' and some authors (including IOC) split N American populations as Cabot's Tern *T. acuflavidus*. We find the molecular studies weak, and unconvincing as evidence for biological species status (Howell 2021); either way, retaining simply 'Sandwich Tern' for one of the taxa (as done for the European birds) is ambiguous and needlessly confusing.

AMERICAN BLACK TERN *Chlidonias [niger] surinamensis* (p. 58). Differences in plumage and provisionally in voice suggest that the *surinamensis* group (New World) and *niger* group (Old World; Eurasian Black Tern) represent separate species.

CAYENNE [SOUTHERN] LAPWING *Vanellus [chilensis] cayennensis* (p. 62). Differences in morphology, plumage, and vocalizations indicate that the widespread *cayennensis* group (S America, spreading to Central America) and allopatric *chilensis* group (Chile and s. Argentina; Chilean Lapwing) are best considered separate species.

WHIMBREL *Numenius phaeopus* (p. 66). Species status has been argued for New World populations (*hudsonicus* group, Hudsonian Whimbrel), based largely on genetic data (Sangster et al. 2011); although Hudsonian Whimbrel is split by IOC, in our view the case remains unproven from a biological perspective.

WILLET *Tringa semipalmata* (p. 68). Differences in ecology, morphology, plumage, and voice (supported by molecular evidence; Oswald et al. 2016) indicate that the *inornata* group (breeding interior w. N America; Western Willet) and *semipalmata* group (breeding coastal e. N America; Eastern Willet) are probably best treated as separate species.

AMERICAN GREAT EGRET *Ardea [alba] egretta* (p. 78). Differences in morphology, seasonal bare-part coloration, and provisionally in voice indicate that the *egretta* group (Americas) is best treated as a species distinct from Old World populations.

BOAT-BILLED HERON *Cochlearius cochlearius* (p. 82). Differences in plumage coloration, crest length of breeding birds, and provisionally in voice (averages higher, more chuckling in Northern), suggest that the *zeledoni* group (Middle America; Northern Boat-billed Heron) and *cochlearius* group (S America; Southern Boat-billed Heron) may represent separate species.

LIMPKIN *Aramus guarauna* (p. 88). Differences in plumage and provisionally in voice suggest the *pictus* group (s. to w. Panama; Northern Limpkin) and *guarauna* group (cen. Panama to S America; Southern Limpkin) may represent separate species.

NORTHERN SUNBITTERN *Eurypyga [helias] major* (p. 100). Differences in plumage and voice suggest that the *major* group (Central America to Andes, including e. Andean *meridionalis*) and *helias* group (lowland S America; Amazonian Sunbittern) represent separate species (Howell & Dyer 2022).

NORTHERN TURKEY VULTURE *Cathartes [aura] aura* (p. 112). Differences in morphology, plumage, and bare-part coloration indicate that Turkey Vulture complex comprises at least 3 groups and at least 2 species: Northern Turkey Vulture (Mexico to Costa Rica); Tropical Turkey Vulture *C. [a.] ruficollis* (Panama to tropical S America); and the distinctive Austral Turkey Vulture *C. [a.] jota* (Andes and s. S America, including *falklandicus*). An undescribed form (shown on plate) occurs from Costa Rica to n. S America, perhaps an intergrade population between Northern and Tropical; study needed.

NORTHERN WHITE HAWK *Pseudastur [albicollis] ghiesbreghti* (p. 126). Differences in voice and morphology indicate that the *ghiesbreghti* group (Mexico to nw. S America) and *superciliaris* group (S America, e. of the Andes; Southern White Hawk) are separate species; also see Lerner et al. (2008).

OSPREY *Pandion haliaetus* (p. 142). Wink et al. (2004) argued that all 3 Osprey taxa they studied (of 4 worldwide) warranted species status, based purely on mitochondrial DNA lineages, whereas Monti et al. (2015) provided a conflicting molecular interpretation based again purely on mitochondrial DNA. Although IOC and others have adopted a two-way split (Western Osprey *P. [h.] haliaetus* vs. Eastern Osprey *P. [h.] cristatus*), we see no biological evidence that offers compelling support for this; a 4-way species split seems equally valid, or all taxa might be maintained as a single species.

NORTHERN MOTTLED OWL *Strix [virgata] virgata* (p. 146). Differences in voice and morphology indicate that the *virgata* group (Mexico to nw. Peru) and *superciliaris* group (S America, e. of the Andes; Amazonian Mottled Owl) are best treated as separate species. Also see Sanchez et al. (2012).

COSTA RICAN [VERMICULATED] SCREECH OWL *Megascops [guatemalae] vermiculatus* and **SKUTCH'S [VERMICULATED] SCREECH OWL** *Megascops [guatemalae]* undescribed (p. 148). Given morphological and vocal differences comparable to those between other accepted species of screech owls, we recognize 5 species of 'Vermiculated Screech Owl' in Middle America, 2 of them in Costa Rica: Costa Rican Screech Owl (e. Nicaragua to nw. Panama) and the formally undescribed Skutch's Screech Owl, from the Pacific slope of Costa Rica (and w. Panama?); on the basis of voice, Skutch's Screech Owl is allied to Choco Screech Owl and is treated within that species by eBird.

FERRUGINOUS PYGMY OWL *Glaucidium brasilianum* (p. 148). Vocal and slight morphological and plumage differences suggest that the *ridgwayi* group (Mexico to nw. Colombia; Ridgway's Pygmy Owl) and *brasilianum* group (S America, e. of Andes; Ferruginous Pygmy Owl) may best be treated as separate species.

BARN OWL *Tyto alba* (p. 150). The Barn Owl *Tyto alba* complex comprises 3 genetic lineages that are treated differently by different authors. American Barn Owl *T. [a.] furcata* is treated as a species by IOC, but critical biological analysis of the situation could help resolve this issue.

SOUTHERN BAND-TAILED PIGEON *Patagioenas [fasciata] albilinea* (p. 164). Differences in plumage and voice indicate a clear species break in Middle America between the *fasciata* group (N America to Nicaragua; Northern Band-tailed Pigeon) and *albilinea* group (Costa Rica to S America).

VERREAUX'S [WHITE-TIPPED] DOVE *Leptotila [verreauxi] verreauxi* (p. 168). Differences in song and bare-part coloration suggest that the *fulviventris* group (Mexico to w. Nicaragua; Lawrence's Dove) and *verreauxi* group (Nicaragua to S America) represent separate species; critical study of the potential sympatry in Nicaragua could be informative.

COMMON SQUIRREL CUCKOO *Piaya [cayana] cayana* (p. 174). Differences in plumage and voice indicate that the *mexicana* group (w. Mexico; Mexican Squirrel Cuckoo) and widespread *cayana* group (e. Mexico to S America) are best treated as separate species; the latter group may include further cryptic species in S America.

AZTEC [OLIVE-THROATED] PARAKEET *Eupsittula [nana] astec* (p. 176). Differences in morphology, plumage, bare parts, and voice indicate that the *astec* group (Mexico to w. Panama) and *nana* group (Jamaica; Jamaican Parakeet) are best treated as separate species; also see Latta et al. (2012).

VERAGUAS [BROWN-THROATED] PARAKEET *Eupsittula [pertinax] ocularis* (p. 176). Differences in plumage, bare parts, and voice indicate that the *ocularis* group (Costa Rica to Panama) is best treated as a species distinct from S American and Caribbean taxa in the Brown-throated Parakeet complex, which may comprise further cryptic species. We favor Veraguas (rather than Veraguan) as a species epithet, as typically done for birds named for geographic entities below (and even at) country level.

NORTHERN BLACK-THROATED TROGON (p. 184). Differences in voice, morphology, and plumage (supported by molecular data) indicate that northern *tenellus* group (Honduras to nw. Colombia) is best treated as specifically distinct from populations in S America (Dickens et al. 2021.

ELEGANT TROGON *Trogon [elegans] elegans* (p. 186). Differences in plumage and voice indicate that the *ambiguus* group (Mexico and sw. US; Coppery-tailed Trogon) and *elegans* group (Guatemala to Costa Rica) are best treated as separate species.

NORTHERN COLLARED TROGON *Trogon [collaris] puella* (p. 186). Differences in plumage and song indicate that the *puella* group (Mexico to Panama) and *collaris* group (e. Panama to S America) are best treated as separate species.

TROPICAL RINGED KINGFISHER *Megaceryle [torquata] torquata* (p. 190). Differences in morphology, plumage, ecology, and voice indicate that the *torquata* group (Mexico to tropical S America) and *stellata* group (s. Chile and adjacent Argentina; Austral Ringed Kingfisher) are best treated as separate species.

LESSER PIED PUFFBIRD *Notharchus [tectus] subtectus* (p. 196). Differences in morphology, plumage, and voice indicate that the *subtectus* group (Central America to nw. S America) and *tectus* group (S America, e. of Andes; Greater Pied Puffbird) are best treated as separate species.

AZURE-HOODED JAY *Cyanolyca cucullata* (p. 210). Differences in plumage and voice suggest that the *mitrata* group (Mexico to Honduras; Northern Azure-hooded Jay) and *cucullata* group (Costa Rica and w. Panama; Southern Azure-hooded Jay) represent separate species.

GRAY-TAILED (WHITE-THROATED) [VARIABLE] MOUNTAIN-GEM *Lampornis [castaneoventris] cinereicauda* and **PURPLE-THROATED [VARIABLE] MOUNTAIN-GEM** *Lampornis [castaneoventris] calolaemus* (p. 220). Taxonomy of the appropriately named Variable Mountain-gem *Lampornis castaneoventris* complex remains unresolved, with 6 taxa involved, one of them formally undescribed (Miller & Rosas, unpubl. data). The main differences are in male gorget and tail color. One option is to lump all taxa into a single variable species; another is to treat various taxa as distinct, which we do here for the 2 main types occurring in Costa Rica, as also done provisionally by Stiles & Skutch (1989).

STRIPE-TAILED HUMMINGBIRD *Eupherusa eximia* (p. 226). Differences in morphology, plumage, and voice suggest that the *eximia* group (Mexico to Nicaragua; Northern Stripe-tailed Hummingbird) and *egregia* group (Costa Rica to Panama; Southern Stripe-tailed Hummingbird) may represent separate species.

SALVIN'S [CANIVET'S] EMERALD *Cynanthus [canivetii] salvini* (p. 228). As explained by Howell (1993a), Salvin's Emerald is distinct from Canivet's Emerald, and both were treated as species by Howell & Webb (1995). The ranges of the 2 taxa approach (or overlap?) in Guatemala and adjacent Mexico, but with no evidence of hybrids. The morphological differences are comparable to (or greater than) those between other accepted species-level taxa of hummingbirds, such as Salvin's Emerald and Garden Emerald *C. assimilis* in Costa Rica.

ALFARO'S/INDIGO-CAPPED HUMMINGBIRD 'Amazilia alfaroana'/Saucerottia cyanifrons. Described as "perhaps the foremost ornithological mystery in Costa Rica" (Stiles & Skutch 1989), a specimen collected in 1895 on Volcán Miravalles has been identified as the lone Central American example of Indigo-capped Hummingbird; as a hybrid; or as possibly a now extinct species (Kirwan & Collar 2016). We are puzzled why a hummingbird would have such a limited distribution in a region (and habitat) not prone to restricted endemics, and consider a unique hybrid to be a more parsimonious explanation (perhaps Blue-vented Hummingbird × Crowned Woodnymph?). Time may yet tell…

WHITE-CHINNED SWIFT *Cypseloides cryptus* (p. 234). Critical study is needed of birds in n. Central America, and of the enigmatic taxon *storeri* in Mexico, to resolve species limits in the White-chinned Swift complex (cf. Howell 1993b).

RICHMOND'S SWIFT *Chaetura [vauxi] richmondi* (p. 236). Differences in morphology, plumage, voice, and ecology indicate that the resident *richmondi* group (Middle America) and migratory *vauxi* group (N America; Vaux's Swift) are best treated as separate species.

HELLMAYR'S [GRAY-RUMPED] SWIFT *Chaetura [cinereiventris] phaeopygos* (p. 236). Differences in morphology, plumage, and voice indicate that the *phaeopgygos* group (Central America) is best treated as a species distinct from the widespread *cinereiventris* group (S America), with the latter likely including further cryptic species.

BROWN-BANDED [BROWN-CHESTED] MARTIN *Phaeoprogne [tapera] fusca* (p. 238). Differences in plumage, ecology, and voice indicate that the migratory *fusca* group (breeding s. S America) and widespread resident *tapera* group (n. and cen. S America; Brown-breasted Martin) are best treated as separate species. Genus *Phaeoprogne* differs from *Progne* in structure, flight manner, lack of sexual dimorphism.

CAVE SWALLOW *Petrochelidon fulva* (p. 240). Differences in morphology, plumage, and voice suggest that the *pallida* group (n. Mexico and sw. US; Northern Cave Swallow) and *citata* group (se. Mexico; Yucatan Cave Swallow) may be separate species; status of Caribbean taxa in Cave Swallow complex also in need of study.

BLUE-AND-WHITE SWALLOW *Pygochelidon cyanoleuca* (p. 242). Differences in morphology, plumage, ecology, and voice suggest that the widespread *cyanoleuca* group (Costa Rica to S America; Mountain Swallow) and migratory *patagonica* group (breeds s. S America; Patagonian Swallow) may be separate species; affiliation of *peruviana* in coastal Peru likely with *cyanoleuca*; study needed.

NORTHERN WEDGE-BILLED WOODCREEPER *Glyphorynchus [spirurus] pectoralis* (p. 244). Differences in plumage and voice indicate that the *pectoralis* group (Mexico to nw. S America) is best treated as a species distinct from other S American populations of Wedge-billed Woodcreeper complex, which may comprise further cryptic species.

GRAYISH [OLIVACEOUS] WOODCREEPER *Sittasomus [griseicapillus] griseus* (p. 244). Differences in plumage and voice indicate that the *griseus* group (Mexico to n. S America) is best treated as a species distinct from other S American populations of the Olivaceous Woodcreeper complex, which comprises further cryptic species.

COSTA RICAN [BLACK-BANDED] WOODCREEPER *Dendrocolaptes [picumnus] costaricensis* (p. 246). Differences in plumage, morphology, and voice suggest that the *costaricensis* group (Costa Rica to w. Panama) is best treated as specifically distinct from other populations of Black-banded Woodcreeper *D. picumnus*, which comprises further cryptic species.

SOUTHERN SPOTTED WOODCREEPER *Xiphorhynchus [erythropygius] aequatorialis* (p. 248). Differences in plumage and voice indicate that the *erythropygius* group (Mexico to Nicaragua; Northern Spotted Woodcreeper) and *aequatorialis* group (Costa Rica to n. Ecuador) are best treated as separate species.

CHERRIE'S [LONG-TAILED] WOODCREEPER *Deconychura [longicauda] typica* (p. 248). Differences in morphology, plumage, and voice indicate that the *typica* group (Honduras to n. Colombia) is best treated as a species distinct from other S American populations of the Long-tailed Woodcreeper complex, which may comprise further cryptic species.

SOUTHERN SPOT-CROWNED WOODCREEPER *Lepidocolaptes [affinis] neglectus* (p. 250). Differences in plumage and voice indicate that the *affinis* group (Mexico to Nicaragua; Northern Spot-crowned Woodcreeper) and *neglectus* group (Costa Rica to w. Panama) are best treated as separate species.

NORTHERN SPOTTED BARBTAIL *Premnoplex [brunnescens] brunneicauda* (p. 252). Differences in song suggest that the *brunneicauda* group (Costa Rica to Panama) and *brunnescens* group (S America; Southern Spotted Barbtail) are best treated as separate species.

PLAIN XENOPS *Xenops [minutus] genibarbis* (p. 252). Differences in plumage and voice indicate that the widespread *genibarbis* group (Plain Xenops, which may contain further cryptic species) is best treated as a species distinct from the *minutus* group of se. Brazil (White-throated Xenops).

MIDDLE AMERICAN [BUFF-THROATED] FOLIAGE-GLEANER *Automolus [ochrolaemus] cervinigularis* (p. 256). Differences in plumage and voice indicate that Buff-throated Foliage-gleaner comprises at least 2 species: the *cervinigularis* group (Mexico to nw. Panama) and *ochrolaemus* group (cen. Panama to S America), in addition to recently split Chiriqui [Buff-throated] Foliage-gleaner *A. [o.] exsertus* (Pacific slope in s. Costa Rica and w. Panama).

NORTHERN RUDDY FOLIAGE-GLEANER *Clibanornis [rubiginosus] rubiginosus* (p. 256). Differences in plumage and voice indicate that the *rubiginosus* group (Mexico to w. Ecuador) is best treated as a species distinct from other S American populations of Ruddy Foliage-gleaner complex, which may comprise further cryptic species.

GRAY-HOODED [GRAY-THROATED] LEAFTOSSER *Sclerurus [albigularis] canigularis* (p. 258). Differences in plumage and song indicate that the *canigularis* group (Costa Rica to w. Panama) is best treated as a species separate from populations of the Gray-throated Leaftosser complex in S America, which, on the basis of songs, comprises at least 3 more cryptic species: *S. [a.] albigularis* of n. S America, *S. [a.] albicollis* of sw. Amazonia, and *S. [a.] zamorae* of e. Ecuador and e. Peru.

WESTERN WHITE-FLANKED ANTWREN *Myrmotherula [axillaris] melaena* (p. 266). Differences in plumage and song indicate that the *melaena* group (Cen America and w. S America) and *axillaris* group (e. S America) are best treated as separate species.

HOFFMANN'S [BLACK-FACED] ANTTHRUSH *Formicarius [analis] hoffmanni* (p. 272). Differences in plumage and song indicate that Black-faced Antthrush comprises at least 3 species (Howell 1994): *hoffmanni* group (Honduras to nw. Venezuela) is here split from Mayan Antthrush (n. Middle America), and *analis* group (widespread in S America).

BLACK-HOODED [BLACK-HEADED] ANTTHRUSH *Formicarius [nigricapillus] nigricapillus* (p. 272). Differences in plumage and song indicate that the *nigricapillus* group (Central America) and *destructus* group (nw. S America; Choco Antthrush) are best treated as separate species.

SPECTACLED [STREAK-CHESTED] ANTPITTA *Hylopezus [perspicillatus] perspicillatus* (p. 274). Differences in plumage and song indicate that Streak-chested Antpitta comprises 2 species whose ranges split in Costa Rica.

TAWNY-FLANKED [STREAK-CHESTED] ANTPITTA *Hylopezus [perspicillatus] intermedius* (p. 274). See above under Spectacled Antpitta.

CENTRAL AMERICAN SHARPBILL *Oxyruncus [cristatus] frater* (p. 276). Differences in plumage and voice indicate that the *frater* group (Costa Rica to nw. Colombia) is best treated as a species distinct from S American populations of Sharpbill, which likely comprise further cryptic species, including *hypoglaucus* group of Peru to n. Brazil, and *cristatus* group of se. Brazil region.

NORTHERN BLACK-AND-WHITE BECARD *Pachyramphus [albogriseus] albogriseus* (p. 282). Differences in song and morphology indicate that *albogriseus* group (Costa Rica to ne. Peru) and *guayaquilensis* group (sw. Colombia to s. Peru; Southern Black-and-white Becard) are probably best treated as separate species; a conclusion also supported by molecular data (Musher & Cracraft 2018).

MIDDLE AMERICAN [BRIGHT-RUMPED] ATTILA *Attila [spadiceus] flammulatus* (p. 284). Differences in plumage and voice suggest that the *flammulatus* group (e. Mexico to w. Ecuador) may best be treated as a species distinct from the *pacificus* group (w. Mexico; West Mexican Attila) and *spadiceus* group (S America, e. of Andes).

WHITE-CROWNED MANAKIN *Pseudopipra pipra* (p. 288). Differences in song suggest that multiple species may be involved in the White-crowned Manakin complex, including the *anthracina* group (Costa Rica to Panama; Zeledon's Manakin) and numerous taxa in S America (see Spencer 2012).

WESTERN WHITE-THROATED SPADEBILL *Platyrinchus [mystaceus] albogularis* (p. 292). Differences in voice, plumage, and morphology indicate that the *albogularis* group (Costa Rica to w. S America) and *mystaceus* group (e. S America) are best treated as separate species, with perhaps further cryptic species involved in S America.

WESTERN SLATY-CAPPED FLYCATCHER *Leptopogon [superciliaris] transandinus* (p. 294). Differences, mainly in voice, suggest that the *transandinus* group (Costa Rica to nw. S America), *superciliaris* group (Venezuela to Peru, e. of Andes), and *albidiventer* group (s. Peru to Bolivia) represent cryptic species. Central American *hellmayri* also differs slightly from S American *transandinus*, and study needed.

OLIVE-STREAKED [OLIVE-STRIPED] FLYCATCHER *Mionectes [olivaceus] olivaceus* (p. 294). Differences in voice, plumage, and morphology indicate that the *olivaceus* group (Costa Rica to w. Panama), *galbinus* group (S America, w. of Andes), and *venezuelensis* group (S America, e. of Andes) may best be treated as separate species.

NORTHERN OCHRE-BELLIED FLYCATCHER *Mionectes [oleagineus] assimilis* (p. 294). Differences in voice, plumage, and morphology suggest that the *assimilis* group (Mexico to n. S America), *pacificus* group (sw. Colombia to nw. Peru), and *oleagineus* group (S America, e. of Andes) may best be treated as separate species.

CENTRAL AMERICAN [SOUTHERN] BEARDLESS TYRANNULET *Camptostoma [obsoletum] flaviventre* (p. 298). Differences in voice and plumage indicate that the Southern Beardless Tyrannulet complex involves multiple species, also including at least the *sclateri* group (w. Ecuador and w. Peru; Western Beardless Tyrannulet); *napaeum* group (Amazonian region; Amazonian Beardless Tyrannulet); and *obsoletum* group (s. S America; Austral Beardless Tyrannulet).

MOUSE-COLORED TYRANNULET *Phaeomyias murina* (p. 298). Differences in voice and morphology suggest that the *incomta* group (Costa Rica to n. S America; Northern Mouse-colored Tyrannulet) and *murina* group (widespread in S America.) may represent separate species.

MISTLETOE TYRANNULET *Zimmerius parvus* (p. 300). Distinct vocal differences between undescribed northern birds (Belize to Costa Rica), 'central' birds *Z. [p.] parvus* (Costa Rica to cen. Panama), and undescribed southern birds (e. Panama) suggest that three cryptic species are likely involved (Howell & Dyer 2022.).

COLOMBIAN [GREENISH] ELAENIA *Myiopagis [viridicata] accola* (p. 302). Differences in voice and morphology indicate that the Greenish Elaenia complex comprises multiple cryptic species, also including *M. [v.] minima* (w. Mexico; West Mexican Elaenia) and *M. [v.] placens* (e. Mexico to Nicaragua; Mesoamerican Elaenia), plus others in S America.

SCLATER'S [YELLOW-OLIVE] FLATBILL *Tolmomyias [sulphurescens] cinereiceps* (p. 302). Differences in voice and morphology indicate that the Yellow-olive Flatbill complex comprises multiple cryptic species, among which the *cinereiceps* group (Mexico to Costa Rica) is quite distinct from other groups, including the adjacent (sympatric?) *flavoolivaceus* group (Panama to nw. Colombia; Panama Flatbill).

COSTA RICAN TUFTED FLYCATCHER *Mitrephanes [phaeocercus] aurantiiventris* (p. 306). Differences in voice and plumage indicate that the *phaeocercus* group (Mexico to Nicaragua; Mexican Tufted Flycatcher) and *aurantiiventris* group (Costa Rica to Panama) are best treated as separate species.

NORTHERN TROPICAL PEWEE *Contopus [cinereus] bogotensis* (p. 308). Differences in voice and plumage indicate that the *bogotensis* group (Mexico to n. S America) and *cinereus* group (e. and s. S America; Southern Tropical Pewee) are best treated as separate species, perhaps with further cryptic species involved.

SOUTHERN YELLOWISH FLYCATCHER *Empidonax [flavescens] flavescens* (p. 312). Differences in voice and plumage indicate that the *salvini* group (Mexico to Nicaragua; Northern Yellowish Flycatcher) and *flavescens* group (Costa Rica to Panama) are best treated as separate species.

BLACK PHOEBE *Sayornis nigricans* (p. 312). Differences in voice and plumage suggest that the *nigricans* group (N America s. to Panama; Northern Black Phoebe) and *latirostris* group (S America; Southern Black Phoebe) may represent separate species.

NORTHERN SOCIAL FLYCATCHER *Myiozetetes [similis] texensis* (p. 316) and **COLOMBIAN SOCIAL FLYCATCHER** *Myiozetetes [similis] columbianus* (p. 316). Differences in voice and morphology indicate that the Social Flycatcher complex comprises at least 5 cryptic species, also including *M. [s.] grandis* (w. Ecuador to nw. Peru; Western Social Flycatcher); *M. [s.] similis* (Amazonian region; Amazonian Social Flycatcher); and *M. [s.] pallidiventris* (e. Brazil to n. Argentina; Austral Social Flycatcher).

NORTHERN STREAKED FLYCATCHER *Myiodynastes [maculatus] maculatus* (p. 318). Differences in voice and morphology indicate that the *maculatus* group (Mexico to S America) and *solitarius* group (breeds s. S America; Austral Streaked Flycatcher) are best treated as separate species.

NUTTING'S FLYCATCHER *Myiarchus nuttingi* (p. 320). Differences in plumage, morphology, and voice between the *nuttingi* group (Guatemala to Costa Rica, possibly also s. Mexico; Nicoya/Ridgway's Flycatcher) and *inquietus* group (Mexico; Mexican/Godman's Flycatcher) suggest that cryptic species may be involved; critical study is needed.

SALVADORAN [NUTTING'S] FLYCATCHER *Myiarchus [nuttingi] flavidior* (p. 320). As noted by Howell (2012), differences in voice, morphology, and ecology indicate that the *flavidior* group (s. Mexico to Nicaragua, perhaps nw. Costa Rica) is specifically distinct from *nuttingi* group (Mexico to Costa Rica; Nutting's Flycatcher, see above). Salvadoran and Nutting's occur in parapatry (Mexico) and sympatry (Honduras; perhaps also Mexico, Guatemala, Nicaragua), and may not even be sister species. The name Ridgway's Flycatcher has been suggested for *flavidior* (Howell 2012), but that name would be more appropriate for nominate *nuttingi* if specifically distinct from *inquietus*, with Nutting's Flycatcher retained for the whole complex.

MIDDLE AMERICAN [TROPICAL] KINGBIRD *Tyrannus [melancholicus] satrapa* (p. 322). Differences in voice (especially dawn song), morphology, and plumage suggest that the *satrapa* group (e. Mexico to nw. S America), *occidentalis* group (w. Mexico; West Mexican Kingbird), and *melancholicus* group (widespread in S America; South American Kingbird) are best treated as separate species.

FORK-TAILED FLYCATCHER *Tyrannus savana* (p. 324). Differences in morphology, ecology, and provisionally in voice suggest that the *monachus* group (Mexico to nw. S America; Northern Fork-tailed Flycatcher) and *savana* group (breeds s. S America; Austral Fork-tailed Flycatcher) may represent separate species.

VIEILLOT'S [TROPICAL] MOCKINGBIRD *Mimus [gilvus] gilvus* (p. 326). Differences in voice and plumage suggest the Tropical Mockingbird complex probably comprises multiple species, including the *gracilis* group (Mexico to Honduras; Mayan Mockingbird, see Howell 2019), *gilvus* group (Nicaragua to n. S America and s. Caribbean, perhaps including further cryptic species), and *antelius* group (e. Brazil; Brazilian Mockingbird).

WHITE-THROATED THRUSH *Turdus assimilis* (p. 328). Vocal differences (most evident in call notes) between populations e. and w. of Isthmus of Tehuantepec, Mexico, hint that cryptic species may be involved; study needed.

SWAINSON'S THRUSH *Catharus ustulatus* (p. 330). Differences in voice, plumage, and ecology suggest that the *ustulatus* group (breeding w. America, wintering Mexico to n. Central America; Russet-backed Thrush) and *swainsoni* group (breeding n. and interior w. N America, wintering s. Central America to S America; Olive-backed Thrush) may represent separate species.

COSTA RICAN [BAND-BACKED] WREN *Campylorhynchus [zonatus] costaricensis* (p. 336). Vocal and morphological differences indicate that the *costaricensis* group (s. Nicaragua to w. Panama) is best treated as specifically distinct from *zonatus* group (Mexico to n. Nicaragua; Mesoamerican Wren) and *brevirostris* group of nw. S America; also supported by molecular data (Vázquez-M. & Barker 2021).

HOUSE WREN *Troglodytes aedon* (p. 344). Differences in voice, plumage, and ecology suggest that the *aedon* group (N America; Northern House Wren), *brunneicollis* group (Mexico; Brown-throated Wren) and *musculus* group (s. Mexico to S America; Southern House Wren) may represent separate species, along with some Caribbean taxa in the House Wren complex.

PLAIN WREN *Cantorchilus modestus* complex (p. 338). Although usually now treated as 3 species (Cabanis's Wren, Canebrake Wren, Isthmian Wren), we find the case for splitting Plain Wren into 3 species unconvincing, another instance of divergent mitochondrial lineages elevated to the level of species by sophistry rather than science. With respect to possible vocal differences, the paper by Saucier et al. (2015) and Saucier's follow-up proposal to NACC were misleading at best, cf. Boesman (2016) and our own analysis. Song differences among taxa are not at all clear, although there may be some differences in scolding calls. Moreover, and perhaps unsurprisingly, Freeman & Montgomery (2017) found *zero* discrimination between 'Isthmian Wren' and 'Cabanis's Wren' in song playback experiments, yet their finding of much greater discrimination led to lumping of Scarlet-rumped Tanager (Howell & Dyer 2022).

MIDDLE AMERICAN [WHITE-BREASTED] WOOD WREN *Henicorhina [leucosticta] prostheleuca* (p. 342). Vocal and morphological differences indicate that the *prostheleuca* group (Mexico to w. Colombia) is best treated as specifically distinct from other S American populations.

WHISTLING [SOUTHERN NIGHTINGALE-] WREN *Microcerculus [marginatus] luscinia* (p. 342) Vocal and morphological differences indicate that the *luscinia* group (Costa Rica to Panama) is best treated as specifically distinct from S American populations.

GRASS [SEDGE] WREN *Cistothorus [platensis] elegans* (p. 344). We follow the study by Robbins & Nyári (2014) who advocated splitting the Sedge Wren complex into 8 species, including *elegans* of Middle America.

ROCK WREN *Salpinctes obsoletus* (p. 344). Differences in voice and plumage suggest that the *obsoletus* group (N America to cen. Mexico; Northern Rock Wren) and *guttatus* group (s. Mexico to Costa Rica; Southern Rock Wren) may represent separate species.

NORTHERN [LONG-BILLED/TRILLING] GNATWREN *Ramphocaenus [melanurus] rufiventris* (p. 346). Differences in voice and plumage indicate that the *rufiventris* group (Mexico to nw. Peru) is best treated as specifically distinct from other S American populations of the *R. melanurus* complex.

CENTRAL AMERICAN [WHITE-LORED] GNATCATCHER *Polioptila [albiloris] albiloris* (p. 346). Differences in morphology and voice between the *vanrossemi* group (w. Mexico; Van Rossem's Gnatcatcher) and *albiloris* group (Guatemala to Costa Rica) indicate that cryptic species are probably involved.

YELLOW-GREEN [SCRUB] GREENLET *Hylophilus [flavipes] viridiflavus* (p. 348). Differences in voice and plumage indicate the *viriflavidus* group (Costa Rica to Panama) and *flavipes* group (n. S America; Scrub Greenlet) are best treated as separate species.

MANGROVE VIREO *Vireo pallens* (p. 350). Differences in voice, morphology, and ecology suggest that the *pallens* group (Mexico to Costa Rica, Pacific coast) and *semiflavus* group (Mexico to Nicaragua; Mayan Vireo) may best be treated as separate species. Differences between them are as great or greater than between other vireo taxa treated as species, such as Red-eyed Vireo and Chivi Vireo *V. chivi*.

SOUTHERN BROWN-CAPPED VIREO *Vireo [leucophrys] leucophrys* (p. 352). Differences in voice and plumage indicate that the *amauronotus* group (Mexico to Nicaragua; Northern Brown-capped Vireo) and *leucophrys* group (Costa Rica to S America) are best treated as separate species.

EASTERN WARBLING VIREO *Vireo [gilvus] gilvus* (p. 352). Differences in voice, morphology, and ecology indicate that the *gilvus* group (breeding in e. N America) and *swainsoni* group (breeding w. N America to Mexico) may best be considered separate species.

MANGROVE WARBLER *Setophaga petechia* (p. 434). Taxonomy of Mangrove Warbler complex remains vexed; taxon *aureola* of Cocos and Galapagos Islands perhaps best treated as a full species, Galapagos Warbler.

BAIRD'S [OLIVE-CROWNED] YELLOWTHROAT *Geothlypis [semiflava] bairdi* and **CHIRIQUI (MASKED) YELLOWTHROAT** *Geothlypis [aequinoctialis] chiriquensis* (p. 368). Differences in voice, morphology, and genetics suggest that both of these taxa are best treated as species. Molecular evidence also indicates that Chiriqui is not closely related to the Masked Yellowthroat group of South America, but instead is sister to Baird's Yellowthroat (Escalante et al. 2009).

STRIPE-CROWNED [GOLDEN-CROWNED] WARBLER *Basileuterus [culicivorus] culicivorus* (p. 370). Differences in morphology and voice indicate that the *culicivorus* group (e. Mexico to Panama) is best treated as a species separate from other taxa in the Golden-crowned Warbler complex in S America and perhaps also from birds in w. Mexico.

PANAMA [ROSY] THRUSH-TANAGER *Rhodinocichla [rosea] eximia* (p. 374). Differences in morphology and voice suggest that the *eximia* group (Costa Rica to Panama) is best treated as a species separate from other populations of the Rosy Thrush-Tanager complex, including Mexican [Rosy] Thrush-Tanager *R. [r.] schistacea* and 2–3 potential species-level taxa in Colombia and Venezuela.

YELLOW-THROATED BRUSHFINCH *Atlapetes [albinucha] gutturalis* (p. 376). Differences in morphology and voice comparable to some other accepted brushfinch species suggest that the *albinucha* group (e. Mexico; White-naped Brushfinch) and *gutturalis* group (s. Mexico to S America) are perhaps better treated as separate species, as done for many years before being lumped with no convincing rationale.

ORANGE-BILLED SPARROW *Arremon aurantiirostris* (p. 378). Distinct differences in both call and song, coupled with minor plumage differences, suggest that the *rufidorsalis* group (Mexico to nw. Panama; Northern Orange-billed Sparrow), *aurantiirostris* group (Costa Rica to nw. Peru; Western Orange-billed Sparrow), and *spectabilis* group (s. Colombia to n. Peru, e. of Andes; Eastern Orange-billed Sparrow) may represent separate species.

OLIVE SPARROW *Arremonops rufivirgatus* (p. 380). Differences in morphology and song suggest that the *superciliosus* group (Honduras to Costa Rica; Southern Olive Sparrow) may be specifically distinct from n. populations of the Olive Sparrow complex, which comprises 4 additional groups. Based on plumage, song, and ecology, the enigmatic taxon *twomeyi* of Honduras is also part of the Southern Olive Sparrow group, despite inexplicably having been described (and still maintained) as a race of Green-backed Sparrow *A. chloronotus*.

WHITE-EARED GROUND SPARROW *Melozone leucotis* (p. 380). Differences in morphology and song suggest that the *occipitalis* group (s. Mexico to El Salvador; Spectacled Ground Sparrow) and *leucotis* group (Honduras to Costa Rica; Black-chested Ground Sparrow) may represent separate species. Also see Sandoval et al. (2017).

STRIPE-HEADED SPARROW *Peucaea ruficauda* (p. 382). Differences in morphology, plumage, and voice suggest that the *acuminata* group (w. Mexico; Northern Stripe-headed Sparrow) and *ruficauda* group (s. Mexico to Costa Rica; Southern Stripe-headed Sparrow) may represent separate species.

NORTHERN [WEDGE-TAILED] GRASSFINCH *Emberizoides [herbicola] sphenurus* (p. 382). Differences in song and morphology suggest that the *sphenurus* group (Costa Rica to n. S America) is specifically distinct from other populations in s. S America.

MIDDLE AMERICAN BUSH-TANAGER *Chlorospingus [flavopectus] ophthalmicus* (p. 384). Dawn songs of the *ophthalmicus* group (Middle America) are distinctly high-pitched vs. the low-pitched songs of the *flavopectus* group (S America), supporting species status for these 2 groups; within each region there are likely further cryptic species, but biological data (notably dawn songs) are sparse or lacking for many regions and taxa.

ASHY-THROATED BUSH-TANAGER *Chlorospingus canigularis* (p. 384). A large range disjunction and plumage differences suggest the *olivaceiceps* group (Costa Rica to w. Panama; Olive-crowned Bush-Tanager) may be specifically distinct from the *canigularis* group (S America) but we have found no song recordings for *olivaceiceps* (calls of the two groups are similar, which may not be saying much with *Chlorospingus*).

HICK'S [VARIABLE] SEEDEATER *Sporophila [corvina] ophthalmica* (p. 392). Differences in plumage and voice indicate that the *ophthalmica* group (Costa Rica to nw. Peru) and *corvina* group (Mexico to Panama; Black Seedeater) are best treated as separate species, with a narrow and apparently stable hybrid zone in cen. Panama (Olson 1981).

BLACK [VARIABLE] SEEDEATER *Sporophila [corvina] corvina* (p. 394). See above under Hick's Seedeater.

BLUE SEEDEATER *Amaurospiza concolor* (p. 396). Based purely on genetic lineages, IOC split the *concolor* group (s. Mexico to Panama) and *aequatorialis* group (sw. Colombia to n. Peru) as species. Morphology and voice of all *Amaurospiza* are similar, and Ecuadorian birds respond aggressively to songs from Mexican birds (Howell, pers. obs.). Moreover, samples used in studies to date are very small, and it seems equally plausible to subsume most or all taxa as subspecies of a widespread Blue Seedeater (Howell & Dyer 2022).

SOUTHERN BLACK-FACED GROSBEAK *Caryothraustes [poliogaster] scapularis* (p. 400). Differences in plumage and voice indicate that the *scapularis* group (e. Honduras to Panama) and *poliogaster* group (Mexico to w. Honduras, Northern Black-faced Grosbeak) are best treated as separate species. Mexican birds ignore Costa Rica recordings but respond strongly to their own vocalizations (R. C. Hoyer, pers. comm.), and vocal differences are appreciably greater than, e.g., those between Rose-breasted and Black-headed Grosbeaks in N America, which are treated as species.

RED-THROATED ANT-TANAGER *Habia fuscicauda* (p. 404). Seemingly minor differences in voice and morphology suggest that the *salvini* group (Mexico to n. Nicaragua; Salvin's Ant-Tanager) and *fuscicauda* group (s. Nicaragua to n. Colombia; Cabanis's Ant-Tanager) may represent separate species.

MIDDLE AMERICAN [RED-CROWNED] ANT-TANAGER *Habia [rubica] rubicoides* (p. 404). Differences in voice and morphology indicate that the *rubicoides* group (e. Mexico to Panama) is best treated as a species separate from populations of the Red-crowned Ant-Tanager complex in S America.

COMMON BANANAQUIT *Coereba [flaveola] luteola* (p. 410). Differences in voice and morphology suggest that the *luteola* group (mainland Americas) may represent a species separate from the *flaveola* group (Caribbean region), which likely comprises multiple species.

BLUE-GRAY TANAGER *Tangara episcopus* (p. 410). Striking plumage differences between the *cana* group (Mexico to nw. Peru; Northern Blue-gray Tanager) and *episcopus* group (S America, e. of Andes; Amazonian Blue-gray Tanager) suggest separate species may be involved.

WHITE-SHOULDERED TANAGER *Loriotus luctuosus* (p. 418). Differences in morphology and provisionally in voice between the *axillaris* group (Honduras to Panama, Caribbean slope; Costa Rican Tanager), *nitidissimus* group (Costa Rica to Panama, Pacific slope; Chiriqui Tanager), and widespread *luctuosus* group (cen. Panama to S America; White-shouldered Tanager) suggest they may represent separate species.

WHITE-THROATED SHRIKE-TANAGER *Lanio leucothorax* (p. 420). Differences in plumage and provisionally in voice suggest that the *leucothorax* group (Honduras to Panama, Caribbean slope) and *melanopygius* group (Costa Rica to Panama, Pacific slope; Black-rumped Shrike-Tanager) may best be treated as species, with a narrow hybrid zone in w. Panama (Kennard & Peters 1927, Wetmore et al. 1984).

GRAY-HEADED TANAGER *Eucometis penicillata* (p. 420). Differences in morphology and voice between the *spodocephalus* group (Mexico to nw. S America; Northern Gray-headed Tanager) and *penicillata* group (widespread in S America) suggest they may represent separate species.

SCARLET-RUMPED CACIQUE *Cacicus microrhynchus* (p. 424). Differences in voice and morphology indicate that the *microrhynchus* group (Honduras to Panama) and *pacificus* group (nw. S America; Pacific Cacique) are best treated as separate species.

YELLOW-BILLED CACIQUE *Amblycercus holosericeus* (p. 428). Differences in voice and morphology suggest that the *holosericeus* group (Mexico to w. Peru; Western Yellow-billed Cacique) and *australis* group (Colombia to Bolivia, e. of Andes; Eastern Yellow-billed Cacique) may represent separate species.

REFERENCES

American Ornithologists' Union (AOU). 1998. Check-list of North American Birds, 7th edition. AOU, Washington, DC.

Boesman, P. 2016. Notes on the vocalizations of Plain Wren (*Thryothorus modestus*) and Canebrake Wren (*Thryothorus zeledoni*). HBW Alive Ornithological Note 294. In: Handbook of the Birds of the World Alive. Lynx Edicions, Barcelona.

Dickens, J. K., P.-P. Bitton, G. A. Bravo, & L. F. Silveira. 2021. Species limits, patterns of secondary contact, and a new species in the *Trogon rufus* complex (Aves: Trogonidae). Zoological Journal of the Linnean Society 193:499–540.

Escalante, P., L. Márquez-V., P. de la Torre, J. P. Laclette, & J. Klicka. 2009. Evolutionary history of a prominent North American warbler clade: The *Oporornis–Geothlypis* complex. Molecular Phylogenetics and Evolution 53:668–678.

Freeman, B. G., and G. A. Montgomery. 2017. Using song playback experiments to measure species recognition between geographically isolated populations: A comparison with acoustic trait analyses. Auk 134(4):857–870.

Garrigues, R., & R. Dean. 2007. The Birds of Costa Rica: A Field Guide. Cornell Univ. Press.

Garrigues, R., & R. Dean. 2014. The Birds of Costa Rica: A Field Guide, 2nd edition. Cornell Univ. Press.

Garrigues, R., P. Camacho-V., M. Montoya, P. O'Donnell, O. Ramírez-A., & J. Zook. 2018. Lista Oficial de las Aves de Costa Rica Actualización 2018. Comité de Especies Raras y Registros Ornitológicos de Costa Rica (Comité Científico), Asociación Ornitológica de Costa Rica. Zeledonia 22(2):53–58. (Versión Online. Incluye ultimos cambios aceptados por el Comité publicados primero en-línea.)

Gill F., D., Donsker, & P. Rasmussen, eds. 2021. IOC World Bird List (v11.2). doi:10.14344/IOC.ML.11.2.

Howell, S. N. G. 1993a. Taxonomy and distribution of the hummingbird genus *Chlorostilbon* in Mexico and northern Central America. Euphonia 2:25–37.

Howell, S. N. G. 1993b. More comments on White-fronted Swift. Euphonia 2:100–101.

Howell, S. N. G. 1994. The specific status of Black-faced Antthrushes in Middle America. Cotinga 1:20–25.

Howell, S. N. G. 2012. M-M-M-Maybe you just ain't seen Nutting yet? Neotropical Birding 10:14–17.

Howell, S. N. G. 2019. To split a mockingbird. https://ebird.org/news/to-split-a-mockingbird

Howell, S. N. G. 2021. What isn't a species? North American Birds 72(1):16–25.

Howell, S. N. G., & D. Dyer. 2022. Costa Rica—even richer than we thought? North American Birds 73(1):22–33.

Howell, S. N. G., & S. Webb. 1995. A Guide to the Birds of Mexico and Northern Central America. Oxford Univ. Press.

Howell, S. N. G., & K. Zufelt. 2019. Oceanic Birds of the World: A Photo Guide. Princeton Univ. Press.

Howell, S. N. G., A. Jaramillo, N. Redman, & R. S. Ridgely. 2012. What's the point of field guides: taxonomy or utility? Neotropical Birding 11:16–21.

Kennard, F. H., & J. L. Peters. 1927. New birds from Panama (*Lanio*, *Psilorhinus*). Proc. New England Zool. Club 10:1–2.

Kirwan. G. M., & N. J. Collar. 2016. The 'foremost ornithological mystery in Costa Rica': *Amazilia alfaroana* Underwood, 1896. Zootaxa 4189(2):244–250.

Lanyon, W. E. 1961. Specific limits and distribution of Ash-throated and Nutting's flycatchers. Condor 63(6):421–449.

Latta, S. C., A. K. Townsend, & I. J. Lovette. 2012. The origins of the recently discovered Hispaniolan Olive-throated Parakeet: a phylogeographic perspective on a conservation conundrum. Caribbean Journal of Science 46(2–3):143–149.

Lerner, H. R. L., M. C. Klaver, & D. P. Mindell. 2008. Molecular phylogenetics of the buteonine birds of prey (Accipitridae). Auk 304(2):304–315.

Monti, F., & 7 co-authors. 2015. Being cosmopolitan: evolutionary history and phylogeography of a specialized raptor, the Osprey *Pandion haliaetus*. BMC Evolutionary Biology 15:255. DOI 10.1186/s12862-015-0535-6.

Musher, L. J., & J. Cracraft. 2018. Phylogenomics and species delimitation of a complex radiation of Neotropical suboscine birds (*Pachyramphus*). Molecular Phylogenetics and Evolution 118:204–221.

Olson, S. L. 1981. The nature of the variability of the Variable Seedeater in Panama (*Sporophila americana*: Emberizinae). Proc. Biol. Soc. Wash. 94(2):380–390.

Olson, S. L., & R. C. Banks. 2007. Lectotypification of *Larus smithsonianus* Coues, 1862 (Aves: Laridae). Proc. Biol. Soc. Wash. 120(4):382–386.

Oswald, J. A., & 8 coauthors. 2016. Willet be one species or two? A genomic view of the evolutionary history of *Tringa semipalmata*. Auk 133(4):593–614.

Robbins, M. B., & A. S. Nyári. 2014. Canada to Tierra del Fuego: species limits and historical biogeography of the Sedge Wren (*Cistothorus platensis*). Wilson Journal of Ornithology 126(4):649–662.

Sánchez, C., & 12 co-authors. 2012. New and noteworthy records from northwestern Peru. Boletín Informativo UNOP 7(2):18–36.

Sandoval, L., P. P. Bitton, A. D. Demko, S. M. Doucet, & D. J. Mennill. 2017. Phenotypic variation and vocal divergence reveals a species complex in White-eared Ground-sparrows (Cabanis) (Aves: Passerellidae). Zootaxa 4291(1):155–170.

Sandoval, L., & C. Sánchez. 2019. Lista de aves de Costa Rica: vigésima octava actualización. Unión de Ornitólogos de Costa Rica. San José, Costa Rica.

Sangster, G., & 6 co-authors. 2011. Taxonomic recommendations for British birds: seventh report. Ibis 153: 883–892.

Saucier, J. R., C. Sánchez, & M. D. Carling. 2015. Patterns of genetic and morphological divergence reveal a species complex in the Plain Wren (*Cantorchilus modestus*). Auk 132(4):795–807.

Slud, P. 1964. The Birds of Costa Rica: Distribution and Ecology. Bulletin of the AMNH 128.

Spencer, A. 2012. White-crowned Manakin vocal variation. URL: http://www.xeno-canto.org/article/108 (downloaded April 2015).

Stiles, F. G., & A. F. Skutch. 1989. A Guide to the Birds of Costa Rica. Cornell Univ. Press.

Vallely, A. C., & D. Dyer. 2018. Birds of Central America. Princeton Univ. Press.

Vázquez-M., H., & F. K. Barker 2021. Autosomal, sex-linked, and mitochondrial loci resolve evolutionary relationships among wrens in the genus *Campylorhynchus*. Molecular Phylogenetics and Evolution 163:107242.

Wetmore, A., R. F. Pasquier, & S. L. Olson. 1984. The birds of the Republic of Panama, part 4. Smithsonian Misc. Coll. 150.

Wink, M., H. Sauer-Gürth, & H.-H. Witt. 2004. Phylogenetic Differentiation of the Osprey *Pandion haliaetus* inferred from nucleotide sequences of the mitochondrial cytochrome b gene. Pp. 511–516 in Raptors Worldwide, edited by R. D. Chancellor & B.-U. Meyburg. World Working Group on Birds of Prey, Berlin.

Yoon, C. K. 2009. Naming Nature: The Clash Between Instinct and Science. W. W. Norton.

INDEX OF ENGLISH NAMES